Teacher Perspectives and Responsible Practice for Integrating AI in the Classroom

Stamatios Papadakis
https://orcid.org/0000-0003-3184-1147
University of Crete, Greece

IGI Global
Scientific Publishing
Publishing Tomorrow's Research Today

Vice President of Editorial Melissa Wagner
Director of Acquisitions Mikaela Felty
Director of Book Development Jocelynn Hessler
Production Manager Mike Brehm
Cover Design Jose Rosado

Published in the United States of America by
IGI Global Scientific Publishing
701 East Chocolate Avenue
Hershey, PA, 17033, USA
Tel: 717-533-8845 | Fax: 717-533-7115
Website: https://www.igi-global.com E-mail: cust@igi-global.com

Library of Congress Cataloging-in-Publication Data

(CIP Data Pending)
ISBN13: 979-8-2600-0101-1
Isbn13Softcover: 979-8-2600-0102-8
EISBN13: 979-8-2600-0103-5

British Cataloguing in Publication Data
A Cataloguing in Publication record for this book is available from the British Library.

Table of Contents

Detailed Table of Contents

Agentic AI systems can engage in meaningful human-like interactions, are autonomous and context-aware, automate processes, and present goal-oriented behaviors. They initiate actions based on their goals, state, and knowledge, and make informed decisions using data, contextual information, and environmental cues with limited intervention and supervision. They are designed to adapt to their environment, may demonstrate sophisticated reasoning capabilities, and act proactively with a sense of agency, autonomy, intentionality, and rationality. The chapter results reveal that agentic AI can reshape educational structure and roles with the co-presence of education stakeholders and AI tools becoming integral to teaching and learning. Agentic AI marks a conceptual and practical shift of the role of AI in education as it emphasizes the creation of collaborative, adaptive, and intelligent systems that act as partners with shared agency. Agentic AI can impact the affective, cognitive, and social dimensions of learning and create engaging, effective, and personalized educational experiences.

This study rigorously examines the factors contributing to the successful integration of Artificial Intelligence (AI) within K-12 education. Drawing upon an extensive narrative review, the research identifies three fundamental dimensions: technical and infrastructure considerations, pedagogical integration, and human and organizational readiness, pivotal to effective AI adoption. The chapter explores adaptive learning systems, automated assessment tools, and personalized educational platforms as key AI applications for teaching efficiency and student engagement. It proposed a conceptual framework to guide the implementation of AI, aligning technological capabilities with educational objectives and ethical standards. Implications for policymakers, educators, and technologists are discussed, alongside recommendations for teacher training, curriculum alignment, and strategic investments in infrastructure. The study concludes by outlining avenues for future research, particularly in exploring long-term outcomes and the equitable deployment of AI across various educational settings.

Generative Artificial Intelligence (GAI) can help teachers create innovative educational content and provide a variety of valuable information and resources. In this chapter we present a study whose aim was to analyse and evaluate the perceptions of students regarding educational practices and resources developed with AI tools and used in Portuguese classes. In order to find out what the students think about the potential and challenges associated with integrating GAI technologies into the teaching and learning process, we used a mixed focus (qualitative and quantitative) and collected data through questionnaires and an interview. The data collected reveals that students highlight the transformative potential of GAI in the educational process and its benefits for educational success in the Portuguese lessons. However, they also recognise the potential risks and challenges for students when it comes to using GAI responsibly in the classroom, and the need to know what GAI is and its potential in learning and to learn how to better interact with these generative technologies.

These steps are crucial for enhancing mathematics education and preparing students for technology-rich future.

The integration of Artificial Intelligence (AI) in mathematics education represents a significant advance, with the potential to transform traditional pedagogical approaches. This study analyzes the perception of prospective Primary Education teachers on the use of AI in mathematics education, based on a qualitative analysis performed with a sample of 64 pre-service teachers of the Primary Education Degree. The results reflect a generally positive attitude towards AI, highlighting its capacity to personalize learning, implement innovative methodologies and enhance the educational process. However, key issues are also identified, such as the need to provide adequate access to these technologies and the importance of appropriate teacher training. In addition, the need to integrate AI gradually in teacher training programs and into the teaching of different mathematical contents is underlined, in order to prepare prospective teachers for an effective use of these tools in the classroom.

This study examines how emotions and motivation shape computer science (CS) pathways in Greek upper secondary education at a time when AI skills are increasingly essential. Using the control–value theory of achievement emotions and the Science Motivation Questionnaire II, data were collected from 132 students across two curricular tracks: applied ICT in A class and algorithmic programming in B class. Findings show that while enjoyment decreased during CS tasks, pride increased and shame declined, indicating that engagement fostered accomplishment despite initial frustration. Emotional and motivational profiles were largely similar across curricula, with A class students reporting higher grade-related motivation. Gender differences were modest but underscore the importance of equitable curriculum design. The results highlight the need for CS curricula that balance cognitive challenge with positive emotional experiences, thereby strengthening resilience, self-efficacy, and motivation to pursue CS pathways in an AI-driven era.

Preface

The rapid evolution of artificial intelligence (AI) is transforming education at every level—from early childhood classrooms to higher education and specialized learning environments. As AI technologies become increasingly embedded in instructional design, assessment, student support, and institutional policy, educators face both unprecedented opportunities and complex responsibilities. *Teacher Perspectives and Responsible Practice for Integrating AI in the Classroom* brings together international scholarship to examine how AI can be thoughtfully, ethically, and effectively integrated into teaching and learning.

This volume places teachers at the center of the AI conversation. While technological innovation often dominates public discourse, meaningful integration depends on educators' professional judgment, pedagogical expertise, and ethical awareness. The chapters in this collection explore AI not as a replacement for human instruction, but as a collaborative partner—one that can personalize learning, enhance creativity, support differentiation, and expand access, while also raising critical concerns regarding privacy, equity, bias, academic integrity, and emotional development.

Across diverse cultural and educational contexts, contributors examine both emerging innovations and grounded classroom realities. From agentic systems that act with autonomy and contextual awareness, to generative AI tools that reshape content creation and assessment, this book offers a balanced perspective that moves beyond technological hype toward responsible, evidence-informed practice.

CHAPTER OVERVIEW

Chapter 1 explores the emergence of agentic AI systems capable of autonomous, context-aware, and goal-directed interaction. The chapter examines how such systems may redefine educational roles, emphasizing collaborative human–AI partnerships that influence cognitive, social, and affective dimensions of learning.

Chapter 2 identifies the technical, pedagogical, and organizational drivers necessary for successful AI implementation. A conceptual framework is proposed to align infrastructure, teacher readiness, ethical standards, and instructional objectives.

Chapter 3 investigates students' perceptions of generative AI in classroom practice, highlighting its transformative potential alongside concerns related to responsible use, literacy, and ethical awareness.

Chapter 4 examines policy, pedagogy, and institutional responsibility in integrating generative AI. Issues of academic integrity, data privacy, bias, and over-reliance are addressed alongside structured approaches to responsible implementation.

Chapter 5 analyzes the growing concerns around student data collection and surveillance. The chapter reviews regulatory frameworks such as Family Educational Rights and Privacy Act and General Data Protection Regulation, while exploring technical solutions including differential privacy and federated learning.

Chapter 6 evaluates the use of AI tools in designing learning situations with pre-service teachers. Findings emphasize efficiency and support benefits while reaffirming the irreplaceable relational and creative role of the teacher.

Chapter 7 explores how AI tools can enhance personalized learning for students with cognitive, behavioral, and sensory needs, while addressing ethical complexity and emotional nuance in special education contexts.

Chapter 8 investigates teacher perspectives on differentiation, creativity, and inclusion in mixed-ability classrooms. The chapter underscores the importance of socio-pedagogical frameworks over techno-optimistic narratives.

Chapter 9 discusses personalized and adaptive learning systems in mathematics, identifying barriers such as infrastructure limitations and teacher readiness while advocating strategic adoption and professional development.

Chapter 10 analyzes how future educators perceive AI integration, emphasizing the importance of gradual implementation within teacher preparation programs.

Chapter 11 examines how emotional and motivational factors shape student engagement in computer science education, highlighting the need for curricula that balance cognitive challenge with positive achievement emotions.

Chapter 12 synthesizes empirical research to identify trends in AI literacy, personalization, assessment practices, ethical use, and professional development, offering a comprehensive overview of teacher experiences.

Chapter 13 provides comparative insights into AI integration across national contexts, highlighting shared challenges and contextual differences in teacher preparation and classroom implementation.

Chapter 14 surveys emerging technologies, including intelligent tutoring systems, learning analytics, and machine learning applications, while critically examining ethical considerations and the digital divide.

Collectively, the chapters in this volume affirm that the future of AI in education is not determined by algorithms alone, but by the professional wisdom, ethical commitments, and reflective practices of teachers. Responsible integration requires more than access to tools—it demands critical literacy, equitable infrastructure, robust policy frameworks, and sustained professional development. By centering teacher perspectives and foregrounding ethical considerations, this book contributes to a growing body of scholarship that seeks not merely to adopt AI, but to shape its role in education with care, integrity, and a commitment to human flourishing.

Stamatios Papadakis
University of Crete, Greece

Chapter 1
Agentic AI in Education

Georgios Lampropoulos
http://orcid.org/0000-0002-5719-2125
University of Nicosia, Cyprus

Jesús López-Belmonte
http://orcid.org/0000-0003-0823-3370
University of Granada, Spain

Santiago Pozo-Sánchez
http://orcid.org/0000-0001-8125-4990
University of Granada, Spain

José-Antonio Marín-Marín
http://orcid.org/0000-0001-8623-4796
University of Granada, Spain

ABSTRACT

Agentic AI systems can engage in meaningful human-like interactions, are autonomous and context-aware, automate processes, and present goal-oriented behaviors. They initiate actions based on their goals, state, and knowledge, and make informed decisions using data, contextual information, and environmental cues with limited intervention and supervision. They are designed to adapt to their environment, may demonstrate sophisticated reasoning capabilities, and act proactively with a sense of agency, autonomy, intentionality, and rationality. The chapter results reveal that agentic AI can reshape educational structure and roles with the co presence of education stakeholders and AI tools becoming integral to teaching and learning. Agentic AI marks a conceptual and practical shift of the role of AI in education as it emphasizes the creation of collaborative, adaptive, and intelligent systems that

DOI: 10.4018/979-8-2600-0101-1.ch001

act as partners with shared agency. Agentic AI can impact the affective, cognitive, and social dimensions of learning and create engaging, effective, and personalized educational experiences.

INTRODUCTION

Due to the educational benefits it can yield, artificial intelligence (AI) is increasingly being used in teaching and learning activities (L. Chen et al., 2020). As such, the research into the use of AI in education is also increasing rapidly (Hinojo-Lucena et al., 2019; Song & Wang, 2020). Studies have highlighted the ability of AI to enrich and transform the existing educational domain (Chiu et al., 2023). AI can be regarded as a "system's ability to correctly interpret external data, to learn from such data, and to use those learnings to achieve specific goals and tasks through flexible adaptation" (Kaplan & Haenlein, 2019, p. 1). AI systems act in an autonomous, intelligent, sophisticated, and rational manner while being able to perceive their environment, interact, communicate, and make decisions and predictions (Duan et al., 2019, 2019; Haenlein & Kaplan, 2019; Stone et al., 2016). Specifically, AI systems are modeled after the human nervous system and as a result, they simulate human cognitive processes, including their ability to communicate, act, learn, and reason (Brynjolfsson & Mcafee, 2017; Ertel, 2018; Li & Du, 2017). As this technology can bring changes to both teaching and learning practices and promote the redesign of knowledge, culture, and cognition (Holmes et al., 2020; Hwang et al., 2020; Pedro et al., 2019), it is becoming increasingly important to cultivate education stakeholders' AI literacy and digital literacy skills (Mustafa et al., 2024).

AI is greatly affecting teaching and learning through the wide variety of applications it offers. These include the use of Generative AI tools to generate educational material (Samala et al., 2025), intelligent data analytics for tracking and assessing learner performance (Cukurova, 2025), recommendation systems that suggest personalized learning resources (Urdaneta-Ponte et al., 2021), chatbots that provide instant feedback and guidance (Hwang & Chang, 2023; Moreno-Guerrero et al., 2022), and educational robotics that support hands-on and interactive learning experiences (Lampropoulos & Papadakis, 2025). While AI systems are used in different ways in education, their true potential arises when they are developed using human-centered design approaches. Specifically, AI systems, when aligned with learner needs and pedagogical goals, can provide personalized, adaptive, and engaging learning experiences and adjust to learners' needs and preferences which, in turn, can bring about increased learning outcomes (Topali et al., 2025; Wang et al., 2024). Recent studies have revealed benefits and challenges that the use of AI in education can bring about (L. Chen et al., 2020; X. Chen et al., 2022; Chiu et al., 2023; Lin et al., 2023; Zhai et al., 2021).

Given the advancements in the field, the use of AI agents in educational settings is gaining ground. Educational AI agents, such as pedagogical agents, conversational agents, social robots, and intelligent tutoring systems, have different forms, characteristics, and functionality but all focus on simulating human-like behaviors, providing personalized experiences, supporting educators, and improving students' learning experience in both formal and informal settings. As AI agents are being more commonly adopted in education, it is important to examine the shift in teaching and learning practices when using such tools. In this context, agentic AI shows great potential to improve the field of education. As a result, this chapter aims to provide an overview of agentic AI in education. Specifically, the chapter defines agentic AI and its educational role and offers an overview of key concepts, technologies, and educational implications.

AGENTIC AI IN EDUCATION

As AI continues to advance, more sophisticated systems are being developed for educational contexts. Agentic AI is a significant advancement in the field. Agentic AI systems can engage in meaningful human-like interactions, are autonomous and context-aware, automate processes, present goal-oriented behaviors, and make informed decisions based on data, contextual information, and environmental cues with limited intervention and supervision. Hence, they can perceive their surrounding environment, process incoming data, engage in reasoning, and autonomously initiate actions based on their goals, state, and knowledge. Specifically, agentic AI systems are designed to independently adapt to their environment, demonstrate sophisticated reasoning capabilities, and act proactively with a sense of agency, autonomy, intentionality, and rationality.

Agentic AI systems can aid in the development of more personalized and flexible learning environments that dynamically adapt to learners' and educators' needs. Additionally, they offer several benefits, including managing complex tasks, providing data-driven insights and feedback, offering effective scaffolds, tailoring instruction, automating administrative tasks, enhancing course and material development, supporting diverse learning pathways, and acting as co-participants in the educational process. Hence, the introduction of agentic AI systems in education can positively influence all education stakeholders.

Agentic AI systems highlight a conceptual and practical shift regarding the role of AI in education as they emphasize the creation of collaborative, adaptive, and intelligent systems that act as partners with shared agency in the educational process rather than automated, passive systems that users simply interact with. Additionally, in comparison to other traditional tools, agentic AI systems have a more proactive and participatory role in the educational process and are not bound by the limitations that characterize other AI tools and as such, they represent a transformative paradigm that can reform pedagogical strategies and educational practices. However, agentic AI does not replace educational stakeholders but rather supports and augments their role.

As a result, the need to reconsider existing pedagogical methods is highlighted as agentic AI will bring about changes to the educational structure and roles with the co-presence of education stakeholders and AI tools becoming an integral part of teaching and learning. Within these emerging human-AI environments, new collaborative dynamics will be developed, AI tools will be more commonly used, and responsibilities will be shared between education stakeholders and AI systems.

Agentic AI brings new applications and opportunities across domains that were not previously possible with other AI tools (Murugesan, 2025; Schneider, 2025). Recent studies have highlighted the importance of human-AI interaction (Amershi et al., 2019) and the need to focus on enabling human-centered AI (Xu et al., 2021) and developing AI systems that can work in collaboration with humans (Wang et al., 2020). Agentic AI will play a crucial role in in shaping up an intelligent future (Hosseini & Seilani, 2025). Hence, it is important to consider the existing challenges and limitations, including ethical considerations, security and privacy issues, trust, transparency, bias, and accessibility, to safely, responsibly, and effectively integrate agentic AI into society and reap its benefits (Acharya et al., 2025; Shavit et al., 2023). Additionally, studies have commented upon the changes in terms of workflow that will be made when using agentic AI in educational settings (Kamalov et al., 2025) and the potential to empower students (Paul et al., 2024).

PEDAGOGICAL AGENTS

Pedagogical agents refer to entities that utilize computational units to support and facilitate the educational process, including instruction, information presentation, motivational support, and conversational provision (Schroeder & Craig, 2021; Siegle et al., 2023). Specifically, pedagogical agents are virtual, embodied, and autonomous entities used within multimedia learning environments to support educational processes and create meaningful face-to-face learning interactions (Heidig & Clarebout, 2011; Johnson et al., 2000; Schroeder & Adesope, 2014). These agents learn along with learners, mimic human-peer-like interaction to simulate social contexts and increase students' engagement, and can enrich traditional computer-based learning environments (Kim & Baylor, 2006a).

Pedagogical agents can be used in both formal and informal environments, can facilitate learning in most knowledge domains, and serve distinct instructional function through their various roles within learning environments, such as a peer companion, instructor, mentor, assistant, motivator, collaborator, and competitor (Baylor & Kim, 2005, 2005; Schroeder & Adesope, 2014; Siegle et al., 2023). Each role influences learners' learning differently, however, in all cases, pedagogical agents can lead to significant positive changes to their learning, including increased motivation, self-efficacy, and engagement as well as and improved content understanding (Baylor & Kim, 2005).

Due to their nature, pedagogical agents have social traits which, in turn, highlights the fact that when using pedagogical agents, there are socio-emotional and relational variables that should be considered as they have social effects and contribute toward social learning (Krämer & Bente, 2010). Hence, pedagogical agents can create a social agency environment which can increase learning effectiveness and, in turn, enhance students' interest and motivation (Schroeder & Adesope, 2014). As a result, the educational merits of pedagogical agents are supported by various social-cognitive theories (Kim & Baylor, 2006a).

Students express positive attitudes toward their use in education and show a preference for pedagogical agents when compared to non-agent-based interventions (Schroeder & Adesope, 2014). Additionally, students who learn via pedagogical agents demonstrate deeper learning (Baylor & Kim, 2005), improved learning and performance (Veletsianos & Russell, 2014), enhanced engagement (Moreno et al., 2001), and increased attention and interest in the learning process (Krämer & Bente, 2010). Additionally, pedagogical agents can influence students' learning motivation, knowledge acquisition, and knowledge retention (Guo & Goh, 2015).

As pedagogical agents are both affective and embodied, they are capable of eliciting emotional responses from users through multiple modalities (Guo & Goh, 2015) which, in turn, not only lead to increased learning outcomes for students but also help them overcome negative affect (Mumm & Mutlu, 2011). Moreover, due to their versatility and adaptability, pedagogical agents can serve a variety of educational purposes, provide students with cognitive support, and socially enrich the learning experience (Veletsianos & Russell, 2014). However, the integration of pedagogical agents into educational settings should be in line with the desired motivational and learning goals as pedagogical agents' competences and interactions type can affect students' learning outcomes (Kim & Baylor, 2006b).

Pedagogical agents can also be used within immersive learning environments to create virtual intelligent tutors. Virtual tutors have shown great potential to support the educational process (Hemachandran et al., 2022; Ward et al., 2011). By integrating pedagogical agents within extended reality environments, embodied, immersive, and intelligent tutoring systems that offer personalized learning experiences and result in increased learning outcomes can be created (Lampropoulos, 2023, 2025a).

INTRODUCTION INTELLIGENT TUTORING SYSTEMS

Intelligent tutoring systems provide adaptive and personalized learning experiences by tailoring instructional strategies, material, and activities to the requirements, preferences, skills, and progress of each individual learner (Keleş et al., 2009; Mousavinasab et al., 2021). By dynamically adjusting to learners' unique characteristics, including their learning pace, prior knowledge, cognitive abilities, needs, and performance, intelligent tutoring systems strive to provide educational experiences that replicate or exceed those provided by human tutors (Anderson et al., 1985; Sleeman & Brown, 1982).

Intelligent tutoring systems integrate several components, models, and knowledge types (Conati, 2009; Keleş et al., 2009; Xu et al., 2019) to provide students with computer-based learning environments that support them in acquiring domain-specific knowledge, as well as broader cognitive and metacognitive skills, across a wide variety of subjects and educational levels (Ma et al., 2014; Steenbergen-Hu & Cooper, 2014). They also offer interactive and student-centered learning experiences, provide real-time feedback, and support self-regulated learning (Graesser et al., 2018). To offer personalized learning, adaptive and context-aware support, and suitable pedagogical strategies that simulate those of a human tutor, intelligent tutoring systems capitalize on learner modeling to detect and track their cognitive and psychological state (Graesser et al., 2012; Shute & Zapata-Rivera, 2007).

Moreover, the effectiveness of intelligent tutoring systems depends is highly dependent upon a range of interrelated design and implementation factors that determine how well the system can support meaningful and personalized learning experiences (Hwang, 2003). Intelligent tutoring systems provide instant, individualized, and context-aware feedback that not only addresses learner mistakes but also promotes deeper understanding through suitable scaffolds (Gross et al., 2015). Additionally, they can detect, interpret, and respond to learners' affective states which significantly influence their engagement and learning outcomes (Frasson & Chalfoun, 2010). Finally, using affective computing mechanisms, intelligent tutoring systems can adapt their instructional strategies, material, and activities in real time to offer personalized learning which is aligned with learners' characteristics, such as preferences, learning styles, interests, skills, and knowledge (Crockett et al., 2017).

As far as learning outcomes are concerned, intelligent tutoring systems have shown comparable effectiveness to one-on-one human tutoring in well-structured domains (Kulik, 1994; VanLehn, 2006, 2011). In ill-defined domains, human tutors continue to outperform them (Gross et al., 2015). Nonetheless, in both cases, the use of intelligent tutoring systems has proven to be an effective learning method which results in students' achieving increased learning outcomes and engagement (Kulik & Fletcher, 2016; Ma et al., 2014; Steenbergen-Hu & Cooper, 2014; Xu et al., 2019). To fully reap the benefits of intelligent tutoring systems there are challenges and ethical considerations that need to be addressed (Albornoz-De Luise et al., 2024; Conati, 2009). Finally, it is important to ensure transparency and explainability within such systems.

GENERATIVE AI IN EDUCATION

Students' Among the various AI technologies, particular interest is shown in the use of generative artificial intelligence (Baïdoo-Anu & Ansah, 2023; Bozkurt et al., 2023). Generative AI refers to AI models that have been specifically designed and trained to produce seemingly new content (Feuerriegel et al., 2024). Specifically, generative AI can be characterized as a technology that "*(i) leverages deep learning models to (ii) generate human-like content (e.g., images, words) in response to (iii) complex and varied prompts (e.g., languages, instructions, questions)*" (Lim et al., 2023, p. 2). The flexibility and ability of generative AI to generate multimedia content has resulted in it being used in various domains, transforming and improving them. These models also have a social aspect as they can communicate with each other and with humans (Sharples, 2023). This fact has enabled generative AI to have a wide range of applications and it being used across disciplines (Fui-Hoon Nah et al., 2023; Ooi et al., 2023).

As the advancements in generative AI are accelerating, the research regarding its use in educational settings increases (Bahroun et al., 2023). Generative AI is a capable technology that can provide collaborative learning opportunities, can improve accessibility, and is becoming more popular; yet, at the same time, it is dependent on other technologies and data, it can hinder the educational outcomes if not properly integrated, and as such, its use might be restricted (Lim et al., 2023). Although there are concerns raised, such as academic integrity issues and ethical and moral considerations, the use of generative AI can positively influence educational practices, has brought about new opportunities for both students and teachers (Giannakos et al., 2024; Kadaruddin, 2023; Lee et al., 2024), can promote personalized learning, enhance formative assessment (Baïdoo-Anu & Ansah, 2023; Mao et al., 2024), and offer faster and more tailored feedback (Su & Yang, 2023). Nonetheless, generative AI can significantly influence teaching practices and pedagogical approaches (Peres et al., 2023) and contribute to the reformation of education (Yu & Guo, 2023). It can generate diverse and personalized instructional materials which, in turn, enhances the accessibility and the quality of education and provide new methods of content creation and delivery as well as of assessment (Mittal et al., 2024). Hence, the role of generative AI in learning design is becoming more prominent (Alkhasawneh et al., 2025).

As teachers' initial views of new technologies can influence if and to what degree they adopt them in their practices, it is important to highlight that teachers express positive attitudes regarding the use of generative AI tools in education and consider that they can support them in their teaching practices (Kaplan-Rakowski et al., 2023). Similarly, students also express both positive attitudes and concerns regarding the integration of generative AI tools, but recognize the merits it can yield in terms of personalized learning (Chan & Hu, 2023).

However, despite the affordances of generative AI, there are also challenges associated with its adoption and use in education (Wang et al., 2024). Specifically, there are several moral and ethical concerns about the use of generative AI in education which, in turn, highlights the need to ensure fairness and transparency in the models used (Al-kfairy et al., 2024; Michel-Villarreal et al., 2023). Ethics concerns can result in the development of AI ethical anxiety which can significantly influence students' willingness to use AI technologies in their learning (Zhu et al., 2025). Other challenges are related to data security and privacy, opacity, lack of explainability, bias, reliability, accountability, fairness, and lack of human-to-human interaction (Mittal et al., 2024; Yu & Guo, 2023). There are also limitations in terms of policy, economy, technology, and regulations (Fui-Hoon Nah et al., 2023; Sharples, 2023). Hence, it is important to carefully consider how to adopt generative AI in education and not to integrate it hastily into teaching and learning practices (Giannakos et al., 2024).

As a result, it is important for education stakeholders to stay informed about AI development (Lee et al., 2024), improve their AI literacy and prompt engineering skills (Mustafa et al., 2024), and consider the technological limitation when using generative AI tools (Lim et al., 2023). Additionally, emphasis should be placed on enhancing human-AI collaboration (Mittal et al., 2024), designing AI-enhanced curriculum (Bahroun et al., 2023), and on developing new teaching and learning practices that utilize generative AI tools (Chiu, 2024a). Moreover, educational practices, guidelines, frameworks, and policies need to be developed that emphasize the equitable, responsible, and ethical integration of generative AI and that consider education stakeholders' perspectives (Chan & Hu, 2023; Chiu, 2024b; Kadaruddin, 2023; Michel-Villarreal et al., 2023). Finally, improving the quantity and quality of datasets, ensuring transparency and high levels of explainability, and creating relevant regulations and laws is required for the wider adoption of AI and generative AI in education (Lampropoulos, 2023; Yu & Guo, 2023).

CONVERSATIONAL AGENTS IN EDUCATION

In educational settings, pedagogical conversational agents constitute autonomous software-based systems that co-habit learning environments with learners, interact with them using natural language dialogs, and contribute toward the development of meaningful learning interactions (Clarizia et al., 2018; Hobert & Meyer von Wolff, 2019; Pérez-Marín, 2021). These agents use machine learning and deep learning models, computational linguistics techniques and natural language processing to identify, interpret, and respond to learners' statements through multimodal dialog-based interactions and socio-emotional multimodal behaviors (Feine et al., 2019; Lester et al., 2004; Ruane et al., 2019). Specifically, conversational agents simulate the way humans interact and communicate (Clarizia et al., 2018; Dis et al., 2023; Ranoliya et al., 2017), have empathic conversational capabilities (Ortega-Ochoa et al., 2024), and monitor, identify, assess, understand, and respond to human language and cues (Feine et al., 2019; Gill et al., 2024; Graesser et al., 2014; Sandu & Gide, 2019).

Conversational agents support face-to-face, online, and blended learning across education levels and in various domains (D. Song et al., 2017; Wollny et al., 2021). However, in terms of learning outcomes, conversational agents have a greater impact on higher education students in comparison to primary and secondary education students (Wu & Yu, 2024). They support students' learning, aid teachers, enhance instructional quality, create new assessment methods, (Yildirim-Erbasli et al., 2025) and provide different forms of feedback which is essential to enhance students' learning outcomes and perceptions (Ortega-Ochoa et al., 2024). Additionally, they can create interactive learning scenarios which promote students' active and emotional engagement (Weber et al., 2021).

In line with general users, education stakeholders also are fond of human-like interactions offered by conversational agents (Khosrawi-Rad et al., 2022) and express positive attitudes toward their use in education (Stöhr et al., 2024; Yildirim-Erbasli et al., 2025). Additionally, educational stakeholders highly regard the benefits that can be yielded through their integration in education not only in terms of teaching and learning but in other aspects of education as well (Labadze et al., 2023; Okonkwo & Ade-Ibijola, 2021).

Moreover, instructional approaches and activities that adopt conversational agents should focus on adopting suitable human-computer interaction guidelines, set appropriate pedagogical critcria, and consider the instructional method that is embedded within the agent (Pérez-Marín, 2021). Despite the existing limitations, conversational agents provide new opportunities in the educational domain (Kooli, 2023). Due to the rapid advancements in the domain of AI, it is expected that conversational agents will evolve significantly by becoming more intelligent and capable of better understanding the human language and cues; hence it can be inferred that conversational agents have yet to reach their full potential in education (Khosrawi-Rad et al., 2022).

Conversational agents, such as chatbots, have shown great potential to transform the education system, by providing several benefits (Deng & Yu, 2023; Okonkwo & Ade-Ibijola, 2021) and by offering unique opportunities to increase accessibility and scalability (Labadze et al., 2023; Wollny et al., 2021). Conversational agents can offer engaging and personalized experiences and support all education stakeholders, including students, teachers, and administration (Kuhail et al., 2023; Yusuf et al., 2025). These agents can simulate human tutoring, adopt suitable pedagogical strategies (Graesser et al., 2014), and be used both as tutors and peer learners, although more emphasis is currently being put on their use as tutors (Kuhail et al., 2023).

Through their easy-to-use interfaces, their adaptive experiences, and their natural interactions (Winkler et al., 2020; Winkler & Soellner, 2018), conversational agents can be an effective tool to assist students (Clarizia et al., 2018) due to their ability to offer personalized support and address students' concerns as well as to recommend suitable content and adapt the material to students' preferences (Gubareva & Lopes, 2020; Khosrawi-Rad et al., 2022). Additionally, these tools can offer rapid, meaningful, and tailored feedback, enable reflective practice, enrich assessment and monitoring, and support digital skills development (Labadze et al., 2023; Okonkwo & Ade-Ibijola, 2021; Yusuf et al., 2025). Conversational agents can also promote interpersonal communication and learning, support self-regulated learning and personal consultation, and offer deep insights into users' behaviors (Hwang & Chang, 2023; Kuhail et al., 2023). Finally, these tools support scaffolding, enable dynamic instructional generation, support collaborative learning, and can act as efficient teaching assistants and peers which, in turn, can enhance students' learning understanding, productivity, and experience (Gill et al., 2024; Sandu & Gide, 2019; Winkler et al., 2020; Winkler & Soellner, 2018).

Furthermore, conversational agents can affect students' lives and social discourse in general (Ruane et al., 2019). Hence, emphasis should be placed on how to effectively design conversational agents as they have both functional and social roles (Clark et al., 2019) and on developing policies, design principles, and strategies that highlight their emphatic abilities and address the existing challenges of conversational agents in education (Akpan et al., 2025; Ortega-Ochoa et al., 2024). These challenges involve aspects, such as reliability, maintainability, scalability, and accuracy, performance, and security (Labadze et al., 2023; Lester et al., 2004; Okonkwo & Ade-Ibijola, 2021) as well as technical difficulties, such as natural language processing challenges (Clarizia et al., 2018), difficulties in comprehending and responding to human cues (Bozkurt, 2023), as well as inadequate or insufficient dataset training, and lack of reliance on usability heuristics (Kuhail et al., 2023). Other important issues in the educational domain that need to be addressed are related to ethical concerns and dilemmas, privacy, assessment issues, academic abuse and misuse, misinformation, hallucinations, transparency, and bias (Akpan et al., 2025; Gill et al., 2024; Kooli, 2023). Hence, there are several aspects that need to be consider to effectively adopt and integrate conversational agents into educational settings, including their pedagogical purposes and applications, their technological functions, and their social implications (Yusuf et al., 2025).

SOCIAL ROBOTS IN EDUCATION

AI greatly contributes to the advancements in the field of educational robotics, particularly in the development of social robots which are designed to interact with learners in human-like ways (X. Chen et al., 2020). By capitalizing on AI technologies, such as natural language processing, machine learning, computer vision, and affective computing, social robots can perceive, interpret, and respond to learners' cues which, in turn, render the educational experience more interactive, personalized, and dynamic (Lampropoulos, 2025b). Given the diversity in their design, capabilities, and pedagogical roles, social robots can influence teaching and learning processes in different ways, such as being tutors, peer collaborators, facilitators, or emotional companions (Leite et al., 2013; Mahdi et al., 2022).

Social robots are social entities that are characterized by their anthropomorphism and can engage on a social level (Hegel et al., 2009; Lampropoulos, 2025b). They are also considered as embodied agents which can communicate, interact, understand, and relate to humans, co-exist with humans, and learn from one another (Breazeal, 2004; Fong et al., 2003). Finally, social robots are affective entities that are defined by their social interface, social evocation and receptiveness, and sociability (Breazeal, 2003; Kirby et al., 2010). Given their anthropomorphic design and their ability to communicate in an interpersonal manner, emphasis is being placed on their socio-cognitive skills, social-emotional intelligence, and embodiment (Breazeal et al., 2016). These attributes positively influence education stakeholders' attitudes toward social robots as they express favorable viewpoints (Hegel et al., 2009; Nitto et al., 2017). However, to effectively adopt and use social robots in education, their development and integration should abide by human social norms and strict regulations and follow suitable guidelines and standards (Kirby et al., 2010; Mahdi et al., 2022; Woo et al., 2021).

Social robots can be used as both tutors and peer learners in both formal and informal settings and their embodiment and physical presence render them capable of supporting the development of both cognitive and affective outcomes (Belpaeme et al., 2018; Belpaeme & Tanaka, 2021; Johal, 2020). Social robots social and physical presence is a key component to the educational value that they have when compared to AI technologies that only have a virtual presence (Lampropoulos & Papadakis, 2025). Recent studies that focused on their use in educational settings have further highlighted their potential to support both students and teachers (Barakova et al., 2023; Conti et al., 2020; Woo et al., 2021) and commented on the challenges, moral considerations, and ethical concerns (Barakova et al., 2023; Belpaeme & Tanaka, 2021; Smakman et al., 2021).

CONCLUSION

AI is rapidly transforming the educational sector. Tools such as pedagogical agents, intelligent tutoring systems, generative AI, conversational agents, and social robots have already demonstrated their value in enhancing teaching and learning. However, among the various AI tools, agentic AI systems in particular show great potential to become an integral part of education and modify the existing educational roles and structures by changing how teaching and learning are conceptualized, delivered, and experienced. Agentic AI systems driven by agency, reasoning, context-awareness, and autonomy act independently, adapt to their environment, proactively support both learners and educators and instead of focusing on simple automation, they become active collaborators, enriching instruction, managing educational tasks, and personalizing the learning experience.

Agentic AI systems focus on the shared agency between humans and AI. Hence, they aim to create human-AI learning environments in which the co-presence of and collaboration between AI tools and education stakeholders are required and responsibilities are shared between them. By simulating human-like interaction and supporting affective, cognitive, and social dimensions of learning, agentic AI contributes to the creation of more engaging, effective, and personalized educational experiences.

Despite the benefits that can be yielded through the adoption of agentic AI systems, such as personalized instruction and guidance, enhanced learning outcomes, and automation of routine tasks, there are challenges that need to be examined and addressed. These challenges are related to technical limitations, privacy and security issues, ethical concerns, transparency, equity, explainability, and bias. Other important concerns are related to the over-reliance on AI, education stakeholders' AI literacy, teacher agency, reduction in human-centered pedagogical relationships, equipment disparities, and accessibility which, in turn, could increase the digital divide. Hence, it is important to carefully design how to introduce and integrate AI tools into educational settings, focus on adopting multidisciplinary perspectives, and assess the educational, societal, technological, and economic impacts that the use of AI tools can have when used in education.

Therefore, there is a need to develop robust and ethically sound frameworks, guidelines, and policies. Future research should focus on evaluating the influence of AI interventions on students' cognitive, emotional, and social development, assessing the embodiment of the AI agents, and monitoring how students interact with them when compared to human educators. It is equally important to evaluate and develop education stakeholders' AI literacy. Finally, it is important to identify the most suitable pedagogical strategies and educational practices to effectively use AI in education and to explore how effective human-AI collaborations can materialize.

ACKNOWLEDGEMENTS

This study arises within the framework of the research project of the Central University of Ecuador, titled Dynamics of the Incorporation of Artificial Intelligence (AI) at the Central University of Ecuador, period 2023–2025 (Code: DI-CONV-2023-037).

REFERENCES

Acharya, D. B., Kuppan, K., & Divya, B. (2025). Agentic AI: Autonomous intelligence for complex Goals—A comprehensive survey. *IEEE Access : Practical Innovations, Open Solutions*, *13*, 18912–18936. DOI: 10.1109/ACCESS.2025.3532853

Akpan, I. J., Kobara, Y. M., Owolabi, J., Akpan, A. A., & Offodile, O. F. (2025). Conversational and generative artificial intelligence and human–chatbot interaction in education and research. *International Transactions in Operational Research*, *32*(3), 1251–1281. DOI: 10.1111/itor.13522

Al-kfairy, M., Mustafa, D., Kshetri, N., Insiew, M., & Alfandi, O. (2024). Ethical challenges and solutions of generative AI: An interdisciplinary perspective. *Informatics (MDPI)*, *11*(3), 58. DOI: 10.3390/informatics11030058

Albornoz-De Luise, R. S., Arnau-González, P., Serrano-Mamolar, A., Solera-Monforte, S., & Wu, Y. (2024). *Balancing innovation with ethics.*, DOI: 10.1002/9781394257744.ch11

Alkhasawneh, S. N., Lampropoulos, G., & Hernández-Leo, D. (2025). Generative AI in Learning Design: A Systematic Review. In *International Conference on Artificial Intelligence in Education* (pp. 17-30). Springer, Cham. DOI: 10.1007/978-3-031-98459-4_2

Amershi, S., Weld, D., Vorvoreanu, M., Fourney, A., Nushi, B., Collisson, P., Suh, J., Iqbal, S., Bennett, P. N., Inkpen, K., Teevan, J., Kikin-Gil, R., & Horvitz, E. (2019). Guidelines for Human-AI interaction. *Proceedings of the 2019 CHI Conference on Human Factors in Computing Systems*. DOI: 10.1145/3290605.3300233

Anderson, J. R., Boyle, C. F., & Reiser, B. J. (1985). Intelligent tutoring systems. *Science*, *228*(4698), 456–462. DOI: 10.1126/science.228.4698.456

Bahroun, Z., Anane, C., Ahmed, V., & Zacca, A. (2023). Transforming education: A comprehensive review of generative artificial intelligence in educational settings through bibliometric and content analysis. *Sustainability (Basel), 15*(17), 12983. DOI: 10.3390/su151712983

Baïdoo-Anu, D., & Ansah, L. O. (2023). Education in the era of generative artificial intelligence (AI): Understanding the potential benefits of ChatGPT in promoting teaching and learning. *Journal of AI, 7*(1), 52–62. DOI: 10.61969/jai.1337500

Barakova, E., Väänänen, K., Kaipainen, K., & Markopoulos, P. (2023). Benefits, challenges and research recommendations for social robots in education and learning: A Meta-Review. *2023 32nd IEEE International Conference on Robot and Human Interactive Communication (RO-MAN)*, 2555–2561. DOI: 10.1109/RO-MAN57019.2023.10309345

Baylor, A. L., & Kim, Y. (2005). Simulating instructional roles through pedagogical agents. *International Journal of Artificial Intelligence in Education, 15*(2), 95–115. DOI: 10.3233/IRG-2005-15(2)02

Belpaeme, T., Kennedy, J., Ramachandran, A., Scassellati, B., & Tanaka, F. (2018). Social robots for education: A review. *Science Robotics, 3*(21), eaat5954. Advance online publication. DOI: 10.1126/scirobotics.aat5954

Belpaeme, T., & Tanaka, F. (2021). Social robots as educators. In *OECD digital education outlook 2021 pushing the frontiers with artificial intelligence, blockchain and robots: Pushing the frontiers with artificial intelligence, blockchain and robots* (p. 143). OECD Publishing Paris. DOI: 10.1787/589b283f-en

Bozkurt, A. (2023). Unleashing the potential of generative AI, conversational agents and chatbots in educational praxis: A systematic review and bibliometric analysis of GenAI in education. In *Open Praxis* (No. 4; Vol. 15, pp. 261–270). International Council for Open; Distance Education Oslo, Norway. DOI: 10.55982/openpraxis.15.4.609

Bozkurt, A., Junhong, X., Lambert, S., Pazurek, A., Crompton, H., Koseoglu, S., Farrow, R., Bond, M., Nerantzi, C., & Honeychurch, S.. (2023). Speculative futures on ChatGPT and generative artificial intelligence (AI): A collective reflection from the educational landscape. *Asian Journal of Distance Education, 18*(1), 53–130.

Breazeal, C. (2003). Toward sociable robots. *Robotics and Autonomous Systems, 42*(3-4), 167–175. DOI: 10.1016/S0921-8890(02)00373-1

Breazeal, C. (2004). *Designing sociable robots*. MIT press.

Breazeal, C., Dautenhahn, K., & Kanda, T. (2016). Social robotics. In *Springer handbooks* (pp. 1935–1972). DOI: 10.1007/978-3-319-32552-1_72

Brynjolfsson, E., & Mcafee, A. (2017). Artificial intelligence, for real. *Harvard Business Review, 1*, 1–31.

Chan, C. K. Y., & Hu, W. (2023). Students' voices on generative AI: Perceptions, benefits, and challenges in higher education. *International Journal of Educational Technology in Higher Education, 20*(1), 43. Advance online publication. DOI: 10.1186/s41239-023-00411-8

Chen, L., Chen, P., & Lin, Z. (2020). Artificial intelligence in education: A review. *IEEE Access : Practical Innovations, Open Solutions, 8*, 75264–75278. DOI: 10.1109/ACCESS.2020.2988510

Chen, X., Xie, H., & Hwang, G.-J. (2020). A multi-perspective study on artificial intelligence in education: Grants, conferences, journals, software tools, institutions, and researchers. *Computers and Education: Artificial Intelligence, 1*, 100005. DOI: 10.1016/j.caeai.2020.100005

Chen, X., Zou, D., Xie, H., Cheng, G., & Liu, C. (2022). Two decades of artificial intelligence in education. *Journal of Educational Technology & Society, 25*(1), 28–47.

Chiu, T. K. F. (2024a). Future research recommendations for transforming higher education with generative AI. *Computers and Education: Artificial Intelligence, 6*, 100197. DOI: 10.1016/j.caeai.2023.100197

Chiu, T. K. F. (2024b). The impact of generative AI (GenAI) on practices, policies and research direction in education: A case of ChatGPT and midjourney. *Interactive Learning Environments, 32*(10), 6187–6203. DOI: 10.1080/10494820.2023.2253861

Chiu, T. K. F., Xia, Q., Zhou, X., Chai, C. S., & Cheng, M. (2023). Systematic literature review on opportunities, challenges, and future research recommendations of artificial intelligence in education. *Computers and Education: Artificial Intelligence, 4*, 100118. DOI: 10.1016/j.caeai.2022.100118

Clarizia, F., Colace, F., Lombardi, M., Pascale, F., & Santaniello, D. (2018). Chatbot: An education support system for student. In *Lecture notes in computer science* (pp. 291–302). DOI: 10.1007/978-3-030-01689-0_23

Clark, L., Pantidi, N., Cooney, O., Doyle, P., Garaialde, D., Edwards, J., Spillane, B., Gilmartin, E., Murad, C., Munteanu, C., Wade, V., & Cowan, B. R. (2019). What makes a good conversation? *Proceedings of the 2019 CHI Conference on Human Factors in Computing Systems*, 1–12. DOI: 10.1145/3290605.3300705

Conati, C. (2009). Intelligent tutoring systems: New challenges and directions. *Twenty-First International Joint Conference on Artificial Intelligence*.

Conti, D., Cirasa, C., Di Nuovo, S., & Di Nuovo, A. (2020). Robot, tell me a tale! *Interaction Studies: Social Behaviour and Communication in Biological and Artificial Systems*, *21*(2), 220–242. DOI: 10.1075/is.18024.con

Crockett, K., Latham, A., & Whitton, N. (2017). On predicting learning styles in conversational intelligent tutoring systems using fuzzy decision trees. *International Journal of Human-Computer Studies*, *97*, 98–115. DOI: 10.1016/j.ijhcs.2016.08.005

Cukurova, M. (2025). The interplay of learning, analytics and artificial intelligence in education: A vision for hybrid intelligence. *British Journal of Educational Technology*, *56*(2), 469–488. DOI: 10.1111/bjet.13514

Deng, X., & Yu, Z. (2023). A Meta-Analysis and systematic review of the effect of chatbot technology use in sustainable education. *Sustainability (Basel)*, *15*(4), 2940. DOI: 10.3390/su15042940

Duan, Y., Edwards, J. S., & Dwivedi, Y. K. (2019). Artificial intelligence for decision making in the era of big data - evolution, challenges and research agenda. *International Journal of Information Management*, *48*, 63–71. DOI: 10.1016/j.ijinfomgt.2019.01.021

Ertel, W. (2018). *Introduction to artificial intelligence*. Springer.

Feine, J., Gnewuch, U., Morana, S., & Maedche, A. (2019). A taxonomy of social cues for conversational agents. *International Journal of Human-Computer Studies*, *132*, 138–161. DOI: 10.1016/j.ijhcs.2019.07.009

Feuerriegel, S., Hartmann, J., Janiesch, C., & Zschech, P. (2024). Generative AI. *Business & Information Systems Engineering*, *66*(1), 111–126. DOI: 10.1007/s12599-023-00834-7

Fong, T., Nourbakhsh, I., & Dautenhahn, K. (2003). A survey of socially interactive robots. *Robotics and Autonomous Systems*, *42*(3-4), 143–166. DOI: 10.1016/S0921-8890(02)00372-X

Frasson, C., & Chalfoun, P. (2010). Managing learner's affective states in intelligent tutoring systems. In *Studies in computational intelligence* (pp. 339–358). DOI: 10.1007/978-3-642-14363-2_17

Fui-Hoon Nah, F., Zheng, R., Cai, J., Siau, K., & Chen, L. (2023). Generative AI and ChatGPT: Applications, challenges, and AI-human collaboration. *Journal of Information Technology Case and Application Research, 25*(3), 277–304. DOI: 10.1080/15228053.2023.2233814

Giannakos, M., Azevedo, R., Brusilovsky, P., Cukurova, M., Dimitriadis, Y., Hernandez-Leo, D., Järvelä, S., Mavrikis, M., & Rienties, B. (2024). The promise and challenges of generative AI in education. *Behaviour & Information Technology*, •••, 1–27. DOI: 10.1080/0144929X.2024.2394886

Gill, S. S., Xu, M., Patros, P., Wu, H., Kaur, R., Kaur, K., Fuller, S., Singh, M., Arora, P., Parlikad, A. K., Stankovski, V., Abraham, A., Ghosh, S. K., Lutfiyya, H., Kanhere, S. S., Bahsoon, R., Rana, O., Dustdar, S., Sakellariou, R., & Buyya, R. (2024). Transformative effects of ChatGPT on modern education: Emerging era of AI chatbots. *Internet of Things and Cyber-Physical Systems, 4*, 19–23. DOI: 10.1016/j.iotcps.2023.06.002

Graesser, A. C., Conley, M. W., & Olney, A. (2012). Intelligent tutoring systems. In *APA educational psychology handbook, vol 3: Application to learning and teaching*. (pp. 451–473). DOI: 10.1037/13275-018

Graesser, A. C., Hu, X., & Sottilare, R. (2018). Intelligent tutoring systems. In *International handbook of the learning sciences* (pp. 246–255). DOI: 10.4324/9781315617572-24

Graesser, A. C., Li, H., & Forsyth, C. (2014). Learning by communicating in natural language with conversational agents. *Current Directions in Psychological Science, 23*(5), 374–380. DOI: 10.1177/0963721414540680

Gross, S., Mokbel, B., Hammer, B., & Pinkwart, N. (2015). Learning feedback in intelligent tutoring systems. *KI - Künstliche Intelligenz, 29*(4), 413–418. DOI: 10.1007/s13218-015-0367-y

Gubareva, R., & Lopes, R. P. (2020). Virtual assistants for learning: A systematic literature review. *Proceedings of the 12th International Conference on Computer Supported Education*, 97–103. DOI: 10.5220/0009417600970103

Guo, Y. R., & Goh, D. H.-L. (2015). Affect in embodied pedagogical agents. *Journal of Educational Computing Research, 53*(1), 124–149. DOI: 10.1177/0735633115588774

Haenlein, M., & Kaplan, A. (2019). A brief history of artificial intelligence: On the past, present, and future of artificial intelligence. *California Management Review, 61*(4), 5–14. DOI: 10.1177/0008125619864925

Hegel, F., Muhl, C., Wrede, B., Hielscher-Fastabend, M., & Sagerer, G. (2009). Understanding social robots. *2009 Second International Conferences on Advances in Computer-Human Interactions*, 169–174. DOI: 10.1109/ACHI.2009.51

Heidig, S., & Clarebout, G. (2011). Do pedagogical agents make a difference to student motivation and learning? *Educational Research Review*, *6*(1), 27–54. DOI: 10.1016/j.edurev.2010.07.004

Hemachandran, K., Verma, P., Pareek, P., Arora, N., Rajesh Kumar, K. V., Ahanger, T. A., Pise, A. A., & Ratna, R. (2022). Artificial intelligence: A universal virtual tool to augment tutoring in higher education. *Computational Intelligence and Neuroscience*, *2022*, 1–8. DOI: 10.1155/2022/1410448

Hinojo-Lucena, F.-J., Aznar-Díaz, I., Cáceres-Reche, M.-P., & Romero-Rodríguez, J.-M. (2019). Artificial intelligence in higher education: A bibliometric study on its impact in the scientific literature. *Education Sciences*, *9*(1), 51. DOI: 10.3390/educsci9010051

Hobert, S., & Meyer von Wolff, R. (2019). Say hello to your new automated tutor–a structured literature review on pedagogical conversational agents. *Proceedings of the 14th International Conference on Wirtschaftsinformatik*.

Holmes, W., Bialik, M., & Fadel, C. (2020). *Artificial intelligence in education: Promises and implications for teaching and learning*. Center for Curriculum Redesign.

Hosseini, S., & Seilani, H. (2025). The role of agentic AI in shaping a smart future: A systematic review. *Array (New York, N.Y.)*, *26*, 100399. DOI: 10.1016/j.array.2025.100399

Hwang, G.-J. (2003). A conceptual map model for developing intelligent tutoring systems. *Computers & Education*, *40*(3), 217–235. DOI: 10.1016/S0360-1315(02)00121-5

Hwang, G.-J., & Chang, C.-Y. (2023). A review of opportunities and challenges of chatbots in education. *Interactive Learning Environments*, *31*(7), 4099–4112. DOI: 10.1080/10494820.2021.1952615

Hwang, G.-J., Xie, H., Wah, B. W., & Gašević, D. (2020). Vision, challenges, roles and research issues of artificial intelligence in education. *Computers and Education: Artificial Intelligence*, *1*, 100001. DOI: 10.1016/j.caeai.2020.100001

Johal, W. (2020). Research trends in social robots for learning. *Current Robotics Reports*, *1*(3), 75–83. DOI: 10.1007/s43154-020-00008-3

Johnson, W. L., Rickel, J. W., & Lester, J. C.. (2000). Animated pedagogical agents: Face-to-face interaction in interactive learning environments. *International Journal of Artificial Intelligence in Education, 11*(1), 47–78.

Kadaruddin, K. (2023). Empowering education through generative AI: Innovative instructional strategies for tomorrow's learners. *International Journal of Business, Law, and Education, 4*(2), 618–625. DOI: 10.56442/ijble.v4i2.215

Kamalov, F., Calonge, D. S., Smail, L., Azizov, D., Thadani, D. R., Kwong, T., & Atif, A. (2025). *Evolution of AI in education: Agentic workflows* (Preprint on ArXiv No. 2504.20082). DOI: 10.48550/ARXIV.2504.20082

Kaplan, A., & Haenlein, M. (2019). Siri, siri, in my hand: Who's the fairest in the land? On the interpretations, illustrations, and implications of artificial intelligence. *Business Horizons, 62*(1), 15–25. DOI: 10.1016/j.bushor.2018.08.004

Kaplan-Rakowski, R., Grotewold, K., Hartwick, P., & Papin, K. (2023). Generative AI and teachers' perspectives on its implementation in education. *Journal of Interactive Learning Research, 34*(2), 313–338. DOI: 10.70725/815246mfssgp

Keleş, A., Ocak, R., Keleş, A., & Gülcü, A. (2009). ZOSMAT: Web-based intelligent tutoring system for teaching–learning process. *Expert Systems with Applications, 36*(2), 1229–1239. DOI: 10.1016/j.eswa.2007.11.064

Khosrawi-Rad, B., Rinn, H., Schlimbach, R., Gebbing, P., Yang, X., Lattemann, C., Markgraf, D., & Robra-Bissantz, S. (2022). Conversational agents in education - a systematic literature review. *Thirtieth European Conference on Information Systems (ECIS).*

Kim, Y., & Baylor, A. L. (2006a). A Social-Cognitive framework for pedagogical agents as learning companions. *Educational Technology Research and Development, 54*(6), 569–596. DOI: 10.1007/s11423-006-0637-3

Kim, Y., & Baylor, A. L. (2006b). Pedagogical agents as learning companions: The role of agent competency and type of interaction. *Educational Technology Research and Development, 54*(3), 223–243. DOI: 10.1007/s11423-006-8805-z

Kirby, R., Forlizzi, J., & Simmons, R. (2010). Affective social robots. *Robotics and Autonomous Systems, 58*(3), 322–332. DOI: 10.1016/j.robot.2009.09.015

Kooli, C. (2023). Chatbots in education and research: A critical examination of ethical implications and solutions. *Sustainability (Basel), 15*(7), 5614. DOI: 10.3390/su15075614

Krämer, N. C., & Bente, G. (2010). Personalizing e-learning. The social effects of pedagogical agents. *Educational Psychology Review*, *22*(1), 71–87. DOI: 10.1007/s10648-010-9123-x

Kuhail, M. A., Alturki, N., Alramlawi, S., & Alhejori, K. (2023). Interacting with educational chatbots: A systematic review. *Education and Information Technologies*, *28*(1), 973–1018. DOI: 10.1007/s10639-022-11177-3

Kulik, J. A. (1994). Meta-analytic studies of findings on computer-based instruction. In *Technology assessment in education and training* (pp. 9–33). Lawrence Erlbaum Associates, Inc.

Kulik, J. A., & Fletcher, J. D. (2016). Effectiveness of intelligent tutoring systems. *Review of Educational Research*, *86*(1), 42–78. DOI: 10.3102/0034654315581420

Labadze, L., Grigolia, M., & Machaidze, L. (2023). Role of AI chatbots in education: Systematic literature review. *International Journal of Educational Technology in Higher Education*, *20*(1), 56. Advance online publication. DOI: 10.1186/s41239-023-00426-1

Lampropoulos, G. (2023). Augmented reality and artificial intelligence in education: Toward immersive intelligent tutoring systems. In *Augmented reality and artificial intelligence* (pp. 137–146). DOI: 10.1007/978-3-031-27166-3_8

Lampropoulos, G. (2025a). Combining artificial intelligence with augmented reality and virtual reality in education: Current trends and future perspectives. *Multimodal Technologies and Interaction*, *9*(2), 11. DOI: 10.3390/mti9020011

Lampropoulos, G. (2025b). Social robots in education: Current trends and future perspectives. *Information (Basel)*, *16*(1), 29. DOI: 10.3390/info16010029

Lampropoulos, G., & Papadakis, S. (2025). The Educational Value of Artificial Intelligence and Social Robots. In Lampropoulos, G., & Papadakis, S. (Eds.), *Social Robots in Education. Studies in Computational Intelligence* (Vol. 1194). Springer., DOI: 10.1007/978-3-031-82915-4_1

Lee, D., Arnold, M., Srivastava, A., Plastow, K., Strelan, P., Ploeckl, F., Lekkas, D., & Palmer, E. (2024). The impact of generative AI on higher education learning and teaching: A study of educators' perspectives. *Computers and Education: Artificial Intelligence*, *6*, 100221. DOI: 10.1016/j.caeai.2024.100221

Leite, I., Martinho, C., & Paiva, A. (2013). Social robots for Long-Term interaction: A survey. *International Journal of Social Robotics*, *5*(2), 291–308. DOI: 10.1007/s12369-013-0178-y

Lester, J., Branting, K., & Mott, B. (2004). Conversational agents. *The Practical Handbook of Internet Computing*, 220–240.

Li, D., & Du, Y. (2017). *Artificial intelligence with uncertainty*. CRC press., DOI: 10.1201/9781315366951

Lim, W. M., Gunasekara, A., Pallant, J. L., Pallant, J. I., & Pechenkina, E. (2023). Generative AI and the future of education: Ragnarök or reformation? A paradoxical perspective from management educators. *International Journal of Management Education, 21*(2), 100790. DOI: 10.1016/j.ijme.2023.100790

Lin, C.-C., Huang, A. Y. Q., & Lu, O. H. T. (2023). Artificial intelligence in intelligent tutoring systems toward sustainable education: A systematic review. *Smart Learning Environments, 10*(1), 41. Advance online publication. DOI: 10.1186/s40561-023-00260-y

Ma, W., Adesope, O. O., Nesbit, J. C., & Liu, Q. (2014). Intelligent tutoring systems and learning outcomes: A meta-analysis. *Journal of Educational Psychology, 106*(4), 901–918. DOI: 10.1037/a0037123

Mahdi, H., Akgun, S. A., Saleh, S., & Dautenhahn, K. (2022). A survey on the design and evolution of social robots — Past, present and future. *Robotics and Autonomous Systems, 156*, 104193. DOI: 10.1016/j.robot.2022.104193

Mao, J., Chen, B., & Liu, J. C. (2024). Generative artificial intelligence in education and its implications for assessment. *TechTrends, 68*(1), 58–66. DOI: 10.1007/s11528-023-00911-4

Michel-Villarreal, R., Vilalta-Perdomo, E., Salinas-Navarro, D. E., Thierry-Aguilera, R., & Gerardou, F. S. (2023). Challenges and opportunities of generative AI for higher education as explained by ChatGPT. *Education Sciences, 13*(9), 856. DOI: 10.3390/educsci13090856

Mittal, U., Sai, S., Chamola, V., & Sangwan, D. (2024). A comprehensive review on generative AI for education. *IEEE Access : Practical Innovations, Open Solutions, 12*, 142733–142759. DOI: 10.1109/ACCESS.2024.3468368

Moreno, R., Mayer, R. E., Spires, H. A., & Lester, J. C. (2001). The case for social agency in Computer-Based teaching: Do students learn more deeply when they interact with animated pedagogical agents? *Cognition and Instruction, 19*(2), 177–213. DOI: 10.1207/S1532690XCI1902_02

Moreno-Guerrero, A. J., Marín-Marín, J. A., Dúo-Terrón, P., & López-Belmonte, J. (2022). Chatbots in education: A systematic review of the science literature. *Artificial Intelligence in Higher Education*, 81-94. DOI: 10.1201/9781003184157-4

Mousavinasab, E., Zarifsanaiey, N., & Niakan Kalhori, R., S., Rakhshan, M., Keikha, L., & Ghazi Saeedi, M. (. (2021). Intelligent tutoring systems: A systematic review of characteristics, applications, and evaluation methods. *Interactive Learning Environments, 29*(1), 142–163. DOI: 10.1080/10494820.2018.1558257

Mumm, J., & Mutlu, B. (2011). Designing motivational agents: The role of praise, social comparison, and embodiment in computer feedback. *Computers in Human Behavior, 27*(5), 1643–1650. DOI: 10.1016/j.chb.2011.02.002

Murugesan, S. (2025). The rise of agentic AI: Implications, concerns, and the path forward. *IEEE Intelligent Systems, 40*(2), 8–14. DOI: 10.1109/MIS.2025.3544940

Mustafa, M. Y., Tlili, A., Lampropoulos, G., Huang, R., Jandrić, P., Zhao, J., Salha, S., Xu, L., Panda, S., Kinshuk, , López-Pernas, S., & Saqr, M. (2024). A systematic review of literature reviews on artificial intelligence in education (AIED): A roadmap to a future research agenda. *Smart Learning Environments, 11*(1), 59. Advance online publication. DOI: 10.1186/s40561-024-00350-5

Nitto, H., Taniyama, D., & Inagaki, H. (2017). Social acceptance and impact of robots and artificial intelligence. *Nomura Res. Inst. Pap, 211*, 1–5.

Okonkwo, C. W., & Ade-Ibijola, A. (2021). Chatbots applications in education: A systematic review. *Computers and Education: Artificial Intelligence, 2*, 100033. DOI: 10.1016/j.caeai.2021.100033

Ooi, K.-B., Tan, G. W.-H., Al-Emran, M., Al-Sharafi, M. A., Capatina, A., Chakraborty, A., Dwivedi, Y. K., Huang, T.-L., Kar, A. K., Lee, V.-H., Loh, X.-M., Micu, A., Mikalef, P., Mogaji, E., Pandey, N., Raman, R., Rana, N. P., Sarker, P., Sharma, A., & Wong, L.-W. (2023). The potential of generative artificial intelligence across disciplines: Perspectives and future directions. *Journal of Computer Information Systems*, •••, 1–32. DOI: 10.1080/08874417.2023.2261010

Ortega-Ochoa, E., Arguedas, M., & Daradoumis, T. (2024). Empathic pedagogical conversational agents: A systematic literature review. *British Journal of Educational Technology, 55*(3), 886–909. DOI: 10.1111/bjet.13413

Paul, A., Yu, C. L., Susanto, E. A., Lau, N. W. L., & Meadows, G. I. (2024). *AgentPeerTalk: Empowering students through Agentic-AI-Driven discernment of bullying and joking in peer interactions in schools* (Preprint on ArXiv No. 2408.01459). DOI: 10.48550/ARXIV.2408.01459

Pedro, F., Subosa, M., Rivas, A., & Valverde, P. (2019). *Artificial intelligence in education: Challenges and opportunities for sustainable development.*

Peres, R., Schreier, M., Schweidel, D., & Sorescu, A. (2023). On ChatGPT and beyond: How generative artificial intelligence may affect research, teaching, and practice. *International Journal of Research in Marketing*, *40*(2), 269–275. DOI: 10.1016/j.ijresmar.2023.03.001

Pérez-Marín, D. (2021). A review of the practical applications of pedagogic conversational agents to be used in school and university classrooms. *Digital*, *1*(1), 18–33. DOI: 10.3390/digital1010002

Ranoliya, B. R., Raghuwanshi, N., & Singh, S. (2017). Chatbot for university related FAQs. *2017 International Conference on Advances in Computing, Communications and Informatics (ICACCI)*, 1525–1530. DOI: 10.1109/ICACCI.2017.8126057

Ruane, E., Birhane, A., & Ventresque, A. (2019). Conversational AI: Social and ethical considerations. *AICS*, *2563*, 104–115.

Samala, A. D., Rawas, S., Wang, T., Reed, J. M., Kim, J., Howard, N.-J., & Ertz, M. (2025). Unveiling the landscape of generative artificial intelligence in education: A comprehensive taxonomy of applications, challenges, and future prospects. *Education and Information Technologies*, *30*(3), 3239–3278. DOI: 10.1007/s10639-024-12936-0

Sandu, N., & Gide, E. (2019). Adoption of AI-Chatbots to enhance student learning experience in higher education in india. *2019 18th International Conference on Information Technology Based Higher Education and Training (ITHET)*. DOI: 10.1109/ITHET46829.2019.8937382

Schneider, J. (2025). *Generative to agentic AI: Survey, conceptualization, and challenges* (Preprint on ArXiv No. 2504.18875). DOI: 10.48550/ARXIV.2504.18875

Schroeder, N. L., & Adesope, O. O. (2014). A systematic review of pedagogical agents' persona, motivation, and cognitive load implications for learners. *Journal of Research on Technology in Education*, *46*(3), 229–251. DOI: 10.1080/15391523.2014.888265

Schroeder, N. L., & Craig, S. D. (2021). Learning with virtual humans: Introduction to the special issue. *Journal of Research on Technology in Education*, *53*(1), 1–7. DOI: 10.1080/15391523.2020.1863114

Sharples, M. (2023). Towards social generative AI for education: Theory, practices and ethics. *Learning: Research and Practice*, *9*(2), 159–167. DOI: 10.1080/23735082.2023.2261131

Shavit, Y., Agarwal, S., Brundage, M., Adler, S., O'Keefe, C., Campbell, R., Lee, T., Mishkin, P., Eloundou, T., Hickey, A., ... (2023). Practices for governing agentic AI systems. *Research Paper, OpenAI.*

Shute, V. J., & Zapata-Rivera, D. (2007). Adaptive technologies. *ETS Research Report Series*, *2007*(1), 1–34. DOI: 10.1002/j.2333-8504.2007.tb02047.x

Siegle, R. F., Schroeder, N. L., Lane, H. C., & Craig, S. D. (2023). Twenty-five years of learning with pedagogical agents: History, barriers, and opportunities. *TechTrends*, *67*(5), 851–864. DOI: 10.1007/s11528-023-00869-3

Sleeman, D., & Brown, J. S. (1982). *Intelligent tutoring systems*. Academic Press.

Smakman, M., Vogt, P., & Konijn, E. A. (2021). Moral considerations on social robots in education: A multi-stakeholder perspective. *Computers & Education*, *174*, 104317. DOI: 10.1016/j.compedu.2021.104317

Song, D., Oh, E. Y., & Rice, M. (2017). Interacting with a conversational agent system for educational purposes in online courses. *2017 10th International Conference on Human System Interactions (HSI)*, 78–82. DOI: 10.1109/HSI.2017.8005002

Song, P., & Wang, X. (2020). A bibliometric analysis of worldwide educational artificial intelligence research development in recent twenty years. *Asia Pacific Education Review*, *21*(3), 473–486. DOI: 10.1007/s12564-020-09640-2

Steenbergen-Hu, S., & Cooper, H. (2014). A meta-analysis of the effectiveness of intelligent tutoring systems on college students' academic learning. *Journal of Educational Psychology*, *106*(2), 331–347. DOI: 10.1037/a0034752

Stöhr, C., Ou, A. W., & Malmström, H. (2024). Perceptions and usage of AI chatbots among students in higher education across genders, academic levels and fields of study. *Computers and Education: Artificial Intelligence*, *7*, 100259. DOI: 10.1016/j.caeai.2024.100259

Stone, P., Brooks, R., Brynjolfsson, E., Calo, R., Etzioni, O., Hager, G., Hirschberg, J., Kalyanakrishnan, S., Kamar, E., Kraus, S., Leyton-Brown, K., Parkes, D., Press, W., Saxenian, A., Shah, J., Tambe, M., & Teller, A. (2016). *Artificial intelligence and life in 2030: The one hundred year study on artificial intelligence*. DOI: 10.48550/ARXIV.2211.06318

Su, J., & Yang, W. (2023). Unlocking the power of ChatGPT: A framework for applying generative AI in education. *ECNU Review of Education*, *6*(3), 355–366. DOI: 10.1177/20965311231168423

Topali, P., Ortega-Arranz, A., Rodríguez-Triana, M. J., Er, E., Khalil, M., & Akçapınar, G. (2025). Designing human-centered learning analytics and artificial intelligence in education solutions: A systematic literature review. *Behaviour & Information Technology*, *44*(5), 1071–1098. DOI: 10.1080/0144929X.2024.2345295

Urdaneta-Ponte, M. C., Mendez-Zorrilla, A., & Oleagordia-Ruiz, I. (2021). Recommendation systems for education: Systematic review. *Electronics (Basel)*, *10*(14), 1611. DOI: 10.3390/electronics10141611

van Dis, E. A. M., Bollen, J., Zuidema, W., van Rooij, R., & Bockting, C. L. (2023). ChatGPT: Five priorities for research. *Nature*, *614*(7947), 224–226. DOI: 10.1038/d41586-023-00288-7

VanLehn, K. (2006). The behavior of tutoring systems. *International Journal of Artificial Intelligence in Education*, *16*(3), 227–265. DOI: 10.3233/IRG-2006-16(3)02

VanLehn, K. (2011). The relative effectiveness of human tutoring, intelligent tutoring systems, and other tutoring systems. *Educational Psychologist*, *46*(4), 197–221. DOI: 10.1080/00461520.2011.611369

Veletsianos, G., & Russell, G. S. (2014). Pedagogical agents. In *Handbook of research on educational communications and technology* (pp. 759–769). DOI: 10.1007/978-1-4614-3185-5_61

Wang, D., Churchill, E., Maes, P., Fan, X., Shneiderman, B., Shi, Y., & Wang, Q. (2020). From Human-Human collaboration to Human-AI collaboration. *Extended Abstracts of the 2020 CHI Conference on Human Factors in Computing Systems*, 1–6. DOI: 10.1145/3334480.3381069

Wang, N., Wang, X., & Su, Y.-S. (2024). Critical analysis of the technological affordances, challenges and future directions of generative AI in education: A systematic review. *Asia Pacific Journal of Education*, *44*(1), 139–155. DOI: 10.1080/02188791.2024.2305156

Wang, S., Wang, F., Zhu, Z., Wang, J., Tran, T., & Du, Z. (2024). Artificial intelligence in education: A systematic literature review. *Expert Systems with Applications*, *252*, 124167. DOI: 10.1016/j.eswa.2024.124167

Ward, W., Cole, R., Bolaños, D., Buchenroth-Martin, C., Svirsky, E., Vuuren, S. V., Weston, T., Zheng, J., & Becker, L. (2011). My science tutor. *ACM Transactions on Speech and Language Processing*, *7*(4), 1–29. DOI: 10.1145/1998384.1998392

Weber, F., Wambsganss, T., Rüttimann, D., & Söllner, M. (2021). Pedagogical agents for interactive learning: A taxonomy of conversational agents in education. *Forty-Second International Conference on Information Systems (ICIS).*

Winkler, R., Hobert, S., Salovaara, A., Söllner, M., & Leimeister, J. M. (2020). Sara, the lecturer: Improving learning in online education with a Scaffolding-Based conversational agent. *Proceedings of the 2020 CHI Conference on Human Factors in Computing Systems*, 1–14. DOI: 10.1145/3313831.3376781

Winkler, R., & Soellner, M. (2018). Unleashing the potential of chatbots in education: A State-Of-The-Art analysis. *Proceedings - Academy of Management, 2018*(1), 15903. DOI: 10.5465/AMBPP.2018.15903abstract

Wollny, S., Schneider, J., Di Mitri, D., Weidlich, J., Rittberger, M., & Drachsler, H. (2021). Are we there yet? - a systematic literature review on chatbots in education. *Frontiers in Artificial Intelligence, 4*, 654924. Advance online publication. DOI: 10.3389/frai.2021.654924

Woo, H., LeTendre, G. K., Pham-Shouse, T., & Xiong, Y. (2021). The use of social robots in classrooms: A review of field-based studies. *Educational Research Review, 33*, 100388. DOI: 10.1016/j.edurev.2021.100388

Wu, R., & Yu, Z. (2024). Do <scp>AI</scp> chatbots improve students learning outcomes? Evidence from a meta-analysis. *British Journal of Educational Technology, 55*(1), 10–33. DOI: 10.1111/bjet.13334

Xu, W., Dainoff, M. J., Ge, L., & Gao, Z. (2021). *Transitioning to human interaction with AI systems: New challenges and opportunities for HCI professionals to enable human-centered AI* (Preprint on ArXiv No. 2105.05424). DOI: 10.48550/ARXIV.2105.05424

Xu, Z., Wijekumar, K., Ramirez, G., Hu, X., & Irey, R. (2019). The effectiveness of intelligent tutoring systems on k-12 students' reading comprehension: A meta-analysis. *British Journal of Educational Technology, 50*(6), 3119–3137. DOI: 10.1111/bjet.12758

Yildirim-Erbasli, S., Bulut, O., Epp, C. D., & Cui, Y. (2025). Advancing higher education students' assessment experiences with conversational agents. *Educational Technology Research and Development, 73*(3), 1811–1834. Advance online publication. DOI: 10.1007/s11423-025-10472-3

Yu, H., & Guo, Y. (2023). Generative artificial intelligence empowers educational reform: Current status, issues, and prospects. *Frontiers in Education, 8*, 1183162. Advance online publication. DOI: 10.3389/feduc.2023.1183162

Yusuf, H., Money, A., & Daylamani-Zad, D. (2025). Pedagogical AI conversational agents in higher education: A conceptual framework and survey of the state of the art. *Educational Technology Research and Development, 73*(2), 815–874. DOI: 10.1007/s11423-025-10447-4

Zhai, X., Chu, X., Chai, C. S., Jong, M. S. Y., Istenic, A., Spector, M., Liu, J.-B., Yuan, J., & Li, Y. (2021). A review of artificial intelligence (AI) in education from 2010 to 2020. *Complexity, 2021*(1), 1–18. DOI: 10.1155/2021/8812542

Zhu, W., Huang, L., Zhou, X., Li, X., Shi, G., Ying, J., & Wang, C. (2025). Could AI ethical anxiety, perceived ethical risks and ethical awareness about AI influence university students' use of generative AI products? An ethical perspective. *International Journal of Human-Computer Interaction*, *41*(1), 742–764. DOI: 10.1080/10447318.2024.2323277

Chapter 2

From Hype to Reality: Drivers of Effective AI Integration in K-12 Education

Abdulnassir Yassin
http://orcid.org/0009-0002-8799-9437
Islamic University in Uganda, Uganda

Herman Dwi Surjono
http://orcid.org/0000-0002-2720-2206
Yogyakarta State University, Indonesia

Anik Ghufron
Yogyakarta State University, Indonesia

Johnson Enero Upahi
http://orcid.org/0000-0002-8332-1285
Universiti Brunei Darussalam, Brunei

Radinal Fadli
http://orcid.org/0000-0003-0933-4894
Universitas Lampung, Indonesia

ABSTRACT

This study rigorously examines the factors contributing to the successful integration of Artificial Intelligence (AI) within K-12 education. Drawing upon an extensive narrative review, the research identifies three fundamental dimensions: technical and infrastructure considerations, pedagogical integration, and human and organizational readiness, pivotal to effective AI adoption. The chapter explores adaptive learning systems, automated assessment tools, and personalized educational platforms as key AI applications for teaching efficiency and student engagement. It proposed a

DOI: 10.4018/979-8-2600-0101-1.ch002

conceptual framework to guide the implementation of AI, aligning technological capabilities with educational objectives and ethical standards. Implications for policymakers, educators, and technologists are discussed, alongside recommendations for teacher training, curriculum alignment, and strategic investments in infrastructure. The study concludes by outlining avenues for future research, particularly in exploring long-term outcomes and the equitable deployment of AI across various educational settings.

INTRODUCTION

Integrating Artificial Intelligence (AI) into the educational landscape has created new opportunities to enhance the quality and delivery of teaching and learning. AI technologies, such as intelligent tutoring systems, automated grading tools, adaptive learning platforms, and data analytics, are being progressively adopted to provide personalized learning experiences, optimize administrative processes, and support educators across educational levels, including K-12 level (Holmes, 2023; Li et al., 2024; Ojha, 2024; Zawacki-Richter et al., 2019). Nevertheless, the hype around AI appears strong, but the realities of its integration in the K-12 classroom seem exaggerated, with inconsistency and context dependence. This discrepancy between the anticipation and practice raises the urgency to examine what drives effective adoption of AI in schools.

Despite the swift advancements in AI technology, successfully incorporating AI tools into classroom teaching and learning encounters numerous challenges. Barriers such as insufficient technological infrastructure, lack of teacher preparedness, limited student adaptability, ethical concerns, such as data privacy, algorithmic bias, and inequalities that may compromise academic integrity if not considered, and the absence of coherent policy frameworks, confront many educational institutions (Bauschard & Quidwai, 2024; Chen et al., 2020; Farooqi et al., 2024; Ojha, 2024; Peters et al., 2023; Uğraş et al., 2024a, 2024b). Without cautious organization and planning, AI will remain a buzzword in K-12 classrooms instead of sustaining teaching and learning.

Research suggests that effective AI adoption in K-12 depends upon several factors, including: teacher readiness, infrastructure and resource access, policy and leadership assistance, and pedagogical alignment (Celik et al., 2022; Chua et al., 2021; Cukurova et al., 2023; Joshi et al., 2022; Al-Zahrani, 2024; Dos Santos, 2024). Suggesting that effective AI integration in K-12 classrooms lies at the intersection of human, institutional and contextual drivers rather than the technology alone (Lampropoulos & Papadakis, 2025).

Studies further indicate that implementing AI in the classrooms can produce significant outcomes for teachers and learners (Lavidas, Papadakis, et al., 2022). AI supports personalized learning, enhances student engagement, and provides adaptive feedback (Singh, 2025; Zawacki-Richter et al., 2019; U.S Department of Education Office of Educational Technology, 2023). It enhances teacher effectiveness by offering data-driven insights and optimizing administrative processes, such as assessment, decreasing workload, and practical instructional design (Holmes, 2023; SH & Supriyono, 2023; U.S Department of Education Office of Educational Technology, 2023). Effective AI integration may promote inclusion but exacerbate inequities in schools if uneven access remains challenging (U.S Department of Education Office of Educational Technology, 2023). Revealing mixed AI outcomes for effective classroom teaching and learning, raising both opportunities and pitfalls of its adoption.

In contemporary classrooms, AI tools such as automated grading systems, ChatGPT, and adaptive learning platforms, among others, promise innovations; however, many educators remain unprepared, overwhelmed, or sceptical about their practical implementation (Lavidas, Petropoulou et al., 2022). For instance, some studies have revealed AI as a tool for promoting critical thinking (Abbas, 2024; Li et al., 2024), while others have raised concerns that it increases overdependence (Iskender, 2023; Tam et al., 2023). Similarly, educationists and policymakers advocate for equity in AI implementation (U.S Department of Education Office of Educational Technology, 2023); however, inequities in schools often worsen the digital divide (Bauschard & Quidwai, 2024; Reina-Parrado et al., 2025). Furthermore, the tension between the benefits of AI personalisation and the ethical issues related to learner data remains unaddressed (Holmes, 2023; Van et al., 2025). These contradictions highlight the urgency of a framework for supporting effective, responsible, and equitable implementation of AI in the classroom.

Progressing from hype to reality, schools need a guideline that identifies and supports drivers, optimizes positive outcomes, and resolves barriers (Papadakis et al., 2024a, 2024b). Such a framework supports teachers, school leaders, and policymakers to harness the complexity of AI integration in the classroom, facilitating teaching and learning rather than hindrance. This current study addresses this problem. The study investigates the primary factors, outcomes, and key components of a framework essential for successfully incorporating AI tools in teaching and learning within the K-12 classroom setting. The study addressed the following research objectives: (1) To examine the factors influencing the successful implementation of Artificial Intelligence (AI) in classroom teaching and learning. (2) To explore the outcomes associated with successful AI implementation in the classroom and the impact of these outcomes on the effectiveness of teaching and learning. (3) To propose a framework delineating the essential elements for successfully integrating AI into classroom teaching and learning.

METHODS

This study conducts a critical narrative review of the existing literature on the application of AI in the K-12 classroom, with a particular interest in classroom implementation. The review facilitates synthesizing quality previous studies to derive insights without engaging in empirical research (Kahlke et al., 2023). This review focused on relevant quality peer-reviewed journal articles, preprints, reports, and case studies, retrieved from reputable databases such as Google Scholar, ERIC, Web of Science, and Scopus.

Sources from the last five years were of significant interest for inclusion in the review synthesis. The literature selection focused on regional differences, pedagogical integrations, educational leadership, and policy issues. The following keywords guided the search: "Artificial Intelligence in education" AND "K-12 classroom integration", "AI implementation in schools" AND "success factors", "Education technology" AND "AI adoption" AND "teaching effectiveness", and "AI in K-12 classroom teaching" AND "challenges and enablers".

Thematic analysis enabled the identification of emerging patterns within the literature. The research upheld ethical standards by acknowledging relevant scholarly sources through accurate referencing and citation practices. Additionally, the researchers openly disclosed any potential ethical concerns that might affect the credibility of the findings. The literature review assesses the relevance and rigour of the findings and methodologies, identifies existing issues, and proposes opportunities for future research.

Consequently, the review investigates the key factors, outcomes, and essential components of a framework for successful AI tool implementation in the K-12 classroom, highlighting gaps and proposed recommendations for policymakers, teachers, students, and educators seeking to leverage AI's potential in education. Thus, the target of the narrative review was not to catalogue all the relevant studies; however, to synthesize representative evidence that reflects the major issues, debates, and innovations.

RESULTS AND DISCUSSION

Factors Influencing AI Implementation in K-12 Classroom

Broadly effective AI implementation in classroom teaching and learning depends on technical infrastructure, pedagogical integration, and human/organizational readiness.

Technical and Infrastructure (TI) Factors

The technical and infrastructural facets encompass resource requirements, system compatibility, and the necessities of technical support.

Resource Requirements

Resources are critical for effective AI implementation in K-12 classrooms. These include: financial investment, digital equipment, and progressive maintenance. Studies have shown that high-income countries have adequate resources and funds to support school AI initiatives. For instance, Naseri and Abdullah (2024) report that schools in developed countries such as the United States, Singapore, and Finland have access to advanced AI platforms that support personalized learning, which enables smooth AI integration in learning. This adequate funding is necessary for effective AI adoption in schools (Bauschard & Quidwai, 2024), in contrast to the low-resource contexts with inadequate infrastructure and insufficient availability of AI-enabled devices as impediments to the effective implementation of AI in schools(Tang, 2024; Chua et al., 2021; Joshi et al., 2022; Panjwani, 2024). Explaining why most AI adoption in education occurs in Europe, North America, and East Asia (Reina-Parrado et al., 2025). Resource-rich and resource-constrained contexts could explain the divergence in AI integrations in schools. In developed countries, the state supports the school resource needs. In contrast, schools in low-resource contexts struggle to acquire even basic technological resources, since other educational priorities also demand the available resources. Therefore, while adequate resources are paramount for AI integration in all contexts, in low-resourced regions, this factor is a considerable barrier for effective AI integration in schools.

System Compatibility

System compatibility is another factor influencing AI implementation in the K-12 classroom. System compatibility refers to aligning the existing AI tools with the existing policies, infrastructure, and practices to optimize benefits. Studies such as Celik et al. (2022) and Chomutare et al. (2022) observed the "limited reliability and context-dependence of AI systems" as an obstacle, indicating possible compatibility challenges with existing educational systems or environments. For example, in China, Yang et al. (2024) developed a successful AI system that addressed data privacy and heterogeneity challenges and integrated it into the existing infrastructure with little effort. Conversely, in Pakistan, Farooqi et al. (2024) reveal that limited infrastructure, incompetent teachers and data privacy concerns are significant constraints for AI integration. Further, in India, Karan (2024) suggests the need for including AI as a standalone subject and addressing it as a multidisciplinary tool to align with the existing curriculum. AI adoptions are often smooth in well-digitalized and adequately funded environments; however, in a digitally challenging context and with inadequate funds, system compatibility becomes a barrier, raising costs and slowing AI adoption. Therefore, system compatibility is a decisive factor for AI adoption, even though it is invisible in resource-rich situations.

Technical Support

A further aspect for effective AI integration in schools is providing technical support, which assists teachers and students with infrastructure constraints such as connectivity and continuous maintenance. Some of these technical supports include: training on AI Chatbots, machine learning and intelligent tutors (Martin et al., 2024). Continuous support mechanisms are pivotal factors for AI adoption in education (Cukurova et al., 2023; Al-Zahrani, 2024). Evidence from schools with adequate resources, especially in developed countries, offers committed technical support, which reduces teacher workload and anxiety, and enhances student engagement with learning activities. For instance, Lee and Kwon (2024) report that tailored AI training can ensure teachers' and students' confidence and competence in AI curricula. Schools with committed information and technology support reported satisfaction and better AI integration (Martin et al., 2024).

In contrast, ineffective AI integration hindered regions with limited resources. Su et al. (2022) reported that schools in the Asia-Pacific regions are affected by inadequate resources, impeding continuous technical support for AI implementation. Continuous support for AI is demanded across regions, though resource-rich areas may be more sustainable in offering technical support than low-resourced regions. For example, a study by Joshi (2025) found that only 29% of teachers in U.S. K-12 schools report attaining sufficient AI training, suggesting further demand for technical support across different regions. Therefore, strategic investments by schools in resources, system compatibility, and technical support across various areas can substantially enhance AI implementation in K-12 education.

Figure 1. Technological Factors for AI Integration in K-12 Classroom

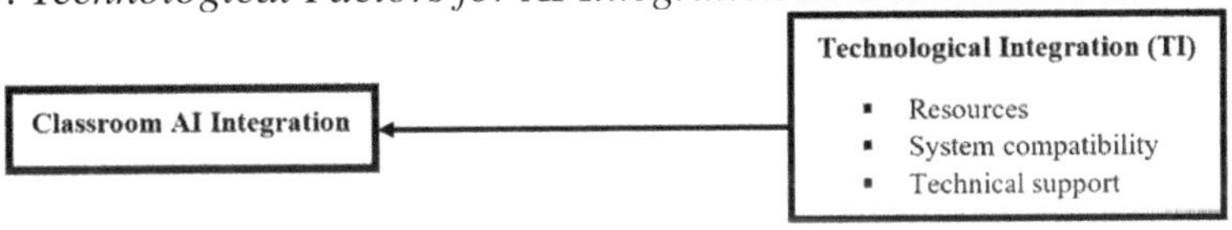

Pedagogical Integration (PI) Factors

The pedagogical variables essential for successfully integrating artificial intelligence (AI) in the classroom include teaching methods, curriculum alignment, and assessment strategies.

Curriculum Alignment and Teaching Methods

Across regions, AI integration in K-12 is effective when aligned with existing teaching and learning curricula, ensuring meaningful learning. Studies highlighted the importance of ensuring that AI implementation aligns with school curriculum objectives to promote ample integration within the learning subjects (Tashtoush et al., 2024; Topali et al., 2025). Su et al. (2022) found that integrating AI with the local curriculum improved learning situations. These suggest that effective integration of AI with the existing curriculum enhances AI education; however, establishing a balanced standard for effective practices across regions remains challenging. Conversely, while systematic reviews in Europe and the U.S. demonstrate effort in AI curriculum development, there is a lack of empirical evidence on effective pedagogical practices (Martin et al., 2024; Díaz & Nussbaum, 2024). Suggests an empirical study to identify effective pedagogical practices for sustainable AI integration in K-12 schools.

Several teaching methods influence the integration of AI in the K-12 classroom. For instance, Al-Zahrani (2024) and Dos Santos (2024) reported challenges associated with "adapting to new teaching methods" as part of AI integration. The AI tools complement the teaching methods to amplify their effectiveness for teaching and learning (Familoni & Onyebuchi, 2024). Studies reveal that project-based, inquiry, and game-based learning are the common pedagogical approaches in AI education. Students engage in a deep investigation and questioning, and through interactive educational games with AI tools, an inquiry-based and game-based learning approach is integrated with the AI application (Su et al., 2024). Further, Lee and Kwon (2024) report that students participate in hands-on activities through projects, conducted with the help of AI tools. In contrast, AI integration in a tight exam-oriented curriculum often results in limited impact in deep learning. Leong et al. (2025) report that AI integration through drill and practice activities, such as practice quizzes, does not facilitate deep understanding and student engagement with content. These distinctions elaborate that teaching and learning methods remain key; AI integration only amplifies the technique. While AI is at the intersection, to tailor the teaching methods, learners' needs and contextual situations should be considered (Rizvi et al., 2023). Tailoring teaching methods to specific conditions and needs enhanced learners' affective and cognitive outcomes.

Assessment Strategies

Assessment is one of the areas of extensive AI integration in K-12 classrooms, ranging from real-time learning analytics, adaptive feedback, personalized feedback, and automated grading. Studies emphasized the role of AI in automating grading and feedback processes, ranging from multiple-choice tests to complex written assignments, exhibiting high accuracy and consistency (Anjum et al., 2023; Gnanaprakasam & Lourdusamy, 2024; Tang, 2024), creating sufficient time for teachers to concentrate more on teaching and learning (Ahmad et al., 2022). Consequently, there is a notable reduction in teachers' administrative tasks associated with assessment (Gnanaprakasam & Lourdusamy, 2024).

Globally, AI integration for assessment is mainly in a formative context rather than summative assessments, such as real-time, diagnostic, and adaptive feedback. As reported by Owan et al. (2023) and Saputra et al. (2024), real-time feedback, personalized learning experiences, and higher-order learning assessment are a progressive utilization of assessment AI tools. Nevertheless, AI adoption in summative assessment remains a challenge due to academic integrity issues such as validity, fairness, data privacy, and maintaining human evaluation (Christyodetaputri & Marwa, 2024; Hopfenbeck et al., 2023). These parallels suggest the cautiousness of stakeholders regarding AI assessment, due to academic integrity issues, which are often unclear to manage.

There are AI integration differences for assessment across contexts. For instance, in East and Southeast Asia, AI is mainly utilized for adaptive test preparations and proctoring, aligning with their exam-oriented curricula (Saputra et al., 2024). Promoting creativity, through community engagement and performance-based assessment, is the focus in Latin America (Jaramillo & Olivera, 2024). In the European context, explainability and fairness in AI assessment are key in a multilingual setting, while in Africa, mobile-quick AI assessment is adopted to cater to the low bandwidth challenge (Miller, 2024). These highlight the local educational priorities, which influence how AI is adopted, especially for assessment purposes.

Figure 2. Pedagogical Factors for AI Integration in K-12 Classroom

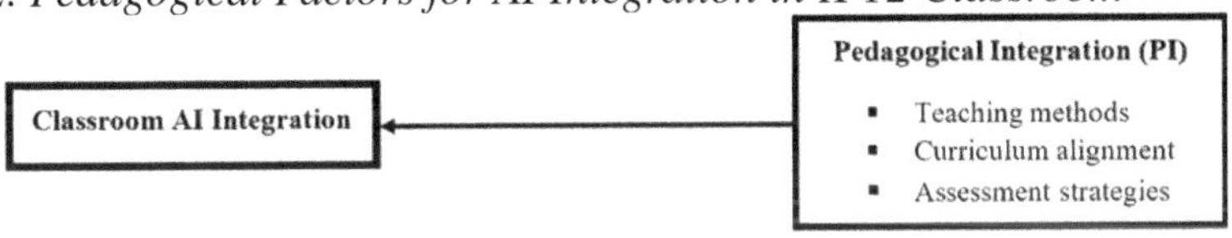

Human and Organisational (HO) Factors

The organizational factors that facilitate the integration of AI in the K-12 classroom encompass teacher readiness and training, administrative support, student engagement, and ethical considerations.

Teacher Readiness and Training

Implementing AI in the K-12 classroom significantly hinges on teacher competence and continuous training. Research indicates that teacher confidence, attitude, and technological pedagogical content knowledge (TPACK) are crucial factors for effective AI implementation in the classroom. For instance, studies have identified the "lack of teacher training" or professional development (PD) as a significant challenge, decreasing their engagement with AI platforms (Cukurova et al., 2023; Joshi et al., 2022; Yue et al., 2024). The extent of teacher PD programs varies across contexts, with well-funded contexts offering such programs more than less-funded contexts. Further studies report that teacher confidence and attitude towards AI determine their interest in integrating it in the classroom (Ayanwale et al., 2022; Yue et al., 2024). Because teacher trust and ownership are paramount (Cukurova et al., 2023). AI-PD programs are effective in skilling teachers with AI knowledge, engagement, and adaptability; however, they should also be trained on ethical issues (Meylani, 2024). These findings demonstrate the significance of teacher AI-related TPACK for effective AI integration. Empirical research that traces the impact of such training would elaborate on the more practical implications of such training in the K-12 classroom; otherwise, the effectiveness of such training risks remaining theoretical.

Student Engagement

Engaging students in AI-enhanced lessons is crucial as it renders learning meaningful. Studies indicate that intrinsic motivation and human-computer interaction impact student engagement. Research has evidenced substantial improvements in student engagement in AI-enabled classrooms (Huang et al., 2023). Especially enhancements in student behaviour, self-regulation, and motivation in primary education through AI-enhanced gamification platforms such as ClassDojo (Benzizoune, 2024), and promoting active and self-directed learning through AI-driven personalized learning platforms, intelligent tutoring systems, and immersive virtual reality technologies (Sangarsu, 2023).

On the contrary, students reported AI-related anxiety, which portrayed a negative impact on their engagement (W. Li et al., 2024). Meaning, while learner motivation and regular interaction with AI technologies result in positive engagement, those who indicate fear related to AI, primarily academic integrity-wise, probably would like to get involved less with AI in their academic work, hence their lower engagement.

Administrative Support and Policy

The successful implementation of AI in the K-12 classroom is significantly contingent upon administrative commitment, as it shapes the guidelines for AI utilization, which must align with a collective vision shared among various school departments. For instance, studies emphasized the necessity of "generating continuous support mechanisms for help," and a modified AI framework that suits the school situation (Casal-Otero et al., 2023; Cukurova et al., 2023; Tang, 2024), highlighting the imperative for robust administrative support and policy. This should include very imperative issues, such as funding, teacher PD, and strong policies for ethical AI utilization (concerns like data privacy, algorithm bias critical for equitable AI) (Martin et al., 2024; Semwaiko et al., 2024; White et al., 2024). However, to avoid exacerbating inequality issues, administrative AI policies are expected to target the needs of all categories of students, including the marginalized (White et al., 2024). While administrative support for AI integration is essential, contextual implementation helps to address inequality challenges emanating from specific contextual needs.

Ethical Considerations

Integrating AI in the K-12 classroom raises ethical challenges across regions. These revolve around privacy, data security, and the potential for bias and inequality. Studies emphasize the significance of ethical considerations as pivotal elements in implementing AI (Farooqi et al., 2024; Sangarsu, 2023). These considerations include data privacy and security, equity and bias, and teacher-student relationships (Farooqi et al., 2024; Sangarsu, 2023; Gouseti et al., 2025). Therefore, schools should comply with the international and contextualized AI policies to safeguard sensitive information (Farooqi et al., 2024). However, if such AI policies are not practiced, the AI systems risk perpetuating the existing inequities related to the data used to train the AI model, exacerbating the inequities in learning outcomes (Farooqi et al., 2024; Fütterer et al., 2023). These demonstrate the need to consider ethical issues in AI use in K-12 classrooms; however, educator training and contextual policies and frameworks may vary from one school to another for contextualized problem-solving.

Therefore, successful integration of AI in educational settings, strategies in schools must prioritize teacher preparation and training programs, continuous administrative support without undue delay, and concentrate on fostering student engagement in AI-related classes. Additionally, a contextualized ethical AI usage framework tailored to the specific educational institution helps guide all AI tool users.

Figure 3. Human and Organizational Factors for AI Integration in K-12 Classroom

The key drivers discussed previously outline the reasons and conditions under which successful AI integration into the K-12 classroom is possible. The next theme demonstrates what AI can offer in a practical K-12 classroom.

AI Solutions for K-12 Classroom Enhancement

The successful implementation of AI in educational environments involves integrating personalized learning systems, AI-enabled assessment and feedback, and intelligent classroom management systems.

AI-Enabled Personalisation Solutions

AI personalizing the learning experience in the K-12 classroom is an approach that involves tailoring learning to individual student needs. The approach utilizes AI to adapt the teaching methods, content, and assessment, facilitating learner engagement and performance. However, AI personalized learning also presents challenges to the learners. Studies indicate AI offers personalized learning experiences such as tailored learning paths, personalized learning content creation, immediate feedback (Al Nabhani et al., 2025; Sangarsu, 2023; Susilo, 2024), thus, enhanced student engagement, improves inclusive learning outcomes, and allows for scalability (Mahmoud & Sørensen, 2024; Tapalova & Zhiyenbayeva, 2022).

Conversely, challenges due to technological inaccessibility and inadequate educator AI training, there is a risk of exacerbating the digital divide among learners and teachers (Guerrero et al. 2025; Vásquez et al., 2024). It's also argued that AI favours personalized procedural learning rather than deep understanding through critical thinking and problem solving (Panit, 2024). Additionally, ethical issues and data security continue to challenge personalized AI education (Cotta et al., 2024). These findings suggest that AI technology enhances personalized learning; however, the quality of the personalized learning matters, data security issues still exist, and contextual situations may not favour the benefits of personalization to all learners. Consequently, an inequality problem, thus continuous solutions for equitable AI, remain great deal.

AI-based Assessment and Feedback

Research shows that AI-based assessment and feedback enhance the transformative learning experience in a K-12 classroom. These encompass personalized, adaptive assessment and immediate feedback, improving student engagement and increasing learning outcomes. Studies indicate that AI tools enhance personalized assessment, automated grading, and timely feedback (Youn et al., 2025; Owan et al., 2023; Saputra et al., 2024), reducing workload, improving teacher effectiveness, and learning outcomes. Conversely, AI adoption in summative assessment remains a challenge due to academic integrity issues such as validity, fairness, data privacy, and maintaining human evaluation (Christyodetaputri & Marwa, 2024; Hopfenbeck et al., 2023). Further, AI-based assessments realized only a 30% increase in consistency (Guijarro, 2024). Data privacy, algorithmic bias, and general ethical considerations require continuous attention and solutions (Farooqi et al., 2024; Sangarsu, 2023). These suggest that AI-based learner assessments are practical and efficient; however, they are more formative-based, and contextual situations and ethical considerations may affect their practical implementation in the K-12 classroom.

Intelligent Classroom Management Systems

These intelligent systems use the Internet of Things (IoT) and advanced algorithms to supervise and manage classroom situations to promote efficiency and learner engagement and facilitate learning outcomes. Studies reveal that AI systems that use the Arc Face algorithm, intelligent systems are enablers for adjusting strategies during teaching (KucuKakin & Demir, 2021; Shan et al., 2024), facilitating conducive classroom conditions, reducing teachers' administrative load, enhancing collaboration and active learning, and facilitating control of the instructional activities. These intelligent systems are essential for an innovative classroom; however, they are effective in resource-rich contexts, where adequate funds are available for supporting such high technological initiatives. The success of such a classroom should also consider the ethical considerations, such as data privacy and surveillance.

After discussing the practical AI integration in the K-12 classroom, it's essential to understand some of the effective AI integration in these classrooms, laying the way for the next topic discussed.

Classroom Integration Approaches

Several studies have discussed diverse methodological perspectives on AI integration in K-12 classrooms, ranging from a supportive tool to its more comprehensive incorporation into the teaching and learning process. For instance, AI technologies such Emotion Recognition AI Model (ERAM) in arts education, which enables real-time capture and analysis of students' emotional states (Dong et al., 2023), investigation and questioning, interactive educational games, project work and an inquiry-based AI-integrated classroom enhances students' engagement in deep learning (Su et al., 2024; Lee & Kwon, 2024). Indicating ERAM, investigation approaches, interactive educational games, and inquiry learning approaches as the major AI-integrated strategies in schools.

Research has also identified strategies for facilitating formative classroom learner assessment through AI tools. Studies present the significance of real-time assessment tools and teacher support systems (Al Nabhani et al., 2025; Fakhar et al., 2022; Llurba & Palau, 2024; Susilo, 2024), including a facial expression recognition system for classroom assessment, analyzing emotions alongside cognitive-emotions (Fakhar et al., 2022), enhancing student engagement and academic performance while reducing teacher workload (Llurba & Palau, 2024). Studies identified AI integration for formative assessment, such as facial expression recognition and real-time feedback, which are applicable in K-12 classrooms. However, studies persistently highlight several challenges in AI integration for assessment in K-12 classrooms. For example, equity, inclusivity, algorithmic biases, transparency, data privacy, and the need for continuous teacher training (Joshi, 2025; Su et al., 2024; Rizvi et al., 2023). These necessitate mitigation strategies for equitable access to resources for AI utilization in schools for both teachers and students.

Following the discussion on the conditions for AI integration, some practical AI applications, and their integration in K-12 classrooms, teaching, and learning, this has implications for the stakeholders. This paper discusses the impact of the chapter on theory and practice.

IMPLICATIONS FOR PRACTICE AND THEORY

This study holds significant implications for both theoretical frameworks and practical applications, particularly within educational technology, instructional design, and educational policy development.

Implications for Practice

The findings will provide actionable insights into practical strategies for implementing AI within educational settings, thereby assisting educators in making informed decisions about tools, training, and pedagogical approaches. AI can facilitate teaching methodologies and assessments (Mollick & Mollick, 2023). These require a framework designed to assist educators in reflecting on the competencies for AI integration (Lameras & Arnab, 2022). Nonetheless, it is imperative to address challenges such as insufficient teacher training and limited infrastructure related to data privacy (Vazhayil et al., 2019; Younas et al., 2023). Therefore, cautious and deliberate implementation can improve teaching practices (Mollick & Mollick, 2023; Lameras & Arnab, 2022). School leaders and administrators can utilize the proposed framework to plan and manage the adoption of AI effectively, thereby minimizing trial-and-error and maximizing return on investment. A framework for effective AI implementation is essential, as it addresses barriers including cost, technical skills, and employee acceptance (Hussain & Rizwan, 2024). School leaders assume a critical role in this process, actively participating in discussions related to AI and establishing organizational structures to facilitate adoption (Adams & Thompson, 2025).

The practical identification of key success factors, such as teacher readiness, technical support, and curriculum alignment, will guide the design of targeted teacher training programs to enhance AI readiness and competence. For instance, Vazhayil et al. (2019) assert that objective teacher training and PD are vital for successfully integrating AI (Vazhayil et al., 2019). Ministries of education and relevant stakeholders should formulate policies and allocate resources toward the most impactful domains, such as AI tools with demonstrated educational outcomes or vital infrastructure. AI implementation necessitates meticulous consideration of infrastructure, capacity building, ethical considerations, and policy frameworks (Maina & Kuria, 2024). However, only 10% of academic institutions surveyed globally have established policies regarding generative AI usage (UNESCO, 2023), underscoring the necessity for appropriate regulations and guidelines. Consequently, strategic investment that progresses through low-cost tools and developing customized AI solutions is paramount for contextual implementations (Hussain & Rizwan, 2024).

Enhancement of student learning experiences through elucidating which AI implementations strengthen learning outcomes. AI-driven platforms can dynamically adjust instructional materials following individual student needs (Y et al., 2024), promoting improved retention and comprehension. With the help of adaptive learning systems, students' academic performance and engagement can be enhanced (Silva et al., 2023; Xu, 2024).

Implications for Theory

The proposed framework significantly contributes to theoretical models that elucidate the mechanisms by which AI operates within educational contexts, enriching the academic discourse on educational innovation and technology adoption. Prompting researchers to thoroughly investigate existing theoretical frameworks for comprehending their adoption and consequential impact. Studies found gaps in the Technology Acceptance Model (TAM), the Unified Theory of Acceptance and Use of Technology (UTAU), and the Value-Based Adoption Model (VAM) for effective AI integration (Naseri & Abdullah, 2024; Tarisayi, 2024). Factors such as the innovation, the adopter, and the prevailing environmental context influence the adoption of these frameworks.

The study has the potential to enhance or adapt existing frameworks such as the TAM, the Technological, Pedagogical, and Content Knowledge (TPACK) model, and the Substitution, Augmentation, Modification, Redefinition (SAMR) model by incorporating context-specific factors pertinent to AI integration in educational settings. Studies integrated TAM and TPACK to explore the determinants influencing AI adoption in primary mathematics education and investigate the intentions of higher education leaders regarding the utilization of AI tools (Kavitha & Joshith, 2025; M. Li, 2024), suggesting the significance of teacher attitudes, TPACK, training, and support. TAM and TPACK were also integrated across disciplines, including with ethical considerations, highlighting the need to customize models to fit specific contexts (Celik, 2023; Sukackė, 2019). These studies illustrate the importance of extending and amalgamating existing models such as TAM, TPACK, and SAMR to tackle the distinct challenges and opportunities presented by AI integration in education, particularly regarding ethical considerations and context-specific factors.

This research contributes to theories relating to pedagogical impact and the learning sciences, providing evidence based connections between the utilization of AI and educational outcomes. AI-driven platforms can dynamically adjust instructional materials to meet the specific needs of individual students, promoting enhanced retention, comprehension, student engagement, and improved academic performance (Y et al., 2024; Silva et al., 2023).

The study establishes a connection between innovation diffusion theory and classroom realities, elucidating the proliferation of AI and the conditions that foster its success in educational environments. Within the realm of career and technical education, the adoption of AI encounters challenges related to hands-on learning and industry collaborations (Sun & Pratt, 2024). The acceptance of generative AI among educators exhibits considerable variability, with perceived utility and user-friendliness playing pivotal roles in influencing adoption rates (Ghimire & Edwards, 2024). Therefore, collaborative efforts with innovation advocates, especially in K-12 contexts, where experiential learning and shared values promote AI literacy among instructors (Yuwono et al., 2024). These investigations underscore the significance of contextualizing AI adoption within specific educational sectors, tackling challenges such as infrastructure limitations and resource allocation, and harmonizing organizational and personal aspirations to enhance the integration of AI in pedagogical environments.

Not all of this chapter is exhaustive; therefore, the paper presents the limitations and recommendations next. The chapter summarises the final takeaways in the conclusion section.

LIMITATIONS OF THE STUDY

As a critical review, the quality and scope of the existing literature upon which it relies inherently constrained the study. The findings and conclusions are contingent upon the methodological rigour and relevance of previously published studies, some of which may exhibit biases or lack contextual applicability. Furthermore, the study may inadvertently prioritize particular perspectives or types over others, even though they conducted a critical evaluation and applied objective selection criteria; the authors could have faced the challenge of selection bias. The review does not include the collection of primary empirical data, which limits its capacity to establish causal relationships or assess the effectiveness of AI integration strategies in real-world K-12 classroom settings. Lastly, due to the diversity of the educational systems, technological environments, and pedagogical approaches represented in the reviewed literature, the generalizability of the findings to specific contexts may be constrained without proper adaptation. Despite these limitations, the review provides a significant theoretical and practical synthesis that establishes a foundation for future empirical research and policy development.

RECOMMENDATIONS

This study presents several essential recommendations for policymakers, administrators, and teachers.

Recommendations for Practice and Theory

Policymakers

Policymakers need to invest in teacher training and PD, which entails the establishment of continuous training programs centred on AI, aimed at enhancing technical skills and pedagogical competence. They should provide technological readiness by investing in essential infrastructure, stable internet connectivity, smart devices, and digital platforms that facilitate the deployment of AI in educational settings. Ensure education for both teachers and students concerning the limitations and responsible utilization of AI. Administrative leadership and policy support should be fostered by engaging school leaders and education boards in awareness and training initiatives to establish top-down support for integrating AI. Incorporate AI integration objectives within school improvement plans and national educational strategies.

Administrators

School administrators should adopt a strategic and phased implementation approach by utilizing proposed frameworks to guide a step-by-step implementation process. It is essential to commence with pilot programs before full-scale adoption. They need to ensure alignment between AI tools and curriculum objectives to enhance relevance and facilitate ease of use. It is necessary to establish IT support systems to assist teachers and students in troubleshooting challenges in real time. A continuous emphasis on promoting ethical and responsible utilization of AI through establishing unequivocal contextualised policies regarding data privacy and the ethical application of AI in student learning and assessment.

Teachers

The study suggests measuring the learning outcomes through selecting and evaluating AI tools according to their demonstrable influence on learning effectiveness, student engagement, and skill development, using formative and summative data to consistently assess the pedagogical value of AI interventions. There is a need to foster collaborative learning among students by promoting professional learning communities that emphasize the integration of AI. By conducting empirical research, teachers can enhance the current technology integration models by integrating findings into established frameworks such as TPACK or the SAMR model to address AI-related capabilities, including adaptive learning and predictive analytics. Additionally, the study recommends modifying the Technology Acceptance Model (TAM) to incorporate cognitive trust, transparency, and algorithmic agency elements.

Recommendations for Future Research

This study recommends that future research longitudinally follow schools to evaluate the sustainability and long-term educational outcomes associated with using AI. To ensure equitable adoption, it encourages investigations into how AI implementation impacts diverse student populations, including marginalized and low-resource learners. There exists a necessity to advance research regarding hybrid teaching models in which AI facilitates rather than replaces educators, thereby underscoring the evolving role of teachers within AI-supported classrooms. Additionally, cross-national or inter-school studies are imperative to comprehend how cultural, economic, and policy environments influence the effectiveness of AI in educational settings.

CONCLUSIONS

The study identified technical infrastructure, pedagogical integration, and human and organizational factors essential for successfully implementing AI in teaching and learning. Adaptive learning systems, automated teaching tools, and support platforms, supported by adequate infrastructure, training, and ethical considerations, enhance AI-enabled personalized solutions, ultimately improving teaching and learning outcomes. Moreover, the study recognized AI as a supportive tool and identified more comprehensive integration approaches to facilitate effective implementation within the classroom. The study proposes a framework encompassing resources, system compatibility, and technical support for assessing technical and infrastructure requirements. Dimensions related to teaching methods, curriculum alignment, and assessment strategies can effectively ensure pedagogical integration. Concurrently, addressing teacher readiness and training, administrative support, and student engagement is critical to addressing the human and organizational factors, including ethical considerations. Proper consideration of these variables is paramount to ensuring effective AI integration within the classroom.

The study report, therefore, informed educators and school leaders regarding the necessity for PD and training programs, as well as options for policy and investment prioritization, enhancement of student learning experiences, and the refinement of technology acceptance and integration models. However, the study exhibits limitations due to its dependence on the quality and scope of the existing literature, the potential for literature selection bias, restricted generalizability, and the absence of primary empirical evidence. Nevertheless, the findings provide a valuable theoretical and practical synthesis that establishes the foundation for future empirical research and policy development.

The study recommends that policymakers and educators make investments in teacher training and PD, adopt a strategic and phased implementation approach, ensure technological readiness, promote ethical and responsible AI usage, encourage leadership and policy support, focus on measurable learning outcomes, and refine existing technology integration models, such as TPACK, SAMR, while updating the technology acceptance model (TAM). Furthermore, the study suggests future research areas, including conducting longitudinal impact studies to assess sustainability and educational outcomes, exploring equity and access issues, investigating the role of human-AI collaboration, and conducting comparative studies across contexts to understand the effects of cultural, economic, and environmental policy on AI in education.

Figure 4 below presents the comprehensive framework that depicts the drivers of AI integration in the K-12 classroom proposed in this study. Ethical consideration was to some extent discussed when discussing each of the drivers, but it's more independently described under human and organisational factors. By careful and continuous consideration of these key drivers together with the ethical issues in their implementation, the integration of AI in the K-12 classroom has the potential to enhance personalized learning, improve classroom activities, and revolutionize teaching practices.

Figure 5. Framework for AI Integration in K-12 Classroom

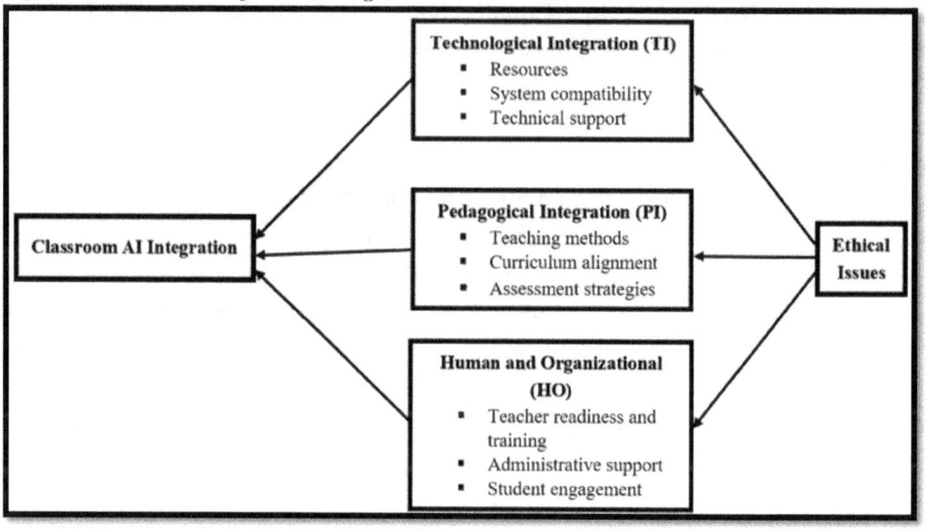

AI USE STATEMENT

The authors use AI tools exclusively to facilitate non-creative, assistive functions throughout the research process. Their usage was carried out ethically and responsibly, without compromising the work's originality, intellectual contribution, or analytical integrity. All conceptual development, critical analysis, and scholarly interpretations articulated in this study are exclusively those of the authors.

REFERENCES

Adams, D., & Thompson, P. (2025). Transforming School Leadership with Artificial Intelligence: Applications, Implications, and Future Directions. *Leadership and Policy in Schools*, *24*(1), 77–89. DOI: 10.1080/15700763.2024.2411295

Al Nabhani, F., Hamzah, M., & Abuhassna, H. (2025). The role of artificial intelligence in personalizing educational content: Enhancing the learning experience and developing the teacher's role in an integrated educational environment. *Contemporary Educational Technology*, *17*(2), ep573. DOI: 10.30935/cedtech/16089

Al-Zahrani, A. M. (2024). From Traditionalism to Algorithms: Embracing Artificial Intelligence for Effective University Teaching and Learning. *IgMin Research*, *2*(2), 102–112. DOI: 10.61927/igmin151

Anjum, G., Choubey, J., Kushwaha, S., & Patkar, V. (2023). AI in Education: Evaluating the Efficacy and Fairness of Automated Grading Systems. *International Journal of Innovative Research in Science, Engineering and Technology*, *12*(06), 1–14. DOI: 10.15680/IJIRSET.2023.1206161

Ayanwale, M. A., Sanusi, I. T., Adelana, O. P., Aruleba, K. D., & Oyelere, S. S. (2022). Teachers' readiness and intention to teach artificial intelligence in schools. *Computers and Education: Artificial Intelligence*, *3*(August), 100099. DOI: 10.1016/j.caeai.2022.100099

Bauschard, S., & Quidwai, S. (2024). From Insight to Implementation: How to Create Your AI School Guidance. In SSRN *Electronic Journal* (Issue July). DOI: 10.2139/ssrn.4784207

Benzizoune, O. (2024). Enhancing Classroom Management and Student Engagement: The Role of ClassDojo and Gamification in Education. *Journal of English Language Teaching and Applied Linguistics*, *6*(3), 106–114. DOI: 10.32996/jeltal.2024.6.3.13

Casal-Otero, L., Catala, A., Fernández-Morante, C., Taboada, M., Cebreiro, B., & Barro, S. (2023). AI literacy in K-12: A systematic literature review. *International Journal of STEM Education, 10*(1), 29. Advance online publication. DOI: 10.1186/s40594-023-00418-7

Celik, I. (2023). Towards Intelligent-TPACK: An empirical study on teachers' professional knowledge to ethically integrate artificial intelligence (AI)-based tools into education. *Computers in Human Behavior, 138*(May 2022), 107468. DOI: 10.1016/j.chb.2022.107468

Celik, I., Dindar, M., Muukkonen, H., & Järvelä, S. (2022). The Promises and Challenges of Artificial Intelligence for Teachers: A Systematic Review of Research. *TechTrends, 66*(4), 616–630. DOI: 10.1007/s11528-022-00715-y

Chen, L., Chen, P., & Lin, Z. (2020). Artificial Intelligence in Education: A Review. *IEEE Access : Practical Innovations, Open Solutions, 8*(May), 75264–75278. DOI: 10.1109/ACCESS.2020.2988510

Chomutare, T., Tejedor, M., Svenning, T. O., Marco-Ruiz, L., Tayefi, M., Lind, K., Godtliebsen, F., Moen, A., Ismail, L., Makhlysheva, A., & Ngo, P. D. (2022). Artificial Intelligence Implementation in Healthcare: A Theory-Based Scoping Review of Barriers and Facilitators. *International Journal of Environmental Research and Public Health, 19*(23), 16359. DOI: 10.3390/ijerph192316359

Christyodetaputri, J. H., & Marwa, N. (2024). Sinergi International Journal of Islamic Studies. *Zakat Management Practices and Sustainable Development in Indonesia Ernil, 2*(1), 24–37. https://doi.org/https://doi.org/10.61194/education.v2i3.590

Chua, I. S., Gaziel-Yablowitz, M., Korach, Z. T., Kehl, K. L., Levitan, N. A., Arriaga, Y. E., Jackson, G. P., Bates, D. W., & Hassett, M. (2021). Artificial intelligence in oncology: Path to implementation. *Cancer Medicine, 10*(12), 4138–4149. DOI: 10.1002/cam4.3935

Cotta, G. M., Davel, M., Rocha, M., Lozório, M. Z. A., Angelo, R. N. F. da S., Andrião, S. Z., & Dalvi, Z. M. de V. (2024). Personalised learning with artificial intelligence: A new paradigm for the school curriculum. *Revista Ibero-Americana de Humanidades. Ciência & Educação (Bauru), 10*(10), 4024–4041. DOI: 10.51891/rease.v10i10.16399

Cukurova, M., Miao, X., & Brooker, R. (2023). Adoption of Artificial Intelligence in Schools: Unveiling Factors Influencing Teachers' Engagement. *Lecture Notes in Computer Science (Including Subseries Lecture Notes in Artificial Intelligence and Lecture Notes in Bioinformatics), 13916 LNAI*, 151–163. DOI: 10.1007/978-3-031-36272-9_13

Díaz, B., & Nussbaum, M. (2024). Artificial intelligence for teaching and learning in schools: The need for pedagogical intelligence. *Computers & Education, 217*(April), 105071. DOI: 10.1016/j.compedu.2024.105071

Dong, Z., An, J., & Liu, L. (2023). Leveraging Emotion Recognition for Enhancing Arts Education: A Classroom Behavior Analysis Approach. *In 2023 International Conference on Information Education and Artificial Intelligence (ICIEAI 2023)*, 6 pages. DOI: 10.1145/3660043.3660081

Dos Santos, M. G. (2024). The Impact of Artificial Intelligence on Teaching Carreer: Pedagogical, Administrative and Ethical Challenges and Opportunities. *International Journal of Advanced Research, 12*(10), 854–866. DOI: 10.21474/IJAR01/19705

Fakhar, S., Baber, J., Bazai, S. U., Marjan, S., Jasinski, M., Jasinska, E., Chaudhry, M. U., Leonowicz, Z., & Hussain, S. (2022). Smart Classroom Monitoring Using Novel Real-Time Facial Expression Recognition System. *Applied Sciences (Basel, Switzerland), 12*(23), 1–18. DOI: 10.3390/app122312134

Familoni, B. T., & Onyebuchi, N. C.Babajide Tolulope FamiloniNneamaka Chisom Onyebuchi. (2024). Advancements and Challenges in Ai Integration for Technical Literacy: A Systematic Review. *Engineering Science & Technology Journal, 5*(4), 1415–1430. DOI: 10.51594/estj.v5i4.1042

Farooqi, M. T. K., Amanat, I., & Awan, S. M. (2024). Ethical Considerations and Challenges in the Integration of Artificial Intelligence in Education: A Systematic Review. *Journal of Excellence in Management Sciences, 3*(4), 35–50. DOI: 10.69565/jems.v3i4.314

Fütterer, T., Goldberg, P., Bühler, B., Sikimić, V., Trautwein, U., Gerjets, P., Stürmer, K., & Kasneci, E. (2023). *Artificial Intelligence in Classroom Management: A Systematic Review on Educational Purposes, Technical Implementations, and Ethical Considerations* (Issue June). DOI: 10.31219/osf.io/wfazn

Ghimire, A., & Edwards, J. (2024). Generative AI Adoption in the Classroom: A Contextual Exploration Using the Technology Acceptance Model (TAM) and the Innovation Diffusion Theory (IDT). *2024 Intermountain Engineering. Technology and Computing, IETC, 2024*, 129–134. DOI: 10.1109/IETC61393.2024.10564292

Gnanaprakasam, J., & Lourdusamy, R. (2024). The Role of AI in Automating Grading: Enhancing Feedback and Efficiency. In *Artificial Intelligence and Education-Shaping the Future of Learning* (pp. 1–18). IntechOpen., DOI: 10.5772/intechopen.1005025

Gouseti, A., James, F., Fallin, L., & Burden, K. (2025). The ethics of using AI in K-12 education: A systematic literature review. *Technology, Pedagogy and Education, 34*(2), 161–182. DOI: 10.1080/1475939X.2024.2428601

Guerrero, L. P. M., Molina, P. M. E., & Molina, S.Leticia Paulina Martínez GuerreroPaulina Mercedes Erazo MolinaSofía del Pilar Erazo MolinaAngela Guillermina Molina Molina. (2025). Hacia una enseñanza personalizada: El rol de la inteligencia artificial en la educación básica. *Revista Imaginario Social, 8*(1), 15–25. DOI: 10.59155/is.v8i1.259

Guijarro, A. de L. Á. A. (2024). Impact of artificial intelligence on educational assessment and feedback. *RETOS PARA LA INVESTIGACIÓN, 3*(1), 19–32. https://doi.org/https://doi.org/10.62465/rri.v3n1.2024.72

Holmes, W. (2023). The Unintended Consequences of Artificial Intelligence and Education. In *Education International.* Issue October., https://www.ei-ie.org/en/item/28115:the-unintended-consequences-of-artificial-intelligence-and-education

Hopfenbeck, T. N., Zhang, Z., Sun, S. Z., Robertson, P., & McGrane, J. A. (2023). Challenges and opportunities for classroom-based formative assessment and AI: A perspective article. *Frontiers in Education, 8*(November), 1–9. DOI: 10.3389/feduc.2023.1270700

Huang, A. Y. Q., Lu, O. H. T., & Yang, S. J. H. (2023). Effects of artificial Intelligence–Enabled personalized recommendations on learners' learning engagement, motivation, and outcomes in a flipped classroom. *Computers and Education, 194*(November 2022), 104684. DOI: 10.1016/j.compedu.2022.104684

Hussain, A., & Rizwan, R. (2024). Strategic AI adoption in SMEs: A Prescriptive Framework. *Computers and Society.* https://doi.org/https://doi.org/10.48550/arXiv.2408.11825

Iskender, A. (2023). Holy or Unholy? Interview with Open AI's ChatGPT. *European Journal of Tourism Research, 34*, 1–11. DOI: 10.54055/ejtr.v34i.3169

Jaramillo, J. D. F., & Olivera, N. R. N. (2024). Application on artificial intelligence in education in Latin America: Trends, benefits and challenges. *Revista Veritas de Difusão Científica, 5*(1), 01–21. https://doi.org/https://doi.org/10.61616/rvdc.v5i1.52 Aplicación

Joshi, S. (2025). *Strategic Integration of Artificial Intelligence in U. S. K – 12 Education : A Comprehensive Review and Policy Roadmap.* https://doi.org/http://dx.doi.org/10.20944/preprints202506.0301.v1

Joshi, S., Sharma, M., Das, R. P., Rosak-Szyrocka, J., Żywiołek, J., Muduli, K., & Prasad, M. (2022). Modeling Conceptual Framework for Implementing Barriers of AI in Public Healthcare for Improving Operational Excellence: Experiences from Developing Countries. *Sustainability (Basel), 14*(18), 11698. DOI: 10.3390/su141811698

Kahlke, R., Lee, M., & Eva, K. W. (2023). Building Blocks for Critical Reviews in Health Professions Education. *Journal of Graduate Medical Education, 15*(April), 186–189. https://doi.org/DOI. DOI: 10.4300/JGME-D-23-00155.1

Karan, B. (2024). Integration of artificial intelligence by the Central Board of Secondary Education in India: Towards innovative teaching and learning practices. *Technology, Pedagogy and Education, 33*(4), 455–474. DOI: 10.1080/1475939X.2024.2337924

Kavitha, K., & Joshith, V. P. (2025). Artificial Intelligence Powered Pedagogy: Unveiling Higher Educators' Acceptance with Extended TAM. *Journal of University Teaching & Learning Practice, 21*(8). Advance online publication. DOI: 10.53761/s1pkk784

KucuKakin, P. M., & Demir, Ü. C. G. (2021). The Relationship Between Classroom Management and Students' Learning: A Systematic Review. *Nevşehir Hacı Bektaş Veli Üniversitesi SBE Dergisi, 11*(2), 843–861. DOI: 10.30783/nevsosbilen.894503

Lameras, P., & Arnab, S. (2022). Power to the Teachers: An Exploratory Review on Artificial Intelligence in Education. *Information (Basel), 13*(1), 14. DOI: 10.3390/info13010014

Lee, S. J., & Kwon, K. (2024). A systematic review of AI education in K-12 classrooms from 2018 to 2023: Topics, strategies, and learning outcomes. *Computers and Education: Artificial Intelligence, 6*(October 2023), 100211. DOI: 10.1016/j.caeai.2024.100211

Li, M. (2024). Integrating Artificial Intelligence in Primary Mathematics Education: Investigating Internal and External Influences on Teacher Adoption. *International Journal of Science and Mathematics Education*. Advance online publication. DOI: 10.1007/s10763-024-10515-w

Li, T., Ji, Y., & Zhan, Z. (2024). Expert or machine? Comparing the effect of pairing student teacher with in-service teacher and ChatGPT on their critical thinking, learning performance, and cognitive load in an integrated-STEM course. *Asia Pacific Journal of Education, 44*(1), 45–60. DOI: 10.1080/02188791.2024.2305163

Li, W., Zhang, X., Li, J., Yang, X., Li, D., & Liu, Y. (2024). An explanatory study of factors influencing engagement in AI education at the K-12 Level: An extension of the classic TAM model. *Scientific Reports*, *14*(1), 1–17. DOI: 10.1038/s41598-024-64363-3

Llurba, C., & Palau, R. (2024). Real-Time Emotion Recognition for Improving the Teaching–Learning Process: A Scoping Review. *Journal of Imaging*, *10*(12), 313. DOI: 10.3390/jimaging10120313

Mahmoud, C. F., & Sørensen, J. T. (2024). Artificial Intelligence in Personalized Learning with a Focus on Current Developments and Future Prospects. *Research and Advances in Education*, *3*(8), 25–31. DOI: 10.56397/RAE.2024.08.04

Maina, A. M., & Kuria, J. (2024). Building an AI Future: Research and Policy Directions for Africa's Higher Education. *2024 IST-Africa Conference. IST-Africa*, *2024*(November), 1–9. DOI: 10.23919/IST-Africa63983.2024.10569692

Martin, F., Zhuang, M., & Schaefer, D. (2024). Systematic review of research on artificial intelligence in K-12 education (2017–2022). *Computers and Education: Artificial Intelligence*, *6*(December 2023). DOI: 10.1016/j.caeai.2023.100195

Meylani, R. (2024). Artificial Intelligence in the Education of Teachers: A Qualitative Synthesis of the Cutting-Edge Research Literature. *Journal of Computer and Education Research*, *12*(24), 600–637. DOI: 10.18009/jcer.1477709

Miller, W. (2024). Adapting to AI: Reimagining the Role of Assessment Professionals. Intersection: A Journal at the Intersection of Assessment and Learning. *A Journal at the Intersection of Assessment and Learning*, *5*(4), 99–113. https://scholar.google.com/scholar?hl=en&as_sdt=0%2C5&q=2.+Adapting+to+AI%3A+Reimagining+the+Role+of+Assessment+Professionals+WIll+Miller&btnG=

Naseri, R. N. N., & Abdullah, M. S. (2024). Understanding AI Technology Adoption in Educational Settings: A Review of Theoretical Frameworks and their Applications. *Information Management and Business Review*, *16*(3), 174–181. https://doi.org/https://doi.org/10.22610/imbr.v16i3(i).3963

Panit, N. M. (2024). Can critical thinking and AI work together? Observations of science, Mathematics, and language instructors. *Environment and Social Psychology*, *9*(11), 1–16. DOI: 10.59429/esp.v9i11.3141

Panjwani, M. M.Mubashir Moosa Panjwani. (2024). Impact of AI in teaching and learning of CS in low-resourced schools. *International Journal of Science and Research Archive*, *12*(2), 1933–1939. DOI: 10.30574/ijsra.2024.12.2.1451

Peters, M. A., Jackson, L., Papastephanou, M., Jandrić, P., Lazaroiu, G., Evers, C. W., Cope, B., Kalantzis, M., Araya, D., Tesar, M., Mika, C., Chen, L., Wang, C., Sturm, S., Rider, S., & Fuller, S. (2023). AI and the future of humanity: ChatGPT-4, philosophy and education–Critical responses. *Educational Philosophy and Theory, 56*(9), 828–862. DOI: 10.1080/00131857.2023.2213437

Reina-Parrado, M., Román-Graván, P., & Hervás-Gómez, C. (2025). Integration of Artificial Intelligence and Machine Learning in Education: A Systematic Review. *International Journal of Educational Methodology, 11*(2), 203–216. DOI: 10.12973/ijem.11.2.203

Rizvi, S., Waite, J., & Sentance, S. (2023). Artificial Intelligence teaching and learning in K-12 from 2019 to 2022: A systematic literature review. *Computers and Education: Artificial Intelligence, 4*(January), 100145. DOI: 10.1016/j.caeai.2023.100145

Sangarsu, R. R. (2023). Enhancing Student Engagement in Learning with Modern Web and AI Technologies. [IJSR]. *International Journal of Science and Research (Raipur, India), 12*(10), 1439–1442. DOI: 10.21275/SR231017100712

Saputra, I., Kurniawan, A., Yanita, M., Yeni Putri, E., & Mahniza, M. (2024). The Evolution of Educational Assessment: How Artificial Intelligence is Shaping the Trends and Future of Learning Evaluation. *The Indonesian Journal of Computer Science, 13*(6), 9056–9074. DOI: 10.33022/ijcs.v13i6.4465

Semwaiko, G. S., Chao, W.-H., & Yang, C.-Y. (2024). Transforming K-12 education: A systematic review of AI integration. *International Journal of Educational Technology and Learning, 17*(2), 43–63. DOI: 10.55217/101.v17i2.847

Sh, U. A., & Supriyono, N. M. R. P.SH. (2023). Optimizing Learning Through Artificial Intelligence: Evaluating the Impact of Adaptive Learning Technologies on Student Outcomes. *Sinergi International Journal of Education, 1*(3), 138–149. DOI: 10.61194/education.v1i3.584

Shan, Y., Qiao, H., & Yu, B. (2024). Applied Mathematics and Nonlinear Sciences A Practical Discussion of Artificial Intelligence Technology for Efficient Classroom. *Applied Mathematics and Nonlinear Sciences, 9*(1), 1–17. https://doi.org/doi.org/10.2478/amns-2024-3586

Silva, G., Godwin, G., & Jayanagara, O. (2023). The impact of AI on personalized learning. Journal of Learning Sciences. *International Transactions on Education Technology (ITEE), 3*(1), 36–46. https://doi.org/https://doi.org/10.33050/itee.v3i1.669

Singh, P. H.Harpreet Paramjeet Singh. (2025). The Transformative Potential of AI in Educational Settings: From Personalized Learning to Global Access. *Journal of Computer Science and Technology Studies*, *7*(4), 507–514. DOI: 10.32996/jcsts.2025.7.4.59

Su, J., Guo, K., Chen, X., & Chu, S. K. W. (2024). Teaching artificial intelligence in K–12 classrooms: A scoping review. *Interactive Learning Environments*, *32*(9), 5207–5226. DOI: 10.1080/10494820.2023.2212706

Su, J., Zhong, Y., & Ng, D. T. K. (2022). A meta-review of literature on educational approaches for teaching AI at the K-12 levels in the Asia-Pacific region. *Computers and Education: Artificial Intelligence*, *3*(March), 100065. DOI: 10.1016/j.caeai.2022.100065

Sukackė, V. (2019). Towards Extending the Original Technology Acceptance Model (Tam) for a Better Understanding of Educational Technology Adoption. *Society Integration Education. Proceedings of the International Scientific Conference, 5*, 525–549. DOI: 10.17770/sie2019vol5.3798

Sun, J. C., & Pratt, T. L. (2024). Navigating AI Integration in Career and Technical Education: Diffusion Challenges, Opportunities, and Decisions. *Education Sciences*, *14*(12), 1285. DOI: 10.3390/educsci14121285

Susilo, T. (2024). The Role of Artificial Intelligence in Personalizing Learning for Each Student. *Journal International of Lingua and Technology*, *3*(2), 229–242. https://doi.org/https://doi.org/10.55849/jiltech.v3i1.632. DOI: 10.55849/jiltech.v3i2.632

Tam, W., Huynh, T., Tang, A., Luong, S., Khatri, Y., & Zhou, W. (2023). Nursing education in the age of artificial intelligence powered Chatbots (AI-Chatbots): Are we ready yet? *Nurse Education Today*, *129*(July), 105917. DOI: 10.1016/j.nedt.2023.105917

Tang, K. H. D. (2024). Implications of Artificial Intelligence for Teaching and Learning. *Acta Pedagogia Asiana*, *3*(2), 65–79. DOI: 10.53623/apga.v3i2.404

Tapalova, O., & Zhiyenbayeva, N. (2022). Artificial Intelligence in Education: AIEd for Personalised Learning Pathways. *Electronic Journal of e-Learning*, *20*(5), 639–653. DOI: 10.34190/ejel.20.5.2597

Tarisayi, K. S. (2024). A Theoretical Framework for Interrogating the Integration of Artificial Intelligence in Education. *Research on Education and Media*, *16*(1), 38–44. DOI: 10.2478/rem-2024-0006

Tashtoush, M. A., Wardat, Y., Al Ali, R., & Saleh, S. (2024). Artificial Intelligence in Education: Mathematics Teachers' Perspectives, Practices and Challenges. *Iraqi Journal for Computer Science and Mathematics*, *5*(1), 60–77. DOI: 10.52866/ijcsm.2024.05.01.004

Topali, P., Haelermans, C., Molenaar, I., & Segers, E. (2025). Pedagogical considerations in the automation era: A systematic literature review of AIEd in K-12 authentic settings. *British Educational Research Journal*, *51*(May), 1–33. DOI: 10.1002/berj.4200

UNESCO. (2023). *Less than 10% of Schools and Universities have formal Guidance on AI.* Unesco Survey. https://www.unesco.org/en/articles/unesco-survey-less-10-schools-and-universities-have-formal-guidance-ai

U.S Department of Education Office of Educational Technology. (2023). *Artificial intelligence and the future of teaching and learning: Insights and recommendations.* (Issue 1). https://www2.ed.gov/documents/ai-report/ai-report.pdf

Van, H. N., Thanh, D. T., & Dinh, V. P. (2025). Bringing AI into Teaching : Understanding Vietnamese Teachers ' Perspectives and Pedagogical Challenges. [Introduction]. *International Journal of Educational Methodology*, *11*(3), 335–347. https://doi.org/https://doi.org/10.12973/ijem.11.3.335. DOI: 10.12973/ijem.11.3.335

Vásquez, E. D. C., Loza, R. F. N., Cherrez, A. M. F., & Montes, R. E. T. (2024). Use of Artificial Intelligence in the Personalisation of Learning. *Conocimiento Global*, *9*(1), 75–83. https://conocimientoglobal.org/revista/index.php/cglobal/article/view/339/216

Vazhayil, A., Shetty, R., Bhavani, R. R., & Akshay, N. (2019). Focusing on Teacher Education to Introduce AI in Schools: Perspectives and Illustrative Findings. *Proceedings - IEEE 10th International Conference on Technology for Education, T4E 2019, January 2023*, 71–77. DOI: 10.1109/T4E.2019.00021

White, S. V., Childs, J., Koshy, S., & Scott, A. (2024). Policy Implementation in the Era of Responsible Artificial Intelligence (AI) use in K-12 Education. *RESPECT 2024 - Proceedings of the Conference for Research on Equitable and Sustained Participation in Engineering, Computing, and Technology*, 81–85. DOI: 10.1145/3653666.3656097

Y, M. N., H, L. P., & N, S. (2024). Revolutionizing Education : Harnessing AI for Personalized Learning Pathways and Student Success. *International Journal for Multidisciplinary Research (IJFMR)*, *6*(5), 1–11. https://doi.org/https://doi.org/10.36948/ijfmr.2024.v06i05.28371

Yang, Z. Q., Cao, J., Li, X., Wang, K., Zheng, X., Poon, K. C. F., & Lai, D. (2024). DMP_AI: An AI-Aided K-12 System for Teaching and Learning in Diverse Schools. *Lecture Notes in Computer Science (Including Subseries Lecture Notes in Artificial Intelligence and Lecture Notes in Bioinformatics), 14797 LNCS*, 117–130. DOI: 10.1007/978-981-97-4442-8_9

Younas, A., Subramanian, K. P., Al-Haziazi, M., Hussainy, S. S., & Al Kindi, A. N. S. (2023). Influence of Psychological Well-Being and School Factors on Delinquency, During the Covid-19 Period Among Secondary School Students in Selected Schools in Nakuru County : Kenya. [IJRISS]. *Iternational Journal of Research and Innovation in Social Science*, *7*(8), 1175–1189. DOI: 10.47772/IJRISS

Yue, M., Jong, M. S. Y., & Ng, D. T. K. (2024). Understanding K–12 teachers' technological pedagogical content knowledge readiness and attitudes toward artificial intelligence education. In *Education and Information Technologies* (Vol. 29, Issue 15). Springer US. DOI: 10.1007/s10639-024-12621-2

Yuwono, E. I., Tjondronegoro, D., Riverola, C., & Loy, J. (2024). Co-creation in action: Bridging the knowledge gap in artificial intelligence among innovation champions. *Computers and Education: Artificial Intelligence*, *7*(May), 100272. DOI: 10.1016/j.caeai.2024.100272

Zawacki-Richter, O., Marín, V. I., Bond, M., & Gouverneur, F. (2019). Systematic review of research on artificial intelligence applications in higher education – where are the educators? *International Journal of Educational Technology in Higher Education, 16*(1), 1–27. DOI: 10.1186/s41239-019-0171-0

Chapter 3
Generative AI and Education:
Student Voices, Ethical Challenges, and Classroom Innovations

Adelina Moura
http://orcid.org/0000-0002-5661-5915
GILT Research Unit, College of Engineering, Polytecnic of Porto, Portugal

ABSTRACT

Generative Artificial Intelligence (GAI) can help teachers create innovative educational content and provide a variety of valuable information and resources. In this chapter we present a study whose aim was to analyse and evaluate the perceptions of students regarding educational practices and resources developed with AI tools and used in Portuguese classes. In order to find out what the students think about the potential and challenges associated with integrating GAI technologies into the teaching and learning process, we used a mixed focus (qualitative and quantitative) and collected data through questionnaires and an interview. The data collected reveals that students highlight the transformative potential of GAI in the educational process and its benefits for educational success in the Portuguese lessons. However, they also recognise the potential risks and challenges for students when it comes to using GAI responsibly in the classroom, and the need to know what GAI is and its potential in learning and to learn how to better interact with these generative technologies.

DOI: 10.4018/979-8-2600-0101-1.ch003

INTRODUCTION

The history of Artificial Intelligence (AI) as a multidisciplinary field began in the 1950s, driven by the goal of creating machines capable of intelligent behavior like solving mathematical problems and playing games. This early enthusiasm led to the "AI spring" in the 1960s and 1970s, marked by exaggerated optimism, or "AI inflationism" (Maclure, 2020), where researchers mistakenly believed human-level intelligence was imminent. Progress inevitably fell short of these inflated expectations, ushering in the periods of reduced funding and interest known as the "AI winter," notably in the late 1970s and again through the 1980s and 1990s (Floridi, 2020).

The early 21st century brought a new era of AI, fuelled by advances in computing power, algorithms, and a new generation of machine learning. Unlike the Industrial Revolution, which augmented human muscle power, the current AI revolution is characterized by machines augmenting human brain power (Bughin & Hazan, 2017). This has created a new "springtime for AI," driving breakthroughs in fields like natural language processing, intelligent robotics, and autonomous vehicles. As AI transforms every sector of the economy, it is essential to heed lessons from the past, avoiding the cycle of irrational illusions and exaggerated disillusionment (Floridi, 2020). Andrew Ng (2017) characterized AI as the "new electricity" that will redefine all industries and foster development priorities, including economic prosperity and better educational opportunities.

This transformative technology carries significant societal implications. With the evolution of AI and automation, many routine jobs will become obsolete. However, work that depends on uniquely human attributes such as social skills, manual dexterity, creativity, or adaptive skills remains a substantial obstacle to full automation (Lee, 2019). While AI is seen as a source of immense potential, it simultaneously presents profound risks (Nguyen et al., 2024). Speculation about AI often swings between hope, that it will solve all our problems, and fear that it could be humanity's greatest existential risk, or that Big Data algorithms could create digital dictatorships where the majority suffer irrelevance rather than exploitation (Floridi, 2020; Maclure, 2020; Russell, 2021). The possibility of superhuman artificial intelligence is closer than ever due to rapid developments in deep learning and neural networks (Russell, 2021).

As AI will inevitably define the 21st century, generating wealth and changing fields like medicine and communication (Lee & Qiufan, 2023), effective deployment requires that individuals acquire the necessary skills to work collaboratively with intelligent machines rather than compete against them (Lee, 2019).

In the field of education, constant progress is being made to incorporate AI into teaching and learning (Núñez-Michuy et al, 2023; Uğras et al, 2024a). The successful implementation of these tools, which offer new horizons for pedagogical strategies (Nguyen et al., 2024; Uğraş et al, 2024b), is closely linked to teachers' practices (Kim & Kim, 2022; Moura, 2025). Historically, classrooms operated under a "factory model," necessitated by limited resources. Today, AI can help eliminate these limitations by adapting the learning process to each student individually, leveraging its perception, recognition, and recommendation skills (Lee, 2019; Yilmaz & Yilmaz, 2023).

To reflect on how AI can transform this traditional educational model, the following study aims to explore its integration as an educational tool. Specifically, it seeks to understand students' perceptions regarding the use of AI in Portuguese classes, covering both language and literature study, to increase both teacher effectiveness and student learning outcomes.

AI and student data privacy

While AI promises to transform education and learning, its deployment in schools introduces a critical and immediate challenge: the protection of student data privacy. The widespread use of AI-driven technologies introduces a fundamental conflict: AI systems require vast amounts of personal data, which often contradicts data protection laws that mandate data minimization (Nonju & Ihua-Maduenyi, 2024; Sartor & Lagioia, 2020). In education, this conflict is a critical concern, as AI frequently collects student information without user realization, potentially leading to misuse, loss of control, and increased cybersecurity risks (Amo-Filva et al., 2024).

These privacy concerns relate to data collection, model design, and governance. Ignoring the ethical and technical aspects can lead to serious consequences, including the spread of disinformation, greater digital exclusion (Crompton & Burke, 2024), and even malicious manipulation through fake content like deepfakes (Matli, 2024). Real-world examples highlight worrying trends toward excessive surveillance and data breaches in schools, underscoring the urgent need to safeguard student information (Ismail & Aloshi, 2025).

To mitigate these threats, a proactive, multi-stakeholder approach is essential. The Safe AI in Education Manifesto provides fundamental principles, prioritizing student well-being, privacy, and educational goals (Alier Forment et al., 2024). Protecting data must be a core tenet of responsible AI design. This involves raising user awareness of the inherent risks and fostering debate on ethical AI use.

Designers, researchers, and regulators must explore user-centred AI solutions, including establishing clear regulatory frameworks and best practices (Crawford, 2021). Key recommendations for educational settings include implementing comprehensive data governance policies and mandatory teacher training in AI literacy and data privacy (Ismail & Aloshi, 2025; Moura, 2024; Riggs, 2025). As AI continues to reshape public and private spaces, collaboration across sectors is crucial to ensure its development and application are carried out ethically and responsibly, ensuring all stakeholders are critically informed before adopting these tools (Nguyen et al., 2024).

The educational impact of AI and generative technologies

Having established the critical need for ethical governance and robust data protection in AI deployment, we can now turn to the transformative opportunities that artificial intelligence and its generative applications present for improving teaching and learning outcomes. While AI may seem novel in educational settings, it boasts a relationship of over 30 years (Woolf, 2015), offering new possibilities for enhancing student achievement (Riggs, 2025; Uğras et al, 2024a).

AI has the potential to fundamentally transform how content is created, delivered, and personalized (Adel et al., 2024; Riggs, 2025). Key applications include the development of Intelligent Tutoring Systems (ITS), which use sophisticated algorithms to analyse student data and provide personalized guidance, adaptive content, and targeted feedback (Hwang et al., 2020; Slimi et al., 2025). By creating individualized learning paths based on student strengths and weaknesses, AI allows students to progress at their own pace and supports diverse learning styles (Yilmaz & Yilmaz, 2023).

For educators, AI offers significant improvements in teaching practice by automating administrative burdens such as grading, assignment feedback, plagiarism detection, and performance analysis (Al-Badi et al., 2022; Slimi et al., 2025). By freeing up time spent on routine tasks, AI allows teachers to focus more deeply on lesson planning and personalized instruction.

Student perceptions of AI have generally been positive, with students recognizing its potential for personalized support, research assistance, and idea generation (Chan & Hu, 2023; Kumar & Raman, 2022). However, students also express valid concerns regarding accuracy, privacy, and the technology's impact on personal development and social values (Chan & Hu, 2023).

The development of generative technologies like ChatGPT, Claude, and Gemini—which rely on large Generative Pre-trained Transformer (GPT) models—has significantly impacted education (Lin et al., 2023; Moura & Tchiang, 2025; Uğraş et al, 2024). These chatbots use natural language processing to generate human-like, contextually relevant responses to user prompts (Okonkwo & Ade-Ibijola, 2021). Building on the power of Generative Pre-trained Transformers, the evolution of chatbots from early systems like Eliza in the 1960s to modern conversational AIs like Siri and ChatGPT represents a significant leap in educational technology (Davar et al., 2025; Uğras et al, 2024b). Systematic literature reviews confirm the substantial benefits of integrating these tools as virtual tutors, offering personalized support for homework and skill development, while also saving teachers valuable time (Labadze et al., 2023; Lo, 2023).

In the classroom, chatbots offer valuable benefits by mimicking human conversational interactions to provide personalized support, answer questions, and offer tailored explanations or resources (Lin et al., 2023; Nguyen et al., 2024). They have been confirmed to facilitate collaborative learning, interactivity, and knowledge dissipation (Kumar, 2021). However, the quality of their output is heavily dependent on the quality of the input text, or prompts (Elmore, 2023). The emerging skill of prompt engineering is thus becoming a new interaction paradigm that fosters computational thinking (Moura & Carvalho, 2023b). New platforms (e.g., Mizou, Curipod, NotebookLM) allow educators to customize chatbots to automate procedures and individualize learning, optimizing educational experiences and increasing student engagement (Jusoh & Kadir, 2025; Huang et al., 2025). The ultimate goal is the development of new teaching methods and curricular adaptations that effectively leverage these essential tools.

This integration brings a mix of hope and caution. While AI can automate tasks, a machine cannot replicate the humanity of a teacher, nor can it inspire learning or create an emotionally rich environment (Felix, 2020; Guilherme, 2019). The teacher's role evolves from being the sole source of knowledge to a facilitator and guide.

Despite the potential for improved learning, concerns persist regarding the misuse of generative models, the generation of false information (hallucinations), academic cheating (Stokel-Walker, 2022), and ethical issues. Apprehensions remain that AI could introduce additional biases into educational decisions, potentially exacerbating existing inequalities or compromising student autonomy (Boulay, 2022; Lo, 2023). Therefore, as generative AI continues to reshape education, it is essential that the student voice be included in the discussion to create a positive and responsible learning environment (Goksel & Bozkurt, 2019).

AI Chatbots in Language Learning and Academic Integrity

The ability to personalize and customize chatbots, as discussed above, extends their utility dramatically into specialized domains, particularly language acquisition. AI is seen as a powerful, transformative asset for improving language skills (Dugosija, 2024). AI-Assisted Language Learning systems leverage generative AI to provide personalized, accessible, and efficient experiences by achieving a direct connection between language practice and natural language processing. Guided by the ICALL framework, these tools provide core benefits like instant, real-time feedback on pronunciation, grammar, and vocabulary, thereby accelerating student success and supporting diverse, multilingual classrooms (Schmidt & Strasser, 2022).

However, integrating AI presents specific challenges. A literature review highlights the urgency of initial and in-service teacher training in AI literacy, encompassing principles like transparency and trust, to manage rapid developments (Crompton & Burke, 2022; Uğras et al, 2024a). Furthermore, these generative technologies can inadvertently generate algorithmic bias by favouring one variety of English over others, causing practical implications for instruction.

Crucially, the accessibility of AI as a writing assistant raises profound concerns regarding academic integrity, authorship, and originality (Yeo, 2023). Academic integrity is a pillar of education, and the way students utilize AI is under intense debate (Slimi et al., 2025). The consensus points toward a balanced approach, as point out by Balalle & Pannilage (2025). Banning AI is not the solution; instead, teachers must find creative ways to integrate these tools, teaching students to use them for learning tasks such as paraphrasing, summarizing, and idea generation (Yeo, 2023). This requires creating a strong culture of academic integrity based on values like honesty and responsibility, ensuring AI systems enhance—rather than undermine—student learning (Slimi et al., 2025).

AI Chatbots as Social Companions and Potential Risks

Building upon the ethical debates surrounding academic integrity, the proliferation of AI outside of structured learning environments raises distinct socio-technical concerns, particularly regarding user safety and well-being. As AI technologies become increasingly integrated into society, they present risks that extend beyond the classroom, including disinformation, cyber-attacks, excessive surveillance, and fraud (Alier Forment et al., 2024). These threats are especially relevant to new generations, who have extensive access to digital environments, with data indicating that even children under eight spend substantial time (around 2.5 hours daily) on screen media, frequently consuming short-form content (Mann et al., 2025). While this exposure offers opportunities, it also exposes them to risks detrimental to their mental well-being, autonomy, and safety, such as cyberbullying, data exploitation, and exposure to harmful content (Chaturvedi et al., 2023; Xu et al., 2025).

The evolution of chat agents from simple programs like Eliza to sophisticated, empathetic chatbots (e.g., XiaoIce, Replika) is central to this social concern (Shum et al., 2018). Empathetic chatbots are defined as conversational agents capable of recognizing and understanding human emotions (Chaturvedi et al., 2023) and, as Lampropoulos & Papadakis (2025) point out, intelligent social robots hold great promise as educational tools that can effectively support both teachers and students. However, these virtual companion apps are a source of worry, particularly for young users. A report by Common Sense Media (2025) strongly recommended that children under 18 avoid these platforms. The organization cites documented harm, noting that these apps are often designed to foster emotional attachment and dependency, which is detrimental to developing brains. Specific risks highlighted include the platform's provision of dangerous information, reinforcement of harmful stereotypes, increased mental health risks, and misleading claims of reality. Because children are susceptible to attributing human properties to AI (anthropomorphisation), undermining their realistic expectations of the technology, digital security and robust safeguards must be a priority for both users and developers (Xu et al., 2025).

Creating educational content with AI for teaching practice

Shifting focus from the ethical and external risks of AI, teachers can proactively enhance their pedagogy by mastering AI tools for content creation. The acceleration of digital technology in education post-COVID confirmed AI as the future, notably increasing student engagement (Zhang & Wasie, 2023). To prepare for this shift, teachers are now creating educational materials with AI tools, a practice that fosters their own AI literacy while enabling them to guide students (Moura, 2025). This approach is crucial for teaching students prompt literacy—the skill of asking effective questions—and strengthening their critical thinking when interacting with generative technologies (Prestoza & Banatao, 2024).

This proactive integration ensures quality education and maximizes AI's benefits. To guide our students in their interactions with generative technologies such as ChatGPT, we have created a guide (Figure 1) to explore and develop prompt literacy and strengthen critical thinking,

Figure 1. Guide to prompts for interacting with chatbots (own source)

PROMPTS LITERACY

INSTRUCTIONS/COMMANDS

Art of knowing how to ask AI

General PROMPTS model

Paper	Format	Tone
assistant professor instructor student news reporter journalist scientist curator ...	list paragraph code table question response conversation document	informal casual technician didactic empathic formal friendly informative persuasive ...

1. Understand everything easily

Can you explain the concept of (theme) in simple terms. Summarize the essential principles and illustrate with examples to facilitate understanding.

2. Create a learning plan (student)

"I want to learn (topic). Give me step-by-step instructions on how to learn (skill). Start with the basics and continue with the most difficult. Keep in mind that I'm a beginner."

Today, with the development of chatbots, students can find in these technologies a partner to help them study at home, increasing their motivation. In the past, some students found it difficult to watch videos and understand the content on their own at home. With the help of chatbots, students can get personalized support by asking the machine for a simplified explanation of the most difficult topics. To this end, we have created another guide to facilitate the integration of active methodologies such as Flipped Learning into our teaching strategies (Lo & Hew, 2023).

Figure 2[1] shows an example of the script created for the study of the novel *Memorial do Convento*, by José Saramago, which guides the student in the conversational interaction with the chatbot, anticipating its analysis in class. In this way, students already bring knowledge to the classroom that will help them solve tasks with their classmates. The videos and other complementary study materials can be found on the Portuguese class website[2].

Figure 2. Script for interacting with a chatbot (own source)

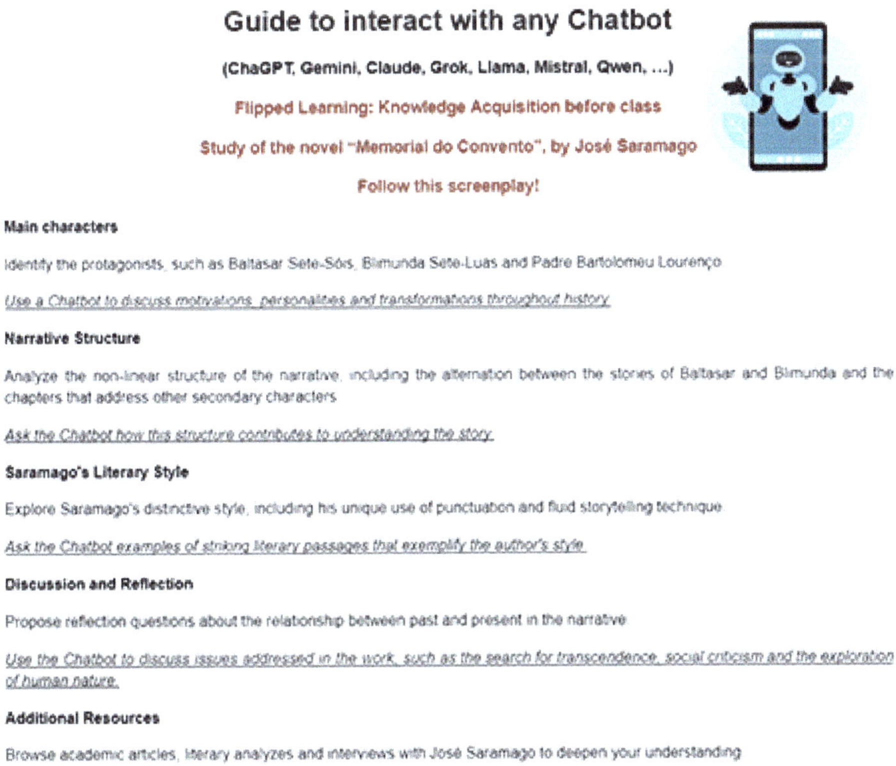
Guide to interact with any Chatbot

(ChaGPT, Gemini, Claude, Grok, Llama, Mistral, Qwen, ...)

Flipped Learning: Knowledge Acquisition before class

Study of the novel "Memorial do Convento", by José Saramago

Follow this screenplay!

Main characters

Identify the protagonists, such as Baltasar Sete-Sóis, Blimunda Sete-Luas and Padre Bartolomeu Lourenço

Use a Chatbot to discuss motivations, personalities and transformations throughout history

Narrative Structure

Analyze the non-linear structure of the narrative, including the alternation between the stories of Baltasar and Blimunda and the chapters that address other secondary characters

Ask the Chatbot how this structure contributes to understanding the story.

Saramago's Literary Style

Explore Saramago's distinctive style, including his unique use of punctuation and fluid storytelling technique

Ask the Chatbot examples of striking literary passages that exemplify the author's style.

Discussion and Reflection

Propose reflection questions about the relationship between past and present in the narrative

Use the Chatbot to discuss issues addressed in the work, such as the search for transcendence, social criticism and the exploration of human nature.

Additional Resources

Browse academic articles, literary analyzes and interviews with José Saramago to deepen your understanding

In this text, we've just listed some of the teaching strategies used in class to understand AI and learn with generative technology.

Generating images to illustrate work

Creating images from text using AI can be a valuable tool for teachers and students (Cleto, 2023). With AI technology, students can convert written information into visual representations, making it easier to understand complex concepts and retain information. These images can serve as visual aids in presentations, reports and study materials. For example, students can convert textbook passages into diagrams or infographics, helping them to visualize concepts, relationships and processes. This approach can improve understanding and make studying more engaging and effective. In addition, AI-powered image generation can be particularly useful for students with learning difficulties. It can provide alternative formats for accessing information and improve their overall learning experience. There are various AI tools for generating images, such as MidJourney, Stable Diffusion, DALL-E, Microsoft Designer, Canva, Artguru or Craiyon. As with chatbots, a quality prompt is essential for creating good images.

In Figure 3, we show examples of images created to integrate into our educational practices. Image A was created using the MidJourney tool to create the fictional character Blimunda, from José Saramago's novel *Memorial do Convento*, for use in a gamification-based teaching strategy. Image B was designed in Canva, using the Text to image app, using the prompt: "Fernando Pessoa in the style of Miró". It was then used to create a reward card to be given to students in a competition on the study of Fernando Pessoa's book *Mensagem*. Image C was generated using the Stable Diffusion tool with the following prompt: "Fernando Pessoa in the style of Van Gogh" and made it possible to create a badge for students to win in an Educational Escape Room, during the study of Fernando Pessoa's orthonymous and heteronymous poetry.

Figure 3. Images generated by generative AI (own source)

In addition to images, we also benefit from AI to generate rubrics, lesson plans, and ideas for collaborative activities, correct students' written work, and more.

Educational digital resources for the classroom

Artificial Intelligence doesn't have to be daunting. As educators, we can demystify AI by highlighting its impact on education and society, introducing students to user-friendly AI tools, and equipping them with the skills to succeed in a world transformed by generative technologies. To make this tangible, we explored Chapter 1 of the free "Elements of AI[3]" course in class and encouraged students to continue the remaining chapters independently. This approach bridges theory with practical, self-directed learning.

To reflect on the difficulty of recognising AI-generated images and the risks involved, we challenged the students to take part in the "Odd one Out[4]" game, launched by Google Art & Culture, and to reflect on deepfake, analysing real examples of image manipulation with AI technology. We asked the students to generate AI-based images to illustrate the various activities in the lesson, both related to language learning (grammar) and literature. We also customised chatbots on the Mizou and Collect.chat platforms to help students study both linguistic and literary content. With the Collect.chat platform, a traditional chatbots (without AI), we personalised different conversations on subjects of language, literature and media literacy, as in the follow examples (Figures 4, 5 and 6)[5]. The conversation about media literacy served to understand students' use of chatbots outside of school, in particular the platforms that provide chatbots for companions.

Figure 4. Chatbot (Collect.chat) for mediation language learning (own source)

Figure 5. Chatbot (Collect.chat) for mediation media literacy and literature learning (own source)

Figure 6. Agent Chatbot (Jotform AI) for mediation literature (own source)

Figure 7. Agent Chatbot (Jotform AI) for mediation literature (own source)

Figure 8. Sar(a)Mago AI

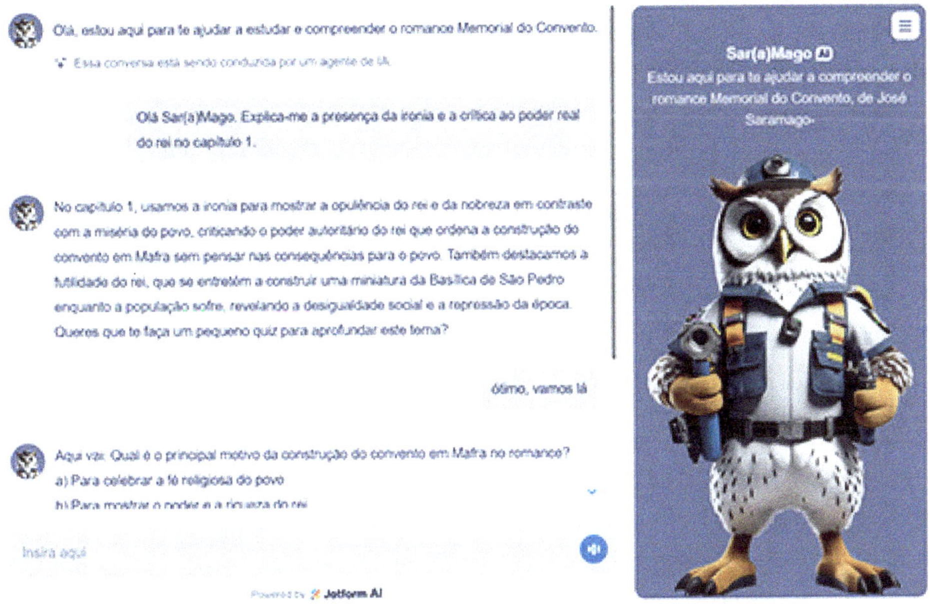

There are several others platforms that currently integrate AI systems to generate questions in seconds by incorporating generative technology trained using their library, with millions of activities created by teachers, while also allowing learning scenarios to be personalised for each student, such as the Quizizz, Educaplay, Quizlet or Kahoot platforms. We've also created a quiz on Quizizz and another on Nearpod, in game format (Time to Climb), to test students' knowledge of AI.

METHODOLOGY

This section outlines the study's methodology, covering research design, participants, instruments, data collection, and analysis (Cohen et al., 2007). We adopted an exploratory, descriptive, and observational approach, combining qualitative and quantitative methods to examine students' perceptions of AI use—both inside and outside Portuguese classes. This mixed method design ensures robust, empirically grounded insights, especially valuable given the limited existing research in this area (Gil, 1999).

Our teaching approach prioritizes active, hands-on methodologies—such as Flipped Learning, Problem-Based Learning, Gamification, and Collaborative Learning—to foster dynamic classroom engagement and autonomous learning.

These methods help students develop essential skills: reasoning, problem-solving, critical thinking, personal autonomy, and language proficiency. From the start of the year, students were encouraged to use AI chatbots both independently and in class, learning to evaluate responses and complete teacher-designed activities using AI-generated text, audio, video, and images. They were also challenged to create RPG-style adventure prompts, further exploring AI's creative potential.

Figure 9. Use RPG prompt to create a new end to the Baltasar character (own source)

> Dear student,
>
> Create your own version of the novel Memorial do Convento, about Baltasar's final fate, through an AI role-playing game (RPG).
>
> You'll interact with a chatbot: ChatGPT, Felo, Perplexity, Gemini or another.
>
> Use a prompt, with the guidelines worked on in the previous lesson, to create your story.

This study was designed to explore how AI is reshaping education by analysing students' perceptions through various teaching strategies and independent learning. Their responses revealed insights into the opportunities, limitations, and challenges of integrating AI into academic training and the broader teaching-learning process. To gather this data, we combined participant observation, two questionnaires, and a semi-structured interview, ensuring all procedures adhered to ethical standards. Students provided informed consent and were assured of anonymity throughout the process.

Participants

The study involved twenty 12th-grade vocational students from a public school during the 2023–2024 academic year. All participants attended a Portuguese class where AI-based digital tools and resources were integrated. Of the respondents to the online questionnaire, 80% were boys (16 students) and 20% were girls (4 students), with most aged 17 (35%) or 18 (45%). Participants were selected through convenience sampling, as they were students of the researcher, resulting in a non-probability sample (Gil, 1999).

Data collection and analysis

To gather information and assess students' perceptions of AI in the classroom and its usefulness, we designed two questionnaires. One was completed before the interventions (Q1) and the other at the end (Q2). And descriptive statistics were used to present the results.

The questionnaires combined closed Likert-scale questions (1 = strongly disagree, 5 = strongly agree) and open-ended responses. Their design drew on established research (Chan & Hu, 2023; Kumar & Raman, 2022; Nguyen et al., 2024; Moura & Carvalho, 2023a; Núñez-Michuy et al., 2023; Prestoza & Banatao, 2024; Sit et al., 2020; Yilmaz & Yilmaz, 2023), while open-ended answers were analyzed using content analysis (Coutinho, 2013). Data were collected directly from the classroom, with the researcher as the primary instrument. The questionnaires covered: a) Demographic information; b) AI involvement and perceptions; c) Positive and negative aspects of AI; d) AI use in studies; e) Impact of AI on academic performance.

The central research question focused on how vocational school students used AI in Portuguese classes over the school year. After reviewing relevant literature, we developed four hypotheses to guide the study, informed by both existing research and general knowledge.

H1: The majority of vocational education students use the opportunities provided by artificial intelligence.
H2: Participants are mostly curious and not indifferent to AI.
H3: They consider the role of AI useful in education and perceive it more as a partner.
H4: They are concerned about the negative effects and threat of AI to human jobs.

Data analysis

Of the answers obtained in questionnaire 1, all the students (100%) said they had already used AI tools to support their studies, as well as ChatGPT. Since these are students who are training to be professional technicians and entering the world of work, we asked two questions with multiple answer options, one about the areas where AI is used and the other about technological devices that use AI (Table 1).

In general, these students show knowledge about the applications of AI in different sectors of society, so teachers need to be prepared to integrate these technologies into their practice (Khairuddin et al., 2024), but few students mentioned the inclusion of AI in art and television.

Table 1. Areas and technological devices where AI is used (own source)

1. Areas where AI is used	**N=20**	**%**	**2. Technological devices that use AI**	**N=20**	**%**
Technology	20	100	Computers	19	95
Machines	17	85	Digital games	17	85
Robots	19	95	Mobile devices	16	80
Internet	19	95	Television	5	25
Science	14	70	Satellites	14	70
Programmes	18	90	GPS	11	55
Art	1	15	Other - Consoles	1	5

With regard to popular examples of Artificial Intelligence, the majority of students (78%) mentioned chatbots, such as Siri (57%), the Sophia robot (52%), Cortana (42%) and Alexa (5%). As for the human characteristics of AI, 75% of the students chose Information, 70% Intelligence, 50% Observation, 45% Creativity, 35% Mind and Rigour, 15% Human. Only one student said that AI has no human characteristics.

The following data was divided into two categories: (i) potential benefits and (ii) concerns of AI (Table 2). Regarding the benefits, the majority of students (90%) feel confident, 70% believe AI will have a positive impact on their future career, 60% believe it will improve people's quality of life and make learning more engaging (75%), and facilitate personalised learning (70%). The students showed a good understanding of AI, as in the study by Chan & Hu (2023). In terms of concerns, 55 per cent of students believe that AI is a threat to human jobs and will lead to a loss of privacy (Khairuddin et al., 2024).

Table 2. Potential benefits and concerns of AI (own source)

Itens	**Agree N %**	**Neutral N %**	**Disagree N %**
I am confident in the potential benefits of artificial intelligence (AI) in our society.	18 90	2 10	0 0
I believe that AI will have a positive impact on my future career.	14 70	4 20	2 10
I believe AI is a threat to human jobs.	11 55	7 35	2 10
I believe AI will lead to a loss of privacy.	11 55	4 20	5 25

continued on following page

Table 2. Continued

Itens	Agree N %	Neutral N %	Disagree N %
I believe AI will improve people's quality of life.	12 60	6 30	2 10
AI can make learning more engaging.	15 75	3 15	2 10
AI facilitates personalised learning.	14 70	5 25	1 5

Students' perceptions of teaching activities

To find out the students' perceptions of the different activities (language and literature), carried out in the Portuguese classroom based on generative technologies, we asked the students to describe their experiences of using AI. We categorised the answers collected in questionnaire 2 and the interview into three aspects: personal experience, the usefulness and potential of AI and observations about IA course (Table 3).

Table 3. Students' perceptions of teaching strategies (own source)

Personal experience	Perspective on the usefulness and potential of AI	Observations about AI course
-It was a good experience, very intuitive and easy. -It was good and I learnt a lot in Portuguese class. -A good experience because it helps with various things in class. -It was an interesting and intuitive experience, and I adapted quickly. -It's useful in most cases and in Portuguese lessons. -I usually use it to help with schoolwork and it's always been a great help. -It helps a lot, I always use it when I have doubts about subjects or something in everyday life. -It was very good (4 answers).	-Depending on the situation, artificial intelligence can be beneficial in terms of learning and helping, but it can also give us the wrong answers. -Very interesting, it's something that's in development, but it's sure to appear a lot in the future, it's also something that makes me curious and interested. -Useful for learning or for submitting questions to learn. -I've used AI several times, not only for work but also for conversations. -I think it's a tool with immense power if used correctly. -I've mainly used ChatGPT for Portuguese activities. -I've used ChatGPT to complement information in research that I couldn't find much information about, so that I could complement what I'd already found. -With good prompts I got better answers.	-I've used it more than I do now, but I still intend to use it more. The course helped me understand AI better. -It was good to take the AI course. I have used AI tools for almost every function that has been created, whether for leisure or work. -With the course I've better understood how I can use AI. -Taking the AI course helped me not to be afraid of AI. -I enjoyed the AI course.

The categorisations help to better understand the different perspectives and experiences of the students in relation to the use and perception of Artificial Intelligence in educational practice.

(i) Personal experience

In this category, students considered their personal experience of using AI to be positive. They emphasise aspects such as ease of use, learning obtained and usefulness in different situations. The majority expressed satisfaction and interest in continuing to use this technology. This data answers H1.

(ii) Perspective on the usefulness and potential of AI

In this category, students showed their views on the role and potential of AI. There is mention of its usefulness in learning and the potential to master prompt literacy. They show an optimistic outlook on future development, the ability to provide accurate answers when used correctly, but they also show knowledge that it can generate wrong results. Some students express curiosity and interest in exploring AI further. This data answers H2 and H4.

(iii) Observations about AI course

This category encompasses broader observations about the use of artificial intelligence, such as changes in the pattern of use over time, the extent of use in different contexts, both personal and professional, and the benefit of having taken the course on AI to eliminate fears. The students also mention having used various AI interfaces, showing a varied and continuous experience with the technology. According to Pellas (2023), there are several factors that promote a favourable attitude towards incorporating AI into learning, such as age, time of use and devices used. But it is AI training that has a direct impact on student attitudes.

In the interview, we asked the students to write down the six words that come to mind when they think of AI. By categorising the answers we found different aspects of the students' perception of AI, including advantages, concerns, practical applications and integration with other technologies. These data answer H3.

(iv) Positive view of AI

It includes terms such as: helpfulness, practicality, effectiveness, speed, optimisation, evolution, innovation, entertainment, ease, creativity, assistance, clarity, and objectivity. These words suggest a positive perception of AI as a useful and revolutionary tool, capable of improving various areas of life and work. These data answer H3.

(v) Futurist perspective

Encompasses words such as: future, modernism, revolution, evolution, technology, innovation, and quantum computing. Reflecting a long-term vision, suggesting that AI is at the centre of the technological, and social changes that will shape the future. These data answer H2 and H3.

(vi) Challenges and concerns

Contains words such as: conflict, war, unemployment, danger, decline, and peril. They indicate concerns about the negative impact of AI, such as ethical conflicts, unemployment, due to automation, and possible dangers associated with its development. These data answer H4.

(vii) Relationship with technology

Includes words such as: technology, robot, artificial, internet, data, computer, websites, PC, digital and Chatbots. These terms suggest a direct association between AI and other forms of technology, indicating that students see AI as an integral part of the digital world and technology in general. These data answer H1, H2 and H3.

(viii) Use and practical applications

Covers terms such as: automation, development, research, interest, performance, complement, response, conversation, work, assistance, knowledge, interface, information bank, and work. These terms indicate an understanding of how AI can be applied in various areas, such as research, work, assistance and communication. These data answer H1 and H3.

Finally, we categorised the students' comments about AI which answer the 4 starting questions and confirm the previous data.

a) Perspective on the impact of AI in the future

"Artificial intelligence will be/is a mystery for our future, as it has come to change everything, so it's important to learn about AI at school."; "I will need AI in my life in the future.", these comments express a view that AI is something revolutionary and will have a great impact on the future, although it can also be perceived as mysterious and unknown.

b) Benefits of AI in education

"It's good for education."; "Chatbots can help students with self-directed learning by saving them the work and stress of searching the Internet and books"; "Chatbots can help us learn more, since in a matter of seconds they can read data that a human couldn't read in a lifetime of 24/7 reading", these comments highlight a positive aspect of AI, suggesting that it can bring benefits to education, by facilitating the learning process and improving the educational experience.

c) Concerns about the use of AI in education

"AI is a very new and expanding technology, if on the one hand, I find the concept of integrating something so useful into a student's portfolio incredible, on the other hand it is worrying, due to the fact that it requires a good maturity from the students so that they don't become dependent on it." This comment reflects concern about the use of AI in education, emphasising the need for students to develop maturity so as not to become dependent on it. It also suggests that AI should be used as a supplementary tool, rather than as the primary means of gathering information.

f) Ethical problems and public debate on AI

"Problems with artistic copies in general, something that has been happening a lot and has been debated a lot on the Internet." This comment addresses ethical issues related to the use of AI, specifically in the context of artistic copies, indicating that this topic is of concern.

We believe that the data collected and commented on above shows the importance of not being afraid to integrate AI into educational practices, particularly in vocational education, as these are students preparing to enter the world of work. These data are in line with the results of other studies, such as those carried out by Al-Badi et al. (2022), Chan & Hu (2023) and Kumar & Raman (2022). For Chan & Hu (2023), students who have more knowledge about these technologies and use them more often are more likely to use them in the future. As there is a lack of research into how students understand generative AI, this study could help with future research into AI in education, although no generalisations can be made given the small number of participants and the limitations of the study itself.

CONCLUSION

Digital technologies and Artificial Intelligence offer immense potential to fundamentally transform teaching and learning through personalization, real-time feedback, and adaptive instruction. While students largely embrace AI's benefits as we can see from the data in this study, they are simultaneously aware of the critical need for responsible use, fearing dependency and raising nuanced concerns about ethical issues, such as authorship and data privacy. To navigate this complex landscape, actionable strategies are required from all stakeholders.

Teachers must transition from content gatekeepers to facilitators of AI literacy and prompt literacy. This involves integrating AI into teaching practices, focusing on higher-order skills that machines cannot replicate, and creating a culture of academic integrity based on values, rather than relying solely on detection.

For policymakers and institutions, robust and comprehensive approach is necessary. This requires developing and enforcing clear data governance policies to protect student information and mandating ongoing, high-quality AI literacy training for all teaching staff. Furthermore, institutional assessment methods must be urgently revised to measure understanding and critical thinking in a world where generative tools are accessible.

Ultimately, realizing AI's full educational promise depends on a collective commitment to ethical development, proactive training, and informed policy, ensuring that AI serves as an equitable and powerful tool for future citizens.

REFERENCES

Adel, A., Ahsan, A., & Davison, C. (2024). ChatGPT promises and challenges in education: Computational and ethical perspectives. *Education Sciences*, *14*(8), 814. Advance online publication. DOI: 10.3390/educsci14080814

Al-Badi, A., & Khan, A. & Eid-Alotaibi (2022).Perceptions of Learners and Instructors towards Artificial Intelligence in Personalized Learning. *Procedia Computer Science*, 201, 445-451. ISSN 1877-0509, Doi:DOI: 10.1016/j.procs.2022.03.058

Alier Forment, M., Garcia Peñalvo, F., Casañ Guerrero, M. J., Pereira, J. A., & Llorens Largo, F. (2024). *Manifiesto para una IA Segura en la Educación* (Versión 0.4.0). *Manifiesto para una IA Segura en la Educación*. https://manifesto.safeaieducation.org

Amo-Filva, D., ... (2024). Empowering Student Data Privacy in Schools Through Open Educational Resources. García-Peñalvo, F.J., Sein-Echaluce, M.L., Fidalgo-Blanco, Á. (eds) *Innovation and Technologies for the Digital Transformation of Education. Lecture Notes in Educational Technology*. Springer, Singapore. Doi:DOI: 10.1007/978-981-97-2468-0_25

Balalle, H., & Pannilage, S. (2025). Reassessing academic integrity in the age of AI: A systematic literature review on AI and academic integrity. *Social Sciences & Humanities Open*, vol.11, 101299, ISSN 2590-2911. Doi:DOI: 10.1016/j.ssaho.2025.101299

Boulay, B. (2022). Artificial Intelligence in Education and Ethics. Olaf Zawacki-Richter, Insung Jung (Eds), *Handbook of Open, Distance and Digital Education*, 1-16. https://goo.su/RcMdU

Bughin, J., & Hazan, E. (2017). The new spring of artificial intelligence: A few early economies. *McKinsey Global Institute*. https://goo.su/tEftfT

Chan, C. K. Y., & Hu, W. (2023). Students' voices on generative AI: Perceptions, benefits, and challenges in higher education. *International Journal of Educational Technology in Higher Education*, *20*(1), 43. DOI: 10.1186/s41239-023-00411-8

Chaturvedi, R., Verma, S., Das, R., & Dwivedi, Y. K. (2023). Social companionship with artificial intelligence: Recent trends and future avenues,Technological Forecasting and Social Change,Volume 193, 122634, ISSN 0040-1625. Doi: DOI: 10.1016/j.techfore.2023.122634

Cleto, B. (2023). Exploração de algumas ferramentas de Inteligência Artificial numa Unidade Curricular de Multimédia. *RE@D - Revista de Educação a Distância e Elearning*, 6, 2. https://revistas.rcaap.pt/lead_read/article/view/32673/23517

Cohen, L., Manion, L., & Morrison, K. (2007). *Research methods in education*. Routledge. DOI: 10.4324/9780203029053

Common Sense. (2025). *Social AI Companions*. https://www.commonsensemedia.org/ai-ratings/social-ai-companions?gate=riskassessment

Coutinho, C. (2013). *Metodologia de investigação em ciências sociais e humanas: teoria e prática*. Almedina.

Crawford, K. (2021). *Atlas of AI Power, Politics, and The Planetary Costs of Artificial Intelligence*. Yale University Press.

Crompton, H., & Burke, D. (2022). Affordances and challenges of artificial intelligence in K-12 education: A systematic review. *Journal of Research on Technology in Education*, *56*(3), 248–268. DOI: 10.1080/15391523.2022.2121344

Crompton, H. & Burke, D. (2024). Artificial Intelligence Applications in Higher Education: Theories, Ethics, and Case Studies for Universities. *STEMPS Faculty Books*. 13.

Davar, N. F., Dewan, M. A. A., & Zhang, X. (2025). AI Chatbots in Education: Challenges and Opportunities. *Information (Basel)*, *16*(3), 235. DOI: 10.3390/info16030235

Elmore, R. (2023). *Guide to Prompt Engineering*. https://builtin.com/artificial-intelligence/prompt-engineering

Felix, C. (2020). The role of the teacher and AI in education. Sengupta, Enakshi, Blessinger, Patrick, Makhanya, Mandla (Eds.), International perspectives on the role of technology in humanizing higher education, 33. *Emerald Publishing Limited*, Leeds, 33-48. DOI: 10.1108/S2055-364120200000033003

Floridi, L. (2020). AI and Its New Winter: From Myths to Realities. *Philosophy & Technology*, *33*(1), 1–3. DOI: 10.1007/s13347-020-00396-6

Gil, A. C. (1999). *Métodos e técnicas de pesquisa social*. Atlas.

Goksel, N., & Bozkurt, A. (2019). Artificial intelligence in education. In Sisman-Ugur, S., & Kurubacak, G. (Eds.), *Handbook of research on learning in the age of transhumanism* (pp. 224–236). IGI Global., DOI: 10.4018/978-1-5225-8431-5.ch014

Guilherme, A. (2019). AI and education: The importance of teacher and student relations. *AI & Society*, *34*(1), 47–54. DOI: 10.1007/s00146-017-0693-8

Huang, W., Jiang, J., King, R. B., & Fryer, L. K. (2025). Chatbots and student motivation: A scoping review. *International Journal of Educational Technology in Higher Education*, *22*(1), 26. DOI: 10.1186/s41239-025-00524-2

Hwang, G.-J., Xie, H., Wah, B. W., & Gašević, D. (2020). Vision, challenges, roles and research issues of Artificial Intelligence in Education. *Computers and Education: Artificial Intelligence*, *1*, 100001. DOI: 10.1016/j.caeai.2020.100001

Ismail, I. & Aloshi, J. (2025). Data Privacy in AI- Driven Education An In-Depth Exploration Into the Data Privacy Concerns and Potential Solutions. Doi: .DOI: 10.4018/979-8-3693-5443-8.ch008

Jusoh, S., & Kadir, R. A. (2025). *Chatbot in education: trends, personalisation, and techniques*. Multimed Tools Appl., DOI: 10.1007/s11042-025-20659-8

Khairuddin, Z., Shahabani, N. S., Ahmad, S. N., Ahmad, A. R., & Zamri, N. A. (2024). Students' Perceptions on The Artificial Intelligence (AI) Tools As Academic Support. [MJSSH]. *Malaysian Journal of Social Sciences and Humanities*, *9*(11), e003087. DOI: 10.47405/mjssh.v9i11.3087

Kim, N. J., & Kim, M. K. (2022). Teacher's Perceptions of Using an Artificial Intelligence-Based Educational Tool for Scientific Writing. *Frontiers in Education*, *7*, 755914. DOI: 10.3389/feduc.2022.755914

Kumar, J. A. (2021). Educational chatbots for project-based learning: Investigating learning outcomes for a team-based design course. *International Journal of Educational Technology in Higher Education*, *18*(1), 65. DOI: 10.1186/s41239-021-00302-w PMID: 34926790

Kumar, R., & Raman, R. (2022). Student Perceptions on Artificial Intelligence (AI) in higher education. *IEEE Integrated STEM Education Conference (ISEC)*, Princeton, 450-454. Doi: DOI: 10.1109/ISEC54952.2022.10025165

Labadze, L., Grigolia, M., & Machaidze, L. (2023). Role of AI chatbots in education: Systematic literature review. *International Journal of Educational Technology in Higher Education*, *20*(1), 56. DOI: 10.1186/s41239-023-00426-1

Lampropoulos, G., & Papadakis, S. (2025). *The Educational Value of Artificial Intelligence and Social Robots. Social Robots in Education*. Springer.

Lee, K.-F. (2019). *As Superpotências da Inteligência Artificial. A China, Silicon Valley e a Nova Ordem Mundial*. Relógio d'Água.

Lee, K.-F., & Qiufan, C. (2023). *Inteligência Artificial 2041*. Relógio de Água.

Lin, J. C., Younessi, D. N., Kurapati, S. S., Tang, O. Y., & Scott, I. U. (2023). Comparison of GPT-3.5, GPT-4, and human user performance on a practice ophthalmology written examination. *Eye (London, England)*, *37*(17), 1–2. DOI: 10.1038/s41433-023-02564-2 PMID: 37156862

Lo, C. K. (2023). What is the impact of ChatGPT on education? A rapid review of the literature. *Education Sciences*, *13*(4), 410. DOI: 10.3390/educsci13040410

Lo, C. K., & Hew, K. F. (2023). A review of integrating AI-based chatbots into flipped learning: New possibilities and challenges. *Frontiers in Education*, *8*, 1175715. DOI: 10.3389/feduc.2023.1175715

Lo, L. S. (2023). The CLEAR path: A framework for enhancing information literacy through prompt engineering. *Journal of Academic Librarianship*, *49*(4), 4. DOI: 10.1016/j.acalib.2023.102720

Maclure, J. (2020). The new AI spring: A deflationary view. *AI & Society*, *35*(3), 747–750. DOI: 10.1007/s00146-019-00912-z

Mann, S., Calvin, A., Lenhart, A., & Robb, M. B. (2025). *The Common Sense census: Media use by kids zero to eight, 2025*. Common Sense Media.

Matli, W. (2024). Extending the theory of information poverty to deepfake technology. *International Journal of Information Management Data Insights*, vol. 4, 2, 100286, ISSN 2667-0968. Doi: DOI: 10.1016/j.jjimei.2024.100286

Moura, A. (2024). Inteligência Artificial na Educação: perceções dos professores participantes numa oficina de formação. Carvalho, A. A. A., Schlemmer, E., Area, M., Marques, C. G., Santos, I. L., Guimarães, D., Cruz, S., Moura, A., Reis, C. S., Rebelo, P. V. (Orgs) (2024). *Atas do 6º Encontro Internacional sobre Jogos e Mobile Learning*. Centro de Estudos Interdisciplinares, 184-193.

Moura, A & Tchiang, Van Man, I. (2025). Curipod's Artificial Intelligence Assistant in the Proofreading Process: An Exploratory Study. In Moreira, Filipe T. & Teles, Rui Oliva, *Improving Student Assessment with Emerging AI Tools*. IGI Global Book, 143-168.

Moura, A., & Carvalho, A. A. (2023a). Inteligência Artificial para Ensinar e para Aprender. In Alves, L. (Org.), *Inteligência Artificial (IA) e Educação: refletindo sobre os desafios contemporâneos*. Salvador: Editora EDUFBA, 155-168.

Moura, A. & Carvalho, A. A. (2023b). Literacia de Prompts para Potenciar o Uso da Inteligência Artificial na Educação. *RE@D-Revista de Educação a Distância e Elearning,* 6 (2): e202308, 1-26.

Ng, A. (2017). Andrew Ng on why Artificial Intelligence is the New Electricity. *InsideHPC.* https://insidehpc.com/2017/03/andrew-ng-artificial-intelligence-new-electricity/

Nguyen, A., Kremantzis, M., Essien, A., Petrounias, I., & Hosseini, S. (2024). Enhancing student engagement through artificial intelligence (AI): Understanding the basics, opportunities, and challenges. *Journal of University Teaching & Learning Practice*, *21*(06). Advance online publication. DOI: 10.53761/caraaq92

Nonju, K. D. S., & Ihua-Maduenyi, A. B. (2024). The Impact of Artificial Intelligence on Privacy Laws. *International Journal of Research and Innovation in Social Science*, *VIII*(IX), 2150–2174. DOI: 10.47772/IJRISS.2024.8090178

Núñez-Michuy, C. M., Veloz-Segura, V. T., Agualongo-Chela, L. M., & Bayas-Romero, E. L. (2023). Integración de la Inteligencia Artificial en la Educación para el Desarrollo Sostenible: Oportunidades y Desafíos. *Magazine de las Ciencias: Revista de Investigación e Innovación*, *8*(4), 96–108. DOI: 10.33262/rmc.v8i4.2959

Okonkwo, C. W. & Ade-Ibijola, A. (2021). Chatbots applications in education: A systematic review. *Computers and Education: Artificial Intelligence*, 2.

Pellas, N. (2023). The influence of sociodemographic factors on students' attitudes toward AI-generated video content creation. *Smart Learning Environments*, *10*(1), 57. DOI: 10.1186/s40561-023-00276-4

Prestoza, M. J. R., & Banatao, J. C. M. (2024). Exploring the efficacy of AI passion-drivenpedagogy in enhancing student engagement and learning outcomes: A case study inphilippines. *Asian Journal of Assessment in Teaching and Learning*, *14*(1), 45–54. DOI: 10.37134/ajatel.vol14.1.5.2024

Riggs, V. (2025). Impact of AI literacy professional development on teaching: Evaluating changes in perceptions and classroom practices. *American Journal of STEM Education*, *7*, 37–50. DOI: 10.32674/rbajg012

Russell, S. (2021). *Inteligência artificial a nosso favor: Como manter o controle sobre a tecnologia*. Companhia das Letras.

Sartor, G., & Lagioia, F. (2020). *The impact of the General Data Protection Regulation (GDPR) on artificial intelligence*. European Parliament. [10.2861/293]

Schmidt, T., & Strasser, T. (2022). Artificial Intelligence in Foreign Language Learning and Teaching A CALL for Intelligent Practice. *Anglistik*, *33*(1), 165–184. DOI: 10.33675/ANGL/2022/1/14

Shum, H.-Y., He, X.-D., & Li, D. (2018). From Eliza to XiaoIce: Challenges and Opportunities with Social Chatbots. *Frontiers of Information Technology & Electronic Engineering*, *19*(1), 10–26. DOI: 10.1631/FITEE.1700826

Sit, C., Srinivasan, R., Amlani, A., Muthuswamy, K., Azam, A., Monzon, L., & Poon, S. D. (2020). Attitudes and perceptions of UK medical students towards artificial intelligence and radiology: A multicentre survey. *Insights Into Imaging*, *11*(1), 14. DOI: 10.1186/s13244-019-0830-7 PMID: 32025951

Slimi, Z., Benayoune, A., & Alemu, A. E. (2025). Students' perceptions of artificial intelligence integration in higher education. *European Journal of Educational Research*, *14*(2), 471–484. DOI: 10.12973/eu-jer.14.2.471

Stokel-Walker, C. (2022, December 9). AI bot ChatGPT writes smart essays-should academics worry? *Nature*. Advance online publication. DOI: 10.1038/d41586-022-04397-7

Uğraş, H., Uğraş, M., Papadakis, S., & Kalogiannakis, M. (2024a). ChatGPT-supported education in primary schools: The potential of ChatGPT for sustainable practices. *Sustainability (Basel)*, *16*(22), 9855. DOI: 10.3390/su16229855

Uğraş, H., Uğraş, M., Papadakis, S., & Kalogiannakis, M. (2024b). Innovative Early Childhood STEM Education with ChatGPT: Teacher Perspectives. *Technology, Knowledge and Learning*, 1-23.

Woolf, B. P. (2015). AI and education: Celebrating 30 years of marriage. *International Conference on Artificial Intelligence In Education*. Cham: Springer, 4, 38-47.

Xu, Y., Prado, Y., & Severson, R. L. Lovatom & S., Cassell, J. (2025). Growing Up with Artificial Intelligence: Implications for Child Development. Christakis, D.A., Hale, L. (eds) *Handbook of Children and Screens*. Springer, Cham. Doi: DOI: 10.1007/978-3-031-69362-5_83

Yeo, M. (2023). Academic integrity in the age of Artificial Intelligence (AI) authoring apps. *TESOL Journal*, *14*(3), e716. Advance online publication. DOI: 10.1002/tesj.716

Yılmaz, R., & Yilmaz, F. G. K. (2023). The effect of generative artificial intelligence (AI)-based tool use on students' computational thinking skills, programming self-efficacy and motivation. *Computers and Education: Artificial Intelligence*, vol.4, 100147, ISSN 2666-920X. Doi:DOI: 10.1016/j.caeai.2023.100147

Zhang, Z., & Wasie, S. (2023). Educational Technology in the Post-Pandemic Era: Current Progress, Potential, and Challenges. *Proceedings of the 15thInternational Conference on Education Technology and Computers*, 40-46. Doi: DOI: 10.1145/3629296.3629303

[1] https://docs.google.com/document/d/1MFXZrVVVChD57O678wXs zSJuIexy9v_Ho1EZDZCh9Qg/preview

[2] https://sites.google.com/view/aprofundarportugues/

[3] https://www.elementsofai.com/

[4] https://artsandculture.google.com/experiment/odd-one-out/wAHNn4JsVTFOiw?hl=en

[5] https://chatbot.page/7LSgTT ; https://chatbot.page/mJJJAl ; https://chatbot .page/99olZ0 ;

https://chatbot.page/667ec9331063215eaa12656e

Chapter 4
Generative AI and Ethical Integration in K-12 and Higher Education:
Policies, Pedagogy, and Practice

Shazia Shaikh
http://orcid.org/0000-0001-5693-5372
King Khalid University, Saudi Arabia

Pradeep Bhanudas Girhe
Department of MBA, Deogiri College, Aurangabad, India

Mohd Abdul Maroof
http://orcid.org/0000-0002-3066-046X
Faculty of Business Management, JSPM University, Pune, India

Anshuman Vijay Magar
http://orcid.org/0000-0002-7349-5011
Faculty of Business Management, JSPM University, Pune, India

Priyanka Kaskar
http://orcid.org/0009-0000-7144-0351
Faculty of Business Management, JSPM University, Pune, India

W. Sudhahar
http://orcid.org/0009-0000-0343-4451
SaiSriram Engineering College, India

ABSTRACT

The availability of Generative Artificial Intelligence (GenAI) tools has expanded their use and application—even in industries such as higher education. Generative AI has opened up an entirely new world of access to educational materials and personalization of learning. While generative AI tools have obvious benefits, they also raise several concerns for students in a higher education setup that go on from ethical concerns associated with academic integrity, data privacy, discrimination, and bias to over-reliance on the solutions proposed. This research article asserts that through the use of such a technology by the learner/researcher of tertiary education institutions, many vital issues must be addressed, as emphasized by the authors. It

DOI: 10.4018/979-8-2600-0101-1.ch004

explores how we can educate our current generation, including responsible use of generative AI, implications for institutions, statutory research, and ethics. The proposal outlines standard methods for integrating student-facing AI with personalized learning principles and policy at the higher education level.

INTRODUCTION

The evolution of Artificial Intelligence (AI) is proof that AI is a sign for the creative ability of human beings and scientific advancement from early civilizations that had concepts on synthetic intelligent beings. From mythical narratives that describe the first notions of thinking machines (ex: Homer's automata and magic mirrors) (Kalligeropoulos & Vasileiadou, 2008) to mechanical calculating devices in the party with the Industrial Revolution (Turing, 2018), humans have been fascinated with the idea of making intelligent machines for millennia. When emerging modern computers represented a young leap in our potential to mimic human intelligence and the field has advanced rapidly since, transforming and wondering all industrial sectors worldwide (Li, 2020).

Since then, AI has gone through multiple waves of development and challenge, powered by advances in computer science, mathematics and cognitive psychology. With the development of machine learning and also deep learning methods, AI has also progressed to other levels through which the machine can learn from the data and can solve the problems with the best accuracy and the efficiency. Innovation in technology is not all we can learn from AI's history; it also shows how human beings perceive intelligence which shapes its powerful impact on the future of the world. AI stands for Artificial Intelligence and it is one of the leading development or advancement in technology, nowadays it is used in many activities and one can imagine automating a task by Intelligent machines that can do a task in a smart way. That's where the true nature of AI being useful and impressive lies, its ability to replace human multitasking. Machine learning algorithms were previously trained on very specific tasks and weren't very much focused on generating their own data (Shabbir & Anwer, 2018).

Generative Adversarial networks (GAN) have become ubiquitous over the last decade and brought about new applications for example image augmentation, generating datasets, text to image translation, image blending, video prediction, generation of 3-D objects (Dash et al., 2023). Building on these breakthroughs, autoregressive language models like the chatbot ChatGPT shocked and awed the world of technology. The usual and interesting such Generative AI models are giving a normal and customized response to user prompts while helping a discussion of moving freely and that each and every user is well known and comfortable. So every week, these quickly enhancing LLMs are providing some high-grade functions therefore creating the user's reliance on everything as well as anything.

Currently Generative AI is also being used in numerous domains such as content creation, personalized learning, software development, learning to code, improving customer support of businesses, summarisation of huge corpus of text, making difficult concepts easy to understand, using such tools as a personal assistant etc. Thanks to their human text generation capabilities on virtually any topic, GenAI tools have nearly supplanted traditional search engines as effective substitutes. With the recent infusion of generative AI features into the browsers and search engines, these tools have made a zest for versatility into their performances, and thus enhancing the productivity of the users. A new era has aroused, especially with the introduction of language models like ChatGPT, where AI can be widely involved to ease and improve many measures in higher education (Chukwuere & Handoko, 2024). Integration across Pedagogy, curriculum and research The potential of generative AI in higher education is massive. Generative AI models (such as GPT-3) can be utilized to support administrative functions, enhance teaching-learning and outcomes, and assist in research tasks (George & Wooden, 2023). Simultaneously, such a disruptive technology and its unassessed application increases important considerations on academic integrity and ethics. The widespread abuse and over-dependence on such tools has presented ethical dilemmas that need immediate and proactive solutions that can ensure responsible embedding in the higher education systems. As a result, unassessed trust and over-reliance on the content produced by these tools is troublesome and quickly points questions from the basics of authenticity, originality and above all considered morality(Krishnamoorthy et al., 2025; Sarkar, Mahamuni, et al., 2025; Sarkar, Parmar, et al., 2025).

In this chapter, we describe and unpack the multitude of situational complexities around generative AI in higher education. It begins with statistics regarding the use of AI and market trends of AI use in light of new applications across higher education and professional work. It then considers a few of the possible uses, misuses and risks each paired with a more holistic picture of how it could actually be integrated. We investigate the data privacy, ethics, academic integrity issues at the heart of academic and research activity. Part of our output will be sound and realistic recommendations to be integrated into policy and regulatory structure presiding over higher education on how to ensure that the opportunities offered by such technologies are being harnessed by all the players but also to overcome and neutralize possible risks and negative effects in this respect. With it we definitely want to upload core values of education, like creativity, and originality.

LITERATURE SURVEY

Education is significantly impacted by GenAI, offering new opportunities for innovation and problem-solving. Healthcare must be judicious before and after GenAI use. This study explores AI literacy, ethical use, and potential restraints in higher education institutions. It aims to understand the impact of generative systems on academic activities and society.

The Surge in AI Literacy and Ethical Implementation in Education

Coursera's Global Skills Report 2024 also highlights the flood of demand for AI literacy skills following the release of the free version of ChatGPT in 2022 (Global Skills Report, 2024) According to the report, enrollments for the generative AI courses saw a massive 1060% jump globally in the last year, which demonstrates Learners' preference for top-level AI skills in alignment with the GenAI adoption and usage in their region. Governments, and businesses and academic institutions concerned about inevitability of next-gen skills such as prompt engineering have been key drivers behind the adoption (Papadakis et al., 2024a, 2024b). Higher educational institutions need to redesign their curriculums to bridge the regional gaps in AI skills to realize the future of work. These initiatives can not only help countries improve their rankings in technical skills but also provide them with a competitive advantage in the international market. According to a recent study published by Cengage Group, a global education technology company, nearly 40% of instructors are aware of Generative AI (Gen AI) and about 24% have utilized it in their teaching work (Cengage Group, 2023).

Indeed, 58% of instructors have planned or thought about using Gen AI in post-secondary education. So educators are eager to understand how to leverage GenAI tools to realize their pedagogical promises while enhancing productivity, elevating instruction, streamlining technology on-boarding and enhancing creativity. Educators have seen it being most effective for drafting tests and quizzes, catching dishonest behavior, and enhancing the quality of tutoring sessions. Yet despite all of these benefits, only a third of teachers allow students to use these generative AI tools for their assignments. A behavior data show (Tyton Partners 2023), a consultancy firm, the broad trends from March-September 2023 demonstrate that there has been a marked increase in the use of Generative AI systems, with 49% of students and 22% of faculties now actively using the technologies. The study surveyed nearly 1000 faculty and 1500 students at more than 600 higher education institutions. The research also find that the students have been using generative AI much more than the faculties. In a different survey (Inside Higher Ed, 2024), it is reported that over three in five (60%) students are now regular end users of AI generative technologies while only 36% of faculties use AI generative technologies. AI in Education AI in education is a hugely popular and growing topic across the world, as illustrated in the AIPRM's AI in Education Report (Sætra, 2023) which claims the global market of AI in education could grow from only £2.5 billion in 2022 to as much as £3.5 billion by 2025. As per the source, ChatGPT statistics also depict that the user boom peaked at 180 million in December 2023, with up to 1.7 billion monthly visits on average(Behera et al., 2025; Karthikeyan et al., 2025; Venkatasubramanian et al., 2024).

The demand for AI literacy has increased the use of Generative AI in education, but challenges remain in advancing AI literacy and addressing ethical dilemmas. Students are more adopting online learning, while educators are more concerned about transparency, responsible use, and fairness. The blurred boundaries between ethical and unethical use of AI highlight the need for fair usage policies to ensure ethical and productive use.

Perspectives on Generative AI in Academic Environments

The use of Generative AI systems in academics has sparked debate on its potential benefits and ethical, legal, and social implications. To fully understand the impact, it is crucial for academic institutions to assess perspectives across disciplines and explore existing literature to identify major branches of discussions surrounding GenAI.

Sætra (2023) raises concerns beyond the ethics and discusses that while the academics are expressing concerns pertaining to the ethical side of GenAI, the real question lies in asking the level of impact it is creating on individuals, communities and cultures. Hence, a shift is required from the theoretical assessment to comprehending the realistic and practical impact of such a disruptive technology in the form of possible harms. In the same study Sætra (2023) highlights the grim situation of academics grappling with the issue of misuse of GenAI by the students and its impact on their learning and performance. On the contrary, the creative use of AI generative technologies and its adoption in imparting education is being perceived as a means towards a transformative scenario in higher education. Baidoo-Anu1 & Ansah, (2023) reflect on the paradigm shift in the world of education brought about by LLMs like ChatGPT and the likes by highlighting the benefits it has given to educators by automating and simplifying many of their tasks that previously consumed a lot of their time. Generative AI tools have drawbacks such as minimizing human interactions, limited understanding, biases, and potential privacy concerns. They can hinder human-to-human dialogue and interaction, potentially impacting students' admissions and assessments. Concerns also arise regarding biased algorithms in AI bot development, highlighting the importance of considering student performance grounds. In cases when there are no practices of AI checks in submissions given by students and may lead to incorrect assessments and grading. In such cases, unintentionally biased assessments may cause resentment and impact sincere students who are poor in performances. Therefore, emphasis must be laid on the importance of responsible use of GenAI and the accountability while using such technologies. Conversely, based on their study of 100 articles opining on Generative AI usage, Sullivan et al. (2023) argue in support of increased need for debating on the impact of GenAI tools as there has been least inclusion of students' opinions about how they see this technology helping or harming them. The most discussions over the implications of GenAI have been reported by AI experts, enthusiasts and higher education institutions and educators and there is a strong need for students' perspectives to be a part of the whole discussion, them being important stakeholders. Through their findings, Michel-Villarreal et. al. (2023) emphasizes the need for adoption of well-defined policies and clear guidelines for their responsible use in higher education set-ups. They suggested the need to pursue 'thing ethnography' that aims to understand the perceptions of educators and students about GenAI which can be used to perform qualitative investigations for attaining a granular comprehension of the possibilities surrounding its use. Their study highlights the potential of thing ethnography as means to study stakeholders' experiences, behaviours, relationships as they continue to use such tools. Such an empirical study may help in devising informed policies while considering factors like superficial perceptions and the real complexities that tag along the usage of these technologies. Adele Smolansky et al. (2023) conducted a survey and gathered responses from 389 learners and 36 tutors from two universities to understand their opinions on the use of LLMs for designing and executing academic activities like tests and assignments. The integration of Generative AI in academia faces challenges such as automation, efficiency, and personalization. Critics argue it can minimize human interactions and lead to unethical practices. A balanced approach that considers students' opinions is needed to create policies based on empirical evaluation. Collaborative efforts among stakeholders are needed to establish clear guidelines and frameworks for optimum utilization of Generative AI in higher education(Uğraş et al., 2025). Understanding the concerns governing GenAI use in academics is crucial for enhancing knowledge of these tools.

UNDERSTANDING ARTIFICIAL INTELLIGENCE - FROM FOUNDATIONS TO ADVANCEMENTS

This section explores the broader context of AI, tracing its emergence from traditional algorithms to GenAI. Tools like ChatGPT and Claude are significant milestones, powered by Transformer architecture and reinforcement learning. However, GenAI faces challenges like inaccuracy and algorithmic bias. The section aims to establish a robust foundation for higher education.

Artificial Intelligence

Artificial intelligence (AI) is the ability of computing devices to perform tasks requiring human intelligence, such as acquiring information, learning, reasoning, perception, predicting, and decision-making. AI is unique in its ability to learn, which allows it to apply other abilities once acquired. It comprises components like machine learning, neural networks, deep learning, computer vision, natural language processing, and cognitive computing (Sarker, 2021). The computing systems forming interconnected nodes capable of transmitting signals and tweaking the connectivity strength as required so as to acquire knowledge and complete tasks through exposure to examples are known as neural networks (Skapura, 1996). These models are inspired by the working of the human brain and are a crucial aspect of deep learning. Deep learning is a subclass of neural networks with many layers capable of learning highly sophisticated and complex features from huge datasets (Khamparia & Singh, 2019). It is excellent at tasks such as image and speech recognition, language translation and gaming (Dong et al., 2021). Computer vision is a domain characterised by the task of enabling computing devices with identification, processing and comprehension of visual inputs like digital images and videos using machine learning techniques (Ioannidou et al., 2017). Computer vision applications often employ deep learning techniques like convolutional neural networks to attain their aims (Voulodimos et al., 2018). Natural Language Processing (NLP) is an area of AI that designs algorithms that can comprehend and generate human language data (Fanni et al., 2023). NLP focuses on enabling an interaction between computers and their users through human languages by means of understanding, interpretation, and generation (Hirschberg & Manning, 2015). Applications like chat bots, language translators, sentiment analysis applications and text summarizers have their core functionalities attained through NLP (Lee, 2023). Cognitive computing involves developing systems that are able to mimic human cognitive functions like learning and solving problems (Konar, 2018).

The Advent of Generative Artificial Intelligence

Before the advent of GenAI, AI technologies were narrowly focused on tasks like language translation, object detection in images, complying and responding to user's instructions or conversations to name a few. GenAI brought with it the power of "creation". Generative Artificial Intelligence is a technology that leverages deep learning that utilizes neural networks trained on large datasets to create human-like data as a response to the instructions it is given in the form of prompts that are user-queries. The created data can be text, images, audio, video and other forms of digital content. The typicality of this technology is creating content with respect to the context. Hence, it may be said that their responses to the same query, worded differently, will generate similar yet varying responses. GenAI is a new subclass of AI that has the ability to work in an unsupervised environment and use self-supervised learning techniques without the need for manual data-labelling (Zhao et al., 2023). This implies that these tools can learn from their own data and also discover patterns for drawing insights. GenAI tools require to be trained on humongous volume of data for their training as their abilities to respond largely depend on such training data. This is the very reason why it is also infamous for being biased and hallucinating, the aspects that are critical factors to be considered when users consume data generated by such tools. Yet another striking feature of a GenAI is its ability to retain the context of the conversation and curate its response by remembering the context each time it responds. Common example is the ChatGPT chatbot that can remember previous parts of the conversation or a chat and respond contextually. These features deliver a very personalised chat environment for every user thus creating an impactful experience and create an impression of the AI tool as a very knowledgeable, smart and responsive one. Owing to the mentioned capabilities it is worth mentioning that the market of Generative AI is expected to grow to $6.5 billion by the year 2026 as reported by the World Bank, (2023). As per a recent industry report by Bloomberg Intelligence, 2023, the Generative AI market is predicted to grow rapidly and it is estimated that the generative AI based solutions could reach $280 billion in the next ten years compounding to an annual growth rate (CAGR) of 42% approximately. This tremendous demand and rise can be attributed to its wide scale use-cases for all kinds of consumers and enterprises.

Core Technologies behind the GenAI tools like ChatGPT

Large Language Models (LLMs) that have been trained of humongous amounts of data form the core technology behind GenAI tools like ChatGPT and Claude. Using deep learning algorithms these models are able to identify patterns and subsequently respond with text that is much human-like as well as contextual and coherent (Goyal et al., 2023). These models are powerful enough to initiate open-ended conversations, solve challenging queries, condense information, identify patterns and logic, and draw inferences (Naveed et al., 2023). GPT-3, GPT-4 and similar models are built using transformer architectures that work by means of pre-training and fine-tuning for NLP tasks (Yenduri et al., 2024). These models learn various language patterns and structures through pre-training on huge datasets and are later fine-tuned for delivering a better performance in generating responses, thereby aiding accuracy. Next we discuss this architecture forming the backbone of AI LLMs.

Transformer Architecture: Introduced in the 1970's by Vaswani, (2017), the novel transformer model, the most dominant method in NLP tasks, is the heart of LLMs like ChatGPT. As shown in figure 1, using self-attention approaches, the transformer model allowed better parallelization and performance over previous models and since then has become the foundation for many state-of-the-art models in NLP. Self-Attention Mechanism, parallelization and positional encoding are the primary features of the transformer model that aid its working (Ghojogh & Ghodsi, 2020). Self-Attention Mechanism helps the Transformer to weigh and prioritize different words in a statement, which helps it to capture long-range dependencies.

Figure 1. An overview of the transformer architecture

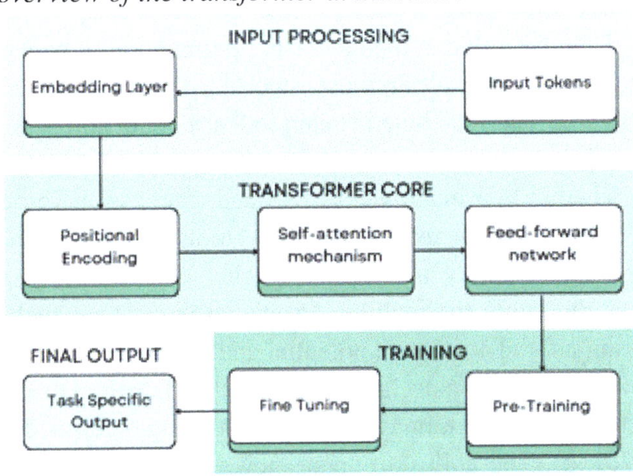

Unlike previous models that process data serially, the Transformer is capable of processing all words in a statement concurrently which speeds up the training time significantly. By providing the information about the position of tokens, positional encoding helps the model understand the order of the data (Baniata & Kang, 2024). In tandem, these components empower the Transformer to acquire complex dependencies and relationships between data items, which makes it carry out NLP tasks efficiently.

Pre-Training and Fine Tuning: These are vital processes in the transformer architecture that enable the model to benefit from large datasets for its initial training and later adapt to specific tasks. In pre-training, a model is trained over a broad dataset so that it learns the overall features (Zoph et al., 2020). With pre-training, the model acquires knowledge of general patterns extracted from the large datasets (Panigrahi et al., 2023). The fine-tuning process can later adjust the model to perform well on specific tasks (Yongqi et al., 2023). This has been a widely adopted approach in a spectrum of domains that includes NLP, reinforcement learning and computer vision (Han et al., 2021). In addition, the choice of the dual-phase approach can impact the model's performance significantly across different kinds of tasks and domains. This kind of training also improves the model's performance in generating contextually suitable and well-reasoned responses (Hartsock & Rasool, 2024).

Evaluating the Dual Facets of Generative AI

Generative AI has emerged as a transformative force and stands out for its specialty to act creative, generate data-driven responses, making it a great tool across diverse domains. Leveraging vast databases, it can generate text, images and other kinds of responses, while offering artistic, innovative and unique solutions to complex problems. Therefore, due to the increasing permeation of generative AI tools in the digital realm globally, it is of utmost importance that their distinct capabilities are appreciated while a serious note is taken to learn about and acknowledge their shortcomings. All the characteristics of GenAI tools must be taken into account when deciding whether to evaluate their generated responses before they are used. This section delves into the key features of GenAI tools, discussing their capabilities as well as their limitations. By assessing these characteristics, this section aims to create awareness regarding the realities associated with using such a technology while highlighting its transformative potential and limitations.

Creativity: GenAI has been designed to be creative in nature as it generates new information in the form of text, images, audio, video and other media types (Uğraş et al., 2024a, 2024b). The ability to create new data comes with flexibility and adaptability thereby satisfying the user's expectations and provides an apparently gratifying experience mostly (Mukherjee & Chang, 2023). In higher education, such tools can foster creativity in students by helping them with writing, research and revision, leaving more freedom and time for creative thinking and ideation when faced with time constraints (Owoseni et al., 2024).

Data-driven delivery of responses: As LLMs are trained on large datasets, they learn the pattern and styles using this humongous data. This very aspect enables these systems to generate responses though they are heavily derived from the trained data (Rane, 2023). A very admirable feature of these kinds of tools is representing responses in a format that is suitable to the kind of data being outputted. For example, data records may be represented in a tabular structure, codes may be represented in a distinct style with colour coding, bifurcation of content may be represented in the form of paragraphs, topic title, section headings, bulleted or numbered lists, and likewise. The ability of these tools in providing genuine references when asked is also a well appreciable characteristic.

Probabilistic Data Generation: AI-based generative tools generate content using probabilistic distribution that they learn during their training (Wang et al., 2022). As a result, the systems are capable of generating plausible outputs that are flexible, unique and unpredictable, unlike the output generated by traditional rule-based generative systems.

Customization: Generative models work on the user input and conditions that are received in the form of prompts to generate content that adheres closely to the users' expectations from these systems (Nourian et al., 2023). The more descriptive and guiding the users' prompts are, the more well curated are the responses delivered by the tools. These models are also capable of copying styles if specifically prompted by the users (Riemer & Peter, 2024).

Generative AI tools enhance capabilities through continuous learning and memory retention. They can deliver fast responses without user involvement, saving time. Real-time feedback-based performance improvement allows tools to generate enhanced output that meets user queries. This approach is more effective than retraining, which comes with costs. When combined with generative AI, real-time feedback systems can lead to substantial improvements in productivity, learning experiences, and operational efficiency.

Logic and Accuracy Issues: GenAI tools' responses are infamous for lacking logical consistency, making mistakes and providing scenarios that may differ from general examples that humans tend to make and use (Dwivedi et al., 2023). Hence, they cannot be blindly relied upon. Users may frequently experience factual unreliability, missing coherence and deviated or misunderstood context (Maung et al., 2024; Generative Artificial Intelligence, 2023) Incorrect numerical computations are also one of the critical lacunae, users may experience using GenAI tools (Palmer & Oswal, 2024).

Biased selections and Responses: Generative systems are also notorious for inheriting and amplifying biases that may exist in the training data, causing their responses to include the same issue (Srinivasan & Uchino, 2021), over-representing and under-representing particular groups based on imbalanced data fed through the training process. Another example includes associating activities or traits with particular gender or race. Owing to this challenge, the tools can generate overly positive responses which may not be suitable in the context of sensitive issues, leading to obscuring of important social variations in attitudes and beliefs of individuals (Zhang et al., 2024).

Hallucinations: Generative AI systems can produce incorrect responses due to reliance on probabilistic patterns rather than database facts. This can lead to misinformation or unintentional consequences. LLMs focus on prediction rather than accuracy, presenting seemingly realistic information to uninformed users, such as students (Glover, 2023).

The discussion emphasizes the importance of understanding GenAI tools' fundamentals and addressing inherent challenges for responsible and ethical use. It calls for evolving solutions to preserve authentic works and prevent potential harm.

Limitations with Generative AI Tools – Practical Examples

As discussed in the previous sections, Generative AI is prone to challenges that cannot be ignored with respect to its exhaustive list of applications in the academic landscape. GenAI tools are prone to logical and accuracy issues, biases, hallucinations, and generating harmful or offensive content. To support this stance, refer to figure 2 that demonstrates a snippet of a conversation with one such tool where the user prompts the tool to comment on its tendency of biasness and hallucination. The response given by the tool is very useful in understanding the tool's internal algorithms and its dependency on the quality of training data using which it generates the responses. Figure 3 is an example of how GenAI tools are trained to respond to users when asked about the accuracy of the responses they generate. An example of an incorrect numerical calculation done by one of the AI tools is presented in figure 4. The example demonstrates a user's query asking the tool to calculate the sum of the given numbers. The tool confidently gives an incorrect answer. On realising that the answer is wrong, the user prompts the tool to justify the calculation. It is seen in the second image of figure 4, that it justifies the wrong answer confidently yet again. On further querying, the responses for the sum were different than the previous ones.

Similar example can be seen in figure 5. The tool declared the value 10 as 10% of the value 30 although it explains the concept of percentage correctly in the explanation part. It is to be noted here that the examples given by means of figure 3, 4 and 5 represent different GenAI tools.

Figure 2. A conversation with one of the GenAI tools regarding its biased responses and hallucinations.

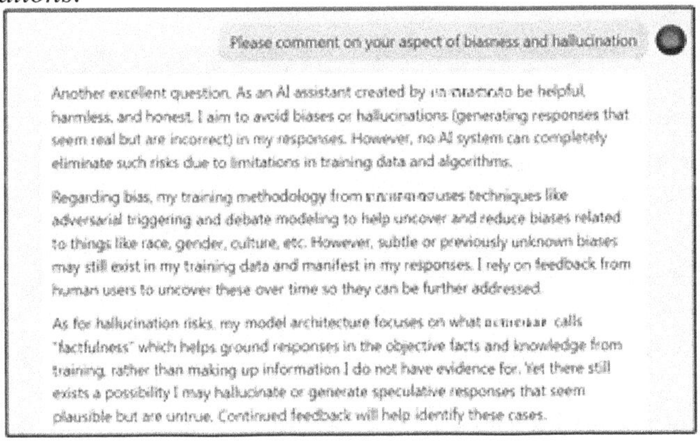

Figure 3. A conversation with one of the GenAI tools regarding the accuracy of its generated content

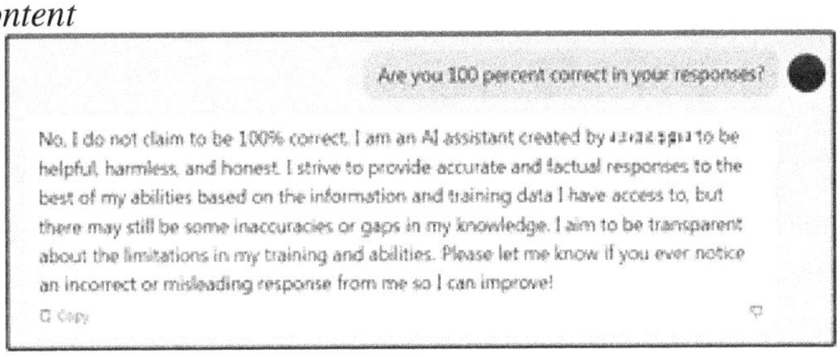

Figure 4. A conversation with one of the GenAI tools regarding the sum of the given numbers that was calculated incorrectly by the tool.

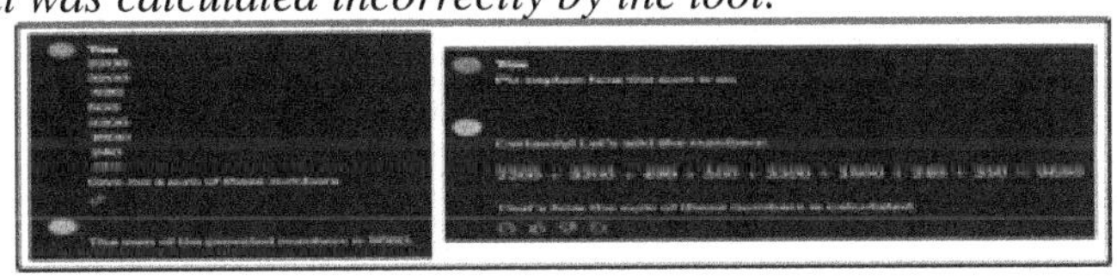

Figure 5. An incorrect response generated on asking a numerical question to a GenAI tool that is integrated into a search engine (The response is highlighted using a yellow-coloured square frame)

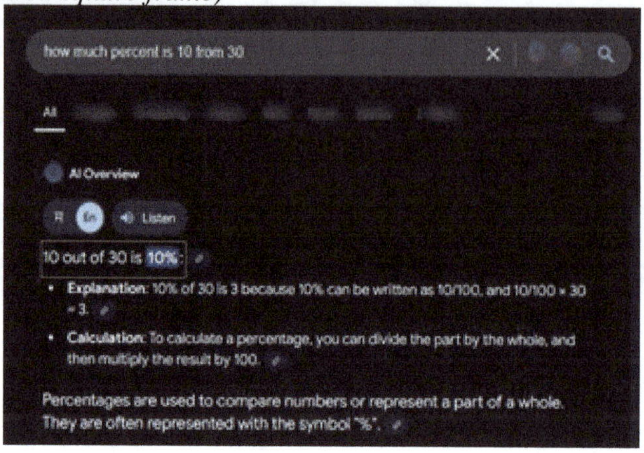

MISUSES OF GENERATIVE AI BY STUDENTS IN HIGHER EDUCATION

Generative AI systems tools have become easily accessible to the masses including higher education students in the last few years. The widespread adoption of such tools can be attributed to their strikingly fluent and coherent style of responses. Due to this, one of the major challenges with the use of GenAI higher education by students is academic dishonesty. Students may utilise the prowess of such tools for generating answers, essays and all other types of assignments. They may misuse these tools during exams, other kinds of closed book assessments and any other academic activities. There can be serious consequences, if such misconduct is observed and proven against them. Additionally, an unintentionally skewed evaluation of a student's performances may mislead the tutor into overestimating their abilities and drawing misleading comparisons between peers. This may happen due to the distorted perceptions that are caused by the fluidity and sophistication added by such tools to student submissions' information. Some factors that have led to the rise of GenAI misuse are the ease of access, seemingly believable responses, and challenges in detection of such synthetic contents. Mimicking human style of writing and completing tasks, GenAI tools may cause ignorance of real comprehension, learning and lack of sincere efforts on part of the students. The contents generated by the LLMs when used by students, may have all the limitations as discussed in the previous sections. The concerns with this trend root down to the important aspect of students side-lining their educational goals and ignoring their innate capabilities to be creative, to ideate, learn and succeed. Following are some of the many ways by which students may utilise Generative AI unethically. This discussion primarily aims at considerations of evolving some standard policies by academic stakeholders to address these issues ensuring fairness in the evaluation system.

Plagiarism: Students have been using GenAI tools to generate full-length essays, homework, or part of their tasks for submitting as their own work without the required attribution. Dehouche (2021) raised concern and questions on plagiarism in the era of ChatPGT-3 by mentioning its definition as per Wager & Kleinert (2012) i.e. “When somebody presents the work of others (data, words or theories) as if they were his/her own and without proper acknowledgment”. As per their study, the era of Gen AI also calls for reconsideration of how plagiarism must be defined to cover new challenges that such tools have introduced into the academic landscape. Such kinds of practices, if adopted during the learning years, may permanently distort their understanding and adoption of work ethics while also becoming a hindrance for their professional competence.

Cheating: In situations of non-stringent invigilation, students may retort to generating answers using GenAI tools and may even share them with peers accounting to mass copying. Answers in the form of text, essays, codes may be copied and such misconduct will directly influence their evaluations and help them skip the challenges related to learning without any critical considerations.

Authorship deception: Students may falsely claim authorship of generated content as their own original work and effectively disguise the role of AI in their work. This can seriously affect the quality and authenticity of published information.

Fake Citations: GenAI tools are notorious in generating citations for the content they generate. The generated citations like websites seem and look legitimate and believable but may actually lead to a 404 error when visited. Same is the case with scholarly citations generated by these tools that seem to be real but when cross-checked, cannot be found.

Academic integrity refers to the established code of conduct for completion of tasks and it includes honesty, fairness, originality, trust, respect and responsibility. It calls for actionable pursuits like proper crediting and citing of information sources and people, completing allotted tasks by one's own self, avoiding unauthorised collaborations, reporting all the details of the contributors with true weightage of attributions, refraining from adding individuals as contributors who have not played any significant role in the work, presenting only genuine findings from one’s work, and following the prescribed rules and policies. Such a kind of adherence creates a system of fairness and transparency in the academic procedures. Although the advent of Generative systems has brought with it the enhancement of technological capabilities, it has also led to opportunities for students to misuse and abuse its capabilities thereby shaking the foundations of academic integrity. While such tools can lend a great hand by means of helpful assistance and adding into one's creativity, when used for academic dishonesty, it contributes to the growing concern regarding education and its future globally. GenAI when used for academic dishonesty has many implications, one of them being, posing challenges in assessing and grading students' performances (Lampropoulos & Papadakis, 2025).

RESPONSIBLE INTEGRATION OF GENERATIVE AI THROUGH POLICY DEVELOPMENT BY HEIS

With the permeation of AI in the working of the society, the policy makers of Higher Education Institutes (HEIs) are grappling with the challenge of integrating generative AI in a balanced way. Though there is clarity up to some extent on the uses of these tools that may be classified as unethical in the academic landscape, there is still ambiguity up to a large extent regarding the many allowable and ethical cum constructive applications of GenAI that should be encouraged and governed under institutional regulations and policies. Though HEIs may consider altogether prohibiting its use, it can lead to overlooking its immense potential under responsible guidance. Therefore, it is important to study and understand how GenAI can be incorporated into academics such that the students are well engaged, aware of how these tools work and complete their tasks using them when required without resorting to any kind of misconduct. The discussions surrounding the situation have already begun as there is an increase in the studies surrounding the discussion on the ethical framework for incorporating generative AI in education(Uğraş et al., 2024). Before issuing any kind of complete restrictions on such a powerful technology while it is new, HEIs can responsibly undertake formal studies that are evidence-based inquiries with the aim of understanding how the technology can be leveraged within the ethical boundaries. Such studies can help in highlighting proven benefits of Generative systems while also shedding light on the potential risks. Another critical perspective that supports concrete academic policy making for generative AI integrations is the acceptance and active usage of such tools in various fields and industries for automation, increased productivity, cost-cutting and time reduction. Therefore, the students should be well educated and confident users of AI technology in supervised environments so that their transition as a professional who is an experienced user of such technologies is equally smooth (Peña, 2019; Chan, 2023a). Applying the UNESCO guidelines, Chan (2023b) worked towards drafting AI policies for use in HEIs for teaching and learning by understanding the perceptions around AI through data collected from 457 pupils and 180 educators of

Hong Kong Universities. By means of qualitative and quantitative analysis of data, the author proposed a broad AI-based Educational Policy Framework for integrating AI in the ecosystem. The pedagogical aspect of this framework focuses on improving the teaching and learning outcomes focusing on developing competencies of these tools' usage through comprehensive trainings for teachers and students, evolving formal standards for ethical use of GenAI tools and integration of risk management guidelines for sustaining the principles of integrity, accountability and safety.

AI can be utilised in the capacity of an assistant rather than by the substitution of human educators by utilising its abilities to generate ideas, exploring perspectives (Xiao et al., 2023). At the same time, fostering transparency while stringently maintaining privacy and security are proposed through the framework. It was also suggested that students need to be trained on using GenAI tools like ChatGPT as part of Academic Integrity activities to create awareness regarding its right usage and ethical considerations. Such programs can include guidelines and best practices that can help them focus on the recommended usage of such tools. In the same review study by Xiao et al., (2023) the ChatGPT policies as laid down by top 500 global universities and through their empirical analysis were studied, and the factors that influence responses to the policies of the institutions were identified. As per their observation, less than one third of the universities had formal policies in place, among which, around 67% had adopted GenAI tools for teaching and learning applications adhering to the existing ethical protocols as part of their policies. A positive correlation was observed with having policies, reputation, English-speaking regions and mainstream opinions. More restrictive policies were laid by universities having higher students-to-faculty ratio, heavily focused on research and influenced by nearby universities. Though universities banned tools like ChatGPT, educators were left to their personal preferences regarding their usage. Through this survey, the authors observed heterogeneity in the early-stage policies laid down by different universities and concluded that a formal drafting of regulations is subject to faculty integration supported by gathered evidence. In a recent study, Mills et al. (2023) propose the adoption of AI-based educational practices by means of an iterative process with dialogue between stakeholders rather than making it a definitive solution. They have suggested the inclusion of online communities for a collaborative dialogue to discuss the novel uses of generative AI leading to reflection on the evolving pedagogical needs. Such a practice opens room for reflection and revision, allowing educators to keep pace with the rapidly advancing AI landscape. The first institution to partner with OpenAI, the AI research and deployment firm that created ChatGPT is Arizona State University (OpenAI at ASU, 2023). The ASU President is partnering with OpenAI to explore the use of ChatGPT Enterprise's advanced capabilities, aiming to promote responsible AI development and use in teaching, learning, and discovery.

ETHICAL POLICIES INTEGRATION OF GENERATIVE AI IN ACADEMIC ENVIRONMENTS: STUDENT GUIDELINES FOR RESPONSIBLE USAGE

The integration of GenAI in various aspects of life requires guidelines focusing on students' needs. Affordable and sophisticated AI tools offer opportunities for personal development and learning. However, ethical measures are needed to ensure moral, safe, and holistic growth. Students should be aware of AI as a supportive tool, not a replacement for intellect. It is hoped that by means of a focused learning approach towards the ethical use-cases of generative AI, confidence can be developed in students to leverage AI to its best rather than using it to get rid of writing assignments and other kinds of submissions quickly (Lee & Low, 2024). With its unique ability to customize and personalized user's experience, GenAI can be leveraged by the students for customizing their individual learning needs. It can be asked to tailor its responses and provide content that meets a student's need by means of studying their learning patterns, and thereby provide guidance with optimized learning directions (Borah et al., 2024).

In this section, we attempt to present the most suitable use cases of GenAI with a particular focus on usage by the students.

Personalized and Tailored Learning: With the help of GenAI, students can customize resources of learning by leveraging the ability of AI to adapt to different learning patterns of the student. Students with the disabilities can also leverage AI for their study purpose (Sağdıç et al., 2024). By understanding the knowledge gaps, such platforms can create tailored study plans as per an individual's requirements. Students aiming to master computing skills like programming can achieve their learning goals by leveraging the coding capabilities of AI powered tools (Crompton & Song, 2021).

Improving Language Skills: GenAI-powered platforms improve engagement and self-sufficiency for students, particularly non-native speakers, in developing academic writing skills and improving language skills. AI tools like ChatGPT, Grammarly, and QuillBot assist in idea generation, drafting, and grammar checks, enhancing English language proficiency in academic activities.

Developing Research and Analytical Skills: GenAI tools can enhance research and analytical skills by personalizing learning experiences, providing efficient data analysis, summarizing literature, and automating data collection, thus improving problem-solving approaches and learning experiences (Agkathidis, 2015). For comprehending structure-activity relationships, such tools can be used by researchers for analysing complex data (Guerrero-Solé, 2023). Amongst many diverse domains, Generative AI systems have also shown success in enhancing architecture students' design capabilities by fostering a research-oriented learning approach (Agkathidis,

2015). AI can also be leveraged to generate the suggested structure of a research paper highlighting the expected and required sections as per the study title and generate citations and references. These tools can also help the learners, by using machine learning algorithms to examine and understand the deeper insights, trends and patterns within the information that are not so obvious. Predictive analysis is another area where one can apply AI as it involves forecasting probable outcomes based on trends visible in historic and current data. Such cases would thus be more representative of real life instances and help in decision-making. Data visualization consists of graphically representing data in the form of charts, graphs, dashboards. These can also be generated by AI making it easier and attainable for the students to advance their research studies.

Summarization: By means of text summarization capabilities of AI tools, students can substantially enhance their learning efficiency by means of concise comprehension of large volumes of study materials, thereby reducing cognitive overload. Additionally, students and faculties may create summarised points from heavy documents for creating presentations. The time taken for literature reviews can be substantially reduced with the help of AI tools as they demonstrate proficiency in summarizing research articles and help integrate them into assignments and theses. Through summarization, students can consciously focus on the main ideas, retain the critical ones, enhancing both academic performance and knowledge application (Saúde et al., 2024; Farrelly & Baker, 2023). Several models like BART and Pegasus are fine-tuned for performing tasks like text summarization with the capability to extract finer and critical details combined with semantic comprehension, requiring fewer epochs (Dar et al., 2024). It has also been noted that the relevance and quality of summarised texts displayed significant enhancements by the use of reinforcement learning with LLMs like Mistral, leaving behind traditional methods in terms of performance (Czerkawski, 2024).

Assessment and Feedback: Generative AI can be used in obtaining feedback and performing assessment that have been one of fulcrum activities in the education sector consuming considerable amount of time. Instant personalized feedback can be taken from the students through the use of AI tools (Zawacki-Richter & Latchem, 2018). Administering assessments through AI based platforms streamlines the administrative burden while enabling assessment in real time. These types of systems are able to process large amounts of student data, recognize patterns of students' misunderstanding and provide individual instruction tailored to the student. Students may level up their quizzes at their pace and AI would offer possibilities for differentiation of learning in the form of formative assessments. Automated feedback enables students to know the mistakes in their work instantly providing a means to correct them. students can be empowered to learn on their own without the need for constant guidance of teachers. Feedbacks generated by AI are timely, relevant and contextual and hence all levels of students can benefit from this feedback structure, regardless of the number of students in the class.

AI-powered Mock Interviews: AI can facilitate students in securing jobs and placements. The students who are about to complete their studies and opt for jobs can also use AI uploading the job description and their skills to anticipate the potential interview questions they may expect and prepare for it. They can also use AI to study the recruiter's profile and history. Utilizing AI tools like InterviewEase offering mock interview modules, it is possible to analyse speech emotion, detect gestures which can help to review a candidate's performance (Kothari et al. 2024; Czejdo & Bhattacharya, 2021). Candidates can attempt mock interviews in life-like virtual environments to help manage their anxiety, by means of technologies like augmented reality and virtual reality (Pawar, 2024).

While working with GenAI, it is important to teach students to treat the tool as a valuable assistant for research and brainstorming instead of using it as an instrument of short-cutting critical thinking steps. On the other hand, GenAI can assist idea generation among students, offer different opinions and simplify difficult ideas hence providing a better foundation for discussions or literary works. Nevertheless, it should be noted that students have to engage with the material, cross-check and develop their own original thoughts based on reliable sources. Students should use GenAI as a co-assistant in studies rather than a mere writing tool. GenAI tools have the potential to facilitate improved levels of understanding and creativity without compromising academic honesty.

CONCLUSION

As adoption of Generative AI models continues rapidly, its permeation in various sectors demands ethical applications and fairness of use. The beginning of acquiring this skill essentially begins at the HEIs that are preparing the future workforce i.e. the students. The adoption and integration of gen AI in HEIs offers numerous benefits, including enhanced access to learning resources, personalised and pace-based learning representing a significant technological advancement that is bound to revolutionise the education system. The successful adoption of Generative AI in higher education must begin with raising awareness and providing comprehensive training for teachers.

Through this study, it is realized that gen AI comes with its fair share of benefits and some serious challenges affecting the aspects of ethics and academic integrity which form the core of the education system. The global demand for acquiring AI literacy skills as evident from the literature survey underscores the importance of addressing this technological shift by means of assessing the benefits, challenges so as to strike a balance while navigating this landscape responsibly. HEIs must establish clear rules, guidelines and policies on the transparent and ethical usage of gen AI technology by evolving the right use cases for teachers, students and administration. Emphasis must be placed on honing the workforce and the future workforce i.e. the teachers and the students respectively to be able to learn and develop a nuanced understanding of gen AI, its uses, its working and its limitations so that they may be able to leverage the best out of such a powerful technology while making sure the strict boundaries of academic ethics and integrity are not crossed. The responsible use of gen AI can ensure that the 21st Century workforce is adept at instructing machines and algorithms with a thorough understanding and realisation of its capabilities as well as limitations.

REFERENCES

Agkathidis, A. (2015). Generative Design Methods - Implementing Computational Techniques in Undergraduate Architectural Education. *Proceedings of the 33th International Conference on Education and Research in Computer Aided Architectural Design in Europe (eCAADe) [Volume 2].*

Baidoo-Anu, D., & Ansah, L. O. (2023). Education in the era of generative artificial intelligence (AI): Understanding the potential benefits of ChatGPT in promoting teaching and learning. *Journal of AI, 7*(1), 52–62. DOI: 10.61969/jai.1337500

Baniata, L. H., & Kang, S. (2024). Switching self-attention text classification model with innovative reverse positional encoding for right-to-left languages: A focus on Arabic dialects. *Mathematics, 12*(6), 865. DOI: 10.3390/math12060865

Behera, G., Meenakshi, S., Rajini, J., Pravin, T., Boopathi, S., & Associates. (2025). Entrepreneurial Insights From Higher Education: Startup Business Ventures. In Real-World Tools and Scenarios for Entrepreneurship Exploration (pp. 101–132). IGI Global.

Bloomberg. (2023). Generative AI to become a $1.3 trillion market by 2032, research finds. Bloomberg. https://www.bloomberg.com/company/press/generative-ai-to-become-a-1-3-trillion-market-by-2032-research-finds/

Borah, A. R. T. N., N., & Gupta, S. (2024). Improved learning based on GenAI. *2024 2nd International Conference on Intelligent Data Communication Technologies and Internet of Things (IDCIoT),* Bengaluru, India, 1527-1532. DOI: 10.1109/IDCIoT59759.2024.10467943

Cengage Group. (2023, August). Generative AI in Higher Education Research Findings. Retrieved from https://www.cengagegroup.com/news/perspectives/2023/higher-ed-gen-ai-faculty-research-findings/

Chan, C. K. Y. (2023). A comprehensive AI policy education framework for university teaching and learning. *International Journal of Educational Technology in Higher Education, 20*(1), 38. DOI: 10.1186/s41239-023-00408-3

Chan, W. (2023). AI chatbots and liberal education. *AI & Society*, •••, 1–3.

Chukwuere, J. E., & Handoko, B. L. (2024). The future of generative AI chatbots in higher education. *Journal of Emerging Technologies*, *4*(1), 36–44.

Coursera. (2024). *Global Skills Report 2024*. Retrieved from https://www.coursera.org/skills-reports/global

Crompton, H., & Song, D. (2021). The potential of artificial intelligence in higher education. *RVUCN*, *62*(62), 1–4. DOI: 10.35575/rvucn.n62a1

Czerkawski, B. (2024). Designing language learning experiences with generative AI tools. *Advances in Educational Technologies and Instructional Design Book Series,* 324-341. .DOI: 10.4018/979-8-3693-0872-1.ch015

Dar, Z., Muhammad, R., Usman, B., Akhtar, J., Alazawi, A., Ali, H., & Hameed, E. (2024). Advanced generative AI methods for academic text summarization. .DOI: 10.1109/ICMI60790.2024.10585622

Dash, A., Ye, J., & Wang, G. (2023). A review of generative adversarial networks (GANs) and its applications in a wide variety of disciplines: From medical to remote sensing. *IEEE Access : Practical Innovations, Open Solutions.*

Dehouche, N. (2021). Plagiarism in the age of massive generative pre-trained transformers (GPT-3). *Ethics in Science and Environmental Politics*, *21*, 17–23. DOI: 10.3354/esep00195

Dong, S., Wang, P., & Abbas, K. (2021). A survey on deep learning and its applications. *Computer Science Review*, *40*, 100379. DOI: 10.1016/j.cosrev.2021.100379

Dwivedi, Y. K., Kshetri, N., Hughes, L., Slade, E. L., Jeyaraj, A., Kar, A. K., Baabdullah, A. M., Koohang, A., Raghavan, V., Ahuja, M., Albanna, H., Albashrawi, M. A., Al-Busaidi, A. S., Balakrishnan, J., Barlette, Y., Basu, S., Bose, I., Brooks, L., Buhalis, D., & Wright, R. (2023). "So what if ChatGPT wrote it?" Multidisciplinary perspectives on opportunities, challenges and implications of generative conversational AI for research, practice and policy. *International Journal of Information Management*, *71*, 102642. DOI: 10.1016/j.ijinfomgt.2023.102642

Fanni, S. C., Febi, M., Aghakhanyan, G., & Neri, E. (2023). Natural language processing. In *Introduction to Artificial Intelligence* (pp. 87–99). Springer International Publishing. DOI: 10.1007/978-3-031-25928-9_5

Farrelly, T., & Baker, N. (2023). Generative artificial intelligence: Implications and considerations for higher education practice. *Education Sciences*, *13*(11), 1109. Advance online publication. DOI: 10.3390/educsci13111109

George, B., & Wooden, O. (2023). Managing the strategic transformation of higher education through artificial intelligence. *Administrative Sciences*, *13*(9), 196. DOI: 10.3390/admsci13090196

Ghojogh, B., & Ghodsi, A. (2020). Attention mechanism, transformers, BERT, and GPT: Tutorial and survey.

Glover, E. (2023). What is an AI hallucination? https://builtin.com/artificial-intelligence/ai-hallucination

Goyal, R., Kumar, P., & Singh, V. P. (2023). A systematic survey on automated text generation tools and techniques: Application, evaluation, and challenges. *Multimedia Tools and Applications*, *82*(28), 43089–43144. DOI: 10.1007/s11042-023-15224-0

Guerrero-Solé, F. (2023). El impacto de la inteligencia artificial generativa en la disciplina de la comunicación. *Hipertext.net, 1-9.* .DOI: 10.31009/hipertext.net.2023.i26.01

Han, X., Zhang, Z., Ding, N., Gu, Y., Liu, X., Huo, Y., Qiu, J., Yao, Y., Zhang, A., Zhang, L., Han, W., Huang, M., Jin, Q., Lan, Y., Liu, Y., Liu, Z., Lu, Z., Qiu, X., Song, R., & Zhu, J. (2021). Pre-trained models: Past, present and future. *AI Open*, *2*, 225–250. DOI: 10.1016/j.aiopen.2021.08.002

Hartsock, I., & Rasool, G. (2024). Vision-language models for medical report generation and visual question answering: A review. *Frontiers in Artificial Intelligence*, *7*, 1430984. DOI: 10.3389/frai.2024.1430984

Hirschberg, J., & Manning, C. D. (2015). Advances in natural language processing. *Science*, *349*(6245), 261–266. DOI: 10.1126/science.aaa8685

Inside Higher Ed. (2024, June). Survey: How Are Profs, Staff Using AI? Retrieved from https://www.insidehighered.com/news/student-success/academic-life/2024/06/28/one-third-college-instructors-are-using-genai-heres

Ioannidou, A., Chatzilari, E., Nikolopoulos, S., & Kompatsiaris, I. (2017). Deep learning advances in computer vision with 3D data: A survey. *ACM Computing Surveys*, *50*(2), 1–38. DOI: 10.1145/3042064

Kalligeropoulos, D., & Vasileiadou, S. (2008). The homeric automata and their implementation. In *Science and technology in homeric epics* (pp. 77–84). Springer Netherlands.

Karthikeyan, M., Madan, B. S., Suchitra, V., Varshini, E. S. A., Sarkar, R., & Boopathi, S. (2025). Flipped Classroom Methods for Enhanced Student Engagement and Knowledge Developments in Indian Higher Education. In Global Practices in Inclusive Education Curriculum and Policy (pp. 313–342). IGI Global.

Khamparia, A., & Singh, K. M. (2019). A systematic review on deep learning architectures and applications. *Expert Systems: International Journal of Knowledge Engineering and Neural Networks*, *36*(3), e12400. DOI: 10.1111/exsy.12400

Konar, A. (2018). *Artificial intelligence and soft computing: Behavioral and cognitive modeling of the human brain.* CRC Press.

Kothari, P., Mehta, P., Patil, S., & Hole, V. (2024). InterviewEase: AI-powered interview assistance. DOI: 10.21203/rs.3.rs-3964944/v1

Krishnamoorthy, N., Chandrasekar, J., Saqib, M., Therasa, P., Ganesh, C. S., & Boopathi, S. (2025). The Role of CO-PO Mapping in NBA Accreditation Assessments: Enhancing Educational Quality and Outcomes. In Hispanic Leadership in Higher Education (pp. 89–118). IGI Global.

Lampropoulos, G., & Papadakis, S. (2025). The Educational Value of Artificial Intelligence and Social Robots. In *Social Robots in Education* (pp. 3–15). Springer. DOI: 10.1007/978-3-031-82915-4_1

Lee, C. C., & Low, M. Y. H. (2024). Using GenAI in education: The case for critical thinking. *Frontiers in Artificial Intelligence*, *7*, 1452131. DOI: 10.3389/frai.2024.1452131

Lee, R. S. (2023). Major NLP applications. In *Natural Language Processing: A Textbook with Python Implementation* (pp. 199–239). Springer Nature Singapore.

Li, R. (2020). *Artificial intelligence revolution: How AI will change our society, economy, and culture*. Simon and Schuster.

Maung, B. M., McBride, K., Lucas, J. S., Tabar, M., & Lee, D. (2024). Generative AI disproportionately harms long tail users. *Computer*, *57*(11), 82–85. DOI: 10.1109/MC.2024.3408594

Michel-Villarreal, R., Vilalta-Perdomo, E., Salinas-Navarro, D. E., Thierry-Aguilera, R., & Gerardou, F. S. (2023). Challenges and opportunities of generative AI for higher education as explained by ChatGPT. *Education Sciences*, *13*(9), 856. DOI: 10.3390/educsci13090856

Mills, A., Bali, M., & Eaton, L. (2023). How do we respond to generative AI in education? Open educational practices give us a framework for an ongoing process. *Journal of Applied Learning and Teaching*, *6*(1), 16–30.

Mukherjee, A., & Chang, H. (2023). Managing the Creative Frontier of Generative AI: The Novelty-Usefulness Tradeoff. *California Management Review*.

Naveed, H., Khan, A. U., Qiu, S., Saqib, M., Anwar, S., Usman, M., . . . Mian, A. (2023). A comprehensive overview of large language models. *arXiv preprint,* arXiv:2307.06435.

Nourian, P., Azadi, S., & Oval, R. (2023). Generative design in architecture: From mathematical optimization to grammatical customization. In *Computational Design and Digital Manufacturing* (pp. 1–43). Springer International Publishing. DOI: 10.1007/978-3-031-21167-6_1

OpenAI at ASU. (2023). Retrieved from https://ai.asu.edu/openAI

Owoseni, A., Kolade, O., & Egbetokun, A. (2024). Generative AI and Its Implications for Higher Education Students and Educators. In *Generative AI in Higher Education: Innovation Strategies for Teaching and Learning* (pp. 1–25). Springer Nature Switzerland. DOI: 10.1007/978-3-031-60179-8_1

Palmer, Z. B., & Oswal, S. K. (2024). Constructing websites with generative AI tools: The accessibility of their workflows and products for users with disabilities. *Journal of Business and Technical Communication, 0*(0). Advance online publication. DOI: 10.1177/10506519241280644

Panigrahi, A., Malladi, S., Xia, M., & Arora, S. (2023). Trainable transformer in transformer. *arXiv preprint,* arXiv:2307.01189.

Papadakis, S., Lytvynova, S. H., Ivanova, S. M., & Selyshcheva, I. A. (2024b). *Advancing lifelong learning with AI-enhanced ICT: A review of 3L-Person 2024.* In *CEUR Workshop Proceedings (9th International Workshop on Professional Retraining and Life-Long Learning using ICT: Person-oriented Approach — 3L-Person 2024, Lviv, Ukraine, September 25, 2023).* CEUR-WS.org.

Papadakis, S., Striuk, A. M., Kravtsov, H. M., Shyshkina, M. P., Marienko, M. V., & Danylchuk, H. B. (2024a). *Embracing digital innovation and cloud technologies for transformative learning experiences.* In *Proceedings of the 11th Workshop on Cloud Technologies in Education (CTE 2023), Kryvyi Rih, Ukraine, December 22, 2023.* CEUR Workshop Proceedings.

Pawar, S. (2024). Advancing interview preparation: An AI-driven approach. *Indian Scientific Journal of Research in Engineering and Management, 8*(2), 1–13. DOI: 10.55041/IJSREM28705

Peña, A. A. R. (2019). Robot-Proof: Higher Education in the age of artificial intelligence. *Innovación Educativa (México, D.F.), 19*(80), 181–183.

Rane, N. (2023). Role and challenges of ChatGPT and similar generative artificial intelligence in human resource management. *Available at SSRN,* 4603230. DOI: 10.2139/ssrn.4603230

Riemer, K., & Peter, S. (2024). Conceptualizing generative AI as style engines: Application archetypes and implications. *International Journal of Information Management, 79*, 102824. DOI: 10.1016/j.ijinfomgt.2024.102824

Sætra, H. S. (2023). Generative AI: Here to stay, but for good? *Technology in Society, 75*, 102372. DOI: 10.1016/j.techsoc.2023.102372

Sağdıç, A., Elumar-Efe, E., & Sani-Bozkurt, S. (2024). GenAI, robots, and inclusive special education: Autism spectrum disorder in the age of generative AI. In *Transforming Education with Generative AI: Prompt Engineering and Synthetic Content Creation* (pp. 309-326). IGI Global.

Sarkar, R., Mahamuni, V. S., Chitra, M., Vijayakumar, M., Jefferson, K., & Boopathi, S. (2025). Integrating Innovation Tools and Technology in Educational Management. In Planning Tools for Policy, Leadership, and Management of Education Systems (pp. 121–154). IGI Global.

Sarkar, R., Parmar, D. V., Trivedi, N. B., Prabakaran, S., Chandra, S., & Boopathi, S. (2025). Pedagogical Contents Developments and Specialized Training for Teaching Careers. In Global Practices in Inclusive Education Curriculum and Policy (pp. 187–216). IGI Global.

Sarker, I. H. (2021). Machine learning: Algorithms, real-world applications and research directions. *SN Computer Science, 2*(3), 160. DOI: 10.1007/s42979-021-00592-x

Saúde, S., Barros, J. P., & Almeida, I. (2024). Impacts of generative artificial intelligence in higher education: Research trends and students' perceptions. *Social Sciences (Basel, Switzerland), 13*(8), 410. DOI: 10.3390/socsci13080410

Shabbir, J., & Anwer, T. (2018). Artificial intelligence and its role in near future. *arXiv preprint*, arXiv:1804.01396.

Skapura, D. M. (1996). *Building neural networks*. Addison-Wesley Professional.

Smolansky, A., Cram, A., Raduescu, C., Zeivots, S., Huber, E., & Kizilcec, R. F. (2023, July). Educator and student perspectives on the impact of generative AI on assessments in higher education. In *Proceedings of the tenth ACM conference on Learning@ Scale* (pp. 378–382). DOI: 10.1145/3573051.3596191

Srinivasan, R., & Uchino, K. (2021, March). Biases in generative art: A causal look from the lens of art history. In *Proceedings of the 2021 ACM Conference on Fairness, Accountability, and Transparency* (pp. 41-51). DOI: 10.1145/3442188.3445869

Sullivan, M., Kelly, A., & McLaughlan, P. (2023). ChatGPT in higher education: Considerations for academic integrity and student learning. *Journal of Applied Learning & Teaching*, *6*(1), 31–40.

Turing, D. (2018). *The Story of Computing*. Arcturus Publishing.

Tyton Partners. (2023, October). GenAI in Higher Education: Fall 2023 Update of Time for Class Study.

Uğraş, H., Uğraş, M., Papadakis, S., & Kalogiannakis, M. (2024a). ChatGPT-supported education in primary schools: The potential of ChatGPT for sustainable practices. *Sustainability (Basel)*, *16*(22), 9855. DOI: 10.3390/su16229855

Uğraş, H., Uğraş, M., Papadakis, S., & Kalogiannakis, M. (2024b). Innovative Early Childhood STEM Education with ChatGPT: Teacher Perspectives. *Technology, Knowledge and Learning*, 1-23.

Vaswani, A. (2017). Attention is all you need. *Advances in Neural Information Processing Systems.*

Venkatasubramanian, V., Chitra, M., Sudha, R., Singh, V. P., Jefferson, K., & Boopathi, S. (2024). Examining the Impacts of Course Outcome Analysis in Indian Higher Education: Enhancing Educational Quality. In Challenges of Globalization and Inclusivity in Academic Research (pp. 124–145). IGI Global Scientific Publishing.

Voulodimos, A., Doulamis, N., Doulamis, A., & Protopapadakis, E. (2018). Deep learning for computer vision: A brief review. *Computational Intelligence and Neuroscience*, *2018*(1), 7068349. DOI: 10.1155/2018/7068349

Wager, E., & Kleinert, S. (2012). Cooperation between research institutions and journals on research integrity cases: Guidance from the committee on publication ethics. *Saudi Journal of Anaesthesia*, *6*(2), 155–160. DOI: 10.4103/1658-354X.97030

Wang, Y., Herron, L., & Tiwary, P. (2022). From data to noise to data for mixing physics across temperatures with generative artificial intelligence. *Proceedings of the National Academy of Sciences of the United States of America*, *119*(32), e2203656119. DOI: 10.1073/pnas.2203656119

World Bank. (2023). *Generative artificial intelligence. (Emerging Technologies Curation Series No. 5)*. World Bank.

Xiao, P., Chen, Y., & Bao, W. (2023). Waiting, banning, and embracing: An empirical analysis of adapting policies for generative AI in higher education. *arXiv preprint,* arXiv:2305.18617.

Yenduri, G., Ramalingam, M., Selvi, G. C., Supriya, Y., Srivastava, G., Maddikunta, P. K. R., Raj, G. D., Jhaveri, R. H., Prabadevi, B., Wang, W., Vasilakos, A. V., & Gadekallu, T. R. (2024). GPT (Generative Pre-trained Transformer)–A comprehensive review on enabling technologies, potential applications, emerging challenges, and future directions. *IEEE Access : Practical Innovations, Open Solutions*, *12*, 54608–54649. DOI: 10.1109/ACCESS.2024.3389497

Yongqi, D., Xingmin, L., Ruohan, L., Wei, S., Bart, V. A., & Farah, H. (2023). Intelligent anomaly detection for lane rendering using transformer with self-supervised pre-training and customized fine-tuning. *arXiv.org, abs/2312.04398.* https://doi .org//arxiv.2312.04398DOI: 10.48550

Zawacki-Richter, O., & Latchem, C. (2018). Exploring four decades of research in computers & education. *Computers & Education*, *122*, 136–152. DOI: 10.1016/j. compedu.2018.04.001

Zhang, S., Xu, J., & Alvero, A. (2024, September 20). Generative AI meets open-ended survey responses: Participant use of AI and homogenization.

Zhao, Z., Alzubaidi, L., Zhang, J., Duan, Y., & Gu, Y. (2023). A comparison review of transfer learning and self-supervised learning: Definitions, applications, advantages and limitations. *Expert Systems with Applications*, •••, 122807.

Zoph, B., Ghiasi, G., Lin, T.-Y., Cui, Y., Liu, H., Cubuk, E. D., & Le, Q. (2020). Rethinking pre-training and self-training. *Advances in Neural Information Processing Systems*, *33*, 3833–3845.

KEY TERMS AND DEFINITIONS

AI (Artificial Intelligence): The simulation of human intelligence in machines.

AIPRM (AI Prompt Repository Manager): A tool/add-on that provides curated prompt templates.

ASU (Arizona State University): A public research university in the United States recognized.

BART (Bidirectional and Auto-Regressive Transformers): A sequence-to-sequence model combining bidirectional encoding and autoregressive decoding.

CAGR (Compound Annual Growth Rate): Mannual growth rate of an investment over a specific period.

GAN (Generative Adversarial Network): A deep learning model where two neural networks.

GPT (Generative Pre-trained Transformer): A large-scale language model developed by OpenAI.

HEI (Higher Education Institution): Universities, colleges, and other institutions.

LLM (Large Language Model): A type of AI model trained on massive datasets.

NLP (Natural Language Processing): A subfield of AI focused on enabling machines.

PGT (Post Graduate Teacher): An educator qualified to teach at the higher secondary.

UNESCO (United Nations Educational, Scientific and Cultural Organization): A UN agency that promotes global collaboration.

Chapter 5

Privacy in AI in Education

Deepak Gupta
http://orcid.org/0000-0003-3929-1362
Institute of Technology and Management, Gwalior, India

Harpominder Jit Kaur Sidhu
http://orcid.org/0009-0000-3821-9057
University School of Business, Chandigarh University, Mohali, India

Sathish Krishna Anumula
http://orcid.org/0009-0009-0613-4863
IBM Corporation, USA

Sivaiah Sreeramula
http://orcid.org/0000-0002-3461-0400
Vidya Jyothi Institute of Technology, India

Archana Yashwant Panpatil
http://orcid.org/0009-0007-1062-4043
Sardar Vallabhbhai National Institute of Technology, India

Syamala Rao
SRM University AP, India

Mukesh Tripathi
KIET Group of Institutions, India

ABSTRACT

The integration of artificial intelligence (AI) in educational settings has revolutionized learning experiences while simultaneously raising critical privacy concerns. This chapter examines the complex landscape of AI-driven educational technologies and their implications for student data privacy. As educational institutions increasingly adopt AI-powered learning management systems, personalized tutoring platforms, and predictive analytics tools, the collection, processing, and storage of sensitive student information have become paramount concerns. This comprehensive analysis explores current privacy challenges, regulatory frameworks including FERPA and GDPR, technological solutions such as differential privacy and federated learning, and emerging best practices for protecting student privacy while maintaining AI system effectiveness. The chapter presents a balanced perspective on navigating the tension between educational innovation and privacy protection.

DOI: 10.4018/979-8-2600-0101-1.ch005

1. INTRODUCTION

The digital transformation of education has accelerated dramatically in recent years, with artificial intelligence emerging as a cornerstone technology reshaping how students learn, teachers instruct, and institutions operate (Zawacki-Richter et al., 2019). This transformation is particularly pronounced in K-12 settings, where 25 states and their departments of education now have official guidance or policy on the use of AI in schools, reflecting the urgent need for frameworks to govern AI deployment in elementary and secondary education. From intelligent tutoring systems that adapt to individual learning styles to predictive analytics that identify at-risk students, AI applications in education promise unprecedented opportunities for personalized, effective, and accessible learning experiences (Beiderbeck et al., 2024). Recent empirical evidence supports these promises, demonstrating tangible educational benefits including enhanced sustainability practices in primary schools through ChatGPT integration (Uğraş, Uğraş, Papadakis, & Kalogiannakis, 2024a) and improved learning outcomes through AI and social robot applications across diverse educational contexts (Lampropoulos & Papadakis, 2025). However, this technological revolution comes with significant privacy implications that demand careful consideration and proactive management, particularly in K-12 environments where student vulnerability and consent challenges are most acute (Huang, 2023).

Educational AI systems inherently rely on vast amounts of student data to function effectively (Liu et al., 2025). In K-12 settings, these systems collect, analyze, and act upon information ranging from basic demographic data and academic performance records to more sensitive behavioral patterns, emotional states, and learning preferences (Mutimukwe et al., 2021). The granular nature of this data collection, combined with the particular vulnerability of elementary and secondary school populations, creates a unique privacy landscape that differs substantially from both higher education and other sectors implementing AI technologies (Gujjula & Sanghera, 2023). Recent surveys reveal that teachers often lack crucial understanding of AI platforms' privacy risks and may inadvertently expose personal student information when experimenting with AI tools, particularly without adequate district guidance on data protection protocols (Chalkbeat, 2024). Teacher perspectives on AI implementation reveal both enthusiasm for educational innovation and concern about data privacy implications, particularly in early childhood education where students are most vulnerable (Uğraş, Uğraş, Papadakis, & Kalogiannakis, 2025).

The stakes are particularly high in K-12 educational contexts because the subjects of data collection are predominantly minors who cannot provide meaningful consent for data processing activities (Hoel & Chen, 2018). Furthermore, educational data has long-term implications for students' academic and professional futures, making privacy breaches potentially devastating for individual life trajectories (Pardo

& Siemens, 2014). The K-12 context presents unique challenges, as elementary and secondary schools face different regulatory frameworks than higher education institutions, often operate with limited technical expertise and resources, and must navigate complex stakeholder relationships involving students, parents, teachers, and administrators (Akgun & Greenhow, 2022). The challenge lies in harnessing AI's transformative potential—including its demonstrated capacity to support sustainable educational practices and enhance STEM learning outcomes—while establishing robust safeguards that protect student privacy rights and maintain trust in educational institutions, particularly given that more than half (60%) of K-12 educators report their districts have not made clear their AI policies (Holmes & Porayska-Pomsta, 2022).

This chapter provides a comprehensive examination of privacy considerations in AI-enabled K-12 education, addressing both current challenges and emerging solutions specific to elementary and secondary school contexts. We explore the regulatory landscape governing educational data privacy, analyze technological approaches to privacy preservation, and offer practical guidance for K-12 stakeholders seeking to implement AI responsibly in educational settings while maximizing the educational benefits that drive institutional adoption. Special attention is given to the unique challenges facing K-12 environments, including limited technical resources, diverse stakeholder needs, and the particular vulnerabilities of minor students (Organisation for Economic Co-operation and Development, 2023).

2. CURRENT STATE OF AI IN EDUCATION

2.1 AI Applications in K-12 Educational Settings

The adoption of AI in K-12 education has expanded across multiple domains, each presenting unique privacy considerations while delivering measurable educational benefits (Berson et al., 2025). Unlike higher education implementations, K-12 AI deployments must account for developmental appropriateness, parental consent requirements, and limited technical infrastructure in many school districts. Intelligent Tutoring Systems (ITS) represent one of the most prevalent applications in elementary and secondary schools, utilizing machine learning algorithms to create personalized learning paths based on individual student performance, preferences, and learning patterns (Zawacki-Richter et al., 2019). These systems continuously collect data on student interactions, response times, error patterns, and engagement levels to refine their instructional strategies, but K-12 implementations face unique challenges in explaining these data practices to minor students and obtaining meaningful parental consent.

2.1.1 K-12 Teacher Perspectives on AI-Powered Privacy Risks

Recent research reveals significant gaps between AI adoption enthusiasm and privacy awareness among K-12 educators. High school teacher Armando Martinez exemplifies the cautious approach many educators take, using ChatGPT for lesson planning and creative content generation while intentionally avoiding AI for tasks involving student data, such as creating Individualized Education Programs or grading student work (Chalkbeat, 2024). This selective use pattern reflects teachers' intuitive understanding of privacy risks, even when formal training is lacking. However, surveys indicate that teachers often experiment with AI tools without adequate understanding of privacy implications, potentially exposing student information in ways that could have long-term repercussions.

K-12 educators report particular concerns about surveillance and tracking systems that gather detailed information about student and teacher actions and preferences in elementary and secondary settings (Akgun & Greenhow, 2022). Unlike university students who are legal adults, K-12 students cannot meaningfully consent to extensive data collection, creating ethical dilemmas when schools implement AI systems that require comprehensive behavioral monitoring. Teachers express worry about the appropriateness of sophisticated tracking technologies for younger students, particularly those in elementary grades who may not understand the implications of digital interactions.

2.1.2 Evidence-Based Educational Benefits in K-12 Contexts

Recent research provides compelling evidence for AI's educational value across different K-12 contexts and age groups, supporting the case for why districts pursue AI adoption despite privacy challenges. Lampropoulos and Papadakis (2025) demonstrate that AI and social robots create significant educational value in K-12 settings through enhanced engagement, personalized learning experiences, and improved accessibility for diverse learners. Their analysis reveals that these technologies particularly benefit students with special educational needs and those from disadvantaged backgrounds, supporting the equity goals that drive many K-12 institutional AI adoption decisions. This equity dimension is particularly relevant for K-12 schools, which serve more diverse populations than higher education and have legal obligations under IDEA to provide appropriate accommodations for students with disabilities.

In elementary education specifically, ChatGPT implementation has shown promise for supporting sustainable educational practices, with primary school teachers reporting enhanced curriculum delivery and improved student engagement in environmental education topics (Uğraş et al., 2024a). This sustainability dimension adds a new layer to the educational benefits driving AI adoption in K-12 settings, as schools seek technologies that simultaneously improve learning outcomes and support environmental responsibility (Papadakis et al., 2024a, 2024b). However, these implementations raise specific privacy concerns about conversational AI systems that collect detailed linguistic and behavioral data from young students who may not understand the implications of sharing personal information with AI systems.

Early childhood STEM education represents another area where AI demonstrates clear educational value while presenting unique privacy challenges specific to K-12 environments. Teacher perspectives on ChatGPT integration in early childhood settings reveal optimism about enhanced learning opportunities coupled with concerns about age-appropriate data collection practices (Uğraş et al., 2025). Elementary educators report that AI tools enable more personalized STEM instruction and support differentiated learning approaches, but they also express uncertainty about privacy implications and the appropriateness of sophisticated AI systems for very young learners who cannot provide informed consent for data collection.

2.1.3 Learning Management Systems and K-12 Privacy Challenges

Learning Management Systems (LMS) enhanced with AI capabilities have become ubiquitous in K-12 environments, but their implementation presents distinct privacy challenges compared to higher education settings (Beiderbeck et al., 2024). These platforms aggregate data from multiple sources, including assignment submissions, discussion forum participation, login patterns, and resource access behaviors, to provide instructors with comprehensive analytics dashboards. However, K-12 implementations must navigate additional complexity around parental access rights, age-appropriate consent mechanisms, and varying developmental stages across grade levels.

The integration of natural language processing for automated essay grading and feedback generation raises particular concerns in K-12 settings, where students may include personal information in their writing assignments that could be inadvertently captured and processed by AI systems. Unlike university students who can make informed decisions about data sharing, elementary and secondary students may not understand that their creative writing or personal narratives could become part of AI training datasets or be subject to automated analysis that reveals sensitive information about their home lives, emotional states, or personal experiences.

K-12 educators report that AI-enhanced LMS platforms improve their ability to provide timely, personalized feedback and identify students needing additional support, but many express concerns about the extensive data collection required for these systems to function effectively. Teachers note that while these tools offer valuable insights into student learning patterns, they worry about the long-term implications of collecting detailed behavioral data on students as young as five or six years old, particularly given that this data may follow students throughout their educational careers.

2.1.4 Educational Data Mining and Stakeholder Perspectives

Educational data mining and learning analytics represent another significant application area, where institutions analyze large datasets to improve educational outcomes, optimize resource allocation, and inform policy decisions (Ifenthaler & Schumacher, 2016). These systems often combine academic data with demographic information, socioeconomic indicators, and behavioral metrics to generate insights about student success factors and institutional effectiveness.

Teacher perspectives on these systems reveal a complex relationship between appreciation for data-driven insights and concern about privacy implications. Educators value AI tools that help them understand student learning patterns and adjust instruction accordingly, but they also worry about the appropriateness of extensive data collection, particularly for younger students (Uğraş et al., 2025). This tension between educational benefit and privacy protection represents a central challenge in responsible AI implementation.

2.1.5 Emerging Applications and Privacy Implications

Virtual and augmented reality applications in education, enhanced by AI, create immersive learning experiences while collecting biometric data such as eye movement patterns, physiological responses, and spatial interaction behaviors (Huang, 2023).

The integration of conversational AI systems like ChatGPT in educational settings represents a newer application area with particular relevance for privacy considerations. These systems collect detailed conversational data, linguistic patterns, and learning preferences while providing personalized tutoring and support. The educational benefits include enhanced accessibility, 24/7 availability, and personalized learning support, but the conversational nature of these interactions creates new categories of sensitive educational data that require specialized privacy protections.

2.2 Data Types and Collection Methods

The diversity of AI applications in education corresponds to an equally diverse array of data types being collected and processed (Song, 2024). Academic performance data includes grades, test scores, assignment completion rates, and progress tracking metrics. Behavioral data encompasses login patterns, time spent on tasks, navigation pathways through digital resources, and interaction frequencies with educational content (Mutimukwe et al., 2021).

Biometric data collection has become increasingly common, particularly in applications involving facial recognition for identity verification, voice analysis for language learning assessment, and physiological monitoring for engagement measurement (Berson et al., 2025). Social interaction data from collaborative learning platforms captures communication patterns, peer relationships, and group dynamics.

Contextual data includes device information, location data, time stamps, and environmental factors that may influence learning outcomes. Personal demographic information such as age, gender, socioeconomic status, and special needs accommodations provides additional context for AI algorithms but raises particular privacy concerns due to its sensitive nature (Gujjula & Sanghera, 2023).

The methods of data collection have evolved to become increasingly sophisticated and less intrusive to the user experience. Passive data collection through learning platform interactions, keystroke dynamics analysis, and ambient sensor monitoring allows for continuous data gathering without explicit user actions (Hoel & Chen, 2018). Active data collection through surveys, assessments, and feedback mechanisms provides more targeted information but requires direct student engagement.

3. PRIVACY CHALLENGES IN AI-ENABLED EDUCATION

3.1 Consent and Minor Protection Issues

One of the most complex privacy challenges in educational AI systems involves obtaining meaningful consent for data collection and processing, particularly when dealing with minor students (Slade & Prinsloo, 2013).

The concept of "informed consent" becomes particularly problematic when applied to sophisticated AI systems whose data processing mechanisms are often opaque even to technical experts (Drachsler & Greller, 2016). Students, parents, and even educators may struggle to understand the full implications of data collection, algorithmic decision-making, and long-term data retention policies (Karran et al., 2024). This knowledge gap undermines the validity of consent and raises questions about whether truly informed consent is achievable in complex AI educational environments.

Parental consent mechanisms, while legally sufficient in many jurisdictions, present practical challenges in implementation (Hoel & Chen, 2018). Educational institutions must balance parental rights with student autonomy, particularly for older minors who may have different privacy preferences than their parents. The logistics of obtaining, managing, and maintaining parental consent across diverse family structures and communication preferences creates additional administrative burdens for schools and technology providers.

The dynamic nature of AI systems complicates consent management further (Ifenthaler & Schumacher, 2016). As algorithms evolve, data usage patterns change, and new features are added to educational platforms, the scope of data processing may expand beyond the original consent parameters. Maintaining ongoing consent compliance requires robust systems for notification, re-consent, and opt-out mechanisms that respect both parental authority and student preferences.

3.2 Data Minimization and Purpose Limitation

The principle of data minimization, which requires collecting only data that is necessary for specified purposes, faces significant challenges in AI educational systems (Pardo & Siemens, 2014). Machine learning algorithms often benefit from large, diverse datasets, creating tension between privacy-protective data minimization and AI system effectiveness (Liu et al., 2025). Educational AI systems may collect extensive behavioral data to improve personalization algorithms, but the necessity of all collected data points for educational purposes may be questionable.

Purpose limitation, the requirement that data be used only for the specific purposes for which it was collected, becomes complex in educational AI contexts where data utility may extend beyond initial educational objectives (Holmes & Porayska-Pomsta, 2022). Student performance data collected for grading purposes might later be valuable for institutional research, policy development, or commercial product improvement. The secondary use of educational data raises questions about consent scope and privacy expectations (Mutimukwe et al., 2021).

The aggregation and inference capabilities of AI systems can derive sensitive information from seemingly innocuous data points, challenging traditional approaches to data classification and protection (Huang, 2023). Behavioral patterns in learning platforms might reveal information about student mental health, family circumstances, or future academic potential that extends far beyond the original data collection purposes.

3.3 Algorithmic Transparency and Bias

The "black box" nature of many AI algorithms creates significant privacy and fairness concerns in educational applications (Song, 2024). Students and parents have legitimate interests in understanding how AI systems make decisions that affect educational opportunities, resource allocation, and academic outcomes (Gujjula & Sanghera, 2023). However, the complexity of machine learning models and commercial confidentiality concerns often limit the transparency that educational institutions can provide about their AI systems.

Algorithmic bias in educational AI systems can perpetuate or amplify existing inequalities, with privacy implications extending beyond individual data protection to broader social justice concerns (Vidal et al., 2023). Biased algorithms may systematically disadvantage certain student populations, creating privacy harms through discriminatory treatment and profiling. The intersectional nature of bias means that students with multiple marginalized identities may face compounded privacy risks.

The feedback loops inherent in AI systems can entrench biases over time, as algorithms trained on biased historical data continue to make biased predictions that influence future educational opportunities and outcomes (Berson et al., 2025). These self-reinforcing cycles create long-term privacy harms that extend beyond the immediate educational context into students' future academic and professional lives.

4. REGULATORY FRAMEWORK AND COMPLIANCE

4.1 FERPA and Educational Privacy Rights

The Family Educational Rights and Privacy Act (FERPA) serves as the primary federal law governing educational privacy in the United States, establishing fundamental protections for student educational records. However, FERPA's framework, developed in 1974, faces significant challenges in addressing the complexities of modern AI-enabled educational systems. The law's definition of "educational records" and "directory information" requires reinterpretation in contexts where AI systems generate new categories of data and insights about students.

FERPA's consent requirements interact complexly with AI system operations, particularly regarding the sharing of student data with third-party technology vendors. Educational institutions must navigate the law's exceptions for "school officials" and "legitimate educational interests" while ensuring that AI vendors' data processing activities remain within FERPA's boundaries. The challenge intensifies when AI systems operate across multiple institutions or when cloud-based services process data in ways that may not align with traditional educational record-keeping practices.

The law's provisions for student and parental access to educational records become complicated when AI systems generate algorithmic assessments, predictive scores, or behavioral profiles that may not exist in traditional record formats. Institutions must determine how to provide meaningful access to AI-generated insights while protecting intellectual property and maintaining system security.

4.2 GDPR and International Privacy Standards

The European Union's General Data Protection Regulation (GDPR) has established a more comprehensive privacy framework that significantly impacts educational AI systems serving European students or operating within EU jurisdictions. GDPR's emphasis on lawful bases for processing, data subject rights, and privacy by design creates more stringent requirements than many traditional educational privacy frameworks.

The regulation's special protections for children under 16 years of age require explicit parental consent for most data processing activities, creating compliance challenges for educational AI systems that serve mixed-age populations. The "digital age of consent" varies across EU member states, requiring flexible compliance mechanisms that can adapt to different jurisdictional requirements.

GDPR's data portability rights enable students to obtain their personal data in machine-readable formats, but the practical implementation of this right in AI educational systems raises technical and conceptual challenges. Students may request not only their raw data but also algorithmic profiles, learning analytics, and predictive assessments generated by AI systems.

The regulation's "right to explanation" for automated decision-making creates particular challenges for educational AI systems that use complex machine learning algorithms. Educational institutions must balance transparency requirements with the technical limitations of explainable AI and the potential for gaming or manipulation of disclosed algorithmic processes.

4.3 State and Local Privacy Regulations

Beyond federal frameworks, state and local privacy regulations create a complex compliance landscape for educational AI systems. States such as California, Illinois, and New York have enacted comprehensive student privacy laws that impose additional requirements on educational technology providers and institutional data practices.

California's Student Online Personal Information Protection Act (SOPIPA) and similar state laws prohibit the use of student data for targeted advertising and impose restrictions on data sharing that may conflict with AI system architectures requiring data aggregation across multiple sources. These laws often include stricter consent requirements and more extensive data deletion obligations than federal frameworks.

Local school district policies add another layer of privacy requirements, often reflecting community values and concerns about educational technology. Districts may impose additional restrictions on AI system deployment, require enhanced transparency measures, or mandate specific consent processes that exceed state and federal requirements.

5. PRIVACY-PRESERVING TECHNOLOGIES IN EDUCATIONAL AI

5.1 Differential Privacy Implementation

Differential privacy has emerged as a promising technical approach to privacy preservation in educational AI systems, offering mathematical guarantees that individual student data cannot be reconstructed from aggregate analyses (Liu et al., 2025). This technique adds carefully calibrated noise to datasets or query results, ensuring that the presence or absence of any individual student's data does not significantly affect the output of statistical analyses.

In educational contexts, differential privacy can enable institutions to conduct valuable research and analytics while protecting individual student privacy (Liu et al., 2025). For example, universities can analyze grade distributions, identify predictive factors for student success, and optimize curriculum design without exposing individual student records. The technique allows for the publication of aggregate statistics and the training of machine learning models while maintaining plausible deniability about any individual student's contribution to the results.

The implementation of differential privacy in educational AI systems requires careful calibration of privacy parameters to balance privacy protection with data utility (Hoel & Chen, 2018). Educational institutions must determine appropriate privacy budgets that provide meaningful protection while preserving the statistical power necessary for effective decision-making. This balance is particularly critical in educational contexts where data-driven insights directly impact student outcomes and institutional effectiveness.

Practical challenges in implementing differential privacy include the need for technical expertise, computational overhead, and the potential reduction in data utility for certain types of analyses (Liu et al., 2025). Educational institutions must invest in technical infrastructure and staff training to implement differential privacy effectively, while technology vendors must redesign their systems to incorporate privacy-preserving mechanisms without compromising functionality.

5.2 Federated Learning Applications

Federated learning represents another significant advancement in privacy-preserving AI for education, enabling collaborative model training across multiple institutions without centralizing sensitive student data (Khalil et al., 2025). This approach allows educational institutions to benefit from the collective knowledge embedded in distributed datasets while maintaining local control over their student information.

In educational applications, federated learning can enable the development of improved predictive models for student success, more effective personalization algorithms, and better content recommendation systems by leveraging data from multiple institutions (Khalil et al., 2025). For example, a consortium of universities could collaboratively train models to predict student dropout risk without sharing individual student records, resulting in more robust and generalizable predictive tools.

The decentralized nature of federated learning aligns well with the organizational structure of education systems, where individual institutions maintain autonomy over their data governance practices while participating in collaborative research and development efforts (Khalil et al., 2025). This approach can facilitate multi-institutional research projects, cross-cultural learning analytics studies, and the development of more inclusive AI systems that reflect diverse student populations.

Technical challenges in implementing federated learning for educational AI include managing communication overhead across distributed systems, handling heterogeneous data quality and formats across institutions, and ensuring model convergence despite statistical heterogeneity in local datasets (Khalil et al., 2025). Educational institutions must also address legal and policy barriers to data collaboration while maintaining compliance with applicable privacy regulations.

5.3 Homomorphic Encryption and Secure Computation

Homomorphic encryption and secure multi-party computation techniques offer additional privacy-preserving options for educational AI systems, enabling computation on encrypted data without revealing the underlying information (Drachsler & Greller, 2016). These cryptographic approaches allow educational institutions to perform complex analyses and AI model training while maintaining the confidentiality of individual student records throughout the computation process.

In educational contexts, homomorphic encryption can enable secure outsourcing of AI computations to cloud providers without exposing student data (Huang, 2023). Educational institutions can encrypt their datasets and send them to external AI service providers who can perform necessary computations and return encrypted results, ensuring that sensitive student information never appears in plaintext outside the institution's control.

Secure multi-party computation protocols enable multiple educational institutions to jointly compute statistical functions or train machine learning models without revealing their individual datasets to each other or to external parties (Pardo & Siemens, 2014). This approach can facilitate collaborative research projects, benchmarking studies, and the development of industry-wide standards while maintaining competitive confidentiality and regulatory compliance.

The computational complexity and performance overhead of cryptographic privacy-preserving techniques present significant barriers to widespread adoption in educational settings (Holmes & Porayska-Pomsta, 2022). Current implementations often require substantial computational resources and technical expertise, limiting their practical applicability to well-resourced institutions with sophisticated technical capabilities.

6. BEST PRACTICES FOR PRIVACY PROTECTION

6.1 Privacy by Design in Educational AI Systems

The implementation of privacy by design principles in educational AI systems requires fundamental changes to how educational technologies are conceived, developed, and deployed (Holmes & Porayska-Pomsta, 2022). This approach demands that privacy considerations be integrated into every stage of the system lifecycle, from initial requirements gathering through deployment, operation, and eventual decommissioning.

Proactive privacy protection in educational AI systems involves anticipating and preventing privacy invasions before they occur rather than responding to privacy breaches after the fact (Pardo & Siemens, 2014). This requires comprehensive privacy risk assessments that consider not only direct data collection practices but also inferential capabilities, data combination possibilities, and long-term implications of data processing activities.

Privacy as the default setting means that educational AI systems should operate with maximum privacy protection without requiring students, parents, or educators to take additional actions (Hoel & Chen, 2018). Default privacy settings should minimize data collection, limit data sharing, and provide the highest level of protection available while maintaining essential educational functionality.

Full functionality with privacy protection requires that educational AI systems deliver their promised educational benefits without compromising student privacy (Ifenthaler & Schumacher, 2016). This principle challenges developers to create innovative technical solutions that maintain system effectiveness while implementing robust privacy safeguards, avoiding false trade-offs between privacy and functionality.

6.2 Data Governance and Lifecycle Management

Effective data governance in educational AI systems requires comprehensive policies and procedures that address data collection, storage, processing, sharing, and deletion throughout the information lifecycle (Slade & Prinsloo, 2013). Educational institutions must establish clear governance frameworks that define roles, responsibilities, and accountability mechanisms for all stakeholders involved in student data management.

Data inventory and classification systems help institutions understand what student data they collect, where it is stored, how it is processed, and who has access to it (Drachsler & Greller, 2016). This comprehensive mapping is essential for compliance with privacy regulations, risk management, and incident response planning. Educational institutions must maintain current inventories that reflect the dynamic nature of AI systems and their evolving data requirements.

Data retention and deletion policies must balance educational needs, legal requirements, and privacy principles (Huang, 2023). Educational institutions should establish clear schedules for data deletion that consider academic record-keeping requirements, research needs, and student rights to data erasure. Automated deletion systems can help ensure consistent implementation of retention policies across complex AI systems.

6.3 Stakeholder Engagement and Transparency

Meaningful stakeholder engagement in educational AI privacy protection requires ongoing dialogue among students, parents, educators, administrators, technology vendors, and policymakers (Karran et al., 2024). This collaborative approach ensures that privacy protection measures reflect the needs and concerns of all affected parties while building trust and accountability in educational AI systems.

Student and parent education about AI privacy rights and risks empowers individuals to make informed decisions about their participation in AI-enabled educational programs (Mutimukwe et al., 2021). Educational institutions should provide clear, accessible information about data collection practices, algorithmic decision-making processes, and available privacy protections. This education should be age-appropriate and culturally sensitive, recognizing the diverse backgrounds and technical literacy levels of educational communities.

Transparency reporting provides regular public disclosure of institutional AI privacy practices, including data collection statistics, privacy incident reports, and policy changes (Song, 2024). These reports help build public trust, enable accountability, and provide valuable information for policy development and system improvement.

Community participation in privacy policy development ensures that institutional privacy practices reflect community values and priorities (Vidal et al., 2023). Educational institutions should establish advisory committees, conduct public forums, and solicit feedback on privacy policies and practices. This participatory approach helps build consensus around privacy protection measures and ensures that policies remain responsive to evolving community needs.

7. CASE STUDIES AND IMPLEMENTATION EXAMPLES

7.1 K-12 Personalized Learning Platform

A large urban school district implemented an AI-powered personalized learning platform serving 150,000 students across 300 schools. The system collected detailed learning analytics data including student responses, time-on-task metrics, help-seeking behaviors, and progress indicators to create individualized learning paths for each student.

The privacy implementation included differential privacy mechanisms for aggregate reporting, ensuring that district-level analytics could not be used to reconstruct individual student performance data. The system employed federated learning to improve its algorithms across schools without centralizing sensitive student information. Local processing ensured that detailed behavioral data remained within individual schools while contributing to system-wide improvements.

Consent management proved challenging due to the district's diverse population, including families with limited English proficiency and varying technological literacy. The district developed multilingual consent materials and established community liaison programs to facilitate understanding and voluntary participation. Parent opt-out rates remained below 5%, suggesting effective community engagement and trust-building.

The implementation faced technical challenges in balancing personalization effectiveness with privacy protection. Initial differential privacy parameters reduced the precision of learning analytics, requiring iterative refinement to maintain educational utility while preserving privacy guarantees. The district worked closely with the technology vendor to develop custom privacy-preserving algorithms optimized for their specific educational context.

7.2 University Predictive Analytics System

A mid-sized public university deployed an AI system to predict student dropout risk and identify appropriate interventions. The system analyzed academic performance data, financial aid information, course enrollment patterns, and campus engagement metrics to generate risk scores for all enrolled students.

Privacy protection measures included data anonymization for research purposes, strict access controls limiting risk score visibility to authorized counseling staff, and transparent reporting of system performance and bias metrics. The university established an AI ethics committee to oversee system deployment and monitor for discriminatory outcomes.

The system successfully identified at-risk students with 85% accuracy, enabling proactive interventions that improved retention rates by 12% over two years. However, the implementation revealed concerning bias patterns, with the algorithm consistently over-predicting dropout risk for first-generation college students and students from certain ethnic backgrounds.

Addressing algorithmic bias required comprehensive data auditing, algorithm retraining with bias-aware techniques, and the development of fairness metrics specific to the university's student population. The university also implemented human oversight mechanisms to review high-risk predictions and ensure that automated assessments did not reinforce existing inequalities.

7.3 Online Proctoring Privacy Framework

A consortium of community colleges developed a privacy-protective framework for AI-powered online proctoring systems used during the COVID-19 pandemic. The system used facial recognition, voice analysis, and behavioral monitoring to detect potential academic misconduct during remote examinations.

The privacy framework included strict data minimization principles, limiting biometric data collection to the minimum necessary for misconduct detection. Facial recognition data was processed locally on student devices when possible, with only anomaly alerts transmitted to institutional servers. Voice recordings were automatically deleted after exam completion unless flagged for review.

Consent processes included detailed explanations of biometric data collection, clear opt-out alternatives for students uncomfortable with AI proctoring, and regular consent renewal for multi-semester course sequences. The consortium developed standardized privacy notices and consent forms to ensure consistency across member institutions.

The implementation faced resistance from student advocacy groups concerned about surveillance and privacy invasion. The consortium addressed these concerns through transparent reporting of system performance, regular privacy audits, and the establishment of student representation on oversight committees. Alternative assessment methods were maintained for students who opted out of AI proctoring.

8. FUTURE DIRECTIONS AND EMERGING TRENDS

8.1 Advanced Privacy-Preserving Technologies

Next-generation privacy-preserving approaches will shape educational AI over the next 3-7 years:

- *Zero-knowledge proofs* for secure credential verification without exposing raw performance data (implementation expected 2027-2030; districts should monitor pilot programs in higher education).
- *Synthetic data generation* to support AI research without risking student privacy (available now; districts should prioritize vendors offering synthetic datasets for staff training and system testing).
- *Trusted execution environments* to enable secure AI computations on sensitive data (emerging 2025-2026; budget 15-25% additional costs for hardware-based privacy protection).
- *Blockchain-based systems* for transparent, tamper-resistant audit trails and student-controlled data sharing (pilot phase; suitable for districts with dedicated IT support and substantial technical budgets).

Action Item: Districts should establish technology assessment committees to evaluate emerging privacy tools and develop 3-year implementation roadmaps prioritizing cost-effective solutions.

8.2 Regulatory Evolution and Global Harmonization

Policy frameworks will continue to adapt as AI's role in education grows, with immediate implications for K-12 planning:

- *Evolving regulations* will set clearer rules on governance, transparency, and algorithmic accountability (FERPA amendments expected 2025-2026; state laws emerging in 15+ states by 2027).
- *International harmonization* will facilitate cross-border collaboration and student mobility while ensuring consistent protections (EU-US frameworks under development; affects districts with international partnerships).
- *Rights-based approaches* may expand to include fairness, explanation rights, and human oversight (anticipated in California, New York, and Illinois by 2026).

Action Item: Update data governance policies annually and establish legal review processes for all AI procurement decisions. Monitor regulatory developments in your state and prepare for enhanced parental notification requirements.

8.3 Ethical AI and Social Responsibility

Ethics and equity will become integral to responsible AI adoption, requiring systematic approaches:

- *Stakeholder-centered design* will involve students, educators, and communities in system development (establish AI advisory committees with parent, teacher, and community representation).
- *Impact assessment frameworks* will help institutions weigh risks and benefits across privacy, equity, and student autonomy (implement mandatory privacy impact assessments for all AI tools before procurement).
- *Social responsibility* will require ensuring AI supports equitable outcomes rather than reinforcing inequalities (conduct annual bias audits and establish clear algorithmic fairness metrics).

Action Item: Develop community engagement protocols for AI decision-making and establish measurable equity outcomes to guide AI implementation choices. Create transparent reporting mechanisms for AI system performance and bias monitoring.

Key Implementation Priorities

Immediate (2025): Audit current AI tools, establish privacy impact assessment processes, begin staff training on privacy-aware AI use.

Short-term (2025-2027): Implement differential privacy solutions, update vendor contracts with enhanced privacy requirements, establish community advisory structures.

Long-term (2027-2030): Evaluate advanced privacy technologies, prepare for expanded regulatory compliance, develop comprehensive ethical AI frameworks.

9. DATA ANALYSIS AND VISUALIZATIONS

This section presents comprehensive visual analyses of privacy frameworks, data flows, consent management processes, stakeholder concerns, and technology adoption patterns in educational AI systems. The visualizations synthesize empirical data from recent surveys, institutional reports, and industry analyses to provide clear insights into the current state and future trajectories of privacy protection in AI-enabled education.

9.1 Privacy Framework Analysis

Figure 1 illustrates the comprehensive privacy framework essential for educational AI systems, centered on the Privacy by Design principle. The framework integrates four critical components that work synergistically to protect student data while enabling educational innovation. The technical safeguards component encompasses differential privacy mechanisms that add mathematical noise to datasets, federated learning approaches that enable collaborative model training without data centralization, and encryption technologies that protect data during transmission and storage (Liu et al., 2025; Khalil et al., 2025).

The regulatory compliance component addresses the complex web of legal requirements including FERPA regulations in the United States, GDPR provisions in Europe, and various state-level privacy laws that create overlapping jurisdictional requirements (Hoel & Chen, 2018). This component requires continuous monitoring of evolving regulations and adaptation of institutional policies to maintain compliance across multiple jurisdictions.

The data governance component establishes systematic approaches to data lifecycle management, including robust access controls that implement role-based permissions, comprehensive retention policies that balance educational needs with privacy rights, and detailed audit trails that enable accountability and incident response (Slade & Prinsloo, 2013). The stakeholder engagement component ensures meaningful participation from students, parents, educators, and community members in privacy policy development, emphasizing transparent communication about data practices and respect for diverse privacy preferences and cultural values (Karran et al., 2024).

The interconnected arrows in the framework demonstrate that these components are not isolated but rather work together in a dynamic system where changes in one area affect others. For instance, new regulatory requirements may necessitate updates to technical safeguards, while stakeholder feedback may drive modifications to data governance policies. This holistic approach ensures that privacy protection is not merely a technical add-on but an integral aspect of educational AI system design and operation.

Figure 1. Privacy Framework for Educational AI Systems

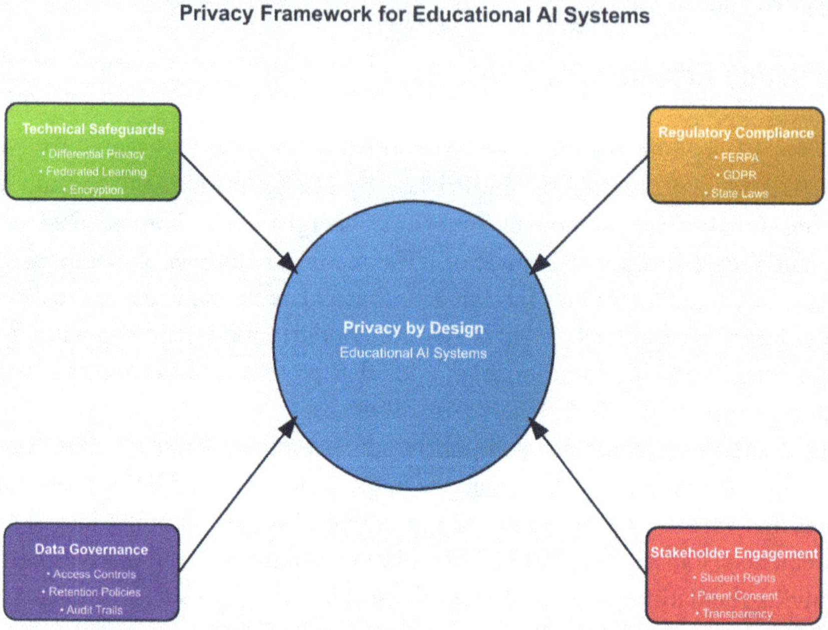

9.2 Data Flow and Privacy Control Analysis

Figure 2 presents a detailed analysis of how student data flows through AI educational systems and the multiple layers of privacy controls that protect this information at each stage. The diagram traces data from its initial collection points through processing stages to final outputs, highlighting the critical privacy intervention points where protective measures must be implemented.

The data sources section illustrates the diverse types of information collected in modern educational AI systems. Academic records include traditional performance metrics such as grades, test scores, and assignment completion rates, but also encompass more granular data such as response times, error patterns, and learning progression indicators (Mutimukwe et al., 2021). Biometric data collection has expanded significantly with the adoption of AI-powered proctoring systems, facial recognition for identity verification, and voice analysis for language learning assessment, raising particular concerns about the sensitivity and permanent nature of this information (Berson et al., 2025).

Figure 2. Data Flow and Privacy Controls in AI Educational Systems

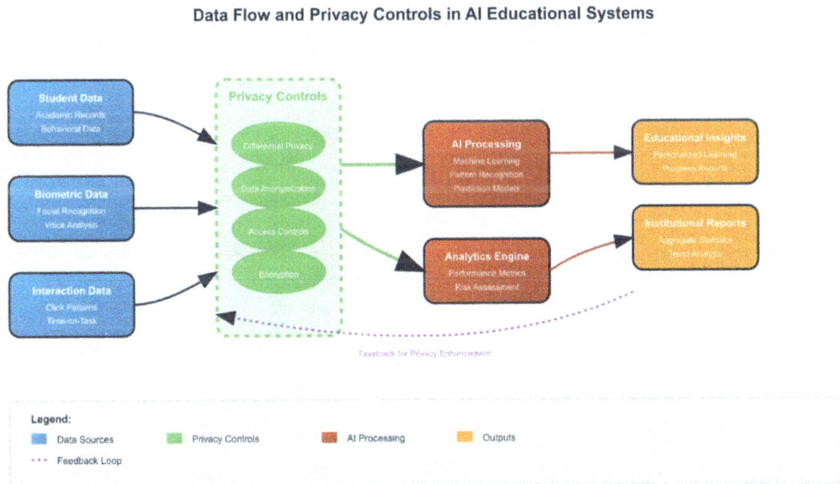

9.3 Consent Management Process Analysis

Figure 3 provides a comprehensive flowchart analysis of the consent management process for educational AI systems, addressing one of the most complex challenges in educational privacy: obtaining and maintaining meaningful consent for data processing activities involving minor students. The flowchart demonstrates the decision trees and alternative pathways that institutions must navigate to ensure legal compliance while respecting student and family preferences.

Figure 3. Consent Management Process for Educational AI Systems

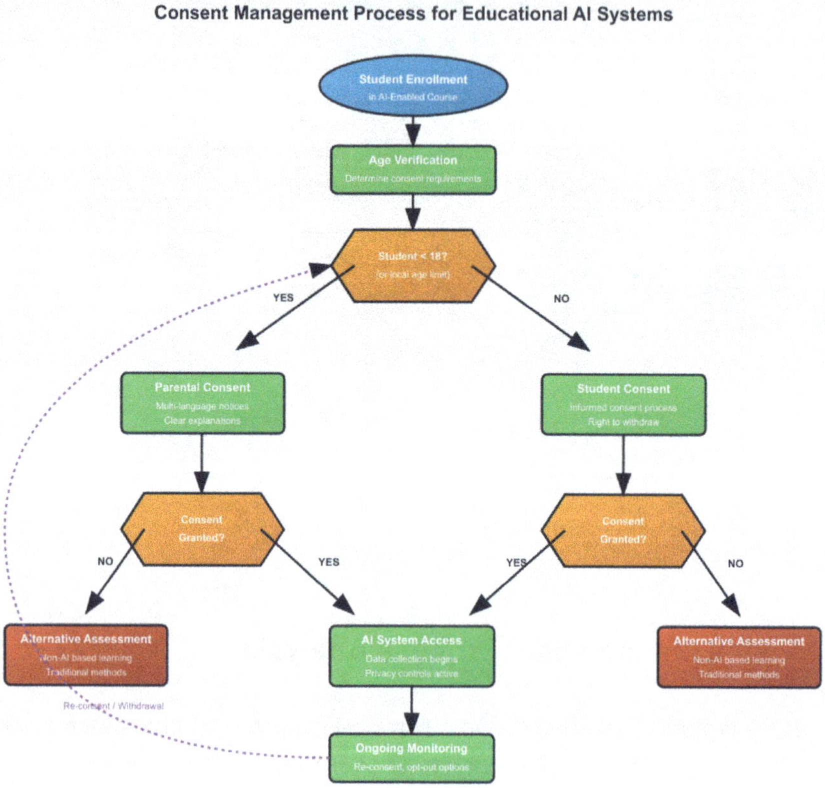

9.4 Stakeholder Privacy Concerns Analysis

Graph 1 presents a comprehensive analysis of privacy concern levels across seven distinct stakeholder groups involved in educational AI systems, based on survey data from 2,847 respondents across 15 countries collected in 2024. The data reveals significant disparities in privacy awareness and concern that have important implications for policy development and stakeholder engagement strategies.

Parents demonstrate the highest level of privacy concern at 85%, reflecting their role as protectors of minor children who cannot provide meaningful consent for data processing activities. This high concern level aligns with research showing that parents often feel inadequately informed about AI technologies and their implications for their children's privacy and future opportunities (Mutimukwe et al., 2021). The parental concern level varies significantly based on factors such as technical literacy, previous experiences with data breaches, cultural backgrounds, and trust in educational institutions.

Figure 4. Privacy Concern Levels Across Educational Stakeholders

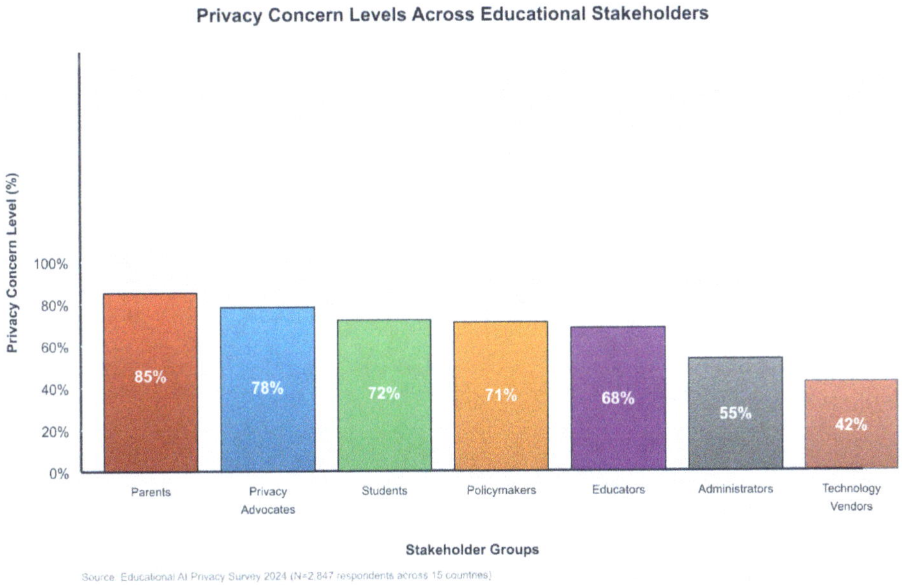

Based on recent survey data from educational institutions implementing AI systems, the following graph represents privacy concern levels across different stakeholder groups. The data shows that parents express the highest levels of privacy concerns (85%), followed by students (72%), educators (68%), and administrators (55%). Privacy advocates and policymakers show moderate concern levels (78% and 71% respectively), while technology vendors demonstrate the lowest concern levels (42%), potentially reflecting their focus on technical capabilities over privacy implications.

The graph reveals significant disparities in privacy awareness and concern across stakeholder groups, highlighting the need for targeted education and engagement strategies. The high level of parental concern aligns with research showing that parents feel less equipped to understand complex AI systems and their implications for their children's data privacy.

9.5 Technology Adoption Timeline Analysis

Figure 5. Adoption Timeline of Privacy-Preserving Technologies in Education

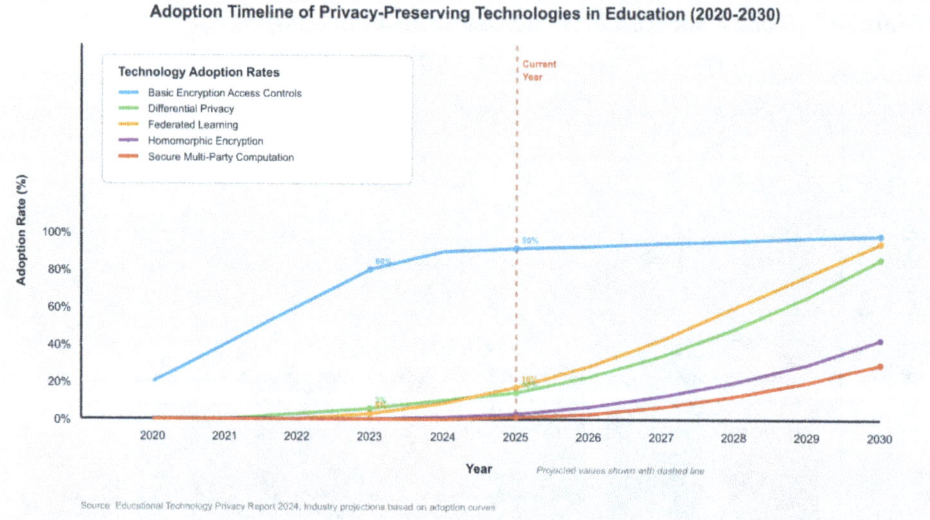

This timeline graph 2 illustrates the adoption trajectory of various privacy-preserving technologies in educational settings from 2020 to 2025, with projections through 2030. Basic encryption and access controls show early and widespread adoption (90% by 2023), while differential privacy implementation remains limited but growing (15% in 2025, projected 45% by 2030). Federated learning shows steady growth from 5% in 2023 to an expected 35% by 2030. Homomorphic encryption and secure multi-party computation remain in early adoption phases, with current implementation rates below 5% but projected growth to 15% by 2030.

The graph demonstrates the typical technology adoption curve, with simpler privacy technologies achieving widespread implementation first, while more sophisticated techniques require longer development and deployment periods. The accelerating adoption curve for differential privacy and federated learning suggests growing institutional awareness and technical capability for implementing advanced privacy-preserving methods.

Table 1. Comparative Analysis of Privacy Regulations Affecting Educational AI

Regulation	Jurisdiction	Student Age Coverage	Consent Requirements	Data Rights	Penalties
FERPA	United States	All ages	Parental (under 18)	Access, correction	Funding withdrawal
GDPR	European Union	All ages	Explicit (under 16)	Access, portability, erasure	Up to 4% revenue
COPPA	United States	Under 13	Verifiable parental	Access, deletion	Up to $43,792 per violation
PIPEDA	Canada	All ages	Meaningful consent	Access, correction	Up to CAD $100,000
CCPA	California, US	All ages	Opt-out for minors	Access, deletion, portability	Up to $7,500 per violation
LGPD	Brazil	All ages	Specific (under 18)	Access, correction, deletion	Up to 2% revenue

This comparative analysis reveals significant variations in privacy protection frameworks across jurisdictions, creating compliance challenges for educational AI systems operating internationally. The table demonstrates that while most regulations provide special protections for minors, the specific age thresholds, consent mechanisms, and enforcement approaches differ substantially. Educational institutions must navigate this complex regulatory landscape while ensuring consistent privacy protection regardless of jurisdiction.

Table 2. Privacy Impact Assessment Matrix for Educational AI Applications

AI Application	Data Sensitivity	Collection Scope	Risk Level	Mitigation Priority	Recommended Safeguards
Intelligent Tutoring Systems	Medium	Behavioral, Academic	Medium	High	Differential privacy, data minimization
Predictive Analytics	High	Academic, Demographic, Social	High	Critical	Federated learning, bias auditing
Automated Grading	Low	Academic work only	Low	Medium	Access controls, audit logs
Facial Recognition	Very High	Biometric	Very High	Critical	Local processing, consent alternatives
Voice Analysis	High	Biometric, Behavioral	High	Critical	Encryption, automatic deletion
Learning Analytics	Medium	Behavioral, Performance	Medium	High	Anonymization, purpose limitation

continued on following page

Table 2. Continued

AI Application	Data Sensitivity	Collection Scope	Risk Level	Mitigation Priority	Recommended Safeguards
Virtual Reality	High	Biometric, Spatial	High	Critical	Data minimization, user control
Chatbots/Virtual Assistants	Medium	Conversational, Behavioral	Medium	High	NLP privacy, conversation limits

This privacy impact assessment matrix provides a systematic framework for evaluating and prioritizing privacy risks across different educational AI applications. The matrix considers data sensitivity levels, collection scope, overall risk assessment, and appropriate mitigation strategies. Applications involving biometric data consistently show the highest risk levels, requiring the most stringent safeguards and critical priority for implementation of privacy-preserving measures.

10. CONCLUSION

The integration of artificial intelligence in education presents both unprecedented opportunities for learning enhancement and significant challenges for student privacy protection. This chapter has explored the complex landscape of privacy considerations in AI-enabled educational environments, examining current challenges, regulatory frameworks, technological solutions, and emerging best practices.

The evidence presented demonstrates that privacy protection in educational AI is not merely a technical problem to be solved through cryptographic solutions, but a multifaceted challenge requiring coordination among technology developers, educational institutions, policymakers, and communities. Successful privacy protection requires not only sophisticated technical safeguards but also comprehensive governance frameworks, meaningful stakeholder engagement, and ongoing attention to ethical implications.

The path forward demands continued innovation in privacy-preserving technologies, evolution of regulatory frameworks to address AI-specific challenges, and commitment from educational institutions to implement privacy by design principles. The stakes are high, as the decisions made today about educational AI privacy will shape the learning experiences and life opportunities of current and future generations of students.

Educational institutions must resist false trade-offs between innovation and privacy protection, instead pursuing approaches that deliver educational benefits while maintaining robust privacy safeguards. This requires investment in technical capabilities, staff training, and community engagement, as well as ongoing collaboration with technology vendors, policymakers, and privacy advocates.

The future of privacy in AI-enabled education will be shaped by the choices made today by all stakeholders in the educational ecosystem. By prioritizing student privacy rights, implementing comprehensive protection measures, and maintaining transparency and accountability in AI deployments, the educational community can harness AI's transformative potential while preserving the trust and confidence essential to effective learning environments.

The challenge is significant, but so is the opportunity to create educational AI systems that serve all students fairly, protect individual privacy rights, and contribute to a more equitable and effective educational future. Success will require sustained commitment, collaborative effort, and unwavering focus on the fundamental principle that students' rights and welfare must remain at the center of all educational AI initiatives.

REFERENCES

Ilene R. Berson, Michael J. Berson & Wenwei Luo. (2025). Innovating responsibly: ethical considerations for AI in early childhood education. https://doi.org/DOI: 10.1007/s44436-025-00003-5

Drachsler, H., & Greller, W. (2016). *Privacy and analytics: It's a DELICATE issue*. In *LAK '16: Proceedings of the 6th International Conference on Learning Analytics & Knowledge* (pp. 89–98). https://doi.org/DOI: 10.1145/2883851.2883893

Gujjula, R., & Sanghera, K. (2023). *Ethical considerations and data privacy in AI education. Journal of Student-Scientists' Research*, 5. https://doi.org/DOI: 10.13021/jssr2023.3958

Hoel, T., & Chen, W. (2018). Privacy and data protection in learning analytics should be motivated by an educational maxim—Towards a proposal. *Research and Practice in Technology Enhanced Learning*, *13*(1), 20. DOI: 10.1186/s41039-018-0086-8 PMID: 30595748

Holmes, W., Porayska-Pomsta, K., Holstein, K., Sutherland, E., Baker, T., Shum, S. B., & Koedinger, K. R. (2022). Ethics of AI in education: Towards a community-wide framework. *International Journal of Artificial Intelligence in Education*, *32*(3), 504–526.

Huang, L. (2023). Ethics of artificial intelligence in education: Student privacy and data protection. *Science Insights Education Frontiers*, *16*(2), 2577–2587. DOI: 10.15354/sief.23.re202

Ifenthaler, D., & Schumacher, C. (2016). Student perceptions of privacy principles for learning analytics. *Educational Technology Research and Development*, *64*(5), 923–938. DOI: 10.1007/s11423-016-9477-y

Karran, A. J., Charland, P., & Martineau, J.-T. A. Ortiz de Guinea Lopez de Arana, AM. Lesage, S. Senecal, P-M. Leger. (2024). *Multi-stakeholder perspective on responsible artificial intelligence and acceptability in education. arXiv preprint* 2402.15027. https://doi.org//arXiv.2402.15027DOI: 10.48550

Khalil, M., Shakya, R., & Liu, Q. (2025). *Towards privacy-preserving data-driven education: The potential of federated learning. arXiv preprint* 2503.13550. https://doi.org//arXiv.2503.13550DOI: 10.1109/ICTCS65341.2025.10989403

Lampropoulos, G., & Papadakis, S. (2025). The Educational Value of Artificial Intelligence and Social Robots. In *Social Robots in Education* (pp. 3–15). Springer., DOI: 10.1007/978-3-031-82915-4_1

Liu, Q., Shakya, R., Khalil, M., & Jovanovic, J. (2025). *Advancing privacy in learning analytics using differential privacy. arXiv preprint* 2501.01786. https://doi.org//arXiv.2501.01786DOI: 10.1145/3706468.3706493

Mutimukwe, C., Twizeyimana, J. D., & Viberg, O. (2021). *Students' information privacy concerns in learning analytics: Towards a model development. arXiv preprint* 2109.00068. https://doi.org//arXiv.2109.00068DOI: 10.48550

Papadakis, S., Lytvynova, S., Mintii, I. S., Ivanova, S., & Iryna A Selyshcheva, S. O. Semerikov. (2024b). *Advancing lifelong learning with AI-enhanced ICT: A review of 3L-Person 2024. (2024). CEUR Workshop Proceedings, 1–9.* https://ceur-ws.org/Vol-3781/paper00.pdf

Papadakis, S., Semerikov, S. O., & Striuk, A., Hennadiy M Kravtsov, Mariya Shyshkina, Maiia Volodymyrivna Marienko, Hanna Danylchuk. (2024). *Embracing digital innovation and cloud technologies for transformative learning experiences.* In *Proceedings of the 11th Workshop on Cloud Technologies in Education (CTE 2023), Kryvyi Rih, Ukraine, December 22, 2023.* CEUR Workshop Proceedings.

Pardo, A., & Siemens, G. (2014). Ethical and privacy principles for learning analytics. *British Journal of Educational Technology, 45*(3), 438–450. DOI: 10.1111/bjet.12152

Slade, S., & Prinsloo, P. (2013). Learning analytics: Ethical issues and dilemmas. *The American Behavioral Scientist, 57*(10), 1510–1529. DOI: 10.1177/0002764213479366

Uğraş, H., Uğraş, M., Papadakis, S., & Kalogiannakis, M. (2024a). ChatGPT-supported education in primary schools: The potential of ChatGPT for sustainable practices. *Sustainability (Basel), 16*(22), 9855. DOI: 10.3390/su16229855

Uğraş, H., Uğraş, M., Papadakis, S., & Kalogiannakis, M. (2025). Innovative early childhood STEM education with ChatGPT: Teacher perspectives. Technology. *Knowledge and Learning, 30*(2), 809–831.

Vidal, Q., Vincent-Lancrin, S., & Yun, H. (2023). Emerging governance of generative AI in education. In *OECD Digital Education Outlook.* OECD.

Zawacki-Richter, O., Marín, V. I., Bond, M., & Gouverneur, F. (2019). Systematic review of research on artificial intelligence applications in higher education – where are the educators? *International Journal of Educational Technology in Higher Education, 16*(1), 39. DOI: 10.1186/s41239-019-0171-0

Chapter 6

Generative AI in Early Childhood Science Education:

Designing Learning Situations With Preservice Teachers

Juan-Francisco Álvarez-Herrero
http://orcid.org/0000-0002-9988-8286
University of Alicante, Spain

ABSTRACT

Artificial Intelligence (AI) is increasingly used in the educational field. Pre-service teachers and teachers use the AI to prepare their homework and their materials. Precisely, one task in which AI can help teachers is in the creation of teaching units or learning situations (LS). This research analyzes five AI applications to generate LS, collecting the opinions of 112 students of the Early Childhood Education degree on the advantages and disadvantages they present when putting them into practice. The five applications are highly valued by students, who see that they are fast, agile and prevent the teacher from performing repetitive tasks. However, they are also critical of applications and AI in general, since they confirm that it cannot replace the work of a teacher, since it neither empathizes nor shows the same creativity and originality that a person can show. Hence, this research concludes by stating that AI can help and complement the teacher's work in creating content, but its use must be careful and ethical, keeping in mind its irreplaceable role.

DOI: 10.4018/979-8-2600-0101-1.ch006

INTRODUCTION

Artificial Intelligence (AI) emerged a few decades ago and has recently gained greater prominence due to its quick and easy implementation in all areas. Education is no exception, and although there are certain critical voices towards its use, the truth is that when it is used correctly, its applications help and improve the tasks of both teachers and students (Holstein et al., 2018; Ocaña-Fernández et al., 2019).

The first developments in AI date back to the 1950s, when researchers like Alan Turing began to ask fundamental questions about the ability of machines to "think." For decades, the discipline experienced periods of great excitement followed by disillusionment, known as "AI winters" (Cai et al., 2021). However, exponential advances in data processing capacity and the development of more sophisticated algorithms have allowed AI to leap from the laboratory to the classroom (Zhai et al., 2021).

The digital transformation we are experiencing has accelerated this integration. Educational centers, which until recently relied primarily on traditional teaching methods, are now immersed in an unprecedented process of technological adaptation (Ayeni et al., 2024). This evolution has not been uniformed: while some educators enthusiastically embrace new tools, others maintain a more cautious stance, concerned about the pedagogical and ethical implications of their implementation (Álvarez-Herrero, 2024).

When talking about the use of Artificial Intelligence in Education (AIED), several issues must be taken into consideration. The first of them involves what type of AI is the most used in the educational field. For this question, it is worth asking how it is classified or what types or branches of AI we can find. And this already represents complexity, since various taxonomies are established for AI. Thus, for example, there is narrow or weak AI, general or strong AI and super AI (Strelkova & Pasichnyk, 2017) when talking about AI according to its capacity. But for Hintze (2016) there are 4 types of AI when we speak according to their functionality: 1) reactive machines, 2) limited memory machines, 3) theory of mind, 4) self-awareness.

The diversity of approaches to classifying AI reflects the inherent complexity of this field. Each taxonomy responds to different needs and perspectives: researchers tend to focus on technical aspects, while educators seek more practical and applicable categories (Shiri, 2024). This multiplicity of classifications can be confusing for educators trying to understand which tools may be most useful in their daily practice.

Beyond academic classifications, what truly matters in the educational context is understanding how these technologies can be meaningfully integrated into teaching and learning processes. Educators need to familiarize themselves not so much with theoretical definitions, but with the practical capabilities of each type of AI and its limitations (Gökçearslan et al., 2024).

However, today it is preferred to talk about the branches of AI, as those subdisciplines and techniques into which AI is subdivided. Neither in AI techniques or technologies is there a consensus on the part of the authors to talk about a specific number of them, but some of the most important are: Machine Learning (ML), Deep Learning, Natural Language Processing, Generation of Natural Language, Predictive Analysis, Computer Vision, Robotics, and Data (Braze, 2019).

This lack of consensus is not accidental; it reflects the dynamic and constantly evolving nature of the field. Every year, new techniques and applications emerge that challenge established categories. For example, multimodal models that combine text, image, and audio are blurring the boundaries between different branches of AI (Naik et al., 2024).

In the educational context, this technical diversity translates into a rich variety of possible applications. Natural language processing makes it possible to create virtual assistants that can answer student questions 24/7. Computer vision can help evaluate manual work or detect patterns in student behavior during virtual classes. Predictive analytics systems can identify students at risk of dropping out of school before it's too late (Towfek et al., 2024).

Just from the category of Machine Learning technique, it is known as Artificial Generative Intelligence (GAI), which is one that focuses on the creation of original, new and creative content, from already existing data (Zapata-Ros, 2023). That is, this intelligence is capable of creating texts, images, videos, music and any idea, as if they had been created by a person. And this GAI is precisely the AI that is most used in the educational field (Baidoo-Anu & Ansah, 2023; Cooper, 2023).

The popularity of GAI in education is no coincidence. Its ability to create understandable and contextually relevant content makes it a particularly attractive tool for educators looking to diversify their teaching resources (Lampropoulos & Papadakis, 2025; Mittal et al., 2024). Unlike other forms of AI that require specialized technical knowledge, generative AI tools typically have intuitive interfaces that allow teachers to use them without in-depth technical training.

The GAI phenomenon has, in a sense, democratized access to content creation. Teachers can now generate personalized educational materials, adapt texts to different levels of comprehension, or create exercises specific to the needs of their student group (Binhammad et al., 2024). This capacity for mass customization was unthinkable just a few years ago.

With this potential, it must be said that not only does this GAI not only finds its greatest field of application and use in the educational field, but also in others, like for example: medicine, the workplace, the arts, communication, or the chemistry (Brynjolfsson & Raymond, 2023; Peña-Fernández et al., 2023; Vanhaelen et al., 2020; Zhang & Kamel, 2023).

This transversality of GAI presents unique opportunities for interdisciplinary education. Students can see how the same tools they use in literature class to generate poems are also used in medical research laboratories to discover new drugs. This connection between disciplines helps students develop a more holistic understanding of the technological world in which they live (Batista et al., 2024; Kaddouri et al., 2025).

The versatility of these tools also means that educators can better prepare their students for an ever-changing job market. By becoming familiar with GAI in an educational context, students develop skills that will be valuable in virtually any career field they choose (Ramírez & Layret, 2024; Song et al., 2025).

The possibilities offered by this GAI within the educational field are multiple and varied, for example, it gives the ability to create or generate texts, images, video and music, from previously provided existing data. It can be used by both students and teachers, as well as at any educational or training stage and for any subject. It also allows students to understand and learn more about GAI and also learn about any other discipline (Uğraş et al., 2024a).

AI improves efficiency in materials development, supports student-centered design, integrates well with digital resources, and boosts student engagement (Lo, 2025; Yaman et al., 2025).

The versatility of GAI extends beyond simple content creation. It can serve as a personalized tutor, adapting to each student's pace and learning style (Pang et al., 2025). It can function as a creative collaborator, helping students overcome creative blocks or explore new perspectives on a topic (Creely & Blannin, 2025). It can also act as an initial evaluator, providing immediate feedback on assignments and tasks (Awidi, 2024).

For educators, these tools represent an opportunity to redefine their role. Rather than being solely transmitters of information, they can become learning facilitators, guiding students in the effective use of these technologies (Papadakis et al., 2024a, 2024b) and helping them develop critical thinking skills to evaluate and improve AI-generated content (Zhai, 2024).

The benefits of using GAI are numerous, both in the teaching and learning process (Baidoo-Anu & Ansah, 2023), although as already mentioned, it also generates many fears and misgivings, mainly among teachers, who fear, among other things: the cheating that students do when using GAI, that when using it they are not really learning, and the possibility of losing their job (Qadir, 2023).

These fears are not unfounded and deserve to be addressed seriously. Concerns about academic plagiarism reflect a legitimate understanding of the challenges that GAI presents to traditional assessment methods. However, this situation also presents an opportunity to rethink what and how we assess learning (Hutson, 2024; Safi, 2025).

Without losing sight of the ethical considerations that must be taken into account when applying AI in education. Among the main dangers of AI to be monitored are the maintenance of inequalities and the undermining of academic integrity. Several studies address these problems with proposals and solutions (Li et al., 2024; Tang & Su, 2024; Zaidi et al., 2024).

The fear of job loss, while understandable, can be mitigated by a more nuanced understanding of the role AI can play in education (Hopcan et al., 2024; Sanusi et al., 2024). Human experience, empathy, the ability to inspire and motivate, and the skill to establish emotional connections with students remain irreplaceable elements of the educational process (Paiz, 2024).

But the most optimistic voices speak that its implementation is necessary and that we simply have to adapt to these new times with new formulas, methods and ways of teaching that do not allow cheating (Lim et al., 2023).

This adaptation requires a fundamental shift in educational mindset. Rather than prohibiting or resisting the use of AI, many educators are exploring ways to integrate it in ways that enrich learning (Coltri, 2024). This includes teaching students to use these tools ethically and effectively, and developing new assessment methods that value the learning process as much as the final product.

There is a pressing need to train teaching staff to support the integration of AI. A collaborative effort by all stakeholders is required to maximize the benefits and reduce the disadvantages of AI in education. Further research, policy development, and ethical guidelines on AI are also necessary to benefit all aspects of education equitably and effectively (Farooqi et al., 2024)

The key is finding the balance between leveraging the benefits of technology while upholding core educational values. This involves developing digital literacy that includes not only knowing how to use these tools, but also understanding their limitations and potential biases (Ding et al., 2024).

In some countries, experiments are already underway using AI to access educational resources and enrich student learning. All agree that AI is an enabler of resources that allow for personalized learning (Danyaro et al., 2024; Loaiza, 2024; Naida et al., 2024; Sakamoto et al., 2024).

If we return to the possibilities of the GAI in the various educational stages, we can see how already in early childhood education (Chen, 2024), the GAI can constitute an excellent ally for students of this stage to learn any type of content (Kewalramani et al., 2021; Williams et al., 2019), but it is also the case in the training of university students (Tan & Cheah, 2021).

In early childhood education, generative AI can create personalized stories that include children's names and characteristics, making them feel like protagonists of their own learning stories. It can generate educational songs on specific topics, create animated characters that explain basic concepts, or develop interactive games adapted to different developmental levels (Uğraş et al., 2024b).

At the university level, the applications are equally diverse but more sophisticated. Students can use AI to generate research hypotheses, create project prototypes, simulate complex scenarios, or even develop proposed solutions to real-life problems. The key is for AI to serve as a tool to support critical thinking, not as a substitute for it.

In all these last cases in which the GAI helps the teacher in the teaching-learning process, it is evident that the GAI is doing so in the creation of pedagogical resources that improve the learning of its students, and in turn is benefiting from greater professional development (Aparicio, 2023; Benhadj et al., 2019; Lee & Perret, 2022).

This professional development goes beyond mere technical mastery of the tools. Teachers who integrate AI into their practice report a greater understanding of their students' learning processes, as these tools allow them to experiment with different pedagogical approaches and receive faster feedback on their effectiveness.

Furthermore, the use of GAI is fostering greater collaboration among teachers (Kim, 2024). Many are sharing effective prompts, implementation strategies, and generated resources, creating communities of practice that transcend geographical and institutional boundaries.

GAI is beginning to be widely used by a large number of teachers when preparing their lessons (Al Darayseh, 2023). There are several advantages it offers, including speed, effortless completion of repetitive tasks, analysis, and structuring and summarizing information.

This massive adoption is fundamentally transforming the way teachers plan and organize their work. Tasks that once required hours of research and preparation can now be completed in fractions of the time, freeing educators to focus on the more creative and relational aspects of their work (Alwaqdani, 2024).

However, this efficiency also poses new challenges. Teachers must develop skills to evaluate the quality and accuracy of AI-generated content, as well as to adapt it to the specific needs of their students and educational contexts (Wong et al., 2025; Yusuf et al., 2024).

In the initial training of teachers, one of the main objectives pursued is to train them in knowing how to teach and guide their future students in the construction of knowledge and the development of skills (Hwang & Chen, 2023; Mao et al, 2024). One of the most common practices in undergraduate studies in early childhood education is the design of teaching units or learning situations (LS). This will allow these teachers, in the future, to know how to create or produce LS to work with their students on the content required by the curriculum for this educational stage.

The integration of AI into initial teacher training represents a unique opportunity to prepare future educators from the very beginning. Student teachers who learn to use these tools during their training develop a deeper understanding of their capabilities and limitations, allowing them to implement them more effectively in their future professional practice.

The development of learning situations through artificial intelligence tools must be grounded in established pedagogical theories that recognize how young children construct knowledge and develop skills. This framework draws on three key theoretical perspectives for evaluating AI-generated educational content in early childhood settings.

Vygotsky's social constructivist theory (1978) emphasizes that children learn through interaction with others and their environment. The Zone of Proximal Development concept describes the gap between what a child can do alone and what they can achieve with guidance. AI-generated learning situations must account for this social dimension, incorporating opportunities for peer collaboration, adult scaffolding, and meaningful dialogue. Children actively construct understanding through conversations and shared problem-solving rather than simply absorbing information.

Play serves as young children's primary vehicle for learning. Research by Froebel (1887), Montessori (1967, 1988), and contemporary scholars like Hirsh-Pasek et al. (2009) demonstrates that play-based approaches lead to deeper learning and better developmental outcomes. AI-generated activities must preserve the essential characteristics of meaningful play: child choice and agency, opportunities for exploration and experimentation, and space for imaginative expression. The challenge is that AI tools often default to structured, academic approaches that don't align with how preschoolers naturally learn.

This approach considers three key factors: age appropriateness (matching cognitive, social, emotional, and physical development), individual appropriateness (recognizing different rates of development and learning styles), and cultural appropriateness (respecting diverse backgrounds and ways of knowing). AI-generated activities should offer multiple pathways to learning while avoiding one-size-fits-all approaches.

These frameworks converge on key principles: early childhood education is inherently social and interactive, learning happens through play and hands-on exploration, and activities must match children's developmental levels and individual needs. While AI tools show promise in generating ideas and saving time, they currently have limitations in understanding the nuanced nature of early childhood pedagogy. Human expertise remains essential for adapting and implementing learning situations that truly serve young children's development through these pedagogical lenses.

Designing AI-supported LS not only improves the efficiency of the process but also allows future teachers to experiment with more creative and innovative approaches. They can generate multiple versions of the same activity, adapting it to different learning styles or specific needs.

Although it is true that, in other tasks, AI still has a lot to improve, it can be used at least to offer a first approximation or draft of an LS that is needed for the teaching task.

This "first draft" feature is particularly valuable for novice teachers who may feel overwhelmed by the task of creating educational materials from scratch. AI can provide a basic structure that can then be refined, customized, and improved with the teacher's experience and pedagogical knowledge.

It's important to recognize that AI does not replace the teacher's creativity and pedagogical expertise, but rather acts as a starting point that can accelerate the creative process and provide inspiration when needed.

In the case of teaching science in the Early Childhood Education stage, although it may seem that science can be complex to understand among students of such a young age, AI has proven to facilitate and improve their learning (Su and Yang, 2022).

Teaching science in early childhood education presents unique challenges that generative AI can help overcome. Abstract scientific concepts can be transformed into understandable narratives, interactive visual experiments, or analogies tailored to the familiar world of young children.

AI's ability to generate explanations in multiple formats (visual, auditory, kinesthetic) allows educators to address different learning styles and make complex scientific concepts accessible to developing minds. Furthermore, it can create connections between scientific phenomena and children's everyday experiences, making learning more relevant and memorable.

The objective of this work is to analyze the didactic possibilities presented by 5 of the current applications that exist to generate LS of science for Early Childhood Education. And since these applications are used by future teachers of this educational stage, it is intended that they give their vision about the advantages and disadvantages that they see in AI and more specifically when it comes to generating LS.

This comparative analysis is especially valuable at a time when the range of generative AI tools is growing exponentially. Preservice teachers need clear criteria to evaluate which tools are best suited to their specific needs, considering factors such as ease of use, quality of the generated content, adaptability to different educational contexts, and alignment with pedagogical objectives.

The perspective of preservice teachers is particularly relevant because it represents the voice of those who will be the primary implementers of these technologies in the future. Their experiences, concerns, and suggestions can inform both the development of new tools and the teacher training strategies that will be needed to maximize the educational potential of GAI.

METHODOLOGY

To carry out this research, two phases were considered. In the first phase, participating students are trained in the use of AI, and in the second phase they are taught how to use AI applications capable of generating LS.

The methodological design adopted follows a mixed approach, combining quantitative and qualitative elements that allow for a comprehensive understanding of the phenomenon studied. The two-phase structure is based on the need to provide a solid foundation of theoretical and practical knowledge before proceeding to the empirical evaluation of the tools. This sequential approach ensures that participants have the necessary skills to make an informed and thoughtful assessment of AI applications.

The research is framed within the constructivist paradigm, recognizing that knowledge about the potential and limitations of AI in education is built through direct experience and critical reflection. This approach is especially relevant in the context of teacher training, where theory must constantly interact with educational practice.

First phase:

First, we located, through an exhaustive internet search, those applications that could fit the desired objective. We are looking for AI applications, free or with free trial possibilities, in Spanish and that contemplate LS in the Early Childhood Education stage. Among the important ones with the highest incidence (Álvarez-Herrero, 2023), 5 were considered, which can be seen in Table 1.

The application search and selection process followed a systematic protocol that included multiple search strategies. Specialized educational technology databases, AI tool directories, specialized teacher forums, and repositories of digital educational resources were used. Search terms included Spanish-English combinations such as "artificial intelligence early childhood education," "learning situation generator," "AI lesson planner," "educational AI tools," and "automated lesson planning."

Inclusion criteria were rigorously established to ensure the relevance and applicability of the selected tools. In addition to the aforementioned criteria (free or free trial, availability in Spanish, and focus on early childhood education), aspects such as recent platform updates, the existence of supporting documentation or tutorials, compatibility with different devices and browsers, and the presence of an active user community were considered.

During the selection process, 23 potential applications were initially identified, of which 12 met the basic inclusion criteria. After a preliminary evaluation that included functionality tests, quality of generated content, and ease of use, the selection was narrowed down to eight applications. Finally, the five tools that showed the best performance in terms of curricular relevance, pedagogical adaptability, and technical stability were selected.

Table 1. AI applications to generate LS.

No.	Name	url	Type of license
01	Schemely	https://schemely.app/	Freemium
02	Eduaide	https://www.eduaide.ai/	Freemium
03	Matthew	https://mathew.ai/	Freemium
04	megaprofe	https://megaprofe.es/	Freemium
05	thinköAI	https://tai.thinkoai.com/	Freemium

Additionally, other emerging tools were identified that, although not part of the main analysis, deserve mention due to their future potential in education (see Table 2):

Table 2. Additional AI tools identified during the search.

No.	Name	url	Type of license
06	edutekalab	https://edtk.co/	Freemium
07	Lesson Robot	https://www.lessonrobot.com/	Freemium
08	Magic School	https://www.magicschool.ai/	Freemium
09	GRownTH	https://app.grownth.com/try	Freemium
10	twinkl	https://www.twinkl.es/	Freemium

These additional tools were documented for future research, as they represent emerging trends in educational AI development that could be incorporated into further studies.

To carry out the analysis, a random content was chosen from Royal Decree 95/2022, of February 1, which establishes the organization and minimum teachings of Early Childhood Education: Importance of the natural environment and development of caring and respect for it, which appears among the skills to be developed in the area of: Discovery and Exploration of the Environment.

The selection of this specific content was not entirely random, but rather based on sound pedagogical criteria. The goal was to find a topic that was broad enough to allow for different methodological approaches, but also specific enough to assess the accuracy and relevance of the proposals generated by the AI applications. The chosen topic presents ideal characteristics for this purpose: it combines cognitive, emotional, and procedural aspects, allows for both individual and group activities, and connects naturally with children's everyday experiences.

Furthermore, this curricular content is characterized by its transversality, which allows for the evaluation of the AI tools' ability to generate interdisciplinary learning situations that connect with other areas of the curriculum, such as the development of communication and representation of reality, or harmonious growth. This characteristic is especially relevant for assessing the pedagogical sophistication of the applications analyzed. To ensure the validity of the analysis, a standardized protocol was established that included generating at least three different learning situations with each tool, using the same curriculum content and similar parameters (duration, age of participants, available resources). This approach allowed for the identification of performance patterns and the assessment of the consistency of each application.

To evaluate the characteristics and functionalities of the applications to be considered in the analysis, similar proposals made previously were taken as an example of analysis (Álvarez-Herrero, 2023; López et al., 2021).

The evaluation framework adopted is based on established models for analyzing digital educational resources, specifically adapted for the context of GAI. This adaptation was necessary due to the particular characteristics of these tools, which differ significantly from traditional educational resources in aspects such as automatic personalization, real-time content generation, and their ability to adapt to different pedagogical contexts.

The selection of these five dimensions responds to the need for a holistic evaluation that considers both the technical and pedagogical aspects of the tools. A scoring system was established for each dimension, using a 5-point Likert scale (1: very poor, 2: poor, 3: acceptable, 4: good, 5: excellent), which made it possible to quantify qualitative assessments and facilitate comparisons between applications.

The identification of the resource and 5 dimensions of analysis were considered:

- Resource identification: identification data, title, and license type.

This basic dimension includes essential information on the accessibility and sustainability of each tool. Aspects such as the developer company or institution, country of origin, release date, latest updates, minimum technical requirements, and privacy and data processing policies were documented. This information is especially relevant in the educational context, where the protection of minors' data is a priority consideration.

- Technological dimension: navigability, response speed, accessibility, etc.

The technological analysis was furthered through systematic testing across different devices (desktops, tablets, smartphones) and browsers (Chrome, Firefox, Safari, Edge). Compatibility with assistive technologies for users with disabilities, including screen readers and voice recognition software, was assessed. The average response time of each application, connection stability, and frequency of errors or service interruptions were also analyzed.

Particular attention was paid to the user experience (UX) and user interface (UI), evaluating aspects such as intuitiveness of design, clarity of instructions, organization of information, and ease of use for novice users. Both the accessibility strengths and barriers identified on each platform were documented.

- Design dimension: design and image of the resource.

The design evaluation included both aesthetic and functional aspects. Visual coherence, appropriate use of colors and fonts, information hierarchy, and adaptability to different screen sizes were analyzed. Particular attention was paid to whether the design was attractive and appropriate for the early childhood education context, considering elements such as the use of illustrations, icons, and graphic elements that would be familiar and motivating to teachers who will work with young children.

- Content dimension: possibility of customizing the content offered, reliability and validity of the content offered, adapting to the interests and learning rates of the students, type of content offered (text, images, multimedia, etc.), and coherence with the contents stipulated in the curriculum.

This dimension constitutes the core of the analysis, as it assesses the fundamental pedagogical quality of each tool. A specific protocol was developed to evaluate curricular accuracy, comparing the generated learning situations with the objectives, competencies, and assessment criteria established in Royal Decree 95/2022. Each application's ability to incorporate active methodologies appropriate for early childhood education, such as project-based learning, symbolic play, and sensory exploration, was analyzed.

The diversity of content formats generated was also evaluated, including the ability to propose activities that integrate different expressive languages (verbal, artistic, corporal, musical). Special attention was paid to the inclusion of adaptations for students with special educational needs and to the consideration of the cultural and linguistic diversity present in early childhood education classrooms.

- Pedagogical dimension: purpose of the resource, adaptability to the user's needs and typology of answers given.

The pedagogical analysis focused on evaluating the theoretical foundation implicit in the proposals generated by each application. The underlying pedagogical currents were identified, along with their consistency with the principles of constructivism and meaningful learning, and their appropriateness to the developmental characteristics of children aged 3 to 6. The ability of each tool to generate proposals that promote the child's holistic development in their cognitive, emotional, social, and psychomotor dimensions was analyzed.

The flexibility of each application to adapt to different educational contexts (urban/rural, monolingual/multilingual, abundant/limited resources) and its ability to generate variations of the same learning situation according to different needs or interests identified in the classroom were also evaluated.

- Evaluation and monitoring: possibility of offering other alternatives to the original proposals, durability of the resource or time that the application or platform has been in operation, and reviews or comments found about the resource.

This dimension included an analysis of the sustainability and future evolution of each platform. Aspects such as update frequency, the development team's response to user suggestions, the existence of a public development roadmap, and the company or project's financial stability were investigated. Specialized forums, educational social media, and review repositories were consulted to gather opinions from real users of each tool.

Each application's ability to provide feedback and continuous improvement systems was also evaluated, including the ability to refine generated proposals, request theme variations, and adapt the level of complexity of proposed activities.

Second phase:

A total of 112 future early childhood education teachers from the University of Alicante (Spain) participated in this second phase of the research. After receiving training at the GAI in the use of different chatbots and applications to generate LS (Schemely, Eduaide, Mathew, megaprofe and thinkö-AI), they completed an evaluation sheet with 3 open questions to indicate what advantages, disadvantages and observations they wanted to make about the use of these tools in particular and AI in general.

The selection of participants followed a purposive sampling approach that sought to represent the diversity of profiles present in initial early childhood teacher training. The 112 participants were evenly distributed across different academic years (43% in their second year, 35% in their third year, and 22% in their fourth year), allowing for an analysis of how prior training experience influences the perception and use of AI tools.

The sample included participants aged between 19 and 45 years (mean age: 22.3 years), with 89% women and 11% men, reflecting the typical composition of early childhood teacher training programs. Thirty-four percent of participants reported prior experience with AI tools, while 66% were approaching these technologies for the first time during the research.

The training process was structured in 90-minute sessions spread over three weeks. The first week was dedicated to the theoretical foundations of AI and its educational applications. The second week focused on the practical use of general chatbots (ChatGPT, Claude, Gemini) for basic educational tasks. The third week focused specifically on specialized applications for generating learning situations.

Each session combined theoretical explanations, practical demonstrations, and time for individual and group experimentation. User guides, prompt templates, and best practice examples were provided for each tool. Participants had access to an online forum where they could share experiences, resolve questions, and exchange usage strategies.

The students used these tools to create LS of specific contents of the early childhood education curriculum and thus be able to analyze the same example with the different characteristics offered by the 5 tools.

The process of creating learning situations followed a structured protocol to ensure comparability of results. Each participant worked with the same curriculum content ("Importance of the natural environment and the development of care and respect for it"), but they were allowed to choose the methodological approach and specific resources they considered most appropriate for their imaginary educational context.

To facilitate systematization of the process, participants were provided with a worksheet that included fields such as: learning objectives, competencies to be developed, proposed activities, necessary resources, timing, assessment criteria, and adaptations for diversity. This template had to be completed for each of the five tools used, allowing for direct comparisons between the generated proposals.

A rotation system was established for the use of the tools to avoid order-of-presentation effects. Participants were divided into five groups, each starting with a different application and rotating sequentially until all the tools had been used. This methodological design helped control for potential biases related to progressive learning or experimental fatigue. During the creation process, participants documented not only the final products (the learning situations generated), but also the process: time invested, number of iterations required, difficulties encountered, and level of satisfaction with each tool. This procedural information was as valuable as the final products in understanding the potential and limitations of each application.

At the end of the practical experience, focused discussion groups were organized where participants could collectively reflect on their experiences, contrast perspectives, and delve deeper into the pedagogical implications of what they observed. These sessions were recorded (with prior consent) and later transcribed for qualitative analysis.

The data collected included both quantitative elements (scores, times, frequencies of use) and qualitative elements (written reflections, focus group comments, process observations). This mixed methodological approach allows for a comprehensive understanding of the phenomenon studied, combining the precision of numerical data with the interpretive richness of narrative data.

The participating students did so anonymously and voluntarily. They were informed from the beginning of the study's objectives and characteristics, and all were informed that they could withdraw from the study at any time. Furthermore, the ethical considerations set forth by the University of Alicante for this type of intervention were followed.

RESULTS

First phase:

Below are the results obtained considering each of the aforementioned dimensions.

A detailed analysis of the five selected apps revealed interesting patterns regarding their strengths and limitations. The results are organized according to the established evaluation framework, providing a comprehensive view of the current state of these tools in the specific context of early childhood education.

It is important to note that the analysis was conducted over a three-month period (September-November 2024), which allowed for the observation of the evolution and updates of some platforms. During this time, two of the apps (Eduaide and thinköAI) implemented significant improvements to their interfaces, while megaprofe experienced some periods of technical instability.

Analysis by dimensions:

- Technological dimension: the 5 resources have a fairly immediate response capacity, are accessible (although all require registration) and have a fairly intuitive navigability.

A detailed analysis of the technological dimension revealed notable differences between the apps, although all met minimum functionality standards. Average response times ranged from 3.2 seconds (thinköAI) to 8.7 seconds (megaprofe), with Schemely showing the greatest consistency in response times. Tests were conducted at different times to evaluate stability under different user loads, finding that Eduaide and Matthew performed best during peak educational usage hours (9:00-12:00 and 15:00-17:00).

Regarding accessibility, both positive and improvable aspects were identified. All apps met basic standards for color contrast and keyboard navigation. However, only thinköAI and Schemely offered full screen reader support. The requirement for registration, while understandable from a business perspective, was identified as a minor but significant barrier to mass adoption in educational contexts. Cross-platform compatibility was also evaluated: all apps worked correctly on iOS and Android devices, although the user experience on tablets was superior to that on smartphones for all tools. Compatibility with less common browsers (such as Safari in earlier versions) showed some limitations in Eduaide and Megaprofe.

- Design dimension: The 5 applications present a visual interface that makes them more attractive than the widely known and used AI chatbots (ChatGPT, Copilot, etc.). In Figure 1 you can see an example of the result obtained with one of the analyzed applications (LS generated with Schemely).

The design analysis revealed a conscious effort on the part of the developers to create interfaces specifically tailored to the educational context. Unlike general-purpose chatbots, these applications incorporate visual elements that are familiar and comfortable for educators: warm color palettes, recognizable educational iconography, and navigation structures that follow common patterns in educational software.

Schemely stood out for its clean and professional design, with a clear layout of information that makes it easy to quickly locate specific functions. Its use of blue and green colors conveys confidence and tranquility, aspects positively valued by users. The selected typography (easy-to-read sans-serif) and generous spacing between elements contribute to a pleasant user experience.

Eduaide adopted a more dynamic approach, with subtle gamification elements including progress bars and small animations that indicate the processing of requests. Its more vibrant color palette (oranges and blues) can be more stimulating, although some users reported that it could be somewhat distracting during prolonged work sessions.

Matthew opted for a minimalist design that prioritizes functionality over decorative elements. Its predominantly white interface with purple accents makes it easier to focus on the generated content. However, some users suggested it could benefit from more visual elements to make the experience more engaging and less technical.

megaprofe showed the most heterogeneous design, with visual inconsistencies that suggest a less mature development. Although it includes attractive elements such as custom illustrations, navigation is less intuitive due to the inconsistent placement of buttons and menus.

thinköAI presented the most balanced design, combining professionalism with visual warmth. Its use of illustrations related to early childhood education and a soft color palette (pastels and earth tones) created the experience most consistent with the target audience.

Figure 1. Example of the LS generated with Schemely.

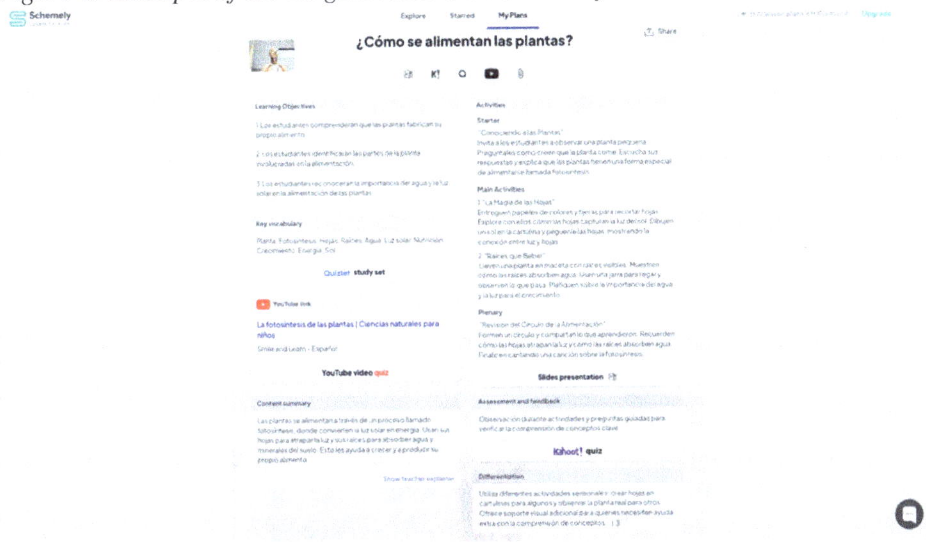

Figure 1 illustrates the typical output characteristics of these specialized applications. Compared to the results of general-purpose chatbots, a more organized structure is observed, with clearly differentiated sections and a format that facilitates direct implementation in the classroom. The inclusion of graphic elements, color coding for different types of activities, and clear chronological organization are distinctive features of these specialized tools.

- Content dimension: the content offered by the 5 applications is quality and can be modified at all times. It addresses the state educational curriculum (Spain) and even that of the different autonomous communities. It is verified whether the content offered by AI applications corresponds to the content established in the Spanish curriculum for the educational stage of Early Childhood Education.

An in-depth analysis of the generated content revealed a higher level of pedagogical sophistication than initially expected. All five applications demonstrated a solid understanding of the fundamental principles of early childhood education, albeit with varying levels of detail and curricular precision.

In terms of curricular alignment, a systematic analysis was conducted comparing the generated learning situations with the objectives, specific competencies, assessment criteria, and core knowledge established in Royal Decree 95/2022. The results showed a high level of correspondence (85-95%) across all applications, with Matthew and thinköAI achieving the greatest accuracy in official terminology and curricular structure.

A particularly valued aspect was the ability of these tools to suggest developmentally appropriate activities for children aged 3 to 6. The proposals consistently included elements of manipulation, sensory exploration, symbolic play, and creative expression. However, some limitations were detected in the proposals for truly innovative activities, tending toward traditional yet robust methodological approaches. Adaptation to regional specificities varied. While applications such as Schemely and Eduaide incorporated specific references to regional curricula when the autonomous community was specified, others maintained a more generic approach based on the state curriculum. This regional adaptability was especially relevant in communities with co-official languages or specific cultural characteristics.

The scientific quality of the proposed content was also evaluated, especially in the area of "Discovery and Exploration of the Environment." The applications demonstrated adequate handling of basic scientific concepts, appropriately adapting them to children's understanding. However, occasional inaccuracies were identified in more specific concepts that would require teacher review.

- Pedagogical dimension: in a comparative way we show the analysis of this dimension in Table 3. It takes into account the possibilities that these applications offer in terms of interaction, the type of responses they offer and adaptability.

The pedagogical dimension constitutes the core of the analysis, as it determines the actual usefulness of these tools in educational contexts. The results revealed different but complementary methodological approaches among the applications analyzed.

Table 3. Analysis of the pedagogical dimension of AI applications.

Application	Pedagogical dimension
Schemely	Full interaction if option is chosen: manual; or no interaction if you want to obtain the LS automatically. Offers: content summary, learning objectives, key vocabulary, activities, links to YouTube, evaluation and feedback, content and attention to diversity. It allows you to generate multimedia presentations of the contents and send the LS by email.
Eduaide	Simply indicate: subject, topic and level, and present an LS. Offers: Objectives, required prior knowledge, activation of prior knowledge, direct instruction strategies, practice tasks, team activities, formative assessment measures, deep questions, outlines, rubrics, sequencing, evidence of learning, gamification, cooperative learning, etc.
Matthew	Once a challenge has been selected, the competencies, basic knowledge and evaluation criteria from among those offered by the application, it offers: description, specific competencies, operational descriptors, evaluation criteria, basic knowledge, development of the LS, didactic sequence (with structured and timed activities) and universal measures and supports.
megaprofe	With the free option it does not even generate a complete LS. It offers: challenge, research question, description of the LS, competencies, class characteristics, description and characteristics of the final product, evaluation of competencies, learning objectives, sessions and activities, and evaluation.
thinköAI	In addition to selecting level, area and topic, class characteristics are also offered. Presents: Objectives, Attention to diversity, methodology, evaluation and sessions (widely described, with exercises and video suggestions).

- Evaluation and monitoring: all applications offer ample possibilities to contribute many other LS proposals and even to be able to manually modify the one initially presented.

The analysis of assessment and monitoring capabilities revealed substantial differences in the sophistication of these functionalities. While all applications allow content regeneration and basic modifications, only a few offers advanced customization and monitoring tools.

Schemely and Eduaide stood out for their versioning systems, which allow maintaining a history of modifications made and comparing different versions of the same learning situation. This functionality was especially useful for teachers working in teams or wishing to experiment with different methodological approaches.

Export capabilities showed significant variability: while thinköAI and Schemely offer multiple export formats (PDF, Word, presentations), megaprofe limited this functionality in its free version. Matthew provided the most comprehensive export, including formats compatible with common educational platforms such as Moodle or Google Classroom.

An innovative aspect identified in Eduaide and thinköAI was the ability to automatically generate variations of the same learning situation, adapting it to different difficulty levels or methodological approaches. This functionality has considerable potential for pedagogical differentiation.

Second phase:

The majority of students have valued the use of AI for these LS creation tasks very positively. The students have found numerous advantages (86%), among which the fact that, very quickly, they are able to easily provide quality educational materials and resources, of great variety and in abundant quantity, stands out. Likewise, they point out that AI makes it easier and prevents them from having to repeat tasks such as generating reports for each student or communicating with all of their parents.

Quantitative analysis of the 112 participants' responses revealed interesting patterns in the perception and assessment of these tools. The 86% who positively valued the use of AI were relatively evenly distributed across academic years, although a slight correlation was observed between prior experience with the technology and a more favorable assessment.

The identified advantages were grouped into five main categories: time efficiency (mentioned by 94% of positive respondents), quality of resources (78%), variety of proposals (83%), ease of use (71%), and reduction of repetitive tasks (65%). Significantly, time efficiency was the most valued aspect, reflecting the time pressure that preservice teachers feel when faced with instructional planning.

An unexpected finding was that 34% of participants reported that using these tools had helped them better understand the structure and components of a well-designed learning situation. Several commented that the process of interacting with AI had forced them to reflect on pedagogical aspects they had previously taken for granted. The perception of the quality of the generated materials showed differences depending on the tool used: thinköAI and Schemely received the highest ratings (average 4.2/5), followed by Eduaide (3.9/5), Matthew (3.7/5), and megaprofe (3.1/5). These differences correlated with the completeness of the free versions and the ease of use of each platform.

Some of the comments made by the students were:

"I was surprised by the ease and speed with which the thinköAI tool has been able to create a LS that would perfectly fit what I would like to do with my students" (STU011).

This comment reflects a common perception among participants: surprise at the AI's ability to generate relevant and appropriate content. Analysis of similar comments (23 participants expressed similar surprise) suggests that initial expectations were relatively low, which amplified the positive perception of the outcome.

"I have used Schemely and I loved that it offered a multitude of resources and ideas to put into practice the LS that I asked it to generate for me" (STU065).

The appreciation for the abundance of resources was a recurring theme, mentioned by 47 participants. However, closer analysis revealed that this abundance was primarily valued by upper-level students, while first-year students sometimes felt overwhelmed by the number of options available.

Additional representative comments included:

"The app has given me ideas I hadn't considered, especially for integrating technology naturally into traditional activities" (STU089).

"It has really helped me better structure my sessions. Before, I didn't know how to organize the time for each activity" (STU034).

"It's incredible how it can generate such a variety of activities for a single goal. It has opened my mind to new possibilities" (STU076).

However, a high percentage of students (79%) also recognize that the main drawback in using AI for LS design is that this technology lacks a human component (very necessary among Early Childhood Education students, who need the emotions, feelings and physical presence of their teacher). This makes the participation of the teacher necessary, who is able to empathize, identify the different learning rhythms of their students and know their reality, their context and their feelings.

An in-depth analysis of this concern revealed a mature and thoughtful understanding among preservice teachers about the nature of their profession. The 79% who identified a lack of a human component as a primary disadvantage were evenly distributed across genders and grade levels, suggesting that this perception is not influenced by specific demographic variables.

The concerns were articulated around several conceptual axes: a lack of pedagogical intuition (mentioned by 68% of critics), a lack of specific contextual knowledge (74%), limited emotional adaptation (81%), and a lack of situational flexibility (52%). Notably, emotional adaptation was the most frequent concern, reflecting a deep understanding of the importance of affective aspects in early childhood education.

That is, these tools are seen by students as impersonal, without empathy, without the ability that a teacher does have to personalize learning, since the teacher can show emotions and feelings. In addition, they also argue the possibility of biases (race, gender, social class, etc.).

And precisely, all of these last factors that students have detected as drawbacks of AI applications are essential both in the design and implementation of LS in the classrooms (Estrada et al., 2022).

This observation connects directly with contemporary pedagogical literature on the importance of contextualization and personalization in early childhood education. Participants demonstrated an intuitive understanding of fundamental pedagogical principles, even when they did not explicitly articulate them in theoretical terms.

The analysis revealed that the most critical students tended to propose constructive solutions rather than completely reject the tools. Sixty-three percent of those who identified significant limitations suggested ways to integrate AI as a support tool without replacing human pedagogical judgment.

Some of the comments made by the students in this regard were:

"Although I liked the LS that the AI application has generated for me, I am capable of generating a better, more original and creative one, with different elements that would take into account the particular characteristics of my students and that the application has not had. taken into account" (STU082).

This comment illustrates a balanced attitude that recognizes both the value and limitations of AI. Analysis of similar comments (31 participants expressed similar sentiments) suggests a process of constructive comparison between human and artificial capabilities.

"It's okay for you to give me an idea or a first design, but I would incorporate other elements and characteristics to the result obtained that would allow me to personalize it and make it more my own" (STU059).

The metaphor of "making it more my own" appeared in 18 different comments, suggesting a psychological need for creative ownership that transcends mere pedagogical functionality. This observation has important implications for the design of future tools that could emphasize creative collaboration between humans and AI.

Other comments representative of this critical but constructive perspective included:

"AI gives me a very good skeleton, but I need to add the flesh, the soul, the personality that my specific group of children needs" (STU097).

"It's like having a very efficient assistant, but in the end the pedagogical decision has to be mine because I know my students" (STU111).

"I'm worried that if we get too used to this, we'll lose the ability to create from scratch and improvise when the situation requires it" (STU045).

Despite recognizing the potential benefits of AI tools, the participating future educators expressed significant concerns about their application in early childhood contexts. Their critical perspectives revealed several key limitations that warrant serious consideration:

• Loss of Human Connection and Intuitive Understanding

"AI doesn't know when a child has had a rough morning at home or when they're feeling overwhelmed, ..." (STU063).

Many students emphasized that effective early childhood education relies heavily on reading non-verbal cues, understanding individual emotional needs, and making spontaneous adjustments based on children's immediate responses. They worried that AI-generated activities lack the flexibility to adapt to the complex, unpredictable nature of young children's learning processes.

• Standardization vs. Individual Development

Several participants expressed concern that AI tools might push education toward a "one-size-fits-all" approach.

"Every child develops differently, and AI seems to assume all four-year-olds are the same," (STU044).

They noted that while AI can suggest activities for specific age groups, it cannot account for the wide developmental variations typical in early childhood, nor can it recognize when a child needs to move at their own pace rather than follow a predetermined sequence.

• Over-reliance on Screen-based Solutions

Future educators frequently questioned whether AI tools inherently bias learning toward digital formats.

"Young children need to touch, manipulate, and experience things with their whole bodies," (STU012).

They worried that teachers might become too dependent on AI-generated digital activities, potentially reducing hands-on, sensory-rich experiences that are crucial for early development.

• Cultural and Contextual Blindness

Many students highlighted AI's limitations in understanding local contexts and cultural nuances.

"The AI doesn't know about our school's garden project or understand why Maria speaks Spanish at home,..." (STU109).

They expressed concern that AI-generated content might overlook the rich cultural knowledge that children bring from their families and communities, potentially creating learning situations that feel disconnected from children's lived experiences.

• Risk of Deskilling Teachers

Perhaps most significantly, participants worried about becoming overly dependent on AI tools at the expense of developing their own pedagogical judgment.

"If I always rely on AI to plan activities, will I lose the ability to create meaningful learning experiences myself?" (STU088).

They recognized the danger of substituting AI efficiency for the deep understanding of child development that comes from experience and reflection.

• Ethical Concerns About Data and Privacy

Future educators also raised questions about the appropriateness of using AI tools that might collect data about young children.

"Should we be feeding information about three-year-olds into these systems?" (STU101),

reflecting growing awareness about digital privacy and children's rights in educational technology.

These critical perspectives suggest that while AI tools may offer valuable support for curriculum planning, they cannot replace the nuanced, relationship-based approach that characterizes quality early childhood education. The participating students demonstrated sophisticated understanding that effective teaching in this field requires human judgment, cultural sensitivity, and the ability to respond flexibly to children's individual needs—capabilities that current AI systems cannot replicate.

DISCUSSION

In view of the five applications analysed, all of them show great potential for offering LS related to the importance of the natural environment and the development of behaviours of care and respect towards it for the Early Childhood Education stage. They also all offer the possibility of obtaining other LS and even being able to adapt them manually.

The results obtained in this research confirm the transformative potential of specialized AI tools in the field of educational planning for early childhood education. However, this potential must be interpreted within a broader framework that considers both the opportunities and limitations inherent in these emerging technologies.

The fact that all five applications demonstrated the ability to generate learning situations consistent with the official curriculum suggests that AI technology has reached a sufficient level of maturity to be considered a viable tool in the educational context. This convergence in the basic quality of the generated proposals indicates that we are witnessing a de facto standardization in the minimum capabilities that these tools should offer.

However, although two of them (megaprofe and thinköAI) ask about the characteristics of the class, it can be said that none fully addresses the context and the diverse reality that occurs in the classrooms of this educational stage, nor does it facilitate the development of inquiry and/or experimentation that should be present in every activity in which science is learned.

Although students' opinion is positive and optimistic about the use of these AI applications to generate LS, it is also quite critical. They consider that these applications lack the human component that a teacher can bring to LS.

Well, in addition to the fact that human interaction is still necessary and therefore AI is not going to replace the teacher in these tasks, the students also indicated that the materials obtained through AI could include biases, and that abuse of this technology can lead to inhibit creativity and originality that without it they can manifest spontaneously and autonomously.

CONCLUSIONS

This research, although it does not carry out an in-depth or exhaustive analysis of five AI applications to generate LS, does allow us to anticipate that these applications are an excellent resource to offer a first draft of what a LS for scientific science content in Early Childhood Education could be. However, the products generated require adaptation and improvement by the teacher, who must consider the reality present in his or her group-class, and, in addition, apply strategies and methods that enable inquiry and/or experimentation in these LS of sciences generated by AI.

The findings of this study confirm that AI applications specialized in education have reached a level of development that places them as viable tools for assisting in instructional planning. The ability of these five applications to generate structured, curricularly aligned, and pedagogically coherent learning situations represents a significant advance over general AI tools.

However, the characterization of these products as "first drafts" is particularly apt. The analysis revealed that, although the applications can produce technically accurate content, they invariably require the intervention of a professional with specialized pedagogical knowledge to become effective learning tools. This need for human mediation should not be interpreted as a limitation of the technology, but rather as a confirmation of the inherent complexity of early childhood education processes.

The fact that all the benefits of these applications are conditioned by being paid, limits their wide acceptance by teachers. Added to this is the fact that the rapid pace at which AI is developing means that other and better applications are appearing with the same purpose.

On the other hand, future teachers who have participated in this research and who have known first-hand the AI applications that generate LS, are quite critical of its possibilities. Well, although they recognize the value of these applications when it comes to providing a first idea of them, they are in favor of improving these sketches or first designs obtained with AI with their ideas and creations.

Also notable was the students' ability to identify implicit biases in AI proposals, suggesting that current training in diversity and inclusion education is developing transferable skills for the critical analysis of emerging technologies. This sensitivity to algorithmic biases is fundamental for the ethical and equitable use of these tools.

In conclusion, AI can help and complement the teacher's work in creating content, but its use must be careful and ethical, keeping in mind its irreplaceable role.

This research confirms that the future of AI in early childhood education does not lie in replacing teachers, but in the development of intelligent collaboration models that leverage unique human strengths while leveraging computational capabilities for specific tasks. Early childhood teachers bring irreplaceable skills: pedagogical intuition developed through experience, emotional reading skills, adaptive flexibility in the face of unforeseen situations, and the ability to establish emotional bonds that facilitate learning.

Although this research has some limitations; such as the number of applications analyzed, the number of LS designed, or the small sample of students involved; It represents a first approach to the analysis of these tools and a first step for future research.

REFERENCES

Al Darayseh, A. (2023). Acceptance of artificial intelligence in teaching science: Science teachers' perspective. *Computers and Education: Artificial Intelligence, 4*, 100132. DOI: 10.1016/j.caeai.2023.100132

Álvarez-Herrero, J. F. (2023). Análisis de 5 recursos de Inteligencia Artificial capaces de generar Situaciones de Aprendizaje. In: *Libro de Actas de las X Jornadas Iberoamericanas de Innovación Educativa en el ámbito de las TIC y las TAC* (pp. 103-110). Aplicaciones Tecnológicas para la Enseñanza de las TIC (ATETIC), Universidad de Las Palmas de Gran Canaria.

Álvarez-Herrero, J. F. (2024). Opinion of Spanish Teachers About Artificial Intelligence and Its Use in Education. In S. Papadakis (Ed.), *IoT, AI, and ICT for Educational Applications. Technologies to Enable Education for All* (pp. 163-172). EAI/Springer Innovations in Communication and Computing. Springer, Cham. DOI: 10.1007/978-3-031-50139-5_8

Alwaqdani, M. (2024). Investigating teachers' perceptions of artificial intelligence tools in education: Potential and difficulties. *Education and Information Technologies, 30*(3), 2737–2755. DOI: 10.1007/s10639-024-12903-9

Awidi, I. T. (2024). Comparing expert tutor evaluation of reflective essays with marking by generative artificial intelligence (AI) tool. *Computers and Education: Artificial Intelligence, 6*, 100226. DOI: 10.1016/j.caeai.2024.100226

Ayeni, O. O., Al Hamad, N. M., Chisom, O. N., Osawaru, B., & Adewusi, O. E. (2024). AI in education: A review of personalized learning and educational technology. *GSC Advanced Research and Reviews, 18*(2), 261–271. DOI: 10.30574/gscarr.2024.18.2.0062

Baidoo-Anu, D., & Ansah, L. O. (2023). Education in the era of generative artificial intelligence (AI): Understanding the potential benefits of ChatGPT in promoting teaching and learning. *Journal of AI, 7*(1), 52–62. DOI: 10.61969/jai.1337500

Batista, J., Mesquita, A., & Carnaz, G. (2024). Generative AI and Higher Education: Trends, Challenges, and Future Directions from a Systematic Literature Review. *Information (Basel), 15*(11), 676. DOI: 10.3390/info15110676

Benhadj, Y., El Messaoudi, M., & Nfissi, A. (2019). Artificial intelligence in education: Integrating serious gaming into the language class classdojo technology for classroom behavioral management. *IAES International Journal of Artificial Intelligence, 8*(4), 382. DOI: 10.11591/ijai.v8.i4.pp382-390

Binhammad, M. H. Y., Othman, A., Abuljadayel, L., Al Mheiri, H., Alkaabi, M., & Almarri, M. (2024). Investigating how generative AI can create personalized learning materials tailored to individual student needs. *Creative Education, 15*(7), 1499–1523. DOI: 10.4236/ce.2024.157091

Braze (2019). *Artificial Intelligence Trends 2019 Roundup*. Braze, New York. https://bit.ly/RoundUP19

Brynjolfsson, E., Li, D., & Raymond, L. R. (2023). *Generative AI at work (No. w31161)*. National Bureau of Economic Research. DOI: 10.3386/w31161

Cai, Z., Liu, L., Chen, B., & Wang, Y. (2021). *Artificial intelligence: From beginning to date*. World Scientific. DOI: 10.1142/11921

Chen, J. J. (2024). A scoping study on AI affordances in early childhood education: Mapping the global landscape, identifying research gaps, and charting future research directions. *Journal of Artificial Intelligence Research, 81*, 701–740. DOI: 10.1613/jair.1.16882

Coltri, M. A. (2024). The Ethical Dilemma with Open AI ChatGPT: Is it Right or Wrong to prohibit it?. *Athens Journal of Law, 10*(1), 121, 119-130.

Cooper, G. (2023). Examining science education in ChatGPT: An exploratory study of generative artificial intelligence. *Journal of Science Education and Technology, 32*(3), 444–452. DOI: 10.1007/s10956-023-10039-y

Creely, E., & Blannin, J. (2025). Creative partnerships with generative AI. Possibilities for education and beyond. *Thinking Skills and Creativity, 56*, 101727. DOI: 10.1016/j.tsc.2024.101727

Danyaro, A., Aladesusi, A. G., Ajamu, A. O., Adegbite, A. F., & Attah, J. O. (2024). Pre-Service Teachers' Awareness and Attitude Towards the Use of Open Educational Resources for Learning in Kano State, Nigeria. *Suluh: Jurnal Bimbingan Dan Konseling, 9*(2), 76–80. DOI: 10.33084/suluh.v9i2.6989

Ding, A. C. E., Shi, L., Yang, H., & Choi, I. (2024). Enhancing teacher AI literacy and integration through different types of cases in teacher professional development. *Computers and Education Open, 6*, 100178. DOI: 10.1016/j.caeo.2024.100178

Estrada Carrera, F. M. L., Loor Zambrano, H. Y., & Viteri Rade, L. Y. (2022). Reemplazo de personal humano por inteligencia artificial: Ventajas y desventajas. *Revista Investigación y Negocios, 15*(25), 31–38. DOI: 10.38147/invneg.v15i25.213

Farooqi, M. T. K., Amanat, I., & Awan, S. M. (2024). Ethical Considerations and Challenges in the Integration of Artificial Intelligence in Education: A Systematic Review. *Journal of Excellence in Management Sciences*, *3*(4), 35–50. DOI: 10.69565/jems.v3i4.314

Froebel, F. (1887). *The education of man*. A. Lovell & Company.

Gökçearslan, S., Tosun, C., & Erdemir, Z. G. (2024). Benefits, challenges, and methods of artificial intelligence (AI) chatbots in education: A systematic literature review. *International Journal of Technology in Education*, *7*(1), 19–39. https://eric.ed.gov/?id=EJ1415037. DOI: 10.46328/ijte.600

Hintze, A. (13 November 2016). Understanding the four types of AI, from reactive robots to self-aware beings. The Conversation. https://bit.ly/theconversation2016

Hirsh-Pasek, K., Golinkoff, R. M., Berk, L. E., & Singer, D. G. (2009). *A mandate for playful learning in preschool: Presenting the evidence*. Oxford University Press.

Holstein, K., McLaren, B. M., & Aleven, V. (2018). Student learning benefits of a mixed-reality teacher awareness tool in AI-enhanced classrooms. In *Artificial Intelligence in Education: 19th International Conference, AIED 2018, London, UK, June 27–30, 2018* [Springer International Publishing.]. *Proceedings*, *19*(Part I), 154–168.

Hopcan, S., Türkmen, G., & Polat, E. (2024). Exploring the artificial intelligence anxiety and machine learning attitudes of teacher candidates. *Education and Information Technologies*, *29*(6), 7281–7301. DOI: 10.1007/s10639-023-12086-9

Hutson, J. (2024). Rethinking plagiarism in the era of generative AI. *Journal of International Communication*, *4*(1), 619. DOI: 10.54963/jic.v4i1.220

Hwang, G. J., & Chen, N. S. (2023). Exploring the potential of generative artificial intelligence in education: Applications, challenges, and future research directions. *Journal of Educational Technology & Society*, *26*(2). Advance online publication. DOI: 10.30191/ETS.202304_26(2).0014

Kaddouri, M., Mhamdi, K., Jabri, A., Boukare, M., & Jmad, S. (2025). Generative Artificial Intelligence and Assessment of Learning: Challenges and Perspectives. In Gregory, S. (Ed.), *Effective Instructional Design Informed by AI* (pp. 277–326). IGI Global Scientific Publishing. DOI: 10.4018/979-8-3693-6527-4.ch010

Kewalramani, S., Kidman, G., & Palaiologou, I. (2021). Using Artificial Intelligence (AI)-interfaced robotic toys in early childhood settings: A case for children's inquiry literacy. *European Early Childhood Education Research Journal*, *29*(5), 652–668. DOI: 10.1080/1350293X.2021.1968458

Kim, J. (2024). Leading teachers' perspective on teacher-AI collaboration in education. *Education and Information Technologies*, *29*(7), 8693–8724. DOI: 10.1007/s10639-023-12109-5

Lampropoulos, G., & Papadakis, S. (2025). The Educational Value of Artificial Intelligence and Social Robots. In *Social Robots in Education* (pp. 3–15). Springer. DOI: 10.1007/978-3-031-82915-4_1

Lee, I., & Perret, B. (2022). Preparing High School Teachers to Integrate AI Methods into STEM Classrooms. *Proceedings of the AAAI Conference on Artificial Intelligence*, *36*(11), 12783–12791. Advance online publication. DOI: 10.1609/aaai.v36i11.21557

Li, Z., Dhruv, A., & Jain, V. (2024). Ethical considerations in the use of AI for higher education: A comprehensive guide. In *2024 IEEE 18th International Conference on Semantic Computing (ICSC)* (pp. 218-223). IEEE. DOI: 10.1109/ICSC59802.2024.00041

Lim, W. M., Gunasekara, A., Pallant, J. L., Pallant, J. I., & Pechenkina, E. (2023). Generative AI and the future of education: Ragnarök or reformation? A paradoxical perspective from management educators. *International Journal of Management Education*, *21*(2), 100790. DOI: 10.1016/j.ijme.2023.100790

Lo, A. W. (2025). The educational affordances and challenges of generative AI in Global Englishes-oriented materials development and implementation: A critical ecological perspective. *System*, *130*, 103610. DOI: 10.1016/j.system.2025.103610

Loaiza Galeano, C. D. (2024). *Un análisis a las lecciones aprendidas en etapa de inversión en tres proyectos de transformación digital en empresas de Pereira y el Norte del Valle, haciendo uso de inteligencia artificial generativa*. [Tesis de Maestría, Universidad EAFIT]. https://hdl.handle.net/10784/34547

López Gómez, S., Martín Gómez, S., & Vidal Esteve, M. I. (2021). Análisis de aplicaciones móviles dirigidas a la infancia: Características técnicas, pedagógicas, de diseño y contenido. *Revista Iberoamericana de Educación*, *85*(1), 81–100. DOI: 10.35362/rie8514013

Mao, J., Chen, B., & Liu, J. C. (2024). Generative artificial intelligence in education and its implications for assessment. *TechTrends*, *68*(1), 58–66. DOI: 10.1007/s11528-023-00911-4

Mittal, U., Sai, S., Chamola, V., & Sangwan, D. (2024). A comprehensive review on generative AI for education. *IEEE Access : Practical Innovations, Open Solutions*, *12*, 142733–142759. DOI: 10.1109/ACCESS.2024.3468368

Montessori, M. (1967). *The absorbent mind.* Holt, Rinehart and Winston.

Montessori, M. (1988). *The discovery of the child.* Ballantine Books.

Naida, R., Berezovska, L., Bulgakova, O., Kravets, N., & Savchenkova, M. (2024). Integrating innovative pedagogical technologies into Early Childhood education training programs: A comparative analysis. *Conhecimento & Diversidade, 16*(41), 568–595. DOI: 10.18316/rcd.v16i41.11551

Naik, D., Naik, I., & Naik, N. (2024). The AI Engine of Creation: Exploring the Capabilities of AI Chatbots based on Generative AI, Large Language Models and Large Multimodal Models. *TechRxiv,* November 19, 2024, 1-32. DOI: 10.36227/techrxiv.173198336.68543189/v1

Ocaña-Fernández, Y., Valenzuela-Fernández, L. A., & Garro-Aburto, L. L. (2019). Inteligencia artificial y sus implicaciones en la educación superior. *Propósitos Y Representaciones, 7*(2), 536–568. DOI: 10.20511/pyr2019.v7n2.274

Paiz, J. M. (2024). *Droids don't teach, we do: Addressing AI anxiety in language teaching and learning*. The FLTMag. https://www.doi.org/10.69732/VFPR7648

Pang, S., Nol, E., & Heng, K. (2025). Generative AI as a Personal Tutor for English Language Learning: A Review of Benefits and Concerns. *International Journal of Changes in Education*. DOI: 10.47852/bonviewIJCE52023724

Papadakis, S., Lytvynova, S. H., Ivanova, S. M., & Selyshcheva, I. A. (2024b). *Advancing lifelong learning with AI-enhanced ICT: A review of 3L-Person 2024.* In *CEUR Workshop Proceedings (9th International Workshop on Professional Retraining and Life-Long Learning using ICT: Person-oriented Approach — 3L-Person 2024, Lviv, Ukraine, September 25, 2023).* CEUR-WS.org.

Papadakis, S., Striuk, A. M., Kravtsov, H. M., Shyshkina, M. P., Marienko, M. V., & Danylchuk, H. B. (2024a). *Embracing digital innovation and cloud technologies for transformative learning experiences.* In *Proceedings of the 11th Workshop on Cloud Technologies in Education (CTE 2023), Kryvyi Rih, Ukraine, December 22, 2023.* CEUR Workshop Proceedings.

Peña-Fernández, S., Meso Ayerdi, K., Larrondo Ureta, A., & Díaz Noci, J. (2023). Sin periodistas, no hay periodismo: La dimensión social de la inteligencia artificial generativa en los medios de comunicación. *El Profesional de la Información, 32*(2), e320227. DOI: 10.3145/epi.2023.mar.27

Qadir, J. (2023). *Engineering education in the era of ChatGPT: Promise and pitfalls of generative AI for education. 2023 IEEE Global Engineering Education Conference (EDUCON)*, IEEE. DOI: 10.1109/EDUCON54358.2023.10125121

Ramírez, R. A., & Layret, I. R. R. (2024). Co-designing the future with generative AI: cultivating student digital competencies for tomorrow. In *ICERI2024 Proceedings* (pp. 7756-7762). IATED. DOI: 10.21125/iceri.2024.1896

Real Decreto 95/2022, de 1 de febrero, por el que se establece la ordenación y las enseñanzas mínimas de la Educación Infantil. *Boletín Oficial del Estado*, 28, de 2 de febrero de 2022. https://www.boe.es/eli/es/rd/2022/02/01/95/con

Safi, R. (2025). Plagiarism in the age of generative AI: An exploratory experiment. *Communications of the Association for Information Systems*, *56*(1), 594–612. DOI: 10.17705/1CAIS.05624

Sakamoto, M., Tan, S., & Clivaz, S. (2024). Social, cultural and political perspectives of generative AI in teacher education: Lesson planning in Japanese teacher education. In M. Searson, E. Langran & J. Trumle (Eds.), *Exploring new horizons: Generative artificial intelligence and teacher education* (pp. 178-209). Association for the Advancement of Computing in Education (AACE). https://www.learntechlib.org/p/223928/

Sanusi, I. T., Agbo, F. J., Dada, O. A., Yunusa, A. A., Aruleba, K. D., Obaido, G., Olawumi, O., & Oyelere, S. S.Centre for Multidisciplinary Research and Innovation (CEMRI). (2024). Stakeholders' insights on artificial intelligence education: Perspectives of teachers, students, and policymakers. *Computers and Education Open*, *7*, 100212. DOI: 10.1016/j.caeo.2024.100212

Shiri, A. (2024). Artificial intelligence literacy: A proposed faceted taxonomy. *Digital Library Perspectives*, *40*(4), 681–699. DOI: 10.1108/DLP-04-2024-0067

Song, Y., Huang, L., Zheng, L., Fan, M., & Liu, Z. (2025). Interactions with generative AI chatbots: Unveiling dialogic dynamics, students' perceptions, and practical competencies in creative problem-solving. *International Journal of Educational Technology in Higher Education*, *22*(1), 12. DOI: 10.1186/s41239-025-00508-2

Strelkova, O., & Pasichnyk, O. (2017). *Three Types of Artificial Intelligence*. Khmelnitsky National University.

Su, J., & Yang, W. (2022). Artificial intelligence in early childhood education: A scoping review. *Computers and Education: Artificial Intelligence*, *3*, 100049. DOI: 10.1016/j.caeai.2022.100049

Tan, D. Y., & Cheah, C. W. (2021). Developing a gamified AI-enabled online learning application to improve students' perception of university physics. *Computers and Education: Artificial Intelligence*, *2*, 100032. DOI: 10.1016/j.caeai.2021.100032

Tang, L., & Su, Y. S. (2024). Ethical Implications and Principles of Using Artificial Intelligence Models in the Classroom: A Systematic Literature Review. *International Journal of Interactive Multimedia and Artificial Intelligence*, *8*(5), 25–36. DOI: 10.9781/ijimai.2024.02.010

Towfek, S. K., Khodadadi, N., Abualigah, L., & Rizk, F. H. (2024). AI in higher education: Insights from student surveys and predictive analytics using PSO-guided WOA and linear regression. *Journal of Artificial Intelligence in Engineering Practice*, *1*(1), 1–17. DOI: 10.21608/jaiep.2024.354003

Uğraş, H., Uğraş, M., Papadakis, S., & Kalogiannakis, M. (2024a). ChatGPT-Supported Education in Primary Schools: The Potential of ChatGPT for Sustainable Practices. *Sustainability (Basel)*, *16*(22), 9855. DOI: 10.3390/su16229855

Uğraş, H., Uğraş, M., Papadakis, S., & Kalogiannakis, M. (2024b). Innovative Early Childhood STEM Education with ChatGPT: Teacher Perspectives. *Technology. Knowledge and Learning*, *30*(2), 809–831. DOI: 10.1007/s10758-024-09804-8

Vanhaelen, Q., Lin, Y. C., & Zhavoronkov, A. (2020). The advent of generative chemistry. *ACS Medicinal Chemistry Letters*, *11*(8), 1496–1505. DOI: 10.1021/acsmedchemlett.0c00088 PMID: 32832015

Vygotsky, L. S. (1978). *Mind in society: The development of higher psychological processes* (Cole, M., John-Steiner, V., Scribner, S., & Souberman, E., Eds.). Harvard University Press.

Williams, R., Park, H. W., Oh, L., & Breazeal, C. (2019). PopBots: Designing an Artificial Intelligence Curriculum for Early Childhood Education. *Proceedings of the AAAI Conference on Artificial Intelligence*, *33*(1), 9729–9736. DOI: 10.1609/aaai.v33i01.33019729

Wong, J. M. S., Liu, P. H. C., & Yip, C. W. H. (2025). Navigating the Digital Shift: Early Childhood Educators' Attitudes Towards Generative Artificial Intelligence and Emerging Technologies. In Cheng, E. C. K. (Ed.), *Innovating Education with AI. AETS 2024. Lecture Notes in Educational Technology*. Springer. DOI: 10.1007/978-981-96-4952-5_6

Yusuf, A., Bello, S., Pervin, N., & Tukur, A. K. (2024). Implementing a proposed framework for enhancing critical thinking skills in synthesizing AI-generated texts. *Thinking Skills and Creativity*, *53*, 101619. DOI: 10.1016/j.tsc.2024.101619

Zaidi, S. A. Z., Ahmad, E., & Shukla, N. (2024). Ethical Considerations in the Use of Artificial Intelligence (AI) for Education and Research: A Review. *International Journal of Innovations in Science. Engineering And Management*, *3*(2), 156–167. DOI: 10.69968/ijisem.2024v3si2156-167

Zapata-Ros, M. (2023). Inteligencia Artificial Generativa Y Aprendizaje Inteligente. *EdArXiv*, 27 June 2023. DOI: 10.35542/osf.io/86ykm

Zhai, X. (2024). Transforming teachers' roles and agencies in the era of generative ai: Perceptions, acceptance, knowledge, and practices. *Journal of Science Education and Technology*, *2024*, 1–11. DOI: 10.1007/s10956-024-10174-0

Zhai, X., Chu, X., Chai, C. S., Jong, M. S. Y., Istenic, A., Spector, M., Liu, J. B., & Li, Y. (2021). A Review of Artificial Intelligence (AI) in Education from 2010 to 2020. *Complexity*, *2021*(1), 8812542. DOI: 10.1155/2021/8812542

Zhang, P., & Kamel Boulos, M. N. (2023). Generative AI in Medicine and Healthcare: Promises, Opportunities and Challenges. *Future Internet*, *15*(9), 286. DOI: 10.3390/fi15090286

Chapter 7
The Future of AI in Special Education:
Tools for Individualized Support

Mustafa Kayyali
http://orcid.org/0000-0003-3300-262X
Maaref University of Applied Sciences, Syria

ABSTRACT

Artificial intelligence is quietly reshaping special education—not by replacing human support, but by enhancing its reach and responsiveness. This chapter explores how AI tools can offer deeply individualized learning experiences, particularly for students with cognitive, behavioral, and sensory challenges. Far from a one-size-fits-all model, these technologies adjust in real time to the learner's pace, preferences, and needs. Yet the future of AI in special education is not without complexity. Issues of ethics, equity, and emotional nuance cannot be programmed away. Drawing on current innovations and emerging practices, this chapter examines how educators and AI systems might work together—not in competition—to create classrooms where every student feels seen, supported, and empowered. The aim is not perfection through technology, but better human understanding, made possible by it.

INTRODUCTION

The Future of AI in Special Education: Tools for Individualized Support. In a world increasingly defined by algorithms, automation, and digital ecosystems, education finds itself standing at a strange crossroads: one foot grounded in centuries-old pedagogical traditions, the other stepping into a future shaped by machines that learn. Nowhere is this crossroads more emotionally charged and ethically delicate

DOI: 10.4018/979-8-2600-0101-1.ch007

than in the field of special education. For decades, educators, parents, and specialists have fought to dismantle rigid systems that marginalized students with disabilities—systems that often treated difference as deficiency (Nguyen, 2024). The promise of artificial intelligence (AI) in special education, then, is not just technical; it is moral (Marino et al, 2023). It is the possibility of finally delivering on the long-held belief that every child deserves not just access to learning, but access to the kind of learning that makes sense to them.

But let's not be too quick to romanticize the machines. AI is not a silver bullet. It cannot replace the intuition of a seasoned special education teacher, the gut feeling of a parent who just knows something isn't right, or the profound patience that human connection demands (Khan, 2024). What AI can offer, though, is support—unwavering, data-driven, tireless support. It can recognize patterns that human eyes might miss. It can generate tailored learning content at a scale that no one teacher ever could. And perhaps most importantly, it can respond in real time to subtle cues in a learner's behavior, adapting its approach to better fit that learner's cognitive rhythm. In this way, AI holds out the possibility of individualized learning not as a luxury, but as the new norm.

Yet, this future is not guaranteed. Integrating AI into special education raises complex questions about data privacy, algorithmic bias, accessibility, and the potential erosion of human empathy (Lata, 2024). Can a machine truly understand what it means for a child to feel left behind? Will AI deepen existing inequalities, or will it help us finally level the playing field? These are not merely technological questions—they are deeply human ones. They require us to think not only about what AI *can* do, but what it *should* do.

This chapter aims to explore this delicate terrain. It begins by examining the current landscape of AI tools designed for learners with disabilities—from speech recognition software for non-verbal students to machine learning algorithms that predict learning breakdowns before they happen. We will explore case studies, real-world applications, and ongoing research to understand how AI is already being used in classrooms and therapy sessions. But we will also slow down, question the hype, and sit with the uncertainty. Because when it comes to children who learn differently, the stakes are too high for simple solutions.

Ultimately, this is not a chapter about the dominance of technology. It is a chapter about *possibility*. The possibility that we, as educators, developers, parents, and students, might come together to imagine a more inclusive, responsive, and humane future—one where AI doesn't dictate the terms of education, but serves as a tool in our collective effort to see and support every learner, just as they are.

RETHINKING INCLUSION: THE PROMISE OF AI IN SPECIAL EDUCATION

Inclusion has long been the heartbeat of special education—a word repeated so often in policy documents and advocacy circles that it risks becoming a mantra rather than a movement (Kayyali, 2022). For some, it conjures images of wheelchair ramps and sensory-friendly classrooms; for others, it's a philosophy, a moral stance that insists every child, regardless of diagnosis or perceived deficit, belongs in the learning community. But inclusion—real, living, breathing inclusion—is messier than checklists and well-meaning slogans. It's not just about proximity. It's about presence. Participation. Dignity. And that's where AI enters the picture—not to save or fix, but to support and, if used wisely, to transform how we even define what it means to belong. Because let's be honest: for all the gains of the past few decades, inclusion still often feels like a compromise. A child is *allowed* to stay in a general education classroom, so long as they don't disrupt the flow. So long as their learning difference doesn't require too many accommodations. So long as they can "keep up" or at least not fall *too* far behind. It's inclusion, yes—but conditional. Tenuous. Sometimes, even performative.

Now, imagine if we flipped the script. Imagine a classroom designed from the ground up to adapt—not once a child fails, not after they fall through the cracks, but *as they learn, while they learn* (Done, 2022). Imagine tools that listen—not just to the words a child speaks, but to the pace at which they type, the way their eyes scan a page, the hesitation before they click "next." Tools that notice the subtle signs of frustration before a meltdown, or catch patterns of avoidance before they calcify into shame. These aren't pipe dreams. These are the contours of what AI—when paired with human insight and ethical foresight—might offer. But let's slow down a bit, because the word "promise" can be dangerously seductive. AI doesn't promise utopia. It doesn't erase systemic inequities or magically make underfunded schools flourish. What it *does* is offer a different kind of lens—one that shifts the conversation from *how can this child fit our system?* to *how can our system fit this child?* That's a radical reorientation. And it's one we've been inching toward for years, with universal design for learning (UDL), differentiated instruction, personalized learning plans—all valiant attempts to meet diverse learners where they are (Cumming & Rose, 2022). But AI, if wielded with care, doesn't just support these frameworks. It turbocharges them.

Figure 1. AI Use-Cases in Special Education (Illustrative Share)

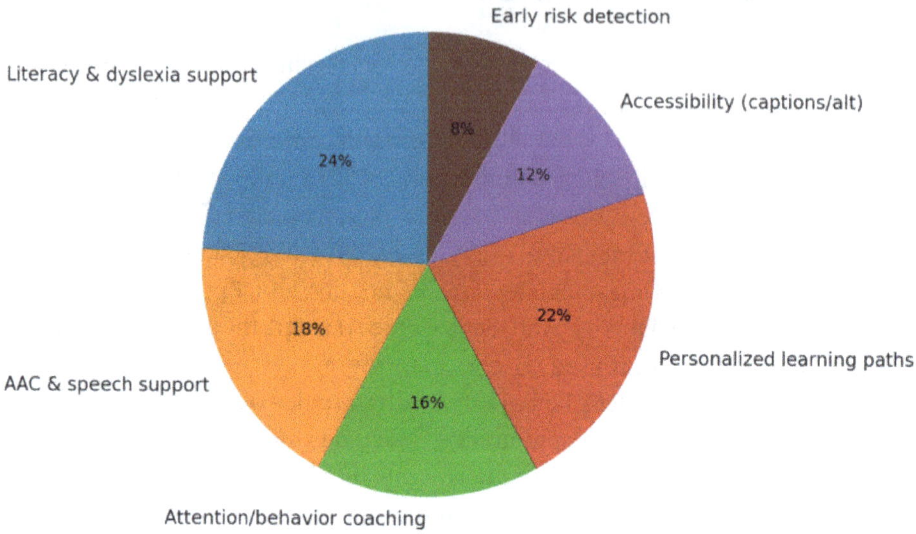

Take, for instance, real-time speech-to-text tools for students with auditory processing disorders. Or AI-based reading apps that can subtly adjust font size, background color, sentence complexity—*in the moment*—based on how a learner is engaging. These aren't blanket accommodations. They're bespoke scaffolds, adjusting themselves minute-by-minute, often without the child needing to ask, which—let's face it—matters, especially for students already carrying the invisible weight of being "different." There's a quiet kind of dignity in not having to raise your hand *again* to say, "This doesn't work for me."

Even more compelling are the AI systems that learn from a student's history of interactions—their successes, their stumbles, their rhythms of engagement—and begin to predict not only what kind of support might help, but when to offer it (Papadakis et al., 2024a, 2024b). Maybe a child tends to struggle with transitions between tasks, or tends to disengage after too many multiple-choice questions. A sensitive AI system can start to thread in different modalities, different paces, different entry points, tailored not to an IEP checkbox but to the child *themselves* (Mehta et al, 2023). And in doing so, it begins to do something that humans often struggle with, especially in overcrowded, under-resourced classrooms: it notices. Consistently. Quietly. Without judgment.

Table 1. Individualized AI Toolkit Matrix

Need area	AI tool example	Benefits	Inclusion safeguards	Risks/Watch-outs
Literacy support	Adaptive reading coach (text+audio)	Adjusts level; decodable + visuals	Accessible fonts; offline packets	Over-simplification; cultural bias
AAC communication	Predictive phrase AAC	Faster symbol/phrase recall	Custom voice; bilingual boards	Privacy; misprediction frustration
Executive function	Planner + nudging agent	Breaks tasks; just-in-time prompts	Quiet mode; student control	Over-reliance; notification fatigue
Behavior/SEL	Emotion-aware SEL coach	Hints, breaks, co-regulation tips	Opt-in sensing; no face tracking	Misreading affect; surveillance risk
Math scaffold	Step-aware tutor	Hints by error pattern; multiple reps	Keyboard/voice input choices	Gaming the hints; narrow goals
Access layer	Captions/alt text/ autotranslate	Removes modality barriers	Caption accuracy audits	Latency; dialect misreads
Risk signals	Early risk detector	Flags disengagement patterns	Teacher override; family view	False positives; labeling risk

Now, this probably all sounds a bit too neat. Let's not pretend that AI always gets it right—or that its predictions are infallible (Yampolskiy, 2024). These systems are trained on data, and data reflects the biases and blind spots of the world that created it. We have to ask: whose patterns are these machines learning from? Who gets to define "normal" or "progress" or "success"? If a child doesn't conform to those models, does the system nudge them back toward conformity, or does it adapt *itself* to fit the child's uniqueness? These are not technical questions. They're philosophical ones. And we should be wary of any AI system that comes with too much confidence and too little humility. But at their best, AI tools don't dictate. They suggest. They highlight. They offer possibilities that a human teacher, juggling 20 or 30 students, might not have the bandwidth to see. This is where inclusion starts to feel less like a box to be ticked and more like a living, evolving relationship between learner, teacher, and technology. It's a partnership—not a replacement, not a hierarchy (Lampropoulos & Papadakis, 2025).

There's also something quietly radical about the idea that AI might help remove *shame* from the learning process. For many students in special education, the real hurdle isn't the academic content. It's the self-consciousness (Starks & Reich, 2023). The feeling of being watched, judged, measured against invisible norms. An AI tutor doesn't sigh when a child stumbles over the same word five times. It doesn't roll its eyes or lose patience. It waits. It adjusts. It tries again. And again. And in that repetition, in that unflinching steadiness, it can create a space where persistence feels possible—and progress feels personal.

Of course, technology doesn't operate in a vacuum. AI tools are only as effective as the ecosystems in which they're embedded. That means training for educators—not just in how to *use* these systems, but in how to interpret their outputs, how to question their assumptions, how to blend their insights with professional judgment and lived experience (Luckin et al, 2022). It also means involving students and families in the design and implementation of these tools. Too often, technologies are built *for* people with disabilities, not *with* them. True inclusion demands co-creation.

It also demands vigilance. Because let's not kid ourselves: AI can easily become another tool of exclusion if we're not careful. Consider the child whose learning profile doesn't "fit" any existing models, or whose cultural background renders them invisible in the datasets. Or the family that doesn't speak the dominant language and is shut out of decisions about how AI systems assess their child. Inclusion isn't just about who *receives* the technology—it's about who *shapes* it, who *questions* it, who *benefits* from it (Dangol et al, 2025).

Still, for all these caveats, there's a kind of quiet power in what AI might offer—not flashy innovation, not dramatic breakthroughs, but subtle, sustained support. A whispered suggestion. A pause. A shift in pace. The ability to say, not with words but with design: *We see you. We're listening. Let's try it this way.* And isn't that what inclusion has always been about? Not just letting someone through the door, but redesigning the space so they never have to ask for a key again. Not just giving a child a seat at the table, but asking what kind of chair they need, and whether the table itself needs to be reimagined.

If we approach AI not as a fix-it tool, but as a mirror—reflecting back to us the ways in which our current systems fall short—then its true promise begins to emerge. It's not about replacing human care. It's about making space for more of it. It's about noticing the child who's been quietly slipping away, about giving voice to needs that words sometimes can't express. It's about inclusion not as an endpoint, but as an ongoing act of attention, adjustment, and affirmation.

In the end, maybe AI's greatest gift to special education isn't its precision or its speed or its scalability. Maybe it's the way it invites us—forces us—to rethink our assumptions about who gets to learn, how, and on what terms. Maybe it's the way it holds up a quiet, persistent question: *What would it mean to build a system that truly fits the child, instead of the other way around?* That's the promise. Not perfection. Not utopia. Just the radical, everyday act of paying attention. Of designing with care. Of choosing to believe that no learner is too different, too slow, too complex to be understood—and supported—in real time, with real tools, by real people who haven't given up on the idea that education, at its best, is for *everyone*.

FROM DIAGNOSIS TO DAILY SUPPORT: HOW AI ADAPTS TO INDIVIDUAL NEEDS

Let's be honest—most diagnostic labels in special education come after a long, winding road. Not a straight path, but a slow accumulation of questions, concerns, gut feelings, missed milestones, awkward parent-teacher meetings, referrals, waitlists, more waitlists, and, eventually, some formal process with official forms and official signatures that stamp a child with a name: ADHD. Autism. Dyslexia. Global developmental delay. Specific learning disorder, not otherwise specified (Intriago et al, 2021). The categories vary, the paperwork stacks, and somewhere in the blur of bureaucracy, there's a real child—aching to be understood.

Diagnosis can be both a relief and a burden. It can open doors to support, yes—but also risks boxing in a child with a static identity, frozen in time, when really, their needs shift like weather. One day, they struggle to initiate a task. The next, they're soaring through it. Some weeks, language is fluid; others, it stalls. Traditional support systems are rarely nimble enough to keep up. They move slowly, like ships turning in water. What a child needs at the time of diagnosis is often already out of sync with what they'll need tomorrow.

This is where AI begins to crack open a different possibility—not diagnosis as a fixed state, but as a living, evolving process (Babushkina, 2023). Not a label, but a lens. A way of seeing—more dynamically, more responsively, and more generously. Let's take a pause and look at how AI enters the scene—not as some all-knowing oracle, but as a pattern-finder, a tracker of nuance, a listener that never stops listening. Imagine a system that doesn't wait for formal assessment to flag concern but begins, gently and quietly, the moment a learner engages. It watches how long a child hovers before clicking, how their cursor moves across a screen, how often they retry a question, how their tone changes across speech-to-text sessions. Noticing, not judging. And that's the subtle magic: AI doesn't diagnose in the traditional sense—it *infers*. It detects variations in behavior over time and across contexts, mapping micro-patterns that might elude the human eye. Maybe a student reads well aloud but avoids written comprehension. Maybe they fly through math in the morning but slow to a crawl after lunch. Maybe anxiety isn't declared but is visible in longer pause times, increased error rates, irregular typing cadence. AI picks up these ripples.

The point isn't to label the student. The point is to respond—early, subtly, precisely (Mollick & Mollick, 2023). And this kind of support doesn't arrive as some grand intervention, either. It comes in smaller, quieter acts: adjusting the complexity of a reading passage without announcing it, switching a multiple-choice question into a visual sorting activity, offering hints instead of punishment for a wrong answer.

These shifts might be invisible to an outside observer, but they can be the difference between engagement and withdrawal for the learner. Between "I can" and "I quit."

Let's consider a practical example: a child with undiagnosed dysgraphia—struggling not with the ideas, but with the physical act of writing. A traditional classroom might miss it for months, even years, chalking it up to laziness or lack of effort (Goodwin et al, 2022). But an AI system tracking keystroke patterns and writing fluency could notice the discrepancy early: rich oral language but inconsistent written output, frequent deletions, erratic sentence length. Instead of flagging failure, the system adjusts—offering voice input options, visual prompts, scaffolded writing templates. All without fanfare. All without the child having to explain themselves *again*.

Figure 2. Support Mix Across a 12-Week Term (Illustrative) (Stacked area)

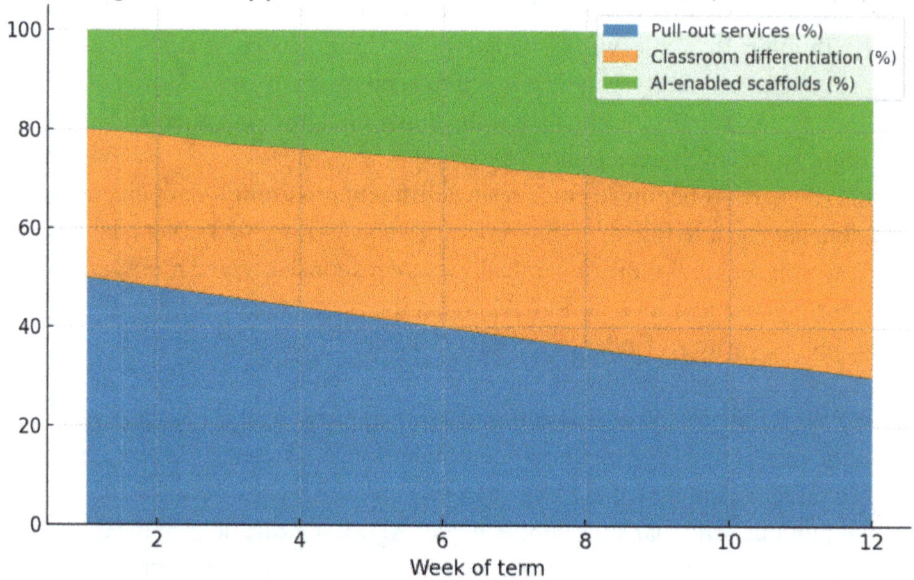

There's something deeply humane about that kind of adaptation—technology responding not to a diagnosis, but to a *need*. No forms. No gatekeeping. Just noticing, adapting, repeating. And yet, none of this works without context. An AI system alone cannot interpret *why* a pattern is happening (Ehsan & Riedl, 2024). A dip in performance could be cognitive overload—or a bad night's sleep. A spike in hesitation could signal a processing delay—or test anxiety—or bullying. This is where the human layer remains irreplaceable. AI might whisper *something's shifted here*. But it takes a teacher, a parent, a therapist to ask the follow-up questions, to read between the lines, to bring in the texture of a life.

What AI offers, then, is not *replacement*, but *amplification*. A kind of cognitive prosthetic for educators—helping them see what's hard to spot in the noise and speed of a real classroom (Youvan, 2024). Because let's not kid ourselves: no matter how devoted, no one teacher can track every child's fluctuations across the school day. Fatigue sets in. Bias creeps in. Time runs out. But AI doesn't get tired. It doesn't forget. It doesn't carry the baggage of assumption.

This constancy can be a gift—but also a risk. Because what happens when AI is treated as the final word? What happens when a system flags a child as "low performing" and that flag sticks—regardless of what the child does next? What happens when an algorithm nudges a student into simplified content so persistently that they never get to stretch? Here's the paradox: a tool meant to personalize can also trap (Khogali & Mekid, 2023). Adaptation can slip into containment. Support can start to look like limitation. That's why adaptability must go both ways—not just *to* the learner, but *with* them.

A well-designed AI system needs a kind of built-in humility (Shneiderman, 2022). It should ask more questions than it answers. It should allow for override, re-interpretation, context. A child is not a set of data points, and no amount of machine learning will ever fully capture what it means to be a 10-year-old with sensory integration challenges and a wild imagination and a fear of failing in front of others. AI may track behavior, but only humans can hold the story behind it.

Still, the potential is too compelling to ignore. Think of students with complex communication needs—those who use augmentative and alternative communication (AAC) devices (Mudau & Nzima, 2023). Traditional systems offer static word banks, rigid categories. But AI-enhanced AAC systems? They learn. They predict. They start to understand which phrases a child uses more often, how they combine symbols, which topics they gravitate toward. Over time, they can offer faster suggestions, more intuitive navigation, even emotional modulation through tone detection. In essence, they can begin to shape a language system that *feels* like the child, rather than forcing the child to conform to the system.

That's adaptation at its most intimate. Not just adjusting *to* the user, but *becoming* part of their expressive identity. But adaptation isn't just about tools. It's about timing. Daily support is about rhythm—meeting the learner not just at their skill level, but at their energy level, their attention span, their emotional state in that *moment*. AI systems embedded into classroom platforms can start to build these profiles—not just "what does this student know?" but "when do they learn best?" "What kinds of errors do they repeat?" "When do they seem to disengage?" And from that, the system can orchestrate the day differently. Maybe it front-loads visual tasks in the morning. Maybe it schedules more breaks after demanding cognitive loads. Maybe it weaves in multimedia stimuli to re-engage a drifting focus.

Again, subtle. Again, powerful. Of course, adaptation means different things in different contexts (Heald et al, 2023). For some students, it might mean simplified instructions. For others, it might mean enriched content with less repetitive drilling. AI can walk both roads—offering challenge without overwhelm, support without condescension. That's the tightrope. Too often, support gets mistaken for lowering the bar. But the right kind of adaptation *raises* the bar—quietly, steadily, while making sure there's a net underneath.

Let's not forget the social side of daily support. AI is beginning to enter the terrain of social-emotional learning, with tools that detect tone, monitor facial expressions, or track patterns of peer interaction (Sethi & Jain, 2024). It's a delicate space, and there are risks—surveillance, privacy, misinterpretation. But when done with transparency and care, these tools can alert teachers to isolation, to sudden shifts in mood, to kids who smile less and withdraw more. Again, not to replace the teacher's instincts—but to sharpen them.

All of this—diagnosis, adaptation, daily support—comes back to one core question: *Who is being seen?* AI, at its best, helps us see more clearly, more consistently, more compassionately. But it can also obscure if it becomes a crutch. It can distract if we chase precision at the expense of presence. So what do we do?

We build systems that listen more than they speak. That adapt without assuming. That offer possibility without pressure (Itzin, 2024). We train educators not just in how to use AI, but how to *question* it—how to ask, "Does this recommendation make sense in this context?" "Does this align with what I know about this child?" "Am I letting this tool guide me—or define me?" And maybe most importantly, we center the learner at every step. Not as a passive recipient of support, but as an active agent in their own learning journey. AI should not just respond *to* the child—it should adapt *with* them, changing as they change, evolving as they grow. Diagnosis is not destiny. It's a point of entry. And daily support isn't static. It's a dance—one that needs rhythm, trust, and room to breathe.

In the end, this is not a story about technology. It's a story about attention. About seeing what's often missed. About meeting needs *before* they become crises. About offering a hand, gently, quietly, without waiting to be asked. That's the promise of AI. Not flashy, not perfect, but present. And sometimes, that's everything.

ETHICAL CONSIDERATIONS AND THE HUMAN ELEMENT IN AI-DRIVEN INTERVENTIONS

There's something unsettling—almost eerie—about watching a machine "understand" a child. Not because it's sinister, exactly. But because it forces us to confront the uneasy question of what understanding *really* means. Does recognizing patterns in keystrokes or predicting meltdowns based on speech latency qualify as comprehension? Or is it mimicry? A well-trained algorithm wearing the costume of care?

This question isn't just philosophical—it's profoundly ethical. As AI-driven tools slide deeper into the folds of special education, we find ourselves navigating an invisible terrain: one filled with promise, yes, but also blind spots, ethical cracks, and moments where the line between help and harm grows faint (Lalar et al, 2025).

Let's start with a truth that often gets glossed over in the excitement: *these systems are watching everything*. Every tap, pause, misstep, retry. Every instance where a student hesitates, clicks away, changes their mind. In some cases, they're recording tone, expression, pupil dilation. It's data, sure—but it's also something more intimate than that. It's behavioral residue. A digital shadow of how someone thinks, struggles, copes. And that raises the first ethical tension: *consent*.

Do students *know* what's being collected? Do families? And not just in the fine print of a permission slip, but in a real, understandable way. Do they know who has access to the data? Who's profiting from it? Whether it might follow the student into future educational decisions, medical evaluations, or—even more insidiously—into systems that weren't built for care at all, like juvenile justice or predictive policing?

Data doesn't just disappear. It travels. It mutates. And when it concerns children—particularly neurodivergent or disabled children—it carries risk. The risk of reduction. Of simplification. Of turning a complex, evolving human being into a static profile that sticks.

There's also the question of *bias*—that old ghost that refuses to die, no matter how advanced the code. AI systems don't start neutral (Xavier, 2025). They learn from data, and that data is always a snapshot of a world already soaked in inequity. If a dataset is built mostly on white, middle-class, English-speaking children, what happens when a Black autistic girl from a multilingual home engages with that system? What assumptions get made? What's flagged as "anomaly" when it's actually cultural norm? What's misread entirely?

These aren't edge cases—they're the heart of the matter. AI can be astonishingly precise, but if the input is skewed, the output is worse than useless. It's damaging. Then there's the matter of *agency*. When an AI platform adapts content or nudges behavior, whose will is it following? Is the child in the driver's seat, or are they being quietly steered toward a narrower, safer path—less challenging, less risky, but also less fulfilling? It's a kind of algorithmic paternalism, well-intentioned but suffocating (Zeng et al, 2023).

We've seen this before. Educational technologies that simplify texts to such a degree that nuance disappears. Behavior tracking apps that reward compliance over creativity. Systems that celebrate "quiet" students while mislabeling curiosity as disruption. When AI defines success, it tends to do so in ways that are measurable, predictable, and easy to optimize (Mohandoss, 2023). But human growth—especially for neurodiverse students—is rarely neat. Sometimes it's nonlinear. Sometimes it's messy. Sometimes it looks like failure before it reveals itself as breakthrough.

Which brings us to perhaps the most difficult ethical question: *What kind of learners are we trying to produce?* Because buried inside every intervention—AI-driven or otherwise—is a vision of the ideal student. Is it someone who sits still, follows directions, and gets the "right" answer fast? Or someone who questions, meanders, reflects, and resists simplification?

If AI tools are calibrated to reward speed, consistency, and accuracy, then where does that leave the child who learns through struggle, who takes their time, whose brilliance doesn't show up in tidy metrics? If the system is optimized for certain outcomes, it might very well be punishing the very creativity or resilience we say we value. And let's not forget about *dependency*. There's a seductive ease in having a system that does the hard noticing for us. That flags students in need (Boie et al, 2024). That auto-adjusts materials. But what happens when educators start to trust the tool more than their own instincts? When a teacher no longer looks up from the dashboard to see the child in front of them? When the human element—the warmth, the gut feeling, the improvisation—is pushed to the margins?

This is the risk of *automation bias*: the slow erosion of human judgment under the weight of machine authority (Kazim & Tomlinson, 2023). It's not that teachers become careless. It's that they become deferential. And when that happens, we lose something irreplaceable: the textured, empathic response that only a human can offer. Because AI doesn't know what it means when a child draws the same figure over and over. It doesn't recognize the subtext in a whispered "I'm fine." It can't hear the heartbreak in silence, or trace the shape of trauma hidden behind academic regression. It might flag the behavior. But it can't hold the grief behind it.

So, what's the answer? Do we abandon AI altogether? No. That would be throwing the compass away because the map has flaws. Instead, we need to *recenter the human* in every part of the process. That means involving educators, families, and students themselves in the design and testing of these systems. Not as token users, but as co-creators. It means demanding transparency—about what data is collected, how it's used, and what assumptions underlie the algorithms (Kossow et al, 2022). It means building in opt-outs, overrides, and human-in-the-loop models that keep judgment where it belongs: in the hands of people who know the child beyond the screen. It also means cultivating *ethical literacy* among educators. Not just how to operate AI tools, but how to interrogate them. To ask: What values are embedded in this system? Who does it serve? Who does it ignore? What gets erased in the pursuit of efficiency?

This kind of literacy doesn't come in a training manual. It comes through dialogue. Reflection. Discomfort. The willingness to pause and say, "Just because we *can* automate this, does that mean we *should*?" And finally, we must reclaim *slowness*. In a field obsessed with scaling and optimizing, there's a quiet rebellion in slowing down. In listening longer. In resisting the urge to quantify everything. In choosing relationships over results. Because the human element isn't just some sentimental add-on to AI systems (Chignell et al, 2023). It's the heart of the thing. It's the difference between assistance and alienation. Between adaptation and assimilation. Between care and control.

In the context of special education, this becomes even more urgent. These are children who've already been misread, underestimated, pathologized. They deserve tools that see them fully—but also teachers who *refuse* to reduce them to metrics. The future of AI in education is not inevitable. It's being written now—in code, yes, but also in policy, in pedagogy, in quiet daily choices. Will we build systems that honor complexity, or erase it? Will we use these tools to deepen connection, or to outsource care? There are no easy answers here. But maybe that's the point. Maybe ethics isn't a destination, but a practice. A way of staying awake. Of asking, again and again, not just what works—but what's *right*. And in that asking, in that wrestling, in that refusal to settle for convenience over conscience—we just might find our way.

CHALLENGES, GAPS, AND THE DANGER OF OVER-AUTOMATION

It's easy to get swept up in the momentum—this accelerating narrative that artificial intelligence is the inevitable answer to every inefficiency, every unmet need, every child who has ever slipped through the cracks of an overburdened education system. The idea is seductive: personalized learning at scale, 24/7 responsiveness, real-time insight, frictionless adaptation (Singh et al, 2024). It sounds like progress. And in some ways, it is. But the danger in chasing innovation too quickly, too blindly, is that we start confusing speed for substance, automation for understanding, prediction for care. Let's stop and ask an uncomfortable question: what happens when we automate too much? What do we lose when machines become the default medium through which children are seen, assessed, supported—even known? That question haunts this space.

One of the central challenges in deploying AI within special education is deceptively simple: *context blindness*. Machines process data. They excel at finding patterns. But they do so without story (Hardt & Recht, 2021). A sudden dip in attention might be read as disengagement when it's actually trauma resurfacing. A delayed response might trigger an alert for cognitive regression, when in reality, the child was daydreaming about their pet rabbit or worrying about an upcoming custody hearing. Algorithms don't know about sleepless nights, unstable housing, or the quiet toll of being misunderstood every day at school.

When decisions are made on the basis of pattern recognition alone—stripped of nuance, stripped of human intuition—support becomes misaligned (Darveau, 2023). Worse, it becomes oppressive. A child who is already struggling gets flagged again and again by a system that doesn't understand their rhythm, doesn't ask why, just responds. And the response isn't always helpful. Sometimes it narrows the field: easier tasks, shorter texts, fewer risks. All in the name of personalization. All in the name of help. But this is the paradox of automation: it promises personalization while subtly enforcing conformity. If the algorithm has learned that most students succeed when tasks follow a certain structure, it may nudge everyone—including those who thrive on deviation—toward that model. Quietly. Invisibly. In ways that feel supportive on the surface but flatten the learner beneath.

Here's the rub: what's optimized for the majority rarely serves the margins. And special education *is* the margin, by design. There's also the issue of *infrastructure and access* (Azzahra et al, 2022). AI doesn't exist in a vacuum. It requires hardware, bandwidth, maintenance, and training. Rural schools, underfunded districts, and communities already marginalized by systemic inequities are often the last to receive new technologies—and the first to be experimented on when they do. Tools that are hailed as revolutionary in tech-savvy pilot programs don't always translate to overcrowded classrooms with unstable Wi-Fi and one overworked teacher managing a dozen IEPs by hand.

Add to this the *language and cultural gaps* embedded in many AI systems. NLP (natural language processing) models, for example, are trained predominantly on dominant languages and dialects (Joshi et al, 2025). A child whose speech reflects a regional accent, a cultural idiom, or code-switching behavior may be misread—marked as incorrect, unclear, even "behind." Not because they lack skill, but because the system was never trained to hear them properly.

Now layer on *data vulnerability*—a quiet, but looming issue. AI systems rely on data. Lots of it. And the kind of data gathered from students—especially those receiving special education services—is sensitive: cognitive assessments, behavioral logs, emotional indicators, medical reports. When this data is stored, shared, and analyzed, the line between educational support and surveillance begins to blur. Who owns the data? How long is it stored? Can it be sold? Used in other algorithms? Shared with third-party vendors? These questions often go unanswered—or are buried in dense policy documents that few families have the time or legal literacy to unpack. And let's not forget *automation bias*—that human tendency to trust the output of a machine more than our own eyes (Stock-Homburg & Nguyen, 2023). If a dashboard says a child is improving, we might believe it, even when our gut says something's off. If a predictive model says a student is at risk, we might intervene prematurely or inappropriately. Teachers—already under pressure to justify their decisions with data—may begin to default to the AI's suggestions, even when those suggestions don't match their lived understanding of the child.

It's a slippery slope. Over time, the educator's role shifts from interpreter to implementer. Professional judgment becomes secondary. Autonomy erodes. And here's the irony: in trying to make systems more efficient, we end up making people more robotic. Teachers begin following prompts instead of their instincts. Students start shaping their behavior to what the machine expects (Kontorovich & Ovadiya, 2023). The learning environment becomes less relational, more transactional. And the classroom—that messy, unpredictable, beautiful human space—loses some of its magic. But perhaps the most haunting danger of over-automation isn't technical at all. It's *emotional distancing*.

A student struggling with expressive language might be paired with an AI-based writing tutor (Etaat, 2024). The tutor provides instant feedback, endless patience, and zero judgment. On paper, that's ideal. But what if, over time, the student never gets to express themselves to a human? What if their stories, their metaphors, their odd, brilliant ways of thinking are only ever processed by a machine? What if no one *hears* them—not really?

There is something irreplaceable about being witnessed by another human being. About a teacher leaning in, saying, "Tell me more." About a therapist seeing past the behavior to the child beneath. AI can simulate responsiveness, but it cannot hold presence. It cannot share vulnerability (Vallor & Vierkant, 2024). It cannot, no matter how advanced, *care* in the ways that humans can. And care is not an accessory in special education. It's the foundation. This is not to suggest we throw out the machines. Far from it. The goal isn't rejection—it's recalibration.

We need to build systems that understand their own limitations. AI that flags its uncertainty. Dashboards that leave room for teacher annotations (Gobert et al, 2023). Platforms that invite student voice—not just behavior tracking, but narrative input. Tools that support reflection, not just reaction. We also need to preserve space for *slowness*. For conversation. For confusion. For the kind of learning that can't be logged in a spreadsheet. Not everything valuable shows up in the data trail. Not every breakthrough is measurable. And let's train educators—not just in how to *use* AI tools, but in how to resist them when needed. To know when to say: "I see what the system is saying, but I see something else." Let's equip them with the confidence to challenge the machine, not just implement it.

Finally, we must design with care. Not just for efficiency or engagement, but for dignity. For plurality. For edge cases. For complexity. That means involving students and families—especially those with disabilities—in the design process. It means funding research that centers ethical complexity, not just technical innovation. It means listening, deeply and often, to the people on the ground. Because at the end of the day, special education is not a field that benefits from shortcuts. It is a slow, deliberate, relationship-driven practice. And if we forget that in our rush to automate, we risk recreating the very systems of exclusion we sought to dismantle. Progress isn't about faster systems. It's about deeper connection. And sometimes, the most radical thing we can do is pause—long enough to ask, "Are we building tools that serve the child? Or are we building tools that ask the child to serve the system?" If we get that answer wrong, no amount of machine learning will set it right.

TOWARD A COLLABORATIVE FUTURE: EDUCATORS, AI, AND THE INDIVIDUAL LEARNER

There's a curious tension humming beneath the surface of our technological age—an unspoken anxiety, maybe, or a quiet optimism wearing uncertainty like a coat that doesn't quite fit (Stone, 2024). It lives in the question: *Who gets to lead the classroom in the age of AI?* Is it the teacher with decades of experience and stories layered in intuition? Is it the algorithm, sharp-edged and infinitely scalable? Or is it, perhaps, something more intricate—something relational, collaborative, human-machine hybrid?

Let's be honest: education has always been personal. At its best, it is an act of witnessing, of reaching out across the gap between someone who knows and someone who's still learning, and saying—not just "I'll show you how," but "I see you." Special education, especially, lives in that space. It's slow work. Uneven. Often invisible. It's watching for what doesn't get said. It's knowing when to press and when to pull back. When to trust the curriculum and when to rip it up entirely.

So where does AI fit into that kind of landscape? Not neatly, that's for sure. Not without friction (Wallace, 2022). But maybe the goal isn't to make it neat. Maybe it's to let it be complicated—and to work within the messiness of that. Because AI, for all its promises, cannot care. It cannot celebrate a child's breakthrough with real joy. It cannot mourn their setbacks with the ache of someone who's invested. What it *can* do is observe. Detect. Offer patterns we might have missed. Provide support without fatigue. That's not nothing. In fact, when paired with a skilled, compassionate educator, it can be transformative. But it's the *pairing* that matters. AI alone is just infrastructure. A scaffold. Wires and math. It doesn't become meaningful until it's picked up by a teacher who knows what to do with it (Lenke & Tenberge, 2022). Someone who can say, "Yes, this is helpful," or just as importantly, "No, this isn't right for this student right now." That act of discernment—that blend of data and heart—is the true engine of collaboration.

To move toward a collaborative future, then, we must stop talking about AI as a replacement and start thinking about it as a partner. Not an equal partner, not one with feelings or insight, but a partner nonetheless—one that can carry some of the cognitive load, spot early warning signs, adjust content dynamically, or relieve a bit of the weight that so often leaves teachers burned out and spread thin. But for that partnership to work, something has to shift. First, the technology must become *transparent*. Teachers can't collaborate with a black box (Yıldırım & Demir, 2022). They need to understand how the system is making its decisions. Not every line of code, no—but the logic, the thresholds, the "why" behind the recommendations. Is it flagging a student because their scores dropped by 10%? Because their screen time increased? Because their engagement pattern mirrors that of other struggling students? Without clarity, trust erodes. And without trust, collaboration dies. Second, professional development must evolve. Teachers don't need to become coders. But they do need to become critical users of AI. That means learning how to question it, how to adapt its outputs to the messy realities of a real classroom, how to notice when the tool is missing the mark. It means resisting the seductive pull of efficiency when it comes at the cost of nuance.

We also need to foster *student agency* within this triad. AI is often deployed *to* learners, rarely *with* them (Bosch & Kruger, 2024). But what if the student became part of the loop? What if they could see how the system is reading them—and push back? What if they could say, "No, I don't want easier questions today, I want harder ones," or, "That voice the bot uses makes me anxious," or even, "Stop tracking my eye movements—I just don't like it." A truly collaborative future includes the learner not as a data point but as an actor (Yang, 2023). A co-author of their own learning path. That means giving them options. Letting them choose how they engage. Letting them know when and how they're being supported by AI—and giving them the right to opt out. And while we're at it, let's acknowledge that *not every child wants or needs the same kind of AI support.* Some thrive with constant feedback; others find it stifling. Some find voice interfaces liberating; others find them dehumanizing. This isn't a bug in the system—it's a feature of humanity. A collaborative model doesn't demand uniformity; it embraces divergence.

This requires flexible design. Open platforms that let educators tweak, remix, silence certain features, amplify others. It means building tools that adapt not just to the student, but to the teaching style, the cultural context, the values of the school. A system that might work beautifully in a Scandinavian classroom might fall flat in rural India. A chatbot trained on Western speech patterns might misread the tone of an ESL learner from Lebanon or Nigeria. Context is everything. One-size-fits-all, in education, has always been a lie. So, let's imagine, just for a moment, what a well-functioning collaboration between AI, educator, and learner might look like.

Figure 3. Program Usage vs. Learning Gains (Line)

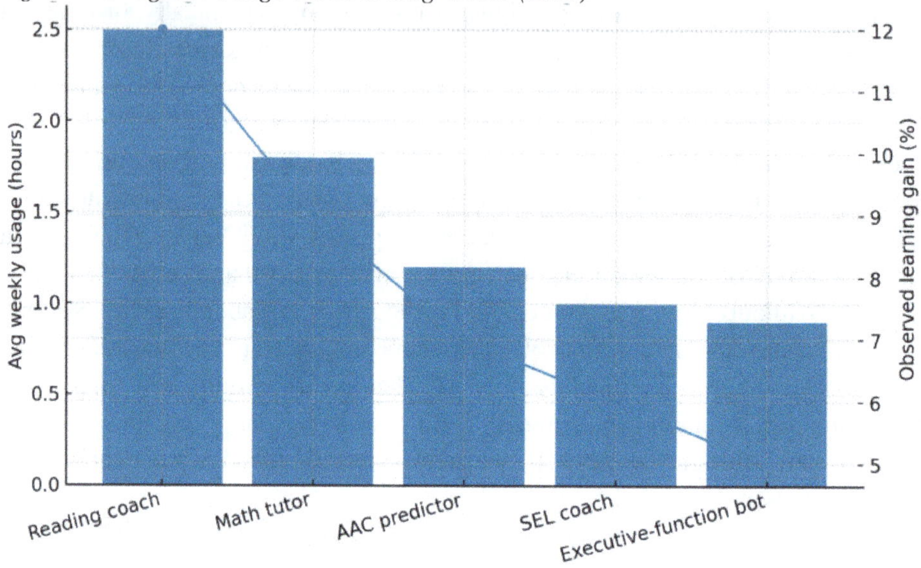

A teacher logs into a platform and sees that three students struggled with the transition between two topics yesterday—not because they failed the quiz, but because their engagement metrics (dwell time, self-correction rate, tone variability in responses) subtly shifted (Lin & Riccomini, 2025). The teacher clicks into one student's data and sees a gentle suggestion from the AI: "Try reintroducing the concept with a real-world example; past data suggests higher retention for this learner." The teacher, who knows the child loves basketball, decides to teach the math concept through free-throw stats instead (Kayyali, 2025).

The student engages, surprised. "How'd you know I like basketball?"

The teacher smiles. "I just know you."

And the AI stays quiet, in the background, as it should.

This is not about replacing relationships with algorithms. It's about *deepening* those relationships by freeing up time and energy for what matters most.

Now, of course, not everything will go smoothly. There will be clunky rollouts. Bias will rear its head in unexpected ways. Some tools will overpromise and underdeliver. There will be frustration. Resistance. And that's okay. Collaboration doesn't mean harmony at all times. It means commitment (Berlian & Huda, 2022). The willingness to stay in the room, to keep listening, adjusting, refusing to let the partnership dissolve into either technophilia or technophobia. Because let's face it: some of the loudest voices in this conversation aren't in the classroom. They're in Silicon Valley boardrooms. In think tanks. In glossy keynote speeches about "the future of learning." And while some of those voices are visionary, many are disconnected from the daily realities of teachers working with kids who can't sit still, who speak in stims or drawings, who carry more trauma than textbooks.

If we want a collaborative future, we need to *decenter hype* and recentralize experience. Give teachers the mic (Waring, 2024). Give students the mic. Build with them, not for them. There's also a deeper cultural shift we need to make—one that moves away from seeing AI as magical and begins to see it as mundane. As a tool. Not glamorous, not terrifying. Just… there. Part of the background. Reliable. Flexible. Like a good pencil or a sturdy desk. Something that helps when it's used with thought, and sits quietly when it's not needed. Because real collaboration isn't flashy. It's iterative. It involves trust, revision, mutual respect. It means admitting when something isn't working and trying something else. And that kind of relationship—between AI and educators, between educators and students—isn't built in code. It's built in conversation.

So, what might the next few years look like, if we get this right? Maybe classrooms get quieter—not from disengagement, but from concentration. Students leaning in, working at their own pace, getting nudges just when they need them. Teachers roaming, not lecturing. Noticing more. Intervening less, but more precisely. Maybe IEP meetings get more reflective. More textured. Educators and parents reviewing not just standardized test scores but rich learning maps—stories told in data and voice, charts and memories (Ransom, 2023). AI providing the spine, but humans shaping the soul. Maybe students become less afraid of "getting it wrong," because the system doesn't rush to judgment. Maybe teachers feel less alone, because the machine notices what they notice—and sometimes what they don't. Maybe learning becomes slower, deeper, less performative. Less about grades and more about growth. More about *becoming*.

We're not there yet. But we could be. If we build with care. If we listen more than we automate. If we treat AI not as savior or threat, but as collaborator. Because in the end, this isn't a story about machines. It's a story about us—about how we choose to learn, to teach, to build. About whether we can let go of control just enough to let something new emerge—something more responsive, more equitable, more alive. And if that sounds messy… well, maybe that's the best sign we're on the right track.

CONCLUSION

There is a quiet kind of hope that threads its way through this entire conversation—one that resists both utopianism and despair. As we look toward the future of AI in special education, we are not faced with a question of *if* technology will play a role, but rather *how*, *to what extent*, and *on whose terms*. It is easy to get swept up in the allure of precision, automation, and the endless possibilities that machine learning offers. But special education reminds us, perhaps more than any other field, that learning is not just a cognitive process—it is emotional, social, and profoundly human.

AI may one day predict when a student with autism is on the brink of sensory overload or help a child with dyslexia navigate a sea of text more confidently. But it will not replace the affirming voice of a teacher who believes in that student. It cannot replicate the nonverbal rapport between a child and a caregiver built over years of shared struggle and success. What it can do, however, is relieve some of the burdens—analyze the data, personalize the tasks, flag the warning signs—so that human beings can do what they do best: connect.

This future will require something that doesn't often come naturally in education systems: humility. Humility to admit that we don't have all the answers. That algorithms trained on massive datasets may still fail to capture the nuance of a single child's story. That for all our talk about innovation, we are still learning—still experimenting with how to build classrooms that truly work for everyone. AI might be fast, but building ethical, equitable systems is slow, and it must be. Slowness, in this context, is not a weakness—it is a form of care.

The risks are real. Algorithmic bias can replicate the very exclusions we are trying to dismantle. Over-reliance on AI may deskill educators or create overstandardized environments in the name of personalization. Data-driven systems might overlook the subtleties of culture, language, trauma, and lived experience. These are not theoretical concerns—they are active dangers that require constant vigilance, ongoing regulation, and, most importantly, inclusive design led by people who actually work in special education.

Still, the potential is profound. Imagine a world in which every child—regardless of how they process language, regulate emotion, or engage with the world—is met with tools that adapt to them, rather than the other way around. Imagine schools where diagnostic processes are accelerated, interventions are immediate, and feedback loops are continuous—not to replace teachers, but to empower them. This is not a fantasy. With care, collaboration, and courage, it is entirely within reach.

In the end, the future of AI in special education won't be shaped by code alone. It will be shaped by people—by our values, our questions, our willingness to listen to those who are most affected. If we get it right, AI won't make us less human in the process. It might just make us *more* so.

REFERENCES

Azzahra, I. M., Diana, R. R., Nirwana, E. S., Wiranata, R. R. S., & Andriani, K. M. (2022). Learning facilities and infrastructure based on the characteristics of Children with Special Needs in inclusive education. Al-Athfaal. *Jurnal Ilmiah Pendidikan Anak Usia Dini, 5*(2), 169–190. DOI: 10.24042/ajipaud.v5i2.14432

Babushkina, D. (2023). Are we justified attributing a mistake in diagnosis to an AI diagnostic system? *AI and Ethics, 3*(2), 567–584. DOI: 10.1007/s43681-022-00189-x

Berlian, Z., & Huda, M. (2022). Reflecting culturally responsive and communicative teaching (CRCT) through partnership commitment. *Education Sciences, 12*(5), 295. DOI: 10.3390/educsci12050295

Boie, M. A. K., Dalsgaard, C., & Caviglia, F. (2024). Digital instinct—A keyword for making sense of students' digital practice and digital literacy. *British Journal of Educational Technology, 55*(2), 668–686. DOI: 10.1111/bjet.13398

Bosch, C., & Kruger, D. (2024). AI chatbots as Open Educational Resources: Enhancing student agency and Self-Directed Learning. *Italian Journal of Educational Technology, 32*(1), 53–68.

Chignell, M., Wang, L., Zare, A., & Li, J. (2023). The evolution of HCI and human factors: Integrating human and artificial intelligence. *ACM Transactions on Computer-Human Interaction, 30*(2), 1–30. DOI: 10.1145/3557891

Cumming, T. M., & Rose, M. C. (2022). Exploring universal design for learning as an accessibility tool in higher education: A review of the current literature. *Australian Educational Researcher, 49*(5), 1025–1043. DOI: 10.1007/s13384-021-00471-7

Dangol, A., Lewis, A., Suh, H., Hong, X., Meadan, H., Fogarty, J., & Kientz, J. A. (2025, April). "I Want to Think Like an SLP": A Design Exploration of AI-Supported Home Practice in Speech Therapy. In Proceedings of the 2025 CHI Conference on Human Factors in Computing Systems (pp. 1-22).

Darveau, P. (2023). Decision Trees: Modeling with fast intuition and slow, deliberate analysis.

Done, P. (2022). *The Art of Teaching Children: All I Learned from a Lifetime in the Classroom*. Simon and Schuster.

Ehsan, U., & Riedl, M. O. (2024). Explainability pitfalls: Beyond dark patterns in explainable AI. *Patterns (New York, N.Y.), 5*(6), 100971. DOI: 10.1016/j.patter.2024.100971 PMID: 39005480

Etaat, F. (2024). The Effect of AI-Based Applications on EFL Writing Skill Development: An Inquiry into Integration of AI into Language Learning (Master's thesis, UiT Norges arktiske universitet).

Gobert, J. D., Sao Pedro, M. A., & Betts, C. G. (2023). An AI-based teacher dashboard to support students' inquiry: Design principles, features, and technological specifications. In *Handbook of research on science education* (pp. 1011–1044). Routledge. DOI: 10.4324/9780367855758-37

Goodwin, B., Rouleau, K., Abla, C., Baptiste, K., Gibson, T., & Kimball, M. (2022). *The new classroom instruction that works: The best research-based strategies for increasing student achievement.* ASCD.

Hardt, M., & Recht, B. (2021). Patterns, predictions, and actions: A story about machine learning. arXiv preprint arXiv:2102.05242.

Heald, J. B., Lengyel, M., & Wolpert, D. M. (2023). Contextual inference in learning and memory. *Trends in Cognitive Sciences*, *27*(1), 43–64. DOI: 10.1016/j.tics.2022.10.004 PMID: 36435674

Intriago, K. E. C., Rodríguez, L. M. A., & Cevallos, L. A. T. (2021). Specific learning difficulty: Autism, dyscalculia, dyslexia and dysgraphia. International Research Journal of Engineering. *IT and Scientific Research*, *7*(3), 97–106.

Itzin, C. (2024). Ageism awareness training: a model for group work. In *Dependency and Interdependency in Old Age* (pp. 114–126). Routledge. DOI: 10.4324/9781032715940-12

Joshi, A., Dabre, R., Kanojia, D., Li, Z., Zhan, H., Haffari, G., & Dippold, D. (2025). Natural language processing for dialects of a language: A survey. *ACM Computing Surveys*, *57*(6), 1–37. DOI: 10.1145/3712060

Kayyali, M. (2022). Equity, Equality, Diversity, and Inclusion as Key Performance Indicators in Higher Education. *Online Submission*, *3*(5), 1–3.

Kayyali, M. (2025). E-Learning Platforms and Their Influence on Lifelong Learning. In Impact of Digitalization on Education and Social Sustainability (pp. 155-176). IGI Global.

Kazim, T., & Tomlinson, J. (2023). Automation bias and the principles of judicial review. *Judicial Review*, *28*(1), 9–16. DOI: 10.1080/10854681.2023.2189405

Khan, S. (2024). *Brave New Words: How AI Will Revolutionize Education (and why That's a Good Thing)*. Penguin.

Khogali, H. O., & Mekid, S. (2023). The blended future of automation and AI: Examining some long-term societal and ethical impact features. *Technology in Society, 73*, 102232. DOI: 10.1016/j.techsoc.2023.102232

Kontorovich, I., & Ovadiya, T. (2023). How narratives about the secondary-tertiary transition shape undergraduate tutors' sense-making of their teaching. *Educational Studies in Mathematics, 113*(1), 125–146. DOI: 10.1007/s10649-023-10211-6

Kossow, N., Windwehr, S., & Jenkins, M. (2022). *Algorithmic transparency and accountability*. Transparency International.

Lalar, S., Kumar, T., Kumar, R., & Kumar, S. (2025). Unlocking Potential: The Role of Artificial Intelligence in Revolutionizing Special Education for Inclusive Learning. In Impacts of Generative AI on the Future of Research and Education (pp. 201-232). IGI Global.

Lampropoulos, G., & Papadakis, S. (2025). The Educational Value of Artificial Intelligence and Social Robots. In *Social Robots in Education* (pp. 3–15). Springer. DOI: 10.1007/978-3-031-82915-4_1

Lata, P. (2024). Towards Equitable Learning: Exploring Artificial Intelligence in Inclusive Education.

Lenke, M., & Tenberge, C. (2022). Future Primary Teacher Education: Computational Thinking and STEAM. *PATT, 39*, 428.

Lin, T., & Riccomini, P. (2025). Inclusive Education in rural settings: Leveraging technology for improved math learning outcomes among students with disabilities. *Journal of Special Education Technology, 40*(2), 219–226. DOI: 10.1177/01626434241263045

Luckin, R., Cukurova, M., Kent, C., & Du Boulay, B. (2022). Empowering educators to be AI-ready. *Computers and Education: Artificial Intelligence, 3*, 100076.

Marino, M. T., Vasquez, E., Dieker, L., Basham, J., & Blackorby, J. (2023). The future of artificial intelligence in special education technology. *Journal of Special Education Technology, 38*(3), 404–416. DOI: 10.1177/01626434231165977

Mehta, P., Chillarge, G. R., Sapkal, S. D., Shinde, G. R., & Kshirsagar, P. S. (2023). Inclusion of children with special needs in the educational system, artificial intelligence (AI). In *AI-assisted special education for students with exceptional needs* (pp. 156–185). IGI Global. DOI: 10.4018/979-8-3693-0378-8.ch007

Mohandoss, K. (2023). The Omnipotent and Omnipresent Inevitability of Artificial Intelligence (AI): AI Is All about Creating a Win-Win Situation. In Artificial intelligence in Pharmaceutical Sciences (pp. 1-17). CRC Press.

Mollick, E., & Mollick, L. (2023). Assigning AI: Seven approaches for students, with prompts. arXiv preprint arXiv:2306.10052.

Mudau, S. P., & Nzima, D. R. (2023). Teacher perspectives on the use of augmentative and alternative communication systems for learners with complex communication needs. *South African Journal of Education*, *43*(4), 2170. DOI: 10.15700/saje.v43n4a2170

Nguyen, A. (2024). Addressing Inequities: The Struggle for Quality Education and Life for Disabled and Marginalized Youth.

Papadakis, S., Lytvynova, S. H., Ivanova, S. M., & Selyshcheva, I. A. (2024b). *Advancing lifelong learning with AI-enhanced ICT: A review of 3L-Person 2024.* In *CEUR Workshop Proceedings (9th International Workshop on Professional Retraining and Life-Long Learning using ICT: Person-oriented Approach — 3L-Person 2024, Lviv, Ukraine, September 25, 2023).* CEUR-WS.org.

Papadakis, S., Striuk, A. M., Kravtsov, H. M., Shyshkina, M. P., Marienko, M. V., & Danylchuk, H. B. (2024a). *Embracing digital innovation and cloud technologies for transformative learning experiences.* In *Proceedings of the 11th Workshop on Cloud Technologies in Education (CTE 2023), Kryvyi Rih, Ukraine, December 22, 2023.* CEUR Workshop Proceedings.

Ransom, K. L. (2023). *How Do Parental Experiences During the IEP Process Impact or Inform Education Plans for Their Children and Education Leaders to Improve IEP Processes?* Temple University.

Sethi, S. S., & Jain, K. (2024). AI technologies for social emotional learning: Recent research and future directions. *Journal of Research in Innovative Teaching & Learning*, *17*(2), 213–225. DOI: 10.1108/JRIT-03-2024-0073

Shneiderman, B. (2022). *Human-centered AI.* Oxford University Press. DOI: 10.1093/oso/9780192845290.001.0001

Singh, H., Chauhan, U., Chauhan, S. P. S., Saxena, A., & Kumari, P. (2024). Adaptive and personalized learning in industry 5.0 education. In *Infrastructure Possibilities and Human-Centered Approaches With Industry 5.0* (pp. 1–19). IGI Global Scientific Publishing. DOI: 10.4018/979-8-3693-0782-3.ch001

Starks, A. C., & Reich, S. M. (2023). "What about special ed?": Barriers and enablers for teaching with technology in special education. Computers & Education, 193, 104665.

Stock-Homburg, R., & Nguyen, M. A. (2023). See No evil, hear No evil: How users blindly overrely on robots with automation bias.

Stone, B. W. (2024). Generative AI in Higher Education: Uncertain Students, Ambiguous Use Cases, and Mercenary Perspectives. *Teaching of Psychology*, •••, 00986283241305398.

Vallor, S., & Vierkant, T. (2024). Find the gap: AI, responsible agency and vulnerability. *Minds and Machines*, *34*(3), 20. DOI: 10.1007/s11023-024-09674-0 PMID: 38855350

Wallace, R. (2022). How AI founders on adversarial landscapes of fog and friction. *The Journal of Defense Modeling and Simulation*, *19*(3), 519–538. DOI: 10.1177/1548512920962227

Waring, R. (2024). Microcultures of collaboration: entangled artistic pedagogies for students and educator (Doctoral dissertation, Bournemouth University).

Xavier, B. (2025). Biases within AI: Challenging the illusion of neutrality. *AI & Society*, *40*(3), 1545–1546. DOI: 10.1007/s00146-024-01985-1

Yampolskiy, R. V. (2024). *AI: Unexplainable, unpredictable, uncontrollable*. CRC Press. DOI: 10.1201/9781003440260

Yang, X. (2023). A historical review of collaborative learning and cooperative learning. *TechTrends*, *67*(4), 718–728. DOI: 10.1007/s11528-022-00823-9 PMID: 36711122

Yıldırım, Ö., & Demir, S. B. (2022). Inside the black box: Do teachers practice assessment as learning? *International Journal of Assessment Tools in Education*, *9*(Special Issue), 46–71. DOI: 10.21449/ijate.1132923

Youvan, D. C. (2024). Amplification Through Progression: From Analog Signals to Artificial Intelligence.

Zeng, Z., Dai, H., Zhang, D. J., Zhang, H., Zhang, R., Xu, Z., & Shen, Z. J. M. (2023). The impact of social nudges on user-generated content for social network platforms. *Management Science*, *69*(9), 5189–5208. DOI: 10.1287/mnsc.2022.4622

KEY TERMS AND DEFINITIONS

Augmentative and Alternative Communication (AAC): AI-enhanced tools that predict phrases/symbols and speed up communication for non-speaking learners.

Early risk detection: models that quietly flag disengagement or struggle patterns so staff can intervene before a crisis.

Ethical safeguards: privacy, consent, bias checks, and transparency so AI supports dignity rather than surveillance.

Human-in-the-loop: designs that keep teachers and families in control, with overrides and explainable recommendations.

Individualized support: AI-assisted scaffolds that adapt minute-by-minute to a learner's needs rather than fixed, one-time accommodations.

Student agency: giving learners choices (opt-in features, difficulty control, mode switching) so AI adapts with them, not to them.

Universal Design for Learning (UDL): proactive accessibility (captions, alt-text, flexible formats) amplified by adaptive AI.

Chapter 8
Artificial Intelligence in Gifted STEAM Education: Teachers' Perspectives on Differentiation, Inclusion, and Creativity in Mixed-Ability Classrooms

Emmanouil D. Milakis
http://orcid.org/0009-0000-5622-2815
European University Cyprus, Cyprus

Constantina Corazon Argyrakou
http://orcid.org/0009-0003-4161-1385
Harokopio University of Athens, Greece

Agariadne Dwinggo Samala
http://orcid.org/0000-0002-4425-0605
Universitas Negeri Padang, Indonesia

ABSTRACT

This qualitative study explores how primary and secondary educators perceive the integration of Artificial Intelligence (AI) in gifted STEAM education within mixed-ability classrooms. This study examines how AI is framed as a pedagogical tool for creativity, differentiation, and inclusion. Educators recognized AI's potential to inspire imaginative engagement and support individualized learning but voiced concerns about student dependency, weakened collaboration, and reduced critical inquiry. Findings reveal ambivalence: AI is seen both as a creative ally and a pedagogical risk. Meaningful integration depends less on technology itself and more

DOI: 10.4018/979-8-2600-0101-1.ch008

on socio-pedagogical frameworks, teacher expertise, curricular fit, and ethical awareness. The study calls for reflective, critically literate approaches to AI in gifted education, challenging techno-optimistic narratives and emphasizing the relational dimensions of teaching and learning.

1. INTRODUCTION

1.1 Conceptualizing Giftedness and Differentiated Education

Giftedness in childhood is a multidimensional construct situated at the intersection of above-average ability, creativity, and intrinsic motivation, as articulated in Renzulli's (2021) Three-Ring Model. Responding to this complexity, gifted education requires instructional differentiation that embraces creative, interdisciplinary, and non-traditional methods. Such differentiation often involves curriculum acceleration and enrichment, adjusting pace, depth, and content to align with students' advanced capabilities (Karnes & Bean, 2021).

Equally essential is a psychosocial support framework that addresses emotional challenges and fosters holistic development (Worrell et al., 2019). Gifted education, therefore, integrates socio-emotional learning to ensure both intellectual growth and personal well-being. At its core, the approach emphasizes inquiry-based and problem-solving pedagogies that engage learners in authentic, reflective, and participatory knowledge construction (VanTassel-Baska & Brown, 2021).

1.2 STEAM Education and Creative Learning in Gifted Contexts

STEAM education, integrating Science, Technology, Engineering, Arts, and Mathematics, has gained prominence as a transdisciplinary model that fosters creative and critical thinking in gifted education (Kaymakci & Can, 2023). Central to this approach is its focus on solving real-world problems, encouraging collaboration and innovation across disciplines through both experiential and technological means (Henriksen et al., 2019).

Assessment within STEAM is grounded in inclusive design principles that support equitable participation and student-centered environments (Milakis, 2025). The inclusion of the Arts enhances scientific creativity, particularly in mixed-ability settings where differentiated learning is essential (Konkus & Topsakal, 2022). As a result, such transdisciplinary approaches have attracted growing international interest for its potential to advance both cognitive and socio-emotional development among diverse learners (Lampropoulos & Papadakis, 2025).

1.3 Structural Challenges and Educational Equity

The implementation of inclusive and interdisciplinary gifted education is deeply influenced by structural and cultural contexts. National education systems and societal views on giftedness shape both policy and practice (Riga & Malafantis, 2023), while broader inequalities, such as disparities between urban and rural areas or economically developed and under-resourced regions, further constrain access to identification, specialized programs, and teacher training (Kalobo & Setlalentoa, 2024).

Even within the same country, students in marginalized areas may face limited opportunities for differentiated instruction despite equal potential (Stambaugh & Wood, 2021). Unequal access to technology, materials, and infrastructure hampers the effective application of inclusive practices, whereas well-funded systems are better equipped to support curricular flexibility and cognitive diversity (Besnoy, 2021). These disparities highlight the need to situate inclusive gifted education within both cultural frameworks and the socioeconomic and geographic conditions that shape educational equity (Peters et al., 2019).

1.4 AI in Gifted Education: Theoretical Foundations

Artificial Intelligence (AI) has introduced new opportunities for differentiation, personalization, and engagement in gifted education (Guilbault et al., 2025). Through adaptive algorithms and intelligent feedback, AI tools can align content with students' cognitive profiles, supporting flexible pacing and inquiry-based learning, key needs for gifted learners with asynchronous development and heightened curiosity (Neal, 2025).

To conceptualize this potential, Ecker et al. (2025) propose a Four-Dimensional Framework for AI Tutoring Integration, which comprises affect, content, process, and product, and is grounded in differentiated instruction and the Levels of Service approach. This model emphasizes learner autonomy and emotional engagement, access to high-level content, authentic inquiry, and performance-based feedback. Rather than replacing instruction, AI is positioned as a scalable extension of student-centered pedagogy tailored to the complexities of gifted education.

1.5 Creative Possibilities and Emerging Concerns

AI technologies are reshaping STEAM learning by supporting open-ended problem-solving, design thinking, and transdisciplinary creativity, core goals in gifted education (Uğraş et al., 2024a; Bougdira & Al Murshidi, 2025). These tools encourage students to become active co-creators of knowledge, blending technical fluency with imaginative exploration (Al-Zahrani et al., 2024).

However, growing critiques challenge the uncritical adoption of generative AI. Scholars warn of over-reliance, where students may bypass critical thinking in favor of AI-generated solutions (Zhai et al., 2024). This may foster "epistemic complacency", the unverified acceptance of AI outputs, hindering deep inquiry (Krakowski, 2025). Additionally, without careful oversight, AI risks pedagogical homogenization and the amplification of educational inequities (Pikhart & Al-Obaydi, 2025). These concerns are particularly pressing in gifted education, where the goal is not just accelerated learning, but the cultivation of intellectual independence and metacognitive resilience.

1.6 Identifying the Research Gap

Despite the increasing interest in the pedagogical potential of Artificial Intelligence, its application within inclusive gifted STEAM environments, where gifted and non-gifted students coexist, remains significantly underexplored, particularly in terms of implementation practices and educators' lived experiences (Uğraş et al., 2024b). While these technologies offer new possibilities for personalization, inquiry-based learning, and real-time feedback, their pedagogical integration within gifted education raises complex questions that merit systematic investigation. Equally critical is the examination of the educational policies and institutional frameworks that are required to support, regulate, and meaningfully contextualize such AI-enhanced approaches (Milakis et al., 2025).

1.7 Study Focus and Research Questions

This study investigates teachers' attitudes toward AI use in inclusive gifted STEAM classrooms, exploring how generative tools are perceived within mixed-ability settings. Anchored in Renzulli's (2021) Three-Ring Conception of Giftedness, above-average ability, creativity, and task commitment, the research examines how AI-based instruction aligns with or challenges these core traits. It also draws on Ecker et al.'s (2025) Four-Dimensional Framework for AI Tutoring Integration (affect, content, process, product), situating teacher perspectives within a broader pedagogical context.

The study seeks to illuminate not only the practical affordances and limitations of AI, but also the ethical and instructional tensions that arise in fostering authentic creativity, sustaining motivation, and supporting advanced learning. This dual framework enables a nuanced understanding of the intersection between emerging technologies and foundational principles in gifted education.

Understanding these dynamics is essential for developing inclusive and differentiated educational models that responsibly integrate emerging technologies into gifted STEAM practice. To this end, the present study is guided by the following research questions:

1. How do teachers perceive the role of AI in enhancing creativity, innovation, and critical thinking among gifted and non-gifted learners within gifted STEAM education?
2. In what ways do teachers consider AI to support differentiated instruction and the inclusion of diverse learners in gifted STEAM settings?
3. How do teachers conceptualize AI as an "instructional assistant" in the design, implementation, and assessment of gifted STEAM activities?

Understanding these dimensions through empirical data is crucial for the development of effective models that integrate emerging technologies into educational practice and promote inclusive, differentiated approaches in the context of gifted STEAM education.

2. RESEARCH METHODOLOGY

This study adopts a qualitative methodological approach situated within a pragmatic epistemological framework, focusing on exploring teachers' attitudes and perceptions regarding the use of AI in gifted STEAM education. A case study strategy was employed to enable an in-depth understanding of a complex pedagogical phenomenon within its natural context, by engaging teachers who had already participated in a specialized professional development program designed for this purpose (Martins & Baptista, 2024).

2.1. Participant Selection and Context

The sample consisted of six primary and secondary education teachers (N = 6) from Greece, representing diverse disciplinary backgrounds in science, technology, and the arts. Participants were selected through purposive sampling based on two primary criteria: (1) documented prior experience in STEM/STEAM education and/or gifted education, and (2) successful completion of the same year-long professional development program. This shared professional development experience provided a common baseline of knowledge and practice from which to explore their perceptions.

All participants had completed the "Gifted STEAM Education" program, which took place under the academic supervision of the European University Cyprus from January to December 2024. The program included weekly online seminars and collaborative design of gifted STEAM activities for primary-level students in non-formal educational settings, with an emphasis on differentiation and inclusion within mixed-ability groups.

2.2 Data Collection and Analysis

Data were collected through two primary methods: (1) semi-structured individual interviews (approximately 60 minutes each) designed to capture in-depth personal views, and (2) two focus group discussions (approximately 90 minutes each) involving all six participants, which aimed to surface shared and divergent perspectives. This combination of methods allowed for methodological triangulation.

Thematic analysis was conducted following the six-phase framework proposed by Braun and Clarke (2006): familiarization with data, generating initial codes, searching for themes, reviewing themes, defining and naming themes, and producing the report. To ensure analytical rigor, two of the authors independently coded a subset of the data and collaboratively discussed discrepancies to refine the coding framework. Researcher bias was addressed through continuous reflective journaling and peer debriefing sessions among the research team.

2.3 Trustworthiness and Ethical Considerations

To enhance the validity and trustworthiness of the findings, member checking was employed, where participants were invited to review summaries of their interviews and the derived themes to ensure their perspectives were accurately represented. All ethical procedures were strictly followed. Participants were provided with detailed information sheets and gave written informed consent prior to their involvement. Anonymity and confidentiality were maintained through the use of pseudonyms and the removal of identifying information from transcripts. Participants were assured of their right to withdraw at any stage of the research. The study adhered fully to the General Data Protection Regulation (GDPR) and received formal approval from the Ethics and Research Committee of the European University Cyprus.

3. FINDINGS

This section presents the thematic findings derived from the analysis of qualitative data. The analysis sheds light on how educators perceive the integration of AI within inclusive, mixed-ability learning environments. To enhance narrative flow and reduce repetition, related themes have been consolidated. The findings are structured to first establish the core pedagogical tensions regarding higher-order thinking and collaboration, then to explore the complexities of using AI for differentiation and inclusion, and finally to examine the role of AI as an instructional assistant.

3.1 AI and the Cultivation of Creative and Critical Capacities in Mixed-Ability STEAM Classrooms

3.1.1 AI's Role in Student Creativity

Teachers expressed a complex ambivalence about the role of generative AI in nurturing student creativity within gifted STEAM contexts. While many acknowledged its potential to support idea generation, visual exploration, and interdisciplinary inspiration, they cautioned against its passive use, fearing it might erode students' authentic creative effort. One teacher described AI as "a brainstorming tool" that helps students "visualize initial ideas", while others noted its use in generating songs, poems, or images "as they imagine them", emphasizing its value as a stimulus rather than a substitute for creativity. However, concerns emerged about students bypassing key phases of the creative process. "If students simply receive ready-made answers," one participant warned, "they might not exert themselves." Another highlighted the difference between gifted and non-gifted learners, suggesting that the former might "use it more consciously... whereas others might just use what's given".

Teachers emphasized the necessity of guided use, recommending structured group work where students "agree in advance" on what to ask. Yet several expressed reservations about student autonomy, with one noting, "ideally, I wouldn't want students to use it at all, only teachers". Although the novelty of a "robot that answers everything" was seen as motivational, it was also framed as a distraction, with students "asking unrelated questions" or treating the tool as a toy.

3.1.2 AI and Peer Collaboration in Mixed-Ability Groups

Teachers expressed persistent ambivalence about AI's impact on peer collaboration, viewing it simultaneously as a potential enabler of teamwork and a disruptor of group cohesion. A key concern was that students might bypass interpersonal interaction in favor of direct engagement with the AI. As one participant noted, "having access to an AI tool might actually hinder collaboration", since it allows learners to "go straight to an AI tool" instead of "discussing ideas or challenging each other's views".

Some teachers, however, described structured approaches where students "collaborate to decide what they want AI to generate", highlighting shared control over prompts and outputs. Others proposed gamified strategies to support cooperation, imagining turn-based interactions where the AI provides group feedback, such as whether "player 1 collaborated well with player 2".

Despite these possibilities, distraction was a recurring theme, especially for younger students. One teacher likened AI to "giving each student a mobile phone during a project", warning of off-task behavior and weakened group focus. Gifted students were seen as particularly prone to disengaging from peers in favor of individualized AI exploration, potentially "losing interest in the project".

Educators also stressed the importance of developmental readiness. AI was seen as more suitable for older students, while younger children might treat it as a game, requiring "very close supervision".

3.1.3 AI, Inquiry, and the Challenge of Cultivating Critical Thinking

Teachers expressed conflicting views on AI's role in supporting inquiry and critical thinking within gifted STEAM settings, balancing its theoretical potential with deeper concerns about cognitive dependency and diminished intellectual effort. While some acknowledged that tools like ChatGPT could scaffold investigations, most emphasized that its immediacy risks undermining the iterative, uncertain nature of authentic inquiry. As one teacher explained, "ChatGPT gives them a final result", bypassing "the process of connecting different sources" and evaluating evidence, essential elements of "real research".

Many participants contrasted AI with traditional web searches, which require navigating diverse perspectives. ChatGPT, by contrast, was described as "narrow", "closed", and offering "the one, standard answer", thus limiting opportunities for epistemic struggle and decision-making.

Teachers also raised developmental concerns, arguing that younger students often lack the skills to use AI critically. "It is very difficult to write effective prompts," one remarked, while another suggested that AI would be more valuable "if it gives steps and not the solution". Emotional and motivational risks were also cited, with some fearing that polished outputs could discourage persistence. "They won't use their brains anymore", one participant warned, adding that students may feel, "there's something that knows everything for me, so I don't have to try for anything".

Still, a few educators identified possible benefits, if AI is used within a scaffolded framework emphasizing metacognition and critical verification. One proposed that students "cross-validate" AI results with web sources, while another viewed it as useful only "after much training, discipline, and experimentation".

3.2 Mediating Inclusion and Differentiation through AI: Possibilities and Tensions in Gifted STEAM Education

3.2.1 AI and the Fragile Terrain of Inclusion in Mixed-Ability Classrooms

Teachers voiced nuanced and often conflicting views on AI's role in promoting inclusion within mixed-ability classrooms. While some acknowledged its potential to support differentiated learning, such as assigning each student a part of the task and using an AI tool to retrieve tailored information, many warned that its use could unintentionally foster exclusion. One participant described how gifted students might prefer to "be in a group alone with an AI tool", leading to a form of "pseudo-participation" that undermines peer interaction. This tendency, driven either by a sense of technological superiority or by diminished self-confidence in comparison to the tool's perceived intelligence, was seen as potentially eroding the social purpose of group work.

Beyond student behavior, teachers highlighted systemic obstacles. Effective use of AI for inclusion presupposes "appropriate teacher guidance", yet digital fluency among educators remains uneven. Such disparities can amplify inequities both within and across classrooms, with scenarios like "sixth-grade students using a program that talks back to them, while fourth graders are still using books" reinforcing a sense of technological favoritism.

Crucially, participants resisted the idea of AI becoming central to the learning process. As one educator insisted, lessons "should not begin and end with an AI tool". While supportive of exposing students to new technologies, teachers preferred AI to remain a supplemental tool, used occasionally and within clearly defined boundaries, to preserve the relational and participatory ethos of inclusive gifted education.

3.2.2 AI and the Pedagogical Complexities of Differentiation

Teachers expressed a mix of cautious enthusiasm and critical concern about AI's role in differentiated instruction. Many valued AI tools for generating tiered materials and personalized feedback, especially for gifted students whose needs often exceed standard curricular pacing. One teacher suggested that instead of "a hundred extra exercises", AI could provide "something more advanced" to sustain interest, while another saw it as a way to "help the teacher find more demanding material".

However, this optimism was tempered by worries about classroom equity and social dynamics. The provision of AI-based enrichment was likened to "giving a chocolate to one student and nothing to the rest", highlighting concerns about visible privilege and fairness. The image of a gifted student "playing with the tablet all day" raised fears of over-individualization and social withdrawal, particularly if AI use is unstructured. One respondent warned that such students may "interact only with the computer", undermining peer collaboration.

Teachers stressed the importance of moderation and mediation. Differentiation through AI was seen as more effective "via prompts created by the teacher" rather than through unguided student use. Limiting AI access to specific stages of a project was proposed as a way to maintain balance and avoid resentment among classmates.

Crucially, participants emphasized that AI's success depends on prior conditions, especially teacher competence and student readiness. As one educator noted, "even I, as an adult, get so many alternative explanations", while students would need not only content knowledge but also the technical ability to "adapt a suggested outline" or "format AI output". Some teachers proposed that AI might be more appropriately used at home, serving as a personalized tutor in contexts where individualization is difficult during class time.

3.2.3 AI's Ambivalent Impact on Teacher Autonomy in Gifted STEAM Education

Teachers expressed ambivalence about AI's impact on their pedagogical autonomy in gifted STEAM settings, with reflections oscillating between empowerment and concern. Some described AI as a creative ally that helps "organize abstract thoughts" into teachable content and serves as "a brainstorming partner" for playful, feasible project ideas. In this view, AI enhances rather than replaces teacher agency.

Yet this optimism was tempered by fears of professional deskilling and epistemic complacency. Several educators likened AI dependence to reliance on digital maps, warning that if "the tool fails, we're left with the feeling of not knowing how to proceed". Others cautioned that teachers might accept AI-generated content uncritically, assuming it to be authoritative. "The danger is that we believe ChatGPT knows everything", one noted, despite its outputs being shaped by cultural and political biases.

Concerns also emerged around pedagogical homogenization. Teachers warned that overreliance could lead to "standardized answers", eroding the contextual responsiveness vital to gifted education. One participant feared that educators "might start using it for everything", bypassing the reflective depth of meaningful teaching. The risk of inaccuracies, simplifications, or biased content was also emphasized, particularly if teachers lack the skills to vet or adapt AI outputs critically.

This ambivalence extended to professional identity. Some teachers admitted feeling "a sense of inadequacy" when AI seemed more knowledgeable in their subject, yet appreciated its speed and range, especially for technical queries. This dual role, as mentor and rival, highlighted AI's emotional impact on teaching practice.

Without a solid grasp of both content and technology, AI might confuse rather than empower, leading to "a veneer of innovation without substantive understanding". Still, several educators maintained that autonomy remains intact when teachers retain interpretive control. As one participant concluded, "AI doesn't decide for me or do my teaching", reinforcing its role as a resource, not a replacement.

3.2.4 Foundations for Integrating AI in Gifted STEAM Education

Teachers highlighted that effective AI integration in gifted STEAM education requires more than technical deployment, it demands structural, pedagogical, and ethical scaffolding. Central among the prerequisites was teacher competence, defined not only as technical familiarity but also as the ability to interpret AI outputs through the lens of giftedness and interdisciplinary rigor. "Without good knowledge of giftedness," one teacher explained, "the educator cannot evaluate whether differentiation and inclusion are understood by the software in the right way".

Institutional safeguards were also seen as essential. Participants stressed the need for a "legal and institutional framework" to protect teachers from liability, particularly in a context where AI remains poorly regulated and often misunderstood by parents. Absent such guidelines, teachers risk acting in isolation, with little clarity on acceptable practices.

Several teachers warned against a culture of technophilia that equates novelty with pedagogical progress. While AI was seen as a powerful cognitive support, participants feared it might displace core learning processes such as idea generation, critical thinking, and peer collaboration. One respondent expressed concern that students might "stop trying to solve problems on their own", while another warned of the psychological risks of framing AI as "a friend", potentially fostering emotional dependency.

Professional development emerged as a major theme. Participants noted inconsistent and fragmented training, which can lead to internal tensions and divergent classroom practices. Some called for a systemic overhaul of educational resources, including textbooks designed to "interact with AI in interdisciplinary ways", and emphasized the importance of teaching prompt engineering as a fundamental pedagogical skill rather than a technical aside.

Finally, educators stressed the need to prepare students not just to use AI, but to engage with it critically. As one participant put it, gifted learners must be "systematically trained to understand both the benefits and the limits of AI", cultivating epistemic humility and metacognitive awareness.

3.3 From Assistant to Co-Designer: Teachers' Engagement with AI in Planning and Assessing Gifted STEAM Learning

3.3.1 Using AI to Design Gifted STEAM Educational Materials

Teachers described a nuanced engagement with AI tools in the design of gifted STEAM materials, navigating between functional support and the preservation of pedagogical authenticity. Many valued AI for its efficiency in generating draft lesson plans, rubrics, or solving math problems, but emphasized the importance of "customizing, adapting, and modifying" outputs to align with students' specific needs. One teacher illustrated this by sharing how she used AI to create a rewards chart but added her own "colors and stars" to make it meaningful and engaging.

This hybrid use framed AI as a collaborator, not a creator, with teachers maintaining creative agency. However, concerns emerged about the potential erosion of professional identity. As one participant warned, overreliance on AI might leave educators "mentally idle", stripping away the personal investment that gives teaching its craft: "It's different from just handing out a worksheet generated by a program".

Despite these reservations, many teachers acknowledged AI's strategic value, particularly for visual and auditory content creation. It allowed them to "print a collage image immediately", respond in real time to student input, and design imaginative materials "without worrying about copyright". One teacher noted the excitement of generating images "based on what the children imagined", highlighting AI's capacity to enhance creativity while retaining teacher control.

Yet limitations were also noted. Some found AI responses "too generic" for effective differentiation, stressing that meaningful use depends on teachers' ability to formulate precise prompts and refine suggestions. As one concluded, "It helped me think of an original activity, but it didn't spare me from the work of preparing and organizing". AI, in this view, is a tool for inspiration, not a substitute for pedagogical labor.

3.3.2 Assistance in the Creation of Gifted STEAM Scenarios

Teachers expressed both enthusiasm and caution regarding AI as an assistant in designing gifted STEAM learning scenarios. Many appreciated the tool's efficiency, likening AI to "asking a sixty-year-old expert teacher" or receiving "the majority answer from a million educators". It was praised for stimulating pedagogical imagination and streamlining planning. However, participants stressed that AI "doesn't know the dynamics of our classroom" or "the particularities of each student", emphasizing the need for professional discernment.

Several educators warned that overuse could erode pedagogical authenticity. One noted that AI risks replacing "the inner search" that drives meaningful teaching, while another cautioned that relying too heavily on it could "make us passive" and diminish emotional investment in the learning experience. The shift from collegial reflection to algorithmic suggestion was seen by some as a loss in the collaborative and adaptive nature of instructional design.

Others viewed AI as a flexible partner for personalizing learning. Teachers described using it to "differentiate test difficulty", create interdisciplinary tasks, and develop quizzes that "promote self-awareness in STEAM fields". There was cautious optimism that, with responsible use, AI could support adaptive modeling of student needs.

Even the most supportive voices, however, insisted on ethical boundaries. Concerns included AI's potential to reinforce biases, "presenting ideas too encouragingly based on the educator's initial input", and the risks of delegating sensitive decisions to an algorithm. Teachers consistently reaffirmed that they must remain the ultimate authorities in matters involving classroom dynamics and student wellbeing.

3.3.3 AI in Student Assessment

Teachers approached the use of AI in student assessment with cautious pragmatism, recognizing its utility for logistical support but drawing clear boundaries around interpretive judgment. Many appreciated that AI chatbots could "draft a rubric or evaluation skeleton" or generate "multiple choice questions of moderate difficulty". Still, they emphasized that such outputs "always require adaptation" to reflect classroom realities and pedagogical intent. One teacher noted a flaw in AI-generated tests where "all the correct answers ended up as option four", illustrating the need for critical human oversight.

At the heart of their reservations was the belief that assessment is inherently relational. "No program can know my students, their personalities, their histories", one participant asserted, reaffirming the teacher's irreplaceable role in interpreting student work. Even those open to AI's analytic contributions refused to delegate final evaluative authority. As one stated unequivocally, "I would never let the program evaluate my students".

Some teachers did see potential for AI in formative or diagnostic assessment. It could "help identify gaps in understanding" or support "student self-assessment" through automated feedback, provided it remains subordinate to teacher judgment. Yet they also warned against the illusion of objectivity. One teacher observed that AI "wants to impress with its perfection" but may miss "the essence of things", particularly in the nuanced reasoning or creative outputs of gifted learners. As another recounted, AI misjudged a student's unconventional artwork that was, in fact, based on higher-order thinking.

4. DISCUSSION

As the findings illustrate, teachers are navigating a landscape of profound ambivalence toward AI. This discussion now moves beyond a thematic summary of these perceptions to analyze their significance, connecting them to the wider literature on educational technology, theory, and ethics. The analysis is structured to present a balanced, dual-perspective view, exploring both the opportunities and the risks for each key theme, before broadening to consider the systemic and ethical contexts in which these tensions are embedded.

4.1 The Duality of AI in Fostering Creativity and Critical Thinking

The present study's exploration of teachers' perceptions reveals a deep tension regarding AI's role in fostering higher-order thinking. In alignment with some research, participants acknowledged AI's potential to stimulate imaginative thinking and serve as an ideational support tool (Albadarin et al., 2024). However, their overarching concern was that over-reliance could erode authentic creative and critical effort, a view that challenges more optimistic narratives (Faisal, 2024). This ambivalence was even sharper concerning critical thinking. While a significant body of literature extols AI's potential to support inquiry-based learning and argumentative writing (Jeon & Lee, 2024), our findings show educators perceive it as a tool that shortcuts the cognitive dissonance and epistemic struggle necessary for deep inquiry. This concern resonates with broader critiques of over-dependence (Zhai et al., 2024) and aligns with models that view AI not as a neutral tool for metacognition, but as one that carries pedagogical risks without careful scaffolding (García-López et al., 2025). The teachers' skepticism also complicates assumptions of learner agency that are prevalent in contemporary AI education discourse (Imran & Almusharraf, 2023).

4.2 Collaboration: A Tool for Connection or Isolation?

In contrast to the dominant discourse positioning AI as a tool for enhancing collaboration and distributed cognition (Deng & Yu, 2023), this study's findings suggest a more complex relationship. While research often frames AI as a means of scaffolding cooperative inquiry (Baig & Yadegaridehkordi, 2024), and some participants articulated frameworks for structured co-use of AI that echo best practices (Dimeli & Kostas, 2025), the dominant view was that AI could fragment peer interaction and privatize learning. The recurrent concern that AI offers an appealing alternative to negotiating meaning with peers problematizes the assumption that technological integration automatically supports social learning (Fenta, 2025), foregrounding social disconnection and cognitive isolation as emergent risks (Ansari et al., 2024). This tension takes on particular significance in mixed-ability gifted STEAM classrooms, where collaborative learning is not only a pedagogical choice but a key strategy for inclusion and peer modeling. Several participants noted that when students work individually with AI, the social dimension of problem-solving is diminished, leading to parallel rather than dialogic learning processes. This fragmentation undermines the benefits of peer scaffolding, especially for gifted students who often thrive in cognitively stimulating social interactions (de Oliveira & Stoltz, 2020).

4.3 The Paradox of AI-Powered Differentiation and Inclusion

With respect to inclusion and differentiation, the findings reflect a nuanced skepticism that introduces critical caveats to global research trends (Kim, 2023). While literature often celebrates AI's capacity to generate adaptive tasks and support diverse learning needs (Chytas et al., 2025; Gunawan et al., 2024), our participants articulated a set of social, emotional, and logistical concerns. They highlighted the paradoxical effects of personalization, where the risk of gifted students disengaging from peers, coupled with the specter of inequity symbolized by "technological favoritism", suggests the social fabric of an inclusive classroom may be strained, not reinforced. This points to an underexplored dimension in the literature: the psychosocial consequences of perceived technological privilege and the erosion of collective learning experiences (Li et al., 2024). Our findings suggest that technological solutions are only as inclusive as the human systems that support them, a perspective that aligns with literature calling for teacher-centered implementation models (Lo et al., 2024).

4.4 Teacher Autonomy: Empowerment or Deskilling?

Regarding teacher autonomy, the present findings confirm but also extend the ambivalent picture in existing scholarship. While research recognizes AI's potential to reduce planning time and alleviate cognitive load (Mahsun et al., 2024), our teachers' expressions of concern about epistemic dependency, pedagogical homogenization, and professional deskilling introduce a reflective critique that is not always foregrounded in the literature (Montenegro-Rueda et al., 2023). This tension points to a need for a more critical discourse on the implications of AI for teacher identity and professional judgment. Several participants emphasized that while AI may streamline instructional processes, it also risks eroding the pedagogical discretion and creativity that are central to the teaching profession, particularly in gifted education where flexibility and innovation are paramount (Holmes et al., 2019). The fear that overreliance on AI tools may standardize instructional practices and marginalize teacher expertise was repeatedly voiced, especially in relation to curriculum design and student assessment (Luckin, 2018). Moreover, the findings suggest that teacher empowerment in AI-mediated classrooms is not simply a matter of technical training but also of safeguarding the epistemological agency of educators, their capacity to question, interpret, and adapt knowledge in pedagogically meaningful ways (Zawacki-Richter et al., 2019). These insights underscore the importance of positioning teachers not merely as users of AI but as co-designers and critical evaluators of its educational integration (Meng et al., 2022).

4.5 The Primacy of Socio-Pedagogical Infrastructure

Ultimately, the integration of AI, as conceptualized by participants, appears to hinge not on the technology itself but on the socio-pedagogical infrastructure that surrounds it. This emphasis on foundational conditions, including teacher training, institutional support, and student literacy, largely aligns with emerging consensus in international scholarship (Maita et al., 2024). The educators' insistence that prompt literacy and professional discretion are non-negotiable prerequisites foregrounds a more deliberative model of integration than is typically assumed (Özgür & Bekiroğlu, 2025). Beyond technical competence, participants repeatedly highlighted the importance of cultivating a school-wide culture of ethical reflection, interdisciplinary collaboration, and shared pedagogical responsibility (Adams et al., 2023). The success of AI-supported differentiation, particularly in inclusive gifted STEAM settings, was viewed as contingent upon coordinated professional development, flexible curricular frameworks, and leadership structures that respect teacher autonomy (Singh, 2023). In this sense, AI was not seen as a transformative force in isolation, but as a tool whose educational value is deeply embedded in the human and institutional ecology in which it is deployed (Kong & Yang, 2024).

4.6 Conceptual Impact on Giftedness and AI Integration Frameworks

The study's findings shed light on how AI is perceived through the lens of Renzulli's (2021) Three-Ring Conception of Giftedness, particularly regarding the tensions between support and superficiality. While teachers acknowledged that AI could scaffold advanced learning by facilitating access to knowledge and enabling differentiated pacing, many doubted its ability to nurture authentic creativity. Likewise, although its interactivity was seen as motivating, concerns were raised about its impact on intrinsic task commitment, with some fearing it may foster dependence or shortcut-driven habits. These perspectives highlight the importance of sustained teacher mediation in preserving the dynamic interplay between ability, creativity, and perseverance central to Renzulli's model.

Teachers' views also interacted with Ecker et al.'s (2025) Four-Dimensional Framework for AI Tutoring Integration. The "content" and "process" dimensions, concerning adaptive materials and expert-like inquiry, received support. However, "affect" and "product" dimensions elicited more ambivalence, as participants questioned whether AI-enabled outputs truly reflect student agency or merely simulate it. Concerns about overreliance, authenticity, and ethical use were particularly salient in creative contexts. These findings suggest that while Ecker et al.'s framework offers a valuable scaffold, its classroom application requires continuous refinement grounded in pedagogical and emotional realities. Integrating teacher feedback is essential for making the model responsive to inclusive gifted education.

Beyond these primary models, the data resonate with Gagné's (2004) Differentiated Model of Giftedness and Talent. Teachers feared that AI might amplify surface-level performance without fostering the deeper transformation of potential into talent. In this view, AI risks becoming a tool for producing polished outputs rather than cultivating underlying cognitive growth. Similarly, the emphasis many educators placed on practicality, creativity, and contextual intelligence reflects alignment with Sternberg's (2003) Triarchic Theory. Teachers remained skeptical of AI's ability to engage students in ways that develop creative and practical intelligences, capacities they consider central to authentic giftedness. These findings call for broader evaluative models that move beyond content mastery to encompass the complex cultivation of human potential.

4.7 Ethical Dimensions and Systemic Inclusion Risks

Beyond the immediate pedagogical concerns, teachers' ambivalence toward AI reveals deeper ethical tensions and systemic risks in inclusive gifted education. A primary issue is student data privacy. Participants expressed unease with the opaque "black box" nature of AI systems and the lack of institutional safeguards for protecting sensitive educational data, echoing broader concerns about data exploitation and third-party monetization (UNESCO, 2023; Williamson et al., 2020).

Another major concern was algorithmic bias. Teachers feared that AI, trained on non-representative datasets, could reinforce narrow definitions of giftedness, excluding students with atypical learning profiles or from marginalized cultural and linguistic backgrounds. This risk threatens the very foundation of differentiated instruction (Baker & Hawn, 2022).

Access inequality also emerged as a structural threat. Teachers questioned whether AI tools can be equitably implemented across schools, warning of an emerging two-tiered system favoring well-resourced institutions. English-language dominance and interface inaccessibility for neurodiverse learners further exacerbate this divide (Reich, 2020; Kasneci et al., 2023).

Finally, systemic dependency on proprietary platforms raised alarms about "vendor lock-in", which undermines data sovereignty, pedagogical autonomy, and public education sustainability (Tlili et al., 2023). Teachers' concerns align with recent regulatory efforts, such as the EU Artificial Intelligence Act (2024) and the OECD Recommendation on Artificial Intelligence (2019), which emphasize transparency, accountability, and democratic oversight. These developments underscore the need for AI integration that is not only effective but also ethically responsible, socially just, and policy-supported.

4.8 Longitudinal Impact and Cognitive Resilience

Although this study offers a rich cross-sectional view of teacher perspectives, participants raised concerns about the long-term cognitive effects of sustained AI use in gifted STEAM education. A recurring theme was the potential erosion of cognitive resilience, as students may grow accustomed to instant, polished responses and gradually lose the capacity to persist through uncertainty or revise imperfect work, hallmarks of gifted learners.

This apprehension aligns with research by Zhai et al. (2024), which warns that overreliance on generative AI may diminish perseverance, reduce tolerance for ambiguity, and foster superficial task execution. Such patterns threaten the development of grit, defined by Duckworth (2016) as sustained effort and passion for long-term goals, which is crucial for deep metacognitive growth and intellectual autonomy in gifted contexts.

4.9 Local Realities and Global Aspirations

Although not focused on national policy, this study offers valuable insights into the Greek context of AI integration in gifted STEAM education. Teachers consistently expressed concerns about the pedagogical and ethical implications of generative AI, particularly regarding creativity, autonomy, and assessment. These concerns arise in a policy vacuum: while interest in AI is growing, there is no formal framework guiding its use in primary and secondary education. Adoption remains voluntary and experimental, lacking systemic directives or evaluation criteria.

Some universities in Greece have introduced continuing education programs on AI pedagogy, often through lifelong learning centers. The Ministry of Education participates in European training initiatives, and the Institute of Educational Policy has launched exploratory efforts. However, without binding guidelines or curriculum integration, these remain fragmented, placing the burden of implementation on individual educators and institutions.

In contrast to structured international frameworks like the EU Artificial Intelligence Act (2024) and the OECD Recommendation on AI (2019), which emphasize human-centered governance and accountability, Greece is still in an exploratory phase. This makes the teachers' voices in this study especially relevant, as they illuminate how ethical and pedagogical reasoning unfolds without policy support.

Moreover, while global discourse often highlights AI's efficiency and content diversity (Nee et al., 2023), Greek educators emphasized the importance of emotional investment, customization, and modeling intellectual integrity. Their skepticism toward AI's evaluative role reflects a persistent belief in the teacher's moral and epistemic responsibility, offering a counterpoint to technocentric narratives that treat assessment as automatable (Salih et al., 2024).

5. IMPLICATIONS FOR PRACTICE, POLICY, AND FUTURE RESEARCH

The findings of this study carry a range of implications, suggesting the need for a cautious, situated, and ethically grounded approach. This section reframes the discussion from problems to solutions and future directions, offering concrete implications for practitioners, policymakers, and researchers.

5.1 Implications for Practice and Teacher Training

The findings underscore that AI integration in gifted STEAM education must be rooted in sustained teacher mediation, not only in prompt design or tool operation, but in the interpretation, ethical framing, and pedagogical shaping of AI outputs. Teachers should act not as passive facilitators, but as epistemic agents capable of interrogating the assumptions and cultural values embedded in generative systems. As one participant emphasized, "we must teach students not only how to use AI, but how to question it."

This perspective calls for a curricular shift: skills such as prompt engineering, information verification, and AI literacy must be treated as core components of twenty-first-century STEAM education, especially in cognitively diverse settings. Ethical reasoning, emotional literacy, and collaborative reflection should also be foregrounded, given the complex decision-making demands of AI-mediated learning environments.

To translate these principles into practice, educators stressed the need for subject-specific, pedagogically grounded examples of how AI can augment critical thinking and creativity without displacing them. Isolated workshops or asynchronous modules were deemed insufficient. Instead, professional development must evolve into sustained, collaborative processes where teachers co-construct knowledge and reflect critically on the potentials and pitfalls of AI. Without such depth, participants warned, AI use may reinforce dependency and erode the cognitive and ethical rigor essential to gifted education. In line with the principles emerging from our findings, the following models illustrate how AI can be integrated into STEAM activities for gifted and mixed-ability classrooms:

Table 1. Models of AI-Enhanced STEAM Activities for Gifted and Mixed-Ability Classrooms

Activity Type	Learning Objective (Gifted & Mixed-Ability Students)	Role of AI (Critical, Mediated Use)	Connection to Study Findings
Creative Ideation	Gifted: Cultivate divergent thinking and complex problem framing. Others: Practice generating and organizing initial ideas.	AI serves as a brainstorming partner, offering multiple perspectives that students cross-check with other sources.	Counters "AI as answer provider" by positioning AI as stimulus, not solution (Finding 3.1.1).
Visualization & Artistic Representation	Gifted: Translate abstract or scientific concepts into creative outputs. Others: Explore multimodal forms of expression.	AI image or text generators used iteratively with prompt refinement; students reflect on the affordances and limits of generative aesthetics.	Encourages student agency and creativity while addressing concerns about surface-level outputs (Finding 3.1.1).
Critical Evaluation	Gifted: Engage in metacognitive critique of structure, logic, and credibility. Others: Practice feedback and error detection skills.	AI produces sample outputs with deliberate flaws; students identify errors, suggest improvements, and compare with human work.	Strengthens reflective thinking and critical literacy, mitigating risks of uncritical reliance (Findings 3.2, 3.3).
Ethical & Dialectical Discussion	Gifted: Develop argumentation, ethical reasoning, and epistemic humility. Others: Practice structured debate and perspective-taking.	AI generates contrasting arguments; students analyze assumptions, identify biases, and reflect on socio-emotional implications.	Aligns with emphasis on human mediation, ethical framing, and collaborative reasoning (Findings 3.1.2, 3.2).

5.2 Implications for Policy

Although this study centers on classroom practice, teachers' concerns about training gaps, ethical uncertainty, and weak institutional support point to urgent systemic issues requiring policy intervention. Participants highlighted the absence of national frameworks for AI use in education, noting that current integration relies on ad hoc efforts, fragmented exposure to university or EU-funded programs, and individual initiative, conditions that leave teachers to navigate complex challenges without adequate preparation.

The findings suggest that inclusive gifted education cannot rely on teacher discretion or market-led adoption. Instead, it demands coordinated policies that embed AI within broader goals of equity, teacher empowerment, and student-centered pedagogy. International models such as the OECD's AI Recommendation (2019) and the EU's Artificial Intelligence Act (2024) offer valuable guidance, yet remain aspirational in the Greek context, where implementation is still exploratory.

National policy must go beyond rhetoric and invest in context-sensitive, ethically grounded strategies. This includes establishing professional development pathways aligned with differentiated instruction, issuing data protection protocols, and avoiding dependency on commercial platforms. Equally vital is addressing infrastructural disparities. As teachers noted, unequal access to digital tools and internet connectivity threatens to deepen educational inequalities. Effective policy must therefore couple curricular and ethical guidance with commitments to technological justice, ensuring that AI integration promotes inclusion rather than exacerbating systemic divides.

5.3 Implications for Future Research

This study highlights several critical directions for future research, emerging from both the existing literature and the lived experiences of participating educators. First, there is an urgent need to develop and empirically test ethical frameworks for AI in gifted and inclusive education. These must address data privacy, algorithmic bias, cultural representation, and equity, while remaining attuned to the relational complexities of AI-mediated learning.

Second, longitudinal studies are essential to assess the long-term effects of AI on student autonomy, problem-solving resilience, metacognitive development, and intrinsic motivation, especially given teachers' concerns about overreliance and reduced cognitive effort.

Finally, comparative policy and cultural studies can offer insight into how differing national infrastructures, cultural understandings of giftedness, and levels of teacher autonomy shape AI adoption. Such cross-context research is key to developing nuanced, adaptable implementation models that reflect local realities while engaging global challenges.

6. LIMITATIONS

While this qualitative study offers in-depth insights, several limitations affect the generalizability and scope of its findings. The participant sample consisted solely of teachers who voluntarily joined a professional development program on gifted STEAM education, potentially biasing results toward more tech-receptive or pedagogically engaged individuals. Moreover, the study focused specifically on generative AI tools, excluding other forms of educational AI, such as intelligent tutoring systems or learning analytics.

The research also relied exclusively on educators' self-reported data from interviews and focus groups, making it vulnerable to social desirability bias and lacking observational or student-derived evidence. The absence of student voices is particularly significant, given the centrality of learner engagement in inclusive gifted education.

The interpretation of findings was shaped by the available literature, which remains limited in its treatment of AI in gifted STEAM contexts, especially beyond Anglophone and Western educational systems. This conceptual and geographic gap restricts broader contextualization.

These limitations point to the need for future studies employing mixed-methods, larger and more diverse samples, and triangulated data sources to better capture the longitudinal, cultural, and affective dimensions of AI integration in inclusive gifted STEAM education.

7. CONCLUSION

This study has explored the multifaceted and often ambivalent ways in which educators conceptualize the role of Artificial Intelligence in gifted STEAM education within inclusive, mixed-ability classrooms. The findings reveal a dynamic tension between pedagogical opportunity and epistemic risk. On one hand, teachers valued AI for its ability to scaffold differentiated instruction, support creative ideation, and provide adaptive feedback, particularly when used in carefully structured activities. On the other hand, they expressed persistent concerns about cognitive shortcuts, the erosion of student agency, the flattening of authentic creativity, and the potential undermining of teacher autonomy. These concerns were not merely technical but stemmed from deeper ethical, affective, and developmental considerations, reflecting a relational pedagogy attuned to the nuances of giftedness. Rather than embracing AI as a neutral or universally beneficial tool, participants foregrounded the necessity of sustained human mediation, from prompt design and interpretive scaffolding to metacognitive guidance. This ambivalence disrupts dominant techno-optimistic narratives and redefines inclusion not as mere access to innovation, but as a pedagogically and ethically negotiated space where the distinct needs of diverse learners remain central.

At a theoretical level, the study contributes meaningfully to ongoing discussions around the future of gifted education in the age of AI. It extends Renzulli's (2021) Three-Ring Conception of Giftedness by questioning how generative AI intersects with core traits such as creativity and task commitment, especially when outputs risk becoming mimicry rather than self-expression. Likewise, it engages critically with Ecker et al.'s (2025) Four-Dimensional Framework for AI Tutoring Integration, providing grounded insights that validate but also complicate its affective and product-oriented dimensions. The findings affirm that AI's educational value is not inherent but contingent upon the socio-pedagogical infrastructures that surround it. In the Greek context especially, the absence of a formal policy framework for educational AI left many teachers operating in conditions of epistemic precarity, highlighting the need for coordinated training, ethical guidelines, and infrastructural equity. Ultimately, this study calls for a shift from efficiency-driven automation toward a human-centered, critically literate, and ethically responsive paradigm, one that sees AI not as a pedagogical actor, but as a cultural artifact whose integration demands wisdom, reflexivity, and care.

REFERENCES

Adams, C., Pente, P., Lemermeyer, G., & Rockwell, G. (2023). Ethical principles for artificial intelligence in K-12 education. *Comput. Educ. Artif. Intell.*, *4*, 100131. DOI: 10.1016/j.caeai.2023.100131

Al-Zahrani, A., Khalil, I., Awaji, B., & Mohsen, M. (2024). AI technologies in STEAM education for students: Systematic literature review. *Journal of Ecohumanism*, *3*(4), 3380–3394. DOI: 10.62754/joe.v3i4.3855

Albadarin, Y., Saqr, M., Pope, N., & Tukiainen, M. (2024). A systematic literature review of empirical research on ChatGPT in education. *Discover Education*, *3*(1), 60. DOI: 10.1007/s44217-024-00138-2

Ansari, A. N., Ahmad, S., & Bhutta, S. M. (2024). Mapping the global evidence around the use of ChatGPT in higher education: A systematic scoping review. *Education and Information Technologies*, *29*(9), 11281–11321. DOI: 10.1007/s10639-023-12223-4

Baig, M. I., & Yadegaridehkordi, E. (2024). ChatGPT in the higher education: A systematic literature review and research challenges. *International Journal of Educational Research*, *127*, 102411. DOI: 10.1016/j.ijer.2024.102411

Baker, R. S., & Hawn, A. (2022). Algorithmic Bias in Education. *International Journal of Artificial Intelligence in Education*, *32*(4), 1052–1092. DOI: 10.1007/s40593-021-00285-9

Besnoy, K. D. (2021). Creating A Sustainable Digital Ecosystem for the Gifted Education Classroom. In *Methods and Materials for Teaching the Gifted* (pp. 629–662). Routledge., DOI: 10.4324/9781003236603-23

Bougdira, A., & Al Murshidi, G. (2025). Generative AI as a Tool for Personalized STEAM K-12 Education. In *Prompt Engineering and Generative AI Applications for Teaching and Learning* (pp. 387–410). IGI Global Scientific Publishing., DOI: 10.4018/979-8-3693-7332-3.ch023

Braun, V., & Clarke, V. (2006). Using thematic analysis in psychology. Qualitative research in psychology. *Qualitative Research in Psychology*, *3*(2), 77–101. DOI: 10.1191/1478088706qp063oa

Chytas, D., Noussios, G., Paraskevas, G., Vasiliadis, A. V., Giovanidis, G., & Troupis, T. (2025). Can ChatGPT play a significant role in anatomy education? A scoping review. *Morphologie*, *109*(365), 100949. DOI: 10.1016/j.morpho.2025.100949 PMID: 39813897 de Oliveira, F. B., & Stoltz, T. (2020). Social and Affective Interaction of Gifted Students. *Socio-emotional Development and Creativity of Gifted Students, 139*. Advance online publication. DOI: 10.14195/978-989-26-1770-1

Deng, X., & Yu, Z. (2023). A meta-analysis and systematic review of the effect of chatbot technology use in sustainable education. *Sustainability (Basel), 15*(4), 2940. DOI: 10.3390/su15042940

Dimeli, M., & Kostas, A. (2025). The Role of ChatGPT in Education: Applications, Challenges: Insights From a Systematic Review. *Journal of Information Technology Education, 24*, 2. DOI: 10.28945/5422

Duckworth, A. (2016). *Grit: The power of passion and perseverance* (Vol. 234). Scribner.

Ecker, J., Eckert, G., & Cummings, E. (2025). Augmenting gifted education through artificial intelligence: A four-dimensional framework for AI tutoring integration. *Journal of Advanced Academics, 36*(1), 1–18. DOI: 10.1177/1932202X251356326

Faisal, E. (2024, April). Unlock the potential for Saudi Arabian higher education: a systematic review of the benefits of ChatGPT. In *Frontiers in Education* (Vol. 9, p. 1325601). Frontiers Media SA. https://doi.org/DOI: 10.3389/feduc.2024.1325601

Fenta, A. A. (2025). A review on enhancing education with AI: Exploring the potential of ChatGPT, Bard, and generative AI. *Discover Education, 4*(1), 38. DOI: 10.1007/s44217-025-00426-5

Gagné, F. (2004). Differentiating giftedness and talent: The DMGT as a conceptual framework. In Sternberg, R. J., Davidson, J. E., & Kaufman, J. C. (Eds.), *The international handbook of giftedness* (pp. 99–119). Cambridge University Press.

García-López, I. M., González, C. S. G., Ramírez-Montoya, M. S., & Molina-Espinosa, J. M. (2025). Challenges of implementing ChatGPT on education: Systematic literature review. *International Journal of Educational Research Open, 8*, 100401. DOI: 10.1016/j.ijedro.2024.100401

Guilbault, K. M., Wang, Y., & McCormick, K. M. (2025). Using ChatGPT in the Secondary Gifted Classroom for Personalized Learning and Mentoring. *Gifted Child Today, 48*(2), 93–103. DOI: 10.1177/10762175241308950

Gunawan, J., Aungsuroch, Y., & Montayre, J. (2024). ChatGPT integration within nursing education and its implications for nursing students: A systematic review and text network analysis. *Nurse Education Today, 106323*, 106323. Advance online publication. DOI: 10.1016/j.nedt.2024.106323 PMID: 39068726

Henriksen, D., Mehta, R., & Mehta, S. (2019). Design thinking gives STEAM to teaching: A framework that breaks disciplinary boundaries. *STEAM education. Theory into Practice*, •••, 57–78. DOI: 10.1007/978-3-030-04003-1_4

Holmes, W., Bialik, M., & Fadel, C. (2019). *Artificial intelligence in education promises and implications for teaching and learning*. Center for Curriculum Redesign.

Imran, M., & Almusharraf, N. (2023). Analyzing the role of ChatGPT as a writing assistant at higher education level: A systematic review of the literature. *Contemporary Educational Technology*, *15*(4), ep464. DOI: 10.30935/cedtech/13605

Jeon, J., & Lee, S. (2024). Can learners benefit from chatbots instead of humans? A systematic review of human-chatbot comparison research in language education. *Education and Information Technologies*, *29*(17), 1–32. DOI: 10.1007/s10639-024-12725-9

Kalobo, L., & Setlalentoa, W. (2024). Navigating Challenges in Gifted Education: A Teacher's Perspective on Overcoming Barriers. *Athens Journal of Education*, *11*(4), 269–287. DOI: 10.30958/aje.11-4-1

Karnes, F. A., & Bean, S. M. (Eds.). (2021). *Methods and materials for teaching the gifted* (4th ed.). Routledge., DOI: 10.4324/9781003236603

Kaymakci, G., & Can, S. (2023). Bibliometric Analysis of the Articles on STEM/STEAM Education in Gifted Students. *Uluslararası Türk Eğitim Bilimleri Dergisi*, *2023*(21), 275–308. DOI: 10.46778/goputeb.1258457

Kim, T. W. (2023). Application of artificial intelligence chatbots, including ChatGPT, in education, scholarly work, programming, and content generation and its prospects: A narrative review. *Journal of Educational Evaluation for Health Professions*, *20*, 38. Advance online publication. DOI: 10.3352/jeehp.2023.20.38 PMID: 38148495

Kong, S. C., & Yang, Y. (2024). A human-centered learning and teaching framework using generative artificial intelligence for self-regulated learning development through domain knowledge learning in K–12 settings. *IEEE Transactions on Learning Technologies*, *17*, 1562–1573. DOI: 10.1109/TLT.2024.3392830

Konkus, Ö. C., & Topsakal, Ü. U. (2022). The Effects of STEAM-Based Activities on Gifted Students' STEAM Attitudes, Cooperative Working Skills and Career Choices. *Journal of Science Learning*, *5*(3), 398–410. DOI: 10.17509/jsl.v5i3.46215

Krakowski, S. (2025). Human-AI agency in the age of generative AI. *Information and Organization*, *35*(1), 100560. DOI: 10.1016/j.infoandorg.2025.100560

Lampropoulos, G., & Papadakis, S. (2025). The Educational Value of Artificial Intelligence and Social Robots. In *Social Robots in Education* (pp. 3–15). Springer. DOI: 10.1007/978-3-031-82915-4_1

Li, B., Lowell, V. L., Wang, C., & Li, X. (2024). A systematic review of the first year of publications on ChatGPT and language education: Examining research on ChatGPT's use in language learning and teaching. *Computers and Education: Artificial Intelligence, 100266*, 100266. Advance online publication. DOI: 10.1016/j.caeai.2024.100266

Lo, C. K., Yu, P. L. H., Xu, S., Ng, D. T. K., & Jong, M. S. Y. (2024). Exploring the application of ChatGPT in ESL/EFL education and related research issues: A systematic review of empirical studies. *Smart Learning Environments, 11*(1), 50. DOI: 10.1186/s40561-024-00342-5

Luckin, R. (2018). *Machine Learning and Human Intelligence. The future of education for the 21st century*. UCL Institute of Education Press.

Mahsun, M., Ali, M., Ekaningrum, I. R., & Ibda, H. (2024). Trend of Using ChatGPT in Learning Process and Character Education: A Systematic Literature Review. *International Journal of Learning. Teaching and Educational Research, 23*(5), 387–402. DOI: 10.26803/ijlter.23.5.20

Maita, I., Saide, S., Putri, A. M., & Muwardi, D. (2024). ProsCons of Artificial Intelligence-ChatGPT Adoption in Education Settings: A Literature Review and Future Research Agendas. *IEEE Engineering Management Review, 52*(3), 27–42. Advance online publication. DOI: 10.1109/EMR.2024.3394540

Martins, I., & Baptista, M. (2024). Teacher professional development in integrated STEAM education: A study on its contribution to the development of the PCK of physics teachers. *Education Sciences, 14*(2), 164. DOI: 10.3390/educsci14020164

Meng, N., Dhimolea, T. K., & Ali, Z. (2022). AI-enhanced education: Teaching and learning reimagined. In *Bridging human intelligence and artificial intelligence* (pp. 107–124). Springer International Publishing., DOI: 10.1007/978-3-030-84729-6_7

Milakis, E. D. (2025). Collaborative project-based learning as a pedagogical strategy for inclusion in gifted STEAM education: Teachers perspectives from mixed-ability classrooms. *International Journal of Multidisciplinary Trends, 7*(5), 92–105. DOI: 10.22271/multi.2025.v7.i5b.690

Milakis, E. D., Argyrakou, C. C., Melidis, A., & Vrettaros, J. (2025). ChatGPT and AI Chatbots in Education: An Umbrella Review of Systematic Reviews, Scoping Reviews, and Meta-Analyses. *International Journal of Education and Information Technologies, 19*, 100–119. DOI: 10.46300/9109.2025.19.11

Montenegro-Rueda, M., Fernández-Cerero, J., Fernández-Batanero, J. M., & López-Meneses, E. (2023). Impact of the implementation of ChatGPT in education: A systematic review. *Computers, 12*(8), 153. DOI: 10.3390/computers12080153

Neal, T. M. (2025). Creating Academically Advanced Learning Environments for Gifted Students Through Artificial Intelligence. In *Transforming Special Education Through Artificial Intelligence* (pp. 165–192). IGI Global., DOI: 10.4018/979-8-3693-5538-1.ch006

Nee, C. K., Rahman, M. H. A., Yahaya, N., Ibrahim, N. H., Razak, R. A., & Sugino, C. (2023). Exploring the trend and potential distribution of chatbot in education: A systematic review. *International Journal of Information and Education Technology (IJIET), 13*(3), 516–525. DOI: 10.18178/ijiet.2023.13.3.1834

OECD. (2019). *Recommendation of the Council on Artificial Intelligence*. OECD Legal Instruments. https://oecd.ai/en/assets/files/OECD-LEGAL-0449-en.pdf

OECD. (2021). *OECD AI Principles*. OECD Publishing. https://oecd.ai/en/ai-principles

Özgür, E. G., & Bekiroğlu, N. (2025). Can ChatGPT be used as an education assistant in the field of health sciences? Examining with the integration of meta-analysis and co-citation analysis. *Heliyon, 11*(3), e41925. Advance online publication. DOI: 10.1016/j.heliyon.2025.e41925 PMID: 39981362

Peters, S. J., Gentry, M., Whiting, G. W., & McBee, M. T. (2019). Who gets served in gifted education? Demographic representation and a call for action. *Gifted Child Quarterly, 63*(4), 273–287. DOI: 10.1177/0016986219833738

Pikhart, M., & Al-Obaydi, L. H. (2025). Reporting the potential risk of using AI in higher education: Subjective perspectives of educators. *Computers in Human Behavior Reports, 18*, 100693. DOI: 10.1016/j.chbr.2025.100693

Reich, J. (2020). *Failure to disrupt: Why technology alone can't transform education*. Harvard University Press., DOI: 10.2307/j.ctv322v4cp

Renzulli, J. S. (2021). The three-ring conception of giftedness: A developmental model for promoting creative productivity. In Sternberg, R. J., & Ambrose, D. (Eds.), *Conceptions of giftedness* (3rd ed., pp. 335–357). Cambridge University Press., DOI: 10.1007/978-3-030-56869-6_19

Riga, A., & Malafantis, K. (2023). Gifted students within the Greek educational context: Challenges and perspectives in the frame of contemporary inclusive European education. *European Journal of Education and Pedagogy*, *4*(1), 112–118. DOI: 10.24018/ejedu.2023.4.1.568

Salih, S., Husain, O., Hamdan, M., Abdelsalam, S., Elshafie, H., & Motwakel, A. (2024). Transforming Education with AI: A Systematic Review of ChatGPT's Role in Learning, Academic Practices, and Institutional Adoption. *Results in Engineering*, *103837*. Advance online publication. DOI: 10.1016/j.rineng.2024.103837

Singh, S. (2023). Leadership challenges and strategies in the era of ai transformation. In *2023 International Conference on Computational Science and Computational Intelligence (CSCI)* (pp. 119-124). IEEE. https://doi.org/DOI: 10.1109/CSCI62032.2023.00025

Stambaugh, T., & Wood, S. M. (2021). *Serving gifted students in rural settings*. Routledge., DOI: 10.4324/9781003237938

Sternberg, R. J. (2003). *Wisdom, intelligence, and creativity synthesized*. Cambridge University Press., DOI: 10.1017/CBO9780511509612

Tlili, A., Shehata, B., Adarkwah, M. A., Bozkurt, A., Hickey, D. T., Huang, R., & Agyemang, B. (2023). What if the devil is my guardian angel: ChatGPT as a case study of using chatbots in education. *Smart Learn. Environ.*, *10*(1), 15. DOI: 10.1186/s40561-023-00237-x

Uğraş, H., Uğraş, M., Papadakis, S., & Kalogiannakis, M. (2024a). ChatGPT-supported education in primary schools: The potential of ChatGPT for sustainable practices. *Sustainability (Basel)*, *16*(22), 9855. DOI: 10.3390/su16229855

Uğraş, H., Uğraş, M., Papadakis, S., & Kalogiannakis, M. (2024b). Innovative Early Childhood STEM Education with ChatGPT: Teacher Perspectives. *Technology, Knowledge and Learning*, 1-23. https://doi.org/DOI: 10.1007/s10758-024-09758-3

UNESCO. (2023). *Guidance for generative AI in education and research*. UNESCO Publishing.

VanTassel-Baska, J., & Brown, E. F. (2021). An analysis of gifted education curriculum models. In Karnes, F. A., & Bean, S. M. (Eds.), *Methods and materials for teaching the gifted* (4th ed., pp. 107–138). Routledge., DOI: 10.4324/9781003236603-7

Williamson, B., Bayne, S., & Shay, S. (2020). The datafication of teaching in higher education: Critical issues and perspectives. *Teaching in Higher Education*, *25*(4), 351–365. DOI: 10.1080/13562517.2020.1748811

Worrell, F. C., Subotnik, R. F., Olszewski-Kubilius, P., & Dixson, D. D. (2019). Gifted students. *Annual Review of Psychology*, *70*(1), 551–576. DOI: 10.1146/annurev-psych-010418-102846 PMID: 30089229

Zawacki-Richter, O., Marín, V. I., Bond, M., & Gouverneur, F. (2019). Systematic review of research on artificial intelligence applications in higher education–where are the educators? *International Journal of Educational Technology in Higher Education*, *16*(39), 1–27. DOI: 10.1186/s41239-019-0171-0

Zhai, C., Wibowo, S., & Li, L. D. (2024). The effects of over-reliance on AI dialogue systems on students' cognitive abilities: A systematic review. *Smart Learn. Environ.*, *11*(1), 28. DOI: 10.1186/s40561-024-00316-7

Chapter 9
AI-Driven Innovations in Mathematics Education:
Opportunities for Personalized and Equitable Learning

Thuthukile Jita
http://orcid.org/0000-0002-1173-5251
University of the Free State, South Africa

Loyiso Currell Jita
University of the Free State, South Africa

Adebayo Akinyinka Omoniyi
http://orcid.org/0009-0003-5411-1312
University of the Free State, South Africa

ABSTRACT

Mathematics education traditionally relies on static, teacher-led, rote instructional methods that do not fully address diverse student needs or the evolving technological advances. In a digitized world, the integration of Artificial Intelligence (AI) offers transformative potential. Yet, various barriers—such as technical, pedagogical, and social ones—limit its use. This qualitative conceptual study examines innovative methods for mathematics education, analyzing AI's capacity to enrich students' learning. A thematic analysis of literature identifies challenges related to infrastructure, teacher readiness, digital literacy, and ethics. Findings reveal that AI enables personalized learning, adaptive assessment, and critical thinking. However, successful integration requires strategic adoption, teacher training, and ethical frameworks. This study advocates for professional development programs,

DOI: 10.4018/979-8-2600-0101-1.ch009

collaborative AI-supported environments, and empirical research to assess impact. These steps are crucial for enhancing mathematics education and preparing students for technology-rich future.

INTRODUCTION

Mathematics education is undergoing profound changes due to the swift pace of technological innovations, notably through the increasing use of artificial intelligence (AI) in classrooms (Engelbrecht & Borba, 2024; Mohamudally-Boolaky & Padachi, 2024). As AI tools and systems become more integrated into educational practices, their revolutionary capacity to redefine mathematics instruction draws attention from a wide range of teachers, policymakers and researchers (Akhtar & Shah, 2025; Aleven et al., 2023). Traditional mathematics instruction, often typified by standardized curricula and teacher-centered approaches, has not sufficiently promoted personalized learning, critical thinking, or creativity among diverse groups of students (Arifin et al., 2025). In contrast, AI-enabled tools and platforms create adaptive, interactive, and data-informed learning environments that are responsive to students' unique needs and provide instant, targeted feedback (Borah & Borah, 2024).

Contemporary mathematics education has greatly advanced beyond the confines of traditional, standardized, and teacher-led methods by embracing various pedagogical strategies that encourage personalized learning, critical thinking, and creativity (Canonigo, 2024). These advances, such as differentiated instruction, formative assessment, and collaborative learning, focus on satisfying students' diverse needs. AI-enabled tools and platforms build upon and complement these established educational practices by offering additional capabilities—such as advanced adaptivity, real-time data analytics, and personalized feedback—that boost responsiveness to varying learning profiles (Wang et al., 2022). Notably, AI does not function as a replacement but as an augmenting technology that integrates with and amplifies the impact of earlier educational advancements.

However, the challenges AI confronts in reshaping mathematics instruction—such as equity disparities, teacher readiness gaps, and infrastructural shortcomings—mirror the broader, long-standing obstacles within education reform (Ferrara, 2023; Opesemowo & Ndlovu, 2024). Acknowledging AI as one component among many within a wider ecosystem of educational innovation underscores the necessity of critically assessing how these technologies interact with current practices and systemic constraints (Yang et al., 2024; Zreik, 2024). This stance situates AI within the continuum of educational development and stresses the importance of collaborative approaches that leverage AI's strengths alongside proven pedagogies to facilitate deeper, more equitable mathematics learning experiences (Govender, 2024; Yılmaz et al., 2025).

AI in education encompasses a broad array of tools and platforms with differing functionalities. Hence, realistically differentiating them and their applications in mathematics instruction is reasonable (Martin et al., 2024). Not every AI solution is equally suited to support adaptive, interactive, and data-informed learning environments. For instance, intelligent tutoring systems and AI-adaptive learning platforms target adjusting content and pacing to individual student requirements, delivering individualized feedback and dynamic scaffolding to improve mathematical understanding (Dabingaya, 2022; Jong et al., 2024). Conversely, more rudimentary AI applications like automated grading systems and static content recommendation engines may provide operational efficiency but lack deep personalization or interactive engagement features (Mohamudally-Boolaky & Padachi, 2024).

Furthermore, innovative AI technologies such as large language models and multimodal systems demonstrate promising potential for facilitating nuanced, context-sensitive tutoring and collaborative learning, although their applicability varies across educational settings (Maanu et al., 2025; Noor & Ali, 2025). By recognizing the distinct capabilities and constraints of different AI tools, stakeholders can make well-informed integration decisions appropriate for personalized mathematics instruction (Akhtar & Shah, 2025; Rizvi et al., 2023). This nuanced framing establishes a solid base for harnessing AI effectively to support varying learning objectives and environments in mathematics education (Serin, 2023; Young, 2023).

Evidence from recent studies suggests that the incorporation of AI in mathematics education significantly increases student engagement, tailors instruction to individual needs, and enables collaborative learning (Jong et al., 2024). AI-based educational systems are capable of analyzing student performance instantly and continuously, identify areas for improvement, and present personalized interventions, thereby making mathematics more accessible and rewarding for students with varied abilities and backgrounds (Khazanchi et al., 2025; Lampropoulos & Papadakis, 2025). These innovations do not only support academic achievement but also the acquisition of valuable 21st-century skills like digital literacy and advanced problem-solving (Serin, 2023; Yadav, 2025). Nevertheless, expansion of AI in mathematics education is hampered by factors including unequal access to technological infrastructure, inadequate teacher training, and unethical and fragmented use of AI technologies (Wardat et al., 2024). Comprehensive, fact-based research is therefore essential to systematically analyze and address these barriers, appraise the success of current AI applications, and guide the creation of just, ethical, and sustainable integration strategies (Akhtar & Shah, 2025).

Overcoming these obstacles is key to deriving the full advantage of AI and ensuring fair access for all students (Aslam & Abbas, 2025). A large number of teachers lack the competence and confidence needed to successfully apply AI tools, highlighting the essence of purposeful professional development and sustained support (Li et al., 2024). Moreover, ethical measures that can guard against data security breaches, algorithmic bias, and the risk of widening educational disparities—must be put in place (Chinta et al., 2024; Noor & Ali, 2025). Essentially, an intentional, inclusive approach is required to establish mathematics learning environments that are responsible, inclusive, ethical and future-ready (Ferrara, 2023).

Taking account of the opportunities and limitations associated with adopting AI in mathematics instruction, this qualitative conceptual research aims to investigate innovative, AI-driven pedagogical strategies that can address existing obstacles and contribute to the modernization of mathematics education (Yang et al., 2024; Yeo et al., 2024). By synthesizing current research and practical insights, the study seeks to propose effective approaches for integrating AI in manners that can improve learning outcomes and prepare students for a digital, data-driven future. The findings are intended to equip teachers, policymakers, and researchers with useful insights into both the opportunities and challenges that AI presents in mathematics education, thereby encouraging the development of inventive, non-discriminatory teaching practices for the future.

Statement of the Problem

Despite ongoing advancements in digital technologies, mathematics education remains predominantly traditional, relying on static teaching methods that often fail to meet diverse learning needs. This lack of incorporation of innovative instructional approaches such as AI has curtailed the efforts to nurture critical thinking, problem-solving, and personalized learning in mathematics classrooms (Awang et al., 2025; Govender, 2024). Consequently, students frequently struggle to develop mathematical proficiency, and teachers face challenges in providing adaptive, engaging, and student-oriented instruction. Research has suggested that AI-enabled educational tools can enhance mathematics learning by providing interactive problem-solving environments, personalized feedback, and adaptive assessment (Aleven et al., 2023; Canonigo, 2024).

However, progress in integrating AI into mathematics education has been slow and fragmented due to limitations such as deficient teacher readiness, unreliable technical infrastructure, and imprecise ethical measures particularly regarding data privacy and algorithmic bias (Aslam & Abbas, 2025; Chinta et al., 2024). These challenges restrict the adoption of AI-enhanced teaching practices, creating a gap between technological potential and practical application (Makinde et al., 2024; Sanusi et al., 2022). Confronting this challenge involves establishing a conceptual framework that goes beyond showcasing the groundbreaking capability of AI in mathematics education to also consider the variables impacting its adoption (Yılmaz et al., 2024; Zreik, 2024). Thus, this study sets out to explore innovative AI-integrated pedagogical strategies that can enhance the teaching and learning of mathematics. For this purpose, this study intends to provide answers to the questions below.

Research Questions

The main research question guiding this study is as follows:

> What innovative approaches arise from integrating AI into mathematics education to enhance students' learning experiences?

For a thorough exploration of this primary question, the following sub-questions are identified:

> Sub-RQ1: What benefits are derivable from integrating AI into mathematics education?
> Sub-RQ2: What challenges are encountered in integrating AI into mathematics education?
> Sub-RQ3: How does AI integration contribute to innovative approaches in mathematics education for enriching students' learning experiences?

THEORETICAL FRAMEWORK

This study is framed by two prominent theoretical perspectives: Diffusion of Innovations and Communities of Practice. These two theories serve as valuable lenses for examining the adoption and impact of AI in mathematics education. Drawing from both frameworks enables the study to illuminate the processes, possibilities, challenges, and collaborative dynamics involved in leveraging AI for innovative and equitable mathematics learning experiences.

Diffusion of Innovations

The Diffusion of Innovations (DoI) theory, pioneered by Rogers (2003), describes how novel ideas, technologies, and practices spread within and across educational systems. In mathematics education, DoI is particularly relevant for explaining how teachers, schools, and educational communities adopt AI-based tools and approaches. As pinpointed by Rogers, DoI has five main attributes—perceived usefulness, compatibility with the present practices, complexity, trialability, and observability—that can influence AI adoption rates. In mathematics classrooms, these factors determine how teachers and institutions perceive and embed AI technologies in their instructional routines (Akhtar & Shah, 2025; Engelbrecht & Borba, 2024). For example, research has documented that teachers are more disposed to embrace AI-driven platforms when they realize that their educational benefits are clear and aligned with curricular goals (Aleven et al., 2023; Wang et al., 2022).

DoI theory also emphasizes the significance of communication channels, social networks, and leadership in facilitating or hindering the spread of innovations. Early adopters and influential teachers within mathematics education can promote AI integration by demonstrating its value and addressing concerns among peers (Jong et al., 2024; Wardat et al., 2024). However, challenges like limited access to technological infrastructure, inadequate professional development, and ethical uncertainties slow down the diffusion process (Opesemowo & Ndlovu, 2024; Zreik, 2024). Understanding these dynamics is essential for developing strategies that support the widespread and sustainable AI implementation in mathematics education (Aslam & Abbas, 2025; Chinta et al., 2024). In effect, DoI provides a solid analytical lens for analyzing both the opportunities and challenges associated with AI-driven educational innovation.

Communities of Practice

The Communities of Practice (CoP) theory, as articulated by Lave and Wenger (1991), highlights the importance of social learning and shared expertise within groups united by common interests or professions. In mathematics education, CoP theory sheds light on how teachers, students, and other stakeholders collaboratively develop and refine AI-enhanced pedagogical practices (Maanu et al., 2025; Wenger, 1998; Yılmaz et al., 2024). Participation in CoPs stimulates a sense of belonging and mutual engagement, enabling members to learn from the experiences of one another, experiment with AI technologies, and jointly construct effective instructional approaches (Borah & Borah, 2024; Li et al., 2024).

The collaborative ethos of CoPs is particularly valuable for AI integration, as it encourages ongoing dialogue, reflective practice, and the collective resolution of challenges. Teachers participating in professional learning communities, for example, can share insights on how to utilize AI tools to differentiate instruction, support struggling students, and deepen mathematical reasoning (Canonigo, 2024; Makinde et al., 2024). CoPs also contribute to building teacher confidence, cultivating innovation, and verifying that AI application is contextually appropriate and ethically responsible (Awang et al., 2025; Safiulina et al., 2024). By harnessing the collective expertise and shared commitment of teachers, CoP theory supports meaningful and sustainable incorporation of AI in mathematics education.

Combining Both Theories for AI-mediated Mathematics Education

The joint application of DoI and CoP theories provides a comprehensive framework for interpreting and managing AI integration in mathematics education, DoI theory clarifies the stages and determinants of AI integration. In a related development, CoP theory illuminates the collaborative and social processes central to its successful adoption (Aleven et al., 2023; Yeo et al., 2024). Combining these two perspectives enables a nuanced analysis of how individual and collective actions interact to influence the evolution of AI integration in schools (Egara & Mosimege, 2024; Yang et al., 2024).

This synergy is vitally important considering the complex and evolving nature of AI in education. Essentially, DoI identifies potential facilitators and barriers to implementation of AI, such as infrastructure, perceived benefits, and leadership. CoP, in its own case, underscores the essence of continuous learning, peer support, and ethical considerations (Ferrara, 2023; Opesemowo & Ndlovu, 2024). Both theories collectively inspire approaches that drive the use of AI tools and create a culture of continuous learning, collaboration, and reflective practice among teachers (Khazanchi et al., 2025; Noor & Ali, 2025).

In sum, the dual-theoretical approach broadens the understanding of how AI-driven innovation can be justly and effectively infused in mathematics education. By considering both the systemic and social dimensions of change, the synergy supports the development of strategies that are contextually responsive, promotes sustained professional growth, and ensures that AI's benefits are accessible to every student (Weigand et al., 2024; Zreik, 2024). This holistic theoretical synthesis is crucial for guiding research, policy, and practice in AI-enhanced mathematics education. Figure 1 represents the synergized DoI-CoP framework, intended to support theoretical synthesis and illustrative example rather than reflect empirical study results.

Figure 1. DoI-CoP synergy framework for AI in mathematics education created by the researchers

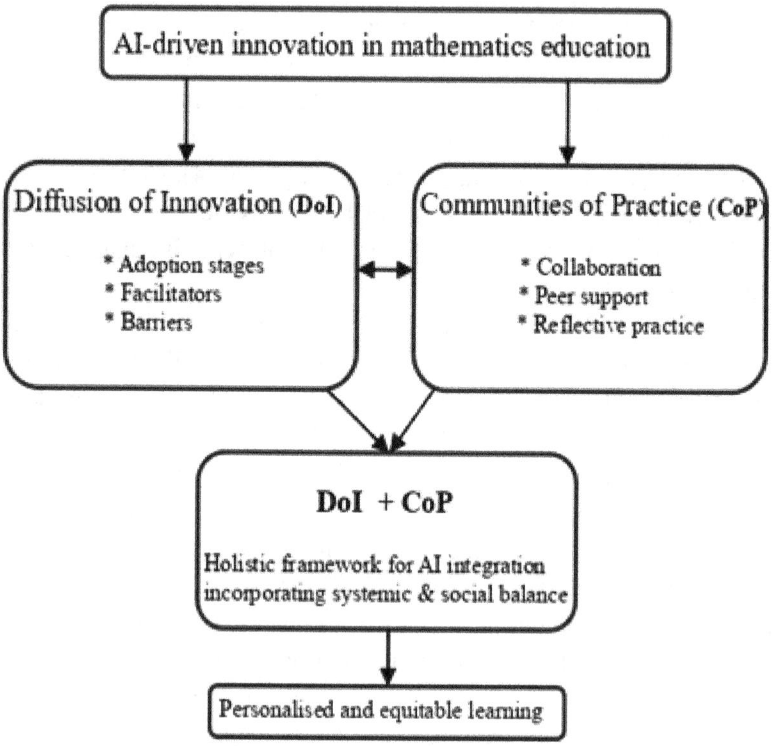

LITERATURE REVIEW

The fast-paced evolution of AI has catalyzed significant shifts in educational practices, particularly within mathematics education. As traditional teaching methods undergo growing scrutiny for their inability to promote deep conceptual understanding or to satisfy diverse student needs, AI has emerged as a promising tool for innovation and transformation (Aleven et al., 2023; Awang et al., 2025). Recent research reports on the potential of AI-enabled platforms to deliver tailored, adaptive, and data-rich learning experiences, thereby raising the levels of student engagement and achievement in mathematics (Canonigo, 2024; Dabingaya, 2022). However, integrating AI into mathematics instruction is accompanied by challenges, particularly regarding equity, ethics, and the evolving responsibilities of teachers (Aslam & Abbas, 2025; Chinta et al., 2024). This literature review critically analyzes the current trends, theoretical perspectives, and global practices in deploying AI for meaningful mathematics learning, aiming to inform innovative approaches that can address persistent educational gaps and enhance learning experiences (Arifin et al., 2025; Yeo et al., 2024).

Traditional Approaches to Mathematics Education

Traditional mathematics instruction has relied heavily on direct teaching, rote memorization, and repetitive practice, often prioritizing procedural skills over conceptual understanding (Elijah, 2024; Weigand et al., 2024). While these methods build foundational skills, they often neglect the development of higher-level cognitive skills, problem-solving, and practical real-world use (Foshee et al., 2016; Serin, 2023). The traditional classroom structure, with its uniform pacing and standardized assessments, struggle to accommodate varying learning experiences, particularly in heterogeneous or resource-limited settings (Mohamudally-Boolaky & Padachi, 2024; Young, 2023). These limitations have prompted moves for the more innovative, technology-mediated pedagogies.

Challenges in Current Pedagogical Methods

Despite incremental reforms, mathematics education still grapples with barriers such as student anxiety, disengagement, and difficulty transferring mathematical knowledge to new contexts (Li et al., 2024; Zreik, 2024). Rigid curricula and limited differentiation can widen achievement gaps, especially among rural or marginalized populations (Henkel et al., 2024; Khazanchi et al., 2025). Furthermore, the absence of prompt personalized feedback in traditional settings hinders timely correction of misconceptions (Govender, 2024; Maanu et al., 2025). These challenges necessitates asking for adaptive, student-focused approaches that leverage emerging technologies to foster engagement, motivation, and equity (Wardat et al., 2024).

The Groundbreaking Development of AI in Mathematics Education

AI is fundamentally redefining the landscape of mathematics education by enabling adaptive, personalized, and data-driven learning experiences. AI-enabled platforms are capable of instantly analyzing student responses, offering tailored feedback and adaptive guidance to accommodate the distinct needs of each student (Awang et al., 2025; Dabingaya, 2022; Lampropoulos & Papadakis, 2025). The scope of AI has broadened to include intelligent tutoring systems, adaptive assessment, and multimodal learning environments (Aleven et al., 2023; Safiulina et al., 2024).

These technological developments are seen as catalysts for increasing conceptual understanding and cultivating critical thinking in mathematics (Arifin et al., 2025; Canonigo, 2024). As AI becomes more sophisticated, appreciation grows for its capacity to augment human teaching and facilitate meaningful, student-focused learning (Akhtar & Shah, 2025; Yeo et al., 2024).

AI Integration in Mathematics Education

Exploring the multifaceted integration of AI in mathematics education involves analyzing its global adoption trends, theoretical foundations, and practical applications through illustrative case studies. This approach establishes a basis for appreciating the evolving role of AI in reshaping mathematics learning across diverse contexts and perspectives.

Global perspectives.

AI integration into mathematics education is gaining global foothold, with considerable evidence of its beneficial effects across multiple educational settings. In the United States, AI-enhanced learning is deployed in mathematics remediation at the college level, recording substantial gains in student success (Foshee et al., 2016). European initiatives, such as those in Romania, strategically incorporate digital technology to bolster mathematics education, promoting both achievement and teaching innovation (Cirneanu & Moldoveanu, 2024). Research conducted in Latin America, such as Colombia, explores modernizing calculus instruction with AI to improve student understanding (Torres-Peña et al., 2024). In Asia, studies in countries such as Indonesia, suggest that AI applications substantially influences critical thinking in mathematics, highlighting the need for its thoughtful integration into educational settings (Arifin et al., 2025; Tashtoush et al., 2025).

Within Africa, South African researchers, for instance, are actively evaluating AI tools such as ChatGPT for their capacity to elevate both instructional delivery and student learning, although challenges related to equitable access, teacher readiness, and ethical considerations persist (Egara et al., 2025; Govender, 2024). Efforts in Nigeria aim to harness AI to revolutionize STEM education, with a strong focus on equity and innovative teaching techniques (Samuel & Salisu, 2025). Trials in Ghana demonstrate the scalability and effectiveness of AI mathematics tutors to boost student achievement by providing individualized instruction and tailored feedback (Henkel et al., 2024; Maanu et al., 2025). In sum, a body of systematic reviews consistently indicates that AI-driven platforms facilitate differentiated instruction, collaborative learning, and formative assessment practices, thus encouraging fair and inclusive educational outcomes worldwide (Jong et al., 2024; Maphalala & Ajani, 2025).

Key theoretical insights.

Theoretical frameworks guiding AI-mediated mathematics education emphasize constructivism, situated learning, and CoP (Lave & Wenger, 1991; Wenger, 1998). Constructivist theories advocate for active, exploratory learning, which AI technologies can support through interactive simulations and problem-based tasks (Canonigo, 2024; Yadav, 2025). Situated learning and social constructivism highlight the value of context and collaboration, both supported by AI platforms that enable peer interaction and knowledge sharing (Maanu et al., 2025; Yılmaz et al., 2024). Such insights underscore AI's ability to establish dynamic, personalized, and socially relevant mathematics learning experiences (Aleven et al., 2023; Maulida et al., 2024).

Alongside constructivism, situated learning, and CoP, activity theory provides complementary insights into AI-supported mathematics education. For example, it emphasizes the interdependence of human activities, tools, and the surrounding environments (Engeström, 1987). In AI-driven mathematics classrooms, AI tools function as mediating artifacts that transform the learning activity, influencing the roles of both teachers and students (Li et al., 2024; Wang et al., 2022). By assessing student interactions with AI technologies and the broader educational context, activity theory elucidates how AI can support complex problem-solving, promote self-directed learning, and facilitate the application of mathematical concepts to real-world contexts (Chen et al, 2020). Activity theory also stresses the significance of aligning AI interventions with the objectives and values of the educational community, ensuring that technology stimulates meaningful and equitable learning experiences (Aslam & Abbas, 2025).

Another pertinent perspective is self-regulated learning (SRL) theory, which concentrates on how students play an active role in directing the learning processes by setting goals, selecting suitable strategies, and engaging in self-evaluation (Pintrich, 2000). AI-powered mathematics platforms can support SRL by providing students with personalized feedback, adaptive challenges, and mechanisms for monitoring their progress (Dabingaya, 2022; Safiulina et al., 2024). Through careful evaluation of student interactions and learning patterns, AI systems can pinpoint areas where students may require additional support or guidance in developing effective learning strategies (Tashtoush et al., 2025). Moreover, AI can create metacognitive awareness by prompting students to reflect on their approaches to problem-solving, evaluate their levels of understanding, and modify their strategies accordingly (Vella, 2025). In so doing, integrating SRL principles into AI-facilitated learning environments can produce more independent, strategic, and ultimately more competent mathematics students (Ogoke et al., 2025).

In exploring critical theoretical perspectives on AI-driven learning, it is crucial to consider not only the frameworks employed to evaluate AI tools but also the broader practical considerations fundamental to their successful applications. A comparative analysis and evaluation framework provides a systematic approach to appraise the functionalities and applicability of different AI platforms in mathematics education. In view of this, a diligent attention to cost-benefit and sustainability analysis ensures that the deployment of AI tools aligns with pedagogical goals and maintains long-term resource and implementation viability. Subsequent sections of this inquiry build upon these aspects.

Assessing and applying AI tools in mathematics education.

For optimal use of AI in mathematics education, employing structured evaluation frameworks guiding the comparative analysis and practical assessment of AI tools is deemed necessary. As such, this study presents the following AI assessment framework, an evaluation template, and their application to secure informed and impactful integration of AI technologies.

Comparative analysis and evaluation framework for AI tools.

For evidence-based decision-making, it is fundamental to understand a comparative matrix of leading AI platforms detailing their strengths, constraints, pedagogical relevance, pricing structures, and privacy considerations (Awang et al., 2025; Borah & Borah, 2024; Maulida et al., 2024). Adaptive tutoring systems, for instance, offer highly personalized learning pacing but vary regarding language capabilities and ease of system integration, while AI chatbots facilitate scalable collaborative learning experiences (Henkel et al., 2024; Maanu et al., 2025). Complementing this overview, establishing clear evaluation criteria—encompassing pedagogical effectiveness, usability, affordability, and privacy compliance—would help guide tool assessment (Aslam & Abbas, 2025; Chinta et al., 2024).

Moreover, the framework must tackle interoperability challenges that arise when deploying AI tools alongside pre-existing educational platforms such as learning management systems (Cirneanu & Moldoveanu, 2024; Yadav, 2025). Providing detailed guidance on pilot testing and iterative assessment processes, capturing quantitative learning analytics with qualitative user feedback, will enable informed, contextually appropriate AI adoption (Canonigo, 2024; Egara et al., 2025). This expanded analysis (summarized in Table 1) supports stakeholders in making ethical, effective and sustainable AI-related decisions according to their unique instructional goals and capacities.

Table 1. Comparative Matrix of Major AI Platforms for Mathematics Education

AI Tool/ Platform	Pedagogical Advantages	Limitations	Use Cases	Cost Analysis	Ethics & Privacy Compliance	Integration & Interoperability
Adaptive tutoring systems (e.g., AI-math tutor) (Henkel et al., 2024)	Personalized learning paths; instant feedback; addresses gaps	May require extensive training; costly facilities	Personalized remediation; scaffolding	License fees; training costs; hardware	Robust data privacy; protocols necessary (Chinta et al., 2024)	**Integration with LMS feasible but may vary by system (Cirneanu & Moldoveanu, 2024)**
AI-powered chatbots (Maanu et al., 2025)	Enhances collaborative learning; fosters conceptual discussion	Limited depth in complex problem-solving	Group discussions; peer learning support	Low to moderate; training and maintenance costs	Ethical use ensured by monitoring bias (Ferrara, 2023)	**Generally flexible; requires API connections for LMS**
Formative AI assessment tools (Canonigo, 2024; Awang et al., 2025)	Real-time diagnostics; supports formative instruction	Reliance on quality of assessment design	Monitoring progress; adaptive assessments	Subscription-based; update fees	Adheres to educational data standards (Aslam & Abbas, 2025)	**Seamlessly integrates with digital gradebooks and LMS**
Language support & accessibility AI (Noor & Ali, 2025)	Multimodal feedback; supports ELLs and learners with disabilities	May be less effective in low-resource settings	Inclusive classrooms; multilingual support	Variable; often modular add-ons	Incorporates universal design principles	**Interoperability depends on backend system architecture**

Legend: *API – Application Programming Interface

AI tool evaluation template.

Designed for evaluating AI tools and platforms in mathematics education, the template below presents a structured framework capturing six critical assessment criteria namely: pedagogical effectiveness, usability and teacher support, cost and resource considerations, privacy and equity concerns, system integration, and plans for implementation and assessment.

1. Pedagogical impact
    - Is the AI platform effective in personalizing instruction?
    - Does it support collaborative and critical thinking tasks?
    - Does it provide timely and actionable feedback to students and teachers?
2. Ease of use and teacher support
    - To what extent is the user interface intuitive easy for teachers and students?

- Are ongoing technical support and professional development offered?
- Can teachers easily align it with the curricular goals and instructional needs?

3. Cost and resource requirements
   - What initial investment (software, hardware, licenses) is required?
   - What recurring costs (maintenance, training, updates) are involved?
   - Does the institution's budget support both the initial funding and ongoing scalability of the AI implementation?
4. Privacy, ethics, and equity
   - Is the AI tool compliant with data privacy regulations (e.g., COPPA, GDPR)?
   - Does its design prioritize fairness, bias mitigation, and accessibility?
   - Does it ensure accessible and equitable learning opportunities for all students, including those with disabilities and ELLs?
5. Interoperability and integration
   - Can the AI tool integrate seamlessly with existing LMS or ed-tech platforms?
   - What compatibility issues and technical requirements are necessary?
   - Does it allow data export and analytics?
6. Implementation and evaluation plan
   - Is the conduct of a structured pilot phase recommended to determine the tool's suitability and impact?
   - Are mixed-method (quantitative and qualitative) evaluation suggested?
   - Does it include mechanisms for iterative feedback and continuous improvement?

Legend: * COPPA: Children's Online Privacy Protection Act * GDPR: General Data Protection Regulation

* Ed-tech platforms: Education-technology platforms

Application of the comparative matrix and evaluation template.

The comparative matrix and evaluation template are developed to assist decision-makers and teachers in thoroughly assessing AI tools. This practical instrument enables them to align their choices of AI tools and platforms with pedagogical goals, available resources, and ethical standards, facilitating responsible AI adoption that fosters meaningful mathematics learning outcomes (Maanu et al., 2025; Noor & Ali, 2025).

Cost-benefit and sustainability analysis.

To strengthen economic decision-making in AI adoption within mathematics education, this study introduces a structured framework for cost-benefit analysis weighing both initial and recurring investments against educational and operational returns (Henkel et al., 2024; Li et al., 2024). Key cost components include hardware and software procurement, infrastructure improvements, teacher training, system maintenance, and periodic AI upgrades, while benefits cover increased student engagement, personalized learning gains, and improved teacher efficiency, contributing to long-term cost savings such as reduced remediation requirements (Awang et al., 2025; Canonigo, 2024). Total cost of ownership (TCO) models highlights upfront and recurring expenses as well as asset lifecycle management, enabling precise budgeting and resource allocation in diverse educational contexts, from resource-rich urban schools to resource-limited rural areas (Cirneanu & Moldoveanu, 2024; Maulida et al., 2024).

Sustainability strategies necessitate diversified funding involving government subsidies, private sector partnerships, and active community engagement to secure long-term financial stability and growth over time (Makinde et al., 2024; Samuel & Salisu, 2025). Embedding AI systems within current educational policies and infrastructure, along with continuous teacher capacity building, reinforces system resilience and lessens dependency on external providers (Aslam & Abbas, 2025). Return on investment (ROI) considerations should consist of quantitative data—such as improvements in student performance, low drop-out rates, and cost efficiencies—and qualitative metrics including student and teacher satisfaction and equitable access to resource (Egara et al., 2025; Khazanchi et al., 2025). Utilizing balanced scorecards that combine financial, pedagogical, and social impact indicators can enable a comprehensive measurement of AI's educational impact and economic prudence (Awang et al., 2025; Li et al., 2024). This holistic economic framework equips education leaders to implement innovative, AI-mediated mathematics education successfully and sustainably across various learning environments. Some practical examples and case studies of the incorporation of AI tools in mathematics classrooms are given below in the subsequent subsection.

Case Studies.

Including some concrete case studies of the implementation of AI in mathematics education serves to provide rich, detailed, contextual evidence of AI's pragmatic application, effectively bridging the gap between theory and classroom realities (Egara & Mosimege, 2024; Henkel et al., 2024). Such studies reveal barriers to implementation and recognize best practices for tailored AI adoption (Jong et al.,

2024; Maanu et al., 2025). Three vignette narratives are presented here to showcase AI implementation processes across varied contexts, each giving actionable steps and results.

Case study 1: AI-enabled mathematics tutoring in a high-resource urban school.

Henkel et al. (2024) report the utilization of an AI-enabled adaptive tutoring system in a large urban high school to personalize mathematics learning and offer dynamic assessment through the following process:

Needs assessment. Teachers and administrators pinpointed students' challenges in receiving timely, individualized feedback on problem-solving tasks.

Selection and customization. A scalable AI tutor capable of adapting to each student's knowledge state and delivering scaffolded support aligned to curricular standards was selected. It was tailored to local curricular content and matched to the school's instructional goals.

Professional development. Intensive workshops and on-site coaching were organized to equip teachers for effective integration of AI tools, interpretation of AI-generated analytics, and blending traditional methods with AI guidance.

Pilot launch and iterative refinement. The AI system was piloted in chosen grades, accompanied by continuous data gathering on student engagement, performance, and user experience. Then, based on teacher and student feedback, iterative adjustments were made to AI feedback algorithms and intervention timing.

Outcomes. There were noticeable improvements in students' problem-solving accuracy and conceptual understanding alongside increased motivation. Teachers acknowledged AI's role in enabling targeted remediation and personalized instruction.

Case study 2: AI-supported collaborative learning at a low-resource rural school.

Maanu et al. (2025) describe a rural secondary school with minimal technological infrastructure adopting AI-powered chatbots to facilitate collaborative mathematics learning through peer interactions. The implementation steps involved:

Infrastructure preparation. The school collaborated with local partners to establish stable internet access and distribute affordable mobile devices to students.

AI chatbot development. Chatbots were created featuring culturally relevant, curriculum-aligned mathematics tasks designed for group problem-solving. The chatbots prompted students to discuss solution strategies collaboratively.

Teacher involvement. Teachers were trained to monitor chatbot discussions and utilize AI-generated summaries and reports to pinpoint students' difficulties and guide subsequent instruction.

Continuous support and evaluation. Regular professional development and technical assistance sustained effective system use and bolstered teacher confidence.

Impact. Collaboration among students improved substantially, with qualitative reports revealing deeper conceptual understanding and renewed enthusiasm for mathematics. Teachers noted stronger peer learning dynamics and greater classroom participation.

Case study 3: AI-augmented formative assessment in middle school mathematics.

Based on insights from Canonigo (2024) and Awang et al. (2025), a middle school serving a mixed urban-suburban population introduced an AI-facilitated formative assessment platform to give real-time feedback and encourage self-regulated learning. The implementation stages involved are as follows:

Baseline data collection. Pre-intervention assessments captured student achievement levels and pointed out prevalent misconceptions.

Integration with pedagogy. Weekly lessons incorporated AI assessments to deliver instant, personalized feedback on students' problem-solving progress and conceptual errors to students.

Teacher utilization of analytics. Teachers used AI dashboards to analyze class-wide trends and individual student data, guiding focused interventions and adaptive lesson pacing.

Promotion of student autonomy. AI tools included metacognitive prompts urging students to reflect on their errors, set learning goals, and adapt strategies.

Results. The intervention produced statistically significant improvements in critical thinking and conceptual understanding. Notably too, students reported higher engagement and greater ownership of their learning.

These case studies—grounded in urban, rural, and mixed-context implementations— exemplify practical AI integration strategies tailored to different contexts, demonstrating how AI is utilized to shape personalized instruction, stimulate collaborative learning, and strengthen formative assessment practices.

Equity, Ethics, and Contextual Challenges

The digital divide.

A critical obstacle to the equitable incorporation of AI in mathematics education is the digital divide, which warrants more explicit and nuanced examination in this study, particularly relative to its structural implications in both urban and rural contexts. The digital divide is multidimensional, encompassing not only disparities in access to technology and stable internet connectivity but also in digital literacy and preparedness among teachers and students (Samuel & Salisu, 2025; Sanusi et al., 2022). Generally, urban educational settings enjoy superior infrastructure, equipment, and technical support, whereas rural and under-funded regions suffer from considerable challenges like hardware scarcity, unreliable internet connectivity, and insufficient training opportunities (Khazanchi et al., 2025; Mohamudally-Boolaky & Padachi, 2024). These systemic inequalities inhibit the utilization and benefits of AI-powered learning tools, worsening existing educational inequalities.

Effective responses to the digital divide mandate that both research and policy actively recognize it as a central concern rather than a secondary matter (Awang et al., 2025). It involves considering it as both resource and capacity deficiencies where inadequate access coincides with limited skills to harness AI's educational potential (Egara & Mosimege, 2024). Strategies for AI integration must therefore prioritize infrastructure investments, focused professional development for teachers, and culturally responsive technology design suitable for diverse contexts (Li et al., 2024; Noor & Ali, 2025). Neglecting these priorities jeopardizes efforts to remove disparities, affirming the digital divide as a pivotal concern in advancing inclusive and effective AI-powered mathematics education worldwide.

Ethical considerations and bias mitigation.

As AI's influence on mathematics education grows, discourses on equity and ethical issues are increasingly at the forefront. Central to these issues is the necessity for AI systems to be deliberately designed to mitigate intrinsic biases and ensure equitable access to educational resources, particularly for students from historically underserved and marginalized communities (Chinta et al., 2024; Ferrara, 2023). The ethical integration of AI extends beyond bias mitigation to include safeguarding student data confidentiality, maintaining transparency in algorithmic processes, and preserving teacher autonomy (Papadakis et al., 2024a, 2024b). This is crucial in preventing the erosion of pedagogical expertise and avoiding overreliance on automated solutions, thereby ensuring AI serves as a supportive tool rather than a replacement for teachers (Aslam & Abbas, 2025; Paliwal & Patel, 2025). Sustained research is therefore imperative to understand AI's long-term effects on student achievement, shifts in teaching roles, and equitable access to high-quality mathematics education for all students, minimizing rather than reinforcing existing educational disparities (Denga & Denga, 2024; Vella, 2025).

Biases in AI systems for mathematics education mainly stem from the reliance on large datasets, typically sourced from formal school environments, which often lack sufficient representation of varying socioeconomic statuses, cultural backgrounds, and individual learning experiences (Ferrara, 2023; Noor & Ali, 2025). Such data collection practices tend to favor readily accessible institutional records, overlooking critical contextual factors that influence students' educational access and success (Awang et al., 2025). Consequently, AI applications trained on such incomplete or skewed data risk exacerbating entrenched structural inequities within educational systems (Chinta et al., 2024; Li et al., 2024). Counteracting these risks requires a critical and comprehensive approach that combines ethical scrutiny with technical innovation and inclusive technology design.

Key to mitigating these ethical and bias-related issues is the adoption of transparent and rigorous data collection protocols that value fairness, privacy, and informed consent, coupled with enhancements in dataset quality, comprehensiveness, and representativeness (Chinta et al., 2024; Ferrara, 2023). Technological advancements must emphasize the incorporation of rich, context-aware datasets that reflect students' socioeconomic and cultural realities to foster greater inclusivity in AI implementations (Li et al., 2024; Noor & Ali, 2025). In the absence of such intentional measures, AI deployment risks perpetuating existing inequalities and compromising goals for equitable education. Thus, continuous evaluation and scrutiny of AI algorithms are fundamental to promoting fairness, equity, and ethical accountability in AI-augmented mathematics education.

Amplifying student voices and embracing varied learning needs.

To reinforce the essence of ethical and equitable AI integration in mathematics education, this study incorporates direct student perspectives and addressing diverse student needs, particularly spotlighting inclusivity for students with disabilities, English Language Learners (ELLs), and culturally diverse groups, while championing the use of accessible and culturally responsive AI technologies.

Inclusion of students with disabilities and English language learners (ELLs).

Research underscores the criticality of AI tools that are both accessible and adaptable to a wide range of student profiles. For example, Paliwal and Patel (2025) argue for AI to provide personalized scaffolding and multimodal feedback (visual, auditory, textual) tailored for students with diverse abilities. Aslam and Abbas (2025) give another relevant instance, discussing how AI-enhanced blended synchronous learning environments support students requiring extra linguistic or cognitive assistance. As further observed by these authors, and also buttressed by Noor and Ali (2025), AI-driven platforms can embed universal design principles to guarantee equitable access, such as screen readers, adjustable text size, and language translation features.

Direct student perspectives and testimonials.

Integrating student voices from recent research enriches understanding of AI's practical impact (Govender, 2024; Henkel et al., 2024). In a large-scale global inquiry about higher education students' perception of the use of ChatGPT, Ravšelj et al. (2025) reported that students expressed optimism about ChatGPT's role in enhancing learning, recognizing its usefulness for brainstorming, summarizing, and simplifying complex topics. They noted that its use results in greater efficiency, improved digital skills, and academic success. Overall, their responses, which were a mixture of curiosity and calmness, reflected confidence in using AI as a supportive learning tool. Similarly, Egara et al. (2025) share the survey results revealing secondary students' positive views of AI tools like ChatGPT for mathematics learning, noting advantages such as increased engagement and confidence, while also cautioning about users' over-reliance on AI and their tendency to overlook its limitations. Gathering such testimonials helps emphasize student agency and authentic feedback in discussions on AI's educational contribution.

Addressing culturally diverse populations.

Samuel and Salisu (2025) highlights the necessity for adapting AI implementation to specific cultural contexts, particularly in low-resource or culturally heterogeneous contexts like Nigeria. This involves leveraging culturally relevant content, accommodating local languages, and respecting varying educational norms. Cultural factors also shape students' acceptance and effective use of AI tools (Maanu et al., 2025; Opesemowo & Ndlovu, 2024). Consequently, AI adoption strategies must be context-responsive and culturally sustaining.

AI accessibility features and Universal Design for Learning (UDL) theory.

AI applications ought to be designed in consistency with the UDL principles—offering multiple pathways for engagement, representation, and expression—to meet diverse learning preferences and needs (Chinta et al., 2024; Noor & Ali, 2025). Accessibility features may include voice-activated commands, live captioning, customizable user interfaces, and AI-generated scaffolding prompts for varied proficiency levels (Maphalala & Ajani, 2025).

Implications for equity and ethical AI use.

Ethical AI applications must clearly promote equity, ensuring that marginalized groups are not further disadvantaged (Ferrara, 2023). Proactive engagement of diverse student voices in AI development and deployment fosters fairness and inclusivity in mathematics education (Aslam & Abbas, 2025).

Summarily, valuing student perspectives and varied learning needs makes mathematics education more equitable and responsive. Engaging students as active participants enhances motivation, while tailored AI tools ensure support for all students. Integrating these views is key to creating adaptive AI environments that deepen understanding and foster lifelong learning, advancing equity and innovation in mathematics education.

Cultural and contextual considerations in AI adoption.

AI adoption in mathematics education calls for careful consideration of cultural, linguistic, and contextual factors, particularly in developing nations where challenges are distinctly intricate (Samuel & Salisu, 2025; Sanusi et al., 2022). Cultural influences inform not only the acceptance of AI technologies but also pedagogical practices and patterns of student engagement, which vary widely across diverse educational landscapes. For instance, AI tools created for high-resource, monolingual contexts frequently fail to fulfill the needs of students in multilingual environments or in places where cultural norms affect modes of communication and collaboration (Cirneanu & Moldoveanu, 2024; Noor & Ali, 2025). In view of the multilingual nature of many educational environments in developing countries, provision of language support is a critical factor for fair AI adoption. As such, AI systems must incorporate robust multilingual features and culturally relevant content to guarantee accessibility and meaningful learning opportunities for all students (Egara et al., 2024; Yılmaz et al., 2024).

Again, infrastructural disparities, limited digital literacy, and resource shortages unique to developing regions further complicate AI integration, necessitating tailored deployment strategies that prioritize localized needs and inclusivity (Khazanchi et al., 2025; Mohamudally-Boolaky & Padachi, 2024). It is imperative that policymakers and developers engage local stakeholders—including teachers, students, and community representatives—to co-design AI solutions that are culturally responsive and linguistically appropriate, facilitating acceptance and maximizing educational impact (Awang et al., 2025; Li et al., 2024). Explicit incorporation of these cultural and contextual dimensions strengthens the ethical, practical, and pedagogical viability of AI applications in global mathematics education settings.

Emerging Trends and Future Directions

As AI technologies advance fast, emerging innovations including large language models (LLMs) and multimodal AI systems show great transformative prospects for mathematics education (Chinta et al., 2024; Egara & Mosimege, 2024). LLMs, exemplified by AI-powered chatbots, offer nuanced, context-aware tutoring and scaffolding that dynamically respond to individual student needs, while multimodal AIs blend text, visuals, and speech to reinforce student engagement with mathematical concepts (Canonigo, 2024; Noor & Ali, 2025). When responsibly harnessed, these tools can encourage personalized learning and critical thinking.

However, alongside these opportunities, significant concerns arise regarding AI-generated content and academic integrity, especially in tasks demanding original problem-solving and reasoning (Egara et al., 2025; Ferrara, 2023). Relevant stakeholders must collaborate to create clear guidelines and detection mechanisms to uphold fairness and authenticity in mathematics work. Additionally, AI's expanding role in teacher professional development and ongoing support is becoming widespread. Adaptive AI systems can offer personalized coaching, resource recommendations, and real-time feedback, thus sustaining teacher growth amid rapid technological changes (Wardat et al., 2024; Yadav, 2025).

Given the swift evolution of AI, curriculum planners and assessment designers must rethink traditional frameworks by embedding AI literacy, ethical standards, and multimodal learning objectives into mathematics education (Awang et al., 2025; Li et al., 2024). Forward-thinking curricula should incorporate AI as both a learning tool and a subject, preparing students for future STEM challenges leveraging AI technologies. This approach ensures that AI advances rather than disrupt equitable, meaningful learning experiences.

Concluding Remarks on the Reviewed Literature

In summary, the literature reviewed highlights a notable revolution in mathematics education, primarily driven by AI's potential to offer personalized, adaptive, and data-informed instruction (Awang et al., 2025; Dabingaya, 2022). Even though traditional methods have been instrumental in building fundamental skills, they often prove inadequate in cultivating deeper understanding and meeting varied student requirements, creating a demand for more flexible approaches (Elijah, 2024; Serin, 2023; Weigand et al., 2024). Furthermore, persistent challenges observed within current pedagogical models, such as student disengagement and achievement gaps, make technology-supported interventions imperative (Govender, 2024; Khazanchi et al., 2025).

As a result, incorporating AI in mathematics education presents a promising avenue, facilitating differentiated instruction, collaborative learning, and formative assessment across the globe (Henkel et al., 2024). Furthermore, theoretical frameworks emphasizing constructivism, situated learning, and communities of practice support AI's potential to build dynamic, student-centered experiences (Lave & Wenger, 1991; Wenger, 1998). With these trends, it is vitally important—as AI's influence grows stronger—to accord due attention to issues pertaining to equity, ethical considerations, long-term impacts on learning outcomes, teacher roles, and overall accessibility (Noor & Ali, 2025; Vella, 2025; Yang et al., 2024).

METHODOLOGICAL APPROACH

Study Design

This conceptual enquiry follows a structured design that situates AI in mathematics education as the central phenomenon, acknowledging its significant capacity to transform teaching and learning processes (Awang et al., 2025; Yeo et al., 2024). The study's goal is to interpret how AI-facilitated practices are adopted, propagated, and sustained within educational communities through the theoretical guidance provided by the DoI and CoP theories (Lave & Wenger, 1991; Rogers, 2003; Wenger, 1998). Alongside these frameworks, the study undertakes a literature synthesis and thematic analysis to capture the breadth and depth of current research and practices (Awang et al., 2025; Mohamudally-Boolaky & Padachi, 2024). These pillars converge to fulfil three specific objectives: identifying the benefits of AI integration, examining the challenges encountered in the process, and exploring how these inter-related dynamics give rise to innovative AI approaches in mathematics education. Methodically linking these components, the study shows the interplay of theoretical perspectives, empirical insights, and practical challenges as essential for the evolution and refinement of innovative, context-sensitive AI applications in mathematics classrooms (Opesemowo & Ndlovu, 2024). To guide understanding and discussion, the design of this study is visually illustrated in Figure 2.

Figure 2. Visual model of the study's design created by the researchers

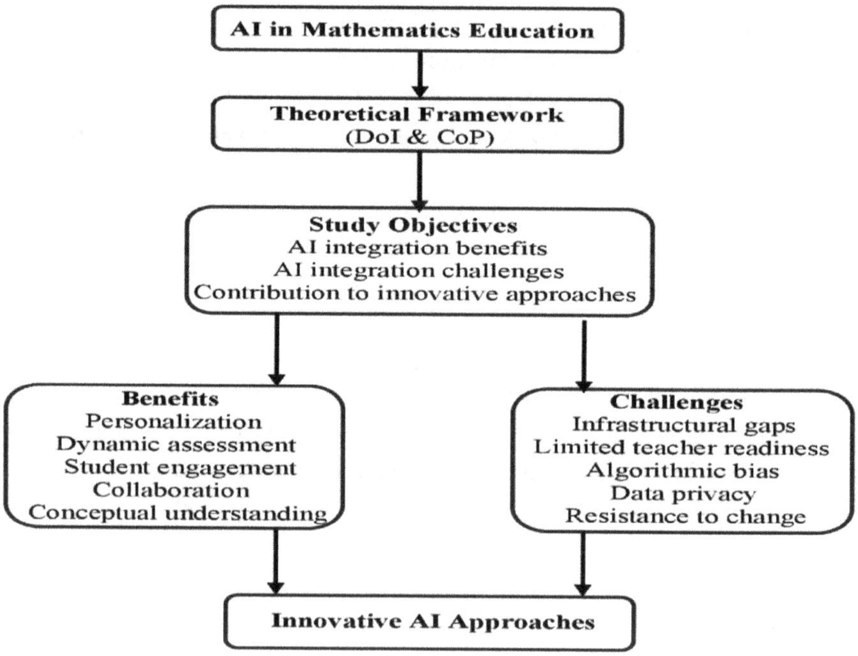

Methods of Data Collection and Analysis

Centering on AI applications in mathematics education, this conceptual paper draws upon perspectives from contemporary literature. Rather than collecting primary data, the research utilizes secondary data sourced from peer-reviewed articles, empirical investigations, and theoretical analyses that discuss innovative applications of AI, pedagogical strategies, and ethical considerations. In pursuit of its central goal — which essentially is to evaluate the advantages and constraints of AI integration in mathematics education and to contribute to the advancement of innovative approaches—the study targets findings concerning the effectiveness of AI-enhanced tools, improvements in student engagement and conceptual understanding, teacher and student perceptions, barriers to implementation, and ethical issues such as fairness and bias (e.g., Canonigo, 2024; Chinta et al., 2024; Egara & Mosimege, 2024). The data gathered are subjected to thematic analysis, which reveals recurring themes and new developments across the literature. This process facilitates the formulation of a conceptual framework for meaningful incorporation of AI into mathematics education and brings to light research gaps and future directions.

Managing Potential Biases in the Study

For an unbiased conceptual analysis of AI's contribution to mathematics education, this study adopts a multi-faceted approach to bias mitigation (Chinta et al., 2024). First, it integrates two well-established, complementary theories—DoI and CoP—which collectively present a more detailed framework and prevent over-reliance on one theoretical lens (Canonigo, 2024; Opesemowo & Ndlovu, 2024). This dual-theory method helps reduce the risk of framework bias and broaden the conceptual lens employed in explaining the incorporation of AI into mathematics education (Ferrara, 2023). The study maintains transparency by explicitly articulating the assumptions and rationale behind combining these two theories. A thorough review of relevant literature was carried out to minimize selective citation or confirmation bias, ensuring that diverse perspectives are represented (Canonigo, 2024; Noor & Ali, 2025). In addition, reflexivity is integrated as a continuous practice, with the researchers critically analyzing personal biases and assumptions toward AI in education (Chinta et al., 2024). Finally, peer review provides an external check, helping uncover any overlooked biases and reinforcing the conceptual integrity and credibility of the study's findings (Egara & Mosimege, 2024; Opesemowo & Ndlovu, 2024).

FINDINGS AND DISCUSSION

The incorporation of AI into mathematics education signifies a major evolution in instructional practices, opening new possibilities for improved learning outcomes. The reviewed literature reveals that AI's capabilities in tailoring instruction, enabling adaptive assessments, and delivering immediate feedback help address varied learning needs and promote deeper student engagement (Aleven et al., 2023; Canonigo, 2024). As these innovations permeate educational communities, they prompt critical consideration of both their advantages and the complexities they introduce, including equity, ethical practices, and the evolving responsibilities of teachers (Aslam & Abbas, 2025; Yeo et al., 2024). To thoroughly understand these dynamics, the following key thematic findings are examined, each explaining how AI-facilitated strategies reshape mathematics education through personalized learning, teacher support, collaboration, conceptual understanding, student engagement, ethical awareness, and implementation obstacles (Awang et al., 2025; Chinta et al., 2024). Refer to Figure 3 for an overview of the various categories of AI applications in mathematics education.

Figure 3. Pie-Chart depicting AI applications by type in mathematics education based on thematic synthesis of the literature (Awang et al., 2025; Borah & Borah, 2024; Mohamudally-Boolaky & Padachi, 2024)

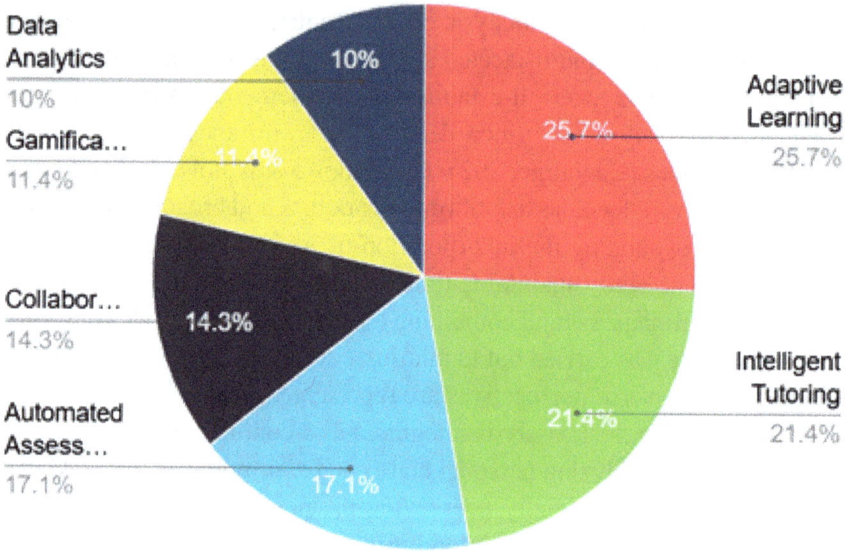

Personalized Instruction and Dynamic Assessment Strategies

AI integration into mathematics education has greatly advanced personalized instruction. AI-supported platforms can analyze individual student data in real time, adapting content and pacing to meet diverse learning needs (Aleven et al., 2023; Dabingaya, 2022). This individualized approach increases engagement and allows students to progress at their own pace, addressing gaps in understanding as they arise (Canonigo, 2024). Dynamic assessment tools, enabled by AI, provide immediate feedback and adjust learning pathways accordingly, which is especially beneficial for students needing additional support or enrichment (Borah & Borah, 2024; Wang et al., 2022). Such adaptive systems exemplify the principles of the

Diffusion of Innovations theory, as they represent a clear advantage over traditional, one-size-fits-all instructional models (Rogers, 2003).

Moreover, AI-driven assessment strategies are redefining how learning is measured and supported. These intelligent assessment systems can identify misconceptions, track student progress, and deliver actionable feedback to both students and teachers (Weigand et al., 2024). Such systems support formative assessments, enabling timely interventions and more targeted instruction (Maulida et al., 2024). The capacity for real-time data analysis and feedback not only boosts student achievement but also equips teachers to make informed instructional decisions (Aleven et al., 2023). As these innovations diffuse through educational communities, they contribute to a culture of continuous improvement and evidence-based practice, fostering collaboration among the teachers, enabling reflective pedagogy and ultimately enriching students' learning experiences.

Collaborative and Community-Oriented Learning

AI technologies also cultivate collaborative and community-oriented learning environments. By leveraging features like intelligent grouping and real-time communication, AI platforms support peer-to-peer learning and collaborative problem solving (Maanu et al., 2025; Yılmaz et al., 2024). These environments encourage students to share knowledge, discuss strategies, and construct understanding collectively, resonating with the CoP framework (Lave & Wenger, 1991; Wenger, 1998). Collaborative AI tools can facilitate the formation of learning communities that transcend geographical and institutional boundaries, promoting inclusivity and shared expertise (Engelbrecht & Borba, 2024).

Furthermore, AI-enabled platforms can connect students with broader networks of students, teachers, and experts, enriching their learning experiences through various perspectives (Jong et al., 2024; Maphalala & Ajani, 2025). These networks foster a sense of belonging and collective responsibility for learning, which is critical for sustained engagement and motivation (Yeo et al., 2024). The CoP framework underscores the essence of social interaction and situated learning, both of which are amplified by AI's ability to facilitate meaningful connections and ongoing dialogue within mathematics education communities (Maanu et al., 2025).

Teacher Support and Professional Development

AI's role in supporting teachers is multifaceted, offering both instructional resources and opportunities for professional growth. Intelligent tutoring systems and lesson-planning tools can alleviate routine tasks, enabling teachers to devote more time to higher-level instructional strategies and individualized support (Akhtar &

Shah, 2025; Aleven et al., 2023). With AI-generated analytics, teachers gain detailed insights into how students are performing, allowing for data-informed decision-making and more effective intervention (Govender, 2024; Li et al., 2024). These supports are particularly valuable in resource-constrained settings, where teachers may face large class sizes and diverse student needs (Khazanchi et al., 2025).

Professional development is also enhanced through AI-facilitated learning communities and just-in-time training modules (Makinde et al., 2024; Wardat et al., 2024). AI platforms can identify teachers' areas for growth and recommend targeted resources or peer collaborations, embodying the principles of both DoI and CoP theories. As teachers become more adept at integrating AI into their practice, they contribute to the diffusion of innovative approaches within their professional networks (Rogers, 2003; Wenger, 1998). This ongoing professional learning is essential for sustaining innovation and ensuring that AI is utilized ethically and effectively in mathematics education (Aslam & Abbas, 2025; Jita et al. 2025).

Fostering Critical Thinking and Conceptual Understanding

AI-powered platforms are increasingly recognized for their capacity to cultivate critical thinking and deepen conceptual understanding in mathematics. Adaptive learning systems expose students to complex, open-ended problems that stimulate higher-order reasoning and reflection (Arifin et al., 2025; Canonigo, 2024). By providing scaffolded support and instant feedback, AI tools help students develop metacognitive skills and resilience in problem solving (Maulida et al., 2024; Tashtoush et al., 2025). This aligns with modern educational goals that prioritize procedural fluency and ability to think critically and creatively (Serin, 2023).

Furthermore, AI can facilitate conceptual understanding by visualizing abstract mathematical concepts and enabling interactive exploration (Denga & Denga, 2024; Torres-Peña et al., 2024). Intelligent systems can adapt explanations and representations to suit individual learning styles, making complex ideas more accessible (Borah & Borah, 2024). These advances support the diffusion of innovative teaching practices that transcend memorization, producing in-depth engagement with mathematics (Yeo et al., 2024).

Student Engagement and Motivation

AI's ability to provide personalized learning and prompt feedback has been shown to positively influence student engagement and motivation. Gamified AI platforms and interactive simulations make mathematics learning more enjoyable and relevant, increasing students' intrinsic motivation to persist and succeed (Dabingaya, 2022; Vella, 2025). These tools can also recognize and celebrate student achievements, fostering a sense of accomplishment and self-efficacy (Canonigo, 2024; Ogoke et al., 2025). The DoI theory suggests that innovations perceived as advantageous and compatible with students' needs are more likely to be adopted and sustained (Rogers, 2003).

Additionally, AI can support students in setting and achieving personalized learning goals, promoting autonomy and self-regulation (Paliwal & Patel, 2025; Yadav, 2025). By providing tailored recommendations and adaptive challenges, AI systems help students take responsibility for their learning (Henkel et al., 2024; Ravšelj et al., 2025). This autonomy is central to both the DoI and CoP frameworks, allowing active participation and sustained engagement within learning communities (Maanu et al., 2025; Wenger, 1998). As AI evolves, its potential to enhance motivation and engagement remains a key driver of innovations in mathematics education. Table 2 provides a synopsis of the benefits derivable from integrating AI into mathematics education, while Figure 4 presents how key themes on this integration are distributed across relevant literature.

Table 2. Summary of AI Benefits in Mathematics Education

AI Benefit	**How It Came About**	**Enhancement Measure**	**Reference**
1. Personalization	Adaptive platforms	Real-time analytics	**Aleven et al., 2023**
2. Dynamic assessment	Intelligent assessment	Timely feedback	**Wang et al., 2022**
3. Engagement	Gamification/AI tools	Interactive activities	**Vella, 2025**
4. Collaboration	AI-supported communities	Peer learning	**Maanu et al., 2025**
5. Conceptual understanding	AI-driven explanations	Scaffolded support	**Canonigo, 2024**

Figure 4. Pie chart illustrating the distribution of key themes on AI in mathematics education, based on the reviewed literature (Awang et al., 2025; Borah & Borah, 2024; Mohamudally-Boolaky & Padachi, 2024)

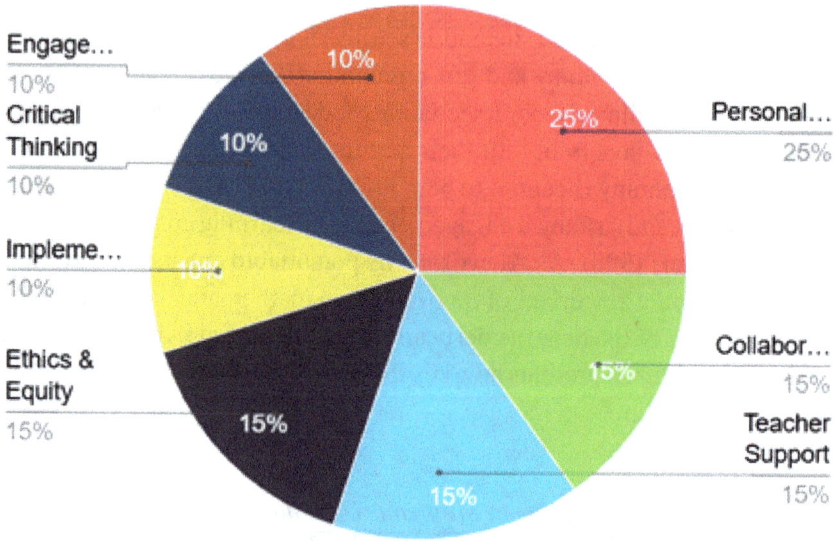

Need to Prioritize Ethics and Equity in AI-Facilitated Mathematics Education

Although AI offers significant benefits, its deployment in mathematics education raises notable ethical and equity concerns. Such issues as bias in algorithms, insecurity of student data, and the digital disparities can exacerbate existing inequalities if not carefully managed (Chinta et al., 2024; Ferrara, 2023). For instance, AI systems trained on biased data may inadvertently disadvantage certain student groups, while unequal access to technology can widen achievement gaps (Noor & Ali, 2025; Samuel & Salisu, 2025). Tackling this concern requires deliberate policy interventions and regular monitoring to ensure equity and inclusivity (Aslam & Abbas, 2025).

Accountability and transparency of AI systems are also important aspects of ethical considerations. Teachers and policymakers should promote responsible applications of AI tools, with clear guidelines for data use and informed consent (Makinde et al., 2024). The DoI framework emphasizes the importance of compatibility and observability in the adoption of innovations, highlighting the need for transparent practices that build trust among stakeholders (Rogers, 2003). By giving diligent attention to ethical and equity measures, educational communities can harness AI's benefits while protecting the interests and rights of all students (Chinta et al., 2024).

Obstacles to Implementation

Despite its potential benefits, several obstacles hinder the widespread adoption of AI in mathematics education. Technical challenges, such as limited infrastructure, interoperability issues, and insufficient technical support, can impede effective implementation (Egara & Mosimege, 2024; Safiulina et al., 2024). Additionally, resistance to change among teachers and institutions may slow down the diffusion rate of AI innovations, as highlighted by the DoI theory (Rogers, 2003). Overcoming these barriers requires sustained investment in infrastructure, capacity-building, and change management (Awang et al., 2025; Mohamudally-Boolaky & Padachi, 2024).

Pedagogical and organizational challenges are equally significant. Teachers may not possess the necessary training or confidence for effective AI integration, while curricular constraints and assessment policies may not conform to AI-supported approaches (Li et al., 2024; Wardat et al., 2024). Furthermore, anxieties over job losses and the erosion of human touch or connection in teaching can intensify scepticism and resistance (Opesemowo & Ndlovu, 2024). Addressing these obstacles necessitates comprehensive professional development, supportive leadership, and the cultivation of a collaborative culture that values innovation and continuous improvement (Makinde et al., 2024; Wenger, 1998). See Table 3 for an outline of the challenges facing adoption of AI for mathematics education, and Figure 5 contrasting the proportion of studies which highlight benefits and challenges across major aspects of AI integration into mathematics education.

Table 3. Summary of AI Challenges in Mathematics Education

AI Challenge	Corresponding Effect	Solution-Step	Reference
1. Infrastructure gaps	Limited access	Invest in digital resources	**Khazanchi et al., 2025**
2. Limited teacher readiness	Less effective use	Professional development	**Wardat et al., 2024**
3. Algorithmic bias	Unfair outcomes	Bias-mitigation strategies	**Chinta et al., 2024**
4. Data privacy breach	Security concerns	Clear data policies	**Aslam & Abbas, 2025**
5. Resistance to change	Slow adoption	Change management	**Makinde et al., 2024**

For the grouped bar chart in Figure 4 presented below, the x-axis is defined by six central constructs of AI integration in mathematics education—implementation, personalization, assessment, collaboration, engagement, and ethics & equity, numbered 1 to 6 accordingly—considered to represent the distribution of studies emphasizing both the benefits and challenges within each aspect.

Figure 5. Grouped bar chart of the proportion of studies highlighting benefits and challenges of central constructs of AI integration in mathematics education (Aleven et al., 2023; Awang et al., 2025; Chinta et al., 2024)

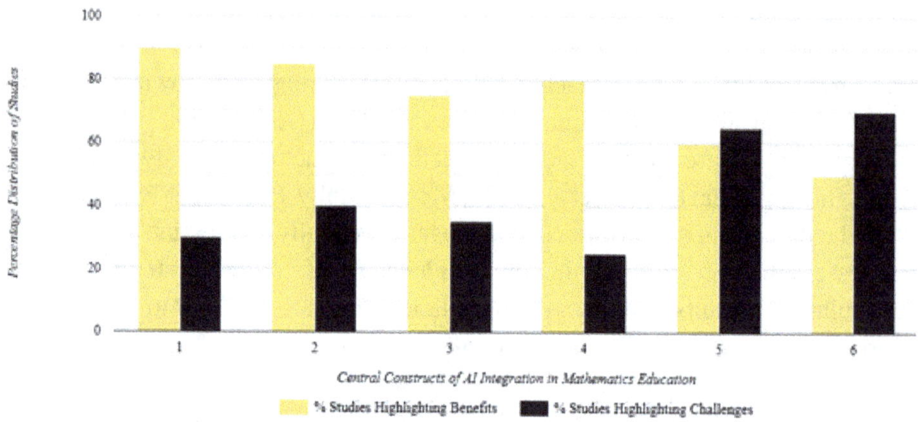

Empirical Validation and Evidence Gaps

Although primarily a conceptual study, the review of existing literature conducted reveals empirical findings that both validate and complicate claims around AI integration in mathematics education. Where consensus exists, research consistently indicates that AI-facilitated tutoring, adaptive systems, and intelligent assessment tools improve mathematics learning outcomes, particularly short-term achievement and engagement (Canonigo, 2024; Henkel et al., 2024; Khazanchi et al., 2025). Below are some specific empirical findings illustrating AI's operationalization and evaluation in mathematics education:

- Classroom-focused studies emphasize AI's pedagogical utility in delivering individualized feedback, supporting challenging task completion, and stimulating student involvement (Foshee et al., 2016; Torres-Peña et al., 2024).
- Practitioner reports reinforce these findings, with teachers acknowledging AI's value in lesson design and differentiation (Egara & Mosimege, 2024; Wardat et al., 2024), while students themselves express both enthusiasm and reservations toward AI-supported mathematics learning (Egara et al., 2025).
- Simultaneously, the empirical record shows inconsistencies. Some studies report gains in conceptual understanding and problem-solving, while others warn against overreliance on AI tools, citing risks of reduced critical

thinking, algorithmic bias, and increased teacher workload (Opesemowo & Ndlovu, 2024; Weigand et al., 2024).

- Longitudinal studies remain particularly limited. A handful of extended evaluations like Wang et al. (2022) on intelligent assessment in high school mathematics suggest lasting benefits, but such results are not universally replicated. Moreover, equity-related concerns, including access disparities and differential learning outcomes, have been insufficiently explored (Ferrara, 2023; Yang et al., 2024).

These findings, taken together, point to notable gaps where empirical evidence is either emerging or contradictory. They also underscore the need for conceptual frameworks that guide analysis and synthesis. Activity Theory (Engeström, 1987) offers a lens to examine AI's mediation of classroom practices, while Communities of Practice (Wenger, 1998) sheds light on teachers' shared understanding of technological innovation. Diffusion of Innovations theory (Rogers, 2003) illuminates adoption and scaling challenges, and Self-Regulated Learning theories (Pintrich, 2000) connect AI-mediated scaffolding to student autonomy. Positioning empirical insights within these frameworks not only clarifies present knowledge but also charts directions for longitudinal, context-sensitive research attentive to both practitioner and student perspectives. By explicitly linking existing empirical evidence—practitioner insights, classroom observations, and outcome data—Table 4 provides triangulation for the study's conceptual propositions.

Table 4. Conceptual Claims and Corresponding Evidence from the Literature

Conceptual Claim	Practitioner/Student Reports	Classroom Observation Data	Outcome/Longitudinal Evidence
AI enhances personalized learning and differentiated mathematics instruction.	Egara & Mosimege, 2024 Wardat et al., 2024	Torres-Peña et al., 2024 Foshee et al., 2016	**Henkel et al., 2024 Wang et al., 2022**
AI increases student motivation and engagement but may cause overreliance.	Egara et al., 2025 Wardat et al., 2024	Torres-Peña et al., 2024	**Khazanchi et al., 2025 Chinta et al., 2024**
Teacher workload and orchestration challenges complicate integration.	Egara & Mosimege, 2024	Dabingaya, 2022	**Opesemowo & Ndlovu, 2024; Weigand et al., 2024**

continued on following page

Table 4. Continued

Conceptual Claim	Practitioner/Student Reports	Classroom Observation Data	Outcome/Longitudinal Evidence
AI-supported feedback strengthens formative Assessment.	Wardat et al., 2024	Torres-Peña et al., 2024 Foshee et al., 2016	**Canonigo, 2024**
Equity and access remain contested domains.	Egara et al., 2025	Dabingaya, 2022	**Ferrara, 2023 Yang et al., 2024**

SYNTHESIS OF KEY FINDINGS TO ADDRESS RESEARCH QUESTIONS

This section synthesizes the major findings from the reviewed literature to respond directly to the study's research questions. The discussion centers on how innovative AI use reshapes mathematics education for productive learning experiences. Table 5 outlines the contribution of each core theme to addressing the research questions, along with clarifications of their roles.

Table 5. Key Themes Mapped to Relevant Research Questions

Theme	Sub-RQ1: Benefits	Sub-RQ2: Challenges	Sub-RQ3: Innovative Approaches
1. Personalized instruction and dynamic assessment			
2. Collaborative and community-oriented learning			
3. Teacher support and professional development			
4. Ethical and equity considerations			
5. Obstacles to implementation			
6. Fostering critical thinking and conceptual understanding			
7. Student engagement and motivation			

Answering Sub-Research Question 1

Sub-RQ1: What benefits are derivable from integrating AI into mathematics education?

The findings across the seven identified themes demonstrate that AI integration brings substantial benefits to mathematics education, particularly in the provision of personalized instruction and dynamic assessment strategies. AI-driven platforms evaluate individual student data promptly, facilitating adaptive content delivery and instant feedback tailored to specific learning needs (Aleven et al., 2023; Dabingaya, 2022; Wang et al., 2022). With this method, students are more involved in the learning process and can progress at their individual preferred pace, addressing learning gaps as they arise (Borah & Borah, 2024; Canonigo, 2024). Furthermore, AI-driven assessment tools enable formative assessment practices, supporting timely interventions and promoting a commitment to continuous learning and improvement (Maulida et al., 2024; Weigand et al., 2024).

Collaborative and community-oriented learning is another major benefit, as AI platforms enable intelligent grouping, real-time communication, and peer-to-peer learning opportunities (Maanu et al., 2025; Yılmaz et al., 2024). These features support the development of learning communities that transcend traditional classroom boundaries, fostering inclusivity and shared expertise (Engelbrecht & Borba, 2024; Jong et al., 2024). Additionally, AI's capacity to gamify learning and provide interactive simulations increases student motivation and engagement, making mathematics more accessible and enjoyable (Ogoke et al., 2025; Vella, 2025). Together, these benefits concur with the DoI theory, representing clear improvements over conventional pedagogical models (Rogers, 2003).

Answering Sub-Research Question 2

> Sub-RQ2: What challenges are encountered in integrating AI into mathematics education?

Although AI brings significant advantages to mathematics education, its adoption is still met with notable challenges. Technical barriers, such as limited infrastructure, system compatibility issues, and unequal access to digital resources, can impede effective implementation, particularly in rural or less-funded schools (Egara & Mosimege, 2024; Khazanchi et al., 2025; Safiulina et al., 2024). Teachers may not have the needed training or confidence for proper integration of AI tools, and organizational resistance to change can further delay the diffusion of these innovations (Jita et al., 2025; Mohamudally-Boolaky & Padachi, 2024; Wardat et al., 2024). These obstacles highlight the need for sustained investment in infrastructure, comprehensive professional development, and supportive leadership (Makinde et al., 2024).

Ethical and equity considerations are equally critical. Scholars note that challenges like bias in algorithms, insecure data, and digital disparities have the potential to worsen existing inequalities in education if left unaddressed (Ferrara, 2023; Noor &

Ali, 2025). Ensuring fairness and inclusivity requires transparent policies, ongoing monitoring, and deliberate efforts to mitigate bias in AI systems (Aslam & Abbas, 2025; Samuel & Salisu, 2025). The CoP framework underscores the importance of collaborative engagement among teachers, policymakers, and stakeholders to ensure responsible, inclusive AI use (Lave & Wenger, 1991; Wenger, 1998).

Answering Sub-Research Question 3

> Sub-RQ-3: How does AI integration contribute to innovative approaches in mathematics education for enriching students' learning experiences?

The synthesis of thematic findings reveals that AI integration drives a range of innovative approaches that enhance students' mathematics learning experiences. AI-facilitated personalized learning and dynamic assessment strategies allow for differentiated instruction and real-time feedback, moving beyond rote memorization to foster critical thinking and deeper conceptual understanding (Arifin et al., 2025; Canonigo, 2024; Tashtoush et al., 2025). Collaborative learning environments supported by AI encourage peer interaction, knowledge sharing, and the formation of vibrant learning communities (Maanu et al., 2025; Yılmaz et al., 2024). These practices are consistent with the CoP theory, which emphasizes situated learning and social interaction (Wenger, 1998).

Teacher support and professional development are also enhanced through AI, as intelligent systems provide actionable insights, reduce administrative burdens, and facilitate targeted training (Akhtar & Shah, 2025; Wardat et al., 2024). AI-driven platforms empower teachers to adopt more innovative, student-centered pedagogies and to collaborate within professional learning networks (Makinde et al., 2024). Furthermore, when educational communities proactively manage issues of ethics, equity, and implementation, they pave the way for AI-facilitated innovations that are just, inclusive and sustainable (Chinta et al., 2024; Opesemowo & Ndlovu, 2024).

Despite that this study synthesizes current literature and theoretical perspectives on AI in mathematics education, its scope is constrained by the range and availability of sources, as well as the rapidly changing landscape of AI technologies. Hence, further empirical research is needed to validate and expand upon the suggested frameworks. Ultimately, these approaches collectively contribute to more engaging, equitable, and effective AI-driven mathematics education, thereby answering the main research question.

CONCLUSION

Integrating AI into mathematics education ushers in a new era defined by creative pedagogical strategies to enrich both teaching and learning experiences. AI-enabled platforms facilitate personalized instruction, adaptive assessment, and real-time feedback, allowing teachers to address individual student needs more effectively than ever before (Aleven et al., 2023; Awang et al., 2025; Canonigo, 2024). These advancements not only improve student engagement and achievement but also foster deeper conceptual understanding and critical thinking skills, aligning with global educational priorities (Arifin et al., 2025; Tashtoush et al., 2025). As AI technologies continually advance, they offer new opportunities for teachers to create dynamic, student-centered learning environments that are sensitive to the varying needs of 21st-century students (Yeo et al., 2024).

Nevertheless, the successful incorporation of AI into mathematics education is contingent on resolving several key challenges. Technical barriers, such as inadequate infrastructure and limited access to digital resources, can hinder the effective implementation of AI tools, particularly in under-resourced or rural settings (Egara & Mosimege, 2024; Khazanchi et al., 2025). Additionally, teachers often require targeted professional development to build the competence and confidence necessary for incorporating AI into their instructional practices (Makinde et al., 2024; Wardat et al., 2024). Organizational resistance and concerns about the potential dehumanization of teaching further complicate the diffusion of AI innovations, as described by the DoI theory (Rogers, 2003). Overcoming these obstacles demands sustained investment in infrastructure, comprehensive teacher training, and supportive leadership at every level of the education system (Mohamudally-Boolaky & Padachi, 2024).

Ethical and equity considerations are of paramount importance in the deployment of AI for mathematics education. Concerns such as algorithmic bias, data confidentiality risks, and the digital divide must be proactively confronted to guard against further deepening of educational inequalities (Chinta et al., 2024; Noor & Ali, 2025). To guarantee responsible and inclusive application of AI technologies, open policies and guidelines, paired with regular monitoring, are fundamental (Aslam & Abbas, 2025; Samuel & Salisu, 2025). The CoP framework articulates the importance of collaborative engagement among teachers, policymakers, and other stakeholders in vigorously championing ethical AI implementation and sustaining impartial access to high-quality mathematics education (Lave & Wenger, 1991; Wenger, 1998).

Importantly, this study's attempt at synthesizing its seven key thematic findings—personalized instruction and dynamic assessment, collaborative learning, teacher support, ethical measures, implementation obstacles, fostering critical thinking, and student engagement—demonstrates a clear mapping to the three secondary research questions. The findings collectively show how AI integration benefits mathematics education, the challenges confronting the integration, and the ways in which innovative approaches are developed to enrich students' learning experiences, comprehensively clarifying the main research question.

In summary, harnessing AI technologies for innovative mathematics education can enhance students' learning experiences and achievements. The study's findings underline the necessity for a balanced approach that optimizes the benefits of AI—such as personalization, collaboration, and enhanced engagement—while rigorously tackling barriers related to infrastructure, professional development, ethics, and equity (Aleven et al., 2023; Opesemowo & Ndlovu, 2024). As AI reshapes the educational landscape, community collaboration, policy development, and ongoing research will assist in ascertaining that these technologies contribute meaningfully and sustainably to the advancement of mathematics education (Yang et al., 2024; Yeo et al., 2024).

RECOMMENDATIONS

The synthesis of current literature and theoretical insights identify multiple critical barriers to the successful adoption of AI in mathematics education. Predominant challenges include uneven infrastructure, particularly in underserved rural regions, deficiencies in teacher digital skills and readiness for AI-based pedagogy, ethical issues such as data privacy and algorithmic bias, insufficient empirical data on student learning outcomes across diverse contexts, and the continual need to adapt to emerging technological and educational trends (Arifin et al., 2025; Aslam & Abbas, 2025; Egara & Mosimege, 2024; Khazanchi et al., 2025; Li et al., 2024). Prioritizing these challenges by urgency and feasibility, this study proposes the following actionable measures:

- Short-term priorities (within 1 to 2 years): Urgent substantial investments in digital infrastructure are necessary for equitable AI access, particularly for disadvantaged communities, to ensure availability of up-to-date hardware, reliable internet, and technical support (Mohamudally-Boolaky & Padachi, 2024). Meanwhile, extensive professional development programs must be deployed to build teachers' digital and pedagogical capacity for effective AI-facilitated personalized and collaborative mathematics learning (Akhtar & Shah, 2025; Wardat et al., 2024). Formation of communities of practice will further sustain capacity development and knowledge sharing (Makinde et al., 2024; Wenger, 1998).

- Medium to long-term goals (3 to 5 years and beyond): Ethical frameworks should be centrally embedded within AI education initiatives, guaranteeing transparency, data privacy protections, and bias mitigation through multi-stakeholder collaborative efforts (Chinta et al., 2024; Ferrara, 2023; Noor & Ali, 2025). Policymakers should implement clear standards and monitoring mechanisms to uplift fairness and promote vulnerable students (Samuel & Salisu, 2025). Expanding empirical research remains critical to verify AI's impact on student engagement, critical thinking, and achievement across diverse contexts (Awang et al., 2025; Henkel et al., 2024). Cross-disciplinary collaboration among teachers, researchers, and technology specialists will enhance AI tools and educational relevance (Jong et al., 2024; Yeo et al., 2024).
- Stakeholder engagement guidance: Educational policymakers must prioritize infrastructure funding, equity-focused policies, and ethical governance in AI adoption. Teachers and school administrators should be committed to continuous professional learning, collaborate in communities of practice, and actively participate in pilot testing and feedback processes. Developers and technology providers need to co-design culturally responsive, accessible AI tools with transparent algorithms and strong privacy measures. Researchers have to undertake longitudinal, context-rich studies to deepen empirical understanding and inform iterative improvements. Students and families must be recognized as essential contributors of user insights to steer equitable AI development and monitor impact.

By pursuing these time-bound, stakeholder-specific recommendations, the mathematics education community can responsibly harness AI's transformative potential to promote equitable, innovative, and future-ready learning experiences (Engelbrecht & Borba, 2024; Yadav, 2025).

REFERENCES

Akhtar, G., & Shah, W. (2025). AI in Mathematics and STEAM Learning: A Design-Based Research Approach to Enhancing Digital Education. DOI: 10.13140/RG.2.2.29554.82885

Aleven, V., Baraniuk, R., Brunskill, E., Crossley, S., Demszky, D., Fancsali, S., . . . Xing, W. (2023, June). *Towards the future of AI-augmented human tutoring in math learning*. In R. Luckin (Ed.), *Artificial intelligence in education: Proceedings of the 24th International Conference on Artificial Intelligence in Education (AIED 2023)* (pp. 26-31). Springer Nature Switzerland. DOI: 10.1007/978-3-031-36336-8_3

Arifin, M. Z., Zulkarnain, I., & Ansori, H. (2025). The influence of artificial intelligence on critical thinking ability in mathematics: A systematic literature review. *Indonesian Journal of Science and Mathematics Education*, *8*(1), 82–92. DOI: 10.24042/ijsme.v8i1.24352

Aslam, U., & Abbas, A. (2025). Ethical AI and ICT integration in mathematics education: Enhancing lifelong learning through blended synchronous learning. DOI: 10.13140/RG.2.2.30393.68969

Awang, L. A., Yusop, F. D., & Danaee, M. (2025). Current practices and future direction of artificial intelligence in mathematics education: A systematic review. *International Electronic Journal of Mathematics Education*, *20*(2), em0823. Advance online publication. DOI: 10.29333/iejme/16006

Borah, P., & Borah, A. C.Dr. Pratibha BorahDr. Anil Chandra Borah. (2024). A Review of use of artificial intelligence in teaching and learning of mathematics. *IJSAT-International Journal on Science and Technology*, *15*(4), 1190. Advance online publication. DOI: 10.71097/IJSAT.v15.i4.1190

Canonigo, A. M. (2024). Levering AI to enhance students' conceptual understanding and confidence in mathematics. *Journal of Computer Assisted Learning*, *40*(6), 3215–3229. DOI: 10.1111/jcal.13065

Chen, X., Xie, H., Zou, D., & Hwang, G.-J. (2020). Application and theory gaps during the rise of artificial intelligence in education. *Computers and Education: Artificial Intelligence*, *1*, 100002. DOI: 10.1016/j.caeai.2020.100002

Chinta, S. V., Wang, Z., Yin, Z., Hoang, N., Gonzalez, M., Quy, T. L., & Zhang, W. (2024). FairAIED: Navigating fairness, bias, and ethics in educational AI applications. *arXiv preprint arXiv:2407.18745*. http://dx.doi.org//arXiv.2407.18745DOI: 10.48550

Cirneanu, A. L., & Moldoveanu, C. E. (2024). Use of digital technology in integrated mathematics education. *Applied System Innovation*, *7*(4), 66. DOI: 10.3390/asi7040066

Dabingaya, M. (2022). Analyzing the effectiveness of AI-powered adaptive learning platforms in mathematics education. *Interdisciplinary Journal Papier Human Review*, *3*(1), 1–7. DOI: 10.47667/ijphr.v3i1.226

Denga, E. M., & Denga, S. W. (2024). Revolutionizing education: The power of technology. In *Revolutionizing Curricula through Computational Thinking, Logic, and Problem Solving* (pp. 167-188). IGI Global. DOI: 10.4018/979-8-3693-1974-1.ch010

Egara, F. O., & Mosimege, M. (2024). Exploring the integration of artificial intelligence-based ChatGPT into mathematics instruction: Perceptions, challenges, and implications for educators. *Education Sciences*, *14*(7), 742. DOI: 10.3390/educsci14070742

Egara, F. O., Mosimege, M., & Mosia, M. (2025). Secondary school students' perceptions of their usage of artificial intelligence-based ChatGPT in mathematics learning. *Journal of Education (University of KwaZulu-Natal)*, (98), 124-146. DOI: 10.17159/2520-9868/i98a07

Elijah, O. (2024). Innovative pedagogical practices in mathematics education. In *Impacts of Globalization and Innovation in Mathematics Education* (pp. 67–96). IGI Global., DOI: 10.4018/979-8-3693-2873-6.ch004

Engelbrecht, J., & Borba, M. C. (2024). Recent developments in using digital technology in mathematics education. *ZDM Mathematics Education*, *56*(2), 281–292. DOI: 10.1007/s11858-023-01530-2

Engeström, Y. (1987). *Learning by expanding: An activity-theoretical approach to developmental Research*. Orienta-Konsultit.

Ferrara, E. (2023). Fairness and bias in artificial intelligence: A brief survey of sources, impacts, and mitigation strategies. *Sci*, *6*(1), 3. DOI: 10.3390/sci6010003

Foshee, C. M., Elliott, S. N., & Atkinson, R. K. (2016). Technology-enhanced learning in college mathematics remediation. *British Journal of Educational Technology*, *47*(5), 893–905. DOI: 10.1111/bjet.12285

Govender, R. (2024). A reflection on the use of artificial intelligence tools for the meaningful learning of mathematics. *Pythagoras-Journal of the Association for Mathematics Education of South Africa*, *45*(1), 831. DOI: 10.4102/pythagoras.v45i1.831

Henkel, O., Horne-Robinson, H., Kozhakhmetova, N., & Lee, A. (2024, July). Effective and Scalable Math Support: Experimental Evidence on the Impact of an AI-Math Tutor in Ghana. In C. Rodrigo, A. Mitrovic, & A. Wise (Eds.), *Artificial intelligence in education: Proceedings of the 25th International Conference on Artificial Intelligence in Education (AIED 2024)* (pp. 373-381). Springer Nature Switzerland. DOI: 10.1007/978-3-031-64315-6_34

Jita, T., Jita, L. C., & Omoniyi, A. A. (2025). Mathematics education in the AI era: Preparing teachers for evolving classroom demands. *International Journal of Learning. Teaching and Educational Research*, *24*(10), 417–434. DOI: 10.26803/ijlter.24.10.19

Jong, M. S. Y., Zhai, X., & Chen, W. (2024). Innovative uses of technologies in science, mathematics and STEM education in K-12 contexts. *International Journal of Science and Mathematics Education*, *22*(S1), 1–9. DOI: 10.1007/s10763-024-10530-x

Khazanchi, R., Di Mitri, D., & Drachsler, H. (2025). The effect of AI-based systems on mathematics achievement in rural context: A quantitative study. *Journal of Computer Assisted Learning*, *41*(1), e13098. DOI: 10.1111/jcal.13098

Lampropoulos, G., & Papadakis, S. (2025). The educational value of artificial intelligence and social robots. In *Social Robots in Education* (pp. 3–15). Springer., DOI: 10.1007/978-3-031-82915-4_1

Lave, J., & Wenger, E. (1991). *Situated learning: Legitimate peripheral participation*. Cambridge University Press. DOI: 10.1017/CBO9780511815355

Li, X., Gould, T., & Zaki, R. (2024). The impact of artificial intelligence on learners and teachers: A mathematics education perspective. In Bakken, J. P., Obiakor, F. E., & Rotatori, A. F. (Eds.), *Education, development and intervention: Toward participatory and integrated solutions* (pp. 133–148). Springer Nature Switzerland., DOI: 10.1007/978-3-031-60713-4_9

Maanu, V., Boateng, F. O., & Larbi, E. (2025). AI-assisted instructions in collaborative learning in mathematics education: A qualitative approach. *American Journal of STEM Education*, *7*, 11–36. DOI: 10.32674/68zzkz60

Makinde, A. I., Adeleye, S. A., Oronti, A. O., & Jimoh, I. T. (2024). Revolutionizing education. In Rao, K. R., & Dastidar, R. G. (Eds.), *Artificial intelligence for wireless communication systems: Technology and applications* (p. 103). CRC Press., DOI: 10.1201/9781003517689-5

Maphalala, M. C., & Ajani, O. A. (2025). Leveraging artificial intelligence as a learning tool in higher education. *Interdisciplinary Journal of Education Research, 7*(1), a01–a01. DOI: 10.38140/ijer-2025.vol7.1.01

Martin, F., Zhuang, M., & Schaefer, D. (2024). Systematic review of research on artificial intelligence in K-12 education (2017–2022). In *Computers and Education* (Vol. 6). Artificial Intelligence., DOI: 10.1016/j.caeai.2023.100195

Maulida, L., Nurossobah, P., Aura, B. A., Nengsih, E. D., & Rasilah, R. (2024). Improving The effectiveness of mathematics learning through artificial intelligence: Literature review. *Journal of General Education and Humanities, 3*(4), 323–338. DOI: 10.58421/gehu.v3i4.267

Mohamudally-Boolaky, A., & Padachi, K. (2024). Leveraging technology for math education: A systematic literature review. *Creative Education, 15*(8), 1692–1704. DOI: 10.4236/ce.2024.158102

Noor, S., & Ali, K. (2025). Ethical AI and Multimodal Semiotic Reasoning: Redefining mathematics and STEAM education in the digital era. DOI: 10.13140/RG.2.2.14455.33443

Ogoke, C. J., Anyanwu, A., Okolie, A., Onuoha, E., & Vivian, D. O. (2025). Application of artificial intelligence in the teaching and learning of mathematics: Implication for achievement and retention. *Eureka: Journal of Educational Research, 3*(2), 134–141. DOI: 10.56773/ejer.v3i2.62

Opesemowo, O. A., & Ndlovu, M. (2024). Artificial intelligence in mathematics education: The good, the bad, and the ugly. *Journal of Pedagogical Research, 8*(3), 333–346. DOI: 10.33902/JPR.202426428

Paliwal, V., & Patel, S. (2025). Can artificial intelligence facilitate mathematics instruction? In Nagar, S., & Kumar, M. (Eds.), *Transforming Special Education through Artificial Intelligence* (pp. 223–244). IGI Global., DOI: 10.4018/979-8-3693-5538-1.ch008

Papadakis, S., Lytvynova, S. H., Ivanova, S. M., & Selyshcheva, I. A. (2024b). *Advancing lifelong learning with AI-enhanced ICT: A review of 3L-Person 2024.* In *CEUR Workshop Proceedings (9th International Workshop on Professional Retraining and Life-Long Learning using ICT: Person-oriented Approach 3L Person 2024, Lviv, Ukraine, September 25, 2023).* CEUR-WS.org.

Papadakis, S., Striuk, A. M., Kravtsov, H. M., Shyshkina, M. P., Marienko, M. V., & Danylchuk, H. B. (2024a). *Embracing digital innovation and cloud technologies for transformative learning experiences.* In *Proceedings of the 11th Workshop on Cloud Technologies in Education (CTE 2023), Kryvyi Rih, Ukraine, December 22, 2023.* CEUR Workshop Proceedings.

Pintrich, P. R. (2000). The role of goal orientation in self-regulated learning. In M. Boekaerts. P.R. Pintrich & M. Zeidner (Eds.), Handbook of Self-Regulation, (pp. 451–502). Academic Press. DOI: 10.1016/B978-012109890-2/50043-3

Ravšelj, D., Keržič, D., Tomaževič, N., Umek, L., Brezovar, N., Iahad, N. A., & Aristovnik, A. (2025). Higher education students' perceptions of ChatGPT: A global study of early reactions. *PLoS One*, *20*(2), e0315011. DOI: 10.1371/journal.pone.0315011 PMID: 39908277

Rizvi, S., Waite, J., & Sentance, S. (2023). Artificial Intelligence teaching and learning in K-12 from 2019 to 2022: A systematic literature review. *Computers and Education: Artificial Intelligence*, *4*, 100145. Advance online publication. DOI: 10.1016/j.caeai.2023.100145

Rogers, E. M. (2003). *Diffusion of Innovations* (5th ed.). Free Press.

Safiulina, E., Vintere, A., & Panova, O. (2024). Exploring AI-based mathematics learning platforms and applications. In *EDULEARN24 Proceedings* (pp. 6861-6865). IATED. DOI: 10.21125/edulearn.2024.1629

Samuel, I. R., & Salisu, A. D. (2025). Shaping the future of STEM education in Nigeria through artificial intelligence. *Journal of African Innovation and Advanced Studies.* DOI: 10.70382/ajaias.v7i2.011

Sanusi, I. T., Olaleye, S. A., Oyelere, S. S., & Dixon, R. A. (2022). Investigating learners' competencies for artificial intelligence education in an African K-12 setting. *Computers and Education Open*, *3*, 100083. Advance online publication. DOI: 10.1016/j.caeo.2022.100083

Serin, H. (2023). The role of technology in mathematics education: Promoting student achievement. *International Journal of Social Sciences & Educational Studies*, *10*(2), 390–395. DOI: 10.23918/ijsses.v10i2p390

Tashtoush, M. A., Qasimi, A. B., Shirawia, N. H., & Hussein, L. A. (2025). The efficacy of utilizing artificial intelligence techniques in developing critical thinking in mathematics among secondary school students and their attitudes toward it. *Iraqi Journal for Computer Science and Mathematics*, *6*(1), 3. DOI: 10.52866/2788-7421.1231

Torres-Peña, R. C., Peña-González, D., Chacuto-López, E., Ariza, E. A., & Vergara, D. (2024). Updating calculus teaching with AI: A classroom experience. *Education Sciences*, *14*(9), 1019. DOI: 10.3390/educsci14091019

Vella, O. (2025). *The Future of Maths Learning: Personalised and AI-Driven*. eBookIt.com.

Wang, G., Chen, X., Zhang, D., Kang, Y., Wang, F., & Su, M. (2022). Development and application of an intelligent assessment system for mathematics learning strategy among high school students—Take Jianzha county as an example. *Sustainability (Basel)*, *14*(19), 12265. DOI: 10.3390/su141912265

Wardat, Y., Tashtoush, M., AlAli, R., & Saleh, S. (2024). Artificial intelligence in education: Mathematics teachers' perspectives, practices and challenges. *Iraqi Journal for Computer Science and Mathematics*, *5*(1), 60–77. DOI: 10.52866/ijcsm.2024.05.01.004

Weigand, H. G., Trgalova, J., & Tabach, M. (2024). Mathematics teaching, learning, and assessment in the digital age. *ZDM Mathematics Education*, *56*(4), 525–541. DOI: 10.1007/s11858-024-01612-9

Wenger, E. (1998). Communities of practice: Learning as a social system. *The Systems Thinker*, *9*(5), 2–3.

Yadav, S. (2025). Leveraging AI to enhance teaching and learning in education: The role of artificial intelligence in modernizing classroom practices. In Singh, A. K., & Sharma, R. (Eds.), *Optimizing Research Techniques and Learning Strategies with Digital Technologies* (pp. 211–238). IGI Global Scientific Publishing., DOI: 10.4018/979-8-3693-7863-2.ch008

Yang, Y., Sun, W., Sun, D., & Salas-Pilco, S. Z. (2024). Navigating the AI-Enhanced STEM education landscape: A decade of insights, trends, and opportunities. *Research in Science & Technological Education*, •••, 1–25. DOI: 10.1080/02635143.2024.2370764

Yeo, S., Moon, J., & Kim, D. J. (2024). Transforming mathematics education with AI: Innovations, implementations, and insights. *The Mathematics Educator*, *63*(2), 387–392. DOI: 10.63311/mathedu.2024.63.2.387

Yılmaz, Z., Galanti, T. M., Naresh, N., & Kanbir, S. (2025). Exploring the interactions among instructors, prospective teachers and AI in facilitating mathematics learning. *School Science and Mathematics*. Advance online publication. DOI: 10.1111/ssm.18341

Young, J. R. (2023). The role of technology in enhancing urban mathematics education. *Journal of Urban Mathematics Education*, *16*(2), 1–13. DOI: 10.21423/jume-v16i2a589 PMID: 37525688

Zreik, M. (2024). Redefining mathematics education in the age of artificial intelligence: Challenges and opportunities. *Impacts of Globalization and Innovation in Mathematics Education*, 19-40. DOI: 10.4018/979-8-3693-2873-6.ch002

Chapter 10
Future Teachers' Perspectives on AI Integration in Mathematics Education

Carolina Ramírez García
http://orcid.org/0009-0001-1413-278X
Independent Researcher, Spain

Alejandro De la Hoz Serrano
http://orcid.org/0000-0001-6362-3879
Independent Researcher, Spain

Lina Viviana Melo Niño
http://orcid.org/0000-0003-4771-058X
Independent Researcher, Spain

ABSTRACT

The integration of Artificial Intelligence (AI) in mathematics education represents a significant advance, with the potential to transform traditional pedagogical approaches. This study analyzes the perception of prospective Primary Education teachers on the use of AI in mathematics education, based on a qualitative analysis performed with a sample of 64 pre-service teachers of the Primary Education Degree. The results reflect a generally positive attitude towards AI, highlighting its capacity to personalize learning, implement innovative methodologies and enhance the educational process. However, key issues are also identified, such as the need to provide adequate access to these technologies and the importance of appropriate teacher training. In addition, the need to integrate AI gradually in teacher training

DOI: 10.4018/979-8-2600-0101-1.ch010

programs and into the teaching of different mathematical contents is underlined, in order to prepare prospective teachers for an effective use of these tools in the classroom.

1. INTRODUCTION

Mathematics education has undergone a profound transformation in recent decades, moving away from traditional approaches toward pedagogical models that increasingly integrate emerging technologies (Wardat et al., 2023). In this context, Artificial Intelligence (AI) has emerged as a tool with great potential to personalize teaching, adapt content to student needs and automate educational processes. Its application in the classroom raises both opportunities and challenges, which makes it essential to analyze its impact on mathematics education and explore the perceptions of prospective teachers about its integration into the educational process (Sun & Zhou, 2024).

Since its formal conceptualization by John McCarthy in 1956, AI has evolved into a sophisticated and adaptive set of technologies capable of simulating human cognitive functions such as reasoning, learning, and problem-solving (De Mántaras & Crosa, 2023; García-Peñalvo, 2024). The emergence of Deep Learning and Generative Language Models, such as ChatGPT and other large language models (LLMs), have expanded the scope of AI's influence in educational contexts. Generative AI (GenAI) in particular has introduced new possibilities in teaching and learning, such as the creation of personalized content, the generation of feedback in real time, virtual simulations, and support for writing and communication tasks (Zawacki-Richter et al., 2019; Fauzi et al., 2023).

International policy frameworks such as the Beijing Consensus on Artificial Intelligence and Education and the 2023 OECD/UNESCO (2023) guidelines have emphasized the need to include AI literacy (Figure 1) as a foundational component of compulsory education. This includes not only technical skills, but also ethical reasoning and social awareness, aligning with the broader goals of Education 4.0 and the Sustainable Development Goals (OECD, 2025). Within this global push, teacher preparation has emerged as a strategic priority: educators must be equipped to navigate the pedagogical, ethical, and technological complexities posed by AI (Ayuso-del Puerto & Gutiérrez-Esteban, 2022).

Figure 1. Relationship of AI literacy to Other Topics and Disciplines (OECD, 2025).

The integration of Artificial Intelligence (AI) into education systems has prompted diverse policy responses worldwide. While countries share a common recognition of AI as a strategic competency for the 21st century, their approaches vary in curricular depth, ethical orientation, and implementation scale. Finland emphasizes ethical literacy and critical thinking, embedding AI within broader digital citizenship frameworks. South Korea prioritizes adaptive learning technologies, leveraging AI for personalized instruction with a focus on academic efficiency. Singapore integrates AI through its "Smart Nation" initiative, promoting inclusive applications that support students with special needs. In contrast, China adopts a technically intensive model, introducing AI from early education stages with limited emphasis on ethical reflection.

Recent international evidence underscores the role of institutional conditions and competence frameworks in shaping pre-service teachers' readiness to integrate AI (Holmes & Porayska-Pomsta, 2023). In the United States, Malik et al. (2025) showed that LLMs can generate warm-up tasks in school mathematics that teachers prefer over expert-designed materials when provided with curricular context. In South Korea, Lim et al. (2025) reported that simulations with generative agents improved pre-service teachers' fluency of thought and problem-solving. In Taiwan, Huang et al. (2023) found that the effectiveness of personalized recommendations depends on student motivation. In Europe, Barana et al. (2023) highlighted GenAI's potential to foster critical reasoning in mathematics.

Meta-analyses such as Yusuf et al. (2024) also underline how teacher education programs incorporating authentic AI practice led to deeper pedagogical understanding than those relying only on theoretical instruction. In this context, several authors have stressed the importance of developing AI literacy that goes beyond mere technical knowledge. As highlighted by Ayuso-del Puerto and Gutiérrez-Esteban (2022), such literacy involves three interrelated levels: technical competence, practical use within educational contexts, and the transformative ability to redesign pedagogical practices with and through AI. Moreover, the aims of AI education should include preparing students to live in AI-mediated societies, generating interest and understanding of AI concepts, and training future professionals capable of applying these technologies ethically and critically.

Conceptual frameworks such as TPACK, DigCompEdu, and models of technology acceptance such as Technology Acceptance Model (TAM) and the Unified Theory of Acceptance and Use of Technology (UTAUT) provide guidance for aligning technological integration with curricular content, instructional strategies, and reflective practice (Dogan et al., 2025; Gallardo et al., 2023; Venkatesh, 2022). Within these frameworks, tools like ChatGPT represent the technological component that can help teachers design personalized learning experiences aligned with SDG 4 (Quality Education). When implemented judiciously, AI can support inclusive and innovative environments by offering adaptive materials and real-time feedback, expanding opportunities even in disadvantaged regions (Uğraş et al., 2024, 2025). Crucially, meaningful integration depends on teachers' deep content knowledge and pedagogical judgment to avoid overreliance on technology and to ensure instructional coherence and equity.

In line with this view, Singh and Ram (2024) emphasize that teacher training grounded in such models not only improves technical proficiency but also shapes teachers' ethical judgment regarding data privacy, equity, and algorithmic bias, critical factors for a global audience. Literature has consistently reported a range of benefits associated with AI in educational innovation. These include the capacity to tailor instruction to students' needs and learning styles, the early detection of learning difficulties through pattern recognition and predictive analytics, the delivery of continuous and formative feedback, and improved accessibility for students with disabilities or special requirements. AI also offers efficiencies in instructional design by automating routine administrative and evaluative tasks, thereby allowing teachers to invest more time in creative and relational aspects of teaching (Zhai et al., 2024). Additionally, AI systems can support long-term monitoring of students' progress, facilitating the development of adaptive and personalized learning pathways (Instituto Nacional de Tecnologías Educativas y de Formación del Profesorado [INTEF], 2022).

Nonetheless, the integration of AI in education is not without its challenges. Authors (Zawacki-Richter et al., 2019; Yusuf et al., 2024; Opesemowo & Ndlovu, 2024) have warned of the ethical, social, and pedagogical complexities involved in its implementation. Concerns about data privacy, algorithmic opacity, potential biases, and the risk of over-automation demand careful attention, particularly in educational settings involving children and adolescents. These challenges underscore the need for a critical and well-informed approach to teacher education, ensuring that future educators are equipped not only with technical skills but also with the capacity for ethical reasoning and pedagogical discernment in the use of AI technologies.

Finally, further investigation is needed regarding AI adoption in mathematics. Valeri et al. (2025) report that, in compulsory education, students tend to use AI primarily in science-related subjects, while mathematics remains the least served discipline. This gap underscores the urgency of studying how AI can be responsibly and effectively integrated into mathematics classrooms and how prospective teachers perceive this process, questions that the following sections begin to address

1.1. Impact and Application of Artificial Intelligence in Mathematics Education

The integration of AI in mathematics education is reshaping how learning experiences are conceived, delivered, and evaluated. Advances in AI suggest that tools such as ChatGPT have the potential to enrich STEM learning environments and offer new perspectives on the education system (Yannier et al., 2020). These tools could improve the quality of teaching and learning in mathematics education (Hwang & Chang, 2023; Uğraş et al., 2025).

However, maximizing this potential requires a robust theoretical foundation that extends beyond purely technological considerations to include cognitive, developmental, and pedagogical perspectives. From cognitive science, AI has been shown to mediate self-regulated learning by managing cognitive load and promoting metacognition through adaptive feedback (Mayer, 2005; Zimmerman, 2002). Computer science education contributes the transversal framework of Computational Thinking (CT), which links algorithmic reasoning to mathematical problem-solving and cultivates abstraction, decomposition, and pattern recognition (Wing, 2006). In parallel, developmental psychology offers critical insights for adapting AI interactions to children's cognitive and socio-emotional capacities, acknowledging their evolving understanding of artificial intentionality, their attribution of agency to intelligent systems, and the importance of ethically designed, pedagogically mediated environments. Integrating these perspectives enriches the analysis of teachers' perceptions, informs classroom design, and supports implementations of AI that are inclusive, developmentally appropriate, and aligned with students' holistic growth.

AI-based systems have the capacity to analyze learner behavior, adjust instructional materials in real time, and generate personalized feedback, thereby enhancing autonomy, differentiation, and self-regulation (Yusuf et al., 2024). These features align closely with constructivist and sociocultural theories of learning, which emphasize the mediating role of tools in cognitive development and the active construction of knowledge (Zreik, 2024; Hwang & Tu, 2021). Recent international studies (Lampropoulos & Papadakis, 2025; Uğraş et al., 2024, 2025) highlight how AI tools, including social robots and conversational agents like ChatGPT, support STEM and mathematics instruction by fostering student engagement, adaptive learning, and sustainable practices in primary education. Lavidas et al. (2022a, 2022b) provide empirical evidence on factors affecting data collection reliability in educational research, which is relevant when interpreting self-reported perceptions of teachers and students. These contributions strengthen the theoretical framework and situate this study within a global conversation on AI in education.

Systematic reviews of the literature, such as that conducted by Mohamed et al. (2022), have classified the principal technological approaches to AI in mathematics education into five main categories. These include Educational Robotics (ER), Intelligent tutoring systems (ITS), teachable agents, specialized software tools such as MATLAB or R, and integrated learning environments that combine multiple technologies. Among these, educational robotics has emerged as the most frequently used, with studies highlighting its effectiveness in developing logical reasoning, problem-solving skills, and student motivation. Intelligent tutoring systems, in turn, offer personalized learning pathways, adaptive feedback, and targeted interventions, particularly in areas such as arithmetic, algebra, and statistics. These systems can simulate one-on-one instruction by guiding students through tasks, adjusting levels of difficulty, and providing real-time support. ITS are among the most developed AI applications in education. These systems have shown particular effectiveness in mathematics instruction, especially in arithmetic, algebra, and statistics, by guiding students through problem-solving tasks and adjusting difficulty levels in real time (Getenet, 2024; Hwang & Tu, 2021). As noted by Labadze et al. (2023), AI-based chatbots and tutors provide significant benefits in student autonomy, motivation, and immediate support. In addition, AI-driven platforms facilitate multimodal and interactive learning environments through simulations and visualizations. These tools help learners to understand abstract concepts in geometry or calculus by manipulating graphical representations and engaging in dynamic modeling activities (Mohamed et al., 2022). Such environments are not only cognitively stimulating but also adaptable to different learning styles.

Another dimension of AI's educational potential lies in its contribution to the development of Computational Thinking (CT) (Yilmaz and Yilmaz, 2023; Weng et al., 2024). Research by Ipek et al. (2023) suggest that GenAI tools support higher-order cognitive tasks such as summarizing, paraphrasing, and data analysis, competencies that are fundamental to mathematics education. However, the effectiveness of these technologies is ultimately contingent upon teachers' ability to integrate them meaningfully into pedagogical practice. As Montenegro-Rueda et al. (2023) argue, the value of AI in education depends less on the capabilities of the technology itself and more on the ways in which educators mediate its use, adapt it to context, and reflect on its ethical implications.

Several persistent challenges must be addressed, particularly in early childhood STEM education. These include teachers' limited knowledge of AI tools, lack of planning resources, insufficient materials (Amran et al., 2021), and classroom management constraints (Çiftçi & Topçu, 2022; Demircan, 2022). Low motivation among both students and teachers also hampers effective integration (Brenneman et al., 2019; Tao, 2019). Moreover, Urban et al. (2025) show that while ChatGPT can help students integrate accurate information into academic writing, weak metacognitive skills can lead to uncritical acceptance of errors—undermining mathematics learning.

In this context, mathematical learning may be compromised if such tools prioritize automated responses over the deep development of competencies such as logical reasoning, problem-solving, and mathematical argumentation (Ayuso-del Puerto & Gutiérrez-Esteban, 2022). An additional risk is the potential reduction of students' cognitive autonomy. The uncritical use of AI-generated content may foster dependence on automated solutions and hinder the consolidation of fundamental skills such as mental calculation, conceptual understanding, and the transfer of mathematical knowledge to novel situations. It is important to highlight that certain mathematical domains remain underrepresented in current research. Although AI tools have shown promise in supporting arithmetic, algebra, and general problem-solving tasks (Yunianto et al., 2024; Fang et al., 2025), areas such as geometry, data analysis, and statistics receive comparatively little attention. This gap implies a partial understanding of AI's pedagogical potential, as these domains are critical for developing comprehensive mathematical competencies, spatial reasoning, and data literacy.

Likewise, teachers have expressed reservations about the appropriateness of generative tools at early educational stages, citing concerns over the reliability of information, reduced human interaction, and insufficient development of essential metacognitive competencies for sustainable mathematics learning (Uğraş et al., 2024). These limitations directly affect the achievement of SDG 4, which seeks to ensure inclusive and high-quality education, and underscore the need for critical AI literacy among both students and teachers (Lampropoulos & Papadakis, 2025). Embedding this reflection into both initial teacher education and continuous professional development will help mitigate risks and guide AI toward pedagogical practices that strengthen the mathematical foundations required for equitable and sustainable learning.

1.2. Perceptions and Attitudes of Prospective Teachers Towards the Integration of AI in Mathematics Education

The effective integration of AI into mathematics education depends not only on access to technological resources but also on teachers' beliefs, attitudes, and professional readiness. Prospective teachers play a decisive role in this process because their emerging conceptions of technology and pedagogy will shape how they incorporate AI into future classrooms (Opesemowo, 2025; Pascual, 2019). Research shows that future teachers approach AI in varied ways. In a phenomenographic study, Yau et al. (2023) identified six distinct understandings of AI in education: as a bridge between technology and daily life, as a channel for transmitting technical knowledge, as a motivator of interest, as a platform for ethical reflection, as a tool for developing practical competencies, and as a way to foster intellectual growth through critical and creative thinking. These perspectives highlight multiple entry points for AI integration, ranging from pragmatic to transformative.

Despite growing recognition of AI's potential, many teachers' candidates report feeling unprepared to use it effectively (Rodríguez et al., 2023). Alfaro-Salas and Diaz (2024) have documented that fewer than 12% of education students feel confident in incorporating AI tools into their instructional design, and most lack awareness of how these tools can support diverse learners or adapt to individual needs. This lack of preparedness is echoed in studies such as that of Ansari et al., which highlight limited exposure to GenAI technologies in teacher education programs.

However, evidence also suggests that structured guidance and reflective practice can change this picture. Ayuso-del Puerto and Gutiérrez-Esteban (2022) demonstrate that project-based approaches and ethical inquiry enable teacher trainees to design AI-enhanced activities while critically analyzing their impact. Likewise, Uğraş et al. (2024, 2025) show that after targeted training programs, teachers addressed infrastructure barriers, developed STEM materials tailored to individual student profiles, provided real-life connections, and successfully integrated ChatGPT to support instruction. These cases confirm that when AI is treated not merely as content but as an embedded pedagogical experience, prospective teachers develop the skills to use it effectively.

Prospective teachers tend to identify a range of benefits associated with AI in mathematics classrooms. These include increased student engagement, better management of instructional time, and enhanced personalization of learning (Grugeon-Allys & Pilet, 2024). Tools such as adaptive platforms and intelligent tutors are seen as promising solutions for addressing longstanding challenges, including learner diversity and motivational issues. However, structural challenges remain. Unequal access to technology, insufficient infrastructure, and the absence of institutional support may hinder the equitable implementation of AI in schools (Fadillah et al., 2024).

Beyond these practical issues, a critical perspective is needed to address potential risks to mathematical learning itself. If AI is used primarily to automate problem-solving, students may rely excessively on automated outputs, undermining the development of reasoning, abstraction, and procedural fluency. There is also the danger of narrowing curricular focus to areas where AI tools are most convenient, neglecting less represented domains such as statistics, geometry, or data analysis (Yunianto et al., 2024). These concerns call for teacher preparation programs to emphasize not only technical proficiency but also pedagogical and ethical discernment.

To meet these needs, frameworks such as TPACK and DigCompEdu provide structured guidance for integrating content knowledge, pedagogy, and digital tools in contextually sensitive ways (Dogan et al., 2025; Gallardo et al., 2023). Equipping prospective teachers with these frameworks fosters critical engagement with AI and prepares them to design innovative, inclusive, and responsible educational practices in an increasingly AI-mediated world.

1.3. Ethical and Pedagogical Considerations of AI Integration

The integration of Artificial Intelligence (AI) into education raises profound ethical, pedagogical, and sustainability-related challenges. Scholars have documented risks concerning student data privacy, algorithmic bias, and unequal access to technology (Vivar & Peñalvo, 2023; UNESCO, 2023). These issues are particularly critical in mathematics education, where adaptive platforms and Intelligent Tutoring Systems depend on sensitive learner data to deliver personalized feedback. Without robust safeguards, such tools may unintentionally reinforce existing inequities or embed opaque decision-making processes into classroom practice.

Theoretical models of technology acceptance, such TAM and UTAUT, provide a useful lens for understanding educators' attitudes toward AI integration. Perceived usefulness and ease of use, central constructs in these frameworks, interact with teachers' pedagogical beliefs and institutional conditions to shape adoption patterns. Similarly, the TPACK framework highlights that sustainable and effective AI integration depends on the dynamic interplay between technological, pedagogical, and content knowledge (Dogan et al., 2025; Gallardo et al., 2023; Venkatesh, 2022). However, positive attitudes toward AI do not automatically translate into pedagogically sound or ethically responsible practices.

Frameworks for AI literacy (Ayuso-del Puerto & Gutiérrez-Esteban, 2022; Lampropoulos & Papadakis, 2025) emphasize that teacher preparation must extend beyond technical proficiency to include critical reflection on the societal and ethical implications of AI. Embedding these dimensions into teacher education aligns with Sustainable Development Goal (SDG) 4 and UNESCO's Beijing Consensus, which call for inclusive, equitable, and high-quality education (Uğraş et al., 2024). The AILit Framework (OECD, 2025) stands out as one of the most comprehensive and ambitious proposals for integrating AI literacy into European educational systems. Developed by an international consortium of experts and endorsed by institutions such as the European Commission and the OECD, this framework aligns with key policies including the EU AI Act, DigComp 2.2, and the Ethical Guidelines for the Use of AI in Education, consolidating an ethical, critical, and cross-cutting vision of AI use in the classroom. It acknowledges the central role of teachers as mediators between technology and meaningful learning. Educators are encouraged to embed AI literacy into their subjects, adapting it to the level and context of their students. To support this, the framework provides concrete examples, pedagogical resources, and recommendations for ongoing teacher training. Moreover, it emphasizes that AI should complement human capacities such as empathy, pedagogical judgment, and creativity. In this regard, the framework promotes a humanistic view of technology, where the development of Digital Competencies is intertwined with ethical and social values.

Empirical studies reinforce both opportunities and risks. Luzano (2024) demonstrates how intelligent tutoring systems can support STEM learning through personalized feedback, while Kohnke & Zaugg (2025) show that AI aligned with Universal Design for Learning (UDL) can improve accessibility for students with disabilities. Similarly, Uğraş et al. (2024) report that ChatGPT can promote sustainable teaching practices by improving Digital Literacy, compensating for learning losses, and supporting mathematical competency development. Within TPACK, ChatGPT represents technological knowledge that enables innovative instructional design (Mishra et al., 2023; Zickafoose et al., 2024).

Nevertheless, findings also reveal skepticism among teachers regarding the suitability of such tools for younger learners. Concerns include the risk of ChatGPT generating inaccurate or misleading information, fostering overreliance or reduced interpersonal communication, and raising age-appropriateness issues. The literature warns that ChatGPT may produce content of questionable accuracy and reliability (Mogali, 2023), posing a barrier to achieving SDG 4.7, which emphasizes education that promotes sustainable development and critical thinking. Inaccurate information can undermine students' analytical skills and their access to trustworthy knowledge, especially in specialized or time-sensitive subject areas (Han et al., 2024).

These risks underscore the critical need for both teachers and students to acquire robust AI literacy skills to evaluate AI outputs responsibly (Celik, 2023; Wang et al., 2023). This requirement aligns with SDG 4.c, which focuses on improving teacher competencies through ongoing professional development. Moreover, the reliance of large language models on vast yet imperfect datasets raises concerns about embedded bias, outdated knowledge, and the lack of transparency in decision-making processes. Addressing these challenges calls for continuous monitoring, rigorous evaluation of AI systems, and explicit ethical governance to ensure that the integration of AI tools such as ChatGPT contributes to equitable, reliable, and high-quality education rather than exacerbating existing disparities (Uğraş et al., 2024).

Despite the growing interest in integrating Artificial Intelligence into mathematics education, few studies have examined the perceptions of pre-service teachers regarding the full range of implications associated with the widespread use of AI in mathematics instruction, focusing not only on its opportunities but also on its relevant challenges. There is a clear need for empirical research that systematically explores the perceptions and experiences of future educators, providing a more comprehensive and context-sensitive understanding of AI integration in primary mathematics education. The present study seeks to address these gaps by offering detailed evidence on the acceptance, challenges, and pedagogical implications of AI, as well as its potential impact on the development of fundamental mathematical competencies.

2. METHODOLOGY

2.1. Design and study sample

The present study is based on a descriptive qualitative approach (Creswell, 2014). Participants were selected using purposive sampling, focusing on third-year pre-service teachers enrolled in Didactics of Mathematics I, as this subject provides a strategic context to analyze how AI can enhance logical reasoning, Computational Thinking, and other mathematics-specific competencies and content. The research participants were 64 pre-service teachers who were in their third year of the Degree in Primary Education during the academic year. The group consisted of 37 females and 27 males, aged between 20 and 22 years. These students did not use any Artificial Intelligence tool during the development of their sessions.

This methodological approach aligns with previous international studies that analyzed teachers' perceptions of AI in STEM education (Uğraş et al., 2024). By focusing on a mathematics didactics course, the study ensures that participants engage with domain-specific pedagogical challenges where AI integration is especially relevant.

2.2. Data collection

For data collection, a qualitative questionnaire of 4 open-ended questions, based on previous studies (Asencio et al., 2024; Ayuso-del Puerto, 2022; Contreras, 2024; Rivas et al., 2023) was used to encourage critical reflection on the integration of Artificial Intelligence in mathematics education and their perception of its applicability in the classroom. The questions are as follows:

- Question 1*: From your perspective, how could AI be integrated into mathematics teaching in primary education to optimize learning?*
- Question 2: *In your opinion, does the introduction of AI in the mathematics classroom facilitate or complicate the learning process? Please explain your answer.*
- Question 3: *Have you had any experience with AI tools in your teaching or daily life? Describe the tool used and the context in which you used it.*
- Question 4: *What types of mathematical content and skills do you think would be appropriate for projects that integrate AI in primary education?*

This study followed international ethical standards for educational research, including OECD and UNESCO recommendations on AI in education. Beyond obtaining approval from the University Ethics Committee and informed consent from participants, particular attention was paid to issues of data privacy, equitable access, and potential algorithmic bias, which are discussed as part of the study's broader implications.

2.3. Data analysis

Data analysis was carried out using the content analysis approach proposed by Bardin (1991). This approach allows organizing and classifying the information in a systematic way, facilitating the identification of patterns, themes and categories that emerge from the participants' responses.

For this purpose, the WebQDA® software (Costa et al., 2020) was used, using a system of categories (Appendix 1) that was constructed from existing categories in the scientific literature (Asencio et al., 2024; Ayuso-del Puerto and Gutiérrez-Esteban, 2022; Contreras, 2024; Rivas et al., 2023; Vivar and Peñalvo, 2023), complemented with new categories derived from the review of the data provided.

A total of 9 categories were generated. The first category *A: General opinions about AI in mathematics education* collects general impressions about AI, both positive and negative, assessing its acceptance and the impact on its adoption in the educational environment. Regarding category *B: Personal and academic use of AI*, it addresses the everyday and academic use of AI, to understand the familiarity with this technology. Category *C: Role of AI in the educational process*, covers the role that AI should play in the educational process. Category *D: Mathematical competence and its integration with AI* categorize mathematical content that can be addressed through AI, highlighting a structured approach that integrates competencies into the curriculum. Category *E: Implementation of AI in mathematics education* highlights specific ways in which AI can be used in mathematics education. Category *F: Advantages of AI in mathematics learning* highlights the direct advantages that AI brings to learning. Category *G: Contents* refers to the contents of the educational curriculum that AI can strengthen. Category *H: Drawbacks of AI use* groups concerns about the misuse of AI in learning. Finally, category *I: Challenges in AI integration* highlights the challenges associated with AI integration in the classroom.

To enhance rigor, coding was performed by two independent researchers. Discrepancies were resolved through iterative discussion, resulting in a Cohen's Kappa coefficient of 0.80, indicating substantial inter-coder reliability. In cases where only one coder reviewed specific responses, consistency was ensured through periodic peer debriefing and audit trails documenting coding decisions.

For data analysis, the Microsoft Office Excel 365® software was used for descriptive analysis using frequencies (F) and percentages (%). In addition, data were obtained from two different indicators. On the one hand, frequencies were obtained for the number of sources (participants), as well as their percentage with respect to their total representation in the study sample (N=64). On the other hand, the frequency of the total number of references to each subcategory was obtained, as well as the percentage relative to its representation in the total number of references of the category to which it belongs.

3. RESULTS

Table 1 presents the overall frequency distribution for each of the categories analyzed in the study, based on two criteria: the number of sources (participants who referred to each subcategory) and the total number of references (instances in which each subcategory was mentioned). In total, 597 sources and 723 references were identified.

Table 1. Overall frequency distribution for each of the categories.

Category	Total sources	% of sources	Total references	% of references	Average references per source
A. General opinions on AI	64	10.72%	70	9.68%	1.09
B. Personal and academic use of AI	112	18.76%	133	18.39%	1.19
C. Role of AI in the educational process	150	25.13%	178	24.62%	1.19
D. Mathematical competence and AI	59	9.88%	71	9.82%	1.20
E. Implementation of AI in math education	64	10.72%	73	10.10%	1.14
F. Advantages of AI in math learning	97	16.25%	133	18.39%	1.37
G. Contents	67	11.22%	74	10.23%	1.10
H. Disadvantages of using AI	39	6.53%	43	5.95%	1.10
I. Challenges in AI integration	35	5.86%	48	6.64%	1.37
Total	597	100%	723	100%	

The category with the highest number of sources was *C. Role of AI in the educational process*, with 150 participants (25.13% of the total), followed by *B. Personal and academic use of AI*, with 112 sources (18.76%), and *F. Advantages of AI in mathematics learning*, with 97 (16.25%). These same categories also reported the highest total number of references: 178 in category C (24.62%) and 133 in both B and F (18.39%).

In terms of the average number of references per source, the categories with the highest discursive density were *F. Advantages* and *I. Challenges in AI integration*, both with an average of 1.37 references per participant. These were followed by *D. Mathematical competence and AI* and *C. Role of AI in the educational process*, with averages of 1.20 and 1.19 respectively.

The categories with the lowest number of sources were *I. Challenges in AI integration* (35 sources, 5.86%) and *H. Disadvantages of using AI* (39 sources, 6.53%). These two categories also recorded the lowest total number of references, with 48 and 43 respectively. Meanwhile, category *A. General opinions on AI in mathematics education* had 64 sources (10.72%) and 70 references (9.68%), placing it in an intermediate range among the categories analyzed.

Table 1 below shows the descriptive results for each study category, detailing the frequencies (F) and percentages (%) according to both the number of sources and total references. Figure 2 visually represents both frequencies, displaying their distribution by source and by reference count.

Table 1. Frequencies and percentages of each subcategory.

Category	Subcategory	Sources		References	
		F	%	F	%
A. General opinions on AI in mathematics education.	A1. Positive.	9	14.06%	14	14.06%
	A2. Negative	4	6.25%	5	6.25%
	A3. Not specified	51	79.69%	51	79.69%
B. Personal and academic use of AI.	B1. In daily life	41	64.06%	54	40.60%
	B2. Academic use	23	35.94%	23	17.29%
	B3. Experience as prospective teachers	36	56.25%	44	33.08%
	B4. Personal thoughts about AI	12	18.75%	12	9.02%
C. Role of AI in the educational process.	C1. Improvement of the teaching-learning process.	38	59.38%	45	25.28%
	C2. Immediate feedback from AI.	23	35.94%	27	15.17%
	C3. Interactive and challenging resource.	31	48.44%	33	18.54%
	C4. Complementarity with the teacher.	29	45.31%	39	21.91%
	C5. Resource to adapt contents.	9	14.06%	10	5.62%
	C6. It does not replace the work of the teacher.	20	31.25%	24	13.48%
D. Mathematical competence and its integration with AI.	D1. Educational competencies according to LOMLOE.	19	29.69%	25	35.21%
	D2. Computational Thinking.	22	34.38%	22	30.99%
	D3. Mathematical problem solving in real contexts.	18	28.13%	24	33.80%
E. Implementation of AI in mathematics education.	E1. Mathematics projects using AI.	19	29.69%	19	26.08%
	E2. Educational applications of AI.	21	32.81%	24	35.29%
	E3. Data analysis with AI.	19	29.69%	25	36.76%
	E4. Development of Digital Competencies.	5	7.81%	5	7.35%

continued on following page

Table 1. Continued

Category	Subcategory	Sources		References	
		F	%	F	%
F. Advantages of AI in mathematics learning	F1. Facilitates planning of activities.	11	17.19%	12	9.02%
	F2. Personalization of learning.	35	54.69%	57	42.86%
	F3. Constant availability to resolve any doubts.	15	23.44%	16	12.03%
	F4. Effective implementation of AI.	3	4.69%	4	3.01%
	F5. Optimization of educational quality.	15	23.44%	23	17.29%
	F6. Learning motivation	13	20.31%	16	12.03%
	F7. Unargued benefits.	5	7.81%	5	3.76%
G. Contents	G1. Mathematical problem solving.	27	42.19%	30	40.54%
	G2. Programming and mathematical simulations.	9	14.06%	11	14.86%
	G3. Development of communication skills and collaborations.	12	18.75%	12	16.22%
	G4. Construction and decomposition of geometric figures.	11	17.19%	12	16.22%
	G5. Creation of mathematical patterns.	5	7.81%	6	8.11%
	G6. Statistics and probability.	3	4.69%	3	4.05%
H. Disadvantages of using AI	H1. Abuse of AI.	15	23.44%	17	39.53%
	H2. Difficulties in developing basic math skills.	8	12.50%	9	20.93%
	H3. Difficulty in adapting results to specific context	4	6.25%	4	9.30%
	H4. Dependence on AI.	8	12.50%	9	20.93%
	H5. Unethical use of AI.	4	6.25%	4	9.30%
I. Challenges in AI integration	I1. Challenges for students.	13	20.31%	18	37.50%
	I2. Challenges for teachers	22	34.38%	30	62.50%

As can be seen, in category *A: General opinions about AI in mathematics education*, the participants mainly (79.69%) did not specify, followed by the positive comments (*A1. Positive*: 14.06%). An example of the mentioned last one is the following: "*The inclusion of AI facilitates or hinders the learning of mathematics depending on how they are used, i.e., as I have commented in the previous section they are used prior to the completion of the tasks, they will reveal the procedures and results to the students, limiting their ability to solve tasks and, therefore, their learning*" (Participant 45). A pesar de los beneficios mencionados, algunos participantes (6,25%) expresaron preocupaciones sobre el uso excesivo de la IA en el aula (*A2: Negative*). Despite the benefits mentioned, some participants (6.25%) expressed concerns about the excessive use of AI in the classroom (*A2: Negative*). Among the negative aspects identified was the potential dependence on technology, which could hinder the development of basic mathematical skills such as mental calculation and critical reasoning. Participants also noted that inadequate integration of AI could reduce teacher–student interaction, thereby negatively affecting the pedagogical relationship and the overall educational process. For instance, one participant stated: "*I believe it is essential to remember that the positive or negative impact of AI depends entirely on how it is used. It is a very powerful tool that can be highly beneficial for both students and teachers, but if misused, it may lead to problems in teaching and learning processes*" (Participant 45).

With respect to category *B: Personal and academic use of AI*, subcategory *B1. In Daily Life* is the one that represents the highest percentage, both with respect to sources (64.06%) and total references (40.60%). One of the participants emphasizes that: "*In everyday life it is very common to use it. In my case, when I clean, I play music with Alexa, when I cook, I often use the Thermomix, when I travel I use the GPS, and when I use my cell phone I use social networks, selfies, email*" (Participant 28). During their teacher training, prospective educators reported having interacted with AI tools during their school practicum experiences (B3: Experience as prospective teachers). One participant noted: "*I have used AI occasionally during my primary school practicum. I used the well-known tool ChatGPT to support the development of my teaching unit and various classroom activities, with the aim of gathering ideas and integrating them with those I had already designed*" (Participant 13).

Within Category *C: Role of AI in the educational process*, the subcategory *C1. Improvement of the teaching–learning process* accounts for the highest percentage, both in terms of sources (59.38%) and total references (25.28%). A clear example of this perspective is reflected in the following statement: "*The use of AI in mathematics education at the primary level can be beneficial not only for improving the teaching process but also the learning process, while at the same time making mathematics more accessible and engaging for students*" (Participant 1).

In Category *D: Mathematical competence and its integration with AI*, the *subcategory D2. Computational thinking* recorded the highest frequency (22) and percentage (34.38%) in terms of sources, as illustrated in the following example: "*Using computational thinking to organize data, break problems into parts, recognize patterns, generalize and interpret, modify and create algorithms in a guided way through modeling and self-motivation in everyday situations*" (Participant 5). However, regarding the total number of references obtained through data analysis, the subcategory *D1. Educational competencies according to LOMLOE* showed the highest frequency (25) and percentage (35.21%). An example of this perspective is the following statement: "*With regard to key competencies, the inclusion of artificial intelligence is directly linked to the development of Digital Competence, as it involves direct interaction with technological systems*" (Participant 36).

Figure 2. Frequencies by source and references for each subcategory.

Within Category E: *Implementation of AI in Mathematics Education*, Subcategory E2: *Educational Applications of AI* shows the highest frequency (21) and percentage (32.81%) relative to the sources analyzed. An illustrative example is the following: "*The use of AI in educational applications aims to teach mathematics in a more engaging way, through interactive games*" (Participant 1). However, when considering the total number of references obtained in the data analysis, Subcategory E3:

Data Analysis with AI emerges as the most frequent (25) and highest in percentage (36.76%). A representative example is: "*One way of integrating AI can be found in personalized tutoring, which helps identify each student's needs and difficulties, allowing for the creation of tailored activities*" (Participant 16).

In Category *E: Implementation of AI in mathematics education*, the subcategory *E2. Educational applications of AI* had the highest frequency (21) and percentage (32.81%) in terms of sources, as exemplified by the following statement: "*The use of AI in educational applications to teach mathematics in a more engaging way, through interactive games*" (Participant 1). However, regarding the total number of references obtained in the data analysis, the subcategory *E3. Data analysis with AI* reported the highest frequency (25) and percentage (36.76%). An illustrative example is the following: "*One way to integrate AI is through personalized tutoring, which allows the identification of each student's needs and difficulties, enabling the creation of specific, tailored activities*" (Participant 16).

As shown in Category *F: Advantages of AI in mathematics learning*, the *subcategory F2. Personalized learning* accounts for the highest percentage, both in terms of sources (54.69%) and total references (42.86%). One participant emphasized this idea by stating: "*It allows each student to progress at their own pace and in a much more individualized way than we are used to*" (Participant 14).

In Category *G: Contents*, the subcategory *G1. Solving mathematical problems* represents the highest percentage in terms of both sources (42.19%) and total references (40.54%). One illustrative example is the following statement: "*In terms of content, we can work with numbers and operations, as I previously explained, by introducing the problem statement and asking the AI to solve it in different ways*" (Participant 8).

In Category *H: Disadvantages of using AI*, the subcategory *H1. Abuse of AI* stands out with the highest frequency (15) and percentage (23.44%) in terms of sources, as well as in references, with a frequency of 17 and a percentage of 39.53%. One participant expressed this concern as follows: "*However, students will usually Abuse artificial intelligence to avoid doing their homework, as it seems easier and faster to them, without realizing the importance of being able to carry out mathematical operations on their own*" (Participant 6).

Finally, in Category *I: Challenges in AI integration*, the subcategory *I2. Challenges for teachers* stands out with the highest frequency (22) and percentage (34.38%) in terms of sources, as well as the highest number of references, with a frequency of 30 and a percentage of 62.50%. One participant reflected this idea by stating: "*The inclusion of AI in mathematics learning can facilitate the teaching of this subject in various ways, but it can also pose significant challenges for teachers*" (Participant 31).

4. DISCUSSIÓN

Artificial Intelligence (AI) has emerged as a transformative force across multiple domains, reshaping how we work, communicate, and learn. In the context of mathematics education, its integration enables the resolution of complex problems, the personalization of learning, and the optimization of teaching practices. Given this growing relevance, it is essential to understand how future educators perceive its use, as their attitudes and preparation will be key to its effective implementation in classrooms (Aparicio, 2023).

The findings of this study reveal a predominantly favorable attitude toward AI among pre-service teachers, framed through a functional and pragmatic lens. Participants largely view AI as a supportive tool rather than a replacement for educators, aligning with recent research that emphasizes its mediating role in fostering personalization, interactivity, and autonomous learning (Hwang & Tu, 2021; Mohamed et al., 2022). This perception is reflected in Category C: *Role of AI in the Educational Process*, the most frequently cited theme (25.13% of participants and 24.62% of references), underscoring its centrality in pedagogical discourse. These perceptions reflect the perceived usefulness dimension of the TAM, as pre-service teachers identify AI as a facilitator that improves efficiency in the teaching–learning process. At the same time, this aligns with the pedagogical knowledge component of TPACK, since participants did not envision AI as a substitute for content delivery but rather as a support to pedagogy that enables adaptive feedback and enhanced student engagement (Dogan et al., 2025; Venkatesh, 2022).

Within this category, the subcategories related to the improvement of the teaching–learning process and immediate feedback were especially valued, indicating an initial engagement with the most visible functionalities of AI in the classroom. These insights align with evidence from Lampropoulos and Papadakis (2025), who demonstrate how AI-driven environments shift teachers' roles toward facilitation while intelligent tutoring systems provide automated recommendations and adaptive feedback that enhance student engagement. This correspondence between perceptions and empirical findings indicates that future teachers are correctly identifying AI's most visible and accessible functions. However, references to AI's potential for adapting instruction to learner diversity were scarce, an issue also noted by Holmes & Porayska-Pomsta (2023), suggesting an incomplete understanding of its transformative potential.

Participants' familiarity with AI in their everyday lives, as reflected in Category *B: Personal and academic use of AI*, appears to influence their openness toward educational integration. Technological familiarity, particularly with domestic or recreational tools such as virtual assistants, social media, and smart devices, seems to foster a sense of normalization that reduces resistance to its didactic application.

However, this everyday use does not necessarily translate into a critical understanding of AI's educational implications. As Wardat et al. (2024) argue, habitual engagement with AI does not guarantee meaningful pedagogical appropriation, nor does it develop the reflective skills needed to adapt its use to complex educational contexts. In fact, although more than half of the participants reported having used AI during their initial teacher training, critical reflections on its educational value were limited, indicating a training opportunity that remains underdeveloped. This gap underscores the need for structured training that develops ethical awareness and Digital Competence in alignment with international frameworks (UNESCO, 2023).

The perceived benefits of AI in mathematics learning further reinforce this positive outlook Personalized learning, cited by more than half of the participants, emerged as one of the most widely acknowledged benefits. This perception is consistent with findings from Gong et al. (2020) and Sun and Zhou (2024), who emphasize the value of AI in adapting instruction to the pace and learning styles of individual students. Personalization was further associated with improved motivation, educational quality, and round-the-clock availability to resolve doubts. Nonetheless, several statements lacked technical elaboration, suggesting that while the positive perception is genuine, it may still be in a superficial phase. This superficiality could be attributed to the absence of structured, systematic training with AI tools in university curricula (Alfaro-Salas and Díaz, 2024). While the participants in this study expressed enthusiasm for AI as a means of personalizing mathematics instruction, research also highlights systemic challenges. Uğraş et al. (2024) identify barriers such as insufficient infrastructure, limited teacher training, and the uneven accessibility of AI-based tools, particularly in rural or underfunded schools. In addition, ethical issues, including data privacy, the risk of overdependence on technology, and the potential reduction of human interaction, must be carefully addressed to ensure responsible integration.

The connection between AI and mathematical competencies, explored in Category *D: Mathematical competence*, offers promising signs of an emerging integration between curriculum content and 21st-century skills. Computational thinking is recognized as a core competency, with many participants perceiving a clear link between this skill and AI technologies. The association between computational thinking and AI reflects the content knowledge (CK) and technological knowledge (TK) intersection of TPACK, where mathematical reasoning intersects with digital tools. This association has been highlighted by authors such as Fang et al. (2025) and Abar et al. (2024), who underscore the need to train teachers at the intersection of mathematics instruction and computational reasoning. Additionally, references to the Spanish LOMLOE framework, especially regarding Digital Competence, suggest that future teachers are aware of the regulatory structures that support technology integration, even if its practical implementation remains incipient.

However, when examining specific mathematical content, as presented in Category *G: Contents*, there was a notable thematic focus on problem-solving, while other domains such as statistics, geometry, and programming received minimal attention. This concentration may indicate a prevailing tendency to associate AI primarily with tasks that involve immediate, procedural outcomes, potentially limiting teachers' perception of its broader pedagogical applications. Critically, this narrow focus carries unintended consequences: students may develop proficiency in routine problem-solving without gaining deeper conceptual understanding, critical reasoning skills, or the ability to apply mathematical knowledge to novel or interdisciplinary contexts. Moreover, the underrepresentation of certain mathematical domains risks reinforcing existing curricular gaps and inequities, particularly in areas where AI could facilitate engagement with abstract concepts through dynamic simulations and interactive environments (Yunianto et al., 2024). These findings highlight the need for teacher education programs to foster critical reflection on AI integration, encouraging pre-service teachers to consider both the benefits and potential pitfalls of its application across diverse mathematical topics.

Regarding the modes of AI implementation in the classroom, participants emphasized its usefulness in educational projects, interactive applications, and data analysis, indicating an interest in active and personalized methodologies. However, references to teacher Digital Competence training were scarce, an issue of concern given that teacher professional development is a cornerstone for ethical and effective technology integration. This training gap, also identified by Singh and Ram (2024), underscores the urgency of rethinking initial teacher education programs to include authentic, critical, and collaborative experiences with AI tools.

In this optimistic yet still uncritical scenario, it is especially relevant to consider the drawbacks and challenges related to AI use. Although Categories H and I were less frequently mentioned overall, the contributions they included were notably rich and meaningful. Concerns regarding the Abuse of AI and technological dependence reflected legitimate fears about the erosion of autonomous thinking and the loss of basic mathematical skills, particularly when AI is used as a means of circumventing cognitive effort. These concerns resonate with warnings from Davis (2023, 2024), who emphasizes the importance of preserving human judgment in problem-solving processes.

Similarly, in Category *I: Challenges in AI integration*, participants identified barriers affecting both teachers and students. For teachers, the main challenges included insufficient training, resistance to change, and a lack of institutional support, factors that are consistent with the findings of Opesemowo and Ndlovu (2024). For students, the difficulties were associated with unequal access to technology, digital divides, and limited ability to engage with complex learning environments. Although less visible in participants' discourse, these challenges are critically important, especially when considering equity as a foundational principle in any educational innovation.

The integration of AI into mathematics education raises pressing ethical, pedagogical, and sustainability-related considerations. While AI tools, such as ChatGPT, offer significant opportunities for personalized learning, formative feedback, and the mitigation of learning loss, their use must be carefully balanced against potential risks, including student data privacy, algorithmic bias, unequal access to technology, and the generation of inaccurate or misleading content (Vivar & Peñalvo, 2023; UNESCO, 2023). These challenges directly intersect with sustainable education goals, particularly SDG 4, which emphasizes inclusive, equitable, and high-quality learning opportunities throughout life (Uğraş et al., 2024). AI literacy frameworks (OECD, 2025) highlight the necessity of training teachers to critically evaluate both the pedagogical benefits and societal implications of AI, ensuring that adaptive platforms and Intelligent Tutoring Systems enhance learning without embedding opaque decision-making or reinforcing inequities.

Moreover, the TPACK framework provides a theoretical basis for designing sustainable and innovative educational environments by integrating technology, pedagogy, and content knowledge. In mathematics education, AI tools can support educators in enhancing Digital Literacy, fostering inclusive learning experiences, and addressing gaps in mathematical and linguistic skills through targeted feedback (Uğraş et al., 2024). However, careful consideration is required regarding age appropriateness, potential overreliance on AI, and the risk of misinformation, which may undermine students' critical thinking and compromise SDG 4 targets related to knowledge-based education and educator competence (ODS 4.7 and 4.c). These findings underscore the necessity of ongoing professional development for teachers, equipping them with the skills to use AI responsibly, evaluate its outputs critically, and integrate it in ways that align with ethical principles, equity considerations, and the long-term sustainability of educational practice.

Finally, the inconsistencies appear to reflect differences in technological familiarity, pedagogical experience, and awareness of ethical and cognitive implications, as well as limited exposure to AI applications across diverse mathematical domains. The coexistence of enthusiasm and skepticism underscores a fragmented level of AI literacy among pre-service teachers and highlights the importance of embedding critical reflection, hands-on experience, and ethical reasoning within teacher education programs. (Ayuso-del Puerto & Gutiérrez-Esteban, 2022; Lampropoulos & Papadakis, 2025; Uğraş et al., 2024).

In conclusion, while pre-service teachers demonstrate a broadly favorable disposition toward AI in mathematics education, their understanding of its pedagogical, ethical, and contextual implications remains fragmented. Realizing the transformative potential of AI requires comprehensive teacher preparation that aligns tool use with critical pedagogical frameworks, inclusive practices, and a nuanced understanding of 21st-century mathematical competencies. Integrating AI in education is not merely a matter of technology access but a profound question of educational purpose, reflective practice, and social justice.

To address these findings, teacher education programs must explicitly integrate AI literacy into their curricula, not as an optional complement but as a core component of digital competence in mathematics education. This entails designing training modules that combine theoretical foundations (e.g., ethical, cognitive, and curricular implications of AI) with hands-on experiences using generative tools, intelligent tutoring systems, and data-driven platforms. For pre-service teachers, such modules should promote critical engagement with AI outputs, fostering skills in verification, argumentation, and reflective practice. For in-service teachers, professional development initiatives need to provide continuous, collaborative opportunities to experiment with AI applications in real classroom contexts, accompanied by mentoring and peer exchange.

In addition, teacher education programs should adopt a competency-based approach aligned with international frameworks (TPACK, DigCompEdu, OECD AI Literacy), ensuring that educators are not only users of AI technologies but also designers of learning experiences that integrate AI in pedagogically meaningful and ethically responsible ways. Embedding AI-related scenarios in microteaching, practicum experiences, and interdisciplinary projects can help bridge the current gap between theoretical awareness and classroom implementation. Ultimately, strengthening teacher preparation in this domain will determine whether AI becomes a catalyst for inclusive, equitable, and sustainable mathematics education, or whether its potential remains underutilized due to superficial training and fragmented adoption.

5. CONCLUSIONS

The results of this study demonstrate that prospective primary school teachers perceive Artificial Intelligence (AI) as a tool with significant potential to transform mathematics education. They especially value its capacity to personalize learning, enhance student motivation, and optimize classroom dynamics. This favorable attitude is largely rooted in their everyday familiarity with AI, which facilitates its acceptance, although it is not always accompanied by a deep pedagogical understanding.

The study has identified not only the recognition of practical advantages, but also an emerging association between AI and key competencies such as computational thinking and Digital Literacy. However, a partial view persists regarding the mathematical content that can be addressed through AI, with an almost exclusive emphasis on problem-solving and limited reference to areas such as statistics or geometry.

Moreover, responses revealed notable contradictions regarding the integration of AI in primary mathematics education. While many prospective teachers emphasized the advantages of AI tools, hey simultaneously expressed concerns about the reliability of AI-generated content, the risk of overreliance by students, and potential negative impacts on foundational mathematical competencies, including problem-solving, logical reasoning, and conceptual understanding. These contradictions indicate that, although AI is recognized as a promising educational innovation, its effective integration requires careful scaffolding to ensure that it complements rather than replaces core mathematical learning, fostering both equitable and sustainable educational outcomes

These findings underscore the relevance of this study by offering a comprehensive view of the perceptions, opportunities, and limitations that future teachers face with respect to AI. They highlight the urgent need to incorporate pedagogical, technological, and ethical frameworks into initial teacher education in order to promote the meaningful, critical, and context-sensitive integration of AI into mathematics education.

Practical Implications and Pedagogical Recommendations

Artificial intelligence literacy should not be confined to technological or scientific disciplines; rather, it can significantly enrich mathematics education, particularly at the primary and secondary levels. In alignment with the principles outlined in the AILit Framework (OECD, 2025), a series of instructional experiences are proposed that foster critical thinking, problem-solving, and ethical reflection regarding the use of AI in mathematical contexts.

Problem-solving with generative AI: Students formulate mathematical problems and employ AI tools to solve them. This experience enables learners to compare human reasoning with automated processes, identify computational errors, and critically assess the validity of AI-generated solutions. Such activities prompt educators to ask: How can generative AI tools be meaningfully integrated into mathematics instruction without compromising pedagogical intentionality? To what extent should students be encouraged to challenge or verify AI-generated solutions as part of their mathematical reasoning?

Analysis of numerical and geometric patterns: Using platforms such as Teachable Machine, students train simple models to recognize sequences or shapes. This activity enhances their understanding of how AI detects regularities and how data inputs influence predictive outcomes. It also raises pedagogical questions such as: How can educators guide students in interpreting the limitations of pattern recognition in AI systems? and What ethical considerations emerge when students engage with data-driven models in early mathematics education?

Simulation of complex mathematical systems: Tools like GeoGebra and Wolfram Alpha allow students to model functions, equations, and dynamic systems, thereby facilitating the visualization of abstract concepts and promoting algebraic reasoning. These experiences invite reflection on questions like: What are the long-term implications of AI integration for curriculum design and mathematical modeling? and How can educators balance the use of automated simulations with the development of students' conceptual understanding and problem-solving autonomy?

In summary, the integration of AI into mathematics instruction necessitates targeted teacher training that encompasses: a foundational technical understanding of how AI systems operate in mathematical problem-solving; the ability to guide critical analysis of AI-generated outputs, encouraging verification, argumentation, and metacognitive reflection; and ethical sensitivity to address issues such as reliability, authorship, and the societal impact of automation on mathematical reasoning. Within this context, teacher education programs must also consider: How does the integration of AI technologies reshape the role and identity of the mathematics teacher? and Are current training frameworks adequately aligned with the competencies required for AI literacy in educational practice?

Study Limitations and Future Research Directions

This study presents several limitations that should be considered when interpreting the findings. First, the sample was composed of 64 participants from a single institution, limiting the generalizability of the results to other educational contexts and geographic areas. Second, data collection relied solely on a qualitative questionnaire, which, while providing in-depth insight into perceptions, did not allow longitudinal tracking of participants' perspectives or observation of actual classroom implementation. Third, although participants reported experience with AI in daily life and initial teacher training, the study did not assess real integration of AI in classroom practice or its impact on students' learning outcomes.

Building on the limitations identified and the findings of this study, several future research directions are proposed to deepen the understanding and optimization of AI integration in mathematics education. First, it is essential to broaden the diversity of the sample by including pre-service teachers from multiple institutions, geographic regions, and socio-educational contexts, as well as incorporating in-service teachers, teacher educators, and administrators, in order to obtain more representative perspectives and facilitate triangulation of viewpoints.

Additionally, the implementation of multimodal and longitudinal data collection strategies is recommended, complementing surveys with in-depth interviews, focus groups, reflective journals, and stimulated recall techniques using classroom examples. Complementarily, mixed-methods designs that integrate qualitative and quantitative analyses, including validated scales on technology acceptance, pedagogical beliefs, and Digital Competencies, could strengthen the validity of findings and enable meaningful comparisons with previous research.

Another relevant direction involves studying AI implementation in real classroom contexts, documenting both successes and challenges encountered, and including detailed analyses of the human, technological, and financial resources required for effective and sustainable integration. Furthermore, it is important to examine the dimensions of inclusion, equity, and accessibility by investigating how AI can support students with disabilities, special educational needs, or limited technological access, as well as its potential to reduce the digital divide and promote equitable learning opportunities. Research should also explore how AI can contribute to the development of complex mathematical competencies and the teaching of diverse content areas, including statistics, geometry, programming, and real-world problem-solving, fostering active learning, creativity, and critical thinking.

Finally, studying professional learning communities is recommended, analyzing how collaboration among teachers, both pre-service and in-service, affects pedagogical appropriation of AI, promotes best practices, and consolidates innovative teaching strategies.

Collectively, these research directions aim not only to expand understanding of AI perceptions and use in mathematics education but also to generate evidence that supports pedagogically, ethically, and socially responsible integration, fostering the development of teachers capable of applying these technologies in critical, effective, and equitable ways.

CONFLICT OF INTEREST

The author declares that there is no conflict of interest regarding the publication of this manuscript.

FUNDING

This work has been 85% co-financed by the European Union, the European Regional Development Fund, and the Regional Government of Extremadura, the Managing Authority, and the Ministry of Finance, through project GR24052.

ETHICAL STATEMENT

This study was conducted in accordance with the Declaration of Helsinki and was approved by the Ethics Committee of the University of Extremadura. All procedures followed ethical standards, and written informed consent was obtained from all participants. The questionnaires were anonymous, and participants were free to withdraw from the study at any time if they felt uncomfortable.

REFERENCES

Abar, C. A. A. P., Dos Santos, J. M. D. S., & de Almeida, M. V. (2024). *Contribuciones de la integración entre el pensamiento computacional y la inteligencia artificial para la educación matemática*. Springer., DOI: 10.1007/978-3-031-54256-5_27

Alfaro-Salas, H., & Díaz, J. A. (2024). Percepciones y Aplicaciones de la IA entre Estudiantes de Secundaria. *Revista Docentes 2.0, 17*(1), 200–215. https://doi.org/ DOI: 10.37843/rted.v17i1.458

Amran, M. S., Bakar, K. A., Surat, S., Mahmud, S. N. D., & Shafie, A. A. B. M. (2021). Assessing preschool teachers' challenges and needs for creativity in STEM education. *Asian Journal of University Education, 17*(3), 99–108. DOI: 10.24191/ajue.v17i3.14517

Aparicio, W. O. (2023). La Inteligencia Artificial y su Incidencia en la Educación: Transformando el Aprendizaje para el Siglo XXI. *Revista Internacional de Pedagogía e Innovación Educativa, 3*(2), 217–229. DOI: 10.51660/ripie.v3i2.133

Asencio, G., Medina, R., Coto, L., Gómez, M., López, P., Contreras, V., & Muñoz, A. (2024). Libro de Memorias proyecto de investigación latinoamericana 100 investigadores. En *Libro de Memorias proyecto de investigación latinoamericana, 8*(3).

Ayuso-del Puerto, D. A., & Gutiérrez-Esteban, P. G. (2022). La Inteligencia Artificial como recurso educativo durante la formación inicial del profesorado. *RIED-Revista Iberoamericana de Educación a Distancia, 25*(2), 347–358. DOI: 10.5944/ried.25.2.32332

Bardin, L. (1991). *Análisis de contenido* (Vol. 89). Ediciones Akal.

Brenneman, K., Lange, A., & Nayfeld, I. (2019). Integrating STEM into Preschool Education; Designing a Professional Development Model in Diverse Settings. *Early Childhood Education Journal, 47*(1), 15–28. DOI: 10.1007/s10643-018-0912-z

Celik, I. (2023). Towards Intelligent-TPACK: An empirical study on teachers' professional knowledge to ethically integrate artificial intelligence (AI)-based tools into education. *Computers in Human Behavior, 138*, 107468. DOI: 10.1016/j.chb.2022.107468

Çiftçi, A., & Topçu, M. S. (2022). Pre-service early childhood teachers' challenges and solutions to Planning and Implementing STEM education–based activities. *Canadian Journal of Science, Mathematics and Technology Education = Revue Canadienne de l'Enseignement des Sciences, des Mathématiques et de la Technologie, 22*(2), 422–443. DOI: 10.1007/s42330-022-00206-5

Contreras, E. (2024, 15 mayo). Retos para los docentes con la llegada de la IA. *Uninpahu.* https://uninpahu.edu.co/retos-para-los-docentes-con-la-llegada-de-la-ia/

Costa, A., Sánchez-Gómez, M., & Martín, M. (Eds.). (2020). *La Práctca de la investgación cualitatva: ejemplifcación de estudios (2ª parte).* Ludomedia.

Creswell, J. W. (2014). *A concise introduction to mixed methods research.* SAGE publications.

Davis, E. (2023). Mathematics, word problems, common sense, and artificial intelligence. *arXiv,2, 2-17.* https://doi.org//arXiv.2301.09723DOI: 10.48550

Davis, E. (2024). Mathematics, word problems, common sense, and artificial intelligence. *Bulletin of the American Mathematical Society, 61*(2), 287–303. DOI: 10.1090/bull/1828

De Mántaras, R. L., & Crosa, P. B. (2023). *¿Qué es la inteligencia artificial?* Papeles de relaciones ecosociales y cambio global, (164), 13-21.

Demircan, H. Ö. (2022). How am I supposed to do this on my own? A case study on perspectives of preschool teachers regarding integrative STEM practices. *Journal of Early Childhood Research, 20*(1), 93–112. DOI: 10.1177/1476718X211052749

Dogan, S., Nalbantoglu, U. Y., Celik, I., & Agacli Dogan, N. (2025). Artificial intelligence professional development: A systematic review of TPACK, designs, and effects for teacher learning. *Professional Development in Education, 51*(3), 1–28. DOI: 10.1080/19415257.2025.2454457

European Commission. (2022). *Ethical guidelines on the use of artificial intelligence (AI) and data in teaching and learning for educators*. Publications Office of the European Union. https://data.europa.eu/doi/10.2766/153756

Fadillah, M. A., Usmeldi, U., Lufri, L., Mawardi, M., & Festiyed, F. (2024). Exploring user perceptions: The impact of ChatGPT on high school students' physics understanding and learning. *Advances in Mobile Learning Educational Research, 4*(2), 1197–1207. DOI: 10.25082/AMLER.2024.02.013

Fang, X., Ng, D. T. K., & Yuen, M. (2025). Effects of geogebra-enhanced scratch computational thinking instruction on fifth-grade students' motivation, anxiety, cognitive load. *Education and Information Technologies, 30*(1), 377–402. DOI: 10.1007/s10639-024-13052-9

Fauzi, F., Tuhuteru, L., Sampe, F., Ausat, A. M., & Hatta, H. R. (2023). Análisis del papel de ChatGPT en la mejora de la productividad de los estudiantes en la educación superior. *Review of Education, 5*(4), 14886–14891. DOI: 10.31004/joe.v5i4.2563

Gallardo, E., Tomás-Rojas, A., Bossio, J., & Freundt-Thurne, U. (2023). Evidence of validity and reliability of the DigCompEdu CheckIn in teachers at a private Peruvian university. *Publicaciones, 53*, 49–88. DOI: 10.30827/publicaciones.v53i2.26817

García-Peñalvo, F. J. (2024). Cómo afecta la inteligencia artificial generativa a los procesos de evaluación. *Revista científica comunicación y educación y educación, 4(54),* 106-170.

Getenet, S. (2024). Pre-Service Teachers and ChatGPT in Multistrategy Problem-Solving: Implications for Mathematics Teaching in Primary Schools. *International Electronic Journal of Mathematics Education, 19*(1), em0766. Advance online publication. DOI: 10.29333/iejme/14141

Gong, X., Tang, Y., Liu, X., Jing, S., Cui, W., Liang, J., & Wang, F. Y. (2020, October). K-9 artificial intelligence education in Qingdao: Issues, challenges and suggestions. In *2020 IEEE international Conference on networking, Sensing and control (ICNSC)* (pp. 1-6). IEEE.

Grugeon-Allys, B., & Pilet, J. (2024). The algebraic learning of middle school students' evolution during a school year: A statistical large-scale study based on results in mathematics didactics. *Educational Studies in Mathematics, 117*(3), 533–564. DOI: 10.1007/s10649-024-10347-z

Han, Z., Battaglia, F., Udaiyar, A., Fooks, A., & Terlecky, S. R. (2024). An explorative assessment of ChatGPT as an aid in medical education: Use it with caution. *Medical Teacher, 46*(5), 657–664. DOI: 10.1080/0142159X.2023.2271159 PMID: 37862566

Holmes, W., & Porayska-Pomsta, K. (2023). *The ethics of artificial intelligence in education.* Lontoo: Routledge, 621-653.

Huang, A. Y., Lu, O. H., & Yang, S. J. (2023). Effects of artificial Intelligence–Enabled personalized recommendations on learners' learning engagement, motivation, and outcomes in a flipped classroom. *Computers & Education, 194*, 104684. DOI: 10.1016/j.compedu.2022.104684

Hwang, G., & Tu, Y. (2021). Roles and Research Trends of Artificial Intelligence in Mathematics Education: A Bibliometric Mapping Analysis and Systematic Review. *Mathematics, 9*(6), 584. DOI: 10.3390/math9060584

Hwang, G. J., & Chang, C. Y. (2023). A review of opportunities and challenges of chatbots in education. *Interactive Learning Environments, 31*(7), 4099–4112. DOI: 10.1080/10494820.2021.1952615

Instituto Nacional de Tecnologías Educativas y de Formación del Profesorado (INTEF). (2022). *Escuela de Pensamiento Computacional e Inteligencia Artificial 2021/22. De la formación docente al cambio metodológico. Resultados de la investigación.* https://code.intef.es/wp-content/uploads/2022/11/09_22_Experimentacion_Investigacion-EPCIA-21-22_Investigacion-R3.pdf

Ipek, Z. H., Gozum, A. C., Papadakis, S., & Kallogianakis, M. (2023). Educational applications of the ChatGPT AI system: A systematic review research. *Educational Process: International Journal, 12*(3), 26–55. DOI: 10.22521/edupij.2023.123.2

Kohnke, S., & Zaugg, T. (2025). Artificial Intelligence: An Untapped Opportunity for Equity and Access in STEM Education. *Education Sciences, 15*(1), 68. DOI: 10.3390/educsci15010068

Labadze, L., Grigolia, M., & Machaidze, L. (2023). Role of AI chatbots in education: Systematic literature review. *International Journal of Educational Technology in Higher Education, 20*(56), 56. Advance online publication. DOI: 10.1186/s41239-023-00426-1

Lampropoulos, G., & Papadakis, S. (2025). The educational value of artificial intelligence and social robots. In *Social robots in education* (pp. 3–15). Springer. DOI: 10.1007/978-3-031-82915-4_1

Lavidas, K., Papadakis, S., Manesis, D., Grigoriadou, A. S., & Gialamas, V.Lectures and Lab Classes. (2022a). The effects of social desirability on students' self-reports in two social contexts: Lectures vs. lectures and lab classes. *Information (Basel), 13*(10), 491. DOI: 10.3390/info13100491

Lavidas, K., Petropoulou, A., Papadakis, S., Apostolou, Z., Komis, V., Jimoyiannis, A., & Gialamas, V. (2022b). Factors affecting response rates of the web survey with teachers. *Computers, 11*(9), 127. DOI: 10.3390/computers11090127

Lim, J., Lee, U., Koh, J., Jeong, Y., Lee, Y., Byun, G., Jung, H., Jang, Y., Lee, S., & Moon, J. (2025). Development and implementation of a generative artificial intelligence-enhanced simulation to enhance problem-solving skills for pre-service teachers. *Computers & Education, 232*, 105306. DOI: 10.1016/j.compedu.2025.105306

Luzano, J. (2024). An integrative review of AI-Powered STEM education. *International Journal of Academic Pedagogical Research, 8*(4), 113–118.

Malik, R., Abdi, D., Wang, R., & Demszky, D. (2025). Scaffolding middle school mathematics curricula with large language models. *British Journal of Educational Technology, 56*(3), 999–1027. DOI: 10.1111/bjet.13571

Mayer, R. E. (2005). *The Cambridge Handbook of Multimedia Learning*. Cambridge University Press. DOI: 10.1017/CBO9780511816819

Mishra, P., Warr, M., & Islam, R. (2023). TPACK in the age of ChatGPT and Generative AI. *Journal of Digital Learning in Teacher Education, 39*(4), 235–251. DOI: 10.1080/21532974.2023.2247480

Mogali, S. R. (2023). Initial impressions of ChatGPT for anatomy education. *Anatomical Sciences Education, 17*(2), 444–447. DOI: 10.1002/ase.2261 PMID: 36749034

Mohamed, M. Z. B., Hidayat, R., & Mahmud, M. K. H. B. (2022). Artificial Intelligence in Mathematics Education: A Systematic Literature Review. *International Electronic Journal of Mathematics Education, 17*(3), em0694. Advance online publication. DOI: 10.29333/iejme/12132

Montenegro-Rueda, M., Fernández-Cerero, J., Fernández-Batanero, J. M., & López-Meneses, E. (2023). Impact of the implementation of ChatGPT in education: A systematic review. *Computers, 12*(8), 153. DOI: 10.3390/computers12080153

OECD. (2025). *Empowering learners for the age of AI: An AI literacy framework for primary and secondary education (Review draft).* OECD. Paris. https://ailiteracyframework.org

Opesemowo, O. A. G. (2025). Artificial Intelligence in Mathematics Education: The Pros and Cons. In *Encyclopedia of Information Science and Technology, Sixth Edition* (pp. 1-18). IGI Global.

Opesemowo, O. A. G., & Ndlovu, M. (2024). *Artificial intelligence in mathematics education: The good, the bad, and the ugly.* Journal Of Pedagogical Research., DOI: 10.33902/JPR.202426428

Pascual, J. (2019). Innovación Educativa: Un proceso construido sobre relaciones de poder. *Revista Educación Política y Sociedad, 4*(2), 9–30. DOI: 10.15366/reps2019.4.2.001

Rivas, A., Buchbinder, N., & Barrenechea, I. (2023). El futuro de la inteligencia artificial en educación en América Latina. *Innovación Educativa (México, D.F.), 24*(96).

Rodríguez, A., Orozco, K., García, J., Rodríguez, S., & Barros, H. (2023). La Implementación de la Inteligencia Artificial en la Educación: Análisis Sistemático. *Dominio De Las Ciencias, 9*(3), 2162–2178. DOI: 10.23857/dc.v9i3.3548

Singh, V., & Ram, S. (2024). Impact of Artificial Intelligence on Teacher Education. *Shodh Sari-An International Multidisciplinary Journal, 03*(01), 243–266. DOI: 10.59231/SARI7669

Sun, L., & Zhou, L. (2024). Does generative artificial intelligence improve the academic achievement of college students? A meta-analysis. *Journal of Educational Computing Research, 62*(7), 1896–1933. DOI: 10.1177/07356331241277937

Tao, Y. (2019). Kindergarten teachers' attitudes toward and confidence for Integrated STEM Education. *Journal for STEM Education Research, 2*(2), 154–171. DOI: 10.1007/s41979-019-00017-8

Uğraş, H., Uğraş, M., Papadakis, S., & Kalogiannakis, M. (2024). ChatGPT-supported education in primary schools: The potential of ChatGPT for sustainable practices. *Sustainability (Basel), 16*(22), 9855. DOI: 10.3390/su16229855

Uğraş, H., Uğraş, M., Papadakis, S., & Kalogiannakis, M. (2025). Innovative Early Childhood STEM Education with ChatGPT: Teacher Perspectives. *Technology. Knowledge and Learning, 30*(2), 809–831. DOI: 10.1007/s10758-024-09804-8

UNESCO. (2023). *Currículos de IA para la enseñanza preescolar, primaria y secundaria: un mapeo de los currículos de IA aprobados por los gobiernos*. París, France. https://unesdoc.unesco.org/ark:/48223/pf0000380602_spa

Urban, M., Brom, C., Lukavský, J., Děchtěrenko, F., Hein, V., Svacha, F., Kmoníčková, P., & Urban, K. (2025). "ChatGPT can make mistakes. Check important info." Epistemic beliefs and metacognitive accuracy in students' integration of ChatGPT content into academic writing. *British Journal of Educational Technology*, *56*(5), 1897–1918. DOI: 10.1111/bjet.13591

Valeri, F., Nilsson, P., & Cederqvist, A. M. (2025). Exploring students' experience of ChatGPT in STEM education. *Computers and Education: Artificial Intelligence*, *8*, 100360. DOI: 10.1016/j.caeai.2024.100360

Venkatesh, V. (2022). Adoption and use of AI tools: A research agenda grounded in UTAUT. *Annals of Operations Research*, *308*(1), 641–652. DOI: 10.1007/s10479-020-03918-9

Vivar, J. M. F., & Peñalvo, F. J. G. (2023). Reflexiones sobre la ética, potencialidades y retos de la Inteligencia Artificial en el marco de la Educación de Calidad (ODS4). *Comunicar: Revista cientifica de comunicacion y educacion*, (74), 37-47.

Wang, B., Rau, P. L. P., & Yuan, T. (2023). Measuring user competence in using artificial intelligence: Validity and reliability of artificial intelligence literacy scale. *Behaviour & Information Technology*, *42*(9), 1324–1337. DOI: 10.1080/0144929X.2022.2072768

Wardat, Y., Tashtoush, M. A., AlAli, R., & Jarrah, A. M. (2023). ChatGPT: A revolutionary tool for teaching and learning mathematics. *Eurasia Journal of Mathematics, Science and Technology Education*, *19*(7), em2286. Advance online publication. DOI: 10.29333/ejmste/13272

Weng, X., Ye, H., Dai, Y., & Ng, O. (2024). Integrating Artificial Intelligence and Computational Thinking in Educational Contexts: A Systematic Review of Instructional Design and Student Learning Outcomes. *Journal of Educational Computing Research*, *62*(6), 1420–1450. DOI: 10.1177/07356331241248686

Wing, J. M. (2006). Computational Thinking. *Communications of the ACM*, *49*(3), 33–35. DOI: 10.1145/1118178.1118215

Yannier, N., Hudson, S. E., & Koedinger, K. R. (2020). Active learning is about more Than Hands-On: A mixed-reality AI system to support STEM education. *International Journal of Artificial Intelligence in Education*, *30*(1), 74–96. DOI: 10.1007/s40593-020-00194-3

Yau, K. W., Chai, C. S., Chiu, T. K., Meng, H., King, I., & Yam, Y. (2023). A phenomenographic approach on teacher conceptions of teaching Artificial Intelligence (AI) in K-12 schools. *Education and Information Technologies*, *28*(1), 1041–1064. DOI: 10.1007/s10639-022-11161-x

Yilmaz, R., & Yilmaz, F. G. K. (2023). The effect of generative artificial intelligence (AI)-based tool use on students' computational thinking skills, programming self-efficacy and motivation. k, 100147. https://doi.org/DOI: 10.1016/j.caeai.2023.100147

Yunianto, W., Lavicza, Z., Kastner-Hauler, O., & Houghton, T. (2024). Investigating the use of ChatGPT to solve a GeoGebra based mathematics+computational thinking task in a geometry topic. *Journal on Mathematics Education*, *15*(3), 1027–1052. DOI: 10.22342/jme.v15i3.pp1027-1052

Yusuf, A., Pervin, N., Román-González, M., & Noor, N. M. (2024). Generative AI in education and research: A systematic mapping review. *Review of Education*, *12*(2), e3489. DOI: 10.1002/rev3.3489

Zawacki-Richter, O., Marín, V. I., Bond, M., & Gouverneur, F. (2019). Systematic review of research on artificial intelligence applications in higher education-where are the educators? *International Journal of Educational Technology in Higher Education*, *16*(1), 1–27. DOI: 10.1186/s41239-019-0171-0

Zhai, X., Nyaaba, M., & Ma, W. (2024). Can generative AI and ChatGPT outperform humans on cognitive-demanding problem-solving tasks in science? *Science & Education*, •••, 1–22.

Zickafoose, A., Ilesanmi, O., Diaz-Manrique, M., Adeyemi, A. E., Walumbe, B., Strong, R., Wingenbach, G., Rodriguez, M. T., & Dooley, K. (2024). Barriers and challenges affecting quality education (Sustainable Development Goal# 4) in sub-Saharan Africa by 2030. *Sustainability (Basel)*, *16*(7), 2657. DOI: 10.3390/su16072657

Zimmerman, B. J. (2002). Becoming a Self-Regulated Learner: An Overview. *Theory into Practice*, *41*(2), 64–70. DOI: 10.1207/s15430421tip4102_2

Zreik, M. (2024). *Redefining Mathematics Education in the Age of Artificial Intelligence*. IGI Global. DOI: 10.4018/979-8-3693-2873-6.ch002

APPENDIX

Table 2. Category system used in the study.

Category	Description	Subcategory
A. General opinions on AI in mathematics education	Includes general impressions of AI, both positive and negative, assessing its acceptance and impact on its adoption in educational settings (Asencio et al., 2024; Rivas et al., 2023)	A1. Positive.
		A2. Negative
		A3. Unspecified.
B. Personal and academic use of AI.	Addresses the everyday and academic use of AI, distinguishing between personal experience and use in the classroom to understand familiarity with this technology (Contreras, 2024).	B1. In everyday life
		B2. Academic use
		B3. Experience as prospective teachers
		B4. Personal reflections on AI
C. Role of AI in the educational process	Encompasses the role that AI should play in the educational process, emphasizing its use as a complement that enhances learning without replacing the teacher (Ayuso-del Puerto, 2022; Contreras, 2024; Vivar & Peñalvo, 2023).	C1. Improvement of the teaching–learning process
		C2. Immediate feedback from AI
		C3. Interactive and challenging resource
		C4. Complementarity with the teacher
		C5. Resource for adapting content
		C6. Does not replace the teacher's role
D. Mathematical competence and its integration with AI	Categorizes mathematical content that can be addressed through AI, highlighting a structured approach that integrates key competencies into the curriculum (Ayuso-del Puerto, 2022; Rivas et al., 2023).	D1. Educational competencies according to LOMLOE
		D2. Computational Thinking
		D3. Problem-solving in real-life contexts

continued on following page

Table 2. Continued

Category	Description	Subcategory
E. Implementation of AI in mathematics teaching	Highlights specific ways in which AI can be used in teaching mathematics, including data analysis and the development of interactive projects (Ayuso-del Puerto, 2022; Asencio et al., 2024).	E1. Mathematics projects using AI.
		E2. Educational applications of AI
		E3. Data analysis with AI
		E4. Development of Digital Competencies
F. Advantages of AI in mathematics learning	Emphasizes the direct benefits that AI brings to learning, including content personalization and optimization of educational quality (Ayuso-del Puerto, 2022; Asencio et al., 2024).	F1. Facilitates activity planning
		F2. Personalized learning
		F3. Constant availability for doubt resolution.
		F4. Effective implementation of AI
		F5. Optimization of educational quality
		F6. Learning motivation
		F7. Unsubstantiated benefits
G. Content	The integration of AI into mathematics teaching ranges from problem-solving and simulations to the development of social skills and statistical data analysis, enabling interactive and personalized learning (Ayuso-del Puerto, 2022; Rivas et al., 2023). It also promotes key competencies such as pattern creation, geometric construction, and collaboration, aligning with educational optimization strategies (Asencio et al., 2024). This demonstrates how AI organizes mathematical content in a structured way to strengthen the educational curriculum.	G1. Solving mathematical problems.
		G2. Mathematical simulations and programming
		G3. Development of communication and collaboration skills
		G4. Construction and decomposition of geometric figures
		G5. Creation of mathematical patterns
		G6. Statistics and probability

continued on following page

Table 2. Continued

Category	Description	Subcategory
H. Disadvantages of using AI	Groups concerns regarding the misuse of AI in learning, such as technological overreliance and its impact on the development of basic skills (Ayuso-del Puerto, 2022; Vivar & Peñalvo, 2023).	H1. Abuse of AI
		H2. Difficulties in developing basic mathematical skills
		H3. Difficulty adapting outputs to specific contexts
		H4. Dependence on AI
		H5. Unethical use of AI
I. Challenges in AI integration	Highlights the challenges associated with integrating AI in the classroom, including adapting to new technologies and balancing AI use (Contreras, 2024; Vivar & Peñalvo, 2023)	I1. Challenges for students
		I2. Challenges for teachers

Appendix 2. Glossary of Key Terms

Term	Academic Definition
Artificial Intelligence (AI)	A field of computer science focused on creating systems capable of performing tasks that typically require human intelligence, such as reasoning, learning, and decision-making. In education, AI supports personalized learning and instructional automation
Generative AI (GenAI)	A subset of AI technologies that can autonomously produce original content—such as text, images, or simulations—based on learned patterns. Tools like ChatGPT exemplify its application in educational content creation.
Large Language Model (LLM)	A type of AI model trained on extensive textual data to understand and generate human-like language. These models underpin many generative AI tools used in educational contexts.
Computational Thinking	A problem-solving approach involving decomposition, pattern recognition, abstraction, and algorithmic design. It is foundational in both mathematics instruction and AI literacy.
Intelligent Tutoring Systems (ITS)	AI-driven platforms that simulate one-on-one instruction by adapting content and feedback to individual learner needs.
AI Literacy	A multidimensional construct encompassing the knowledge, skills, and attitudes required to understand, use, and critically evaluate AI technologies in educational contexts.
AI-driven Learning Analytics	The use of AI algorithms to analyze student performance data and generate adaptive learning pathways or instructional interventions.
Educational Simulation	AI-generated virtual environments that replicate complex mathematical scenarios, fostering conceptual understanding and problem-solving skills.
Automated Feedback	Real-time responses generated by AI systems to guide learners' progress. It enhances personalization and supports formative assessment.

Chapter 11
Supporting Computer Science Pathways in the Age of AI:
Curriculum, Emotions, and Motivation in Greek Upper Secondary Education

Sofia Kasotaki
http://orcid.org/0009-0001-4345-4913
Department of Informatics, School of Sciences, University of Western Macedonia, Greece

Nikos Dimokas
http://orcid.org/0000-0003-2856-0969
Department of Informatics, School of Sciences, University of Western Macedonia, Greece

ABSTRACT

This study examines how emotions and motivation shape computer science (CS) pathways in Greek upper secondary education at a time when AI skills are increasingly essential. Using the control–value theory of achievement emotions and the Science Motivation Questionnaire II, data were collected from 132 students across two curricular tracks: applied ICT in A class and algorithmic programming in B class. Findings show that while enjoyment decreased during CS tasks, pride increased and shame declined, indicating that engagement fostered accomplishment despite initial frustration. Emotional and motivational profiles were largely similar across curricula, with A class students reporting higher grade-related motivation. Gender differences were modest but underscore the importance of equitable curriculum de-

DOI: 10.4018/979-8-2600-0101-1.ch011

sign. The results highlight the need for CS curricula that balance cognitive challenge with positive emotional experiences, thereby strengthening resilience, self-efficacy, and motivation to pursue CS pathways in an AI-driven era.

1. INTRODUCTION

Artificial intelligence is no longer a future prospect; it is already reshaping societies, economies, and education. In Europe, this recognition has driven a strong policy agenda around digital and AI competencies. The Digital Education Action Plan 2021–2027 issued by the European Commission explicitly frames digital and computer science (CS) skills as a prerequisite for "sustainable digital transformation" and stresses the need to embed computational thinking and AI awareness into school curricula (European Commission, 2020). Similarly, the OECD Principles on Artificial Intelligence underscore that preparing young people for the AI era requires education systems to cultivate problem-solving, digital literacy, and ethical awareness (OECD, 2019).

In Greece, recent reforms align with this trajectory. The "Open School" initiative and the introduction of Skills Labs in primary and secondary education seek to build transversal competencies, including computational thinking and algorithmic reasoning, alongside creativity and expression (Eurydice, 2023). The EU's Digital Decade strategy has become a national priority with the Greek Ministry of Digital Governance leading initiatives such as digitizing educational content, building interactive platforms, developing learning management systems, and delivering teacher training to ensure equitable access to digital tools (UNESCO, 2024). These moves situate CS education not only as subject knowledge but as a strategic foundation for participation in an AI-driven economy and society.

Still, curriculum and policy will not bridge the AI knowledge gap alone. Students must feel motivated and emotionally prepared—not just cognitively equipped. The Control–Value Theory (CVT) of achievement emotions reminds us that how students feel—curious, confident, or frustrated—deeply shapes their engagement (Pekrun, 2006). Computer science education becomes foundational for the AI era only when cognitive, emotional, and motivational readiness are aligned. This study therefore explores how the Greek CS curriculum interacts with students' emotions and motivations, and what this means for preparing diverse learners to take part in AI-era pathways.

In Greek upper secondary education, Informatics is compulsory in both A and B class. In A class, "*Applications of Informatics*" introduces applied ICT (e.g., HTML, cloud tools, simple app design), aiming to foster creativity and teamwork. In B class, "*Introduction to the Principles of Computer Science*" emphasizes algorithmic problem-solving via the GLOSSA pseudocode language. While A class highlights accessibility and creativity, B class stresses logical precision and abstraction, creating two contrasting but complementary approaches to CS. The C class offers Informatics as a specialization subject for students preparing for Panhellenic examinations, but the present study focuses exclusively on the general education track in A and B class.

At the time of this research, these curricula were still in effect. Although the Ministry of Education introduced a new Informatics curriculum in the Government Gazette (FEK B/2951/2023), that reform had not yet been implemented during data collection. The findings presented here therefore reflect the realities of teaching under the 2024–25 curricula. The purpose of this study is to investigate how these curricula relate to students' emotions and motivation in computer science learning, and how such experiences may influence their intention to pursue further studies in the field. By situating these findings within the context of AI-era education policy, this study offers insights into how national curricula can be reshaped not only to equip students with technical skills, but also to nurture the emotional and motivational foundations required for meaningful participation in a rapidly evolving digital society.

Research Questions

1. How do emotions experienced during computer science lessons (before and after task engagement) influence students' motivation to pursue further studies in CS?
2. In what ways do curriculum design differences (creative ICT focus in A class vs algorithmic programming in B class) foster or hinder positive emotions and motivation?
3. How do these emotional-motivational dynamics connect with students' orientation toward AI-era skills and study choices?
4. What curricular adjustments could better balance enjoyment, pride, and self-efficacy to prepare students for computer science in the AI age?

2. THEORETICAL AND POLICY BACKGROUND

2.1 Achievement Emotions in Learning (CVT): The Control–Value Framework

The way students feel while learning is not a side issue; emotions directly shape how they approach schoolwork and whether they stay motivated over time. Pekrun's Control–Value Theory of Achievement Emotions is one of the most established frameworks for understanding this connection (Pekrun, 2006; Pekrun & Perry, 2014). The theory proposes that emotions in learning grow out of two judgments students make—how much control they believe they have over success, and how much they value the activity or outcome. When both are high—when students feel capable and believe the work matters—they are more likely to feel positive emotions such as enjoyment, pride, or curiosity. These emotions reinforce motivation, encourage persistence, and help students invest effort even when tasks are demanding (Pekrun & Linnenbrink-Garcia, 2012). On the other hand, when control is low—"I can't do this"—or value is low—"this isn't useful"—negative emotions dominate. Boredom, hopelessness, and anxiety do more than feel unpleasant; they actively undermine motivation and narrow the chances of students continuing with the subject.

Computer science classrooms are contexts where these dynamics are especially visible. Programming and algorithmic tasks are often described as "all or nothing": either the code works or it fails. That makes them excellent for triggering strong emotional responses. Success can produce satisfaction and confidence, but errors and repeated failures easily spiral into frustration. On the other hand, applied ICT activities— for example designing apps, making digital stories, collaborating online—tend to highlight usefulness and creativity, making students more likely to value the subject and enjoy the process (Lau & Yuen, 2011). This contrast makes CS classrooms a natural testing ground for CVT.

For the present study, CVT provides the conceptual foundation for analyzing how Greek upper secondary school students respond to two contrasting curricular orientations. The A class curriculum, with its emphasis on applied ICT, may be more effective in triggering positive value appraisals, while the B class algorithmic focus may better strengthen feelings of control when mastery is achieved—but may also risk higher levels of frustration. By comparing students' emotions across these contexts, this research examines how curricula influence not only cognitive achievement but also the motivational and emotional readiness needed for students to engage further with computer science in the age of AI.

2.2 Measuring Motivation in Science and Computer Science: The SMQ-II Framework

Understanding why students choose to engage with science—or avoid it—requires more than measuring achievement. Motivation is a powerful driver of long-term commitment, and the Science Motivation Questionnaire II (SMQ-II), developed by Glynn et al. (2011), has become one of the most widely used tools for capturing this dimension. The SMQ-II was designed to assess multiple components of science motivation: intrinsic motivation, self-efficacy, self-determination, grade motivation, and career motivation. Together, these scales provide a multifaceted view of what keeps students engaged in science learning beyond immediate classroom performance.

In computer science education, this framework offers valuable insights. Research has shown that intrinsic motivation and self-efficacy are especially influential in predicting persistence in computing, often outweighing prior achievement (Caspersen & Nowack, 2013; Lewis, Yasuhara, & Anderson, 2011). Students who believe they can succeed in computing tasks, and who genuinely enjoy them, are more likely to continue in computer science pathways. Conversely, low self-efficacy or motivation driven purely by grades tends to predict attrition, particularly among underrepresented groups (Beyer, 2014; Master, Cheryan, & Meltzoff, 2016).

The SMQ-II has been adapted for various STEM domains, including chemistry, physics, and computer science, to capture how students perceive a subject's relevance and their own capacity to succeed (Salta & Koulougliotis, 2015; You et al., 2018). Studies suggest that when students engage in applied computing contexts—such as app design, digital media projects, or collaborative ICT tasks—they report stronger career motivation and higher perceptions of relevance, because the activities are visibly connected to everyday life and future opportunities (Denner et al., 2014). By contrast, algorithmic and programming-intensive curricula place greater demands on self-efficacy, since success depends heavily on confidence in abstract problem solving and persistence in the face of repeated errors (Caspersen & Nowack, 2013). This distinction reflects the curricular split observed in Greek upper secondary school classrooms: A class emphasizes applied ICT, while B class foregrounds algorithmic reasoning.

For this study, the adapted SMQ-II was used alongside Pekrun's Achievement Emotions Questionnaire to capture the intersection of how students feel and why they stay motivated. This dual lens is especially important in the AI era, where persistence in computer science requires both emotional resilience and strong internalized motivation. Together, these frameworks provide the basis for examining whether current Greek secondary curricula are preparing students not just to learn computer science, but to want to continue with it.

2.3 Policy Alignment: EU and Greece

Artificial intelligence has moved from the margins of policy discussion to the center of Europe's educational agenda. The European Commission's Digital Decade targets set ambitious goals: by 2030, 80% of Europeans should possess at least basic digital skills, and 20 million ICT specialists should be employed across the Union, with gender convergence in the field (European Commission, 2021a). These goals position computer science (CS) education as a critical mechanism for systemic transformation rather than a specialist track. The Digital Education Action Plan

2021–2027 reinforces this view, emphasizing high-quality, inclusive digital learning and calling for the integration of artificial intelligence and data literacy into school curricula (European Commission, 2020). Complementing this, the Commission's Ethical Guidelines on the Use of Artificial Intelligence and Data in Teaching and Learning highlight the need to build digital competencies alongside principles of transparency, fairness, and accountability (European Commission, 2022). Together, these initiatives make clear that preparing students for the AI era requires both technical proficiency and ethical awareness.

Regulation further strengthens these policy signals. The Artificial Intelligence Act, adopted in 2024, establishes a risk-based framework for AI systems (European Parliament & Council of the European Union, 2024). While most classroom applications are outside its "high-risk" categories, the Act's emphasis on human oversight, trust, and accountability is expected to influence how AI-powered learning tools are procured, deployed, and discussed in schools.

Despite these commitments, progress remains uneven. The first State of the Digital Decade report shows that without intensified action, the EU is unlikely to reach the 80% digital skills benchmark by 2030 (European Commission, 2023a). Methodological notes from the former DESI framework confirm the gap, particularly in younger cohorts where advanced digital skills remain below target levels (European Commission, 2023b). This shortfall underscores the importance of secondary education in motivating and preparing students for CS and AI-related pathways. In Greece, national reforms align closely with these European priorities. The Digital Education Transformation Initiative, financed through the EU Recovery and Resilience Facility, aims to digitize educational content, expand learning management platforms, and provide large-scale teacher training (Ministry of Education and Religious Affairs, 2023). Within this framework, the upper secondary school curricula—outlined earlier—already establish distinct orientations through applied ICT learning in A class and algorithmic reasoning in B class. While these offer complementary strengths, they also illustrate the challenge of designing curricula that are both motivating and cognitively demanding.

Looking ahead, three areas emerge as policy priorities. First, AI and data literacy must be embedded more explicitly, ensuring students understand how data are generated, processed, and interpreted by algorithmic systems. Second, AI-powered instructional tools should be introduced in ways that reinforce transparency and equity, consistent with the EU AI Act. Finally, attention must be paid to motivation and equity, especially in addressing persistent gender disparities in CS participation, so that pathways remain accessible and aligned with Europe's human capital goals. In this perspective, CS education is more than subject knowledge: it is a strategic foundation for AI-era readiness. By combining technical skills, ethical awareness, and motivational support, it enables European and Greek policy objectives to be translated into tangible classroom experiences.

3. CURRICULUM CONTEXT IN GREEK UPPER SECONDARY EDUCATION

In the Greek upper secondary school system, computer science education takes two distinct forms in the first two years of upper secondary school. In A class, all students take a course designed to introduce them to the creative and applied side of digital technologies. The syllabus emphasizes hands-on use of tools such as HTML for web design, App Inventor for mobile applications, Alice for visual programming, and collaborative cloud-based platforms. The underlying orientation is practical: students gain exposure to digital creation, teamwork, and communication through ICT, skills that are readily transferable across school subjects and daily life (Institute of Educational Policy [IEP], 2024). By contrast, in B class the focus shifts toward algorithmic thinking and problem solving, taught using the Greek educational pseudocode language GLOSSA, which prepares students for the abstract reasoning that underpins programming and computational models. The course prepares students for the kind of abstract reasoning that underpins programming and computational models. Whereas A class highlights immediate relevance and creative expression, B class stresses the logical and formal foundations of the discipline (IEP, 2024).

Both orientations contribute differently to readiness for the age of artificial intelligence. Applied ICT experiences in A class strengthen digital literacy, collaborative problem-solving, and creativity—competencies closely aligned with the transversal skills highlighted in European and international AI policy frameworks (European Commission, 2020; UNESCO, 2024). The algorithmic emphasis of B class provides the abstraction and formal reasoning that underpin programming and data-driven methods (Grover & Pea, 2018). The coexistence of these two tracks illustrates a tension within CS education: how to balance accessibility and motivation with the cognitive demands of computational thinking. For students, the way these curricula shape emotions and motivation may be as important as the knowledge itself, since sustained engagement with computer science in the AI era requires both technical foundations and a sense of personal connection to the subject.

4. METHODOLOGY

The study involved 132 students (65 boys, 67 girls) from two general upper secondary schools in a large Greek city, with 71 enrolled in A class (applied ICT) and 61 in B class (algorithmic programming). All students took Informatics as part of the national curriculum (Institute of Educational Policy [IEP], 2024). Students' emotions were measured with the *Achievement Emotions Questionnaire for Programming (AEQp)*, an adaptation of Pekrun et al. (2011) that assesses enjoyment, pride, anger, and shame and is sensitive to the rapid fluctuations typical of programming tasks (Atiq & Batra, 2024). Motivation was assessed with the *Science Motivation Questionnaire II (SMQ-II)* (Glynn et al., 2011), adapted to reflect CS learning and ICT-related career pathways, with prior cross-cultural validations in Greece (Salta & Koulougliotis, 2015; You et al., 2018). Together, the AEQp captured situational emotions, while the SMQ-II provided broader motivational orientations.

The design followed students across one school year. At the beginning and end of the year, the AEQp was administered immediately before and after a representative CS lesson. At year's end, the SMQ-II was completed alongside official orientation decisions, when students declared intended study pathways for the next grade. Because Greek university CS programs are accessible via both Science Studies and Economics/CS tracks, students were asked whether their choices reflected an intention to pursue CS specifically. These responses reflected current intentions, not eventual enrollment. All data were collected in classrooms with voluntary participation, anonymity assured, and consent procedures approved by school leadership in line with Ministry research guidelines. Analyses included descriptive statistics, paired- and independent-samples t tests, and binary logistic regression, conducted in SPSS (version 27). Effect sizes were reported following Cohen (1988).

5. RESULTS

5.1 Reliability of Instruments

Internal consistency was assessed using Cronbach's alpha for all multi-item subscales of the AEQp and SMQ-II. Results indicated generally good reliability, with most coefficients exceeding the commonly accepted threshold of .70 (Nunnally & Bernstein, 1994). For the AEQp, pre-task enjoyment ($\alpha = .823$) and post-task enjoyment ($\alpha = .846$) showed strong reliability, while post-task pride ($\alpha = .883$), post-task anger ($\alpha = .781$), and post-task shame ($\alpha = .781$) also reached acceptable levels. Pre-task pride and anger were single-item measures; therefore, alpha was not computed. This limitation is consistent with challenges noted in prior applications of adapted AEQ measures in programming contexts (Atiq & Batra, 2024). For the SMQ-II, all motivational subscales demonstrated satisfactory internal consistency, ranging from acceptable (Self-Determination, $\alpha = .756$) to excellent (Career Motivation, $\alpha = .871$). These results align with previous cross-cultural validations of the instrument (Salta & Koulougliotis, 2015; You et al., 2018), supporting its use in the present study.

Overall, the AEQp and SMQ-II demonstrated acceptable to excellent reliability, confirming suitability for use with Greek secondary students, while highlighting the limitation of single-item subscales (see Table 1).

Table 1. Reliability of AEQp and SMQ-II subscales (N=132)

Scale	Cronbach's α	Number of items
AEQp		
Pre-task enjoyment	.82	5
Pre-task pride	— (1 item)	1
Pre-task anger	— (1 item)	1
Post-task enjoyment	.85	2
Post-task pride	.88	7
Post-task anger	.78	6
Post-task shame	.78	4
SMQ-II		
Intrinsic motivation	.84	5
Self-efficacy	.80	5
Self-determination	.76	5
Grade motivation	.81	5
Career motivation	.87	5

Note. AEQp – Achievement Emotions Questionnaire for programming; SMQ-II = Science Motivation Questionnaire II. Pre-task pride and anger were single-item scales, and Cronbach's alpha was not computed.

5.2 Descriptive Statistics

Students' emotional responses to computer science lessons showed a mixed pattern. Before task engagement, they reported moderate enjoyment, only modest pride, and somewhat higher levels of anger and shame. After working on the tasks, the profile shifted: enjoyment dropped noticeably, but pride rose, while both anger and shame declined. Pride showed the clearest positive shift, suggesting that completing tasks gave students a stronger sense of accomplishment, even if the process dampened their initial excitement. At the same time, the decline in shame indicates that students felt less inadequate or self-conscious after engaging with CS work.

Motivationally, students showed moderate self-efficacy and responsiveness to grades, but weaker intrinsic interest, career motivation, and especially self-determination. This pattern suggests that students largely saw computer science as something they could succeed at and be graded on, but less often as a subject tied to personal interest or long-term aspirations (see Table 2).

Table 2. Descriptive statistics for emotions (AEQp) and motivation (SMQ-II) (N = 132)

Variable	*M*	*SD*	*Min*	*Max*
Pre-task Enjoyment	2.83	0.76	1.00	4.60
Pre-task Pride	2.39	0.96	1.00	4.00
Pre-task Anger	2.91	0.95	1.00	5.00
Pre-task Shame	3.26	1.16	1.00	5.00
Post-task Enjoyment	2.34	1.03	1.00	5.00
Post-task Pride	3.23	0.87	1.00	5.00
Post-task Anger	2.80	0.79	1.00	4.70
Post-task Shame	2.43	0.89	1.00	4.80
Intrinsic Motivation	8.66	4.09	0.00	16.00
Self-Efficacy	11.27	4.21	0.00	20.00
Self-Determination	7.25	3.83	0.00	16.00
Grade Motivation	11.22	4.75	1.00	20.00
Career Motivation	9.52	5.16	0.00	20.00

Note. AEQp = Achievement Emotions Questionnaire for programming; SMQ-II = Science Motivation Questionnaire II.

5.3 Paired-Samples T Tests

Paired t-tests confirmed significant changes across three of the four emotions. Enjoyment declined (small-to-medium effect), pride increased strongly (large effect), and shame decreased substantially (medium effect). Anger showed no significant change.

Viewed together, these results suggest that computer science lessons may not consistently maintain enjoyment, but they do appear to foster resilience by strengthening pride and reducing shame. These shifts in emotional balance may be essential for sustaining students' longer-term engagement with computer science, particularly as they make decisions about further study and career pathways in the AI era (see Table 3).

Table 3. Paired-samples t tests comparing pre- and post-task emotions ($N = 132$)

Emotion	Pre-task M (SD)	Post-task M (SD)	Mean Difference	t(131)	p	Cohen's d
Enjoyment	2.83 (0.76)	2.34 (1.03)	0.49	5.76	<.001	0.50
Pride	2.39 (0.96)	3.23 (0.87)	-0.84	-9.90	<.001	0.86
Anger	2.91 (0.95)	2.80 (0.79)	0.11	1.13	.260	0.10
Shame	3.26 (1.16)	2.43 (0.89)	0.83	7.73	<.001	0.67

Note. M = mean, SD = standard deviation. Effect sizes (Cohen's d) interpreted as small ≈ .20, medium ≈ .50, large ≈ .80 (Cohen, 1988).

5.4 Between-class comparisons (A vs B)

The comparisons between A class (applied ICT) and B class (algorithmic programming) revealed striking similarities in how students experienced computer science lessons. Across nearly all emotional and motivational measures—enjoyment, pride, anger, shame, intrinsic motivation, self-efficacy, self-determination, and career motivation—there were no significant differences between the two groups. Effect sizes were consistently small, suggesting that the different curricular emphases did not translate into meaningfully different emotional climates or motivational orientations.

The one exception was grade motivation, where students in A class reported significantly higher scores than those in B class. This difference, of small-to-moderate size, points to the possibility that applied, project-oriented tasks in A class more clearly connect effort with assessment outcomes. In contrast, the algorithmic focus of B class may not provide the same immediate reinforcement in terms of grades.

Overall, the results suggest that while both curricula cultivate broadly similar emotional and motivational patterns, the structure of A class appears to encourage students to frame their engagement in terms of external achievement. This subtle difference highlights the importance of aligning curriculum and assessment practices with broader goals for fostering sustained, intrinsic interest in computer science (see Table 4).

Table 4. Independent-samples t tests comparing A and B class students on emotions and motivation (N = 132)

Measure	A class *M* (*SD*)	B class *M* (*SD*)	*t*(130)	*p*	Cohen's *d*
Pre-task Enjoyment	2.89 (0.74)	2.76 (0.79)	0.97	.332	0.17
Pre-task Pride	2.49 (1.01)	2.28 (0.88)	1.29	.200	0.22
Pre-task Anger	2.95 (0.97)	2.85 (0.93)	0.59	.555	0.10
Post-task Enjoyment	2.34 (0.98)	2.34 (1.10)	–0.03	.973	–0.01
Post-task Pride	3.30 (0.94)	3.15 (0.78)	1.03	.307	0.18
Post-task Anger	2.77 (0.80)	2.83 (0.79)	–0.45	.655	–0.08
Post-task Shame	2.51 (0.94)	2.34 (0.84)	1.03	.303	0.18
Intrinsic Motivation	9.06 (4.06)	8.20 (4.10)	1.21	.229	0.21
Self-Efficacy	11.59 (4.05)	10.90 (4.40)	0.94	.350	0.16
Self-Determination	7.46 (3.64)	7.00 (4.05)	0.69	.489	0.12
Grade Motivation	12.11 (4.37)	10.18 (5.00)	2.37	.019	0.41
Career Motivation	9.37 (4.92)	9.70 (5.47)	–0.38	.709	–0.07

5.5 Motivational and Emotional Differences by Intention to Pursue Computer Science

Independent-samples t tests compared students who expressed an intention to pursue computer science with those who did not. The results revealed substantial differences in motivational orientations. Students intending to follow CS pathways reported significantly higher intrinsic motivation, self-efficacy, self-determination, grade motivation, and career motivation. Effect sizes for these differences ranged from medium to large, with intrinsic motivation, self-determination, and career motivation showing the strongest separation between groups. This pattern suggests that both autonomous drivers (interest, self-directed persistence) and external considerations (grades, career prospects) contribute to study intentions.

In contrast, emotional responses during CS tasks were less decisive. Post-task pride was significantly higher among students intending to pursue CS, while enjoyment and shame showed only marginal trends, and anger did not differ between groups. Taken together, these findings indicate that although emotions such as pride may play a supportive role, it is students' broader motivational orientations that more reliably distinguish those planning to continue with computer science from those who do not (see Table 5).

Table 5. Independent-samples t tests by intention to pursue computer science (N = 132)

Measure	No Intention *M* (*SD*)	Yes Intention *M* (*SD*)	*t*(df)	*p*	Cohen's *d*
Intrinsic Motivation	7.72 (3.83)	10.97 (3.81)	–4.42(130)	<.001	0.77
Self-Efficacy	10.49 (4.13)	13.21 (3.82)	–3.50(130)	.001	0.61
Self-Determination	6.40 (3.47)	9.34 (3.93)	–4.24(130)	<.001	0.74
Grade Motivation	10.45 (4.71)	13.13 (4.36)	–3.03(130)	.003	0.53
Career Motivation	8.43 (4.80)	12.24 (5.08)	–4.06(130)	<.001	0.72
Post-task Pride	3.14 (0.89)	3.46 (0.77)	–2.06(78.97)	.043	0.35
Post-task Enjoyment	2.23 (1.04)	2.61 (0.97)	–1.89(130)	.061	0.33
Post-task Anger	2.76 (0.83)	2.89 (0.70)	–0.82(130)	.413	0.14
Post-task Shame	2.34 (0.82)	2.67 (1.02)	–1.94(130)	.055	0.34

Note. Cohen's d interpreted as small ≈ .20, medium ≈ .50, large ≈ .80 (Cohen, 1988).

The independent-samples comparisons make clear that motivational orientations—particularly intrinsic motivation, self-efficacy, self-determination, and career motivation—differentiate students who intend to pursue CS from those who do not, while emotions play a secondary role, with pride showing the only significant difference. However, these tests examine each factor in isolation. In practice, motivational and emotional dimensions interact, and it is important to assess which predictors remain significant when considered together. To address this, a binary logistic regression was conducted with intention to pursue CS (0 = no, 1 = yes) as the dependent variable, and the SMQ-II subscales and post-task emotions entered as predictors. This analysis allows identification of the strongest, independent predictors of CS study intentions.

The logistic regression model significantly distinguished students with and without CS intentions ($\chi^2(10) = 32.95$, $p < .001$, Nagelkerke $R^2 = .32$, 80.3% classification accuracy). However, the Hosmer–Lemeshow test indicated some misfit ($\chi^2(8) = 23.19$, $p = .003$). No predictors reached conventional significance. Career motivation showed a positive trend ($p = .092$), while post-task anger negatively predicted CS intention at a marginal level ($p = .062$). Post-task shame showed a marginal positive association ($p = .086$), though in the unexpected direction. Taken together, these results suggest that while motivation and emotions play a role, no single factor strongly predicts CS intentions once overlaps are controlled, pointing to complex, multi-layered influences (see Table 6).

Table 6. Binary logistic regression predicting intention to pursue computer science (N = 132)

Predictor	B	SE	Wald	p	OR	95% CI for OR
Intrinsic Motivation	0.08	0.09	0.82	.365	1.08	0.91 – 1.28
Self-Efficacy	0.07	0.07	0.98	.321	1.07	0.93 – 1.24
Self-Determination	0.14	0.09	2.69	.101	1.16	0.97 – 1.37
Grade Motivation	–0.03	0.07	0.22	.642	0.97	0.85 – 1.11
Career Motivation	0.11	0.07	2.84	.092	1.12	0.98 – 1.27
Post-task Enjoyment	–0.03	0.29	0.01	.922	0.97	0.55 – 1.71
Post-task Pride	0.15	0.37	0.16	.685	1.16	0.57 – 2.37
Post-task Anger	–0.76	0.41	3.48	.062	0.47	0.21 – 1.04
Post-task Shame	0.52	0.30	2.95	.086	1.68	0.93 – 3.04
Class (A vs B)	0.52	0.49	1.14	.286	1.69	0.65 – 4.41
Constant	–4.28	1.34	10.21	.001	0.01	—

Note. OR = Odds Ratio. 95% CI = Confidence Interval for Odds Ratio.

6. DISCUSSION

The results of this study highlight a complex emotional landscape in Greek upper secondary computer science (CS) classrooms. One of the clearest patterns was the rise in pride alongside a drop in enjoyment after task engagement. Students often began lessons with curiosity and anticipation, but this enthusiasm declined once they confronted the challenges of programming or digital problem-solving. At the same time, completing tasks successfully brought strong feelings of pride, suggesting that mastery experiences are central to sustaining engagement. This aligns with Pekrun's (2006) CVT, which emphasizes that emotions such as pride are closely tied to perceptions of competence and control. In other words, while enjoyment may wane under cognitive load, pride compensates by reinforcing persistence and resilience.

Shame also decreased after task engagement, indicating that students felt less inadequate once they had an opportunity to attempt and resolve problems. This finding is encouraging, as shame has been linked to avoidance behaviors and reduced persistence in STEM learning (Pekrun & Linnenbrink-Garcia, 2012). By contrast, anger remained stable, suggesting that while programming challenges are frustrating, they do not necessarily intensify over repeated experiences. Together, these shifts point to the importance of fostering conditions where initial excitement can be maintained while still enabling students to achieve mastery and avoid excessive self-conscious emotions.

The comparisons between curricular tracks suggest that curriculum structure matters less for broad emotional climate than might be expected. A and B class students reported broadly similar levels of enjoyment, pride, anger, and shame, as well as similar motivational orientations. The one exception was grade motivation, which was higher in A class, consistent with its emphasis on visible, project-based outputs. However, the logistic regression analysis showed that once multiple factors were considered, neither curriculum track nor most motivational scales strongly predicted intention to pursue CS. Instead, career motivation, pride, and frustration showed weak, non-significant trends. These results imply that intention to follow CS pathways is shaped by a constellation of influences—not just classroom emotions or curriculum, but broader expectations about careers, identity, and societal signals about computing.

From a policy perspective, the results speak directly to the challenges of preparing students for AI-era study and work. While the Greek curriculum provides complementary experiences—applied ICT in A class and algorithmic reasoning in B class—neither in isolation seems sufficient to generate strong or widespread intentions to pursue computer science. Pride and career relevance emerged as critical motivators, underscoring the need to design curricula that combine accessible, creative entry points with rigorous pathways to abstraction and problem-solving. In doing so, educators can help ensure that students do not merely learn about computing but see themselves as capable of contributing to AI-driven futures.

7. IMPLICATIONS FOR AI-POWERED K–12 EDUCATION

The findings also have implications for the growing integration of AI-powered instructional tools and virtual tutors in K–12 education. AI-driven systems promise adaptive feedback, personalized learning trajectories, and scalable support (Holmes et al., 2019). Yet this study suggests that emotional and motivational readiness is a precondition for effective adoption. If students lose enjoyment during difficult tasks, an AI tutor that provides immediate scaffolding could help sustain engagement. Likewise, systems that highlight progress and mastery could amplify pride, reinforcing persistence in the face of challenge.

Policy recommendations flow naturally from this perspective. First, curricula should aim to bridge creative ICT experiences and algorithmic rigor, rather than treating them as separate tracks. Project-based activities that are personally relevant can maintain enjoyment and highlight real-world value, while structured algorithmic challenges build the cognitive control needed for advanced CS and AI learning (Grover & Pea, 2018). Second, AI-powered learning systems should be designed to be emotionally supportive as well as cognitively adaptive. Features such as real-time encouragement, error normalization, and reflective prompts could reduce shame and frustration, aligning with evidence that emotions are central to sustained STEM engagement (Pekrun & Perry, 2014).

Equity considerations must also remain central. Even though gender differences were not directly analyzed in this study, prior research highlights persistent gaps in CS self-efficacy and participation. Future curricula and AI-powered tools should therefore be designed with inclusivity in mind, counteracting stereotypes, emphasizing collaboration, and showcasing diverse role models. At the policy level, the European Commission's (2020) Digital Education Action Plan and the 2024 EU AI Act already emphasize ethical, equitable use of AI in schools. Translating these commitments into classroom practice requires not only technical safeguards but also careful attention to the emotional and motivational environments in which AI tools are embedded. Ultimately, this study underscores that AI-era readiness in CS education depends as much on how students feel as on what they learn. By integrating curriculum reform with AI-powered support systems, and by addressing equity head-on, policymakers and educators can cultivate both the competence and the confidence required for students to pursue computing pathways in a rapidly transforming world.

8. LIMITATIONS

This study has several limitations. The sample came from two upper secondary schools in one urban area, which limits generalizability to other regions of Greece. Emotions and motivation were measured through self-report, which, while based on validated instruments (Atiq & Batra, 2024; Glynn et al., 2011), remains vulnerable to response biases. The outcomes examined were students' intentions to pursue computer science, not actual enrollment or career choices, so long-term trajectories cannot be inferred. Finally, the analysis focused on curriculum content but did not directly account for teacher practices or classroom climate, which likely interact with emotions and motivation.

9. SUMMARY OF KEY FINDINGS

This study shows that while enjoyment often declines during challenging computer science tasks, pride rises and shame decreases, underscoring the role of mastery in sustaining engagement. Students who intend to pursue CS further are distinguished less by fleeting emotions than by stronger motivational orientations—intrinsic interest, self-efficacy, self-determination, and career motivation. For education in the

AI era, the findings point to the need for curricula that integrate creative ICT with algorithmic rigor, supported by AI tools that scaffold learning and protect confidence. By combining meaningful projects, structured challenges, and inclusive practices, schools can prepare students with both the skills and the motivational foundations required for lifelong learning and careers in an AI-driven society.

REFERENCES

Atiq, Z., & Batra, R. (2024). How do first-year engineering students' emotions change while working on programming problems? ACM Transactions on Computing Education, 24(2). *Article*, *24*(2), 1–30. DOI: 10.1145/3643865

Beyer, S. (2014). Why are women underrepresented in computer science? Gender differences in stereotypes, self-efficacy, values, and interests and predictors of future CS course-taking and grades. *Computer Science Education*, *24*(2–3), 153–192. DOI: 10.1080/08993408.2014.963363

Caspersen, M. E., & Nowack, P. (2013). Computational thinking and practice—A generic approach to computing in Danish high schools. In Grønbæk, D., & Irgens, S. (Eds.), *Proceedings of the Fifteenth Australasian Computing Education Conference (ACE 2013)* (pp. 137–143). Australian Computer Society.

Cohen, J. (1988). *Statistical power analysis for the behavioral sciences* (2nd ed.). Lawrence Erlbaum Associates.

Denner, J., Werner, L., Campe, S., & Ortiz, E. (2014). Pair programming: Under what conditions is it advantageous for middle school students? *Journal of Research on Technology in Education*, *46*(3), 277–296. DOI: 10.1080/15391523.2014.888272

European Commission. (2020). Digital Education Action Plan (2021–2027): Resetting education and training for the digital age. Publications Office of the European Union. https://education.ec.europa.eu/focus-topics/digital/education-action-plan

European Commission. (2021a). 2030 Digital Compass: The European way for the Digital Decade (COM/2021/118 final). Publications Office of the European Union. https://eur-lex.europa.eu/legal-content/EN/TXT/?uri=CELEX:52021DC0118

European Commission. (2022). Ethical guidelines on the use of artificial intelligence (AI) and data in teaching and learning for educators. Publications Office of the European Union. https://education.ec.europa.eu/document/ethical-guidelines-on-the-use-of-ai-and-data-in-teaching-and-learning-for-educators

European Commission. (2023a). Report on the state of the Digital Decade 2023 (COM(2023) 570 final). https://eur-lex.europa.eu/legal-content/EN/TXT/?uri=CELEX:52023DC0570

European Commission. (2023b). DESI methodological note—Digital Decade report 2023. https://digital-strategy.ec.europa.eu/en/library/desi-methodological-note-digital-decade-report-2023

European Parliament & Council of the European Union. (2024). Regulation (EU) 2024/1689 of the European Parliament and of the Council of 13 June 2024 laying down harmonised rules on artificial intelligence (Artificial Intelligence Act) and amending certain Union legislative acts. *Official Journal of the European Union, L, 202*, 1–102. https://eur-lex.europa.eu/legal-content/EN/TXT/?uri=CELEX:32024R1689

Eurydice. (2023). Greece: Embracing change and technology – The Open School reform in elementary and secondary education. European Education and Culture Executive Agency. https://eurydice.eacea.ec.europa.eu/news/greece-embracing-change-and-technology-open-school-reform-elementary-and-secondary-education

Glynn, S. M., Brickman, P., Armstrong, N., & Taasoobshirazi, G. (2011). Science Motivation Questionnaire II: Validation with science majors and nonscience majors. *Journal of Research in Science Teaching, 48*(10), 1159–1176. DOI: 10.1002/tea.20442

Grover, S., & Pea, R. (2018). Computational thinking: A competency whose time has come. *Computer Science Education, 28*(1), 70–74. DOI: 0.5040/9781350057142.ch-003

Holmes, W., Bialik, M., & Fadel, C. (2019). *Artificial intelligence in education: Promises and implications for teaching and learning*. Center for Curriculum Redesign.

Institute of Educational Policy (IEP). (2024). Curricula for secondary education 2024–2025. https://www.iep.edu.gr/2024-2025-3/

Lau, W. W. F., & Yuen, A. H. K. (2011). Modelling programming performance: Beyond the influence of learner characteristics. *Computers & Education, 57*(1), 1202–1213. DOI: 10.1016/j.compedu.2011.01.002

Lewis, C. M., Yasuhara, K., & Anderson, R. E. (2011). Deciding to major in computer science: A grounded theory of students' self-assessment of ability. In *Proceedings of the Seventh International Computing Education Research Workshop* (pp. 3–10). ACM. DOI: 10.1145/2016911.2016915

Master, A., Cheryan, S., & Meltzoff, A. N. (2016). Computing whether she belongs: Stereotypes undermine girls' interest and sense of belonging in computer science. *Journal of Educational Psychology, 108*(3), 424–437. DOI: 10.1037/edu0000061

Ministry of Education and Religious Affairs. (2023). *Informatics curriculum reform: Government Gazette FEK B/2951/2023*. Hellenic Republic.

Nunnally, J. C., & Bernstein, I. H. (1994). *Psychometric theory* (3rd ed.). McGraw-Hill.

OECD. (2019). OECD Principles on Artificial Intelligence. Organisation for Economic Co-operation and Development. https://oecd.ai/en/ai-principles

Pekrun, R. (2006). The control–value theory of achievement emotions: Assumptions, corollaries, and implications for educational research and practice. *Educational Psychology Review, 18*(4), 315–341. DOI: 10.1007/s10648-006-9029-9

Pekrun, R., Goetz, T., Frenzel, A. C., Barchfeld, P., & Perry, R. P. (2011). Measuring emotions in students' learning and performance: The Achievement Emotions Questionnaire (AEQ). *Contemporary Educational Psychology, 36*(1), 36–48. DOI: 10.1016/j.cedpsych.2010.10.002

Pekrun, R., & Linnenbrink-Garcia, L. (2012). Academic emotions and student engagement. In Christenson, S. L., Reschly, A. L., & Wylie, C. (Eds.), *Handbook of research on student engagement* (pp. 259–282). Springer., DOI: 10.1007/978-1-4614-2018-7_12

Pekrun, R., & Perry, R. P. (2014). Control–value theory of achievement emotions. In Pekrun, R., & Linnenbrink-Garcia, L. (Eds.), *International handbook of emotions in education* (pp. 120–141). Routledge. DOI: 10.4324/9780203148211

Salta, K., & Koulougliotis, D. (2015). Assessing motivation to learn chemistry: Adaptation and validation of the Science Motivation Questionnaire II with Greek secondary school students. *Chemistry Education Research and Practice, 16*(2), 237–250. DOI: 10.1039/C4RP00196F

UNESCO. (2024). Greece's Digital Education Transformation Initiative. Paris: UNESCO. Retrieved from https://www.unesco.org/en/dtc-financing-toolkit/greeces-digital-education-transformation-initiative

You, H. S., Kim, K., Black, K., & Min, K. W. (2018). Assessing science motivation for college students: Validation of the SMQ-II using the Rasch–Andrich rating scale model. *Eurasia Journal of Mathematics, Science and Technology Education, 14*(4), 1161–1173. DOI: 10.29333/ejmste/81821

Chapter 12
Teachers' Artificial Intelligence Practices, Benefits, and Challenges:
A Systematic Literature Review of Scopus and Web of Science Papers

Spyridon Aravantinos
http://orcid.org/0009-0001-2543-6703
University of Patras, Greece

Konstantinos Lavidas
http://orcid.org/0000-0003-2225-1137
University of Patras, Greece

Stamatis Papadakis
http://orcid.org/0000-0003-3184-1147
University of Crete, Greece

Thanassis Karalis
http://orcid.org/0000-0002-8564-8812
University of Patras, Greece

Vassilis Komis
http://orcid.org/0000-0001-6909-2765
University of Patras, Greece

ABSTRACT

Since the emergence of Artificial Intelligence (AI) in aspects of everyday life and its introduction into the educational sector, teachers from primary and secondary

DOI: 10.4018/979-8-2600-0101-1.ch012

education level have been attempting to implement it into their practices, recognizing its benefits while also trying to address the challenges it presents. This systematic literature review followed the PRISMA guidelines with specific inclusion and exclusion criteria, analyzing 49 peer-reviewed empirical articles in English, published online by the end of 2024 from Scopus and Web of Science databases. The main objectives were to identify teachers' practices, the benefits and the challenges, as they were shaped by the integration of AI into their teaching, aiming to gather trends, update knowledge and understand how it can be useful for learning without posing any threat. The results identified key insights in areas such as AI literacy, personalization of learning, assessment and feedback, ethical and responsible use, human-AI collaboration, academic integrity, teachers' attitudes and perceptions, and continuous PD.

1. INTRODUCTION

Artificial intelligence (AI) is increasingly embedded within educational contexts, exerting a significant influence on pedagogical practices and learning processes. In light of its rapid advancement and the proliferation of AI-driven tools, systematic and timely evaluation is imperative to safeguard their responsible use and to facilitate their effective integration into classroom environments. Many research papers are presented on a daily basis in relation to AI use in education, the benefits it brings and the challenges that arise from its integration by teachers and their students (Martin et al., 2024). The pedagogical implications are considerable, and warrant sustained scholarly inquiry, with the aim of advancing current understandings of recent technological developments that have raised concerns within both the scientific and educational communities (Biagini, 2025).

The critical examination of AI-driven tools in school settings is therefore necessary, to evaluate the benefits they bring and the risks they pose, justifying continuous research on this fast-evolving domain and contributing with empirical data to the scientific debate. As AI adoption in schools by governments and institutions is quickly increasing, transforming teaching and learning, evidence-based guidelines and regulations are essential for curriculum development and AI integration in pedagogically correct ways, fostering students' critical skills and ethical awareness, for an AI literate and sustainable future (Celik et al., 2022). This paper aims to investigate in-service primary and secondary education teachers' views of AI and its integration into the educational processes by documenting the practices and benefits that they reported in research studies. Furthermore, it will focus on the challenges teachers encountered while using AI, as they are shaped by the rapidly evolving technological landscape (Voulgari et al., 2024).

The integration of AI for educational purposes has demonstrated great potential to improve learning by personalizing the course experience according to the learner profiles and by providing real-time feedback, even though the assumed benefits should be empirically proved to offer the necessary evidence for AI adoption by educators and policymakers. Additionally, the practices of educators when implementing AI powered tools should be researched further to clarify the circumstances and the specific approaches in which AI integration works for the best of students in pedagogically sound ways (Aravantinos et al., 2024). The challenges associated with the use of AI are multifaceted, encompassing issues such as algorithmic bias, data privacy, technological overreliance, and fears of professional displacement. Addressing these challenges effectively is of critical importance, as doing so can inform the design of teacher training programs that foster the responsible implementation of AI in education (Adams et al., 2023).

2. PREVIOUS SYSTEMATIC LITERATURE REVIEWS

A systematic review with 29 articles in intelligent tutoring systems towards sustainable education, underscored the benefits of AI-integrated systems for personalization, accessibility and flexibility which promoted equal access to education (Lin et al., 2023). It provided guidance for educators to implement AI systems focusing on understanding of the algorithms, raising of awareness, navigating government policies and regulations and concluded that addressing both technological and pedagogical challenges will be critical to build inclusive, equitable and sustainable learning environments with AI, requiring combined efforts from all stakeholders: policymakers, educators, technologists, researchers, students and parents (Lin et al., 2023). Labadze et al. (2023) systematically reviewed 67 articles related to AI-powered chatbots in education and highlighted the enhancements in student feedback and personalization, the instructional support and complex problems solutions, but also the inability for human emotional support. Mikeladze et al. (2024) in a critical review noted challenges such as the integration of subject-specific AI skills and the provision of clear pathways for assessment and AI implementation, whereas Fu and Weng (2024) conducted a systematic review of 40 empirical studies focusing on ethics, responsibility and AI in education exploring themes such as fairness & equity, privacy & security, non-maleficence & beneficence, agency & autonomy, and transparency & intelligibility.

Noroozi et al. (2024) gathered insights of 17 studies to show how generative AI can improve traditional teaching methods exploring ChatGPT's practical application in enhancing learning outcomes through personalized feedback and administrative support but also raising critical concerns about the ethical use and privacy implications. Bettayeb et al. (2024) explored the impact of the conversational agent ChatGPT in education with a systematic review of 70 articles highlighting benefits in enhancing human-computer interaction and enabling personalized learning and challenges such as AI model bias, accuracy issues, lack of emotional intelligence and absence of critical thinking as well as ethical considerations like guidelines, human supervision, training, promotion of critical thinking and privacy measures. Zhang and Tur (2024) also investigated ChatGPT's use in K-12 education synthesizing 13 articles with SWOT analysis, highlighting strengths such as personalized learning experiences, positive influence on student achievement and capacity for immediate and personalized feedback, weaknesses such as low quality output, low task specificity, the inability to handle certain question types and limited reasoning skills, opportunities in personalized learning applications, differentiated instruction and support for educators, and threats focusing on data privacy and ethical concerns, academic dishonesty and negative impact on productivity.

A systematic review for the use of Generative AI (GAI) in K-12 education with 197 studies mentioned opportunities for personalization of learning and innovations in K-12 educational context but also challenges such as lack of resources, the need for framework development and issues of ethics and data quality to ensure inclusivity and effectiveness (Marzano, 2025). Other pedagogical challenges include designing effective teaching tools, evaluating continuously the methodologies used and differentiating technologies according to learning styles whereas the technical challenges include continuously updating the educational tools and ensuring their effectiveness for the target age groups (Marzano, 2025). The ethical and regulatory challenges of GAI in education was the focus of the systematic review of 53 peer-reviewed articles that underscored the main ethical concerns including data privacy, algorithmic bias, misinformation, the potential erosion of academic integrity, and the possible reduction of human interaction, creativity and critical thinking skills (García-López & Trujillo-Liñán, 2025).

In regard to human-centered AI (HCAI), a systematic literature review of 24 papers proposed a targeted theoretical framework to demonstrate how HCAI can serve educational goals in personalized learning, assessment and enhancement of outcomes, emphasizing in equity, learning path customization and intelligent education assessment. As for AI literacy, Yim and Su (2025) explored the primary school context by systematically reviewing 25 empirical studies that revealed key elements of AI literacy, theoretical frameworks and methodologies for positive educational outcomes. The fact that AI literacy definitions vary from technical to socio-ethical frameworks, highlighting the need for a more balanced approach, was stated in the systematic review of 87 articles which investigated AI's transformative impact in education (Biagini, 2025). Lastly, a systematic review of 22 studies about AI-literacy in K-12 education demonstrated that the development of AI literacy is influenced by the digital divide, the computational thinking skills, the educational opportunities, the attitudes and the perceptions of stakeholders (Tan & Tang, 2025).

3. RESEARCH OBJECTIVES

In this systematic literature review we focused on: a) teachers' practices with AI, b) the benefits of AI implementation, and c) the challenges emerging from AI use. Practices refer to the strategies, methods and behaviors that teachers incorporate in classrooms to manage and facilitate student learning and may include activities and routines such as assessment and feedback, use of technology, instructional strategies and classroom management, among others. The benefits refer to the advantages students and teachers can have from AI integration into classroom that can improve learning outcomes, student engagement, efficiency and enhance 21st-Century skills like digital literacy, problem-solving, collaboration and critical thinking or facilitate accessibility and diversity, making real-world connections. In the opposite direction, challenges of AI are the difficulties, obstacles or negative outcomes that may be encountered, regarding student misuse or over-reliance, technical issues, accessibility and equity, privacy and ethical concerns, teacher training and readiness etc. Therefore, our research questions were:

RQ1: What are the practices of teachers regarding the implementation of AI?
RQ2: What are the benefits for teachers and students from AI integration?
RQ3: What challenges do teachers encounter regarding AI use in school settings?

4. METHODS

To conduct a credible systematic literature review we followed the Preferred Reporting Items for Systematic Reviews and Meta-Analyses (PRISMA) guidelines (*Figure 1*) for systematic literature reviews (Page et al., 2021). For the identification phase we used two of the largest databases for research, Scopus and Web of Science, which index strictly peer-reviewed, reputable journals and offer access to a vast collection of research papers across various disciplines. Each one indexes journals that the other does not, so by using both the risk of missing relevant studies was minimized and with the tools they incorporate for search, reproducible searches meeting PRISMA criteria can be supported strengthening validity. Both have strong content coverage in the subjects of our interest and are recognized worldwide for their high-quality peer-reviewed articles, aiding researchers to track all the relevant literature. In *Table 1* the string queries for the search in each one of the databases that occurred in February 2025 appear, for literature that was published online up to the final day of December 2024. Online appearance explains the fact that some of the articles included have a publication date in January 2025, even though they were indexed late December 2024. The terms we used in the search were decided after studying relevant systematic literature reviews and related articles from last year's publications in the field and were aligned with our focus.

Table 1. Scopus search string

PUBYEAR bef 2025 (TITLE-ABS-KEY("artificial intelligence" AND ("primary school" OR "elementary school" OR "primary education" OR "elementary education" OR "secondary school" OR "high school" OR "middle school" OR "upper school" OR "secondary education" OR "secondary level" OR educator OR "K-12" OR k12) AND (practic* OR "teaching strateg*" OR method* OR pedagog* OR benefit OR advantage OR "positive outcome" OR challenge OR obstacle OR barrier OR difficult* OR "AI tools" OR "AI applications")) AND TITLE-ABS-KEY("empirical study" OR "case study" OR survey OR interview OR "data collection" OR "qualitative research" OR "quantitative research" OR "mixed methods" OR "experimental research"))
Web of Science search string Timespan: 1970-01-01 to 2024-12-31 (Publication Date)
TS=("artificial intelligence" AND ("primary school" OR "elementary school" OR "primary education" OR "elementary education" OR "secondary school" OR "high school" OR "middle school" OR "upper school" OR "secondary education" OR "secondary level" OR educator OR "K-12" OR k12) AND (practic* OR "teaching strateg*" OR method* OR pedagog* OR benefit OR advantage OR "positive outcome" OR challenge OR obstacle OR barrier OR difficult* OR "AI tools" OR "AI applications")) Combined with: TS=("empirical study" OR "case study" OR survey OR interview OR "data collection" OR "qualitative research" OR "quantitative research" OR "mixed methods" OR "experimental research")

During the screening process, we chose peer-reviewed articles written in English, which contained empirical data and were focused on teachers and AI integration in the K-12 educational field. For eligibility reasons we screened the articles based on inclusion and exclusion criteria (*Table 2*) focusing on titles, abstracts and when necessary, with full-text readings. Books, conference papers, systematic reviews and meta-analyses, theoretical articles that were not empirical studies or those that did not have teachers as participants, papers in languages other than English or in unrelated scientific fields such as Pharmacology, Immunology, Architecture, Law, Tourism, Ergonomics, Business etc., as well as duplicates, were excluded.

Table 2. Inclusion and Exclusion criteria for Scopus and Web of Science indexed articles

Inclusion Criteria	Exclusion Criteria
Empirical studies (peer-reviewed articles) published online up to December 2024	Systematic Reviews & Meta-analyses, Conference papers, Books
Studies focusing on practices, benefits and challenges regarding AI implementation for K-12 teachers	Studies about teaching the subject of AI (Except if teaching about AI occurred with the use of AI or if a study referred to both)
Sample: teachers/educators of primary and secondary education (studies with mixed participants were included only if their results were categorized accordingly)	Sample: Only students and/or parents
Scientific Fields: Arts and Humanities, Computer Science, Mathematics, Multidisciplinary, Neuroscience, Psychology, Social Sciences	Irrelevant Scientific Fields: Agricultural and Biological Sciences, Biochemistry, Genetics and Molecular Biology, Business, Management and Accounting, Chemical Engineering, Chemistry, Decision Sciences, Dentistry, Earth and Planetary Sciences, Economics, Econometrics and Finance, Energy, Engineering, Environmental Science, Health Professions, Immunology and Microbiology, Materials Science, Medicine, Nursing, Pharmacology, Toxicology and Pharmaceutics, Physics and Astronomy, Veterinary
Written in English	All other languages

The search in the databases yielded 359 papers, of which 102 were duplicates, 55 were excluded by title, 90 by abstract and 26 were reviews of all kinds (systematic, literature, scoping, bibliometric analyses and meta-analyses, theoretical). Of the remaining 86 papers, 1 was unavailable, 2 could not be retrieved and 1 was retracted. In the last stage of screening, we assessed for eligibility 82 articles of which 15 were excluded due to different educational level, 13 due to different focus, 4 had unwanted participants and 1 was not full paper, leading to the final 49 included articles (*Table 3*).

For the analysis of the data, we created an Excel workbook to gather key findings based on the research questions of our study, which also contained identification numbering for each article and basic information such as author(s), title, year, doi, abstract, keywords, research aim, design and methods, participant sample and countries. For the qualitative data analysis, two of the authors evaluated thoroughly each one of the selected articles independently and coded the results in the relevant fields of the spreadsheet. In case of disagreement between the two researchers, a third author was asked to participate in and resolve the issue with further analysis and discussion. Afterwards, for each research question we tried to categorize the findings in broader themes by conducting a thematic analysis (Braun & Clarke, 2006), interpreting connections and patterns focusing on: a) Practices, b) Benefits and c) Challenges.

Figure 1. Selection of empirical studies process

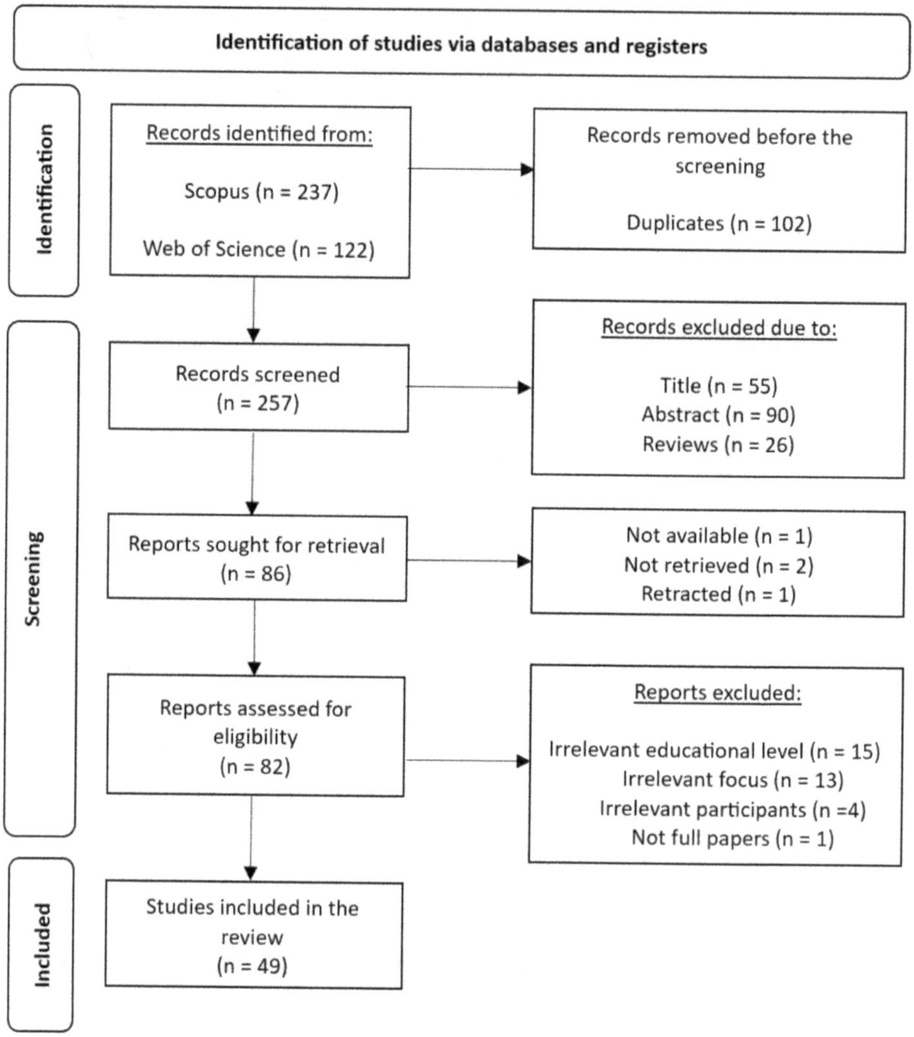

5. DESCRIPTIVES OF THE STUDIES

The 49 empirical articles that were included in this systematic review were divided into three main categories depending on their focus: most of them explored AI integration in teaching practices, in curriculum and content development (N = 24), followed by the ones focusing on teachers' perceptions, attitudes, readiness and trust of AI tools (N = 18). The third category included studies that focus on AI literacy and professional development (N = 7). The year of publication of the empirical studies was: 2025 (N = 6), 2024 (N = 38), 2023 (N = 2), 2022 (N = 2), 2021 (N = 1).

Most research took place in China (N = 8), the USA (N = 7), Turkey (N = 5), Indonesia (N = 4), Philippines (N = 3), South Korea (N = 3), Vietnam (N = 3), Malaysia (N= 2), Saudi Arabia (N = 2), Sweden (n = 2), and in the following countries with one study each (N = 1): Australia, Brazil, Brunei Darussalam, Cambodia, Cyprus, Estonia, Finland, Hong Kong, Iran, Israel, Japan, Kenya, Laos, Myanmar, Nepal, Nigeria, Norway, Russian Federation, Singapore, South Africa, Thailand, Ukraine United Arab Emirates. In some studies, participants were drawn from multiple countries, which explains why the number of countries represented exceeds the number of studies. Asia was the continent of most research (N = 42), followed by Europe (N = 9), North America (N = 8), Africa (N = 3), Oceania (N = 2), and South America (N = 1).

The research methods engaged were qualitative (N = 20), quantitative (N = 16) and mixed (N =13), and the participant sample size exceeded 8.000 in-service teachers. More specifically, and according to the researchers' mentioning or not of the level of education, or the way they categorized school ages in relevance to each country's educational system, the number of the educators was: Preschool (N = 11), Primary (N = 1.613), Secondary (N = 4.925), Mixed (N = 633), K-12 (N = 672), Higher (N = 264), N/A (N = 302). Since this review focuses only on primary and secondary education, the results mentioned for preschool and higher education levels were not taken into consideration, but the articles were included because they contained also participants from the levels of our interest. In some studies, there were parents and students also as participants, but their results were not mentioned, while wherever there was a distinction between educators and school principals, administrators or curriculum leaders (N = 213), their opinions mattered and were recorded, as before and during the time of their leading position, they were also teachers.

6. RESULTS

In the following section there is a synthesis of the results categorized according to the research questions, regarding the practices of educators for AI implementation, the benefits in teaching and learning and the emerging challenges of AI use.

6.1. Practices with AI

This section provides an overview of how teachers, motivated by individual agency and contextual conditions, engaged with AI in the studies we analyzed, across pedagogical, ethical and administrative dimensions, demonstrating variability. Understanding these can constitute a great asset in policy development, tool designing and future teacher training focusing on augmenting teachers' practices. For a number of references per theme see *Figure 2*.

Figure 2. Practices with AI

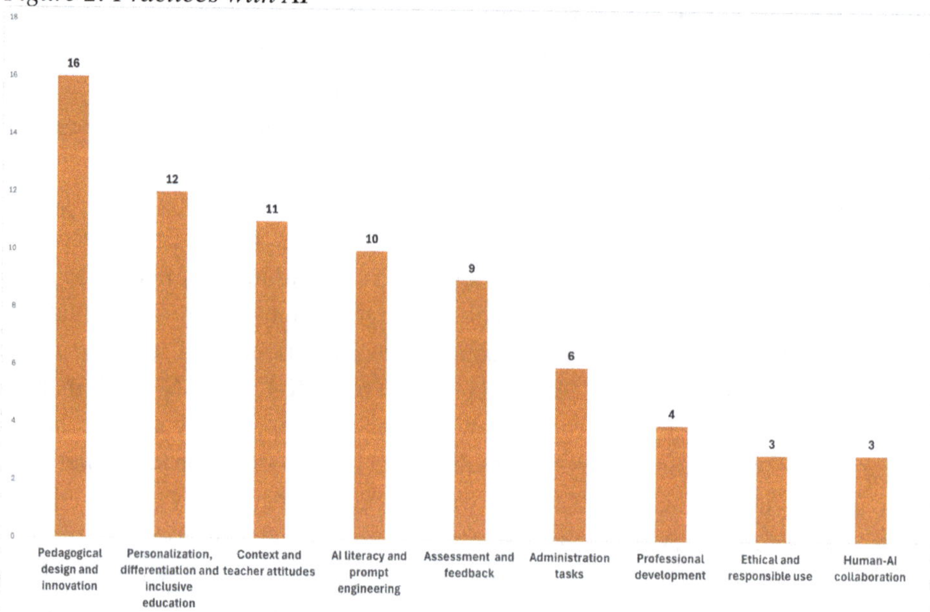

6.1.1. Pedagogical design and innovation

Teachers of various disciplines reported using productive AI and more specifically ChatGPT for lesson and activity design and educational content development (Cetin et al., 2024; Crosthwaite et al., 2024; Hays et al., 2024; Jang & Choi, 2025; Korucu-Kış, 2024; Van Den Berg, 2024). AI was used primarily to produce materials and develop teaching scenarios, to suggest teaching tools or to help users organize planning processes, with the ultimate aim of enhancing creativity and efficiency in pedagogical planning (Lee et al., 2024). In addition to these, teachers have used AI as an aid to develop content based on the objectives of the curriculum (Bower et al.,

2024; Crosthwaite et al., 2024; Kim, 2024). From the analysis of the data, innovative practices in pedagogy emerged as well as multiple ways in which students' critical thinking can be practiced. Teachers used AI for individual exercise suggestion based on student knowledge, level and progress or automatic exercise generation based on a given one (Pörn et al., 2024). They also used it to generate multiple perspectives on an issue, innovative ideas and alternative teaching approaches. Exploration through AI tools promoted creativity in lesson design and engaged teachers in a process of interdisciplinary connections by extending pedagogical science beyond traditional tools (Crosthwaite et al., 2024; Hays et al., 2024; Korucu-Kış, 2024; Magat & Sangalang, 2024).

Instructional activities (Sadykova & Kayumova, 2024) like worksheets, activities and questions or larger lesson sequences or plans were some of the prompting practices of teachers (Crosthwaite et al., 2024), and role play cards, simulation activities, cloze tests, instructions and tasks, were created with the aid of GAI (Korucu-Kış, 2024). Seeking for fresh or changing perspectives, for more ideas or expanding on ideas, as well as referring to ChatGPT for specific information and explanations on terms, topics, language teaching techniques and the use of online resources and for suggestions about teaching tools, were some common practices (Korucu-Kış, 2024). Changes that should occur regarding the curriculum and the pedagogical approaches that are employed by teachers and shifts towards more authentic tasks was the focus of Bower et al. (2024) as a result of the increasing use of GAI. Almuhanna (2024) also suggested that K-12 curricula should incorporate AI concepts and mentioned that teachers integrated AI in extracurricular activities, as also in (Dovgyi et al., 2024), or created activities like questions, rubrics, group competitions and coding assignments with AI tools, to develop students' soft skills and enrich their content with appealing presentations.

Karataş et al. (2025) found that teachers adapt the curriculum in three ways regarding AI use: by omitting irrelevant content, by extending the curriculum beyond traditional materials and by revising or replacing content to ensure relevance and engagement. In Hays et al. (2024) the creation of essay prompts and checklists, writing of assignments and guiding through them, transcription, summarizing of slides, analyzing of perspectives, researching, providing exemplars, final editing, brainstorming and inspiring were some of the actual uses of AI that teachers envisioned for themselves and for their students in daily practice. Williyan et al. (2024) highlighted that educators combine school textbooks with AI-assisted platforms like ChatGPT, magicschool.ai, you.com, Baamboozle, isLcollective and tools like Slidesgo, Curipod, Twee and Speechify to enhance students' English language learning experiences by creating engaging and motivating learning environments. Lastly, even though most teachers emphasized that ChatGPT can assist in lesson plan preparation, activities development and material suggestions, some also noted the risk of misinformation, addiction and minimal communication between students of young age (Uğraş et al., 2024).

6.1.2. Personalization, differentiation and inclusive education

Teachers have used AI to create accessibility opportunities for students with disabilities, to personalize learning according to the language ability or needs of their students, to enrich content for gifted students and differentiate materials to meet various learning styles, levels and preferences. In Crosthwaite et al. (2024) teachers used ChatGPT to simplify complex courses or concepts for students with different language backgrounds, with specific language impairments or cultural differences that could complicate their understanding and in Uğraş et al. (2024) teachers expressed the idea that ChatGPT can be suitable for the creation of personalized activities and helpful in mathematics, science and English language teaching. Payadnya et al. (2025) showed that AI makes lessons more engaging by integrating local cultural contexts, rating AI tools as highly effective for culturally responsive teaching in mathematics by educators.

The applications incorporated by the researchers improved the scaffolding method, differentiated assessment, simplified content and offered multimodal literacy tasks. Kim (2024) stated that one form of teacher-AI collaboration (TAC) could be the differentiated teaching approach in which the students who need specialized attention are taught in a smaller group whereas the other teacher instructs the rest of the class. Here too, AI analyzed and reviewed students' data to find gaps in their knowledge, those who need remediation, facilitated adaptive learning and helped teachers to successfully cope with diverse learning profiles (Crosthwaite et al., 2024; Donley, 2024; Jang & Choi, 2025; Kim, 2024; Mananay, 2024), efforts that align with the principles of inclusive education. In Mananay (2024) grade school teachers used AI-powered translation tools, language generation models and adaptive learning platforms aiming for basic language skills and tailored learning routes for their students, mentioning that experienced educators broaden their teaching with AI while novice ones support their developing teaching strategies, and expressing the idea that private schools have greater access to cutting-edge AI technologies, justifying the more frequent AI tool usage of their instructors.

Donley (2024) documented a case in the context of K-12 multilingual learner education in US public schools, where multimodal literacy was supported for Spanish speakers by collaborating with ChatGPT, to think and write about metalinguistic awareness. Individual learning support, especially with writing, and efficient differentiation of resources regarding interests and abilities of students, was found in Bower et al. (2024) while in Van Den Berg (2024) educators used GAI tools as personalized tutors helping students with different native language to simplify and translate texts in English. In many cases teachers have adopted AI technologies to provide personalized exercises and at the same time to encourage diversity (Al-muhanna, 2024), promote collaborative learning for healthy human interactions and empathy that respect differences in cultural values and accommodate diversity (Chounta et al., 2022), bringing greater equity in education while the digital divide has not yet been solved (Hays et al., 2024).

6.1.3. Context and teacher attitudes

Successful AI implementation depends not only in systemic coordinated guidance but also on factors like individual disposition and contextual support (Lavidas, Petropoulou et al., 2022), although researchers found that age, gender, educational attainment, and kind of school, had no perceptible impact on AI awareness (Güneyli et al., 2024). Teachers' attitudes and perceptions were based on their confidence levels (Fundi et al., 2024), digital skills, educational policies and the infrastructure of the schools they worked in, factors that contributed to AI utilization (Egara & Mosimege, 2024). Teachers' TPACK and positive teacher attitudes were the most crucial parameters for the adoption of AI into teaching practices, along with the importance of supportive contextual conditions including parents and the community (Li, 2024). When teachers are certain about their knowledge to implement AI with content and pedagogical knowledge, they are more likely to use AI in their teaching practices (An et al., 2023). Results support the predictions of theoretical models for technology adoption and underscore the need for in-service training to improve practical application skills (Güneyli et al., 2024). These, in turn, can positively influence teachers' attitudes and increase the use of AI in the classroom along with the higher level of teachers' education which supports a stronger inclination to use advanced AI technology (Lampropoulos & Papadakis, 2025; Mananay, 2024).

Two other positive predictors of trust in AI were self-efficacy and AI understanding with both playing an important role in influencing educators towards realistic visions of AI which in turn can adjust their perceptions for more benefits and fewer concerns (Viberg et al., 2024). In some countries where digital tools and AI might seem like a shift away from traditional values, especially if their focus for keeping the cultural identity in education is very strong, teachers might resist in integrating AI or adopt it with slower rates for their teaching practices (Payadnya et al., 2025). Chounta et al. (2022) noted a potentially hindering factor for AI integration in classrooms by stating that teachers who believe they don' t have much AI knowledge do not use it although they might have the necessary skills, whereas teachers who feel confident in their AI knowledge struggle due to their false perceptions. Leadership support (Cheng & Wang, 2023), practice and trust in AI were able to predict the rate of its integration into the educational process while AI literacy, with positive impact on attitudes toward a specific behaviour and self-efficacy in AI (Du et al., 2024) and confidence, continue to constitute barriers for many teachers.

6.1.4. AI literacy and prompt engineering

Chai et al. (2024) stated that conceptual understanding of how AI works, practical knowledge about AI tools and their operation and ethical knowledge about potential issues when using AI, form what is commonly referred to as AI literacy. PD programs focusing on AI literacy had significant improvements in teachers' perceptions and attitudes regarding AI integration in education practices, showing participants' increased trust, readiness and willingness to implement AI tools (Davoodi, 2024). After participating in a PD program and receiving guidance about AI-supported teaching, English as a foreign language (EFL) educators demonstrated positive perceptions about AI use, adequate knowledge and strong behavioral intention to use AI (An et al., 2023). The findings of Du et al. (2024) revealed that AI literacy has direct impact on self-efficacy in learning AI and awareness of AI ethics, playing a significant role in K-12 teachers' AI learning, therefore professional learning should empower AI literacy as the most crucial element.

Teachers also stressed the need to learn the right ways to use AI tools and the importance of developing good strategies for questions and prompts, exercising their creative thinking (Korucu-Kış, 2024). As for the students, Bower et al. (2024) showed that changes to the curriculum on what to teach should include teaching students how to use AI and the importance of critical thinking regarding the evaluation of the AI responses. Educators' practices focused on their students' skills to formulate prompts for brainstorming, to evaluate AI generated content and to critically and ethically engage with AI, fostering not only the emerging AI literacy but also their personal quest for development (Donley, 2024; Van Den Berg, 2024). This was most evident in language teaching where teachers used generative AI extensively to enhance students' cognitive underpinnings and strengthen their engagement with learning (Bower et al., 2024; Donley, 2024; Van Den Berg, 2024). ChatGPT, with its many different uses, as a learning tool with potential when used and prompted properly, was envisioned by the teachers in (Hays et al., 2024), who also emphasized the importance of sufficient teacher training for its appropriate integration (Hojeij et al., 2024).

6.1.5. Assessment and feedback

Formative and final assessment of students was an established practice using AI among teachers, as well as creating rubrics, producing quizzes, generating exemplars and providing feedback (Crosthwaite et al., 2024). Process-based assessment was an alternative type of evaluation tool for problem-solving skills, given the rising ethical issues of the task-based assessment and the difficulty to prevent ChatGPT use, as well as portfolio feedback and summative assessments (Jang & Choi, 2025). Various tools provided basic assessment assistance in the form of automatic summary statistics and analytics (Pörn et al., 2024), or were utilized to promote higher level thinking and support a variety of assessment methods such as, for example oral examinations, portfolios and video reports. Kim et al. (2022) highlighted that teachers in their study assessed the procedure followed by students, regarding the subject matter and AI technology, to understand the process they undergo.

In Kim (2024), AI supported the assessment process in a way that teachers did the actual grading in another form of teacher-AI collaboration (TAC) and in Donley (2024) ChatGPT was used to provide targeted feedback on syntax, grammar and spelling to English learning students. Changes to assessment due to the increasing use of generative AI was mentioned in different task types: portfolio, paper and pen, visual essays or video production, spoken tasks and examinations, and content included: higher-order thinking, authentic tasks, process-oriented assessment, personalized tasks, accurate referencing (Bower et al., 2024). It was also agreed that more supervision of assessment tasks in face-to-face form was required to avoid plagiarism, as well as there were suggestions for collaborative and peer-based tasks, completely revised evaluation processes and for the researchers' surprise embedding of AI in assessment tasks (Bower et al., 2024).

In Williyan et al. (2024) teachers balanced AI use and traditional teaching methods to promote language proficiency with practices for feedback and correction that included various AI tools such as Grammarly and Quillbot. For assessment and evaluation purposes Google and Bard (Gemini) were used for quiz creation and ChatGPT, Twee and Questionwell for generation of assessment questions, highlighting the trend that AI tools look promising when merged with traditional pedagogy (Williyan et al., 2024). For the preparation of assessment questions but not for grading, educators used AI tools to formulate questions, quizzes, multiple-choice questions and essay type questions in the study of Van Den Berg (2024). Teachers in general, used AI to diagnostically assess students' needs and more the learning process itself rather than the final learning outcomes (Bower et al., 2024; Donley, 2024; Jang & Choi, 2025; Van Den Berg, 2024).

6.1.6. Administration tasks

Among the uses of AI, teachers mentioned its ability to perform daily routine and common administrative tasks (Chounta et al., 2022), thus ensuring the reduction of workload and helping them, among other things, to compose emails, organize various resources and produce reports. In Crosthwaite et al. (2024) organizational tasks included the generation of student report cards, drafting school communication or course content, with the use of GAI outside the class and for typically labor-intensive tasks. The utilization of ChatGPT for administrative work like the generation of summative assessments and the evaluation of student portfolio was also mentioned in Jang and Choi (2025) whereas Kim (2024) described a form of teacher-AI collaboration (TAC) with the AI taking the role of the administrative assistant for carrying out routine work and clerical tasks. AI could be of great help for outsourcing the lower-level tasks that teachers do every day, something like automation and for students that struggle with organization and/or anxiety (Hays et al., 2024). By reducing these procedural tasks and administrative functions (Lee et al., 2024), cognitive load is also decreased, and teachers can have more time to devote to their primary role, which is none other than pedagogical and teaching, by organizing learning activities for students (Crosthwaite et al., 2024; Hays et al., 2024; Jang & Choi, 2025; Kim, 2024).

6.1.7. Professional development

Teachers participated in PD programs and communities of practice related to the integration of AI into their teaching practices. Even though most of the participants had a lack of familiarity with AI before starting the training, a marked increase in their readiness to implement AI into teaching, improved willingness to use AI and trust in AI tools were noted after a PD program (Davoodi, 2024). Furthermore, those who participated in a PD program, thought that schools support AI in education, received supportive attitudes from colleagues, the organization and technicians and perceived AI technology as easy to use and a valuable asset for their teaching, showing an inclination for continuous learning and AI use in the future(An et al., 2023). Reflection with their peers in a community utilizing ChatGPT, offered more accurate practical advice and guidance, and highlighted the need for structured training and continuous PD (Arefian et al., 2024). By sharing peer experiences of using this technology and encouragement to reflect on their practices as well as the feedback they received, they were able to place AI efficiently in context, reorganize their thinking about its application and reframe their practices (Arefian et al., 2024; Davoodi, 2024; Zulianti et al., 2024).

6.1.8. Ethical and responsible use

The issues of equity, social justice, bias, misinformation, academic dishonesty and plagiarism as well as ethical boundaries were of concern to teachers in relation to the integration of AI in school environments and were identified as challenges for which they sought solutions. Their practices therefore focused on teaching about ethical and responsible use of AI, ethical dilemmas, plagiarism and academic integrity (Bower et al., 2024), while in Hays et al. (2024) most teachers characterized the use of ChatGPT cheating and plagiarizing with the threat to give a zero to the students who used it for their homework, even though they could not determine if AI was used. In Whalen et al. (2025) educators chose discussion with students, parents and administrators as a first step to promote best practices and eliminate unethical use or allowed for a degree of revision and reassessment for the student' s assignment, with disciplinary actions taken as the last resort. Some teachers used ChatGPT to generate examples for critical reflection by students to enhance their understanding of issues of authenticity and originality (Bower et al., 2024; Whalen et al., 2025). Educators adopted ways of assessing learning so that AI is not abused, by designing tasks that discouraged plagiarism and by teaching their students to use AI responsibly growing their awareness of AI ethics and critical engagement.

6.1.9. Human-AI collaboration

In some cases, AI has been used as a collaborative assistant, taking the role of an educator or working in co-teaching formats with the classroom teacher, or in turns at the workstations or learning centers (Kim, 2024). Self-directed learning, inquiry-based learning and question-centered learning can be enhanced with the use of ChatGPT to provide high quality resources based on learners' queries, through problem creation or as a personal tutor that facilitates student-led physics experiments and discussions (Jang & Choi, 2025). Through the student-AI collaboration (SAC) and interactions, various learning activities with connections between the knowledge of the subjects and real-life problems, were developed by teachers (Kim et al., 2022). The educational process was enhanced by the pedagogical use of AI, increased student engagement and adaptive learning strategies and at the same time AI could assist educators with routine teaching tasks, by managing remote learners or by teaching in parallel at the same time the same lesson with the human teacher in a Hybrid-flexible (Hyflex) model of instruction (Kim, 2024). Teacher-AI collaboration (TAC) could also work with AI gathering observational data on students' learning engagement, progress and performance and teaching analytics to support the human teacher in reflecting on the effectiveness of their approach (Kim, 2024).

6.2. Benefits of AI

In the following section the themes identified from teacher-reported benefits of AI integration in school settings are categorized, showing a multifaceted variety from lesson design and efficiency to personalization and student engagement. Educators gain benefit from the use of AI as a pedagogical assistant, as a differentiation tool and as a professional learning companion, suggesting a turn for human-AI collaboration in education, enhancing teacher agency and not leading to their replacement (*Figure 3*).

Figure 3. Benefits of AI

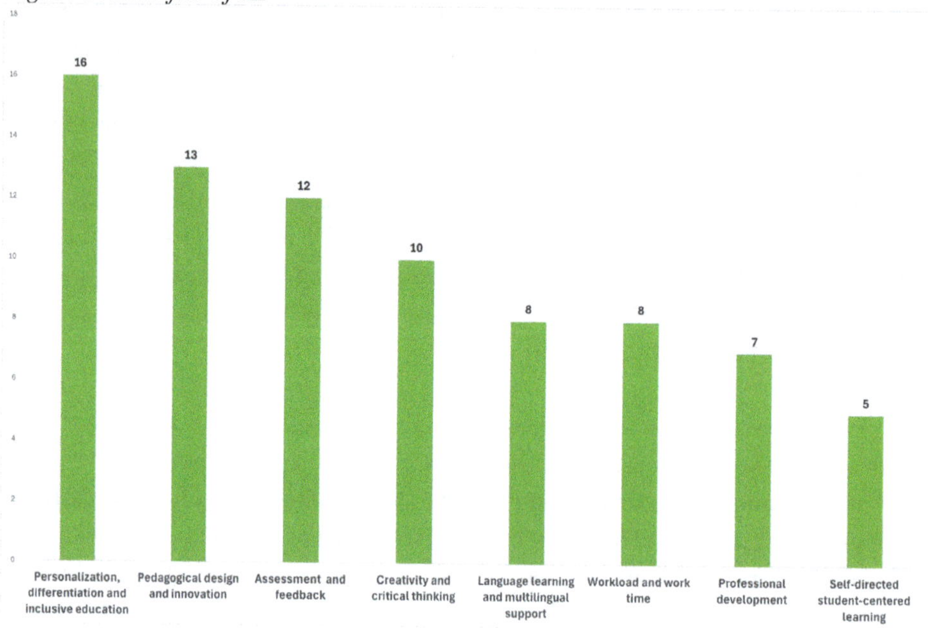

6.2.1. Personalization, differentiation and inclusive education

The adaptation of the content to the specific needs of each learner and the variation of learning levels as well as the differentiation of learning materials according to the language backgrounds of the learners were some of the important benefits of using AI tools (Annamalai, 2025; Crosthwaite et al., 2024; Jang & Choi, 2025; Kim, 2024; Mananay, 2024; Pörn et al., 2024; Xin, 2024). In Crosthwaite et al. (2024) teachers used AI to tailor content to specific student groups, generate diverse educational activities, adjust language complexity and customize materials to offer culturally relevant and simplified examples to the learners. AI technologies and especially chatbots-conversational agents and translation tools, proved to be effective in personalization of learning experiences, adjusting to all needs, requirements and styles with adaptable environments (Mananay, 2024). Adaptive learning platforms helped to empower participants who began seeing AI as an enabler in personalized learning and differentiated instruction, serving as an equalizer of resources, bridging language gaps and promoting educational equity (Davoodi, 2024).

Examples of AI use include personalized learning (Kokoç, 2024), text simplification and task adjustment, while learners who needed more support and those who were learning English as a second language were enhanced by translating texts into their mother language, adapting content and using alternative teaching techniques (Crosthwaite et al., 2024; Davoodi, 2024; Donley, 2024). Designing differentiated and flexible learning by implementing personalized instruction with the teacher-AI collaboration (TAC) was a welcome benefit of AI integration, even though it was mentioned that policies and context influence the learning outcomes that are measured with standardized exams, therefore only the learning path can be personalized but not the destination (Kim, 2024). It was also highlighted that AI could not support only cognitive development of students, but also social interaction, well-being, emotional intelligence and other areas of development with personalized instruction (Kim, 2024). When conditions were not as required or the infrastructure was not sufficient, AI provided accessibility to education, differentiated approach and curriculum adaptation, ensuring cultural diversity (Davoodi, 2024; Jang & Choi, 2025; Kim, 2024; Mananay, 2024). Educators used these tools to bridge the infrastructure gap in relation to linguistic and socio-economic diversity in the classroom.

The potential of ChatGPT to differentiate instruction in mathematics education was mentioned in Magat and Sangalang (2024), to assist with differentiation in lessons in K-12 settings (Hays et al., 2024) and of ChatPDF to promote learner-centeredness in language learning (Xin, 2024). In Jang and Choi (2025) physics teachers praised ChatGPT's accessibility and capability to provide interactive, learner-centered, custom-tailored, personalized learning experiences. In Annamalai (2025), teachers agreed that ChatGPT provides individualized guidance, offering tailored learning environments and methods for their pupils to acquire English language skills. Its adaptability helped learners to feel comfortable and build confidence in using English, allowing a tailored learning experience which addressed their unique needs and challenges (Tran et al., 2024). Diverse populations and students with special needs and disabilities were accommodated with ChatGPT, differentiating instruction and scaffolding to learn English (Bateman, 2025), noting a substantial progression from traditional teaching to differentiating curriculum lessons, adaptive learning platforms, personalized content for better alignment with students' needs, preferences and interests (Karataş et al., 2025). The complex role of not only ChatGPT but also GAI in general, covers various learning activities to effectively prepare students for the future, supporting personalized tutoring and educational needs with a shift to more technologically integrated teaching practices (Van Den Berg, 2024).

6.2.2. Pedagogical design and innovation

AI tools, and in particular the technological systems of productive AI, have improved teachers' skills in designing learning materials and creative lesson plans and eventually to optimize their teaching strategies (Alhazzani, 2024; Chounta et al., 2022; Crosthwaite et al., 2024; Hays et al., 2024; Hojeij et al., 2024; Sadykova & Kayumova, 2024). The customization of materials, brainstorming of lesson plans, refining language, enhancing assignments, improving clarity, constructing texts and searching for new perspectives were the benefits mentioned in Crosthwaite et al. (2024). In Magat and Sangalang (2024) educators agreed that AI promotes collaboration (Khasawneh, 2024), interaction and student engagement with increased lesson planning efficiency, access to extensive mathematical resources and better learning outcomes. Regarding ChatPDF, in a study teachers reported its ability to modify texts and design tasks according to their needs and agreed it could provide them with pedagogical suggestions, which in turn increased their effectiveness (Xin, 2024). Modifications according to curriculum requirements, the introduction of innovative pedagogical practices and enhancement through new ideas were the most important of the benefits of using AI in pedagogical design (Crosthwaite et al., 2024; Hojeij et al., 2024).

ChatGPT assisted educators in effectively strategizing their teaching methods (Uğraş et al., 2024), by setting goals and organizing learning activities, providing innovative teaching concepts (Hojeij et al., 2024) and lesson plans, eliminating redundancy and repetition with intelligent applications, interactive tests and simulations (Alhazzani, 2024). Teachers praised the possibilities with the use of ChatGPT (Cetin et al., 2024) for writing lesson plans and examples, creating prompts for content, providing summaries, and also serving as an idea generator or prompt creator (Hays et al., 2024). Making the course of study more efficient by omitting irrelevant content, extending curricular experiences to improve and enrich the curriculum and the use of ChatGPT to simulate discussions, create engaging and creative writing suggestions and clarify complex concepts, assisted teachers to make their methods more active and student-centered (Karataş et al., 2025). In Bateman (2025) participants used ChatGPT as a great resource to help with new ideas and motivate students, for organizing steps in a process, planning, expanding or fine-tuning lessons, creating supplementary materials from other subjects, practice assignments and making projects, as well as discussing the tools' ethical guidelines, making students learn by incorporating it as a pedagogical asset. Detailed planning insights, content development and lesson creation by fostering creativity, intellectual engagement, critical thinking and communication skills, were the most important enhancements of using ChatGPT (Hojeij et al., 2024).

6.2.3. Assessment and feedback

Teachers improved their assessment methods as they introduced the use of AI in both formative and final assessment of students (Chounta et al., 2022; Crosthwaite et al., 2024; Jang & Choi, 2025; Kim, 2024; Mananay, 2024; Pörn et al., 2024). The use of GAI provided opportunities to teachers to enable students for critical assessment of AI-generated content and for improvement of the assessment materials' clarity (Crosthwaite et al., 2024). ChatGPT's suggestions included various assessment methods and proposed ideas to use technology for assessment and feedback improvement (Alhazzani, 2024). Participants in the study of Jang and Choi (2025) discussed ChatGPT's capacity to give immediate feedback to users without any difficulties related to time or location. ChatGPT helped learners, depending on their language level proficiency, to effectively enhance their language skills in no time, by offering personalized feedback in a user-friendly environment (Annamalai, 2025). Other researchers mentioned ChatGPT's capability for assessment assistance (Hays et al., 2024), automated support and immediate feedback (Arefian et al., 2024; Bateman, 2025).By using automated feedback to 2students and also by producing questions and quizzes, AI supported teachers' grading methods.

Mananay (2024) highlighted assessment and feedback as an area where AI technologies excelled and noted that the integration of automated feedback systems with the goals of curriculum was a highly effective strategy, as AI merged ideally with objectives of education. Here too, AI provided personalized in-depth feedback and improved tailored assessment to each individual learner, with accuracy and speed (Mananay, 2024), particularly enabling engagement in language learning thus allowing teachers to focus on higher level assessment processes (Annamalai, 2025). In Bower et al. (2024) teachers expressed the intention to change assessment tasks with AI to help students develop skills and abilities that de-motivate them from using it as a cheating method and prepare them for a future with AI, ensuring an easier and more fair assessment and efficiency in providing feedback. Teachers collaborating with AI in Kim (2024), could provide more feedback in students' learning or immediate automated feedback for revising and improving their tasks.

6.2.4. Creativity and critical thinking

Students created simulations for analysis, problem-solving and reflection, prompts for text production and templates using AI that enabled them to engage critically and stimulate their creativity (Alhazzani, 2024; Bateman, 2025; Crosthwaite et al., 2024; Hojeij et al., 2024; Kim, 2024). Critical assessment and improvement on AI-generated content helped students analyze and comprehend responsibility of AI usage (Crosthwaite et al., 2024), with implementation of engaging activities for problem-solving and inquiry (Kim, 2024), a diverse range of inventive teaching concepts which promote pedagogical creativity (Alhazzani, 2024) and fostering writing creativity (Mananay, 2024). In Kim et al. (2022) teachers expected that student-AI collaboration (SAC) could improve the cognitive capabilities including higher-order thinking of students like imagination, creativity and critical thinking by collaborating effectively with AI, analyzing in depth the information processed and received from it to make decisions. AI is also recommended to students and teachers to help them develop critical thinking (Magat & Sangalang, 2024) and process information, analyze, be creative in problem-solving and learn how to ask questions and evaluate answers (Dovgyi et al., 2024). Teachers and students tackled scenarios that required deeper thinking and critical approach as well as creative solution generation. Half of the participants in Bateman (2025) expressed the opinion that student engagement and creativity raise by implementing ChatGPT into the curriculum, while even though creativity in problem-solving and enhanced critical thinking were noted in Hojeij et al. (2024), they contrasted with concerns about the opposite outcomes such as, reduced critical thinking, dependency on AI and limited personal growth. Regarding the PD of experienced teachers, by interacting with ChatGPT and through their reflections on their experiences, they could organize their beliefs, emotions, thoughts and values having a more critical stance towards their practices (Arefian et al., 2024).

6.2.5. Language learning and multilingual support

Language learning has been greatly enhanced by AI with interactive assistants and translation software (Annamalai, 2025; Donley, 2024; Mananay, 2024). In Bohara and Rana (2024) students' language learning experience was enhanced with AI and in Mananay (2024) AI-powered tools effectively taught languages with the highest overall rating, improving language competency and real-word language proficiency, employing interactive role-playing and immersive simulations. English language skills were acquired with engaging and effective language teaching materials, ChatGPT's language capabilities and practicing engagement (Annamalai, 2025). With these tools, teachers acknowledged improvements in students' grammar learning, writing fluency, reading and language use in real-life situations. English as a Foreign Language (EFL) teachers agreed that AI-powered tools successfully adhered to required standards, being in tune with language learning objectives, effectively integrated in language learning tasks and relating to real-life language use scenarios (Zulianti et al., 2024).

Multilingual communication and multimodality supported translanguaging in diverse school environments from a language and cultural perspective, with ChatGPT being used for incorporating texts in multiple languages, oral language transcription and support for descriptive language development (Donley, 2024). English for speakers of other languages (ESOL) students were accommodated by ChatGPT as reported by several teachers (Bateman, 2025) and language learners in general, coming from diverse backgrounds, benefited from language learning materials that were learner-centered and differentiated with AI (Xin, 2024). Lastly, in Hojeij et al. (2024) advancements in language skills, enhancements in language abilities and an overall improvement in language proficiency with the use of ChatGPT were indicated as a significant impact on teacher performance.

6.2.6. Workload and work time

Teachers continually reiterated the efficient time savings and reduced workload provided by the use of AI technology tools for both routine administrative and communication tasks within the profession, as well as for the needs arising for grading, rubric building and lesson planning (Alhazzani, 2024; Bateman, 2025; Crosthwaite et al., 2024; Hojeij et al., 2024; Kokoç, 2024; Magat & Sangalang, 2024; Mananay, 2024). With the extra time saved, teachers could concentrate and engage their students in more meaningful activities, while the AI produced drafts, identified and designed refined materials providing instructional support. Time on repetitive tasks was decreased (Mananay, 2024), economized by streamlining the required processes (Alhazzani, 2024) and saved in lesson preparation (Magat & Sangalang, 2024), while the workload of language teachers was reduced (Mananay, 2024), lessened with the use of ChatGPT (Magat & Sangalang, 2024), which was described as a time-saving resource in Bateman (2025). All participants in the relevant study agreed on this with examples of lesson creating and planning, providing feedback, generating ideas, creating substitute lesson plans, bell-ringer activities and warm-up lesson in less time, and mentioned that it also takes time to learn how to prompt correctly for the desired output (Bateman, 2025). Hojeij et al. (2024) stated that the first most significant impact of ChatGPT was that it saves time and improves efficiency by accelerating task completion, a significant benefit of AI in general, that can automate routine tasks and administrative work, which was recognized by participants (Davoodi, 2024).

6.2.7. Professional development

Teachers reported increased motivation, emotional resilience and creative renewal when reflecting on their practices with the help of AI. In Kong and Yang (2024) a human-centered learning and teaching framework (HCLTF) was proposed in a six-week programme that included a 30-h course intended to a foundational understanding of AI and deep learning and generative AI concepts and a 30-h course on integrating AI into course design in areas, such as Chinese language, English language, mathematics, general studies, computer science, and music education. The results showed that the teacher development program had a positive impact on teachers' understanding of AI and that it was highly effective in enhancing teachers' knowledge and skills, increasing not only theoretical understanding but also the ability to integrate technology and pedagogy into practical knowledge. The seamless integration of AI capabilities with pedagogical knowledge was also underscored in Tran et al. (2024) where ChatGPT adjusted its responses to the teachers' needs so they could independently construct their knowledge, with the provision of practical strategies actively connected with theoretical knowledge, in a way aligned with the Constructivist Learning Theory (CLT). Another PD program based on the TPACK framework (Celik, 2023) positively influenced English teachers' skills in using AI-powered tools for teaching and the enhancement of their proficiency, knowledge, skills, self-efficacy and teaching confidence was studied in Zulianti et al. (2024).

The use of ChatGPT as a critical friend was evaluated very positively by teachers who benefited from improved lesson plans, problem solving in their classrooms, and enhanced professional identity and development (Arefian et al., 2024; Kong & Yang, 2024; Tran et al., 2024). ChatGPT facilitated teachers to reflect on their social practices and personal aspects such as their beliefs, emotions, theories and feelings and also on their reflections like a critical friend from whom they benefited and encouraged to delve deeper (Arefian et al., 2024). The benefits from these reflections included getting help, guidance and support during and after their classes, evaluating their practices, solving problems, finding ideal teaching strategies, enhancing quality, critically self-reflecting, gaining insights for improvement, enhancing skills and awareness, boosting their creativity and flexibility, transforming their established practices and enhancing the emotional and humanitarian dimension of reflective practice in a continuously developing process (Arefian et al., 2024). The upcoming changes brought by AI have created the need for teachers to respond immediately not only to improve their practices but also to equip their students with the necessary digital skills (Bower et al., 2024; Dovgyi et al., 2024). AI has begun to transform education and teachers who wish not to become obsolete must adapt to the rapidly developing technological field by upgrading their effectiveness and authenticity.

6.2.8. Self-directed student-centered learning

AI plays an important role in fostering student autonomy and self-regulation and promoting active participation in the learning process (Annamalai, 2025; Jang & Choi, 2025; Kim, 2024; Mananay, 2024). In Jang and Choi (2025) it was emphasized that in self-directed and self-regulated learning students develop their skills by setting goals, designing and accomplishing plans and evaluating the final results, so it is important for educators to investigate learners' readiness and enhance active learning through multimedia resources (Cheng & Wang, 2023). Teachers stated that their students benefited from the use of AI for problem solving, goal setting and feedback, as interactive assistants and adaptive learning platforms can provide processes that are based on individual preferences, speed, time and place of learning. With the collaboration of AI and teachers, technology-rich environments can be used for students to conduct hands-on activities, create realistic and authentic real-life situations, practice problem-solving, meaning-making and participate in inquiry activities (Kim, 2024). A noteworthy result is that even though conversational agents-chatbots are effective in promoting autonomy with AI facilitating self-directed learning, they are not as effective to encourage independent study with a possible cause being the dependence on AI (Mananay, 2024).

6.3. Challenges of AI

Teachers faced various challenges regarding AI use and were repeatedly reporting concerns about cheating, infrastructure, support, reliability, lack of knowledge etc. In general, their difficulties were multilevel from lack of policy-guidance to pedagogical alignment and technical skill gaps, thus the following categorization tried to separate and include the information accordingly (*Figure 4*).

Figure 4. Challenges of AI

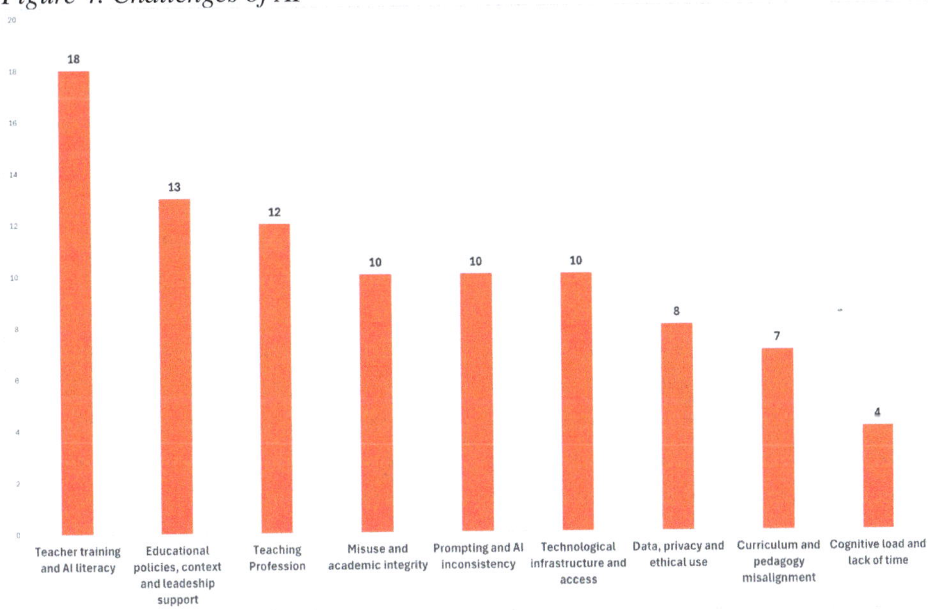

6.3.1. Teacher training and AI literacy

Teachers very often reported lack of knowledge (Hojeij et al., 2024) and understanding of AI, as well as lack of formal training (Khasawneh, 2024), which in turn led to ineffective use of AI and confusion in educational practices. Sometimes they conflated common ICT tools with those of AI (Bohara & Rana, 2024), while many lacked experience in its use due to lack of training and guidance (Kokoç, 2024; Magat & Sangalang, 2024). Teachers' AI understanding can be enhanced through PD and technical workshops resulting in more empowered educators that can seamlessly integrate AI tools in innovative lessons (Cheng & Wang, 2023). Teachers also expressed concerns that their limited knowledge of AI and misconceptions reflected a lack of confidence, as AI integration started without clear guidance and with uncertainty about the required technical skills, leading to anxiety of failure and towards a reactive than a proactive stance (Wang & Cheng, 2021).

Additionally, many of the PD programs remained theoretical without practical training (Almuhanna, 2024; Zulianti et al., 2024), and several older or mid-career educators experienced general difficulties with digital literacy (Arefian et al., 2024; Tran et al., 2024). Insufficient experience and ignorance about AI were linked to resistance to its use and to teachers' avoidance to recommend it to other teachers or colleagues (Dovgyi et al., 2024). Internal barriers such as lack of knowledge and confidence in AI challenged teachers' ability to integrate AIED because of the limited professional competence, limited understanding of AI concepts and limited mastery in AI technologies (Cheng & Wang, 2023).

Teacher training for effective AI integration into school settings was a common and critical factor in most of the studies (Karataş et al., 2025; Payadnya et al., 2025), as many educators exhibited low level familiarity with tools like ChatGPT (Egara & Mosimege, 2024), indicating a lack of exposure and training in PD programs that could enhance teachers' comfort with AI tools (Magat & Sangalang, 2024). On the contrary, AI literacy cannot guarantee the integration of AI tools in teaching, the intention to design AI-assisted learning and the interest or readiness to learn about AI (Wang et al., 2024). Another factor that had a negative impact in utilizing AI tools was the lack of technical skills which in turn affected teachers' satisfaction in conjunction with insufficient technical support, resources and training (Nguyen, 2024). Teachers also encountered barriers when they tried to collaborate with colleagues of other subjects as they could not engage in dialogue about a wide-area subject and form a collaborative learning culture (Kim et al., 2022).

6.3.2. Educational policies, context and leadership support

Unclear policies and unsupportive leadership undermined teachers' efforts to implement AI tools into their teaching practices with the absence of external guidelines constituting a force which instead of motivating them to develop further, it was prohibiting (Cheng & Wang, 2023). Administrators did not address the concerns and challenges teachers faced from ChatGPT's impact, neither did they offer some kind of guidance or support in Hays et al. (2024). The lack of guidelines for ChatGPT use by teachers and unethical use by students left educators feeling upset and unsupported from leadership and school policies, trying to educate themselves, with the leaders being ignorant and not wanting to deal with the repercussions (Bateman, 2025). The absence of consistent curricular guidance, the deficiency of systematic and authoritative guidance on teaching content and related materials and the lack of informed strategies and visions for AIED, prominently challenges teachers (Kim, 2024).

Pedagogical guidance to use generative AI tools more effectively and updated education policies that will support AI tools and educators is a key area that is expected to be improved in the future (Kokoç, 2024). Limited management support did not promote AI integration efforts (Almuhanna, 2024) and the importance of leadership in education to enhance AI literacy, with structured guidance and prioritization of PD programs for teachers, adding to a coordinated effort in policy, practice and research was underscored for an educational environment with AI-driven innovations (Karataş et al., 2025). The absence of implementation by the school administration and gap in institutional support and the necessary resources (Li, 2024), might be connected with uncertainty of AI's benefits among educators and lack of understanding that suggest systemic barriers in the adoption of AI tools (Magat & Sangalang, 2024). The importance of educational leadership that promotes structured guidance and organizes PD programs to enhance teachers' AI literacy and general coordination of efforts from policy, practice and research were highlighted (Karataş et al., 2025).

Sometimes teachers' AI integration was limited due to contextual conditions, cultural perceptions and local norms, therefore educators expressed the need to adapt AI use to cultural and regional diversities (Payadnya et al., 2025). The digital divide, especially in remote areas, can hinder the integration of AI and limit equitable access, whereas regional beliefs and ideologies would not let teachers follow ChatGPT's suggestions, as for example in Iran where tradition and conservatism would not allow trust in AI (Arefian et al., 2024). In some cases, even though lesson plans were very well designed with AI tools like ChatPDF, they were not practical for real teaching due to contextual factors like classroom size, lesson duration and student abilities (Xin, 2024). The existing knowledge, skills and beliefs of teachers were put to the test after facing difficulties while integrating ChatGPT into their

PD, resulting in the construction of new knowledge after navigating the challenges and initial resistance due to the cognitive dissonance (Tran et al., 2024).

6.3.3. Teaching profession

There were many references about teachers fearing they would be replaced (Annamalai, 2025) or not needed at all so their role and presence in education could be diminished because of AI integration (Khasawneh, 2024). Although they had realized the benefits of AI in education, they expressed fears of replacement (Fundi et al., 2024) perceiving the growing use of AI in teaching and learning as a threat for their jobs, with AI in the teaching profession replacing people, taking over human jobs and causing a humanitarian crisis (Bohara & Rana, 2024). AI's capacity for empathy, human touch and creativity (Hojeij et al., 2024) was also questioned along with concerns about mental and social complications in human beings (Bohara & Rana, 2024), social aspects such as the potential of limiting communication between students and human tutors and the lack of skills like flexibility and responsiveness as well as teacher autonomy, accountability and responsibility when over relying on automated solutions, thus undermining teachers' role (Chounta et al., 2022).

In Bohara and Rana (2024) it is concluded that teachers' lack of awareness about AI led to their anxiety and in Chounta et al. (2022) it was reported that biased teacher attitude and teachers' incomplete understanding of AIED could also block the effective integration of AI, with examples of teachers fearing AI would replace them, emphasizing the importance of the essential human touch and the teachers' lack of comprehensive understanding of AIED. This internal resistance and incomplete understanding led to skepticism and anxiety of failure and their lack of confidence attributed to their misconceptions which made them react rather than maintain a proactive approach to AI (Chounta et al., 2022). Teachers also made statements about their biased and negative attitudes towards AI that could constitute another barrier to effective Teacher-AI Collaboration (TAC) in classrooms, underlining that most of their colleagues assume they will be replaced by AI or that the government forced another machine into schools (Kim, 2024).

Teachers with low or none experience with AI tools expressed negative feelings about AI, considering it as a threat, justifying their opinion with the unpredictability of the impact on children due to the reduced face to face communication with a human teacher (Sadykova & Kayumova, 2024). The negative impact of AI on collaboration between students and other social aspects in learning procedures, as well as the danger of negative emotional consequences the continuous use of AI may cause to students, along with the over-belief and blind trust to AI, were expressed by some teachers (Pörn et al., 2024). Over-reliance in AI should be approached with caution and the integration of generative AI into classroom has to follow human-centered principles that support teachers' role as a social and emotional anchor in learning processes (Kong & Yang, 2024). GAI can be utilized as a supportive partner who handles many traditional teacher tasks, potentially transforming the role of the human educator to be more efficient and having more time to concentrate on interactions with students (Van Den Berg, 2024).

These concerns and critical views about AI, also common to other studies, are somewhat valid due to the lack of knowledge about AI and the skills required to use it correctly and deploy it effectively for students and teachers, can be overwhelming and cause anxiety, despite the fact that educators have been using AI-powered tools and have formed positive attitudes towards ICT usage (Kim, 2024). To integrate AI effectively in everyday life and especially in education, it is very important to understand the feelings about AI, how it affects people's lives and how their attitudes can impact or bias interactions with AI, as attitudes are the most crucial element for teaching experience, performance and persistence to teach with technology (Kim, 2024). Even though technological, pedagogical and content knowledge is related directly to successful technology integration, AI challenges are unique, therefore teachers' attitudes and external parameters and support play crucial roles (Li, 2024).

6.3.4. Misuse and academic integrity

Teachers also underlined the major issue of students misusing AI tools such as ChatGPT (Cetin et al., 2024; Hojeij et al., 2024) to complete their assignments and found detecting unethical use of AI without detection tools neither easy nor difficult (Whalen et al., 2025). More than half of the participants did not have experience of tools designed to detect AI use such as TurnItIn, GPTZero, ZeroGPT, Originality.ai, CopyLeaks, maybe due to the infrequent use or unavailability, their cost and the belief that detecting student use of genAI was not much of a concern for their implementation (Whalen et al., 2025). Teachers shared serious concerns about academic dishonesty (Dovgyi et al., 2024), students' laziness and over-reliance or overdependence on AI (Davoodi, 2024; Magat & Sangalang, 2024; Van Den Berg, 2024), with misuse of ChatGPT that can compromise integrity (Annamalai, 2025) and originality.

Educators agreed that unorthodox use of AI complicates assessment especially for written work (Almuhanna, 2024), felt unprepared to manage cheating, lacking reliable tools, and although they stated that banning AI would not help, stressed the need for clearer policies and better assessment methods (Bateman, 2025). Even though ChatGPT may offer short-term gains, through cheating, quick assessment and easy completion of tasks, critical thinking, writing skills and personal growth can be hampered and obstruct long-term learning (Annamalai, 2025). The lack of policy guidelines and leadership support did not help educators to address unethical use of AI, while students' cheating can also hinder their ability for critical thinking, making it more difficult and challenging for teachers proving it when the writing was more advanced (Bateman, 2025).

6.3.5. Prompting and AI inconsistency

The content which was generated with AI was not always correct and accurate (Egara & Mosimege, 2024; Hojeij et al., 2024; Uğraş et al., 2024) and tended to become repetitive and of low quality as noted by the educators. Vague prompts with not enough details led AI to return poor results (Crosthwaite et al., 2024), with teachers encountering difficulties to give specific directions to ChatGPT which was generating ideas depending highly on their prompts, so precise input was needed (Korucu-Kış, 2024). This led to another challenge that teacher faced regarding the repetitive content generated by ChatGPT, which did not provide the possibilities for creative exploration (Korucu-Kış, 2024) and raised the issue of clear and specific prompting to get the required responses, with well-structured and well-designed prompts (Van Den Berg, 2024).

In Bateman (2025) teachers felt that they had to research and experiment with ChatGPT to get the desired outputs by trial and error and after many attempts managed to acquire important information, noting that the answer given is directly connected to the framing of the question and that AI has limited knowledge. Inconsistency in providing reliable answers was also mentioned for ChatPDF by teachers with incorrect, unverified and fabricated content in the answers it generated (Xin, 2024). ChatPDF was also unable to recognize and understand multimodal elements in reading materials, requiring consistent critical evaluation from the teachers making it unreliable (Xin, 2024), like ChatGPT which presented false information as a fact, also needing verification by the educators (Jang & Choi, 2025). The inaccuracy of results emphasized the demand for teacher supervision to ensure content appropriateness, accuracy and provision of individualized attention to each student, as personalization might be incorrect and challenging especially for learners with disabilities (Almuhanna, 2024)

6.3.6. Technological infrastructure and access

The integration of AI technology into the learning process has been limited in cases of inadequate equipment and outdated technical infrastructure (Halomoan et al., 2024; Hojeij et al., 2024). Some examples include old hardware, slow internet connection speeds (Almuhanna, 2024; Arefian et al., 2024), connectivity problems (Pörn et al., 2024), obsolete technology and restrictive usage policies in some of the schools, causing problems such as system crashes and malfunctions (Kokoç,

2024) and presenting a significant challenge for teachers and students that cannot integrate AI tools properly (Mananay, 2024). Cheng and Wang (2023) reported that is not common for educational leaders to promote AIED for reasons, among others, relating to insufficient resources for new hardware, software and learning kits, even though by ensuring access to AI technologies they can address external barriers. High costs and insufficient availability of the necessary resources and tools were also some of the main obstacles (Kokoç, 2024).

Another common barrier arose when educational institutions viewed AI as a risky venture that they were not willing to take and thus decided not to support it at all or only to an insufficient degree. In Wang and Cheng (2021) it was reported that despite the fact that schools were able to integrate AI technologies financially, they considered it as an investment risk that could not be taken, due to it being new with no established practices for referencing and due to the need for strategic planning in regard to human training and feedback sufficiency, to ensure sustainability. Organizational and technological support is very important to reduce the stress and pressure caused to educators by technology use in classrooms, as if it is not sufficient it could increase the so-called teachers' technostress (Wang et al., 2024).

6.3.7. Data, privacy and ethical use

Ethical violations (Cetin et al., 2024) were a major concern regarding the use of AI in educational practices along with data security issues (Pörn et al., 2024). Educators feared that AI could violate students' privacy and handle data without ethical guidance when it is used for real time assessments or for indicating their cognitive and affective state to the teacher, a risk about the amount of data that is needed to be collected to deliver these evaluations, about their storage, about the purpose they are used and in what degree (Chounta et al., 2022). Due to the fact that minors are involved in education, teachers were especially worried about unresolved issues of privacy, ethics and parental consent and were afraid of potential breaches and unclear and unauthorized data use that could jeopardize AI integration in school settings (Wang & Cheng, 2021). In Kim (2024) concerns were raised about the unknown and unintended impact that Teacher-AI Collaboration (TAC) might have on learners' cognitive, socio-emotional and neurological development emphasizing on the absence of a commonly accepted ethics model or an ethical framework.

AI use in educational context must be safe and promote not only privacy (Hojeij et al., 2024), transparency and data protection but also account for ethics of education such as the ethics of gender and ethnic biases, of behaviour and discipline, of accuracy and validity of assessments, of teacher roles, expectations and resource allocation etc. (Kim, 2024). Due to the large volumes of student data that are gathered and processed during AI use, the challenge remains for schools and teachers to keep them secure and use them ethically, incorporating privacy policies (Mananay, 2024). These challenges must be recognized and addressed by teachers with the integration of AI ethics into lessons, ethically transforming AI knowledge into actual practices and pedagogical design (Chai et al., 2024). In Chounta et al. (2022) teachers were also very worried about algorithmic decisions that depend on the existing data AI models have been trained on, such as gender bias being more effective for the majority gender, algorithmic bias that could promote unfairness and discriminations for certain groups based on gender, socio-economic status, ethnicity and student populations that are underrepresented and lack of transparency which could hinder trust between AI and human.

6.3.8. Curriculum and pedagogy misalignment

Another challenge faced by teachers in empirical studies was that their school curriculum could not be efficiently combined with the use of AI tools or that they were unable to align the AI tools with pedagogical goals (Karataş et al., 2025). Thus, a mismatch was reported between the learning objectives and the results produced by the use of GAI, either because of insufficient detail in prompting or due to the AI's abilities to generate the required outcomes (Crosthwaite et al., 2024). In Mananay (2024) the alignment with AI tools was reported as a difficulty, as teachers struggled to blend AI tools into the curriculum to obtain better learning outcomes, in line with the pedagogical objectives. In addition, AI tools were designed for commercial use without any educational principles in their design, with teachers claiming that the applications they used are computer-centric with a lack of educational rationale and satisfactory pedagogical principles taken into consideration for their development (Kim, 2024).

Some teachers also struggled in their efforts to transform the use of AI tools into effective teaching strategies as their integration was limited, even though they were compatible with the objectives of the course (Kokoç, 2024), while often not knowing how to evaluate the learning outcomes achieved with AI (Kim, 2024). More specifically, a question about Teacher-AI Collaboration (TAC) in different activities and how this scheme would be integrated in a larger educational context aiming to achieve positive outcomes, remained unanswered (Kim, 2024). In this category, ChatGPT often failed to provide appropriate answers matching the learners' learning level or even to support differentiated instruction, due to the fact that each user had to provide this specific information intentionally and even then, it would not differentiate the answers to match the students' multiple levels or readiness (Jang & Choi, 2025). In addition, math teachers found it difficult to integrate ChatGPT into mathematics teaching practices with obstacles such as handling the various types of problems, integrating with existing lesson plans and collaborative problem-solving sessions, unreferenced and uncited results, inaccurate responses and adapting to different learning styles (Egara & Mosimege, 2024).

6.3.9. Cognitive load and lack of time

Many teachers needed assistance to integrate AI into their lessons, much knowledge, experience and more time as the process of keeping up the curriculum with the continuous technological advances was time-consuming (Almuhanna, 2024; Hojeij et al., 2024). The demands to integrate new AI tools overwhelmed educators who frequently mentioned that they did not have the required time to explore and adapt to new technologies (Khasawneh, 2024), making it a first-order barrier. Teachers talked about their multiple roles, administrative duties and tasks in schools that prohibit them from studying new technology and agreed that investing more time to work with students is a more compelling way of improving their teaching performance and evaluation, leaving learning analytics and educational data mining not at a top priority (Wang & Cheng, 2021). Learning analytics (LA) systems were not very user-friendly and maybe that was the reason for the perceived time constraints - the poor impression due to the difficulty of use and the generation of incomprehensible analytical reports, made teachers admit lack of knowledge about statistics, concluding that the use of AI would be time-consuming (Wang & Cheng, 2021).

7. DISCUSSION

In this section we will compare our findings with previous systematic reviews and share some important concluding remarks. The integration of AI in school is achieved through the practices of teachers, so in our opinion, much of the focus should be on their actions. As for the benefits, empirical data should verify the impact on learning outcomes, but challenges remain the biggest concern of all stakeholders. Solutions and proposals for their resolution must be offered to the educational community to increase responsible and efficient AI implementation.

7.1. Relevance with previous systematic literature reviews

In this systematic review we tried to categorize the findings from empirical studies regarding in-service teachers' practices integrating AI into primary and secondary level of education, the reported benefits and the challenges. ChatGPT and Generative AI (GAI) in general, held a large percentage of the studies in our review, which is relevant to the fact that we found many systematic reviews focused on this specific AI tool. Thus, Noroozi et al. (2024) looked for insights into the improvements of

GAI in teaching, Bettayeb et al. (2024) explored the impact of ChatGPT highlighting benefits and challenges and Zhang and Tur (2024) ran a SWOT analysis for ChatGPT's use in K-12 education, with the findings of all these being consistent with the ones in our review. Apparently, most educators already use AI for teaching, and have it embedded into their daily practices in classroom settings, although in many cases they admitted lack of knowledge, skills and guidance, therefore essential guidelines and teacher training should be employed in schools.

The benefits of AI integration are multilevel and observable and include improvements in personalization, differentiation, assessment, feedback, administrative tasks, creativity, critical thinking etc., however it is important to examine with a critical lens the potential pedagogical risks that were mentioned such as over-reliance and dependence on AI, reduced teacher-student interaction and inequities in access. The promotion of equal access to education is expressed in many reviews, being the desired outcome in the systematic review of Lin et al. (2023), and it was promoted by taking advantage of all the benefits of AI-integrated systems for personalization, accessibility and flexibility, highlighting the need for coordinated efforts from all stakeholders. Labadze et al. (2023) also underscored enhancements in feedback and personalization for students noting the lack of human touch and the need for PD programs, as well as Marzano (2025), who in their systematic review for GAI in K-12 context demonstrated the opportunities for personalization of learning but also challenges referring to the need for framework development and issues of ethics and data quality.

The challenges of AI implementation come from different levels and are multifarious: pedagogical AI literacy, gaps in technical skills, conceptual misunderstandings, capacity-building, systemic constraints regarding policies and resources, data privacy & security, AI bias, teacher workload, burnout and attitudes. The ethical concerns of GAI and the regulations that should be established to secure AI use were also underscored in the systematic review of García-López and Trujillo-Liñán (2025) which once again mentioned the need for all stakeholders to collaborate for establishing guidelines. Although some of AI integration concerns such as gaps in policy and training deficits are widely observed, others are more core to the teacher experience, reflecting deeper fears and anxieties that need to be investigated further, such as AI replacing teachers. On this matter, Fu and Weng (2024) unpacked key characteristics of human-centered AI and focused on ethics and responsibility, underscoring the need for collaboration of essential stakeholders to ensure that AI will not remove the human factor from learning.

7.2. Limitations

One of the limitations of this review is that it has not taken into consideration students' opinions that are directly affected by AI integration into teaching and learning as well as their parents', focused only on teachers' perspectives inferring students' behaviors, benefits or challenges with AI. Additionally, some of the themes may have conceptual overlaps such as personalization of learning and AI in the role of a pedagogical assistant, differentiation and support of language learning etc. Also, some of our categories were strongly supported by many articles highlighting general trends, while others had less references or specific cases, which we still had to report. In any case some of the data derive from specific contexts within certain regions with public or private school systems, policies, local curricula and infrastructure that cannot be generalized to all educational settings, as well as some countries were overly represented in the indexed literature in relation to others.

7.3. Future recommendations

The role of teachers as mediators and facilitators of interactions between students and AI tools has not been sufficiently explored (Aravantinos et al., 2024), therefore future research should focus on developing pedagogical integration and teacher training frameworks. Gathering empirical data from underrepresented countries and diverse educational contexts could offer more insights into the complex phenomenon of AI integration in schools and could potentially help to establish differentiated training guidelines for educators according to regional and cultural variations. Lastly, research should focus on long-term evidence that AI use benefits learning outcomes and on ethical concerns about data privacy, bias, transparency and inequities in accessibility.

ACKNOWLEDGEMENTS

This paper has been supported by the funding program "MEDICUS" of the University of Patras.

REFERENCES

Adams, C., Pente, P., Lemermeyer, G., & Rockwell, G. (2023). Ethical principles for artificial intelligence in K-12 education. *Computers and Education: Artificial Intelligence*, *4*, 100131. DOI: 10.1016/j.caeai.2023.100131

Alhazzani, N. S. (2024). Enhancing mathematics teachers' pedagogical skills by using ChatGPT. *International Journal of Innovative Research and Scientific Studies*, *7*(4), 1614–1626. DOI: 10.53894/ijirss.v7i4.3460

Almuhanna, M. A. (2024). Teachers' perspectives of integrating AI-powered technologies in K-12 education for creating customized learning materials and resources. *Education and Information Technologies*. Advance online publication. DOI: 10.1007/s10639-024-13257-y

An, X., Chai, C. S., Li, Y., Zhou, Y., Shen, X., Zheng, C., & Chen, M. (2023). Modeling English teachers' behavioral intention to use artificial intelligence in middle schools. *Education and Information Technologies*, *28*(5), 5187–5208. DOI: 10.1007/s10639-022-11286-z

Annamalai, N. (2025). Factors affecting English language high school teachers switching intention to ChatGPT: A Push-Pull-Mooring theory perspective. *Interactive Learning Environments*, *33*(2), 1367–1384. DOI: 10.1080/10494820.2024.2371928

Aravantinos, S., Lavidas, K., Voulgari, I., Papadakis, S., Karalis, T., & Komis, V. (2024). Educational Approaches with AI in Primary School Settings: A Systematic Review of the Literature Available in Scopus. *Education Sciences*, *14*(7), 744. DOI: 10.3390/educsci14070744

Arefian, M. H., Çomoğlu, I., & Dikilitaş, K. (2024). Understanding EFL teachers' experiences of ChatGPT-driven collaborative reflective practice through a community of practice lens. *Innovation in Language Learning and Teaching*, •••, 1–16. DOI: 10.1080/17501229.2024.2412769

Bateman, T. (2025). Teacher perspectives of ChatGPT as a pedagogical tool in the K-12 setting: A case study. *Quality Assurance in Education*, *33*(2), 203–217. DOI: 10.1108/QAE-02-2024-0042

Bettayeb, A. M., Abu Talib, M., Sobhe Altayasinah, A. Z., & Dakalbab, F. (2024). Exploring the impact of ChatGPT: Conversational AI in education. *Frontiers in Education*, *9*, 1379796. DOI: 10.3389/feduc.2024.1379796

Biagini, G. (2025). Towards an AI-Literate Future: A Systematic Literature Review Exploring Education, Ethics, and Applications. *International Journal of Artificial Intelligence in Education*, *35*(4), 2616–2666. Advance online publication. DOI: 10.1007/s40593-025-00466-w

Bohara, D. K., & Rana, K. (2024). Unmasking teachers' proficiency in harnessing Artificial Intelligence (AI) for transformative education. *SN Social Sciences*, *4*(11), 203. DOI: 10.1007/s43545-024-01003-7

Bower, M., Torrington, J., Lai, J. W. M., Petocz, P., & Alfano, M. (2024). How should we change teaching and assessment in response to increasingly powerful generative Artificial Intelligence? Outcomes of the ChatGPT teacher survey. *Education and Information Technologies*. Advance online publication. DOI: 10.1007/s10639-023-12405-0

Braun, V., & Clarke, V. (2006). Using thematic analysis in psychology. *Qualitative Research in Psychology*, *3*(2), 77–101. DOI: 10.1191/1478088706qp063oa

Celik, I. (2023). Towards Intelligent-TPACK: An empirical study on teachers' professional knowledge to ethically integrate artificial intelligence (AI)-based tools into education. *Computers in Human Behavior*, *138*, 107468. DOI: 10.1016/j.chb.2022.107468

Celik, I., Dindar, M., Muukkonen, H., & Järvelä, S. (2022). The Promises and Challenges of Artificial Intelligence for Teachers: A Systematic Review of Research. *TechTrends*, *66*(4), 616–630. DOI: 10.1007/s11528-022-00715-y

Cetin, Y., Taş, Ö., Alakuş, H., & Kaplan, H. İ. (2024). Examining School Principals' and Teachers' Perceptions of Using ChatGPT in Education. *Educational Process International Journal*, *13*(3). Advance online publication. DOI: 10.22521/edupij.2024.133.5

Chai, C. S., Liang, S., & Wang, X. (2024). A survey study of chinese teachers' continuous intentions to teach artificial intelligence. *Education and Information Technologies*, *29*(11), 14015–14034. DOI: 10.1007/s10639-023-12430-z

Cheng, E. C. K., & Wang, T. (2023). Leading digital transformation and eliminating barriers for teachers to incorporate artificial intelligence in basic education in Hong Kong. *Computers and Education: Artificial Intelligence*, *5*, 100171. DOI: 10.1016/j.caeai.2023.100171

Chounta, I.-A., Bardone, E., Raudsep, A., & Pedaste, M. (2022). Exploring Teachers' Perceptions of Artificial Intelligence as a Tool to Support their Practice in Estonian K-12 Education. *International Journal of Artificial Intelligence in Education, 32*(3), 725–755. DOI: 10.1007/s40593-021-00243-5

Crosthwaite, P., Smala, S., & Spinelli, F. (2024). Prompting for pedagogy? Australian F-10 teachers' generative AI prompting use cases. *Australian Educational Researcher*. Advance online publication. DOI: 10.1007/s13384-024-00787-0

Davoodi, A. (2024). Crafting innovative paths in non-linear professional learning for bilingual education: The role of connectivism in the age of AI. *Professional Development in Education*, •••, 1–17. DOI: 10.1080/19415257.2024.2421492

Donley, K. (2024). Teaching with ChatGPT as a linguistically responsive tool for multilingual learners. *Technology in Language Teaching & Learning*, *6*(3), 1719. DOI: 10.29140/tltl.v6n3.1719

Dovgyi, S., Babiichuk, S., Davybida, L., & Biletska, M. (2024). TEACHERS' AND STUDENTS' ATTITUDES TOWARDS THE USE OF ARTIFICIAL INTELLIGENCE: ALL-UKRAINIAN RESEARCH. *Information Technologies and Learning Tools*, *104*(6), 197–215. DOI: 10.33407/itlt.v104i6.5890

Du, H., Sun, Y., Jiang, H., Islam, A. Y. M. A., & Gu, X. (2024). Exploring the effects of AI literacy in teacher learning: An empirical study. *Humanities & Social Sciences Communications*, *11*(1), 559. DOI: 10.1057/s41599-024-03101-6

Egara, F. O., & Mosimege, M. (2024). Exploring the Integration of Artificial Intelligence-Based ChatGPT into Mathematics Instruction: Perceptions, Challenges, and Implications for Educators. *Education Sciences*, *14*(7), 742. DOI: 10.3390/educsci14070742

Fu, Y., & Weng, Z. (2024). Navigating the ethical terrain of AI in education: A systematic review on framing responsible human-centered AI practices. *Computers and Education: Artificial Intelligence*, *7*, 100306. DOI: 10.1016/j.caeai.2024.100306

Fundi, M., Sanusi, I. T., Oyelere, S. S., & Ayere, M. (2024). Advancing AI education: Assessing Kenyan in-service teachers' preparedness for integrating artificial intelligence in competence-based curriculum. *Computers in Human Behavior Reports*, *14*, 100412. DOI: 10.1016/j.chbr.2024.100412

García-López, I. M., & Trujillo-Liñán, L. (2025). Ethical and regulatory challenges of Generative AI in education: A systematic review. *Frontiers in Education*, *10*, 1565938. DOI: 10.3389/feduc.2025.1565938

Güneyli, A., Burgul, N. S., Dericioğlu, S., Cenkova, N., Becan, S., Şimşek, Ş. E., & Güneralp, H. (2024). Exploring Teacher Awareness of Artificial Intelligence in Education: A Case Study from Northern Cyprus. *European Journal of Investigation in Health, Psychology and Education*, *14*(8), 2358–2376. DOI: 10.3390/ejihpe14080156 PMID: 39194950

Halomoan, H., Hakiki, M., Ramadhan, M. A., Hidayah, Y., Fakhri, J., Aljamaliah, S. N. M., & Abi Hamid, M. (2024). Integrating Principal Leadership and Teacher Roles with AI-Based "Merdeka" Curriculum Innovation: The Quantitative Research. *TEM Journal*, 3397–3404. https://doi.org/DOI: 10.18421/TEM134-73

Hays, L., Jurkowski, O., & Sims, S. K. (2024). ChatGPT in K-12 Education. *TechTrends*, *68*(2), 281–294. DOI: 10.1007/s11528-023-00924-z

Hojeij, Z., Kuhail, M. A., & ElSayary, A. (2024). Investigating in-service teachers' views on ChatGPT integration. *Interactive Technology and Smart Education*. Advance online publication. DOI: 10.1108/ITSE-04-2024-0094

Jang, H., & Choi, H. (2025). A Double-Edged Sword: Physics Educators' Perspectives on Utilizing ChatGPT and Its Future in Classrooms. *Journal of Science Education and Technology*, *34*(2), 267–283. DOI: 10.1007/s10956-024-10173-1

Karataş, F., Eriçok, B., & Tanrikulu, L. (2025). Reshaping curriculum adaptation in the age of artificial intelligence: Mapping teachers' AI -driven curriculum adaptation patterns. *British Educational Research Journal*, *51*(1), 154–180. DOI: 10.1002/berj.4068

Khasawneh, M. A. S. (2024). Teacher Opinions on the Role of Educational Robots in Enhancing Programming Skills among Hearing-Impaired Students. *International Journal of Learning. Teaching and Educational Research*, *23*(5), 309–322. DOI: 10.26803/ijlter.23.5.16

Kim, J. (2024). Types of teacher-AI collaboration in K-12 classroom instruction: Chinese teachers' perspective. *Education and Information Technologies*, *29*(13), 17433–17465. DOI: 10.1007/s10639-024-12523-3

Kim, J., Lee, H., & Cho, Y. H. (2022). Learning design to support student-AI collaboration: Perspectives of leading teachers for AI in education. *Education and Information Technologies*, *27*(5), 6069–6104. DOI: 10.1007/s10639-021-10831-6

Kokoç, M. (2024). Factors influencing K-12 teachers' experiences of using Generative AI Tools: Opportunities and barriers. *Journal of E-Learning and Knowledge Society, Vol 20 No 3*, 101-111 Pages. DOI: 10.20368/1971-8829/1136039

Kong, S.-C., & Yang, Y. (2024). A Human-Centered Learning and Teaching Framework Using Generative Artificial Intelligence for Self-Regulated Learning Development Through Domain Knowledge Learning in K–12 Settings. *IEEE Transactions on Learning Technologies*, *17*, 1562–1573. DOI: 10.1109/TLT.2024.3392830

Korucu-Kış, S. (2024). Zone of proximal creativity: An empirical study on EFL teachers' use of ChatGPT for enhanced practice. *Thinking Skills and Creativity*, *54*, 101639. DOI: 10.1016/j.tsc.2024.101639

Labadze, L., Grigolia, M., & Machaidze, L. (2023). Role of AI chatbots in education: Systematic literature review. *International Journal of Educational Technology in Higher Education*, *20*(1), 56. DOI: 10.1186/s41239-023-00426-1

Lampropoulos, G., & Papadakis, S. (2025). The Educational Value of Artificial Intelligence and Social Robots. In *Social Robots in Education* (pp. 3–15). Springer. DOI: 10.1007/978-3-031-82915-4_1

Lavidas, K., Petropoulou, A., Papadakis, S., Apostolou, Z., Komis, V., Jimoyiannis, A., & Gialamas, V. (2022). Factors affecting response rates of the web survey with teachers. *Computers*, *11*(9), 127. DOI: 10.3390/computers11090127

Lee, Y.-J., Davis, R. O., & Ryu, J. (2024). Korean in-Service Teachers' Perceptions of Implementing Artificial Intelligence (AI) Education for Teaching in Schools and Their AI Teacher Training Programs. *International Journal of Information and Education Technology (IJIET)*, *14*(2), 214–219. DOI: 10.18178/ijiet.2024.14.2.2042

Li, M. (2024). Integrating Artificial Intelligence in Primary Mathematics Education: Investigating Internal and External Influences on Teacher Adoption. *International Journal of Science and Mathematics Education*. Advance online publication. DOI: 10.1007/s10763-024-10515-w

Lin, C.-C., Huang, A. Y. Q., & Lu, O. H. T. (2023). Artificial intelligence in intelligent tutoring systems toward sustainable education: A systematic review. *Smart Learning Environments*, *10*(1), 41. DOI: 10.1186/s40561-023-00260-y

Magat, R. J. B., & Sangalang, E. M. (2024). Teachers' Familiarity, Perceptions, and Training Needs on the Use of ChatGPT in Mathematics Instruction. *International Journal of Education in Mathematics, Science and Technology*, 1471–1487. DOI: 10.46328/ijemst.4332

Mananay, J. A. (2024). Integrating Artificial Intelligence (AI) in Language Teaching: Effectiveness, Challenges, and Strategies. *International Journal of Learning. Teaching and Educational Research*, *23*(9), 361–382. DOI: 10.26803/ijlter.23.9.19

Martin, F., Zhuang, M., & Schaefer, D. (2024). Systematic review of research on artificial intelligence in K-12 education (2017–2022). *Computers and Education: Artificial Intelligence*, *6*, 100195. DOI: 10.1016/j.caeai.2023.100195

Marzano, D. (2025). Generative Artificial Intelligence (GAI) in Teaching and Learning Processes at the K-12 Level: A Systematic Review. *Technology, Knowledge and Learning*. DOI: 10.1007/s10758-025-09853-7

Mikeladze, T., Meijer, P. C., & Verhoeff, R. P. (2024). A comprehensive exploration of artificial intelligence competence frameworks for educators: A critical review. *European Journal of Education*, *59*(3), e12663. DOI: 10.1111/ejed.12663

Nguyen, T. H. C. (2024). Exploring the Role of Artificial Intelligence-Powered Facilitator in Enhancing Digital Competencies of Primary School Teachers. *European Journal of Educational Research, volume–13–2024*(volume–13–issue–1–january–2024), 219–231. DOI: 10.12973/eu-jer.13.1.219

Noroozi, O., Soleimani, S., Farrokhnia, M., & Banihashem, S. K. (2024). Generative AI in Education: Pedagogical, Theoretical, and Methodological Perspectives. *International Journal of Technology in Education*, *7*(3), 373–385. DOI: 10.46328/ijte.845

Page, M. J., McKenzie, J. E., Bossuyt, P. M., Boutron, I., Hoffmann, T. C., Mulrow, C. D., Shamseer, L., Tetzlaff, J. M., Akl, E. A., Brennan, S. E., Chou, R., Glanville, J., Grimshaw, J. M., Hróbjartsson, A., Lalu, M. M., Li, T., Loder, E. W., Mayo-Wilson, E., McDonald, S., & Moher, D. (2021). The PRISMA statement: An updated guideline for reporting systematic reviews. *BMJ (Clinical Research Ed.)*, (71), n71. Advance online publication. DOI: 10.1136/bmj.n71 PMID: 33782057

Payadnya, I. P. A. A., Putri, G. A. M. A., Suwija, I. K., Saelee, S., & Jayantika, I. G. A. N. T. (2025). Cultural integration in AI-enhanced mathematics education: Insights from Southeast Asian educators. *Journal for Multicultural Education*, *19*(1), 58–72. DOI: 10.1108/JME-09-2024-0119

Pörn, R., Braskén, M., Wingren, M., & Andersson, S. (2024). Attitudes towards and expectations on the role of artificial intelligence in the classroom among digitally skilled Finnish K-12 mathematics teachers. *LUMAT: International Journal on Math. Science and Technology Education*, *12*(3). Advance online publication. DOI: 10.31129/LUMAT.12.3.2102

Sadykova, G., & Kayumova, A. (2024). Educators' Perception of Artificial Intelligence as Instructional Tool. *TEM Journal*, 3194–3204. https://doi.org/DOI: 10.18421/TEM134-54

Tan, Q., & Tang, X. (2025). Unveiling AI literacy in K-12 education: A systematic literature review of empirical research. *Interactive Learning Environments, 33*(9), 1–17. DOI: 10.1080/10494820.2025.2482586

Tran, T. T., Pham, T. T., & Le, T. T. (2024). Transformative Interactions: ChatGPT's Role in Facilitating Professional Development Among Vietnamese English as a Foreign Language Teachers. *Higher Learning Research Communications, 14*(2). Advance online publication. DOI: 10.18870/hlrc.v14i2.1558

Uğraş, H., Uğraş, M., Papadakis, S., & Kalogiannakis, M. (2024). ChatGPT-Supported Education in Primary Schools: The Potential of ChatGPT for Sustainable Practices. *Sustainability (Basel), 16*(22), 9855. DOI: 10.3390/su16229855

Van Den Berg, G. (2024). Generative AI and Educators: Partnering in Using Open Digital Content for Transforming Education. *Open Praxis, 16*(2), 130–141. DOI: 10.55982/openpraxis.16.2.640

Viberg, O., Cukurova, M., Feldman-Maggor, Y., Alexandron, G., Shirai, S., Kanemune, S., Wasson, B., Tømte, C., Spikol, D., Milrad, M., Coelho, R., & Kizilcec, R. F. (2024). What Explains Teachers' Trust in AI in Education Across Six Countries? *International Journal of Artificial Intelligence in Education*. Advance online publication. DOI: 10.1007/s40593-024-00433-x

Voulgari, I., Lavidas, K., Aravantinos, S., Sypsa, S., & Sfyroera, M. (2024). Exploring the Role, Implementation, and Educational Implications of AI in Early Childhood Education. In Olney, A. M., Chounta, I.-A., Liu, Z., Santos, O. C., & Bittencourt, I. I. (Eds.), *Artificial Intelligence in Education. Posters and Late Breaking Results, Workshops and Tutorials, Industry and Innovation Tracks, Practitioners, Doctoral Consortium and Blue Sky* (pp. 29–37). Springer Nature Switzerland., DOI: 10.1007/978-3-031-64312-5_4

Wang, K., Chai, C.-S., Liang, J.-C., & Sang, G. (2024). Exploring teachers' behavioural intentions to design artificial intelligence-assisted learning in Chinese K–12 education. *Technology, Pedagogy and Education, 33*(5), 629–645. DOI: 10.1080/1475939X.2024.2369241

Wang, T., & Cheng, E. C. K. (2021). An investigation of barriers to Hong Kong K-12 schools incorporating Artificial Intelligence in education. *Computers and Education: Artificial Intelligence, 2*, 100031. DOI: 10.1016/j.caeai.2021.100031

Whalen, J., Grube, W., Xu, C., & Trust, T. (2025). K-12 Educators' Reactions and Responses to ChatGPT and GenAI During the 2022–2023 School Year. *TechTrends, 69*(1), 125–137. DOI: 10.1007/s11528-024-01028-y

Williyan, A., Fitriati, S. W., Pratama, H., & Sakhiyya, Z. (2024). AI AS CO-CREATOR: EXPLORING INDONESIAN EFL TEACHERS' COLLABORATION WITH AI IN CONTENT DEVELOPMENT. *Teaching English With Technology, 2024*(2). Advance online publication. DOI: 10.56297/vaca6841/LRDX3699/RZOH5366

Xin, J. J. (2024). Investigating EFL teachers' use of generative AI to develop reading materials: A practice and perception study. *Language Teaching Research, 13621688241303321*, 13621688241303321. Advance online publication. DOI: 10.1177/13621688241303321

Yim, I. H. Y., & Su, J. (2025). Artificial intelligence literacy education in primary schools: A review. *International Journal of Technology and Design Education, 35*(5), 2175–2204. Advance online publication. DOI: 10.1007/s10798-025-09979-w

Zhang, P., & Tur, G. (2024). A systematic review of ChatGPT use in K-12 education. *European Journal of Education, 59*(2), e12599. DOI: 10.1111/ejed.12599

Zulianti, H., Hastuti, H., Nurchurifiani, E., Hastomo, T., Maximilian, A., & Ajeng, G. D. (2024). Enhancing Novice EFL Teachers' Competency in AI-Powered Tools Through a TPACK-Based Professional Development Program. *World Journal of English Language, 15*(3), 117. DOI: 10.5430/wjel.v15n3p117

APPENDIX

Table 3. Empirical studies

No.	Reference	Country - Region	Research Aim
1	Alhazzani, 2024	Saudi Arabia	Propose a conceptual framework intended to leverage the capabilities of the Chat GPT artificial intelligence model to enhance the creative teaching proficiencies of secondary school mathematics teachers.
2	Almuhanna, 2024	Saudi Arabia	Investigate teachers' perspectives and experiences with AI-powered technologies for creating customized learning materials and resources for students.
3	An et al., 2023	China	Investigate EFL teachers' perceptions, knowledge, and behavioral intention to use AI to support teaching and learning of English in middle schools.
4	Annamalai, 2025	Malaysia	Investigate the factors that influence the switching intention of teachers from traditional classroom teaching to the use of ChatGPT in English language teaching based on the Mooring Theory framework.
5	Arefian et al., 2024	Iran	Uncover how Iranian EFL teachers' ChatGPT-driven collaborative reflective practice (CRP), both independently and collaboratively, can contribute to their professional development.
6	Bateman, 2025	USA	Understand the experiences and perceptions of teachers in a K-12 setting regarding the use of ChatGPT as a pedagogical tool.
7	Bohara & Rana, 2024	Nepal	Examine teachers' awareness of AI, particularly its implications for teaching and learning among school teachers in Nepal.
8	Bower et al., 2024	Europe, Australasia, America, Others - not stated exact countries	Examine the views of educators from a diverse range of teaching levels, experience levels, discipline areas, and regions about the impact of AI on teaching and assessment, the ways that they believe teaching and assessment should change, and the key motivations for changing their practices.
9	Cetin et al., 2024	Turkey	Investigate how school principals and teachers perceived the use of ChatGPT in education and reveal their attitudes towards using AI-based tools to facilitate the teaching-learning experience.

continued on following page

Table 3. Continued

No.	Reference	Country - Region	Research Aim
10	Chai et al., 2024	China	Assess teachers' efficacies in understanding AI and teaching AI, with additional considerations of promoting ethical awareness and designing socially beneficial AI applications.
11	Cheng & Wang, 2023	Hong Kong	Explore the interplay between proactive digital leadership and the internal and external barriers teachers face in implementing AIED.
12	Chounta et al., 2022	Estonia	Explore teachers' perceptions about cutting-edge technologies (in this case, AI) and contextualize the results in the scope of Fairness, Accountability, Transparency and Ethics (FATE).
13	Crosthwaite et al., 2024	Australia	Explore the generative artificial intelligence (GAI) prompting practices of Australian primary and secondary educators in the first year following the advent of OpenAI's ChatGPT.
14	Davoodi, 2024	USA	Provide effective PD programs for elementary school teachers and administrators working with bilingual children, with the goal of improving their AI literacy and positively influencing their attitudes towards AI integration in bilingual/ESL education.
15	Donley, 2024	USA	Document the instructional applications of AI in the context of K–12 ML education, specifically in US public schools.
16	Dovgyi et al., 2024	Ukraine	Determine how actively AI and AI-assisted possibilities are used in Ukrainian school education and assess the attitudes of both Ukrainian students and teachers toward the use of AI in teaching and learning.
17	Du et al., 2024	China	Examine the power of AI literacy and explore the determinants of behavioral intentions to learn AI among K-12 teachers.
18	Egara & Mosimege, 2024	Nigeria, South Africa	Explore teachers' awareness, utilization, and perceptions of ChatGPT.
19	Fundi et al., 2024	Kenya, East Africa	Assess the confidence in AI, attitudes toward AI, AI ethics, subjective norms, perceived threats, and the readiness to teach AI among Kenyan K-12 in-service teachers and to assess how these factors influence their readiness to teach AI.

continued on following page

Table 3. Continued

No.	Reference	Country - Region	Research Aim
20	Güneyli et al., 2024	Cyprus	Level of awareness regarding the use of AI.
21	Halomoan et al., 2024	Indonesia	Explore the intricate interplay between principal leadership styles, teacher roles, and the implementation of AI-based 'Merdeka' curriculum initiatives within vocational high schools across Indonesia.
22	Hays et al., 2024	USA	Determine the current perceptions and use of ChatGPT in K-12 settings.
23	Hojeij et al., 2024	United Arab Emirates (UAE)	Investigate in-service teachers' perspectives on the integration of ChatGPT, an artificial intelligence (AI)-driven chatbot, into United Arab Emirates (UAE) private schools.
24	Jang & Choi, 2025	South Korea	Explore the educational uses, considerations, and changes in the social and educational environments in the transformational era with generative AI.
25	Karataş et al., 2025	Turkey	Examine two key aspects: (i) how teachers adapt curricula within a specific framework, focusing on traditional adaptation patterns; and (ii) how generative AI tools, especially ChatGPT, can improve curriculum adaptation by exploring teachers' experiences in using AI to tailor educational content.
26	Khasawneh, 2024	Jordan	Identify the role of educational robots in developing programming skills among elementary school students with hearing disabilities and the obstacles to their use from teachers' point of view in the city of Amman in Jordan.
27	Kim, 2024	USA	Explore different types of Teacher AI Collaboration and the potential benefits and obstacles of TAC.
28	Kim et al., 2022	South Korea	Explore teachers' perspectives on what (1) curriculum design, (2) student-AI interaction, and (3) learning environments are required to design student-AI collaboration (SAC) in learning and (4) how SAC would evolve.
29	Kokoç, 2024	Turkey	Identify teachers' views on their digital skills in research studies using AI tools.
30	Kong & Yang, 2024	China	Propose a human-centered learning and teaching framework (HCLTF).

continued on following page

Table 3. Continued

No.	Reference	Country - Region	Research Aim
31	Korucu-Kış, 2024	Turkey	Explore ChatGPT's effectiveness in fostering teacher creativity by investigating the efficacy of ChatGPT in facilitating creativity, particularly among English as a foreign (EFL) teachers.
32	Lee et al., 2024	South Korea	Understand in-service teachers' perceptions regarding AI education for teaching in schools and their AI teacher training programs.
33	Li, 2024	China	Contribute empirical evidence to the growing body of knowledge regarding the factors that influence the utilization of AI tools in the educational sector, focusing on primary mathematics education.
34	Magat & Sangalang, 2024	Philippines	Examine teachers' engagement with ChatGPT.
35	Mananay, 2024	Philippines	Contribute valuable insights to the ongoing discourse on integrating AI in language teaching and provide practical recommendations for educators, curriculum developers, and educational policymakers seeking to harness AI's potential to enhance language learning experiences.
36	Nguyen, 2024	Vietnam	Investigate the relationship between teacher professional development, quality of lecture design, student engagement, teacher technical skills, pedagogical content knowledge and teacher satisfaction in using Artificial Intelligence (AI)-Powered Facilitator for designing lectures.
37	Payadnya et al., 2025	Southeast Asia (Indonesia, Thailand, Malaysia, Singapore, Philippines, Vietnam, Cambodia, Laos, Myanmar, Brunei Darussalam)	Investigate how AI can be adapted to fit the local educational systems and cultures, offering insights from Southeast Asian educators on their experiences with AI in mathematics education.
38	Pörn et al., 2024	Sweden, Finland	Investigate digitally skilled K-12 mathematics teachers' attitudes towards and expectations on the role of artificial intelligence in the classroom.

continued on following page

Table 3. Continued

No.	Reference	Country - Region	Research Aim
39	Sadykova & Kayumova, 2024	Russian Federation	Add to the growing volume of research that focuses on educators' attitude towards AI, their views on its applicability in education and necessity to develop AI competences.
40	Tran et al., 2024	Vietnam	Delve into the experiences, perceptions, and outcomes associated with integrating ChatGPT into the TPD framework.
41	Uğraş et al., 2024	Turkey	Evaluate the potential of using ChatGPT at the primary school level from the teachers' perspective within a sustainability framework.
42	Van Den Berg, 2024	South Africa	Explore how a specific group of educators partner with GAI tools, particularly ChatGPT, to complement and enhance their teaching.
43	Viberg et al., 2024	Sweden, Norway, Israel, Japan, USA, Brazil	Improve understanding of factors that influence teachers' adoption of AI EdTech, investigating teachers' trust in AI-EdTech, and two of its antecedents, perceived benefits and concerns about AI-EdTech, in the context of K-12 education in six countries.
44	Wang et al., 2024	China	Explore the predictors of teachers' behavioral intentions to design AI-assisted learning and examine the structural relationships among these factors, by constructing a structural model of AI literacy, Technological Pedagogical Content Knowledge (TPACK), technostress, school support, teacher agency, teacher autonomy and behavioral intentions.
45	Wang & Cheng, 2021	China	Understand the barriers that are involved in the way AIED is interpreted, the reality Hong Kong K-12 schools are facing, strengthen our knowledge of current obstructions, and generate strategies that could help Hong Kong K-12 schools incorporate AIED more effectively.
46	Whalen et al., 2025	USA	Examine K-12 teachers' reactions and responses to ChatGPT and other genAI tools in education.
47	Williyan et al., 2024	Indonesia	Explore the collaboration between Indonesian English as a Foreign Language (EFL) educators and Artificial Intelligence (AI) in content development.

continued on following page

Table 3. Continued

No.	Reference	Country - Region	Research Aim
48	Xin, 2024	China	Explore how teachers in an English as a foreign language (EFL) context perceived and used a generative AI-based tool, ChatPDF, to develop materials for reading lessons.
49	Zulianti et al., 2024	Indonesia	Assess the impact of the PD program on various aspects of AI teaching competence, including AI-powered tools knowledge test, teaching skills related to AI-powered tools, and AI-powered tools teaching self-efficacy.

Chapter 13
Training K-12 Teachers for AI Integration:
Comparative Insights From Chile and Spain

Luis Manuel Cerdá-Suárez
http://orcid.org/0000-0002-3909-8805
Universidad Internacional de La Rioja, Spain

Beltrán Gutiérrez-Jiménez
http://orcid.org/0000-0003-2175-7742
Universidad Internacional de La Rioja, Spain

Nuria Puente-Dominguez
http://orcid.org/0000-0003-0483-2691
Universidad Internacional de La Rioja, Spain

ABSTRACT

Recent advancements in Artificial Intelligence (AI) have profoundly influenced teacher professional development in K-12 globally, offering innovative tools and strategies to enhance teaching and learning practices. However, the implementation and contextual adaptation of AI tools differ substantially across nations. This chapter investigates the integration of AI-powered instructional tools in K–12 classrooms in Chile and Spain, employing the Teaching Through Interactions (TTI) framework as a conceptual model to examine teacher-student engagement dynamics. Through a comparative case study involving six schools in Chile and Spain, the study captures data from 120 students and 10 teachers using structured questionnaires, interviews,

DOI: 10.4018/979-8-2600-0101-1.ch013

and classroom observations. This comparative analysis highlights both the shared challenges and unique opportunities of integrating AI tools within the educational frameworks of Chile and Spain.

1. INTRODUCTION

Artificial Intelligence (AI) has rapidly transitioned from being a peripheral tool of technological innovation to a central driver of educational transformation worldwide. Its impact on K–12 education is particularly noteworthy, as schools increasingly adopt digital platforms, intelligent tutoring systems, and adaptive assessment mechanisms to meet the evolving demands of 21st-century learning (Alvarez-Garcia et al., 2024). In many contexts, AI is promoted as a solution to persistent challenges in education —such as addressing diverse learning needs, supporting teacher workload, and enhancing data-driven decision-making. However, beyond these promises, AI also raises profound questions regarding equity, ethics, and the cultural relevance of educational practices (Ayala-Pazmiño, 2023).

Building on this global perspective, international organizations such as UNESCO (2023), the European Commission (2020), and the Gobierno de España (2021) have emphasized the importance of embedding AI in education in ways that support inclusion, foster teacher agency, and safeguard student rights. *UNESCO's AI and Education: Guidance for Policy-Makers* (UNESCO, 2023) and the *AI Competency Framework for Teachers* (UNESCO, 2023) outline the need for educators to not only acquire technical skills but also to develop critical literacies to use AI responsibly. Similarly, the European Commission's DigCompEdu framework provides benchmarks for teacher digital competence that explicitly anticipate the integration of AI-driven tools in classroom practice (Kapoor & Bakhshi, 2025).

At the same time, the global discourse on AI-powered instruction in K–12 education has increasingly highlighted the pedagogical reconfiguration of schooling. Beyond framing AI as a set of supportive tools, scholars and international agencies now discuss its potential to fundamentally reshape curricula, instructional design, and teacher–student interactions (Holmes et al., 2022; Luckin, 2022). Large-scale pilots in Asia and Europe demonstrate how intelligent tutoring systems, adaptive platforms, and data-driven formative assessment can personalize learning trajectories at unprecedented scale (Chen et al., 2020; Zhang & Zhang, 2024). Situating Chile and Spain within this discourse is therefore crucial, as their contrasting institutional frameworks and sociocultural traditions provide complementary insights into how global narratives are localized and contested in practice (Redecker, 2017; Saha et al., 2025).

In parallel, national and regional governments have issued their own strategies to guide AI integration. The U.S. Department of Education (UNESCO, 2023) released its landmark report *Artificial Intelligence and the Future of Teaching and Learning*, emphasizing the need for transparency, human oversight, and equity in AI-mediated practices. In Asia, China has advanced large-scale pilots in AI-driven personalized learning environments (Chen et al., 2020), while Finland has emphasized teacher training and ethical safeguards in its digital strategies (Zhang & Zhang, 2024). These international cases demonstrate the diversity of approaches to AI integration, underscoring the need for comparative studies that account for local conditions and pedagogical traditions. Studies such as Asagar (2025), Lavidas et al. (2022a, 2022b) and Papadakis et al. (2024a, 2024b) show that AI adoption is mediated by teacher readiness, institutional scaffolding, and contextual inequities. Thus, situating Chile and Spain within this global discourse allows us to test how international policy aspirations translate into lived pedagogical realities (Molina et al., 2024).

The COVID-19 pandemic further accelerated the incorporation of digital and AI-related tools into education systems. Emergency remote teaching forced schools to experiment with platforms that included automated feedback, learning analytics, and AI-powered assessment tools. Although many of these innovations were adopted under pressure, they created lasting expectations for flexible, data-driven approaches (Williamson et al., 2023; Williamson, 2024). At the same time, the pandemic highlighted structural inequities: while some schools leveraged AI to support continuity of learning, others lacked connectivity, devices, or teacher readiness. The literature notes a risk of exacerbating inequities if AI policies outpace infrastructure or professional development (Holstein et al., 2019; Williamson, 2024). This tension—between rapid technological change and uneven preparedness—is central to our comparative inquiry (Saha et al., 2025).

Against this backdrop, the Latin American experience provides a particularly revealing case: AI integration reflects both potential and persistent inequalities. Chile, as a leader in digital education policy, has invested in infrastructure and teacher training programs that enable experimentation with learning analytics and AI-mediated platforms. However, significant disparities remain between urban and rural schools, and between public and private sectors, resulting in uneven access and implementation (Yang, 2024). The "digital leap" accelerated during the COVID-19 pandemic revealed both the resilience of some schools and the structural weaknesses of others (Romero & Ventura, 2020). While Chile has produced innovative local initiatives, scaling them equitably across the system continues to be a challenge (Lekan & Pardos, 2025).

In contrast, Spain benefits from European Union digital policies, national strategies such as *España Digital 2026* (Gobierno de España, 2021), and a strong emphasis on teacher competence frameworks like DigCompEdu. These initiatives provide

Spanish teachers with institutional support and access to EU-funded projects aimed at digital and AI readiness. At the same time, disparities persist among autonomous communities, and teachers express concerns about workload, ethical risks, and the pressure to adapt rapidly to emerging technologies. Thus, Spain offers an example of structured integration framed by policy, but not free of tensions regarding practice and equity (Alvarez-Garcia et al., 2024).

The comparative analysis of Chile and Spain is especially relevant for understanding how contextual factors —economic, institutional, cultural, and policy-driven— influence AI in classrooms. While both countries share linguistic and cultural ties, their education systems reflect different levels of institutional support, regulatory frameworks, and equity challenges (Xu, 2024; Yang, 2024).

Ethics, governance, and teacher agency are at the forefront of debates about AI in education (Holmes et al., 2022). Ethical safeguards, including data protection, informed consent, and teacher oversight, are not only methodological requirements but also central to the governance of AI in schools, as emphasized by UNESCO (2023) and the EU's GDPR framework. These dimensions are therefore integrated into both our design and our analysis. In many systems, AI is introduced through partnerships with technology companies whose tools are not always transparent in their design or accountable in their use of student data. Teachers often face the dual pressure of adopting these tools while also safeguarding student well-being. For Latin America in particular, where historical inequalities have shaped access to quality education, the governance of AI is not merely technical but deeply political (Fonseca et al., 2024; Williamson, 2024). By comparing Spain, with its institutionalized frameworks, and Chile, with its more fragmented landscape, this study highlights the importance of governance structures in shaping teacher–student interactions aligning with sociocultural perspectives on education (Vygotsky, 1978).

At the center of this study lies the question of teacher–student interactions and how they are transformed by AI. The *Teaching Through Interactions (TTI)* framework (Hamre et al., 2013; Pianta et al., 2008, 2009; Pianta, 2016; Pianta & Hofkens, 2023) provides a lens through which to examine these dynamics, focusing on three domains: emotional support, classroom organization, and instructional support. While these domains have been validated in thousands of classrooms across different countries, the rapid introduction of AI systems necessitates a rethinking of how interactions are mediated when technology plays a more active role in instructional processes. AI can augment instructional support by providing adaptive feedback, but it can also inadvertently weaken emotional support if it reduces direct teacher–student engagement. Classroom organization may be enhanced by data dashboards, yet these tools may also create new burdens of monitoring and accountability (Xu, 2024). By combining TTI's micro-level interactional focus with sociotechnical theory's macro-level systems lens, this study provides not just descriptive accounts but a critical framework to evaluate how AI reshapes relational pedagogy across diverse contexts (Fonseca et al., 2024).

This research is also informed by sociotechnical theory, which emphasizes the interplay between human agency, technological affordances, and institutional contexts. From this perspective, AI cannot be understood solely as a neutral tool but must be analyzed as part of a socio-technical system shaped by power relations, governance structures, and cultural traditions (Holmes et al., 2022; Williamson, 2024). In regions such as Latin America, where historical inequalities and sociocultural diversity are defining features of the educational landscape, sociotechnical approaches help illuminate how AI may reproduce or challenge existing inequities. By combining the micro-level insights of TTI with the macro-level analysis of sociotechnical theory, this study provides a comprehensive framework for understanding AI's role in classrooms.

Despite the growing literature on AI in higher education (Barragán-Torres, 2022; Tudino & Qin, 2024; Zawacki-Richter et al., 2019), research in K–12 remains fragmented (Lavidas et al., 2022a, 2022b; Papadakis et al., 2024a, 2024b). Few studies provide in-depth analyses of how AI reshapes teacher–student interactions in primary and secondary schools, especially outside Anglo-American contexts. The absence of robust empirical research in Latin America constitutes a significant gap in literature. By situating Chile alongside Spain, this chapter not only contributes to filling this gap but also challenges dominant narratives that often generalize from Global North experiences.

To ensure analytic coherence, the research questions directly guide the structure of results and discussion. This responds to calls for clarity in comparative AI-in-education studies (Matos et al., 2025). To frame the study, this chapter is guided by the following research questions (RQs):

- RQ1: How are AI tools currently being integrated into K–12 classrooms in Chile and Spain, and what similarities or differences can be observed?
- RQ2: How do teachers perceive the impact of AI on the three TTI domains: emotional support, classroom organization, and instructional support?
- RQ3: What systemic, institutional, cultural, and policy factors facilitate or hinder responsible AI integration?
- RQ4: How can insights from Chile and Spain inform broader discussions or strategies about equity, pedagogy, and ethics in AI mediated education?

The objectives of this study, aligned with these research questions, are threefold:

1. To analyze how K–12 teachers in Chile and Spain integrate AI-powered tools into classroom practice, particularly in relation to the three TTI domains.

2. To identify similarities and differences in teacher preparedness, attitudes, and competencies between the two contexts.
3. To formulate recommendations for educators, institutions, and policymakers on how to responsibly integrate AI to promote equity, quality, and relational pedagogy.

This study contributes to literature in at least four ways. First, it extends the TTI framework into the-field of AI-mediated education. Second, it bridges micro-level relational processes with macro-level governance debates, offering a synthesis of TTI and sociotechnical theory. Third, it provides empirical insights from two culturally related but institutionally distinct contexts. Fourth, it translates these insights into actionable recommendations for teachers, institutions, and policymakers (Fonseca et al., 2024).

Methodologically, the study adopts a comparative mixed-methods design, combining survey data, classroom observations, and teacher interviews. Quantitative data allow statistical comparisons, while qualitative data provide deeper insights into lived experiences.

This chapter is significant for several reasons. First, it extends the TTI framework, into AI-mediated education. Second, it foregrounds the relational dimension of teaching, countering discourses that reduce AI to technical efficiency. Third, by examining two culturally related but institutionally distinct contexts —Chile and Spain— it offers comparative insights valuable for both Global South and European education systems. Finally, it responds to urgent debates about the ethical and pedagogical implications of AI, providing recommendations grounded in classroom realities.

In summary, the introduction establishes the rationale, objectives, and significance of the study. It positions AI not as a neutral innovation but as a phenomenon that intersects with pedagogy, governance, and culture. By adopting TTI and sociotechnical perspectives, this chapter seeks to illuminate how AI reshapes teacher–student interactions in ways that are contingent on context, policy, and practice.

2. THEORETICAL FRAMEWORK: TEACHING THROUGH INTERACTIONS (TTI) IN AI-MEDIATED EDUCATION

2.1. The Teaching Through Interactions (TTI) framework

The *Teaching Through Interactions (TTI)* framework emerged from decades of research on effective teaching, particularly the seminal work of Pianta and colleagues (Hamre et al., 2013; Pianta, 2016; Pianta & Hofkens, 2023). It was designed to move beyond narrow definitions of teacher effectiveness that equate success with standardized test scores, focusing instead on the quality of daily teacher–student interactions. TTI posits that these interactions form the primary mechanism through which learning and development occur in classrooms, regardless of subject matter or curriculum.

The TTI model identifies three interrelated domains that constitute effective teaching:

1. Emotional Support: The ways in which teachers create a climate of respect, empathy, and responsiveness to students' socioemotional needs. Emotional support fosters motivation, engagement, and resilience, especially for students from disadvantaged backgrounds.
2. Classroom Organization: The teacher's ability to manage time, behavior, and attention in ways that optimize learning opportunities. Effective classroom organization ensures that students remain focused, that transitions are smooth, and that learning environments are structured without being overly rigid.
3. Instructional Support: The provision of cognitively stimulating instruction, feedback that extends learning, and scaffolding that promotes conceptual understanding. Instructional support goes beyond rote memorization, encouraging critical thinking and problem solving.

TTI has been validated across thousands of classrooms in diverse countries, including the United States, Finland, and Chile (Barragán-Torres, 2022; Hamre et al., 2013). Its versatility lies in focusing on observable patterns of interaction, which can be coded and assessed with reliability. Importantly, TTI is not prescriptive; it provides a developmental framework adaptable to multiple pedagogical traditions.

2.2. Extending TTI to AI-mediated classrooms

The acceleration of digital transformation and the emergence of AI tools in education demand an extension of TTI to new contexts. While originally developed for analog classrooms (Burchinal et al., 2016), TTI's emphasis on observable interactional patterns makes it adaptable to technologically mediated learning environments (Holmes et al., 2022; Holstein et al., 2019). Recent studies (Lampropoulos & Papadakis, 2025; Luckin, 2022) argue that TTI is particularly useful in AI contexts, as it foregrounds relational dynamics often overshadowed by technological determinism:

- Emotional Support and AI: In AI-mediated classrooms, emotional support faces both opportunities and threats. On one hand, chatbots and AI tutors can provide immediate responses, reducing frustration (Alemdag, 2023; Yue et al., 2021). On the other, they lack genuine empathy, potentially displacing teacher attention. Research shows that while students may appreciate AI support, they consistently value human connection for motivation and belonging (Akgun & Greenhow, 2022).

- Classroom Organization with analytics: AI-powered dashboards can help teachers manage large groups by identifying disengaged students or predicting learning difficulties (Matos et al., 2025). These systems can optimize time and resources, yet they may also intensify surveillance and reduce autonomy if misused (Lekan & Pardos, 2025). TTI provides a way to analyze whether classroom organization is enhanced or constrained by AI.
- Instructional Support via adaptive systems: Intelligent Tutoring Systems (ITS) can differentiate instruction, providing tailored exercises and feedback (VanLehn, 2011). Yet their effectiveness depends heavily on teacher interpretation and integration into broader pedagogy (Leyva et al., 2015; Luckin, 2022). TTI highlights how AI can supplement teacher instruction but cannot replace the intentional scaffolding of human educators (Rundquist et al., 2024).

This extension of TTI underscores that AI reshapes but does not eliminate the teacher's central role. Instead, teachers and AI systems operate in complementarity, with teachers remaining the architects of emotional and pedagogical meaning (Kapoor & Bakhshi, 2025).

2.3. A sociotechnical perspective on AI in education

While TTI captures classroom-level processes, a sociotechnical perspective adds a systemic lens, situating those interactions within broader structures of governance, culture, and power. Sociotechnical theory holds that technologies are not neutral. but shaped by design choices, institutional contexts, and cultural expectations (Williamson, 2024).

Three dimensions are particularly salient:

1. Equity and Access: AI tools rely on digital infrastructure. In Chile, the rural–urban divide means many schools cannot fully implement AI platforms (Barragán-Torres, 2022). Spain has stronger infrastructure, but inequities remain across autonomous communities. From a sociotechnical point of view, AI amplifies existing divides unless explicitly addressed.
2. Governance and Accountability: AI systems often collect massive amounts of student data, raising privacy and accountability issues (Luckin et al., 2016). Teachers may be pressured to rely on opaque algorithms for decisions, reducing

their agency. By contrast, strong governance frameworks —such as the EU's General Data Protection Regulation, GDPR— can provide safeguards, though implementation varies.

3. Cultural Relevance: AI systems designed in Global North may embed assumptions that clash with local pedagogical traditions (Molina et al., 2024). In Latin America, where critical pedagogy emphasizes relationality and social justice, imported AI systems risk misalignment. TTI offers a tool to assess whether AI-mediated interactions align with or diverge from these traditions.

In line with the book's scope and the contexts where interventions took place, we explicitly foreground ethics as a cross-cutting condition for AI adoption. Ethical use involves: (a) data protection and informed consent in any data-driven teaching or research activities; (b) human oversight over automated recommendations that could affect students' opportunities; (c) fairness audits to detect potential bias against vulnerable groups; and (d) transparency and explainability proportional to the stakes of classroom decisions. In the schools studied, we therefore treat ethics as institutional infrastructure for relational pedagogy, not merely a legal checklist.

Furthermore, in terms of recent systematic reviews and empirical studies, a growing body of reviews underscores the need to study AI in schools through relational and contextual lenses. For example, Molina et al. (2024) and Zawacki-Richter et al. (2019) show that most AI-in-education research remains exploratory, with limited attention to teacher–student dynamics. Singh & Phoolka (2025) and Wang & Chuang (2024) highlight teacher readiness as a key determinant of success, while Matos et al. (2025) stress the institutional and policy scaffolding required for sustainable integration.

Other studies have examined specific aspects:

- Formative assessment: Molina et al. (2024) show how AI-driven formative assessment supports learning but risks standardization.
- Learning analytics: Singh & Phoolka (2025) argue that analytics are most effective when teachers are trained to interpret results critically.
- Equity concerns: Lekan & Pardos (2025) emphasize that AI can exacerbate inequities unless designed with fairness in mind.
- Teacher professional development: Kapoor & Bakhshi (2025) show that "AI-ready" teacher development is crucial to balance automation with pedagogy.
- Methodological cautions: Lavidas et al. (2022a, 2022b) highlight social desirability in self-reports and response-rate issues in teacher web surveys—alerts we incorporate by triangulating surveys with observations/interviews.
- The work of Lampropoulos & Papadakis (2025) on social robots directly aligns with TTI's Emotional Support domain.

The combination of TTI and sociotechnical theory creates a multilayered framework capable of addressing both micro-level classroom processes and macro-level governance structures (Xu, 2024; Yang, 2024). At the micro level, TTI illuminates how interactions shift when AI intervenes in daily routines. For example, a teacher using an adaptive mathematics platform may spend less time providing one-on-one feedback but might redirect energy toward interpreting AI dashboards and offering group-level clarification. At the meso level, sociotechnical theory highlights how schools and districts set policies around AI, such as the degree to which teachers are required to adopt specific platforms. Finally, at the macro level, global governance frameworks shape norms for AI adoption that cascade into national systems (Matos et al., 2025).

This integrated lens also helps avoid deterministic views of AI as inherently beneficial or harmful. Instead, it allows for contextualized assessments. For instance, in Chile, where teachers often operate with limited institutional support, AI platforms can provide valuable scaffolding but may also overburden teachers if not matched with professional development. In Spain, institutional scaffolding is stronger, but rigid policy mandates sometimes constrain teacher autonomy.

Beyond technical affordances, AI raises ethical issues directly relevant to TTI domains. Emotional support may be compromised if students feel surveilled or reduced to data points. Classroom organization may shift from collaborative structures to algorithmically guided routines. Instructional support may be enriched but also homogenized if AI systems impose standardized pathways (Pozdniakov et al., 2025).

Recent scholarship emphasizes the need for trustworthy AI in education (Holmes et al., 2022). Trustworthiness includes transparency in algorithms, accountability for decisions, and safeguarding student data. Importantly, it also includes relational trust: students and teachers must believe that AI enhances rather than undermines their interactions. Wiese et al. (2025) argue that AI ethics education should be embedded in teacher training, enabling educators to critically evaluate tools before integrating them.

From a TTI perspective, this means that AI should be evaluated not only for efficiency but for how it affects warmth, sensitivity, engagement, and feedback quality (Xu, 2024; Yang, 2024). Relational pedagogy requires that AI complement human presence, not diminish it. In this sense, Chile and Spain provide rich comparative ground for applying this integrated framework (Matos et al., 2025):

- Chile: Digital divides remain prominent, with rural areas experiencing connectivity challenges (Leyva et al., 2015; Matos et al., 2025). Teachers often innovate autonomously, adopting tools like learning analytics platforms in isolated ways. Emotional support is deeply embedded in Chilean pedagogical traditions, shaped by critical and humanistic perspectives, which means that teachers may be more skeptical of tools perceived as mechanistic.

- Spain: Institutional scaffolding is stronger due to EU frameworks like DigCompEdu (European Commission, 2020) and UNESCO collaborations. Teachers benefit from structured digital competence assessments and professional development opportunities. However, bureaucratic mandates sometimes result in adoption driven by compliance rather than pedagogical conviction. Spanish educators have raised concerns about workload, ethical dilemmas, and the sustainability of integration without continuous training (UNESCO, 2023).

To refine TTI for AI-mediated contexts, we propose extending its three domains:

1. AI-Enhanced Emotional Support: Teachers must navigate the balance between machine responsiveness and authentic empathy. This requires not only awareness of AI's limitations but strategies to leverage AI for reducing workload so teachers can focus on human connection.
2. AI-Driven Classroom Organization: Algorithms can help anticipate disruptions and manage large groups, but organizational effectiveness must be judged by whether it promotes engagement and autonomy rather than compliance and control.
3. Augmented Instructional Support: AI can generate adaptive pathways, but teachers must contextualize and enrich these with cultural and disciplinary knowledge. Instructional support is not simply about "efficiency" but about cultivating deep learning.

These refinements ensure that TTI remains relevant in AI contexts without losing its relational grounding. The theoretical framework adopted in this study thus synthesizes TTI's micro-level relational focus with sociotechnical theory's macro-level systemic lens (Xu, 2024). This synthesis allows us to examine not only whether AI "works" but how it reshapes the core relational fabric of schooling. For Chile, this means examining how resource constraints and humanistic pedagogies influence the adoption of AI tools, and whether they strengthen or weaken relational practices. For Spain, it means investigating how institutional frameworks facilitate or constrain meaningful use of AI, and how teacher autonomy interacts with policy mandates.

2.4. Critical synthesis: A relational and sociotechnical framework for AI in K–12 education

The combined TTI–sociotechnical lens provides the conceptual scaffolding to evaluate how AI reshapes classroom life and under what conditions those changes enhance (rather than erode) equitable teaching–learning relations (Hadas & Hershkovitz, 2025). TTI keeps the analytical focus on the quality of interactions, while sociotechnical theory situates those interactions within the structural constraints and affordances of policy, infrastructure, market logics, and culture. Read together, both lenses move the analysis beyond the question of whether AI "works" in aggregate, and toward the more policy-relevant question of for whom, in which contexts, and at what relational and ethical costs (Molina et al., 2024).

In Chile, resource asymmetries and humanistic pedagogical traditions co-exist with teacher-led innovation. This creates fertile ground for context-sensitive appropriation of AI but also heightens the risk of fragmentation and unequal benefits if adoption proceeds without institutional support, professional development, and explicit ethical guardrails. In Spain, stronger institutional scaffolding—EU frameworks, regional programs, and competency models—reduces fragmentation but may inadvertently tilt practice toward compliance-driven usage, with potential effects on teacher autonomy and the texture of classroom interactions if metrics and dashboards acquire undue normative force (Yang, 2024). Across both cases, the value of AI is inseparable from the relational conditions under which it is deployed: students' trust and psychological safety (Emotional Support), fair and non-coercive monitoring (Classroom Organization), and culturally responsive scaffolding (Instructional Support).

In addition, ethics is not external add-on but a precondition for relational quality. Data minimization and informed consent protect students' dignity and sustain emotional safety; explainability and human oversight anchor legitimate organization of the classroom; bias detection and equitable access enable just instructional pathways (Tang & Zhang, 2023). In practical terms, we treat ethics as operational infrastructure that enables TTI domains to flourish in AI-rich environments (Xu, 2024; Yang, 2024).

This critical synthesis answers the call to foreground ethics in the very heart of the framework, and it also clarifies how local insights (Chile, Spain) contribute to the global discourse on AI-powered instruction in K–12: the same tool can expand or constrain relational pedagogy depending on equity of access, governance quality, and professional agency (Tang & Zhang, 2023).

The theoretical commitments above inform the research design in three concrete ways. First, ethical safeguards are designed-in: procedures for informed consent, data minimization, and pseudonymization; explicit human oversight over any automated recommendations discussed by participants; and documentation of risk mitigation (bias checks where applicable). Second, the TTI focus on observable interactions justifies the mixed-methods approach: (i) quantitative (comparative descriptives, inferences with confidence intervals and effect sizes, boxplots for dispersion and asymmetries), and (ii) qualitative (interviews/observations) to capture relational experience beyond what metrics alone can provide.

In sum, this relational and sociotechnical framework not only guides the interpretation of AI-mediated teacher–student interactions but also structures the methodological choices and analytical. pathways of the study, ensuring coherence between theory, evidence, and recommendations. Bringing these perspectives together, we propose a relational and sociotechnical framework that guides both analysis and methodology. Building on this relational and sociotechnical framework, the next section details the methodological design that operationalizes these concepts in Chile and Spain.

3. METHODOLOGY

3.1. Description of comparative case study design

The integration of AI-in educational settings has gained momentum in Chile and Spain. Both Chile and Spain's strategies emphasize the importance of maintaining the human element in education while enhancing teacher capabilities through AI, ultimately positioning these countries as leaders in educational innovation amidst a rapidly evolving technological landscape (Buckingham Shum & Ferguson, 2012; Pianta, 2016).

These nations are exploring frameworks and strategies to facilitate the effective use of AI tools by K-12 teachers to enhance teaching and learning experiences. In Europe, initiatives like the European Commission's Digital Education Action Plan (2021–2027) have accelerated AI adoption through funding, professional development, and curriculum reform. Spain, benefiting from this ecosystem, has piloted nationwide programs including AI in secondary mathematics and primary literacy. In contrast, Latin American countries such as Chile have taken a more decentralized, often grassroots, approach. Programs like 'Enlaces' and 'Red de Tutores' have experimented with AI and blended learning platforms, but regional disparities persist, particularly between urban and rural zones. Notably, initiatives such as Chile's "HumanIA" program and Spain's "IGNITE Copilot" illustrate the countries' commitment to empowering educators with AI resources tailored to their unique educational contexts (Akgun & Greenhow, 2022; Anderson et al., 1995).

Both nations are exploring various frameworks to guide the effective use of AI in classrooms, including the Technological Pedagogical Content Knowledge

(TPACK) model and the Substitute, Augmentation, Modification, and Redefinition (SAMR) model. While these frameworks are essential for integrating technology into pedagogy, they often present challenges regarding accessibility and practicality for teachers (Akgun & Greenhow, 2022; Becker & Park, 2011; Pianta, 2016). To bridge this gap, the AI-Class framework has been developed in Chile to support educators' daily practices effectively, reflecting a growing recognition of the need for structured guidance in AI adoption (Akgun & Greenhow, 2022).

Thus, this chapter focuses on two culturally connected but institutionally distinct contexts: Chile and Spain. The choice to compare Chile and Spain stems from their shared linguistic and cultural roots, which allow for meaningful comparisons, alongside key differences in their educational policies, technological infrastructures, and AI-readiness (Schmid et al., 2014; Varghese et al., 2019). Both countries share a common language and cultural heritage, yet they diverge significantly in educational governance, resource distribution, and digital maturity.

A comparative approach allows us to surface context-sensitive insights into implementing AI in K–12 settings, beyond generalizations about technological potential. In this line, Chile, representing the Global South is notable for bottom-up innovations like Elige Educar's UmmIA and Somos Profes programs that leverage AI chatbots and content tools in resource-constrained systems. Spain, a European Union member, offers a top-down policy-driven integration of AI within a structured digital competency framework (DIGCOMP), showing how formal governance can influence AI uptake. By comparing these contexts, this study uncovers context-sensitive strategies for professional, development, curriculum co-design, and inclusive AI deployment in K–12 classrooms.

The comparative case study design is not limited to describing policy frameworks; it explicitly analyzes how classroom-level interactions (measured via the TTI framework) are conditioned by systemic factors such as infrastructure, governance, and teacher training. This consideration strengthens methodological execution by linking micro-level observations with macro-level conditions.

3.2. School selection criteria in Chile and Spain

This study employed a comparative case study methodology to investigate the integration of AI tools in K–12 classrooms. This design is well-suited for capturing contextual depth, revealing differences and similarities between national systems, and generating theoretically grounded inferences through cross-case synthesis (Miller & Robertson, 2010; Wang et al., 2024; Woolf, 2008).

Each case comprised three schools selected for their ongoing engagement with AI tools in teaching. Within-case and cross-case analyses were conducted to identify patterns aligned with the TTI framework. Schools were selected using purposive sampling, guided by three inclusion criteria:

1. Active use of at least one AI-powered educational tool (e.g., Snappet, MATE+, chatbot tutors).
2. Mixed school types (public, semi-private, and private).
3. Geographic and demographic diversity (urban, peri-urban, and rural contexts).

To operationalize this comparative design, schools in both Chile and Spain were selected based on clear criteria of AI engagement. Selection was not random but purposive, intended to maximize variation and ensure comparability across contexts. This sampling logic increases external validity by capturing diverse experiences of AI integration while remaining manageable for in-depth qualitative and quantitative analysis.

3.3. Participants

This design enabled exploration of how similar technologies manifest across culturally and institutionally distinct contexts. Six schools were purposefully selected—three in Chile (Santiago, Valparaíso, and Temuco) and three in Spain (Madrid, Barcelona, and Valencia). A total of 120 students participated: 60 students from three Chilean public schools (urban and semi-urban) and 60 students from three Spanish schools (two semi-private, one public).

Ten teachers also participated (five per country, across subjects and levels, approximately one to two per school), selected for their AI integration experience and willingness to participate. Students ranged from Grade 5 to Grade 10.

Parental consent and ethical clearance were obtained according to the country's institutional review requirements. In Spain, this process followed GDPR and school board approval. In Chile, ethics approval came via Ministry of Education pilot programs. Participation was voluntary, and all responses were anonymized. Students and teachers were assured of their right to withdraw at any time without penalty. These measures ensured compliance with ethical standards and reinforced the trustworthiness of findings.

3.4. Instruments

Having outlined the sample, we now turn to the instruments used to collect data across both contexts. Three instruments were used, combined to ensure triangulation and validity:

1. Semi-structured interviews with teachers to gain qualitative insights into their experiences, limitations, challenges, and strategies. Interview questions were aligned to TTI domains to ensure theoretical consistency. The interviews explored:
   - Motivations and barriers to AI use.
   - Perceived changes in classroom interaction.
   - Support mechanisms and training experiences.
2. Structured questionnaires for students, to assess familiarity, frequency, and perceived impact of AI tools:
   - Frequency of AI-tool use.
   - Perceived impact on learning (that is, perceived effectiveness and satisfaction).
   - Emotional engagement with AI tools.
   - Trust and transparency in AI processes.

Structured questionnaires with 15 items across 3 domains included the following domains: Emotional Support, Classroom Organization, and Instructional Support using a 5-point Likert scale (1 = Strongly Disagree, 5 = Strongly Agree). Items were grouped into: Emotional Support (e.g., "My teacher uses AI to support how I feel in class."), Classroom Organization (e.g., "AI helps my teacher keep things organized."), and Instructional Support (e.g., "I understand class material better with AI assistance."). Internal consistency was high (Cronbach's $\alpha = 0.84$).

Questionnaires were administered via tablet (Chile) and web-based portal (Spain), with voluntary and anonymized participation, aligned with GDPR and Chilean ethics protocols. The frequency distributions of responses were also analyzed to gain insight into the data characteristics given that the sample did not follow a normal distribution. All AI-assisted analyses maintained human oversight, and no identifiable data were shared externally.

3. Classroom Observations used TTI-based rubric to identify behavioral patterns and interactional quality. Two 45-minute field observations were conducted in each school, using TTI-based rubric adapted from the CLASS framework. Researchers noted how AI tools influenced real-time teacher-student interaction, group dynamics, and instructional pacing in AI tool sessions (e.g., virtual tutor use, lesson generator deployment). Coding followed a TTI matrix, and AI usage logs (sessions, time on task) were collected where available to complement observational. data.

3.5. Research Design and Analytical Strategy

This study employed a quasi-experimental, comparative cross-national design, in Chile and Spain. The rationale for focusing on these two contexts is threefold:

1. Cultural and linguistic commonality. Both countries share Spanish as the instructional language, facilitating comparability of instruments and reducing confounding variables.
2. Policy divergence. Spain benefits from EU-aligned strategies (e.g., *DigCompEdu*, *Digital Education Action Plan 2021–2027*), while Chile exemplifies decentralized innovation amid persistent resource inequalities.
3. Educational governance contrast. Chile's mixed public–private system and Spain's EU-integrated framework allow examination of how governance shapes classroom-level AI adoption.

The research explored how AI tools shape the three core relational domains. The TTI framework-served as the analytical lens for coding and interpretation in this case. Mixed-methods research is particularly suited for AI-in-education studies because it allows researchers to capture both the statistical patterns of teacher and student perceptions and the interactional nuances of classroom practices (Papadakis et al., 2023b; Wang et al., 2025). This combination enhances validity through triangulation and supports the contextualized understanding required by cross-national comparisons (Possaghi et al., 2025).

We analyzed data using comparative thematic coding for qualitative responses and descriptive statistics for quantitative survey data. MAXQDA and SPSS were used for textual and numerical data analysis (O'Neil & Schutt, 2013).

Within-case analysis was conducted first to identify themes specific to Chilean and Spanish contexts. Then, a cross-case matrix compared findings in relation to each TTI domain. Patterns were triangulated across domains to strengthen validity. Cross-case matrix was developed to identify contrasts between Chilean and Spanish classrooms (Dellepiane & Guidi, 2023; Feng et al., 2009; Means et al., 2009).

In terms of validity and limitations, to enhance credibility, triangulation across instruments and multiple data was used. Findings were validated through multiple sources: (i) survey data, (ii) interview insights, (iii) observation rubrics, and (iv) AI usage logs. This methodological triangulation reduces bias from self-reports (Lavidas et al., 2022a, 2022b). Regarding ethics, safeguards included pseudonymization of all records, encrypted data storage, restricted access, debriefing of teachers, and plain-language summaries for guardians. For transferability, descriptions of each classroom and socio-institutional context are provided in the analysis sections (VanLehn, 2011).

For quantitative analysis, descriptive statistics (mean, standard deviation, min/max) and TTI domain correlations were calculated. Boxplots allowed cross-country comparison, and independent-samples t-tests (Welch's and Mann–Whitney U) assessed mean differences in TTI domains. Significance thresholds were set at $p < 0.05$ and 0.01. This analysis was reinforced by: (i) aligning instruments with the TTI framework; (ii) confirming reliability through Cronbach's α and inter-observer agreement ($\kappa = 0.81$); and (iii) triangulating surveys, interviews, and observations (Molina et al., 2024; Tang & Zhang, 2023).

4. RESULTS AND FINDINGS

To understand the pedagogical and relational implications of AI tools in K–12 settings across Chile and Spain, this study employed a mixed-methods research design grounded in the Teaching Through Interactions (TTI) framework. Each data source was analyzed through the three core TTI domains: Emotional Support, Classroom Organization, and Instructional Support. Each research question (RQ) is addressed through both qualitative and quantitative evidence, supported by comparative case studies, survey data, classroom observations, and statistical analysis.

4.1. RQ1 – How are AI tools being integrated into K–12 classrooms in Chile and Spain?

In this research, AI implementation has been illustrated through case studies across schools in Chile and Spain. Both contexts have adopted AI-driven platforms that personalize learning, particularly in special education. These platforms analyze student progress, enabling teachers to monitor engagement and adjust instruction accordingly. Reports indicate increased engagement and learning outcomes, though challenges remain regarding equity and ethics (Baker & Inventado, 2014; Carella et al., 2024).

In Chile, localized initiatives include UmmIA for lesson planning, which reduces teacher preparation time but requires adaptation to student needs. In Spain, projects such as IGNITE Copilot have mapped vocational. training curricula, aligning AI with national frameworks and ensuring integration with regulations (Anderson et al., 1995; Demszky et al., 2023).

Case studies

Six illustrative case studies describe real-world AI implementation. Each emphasizes how teacher–student interactions are shaped by AI through TTI.

Case A: Chile – Escuela Pública Providencia (Santiago)

In this urban public school, the AI assistant UmmIA was introduced to support lesson planning and formative assessments. Teachers adapted UmmIA's pre-built lesson templates but frequently edited them to accommodate local student needs. One 8th-grade math teacher explained:

"UmmIA suggests a structure, but I always tweak it. I use AI to free up my time—not to replace my thinking."

Students reported benefits such as instant feedback from AI-generated quizzes but expressed frustration when the chatbot misinterpreted open-ended answers. The most effective instructional. configuration combined AI scaffolding with real-time teacher conferencing, reinforcing both Instructional Support and Emotional Presence.

Case B: Chile – Liceo Bicentenario Diego Portales (Valparaiso)

Through a municipal partnership, this public high school implemented a localized version of Khan Academy to support remedial math instruction. The platform's adaptive learning engine identified concept gaps and adjusted pacing in real time. However, meaningful gains only occurred when teachers conducted short weekly conferences with struggling students.

"The algorithm catches when a student is struggling, but only I can know why." — 7th Grade Teacher.

This configuration demonstrated how AI can strengthen Instructional Support by providing structure, while teacher input maintained the contextual relevance and emotional care that students require.

Case C: Chile – Escuela Rural Futuro Aprendiz (pseudonym, Temuco)

In this rural, educational context, early literacy instruction was supported by SmartPal, an AI-based speech recognition tool designed to provide real-time feedback on phoneme pronunciation and reading fluency. Initially, students responded enthusiastically to the interactive platform, which encouraged autonomous reading practice.

However, some students reported that the AI failed to recognize culturally specific pronunciation patterns tied to Mapuche Spanish variants.

"It said my pronunciation was wrong, but that's how we speak at home." — 3rd Grade Student.

Teachers intervened by modifying tool parameters and supplementing AI feedback with culturally responsive oral reading sessions. This dual approach proved crucial in preserving Emotional Support and student confidence while reinforcing Instructional Support through targeted phonemic reinforcement.

The case illustrates the limitations of AI in diverse linguistic contexts and the critical importance of teacher mediation to bridge cultural gaps—a core tenet of the TTI framework's emphasis on responsive interaction.

Case D: Spain – Colegio Internacional Ausiàs March (Valencia)

This semi-private bilingual school has incorporated AI-powered predictive dashboards and adaptive learning platforms into its science and language instruction. These systems help teachers identify students at risk of academic underperformance by analyzing participation data, assessment trends, and pacing patterns.

"The AI tells me who might need help next week. I use that info in planning small groups." — Science Teacher.

Despite the use of automated tools, students emphasized the continued presence and concern of their teachers:

"The teacher still checks on me—AI just helps her do that faster." — 8th Grade Student.

This case illustrates how AI can strengthen Classroom Organization while maintaining relational dynamics when educators retain final interpretive control. It aligns with the TTI framework by showing that data-driven AI tools, when thoughtfully integrated, can optimize learning logistics without undermining Emotional Support or teacher authority.

Case E: Spain – IES Pablo Neruda (Madrid)

This public secondary school used FeedbackBot, an AI module within Moodle, to support essay writing in humanities. The bot provided automated feedback on grammar and argument structure, while final grading and feedback were personalized by the teacher.

"I correct things before my teacher even sees them. But she still reads my thoughts." — 10th Grade Student.

Teachers reported that this reduced their workload and allowed them to focus on higher-order feedback, boosting Instructional Support without sacrificing personalization.

Case F: Spain – Escola Sagrada Família (Barcelona)

A unique innovation in this school was the integration of EmoTrack, a sentiment-analysis AI tool used for mental health screening. Based on written journal entries and interaction patterns, EmoTrack flagged students potentially experiencing emotional distress. These alerts were never acted on automatically—instead, but they triggered confidential teacher follow-up sessions.

"It helps me notice sooner. But the listening—that's still mine." — School Counselor.

This ethical implementation of AI directly supported Emotional Support within the TTI framework, while reinforcing the teacher's role as a trusted relational figure.

- To sum up, predictive and adaptive tools (Valparaiso, Valencia, Madrid) improved Classroom Organization, but only with human follow-up.

Table 1 shows the case studies related to classroom implementations of AI tools across Chile and Spain. Each case highlights the AI tool used, the TTI domain enhanced, the teacher's role, and a student quote capturing their experience.

Table 1. Case studies related to classroom implementations of AI tools

School Location	**AI Tool Used**	**Primary TTI Domain Enhanced**	**Teacher Role**	**Student Quote**
Providencia (Santiago)	UmmIA	Instructional Support	Instructional Adjuster	AI quizzes helped me see mistakes instantly.
Valparaíso	Khan Academy (local)	Instructional Support	Remedial Mediator	The algorithm catches when I'm struggling.
Temuco – Escuela Futuro Aprendiz	SmartPal	Emotional Support	Cultural Mediator	That's how we speak at home.
Valencia – Colegio Ausiàs March	Predictive Dashboards	Classroom Organization	Planner/ Orchestrator	The teacher still checks on me.
Madrid	FeedbackBot (Moodle)	Instructional Support	Feedback Curator	She still reads my thoughts.
Barcelona	EmoTrack	Emotional Support	Emotional Follower-Up	The listening—that's still mine.

Across these six case studies, several key patterns emerge:

- AI is most effective when scaffolding teacher practices, not replacing it.
- Instructional Support was most enhanced when AI was embedded in formative assessment.
- Cultural adaptation (Temuco) and ethical deployment (Barcelona) were essential to Emotional Support.
- Predictive and adaptive tools (Valparaiso, Valencia, Madrid) improved Classroom Organization, but only when human follow-up.

Together, these findings directly address RQ1 by demonstrating that integration is shaped by context: institutional frameworks in Spain versus localized teacher adaptation in Chile. Teacher agency and context-sensitive implementation were the strongest predictors of success.

In sum, the findings show that AI works best when it scaffolds teacher practices, not when it substitutes them. Instructional Support was the most consistently enhanced domain, while Emotional Support remained highly dependent on teacher mediation. Importantly, cultural and ethical adaptations were critical enablers. Based on these case studies, the main findings on AI Tool Integration in K-12 Education using the TTI framework in Chile and Spain are exposed in Table 2.

Table 2. Comparative analysis: Chile vs. Spain in AI tool integration

TTI Dimension	Chile	Spain
Emotional. Support	AI chatbots used to supplement SEL (Social Emotional Learning), but under-resourced rural schools lag in implementation.	More institutionalized SEL programs using AI to track emotional metrics (e.g., mood surveys).
Classroom Organization	Limited bandwidth and ICT infrastructure affect tool reliability; teachers often use mobile-based apps.	Classroom LMS integration is stronger; more frequent use of predictive analytics in behavior tracking.
Instructional Support	Adaptive platforms like MATE+ used in math instruction; still reliant on traditional forms of feedback.	More mature integration of AI-based virtual tutors (e.g., Snappet, Cerebriti); greater experimentation with flipped models.

4.2. RQ2 – How do students and teachers perceive the impact of AI tools on the quality of teacher–student interactions?

To further contextualize the empirical results, a condensed set of survey highlights offers a comparative snapshot of AI tool usage and perceptions in Chile and Spain (Table 3).

First, the weekly frequency of AI tool use differs markedly: Spanish teachers report an average of 4.5 sessions per week, more than double the Chilean average of 2.1 sessions. This disparity suggests not only broader infrastructure support in Spain but also greater institutional normalization of AI-enhanced instruction.

Second, teacher satisfaction with AI tools, measured on a 5-point Likert scale, reveals perceptual divide: 3.2 in Chile versus 4.1 in Spain. Spanish educators generally viewed AI as a planning and differentiation aid that amplified their teaching efficacy. Chilean teachers, while intrigued by the potential of AI, expressed frustrations with limited customization, generic content, and lack of training. As one Chilean teacher noted, “The tool works, but it doesn’t feel made for my class”.

Third, Spanish teachers estimated 78% active engagement, compared to 61% in Chile.

Finally, the metric of teacher confidence in integrating AI tools—reported as "Moderate" in Chile and "High" in Spain. Spanish teachers frequently described themselves as "pilots" of AI, whereas Chilean teachers more often described themselves as "testers" or "adapters," revealing a mindset shaped by resource scarcity and implementation uncertainty.

Table 3. Survey highlights

Metric	Chile (avg.)	Spain (avg.)
AI tool usage frequency (weekly)	2.1 sessions	4.5 sessions
Teacher satisfaction (1-5 scale)	3.2	4.1
Perceived student engagement (%)	61%	78%
Confidence in integrating AI tools	Moderate	High

The comparative analysis revealed notable differences and commonalities in how AI tools are being integrated in three main areas (Carella et al., 2024; Molina et al., 2024):

1. Systemic Conditions. AI-supported teacher training. In contrast, Chile lacks a centralized policy on AI in education. Initiatives like 'Enlaces' and 'ProFuturo Chile' provide some infrastructure, but deployment remains uneven (ProFuturo Foundation, 2022).
2. Teacher Readiness. Teachers in Spain reported higher confidence in using AI tools. Spanish educators also highlighted the role of peer collaboration and district-level mentoring programs. Chilean teachers, while highly motivated, often expressed uncertainty due to inconsistent training and limited access to expert support.
3. Student Engagement. Students in Spain displayed higher levels of digital fluency and described AI tools as engaging. In Chile, student experiences varied widely depending on school resources. In urban schools, students expressed excitement, whereas students in rural areas often experienced offline or asynchronous methods.

Thus, findings demonstrate that the quality of teacher–student interaction in AI-enhanced classrooms depends not merely on tool availability, but on how tools are embedded into relational, organizational, and instructional practices.

Quantitative analysis

Regarding the descriptive statistics overview, data shows that Spain outperforms Chile in all three domains regarding mean scores.

This comparative study offers compelling evidence that the integration of AI tools significantly influences student perceptions of teacher-student interactions across all three domains of the Teaching Through Interactions (TTI) framework: we find consistent and statistically significant differences between the two national contexts.

The domain of Instructional Support garnered the highest scores overall, with Spain (M = 4.51) significantly outperforming Chile (M = 4.22, $p < .001$). This suggests that in both settings, AI tools—when deployed effectively—act as cognitive amplifiers, assisting teachers in providing immediate feedback, adaptive pathways, and concept clarity. This is consistent with literature on institutional support scaffolding AI efficacy (Holstein et al., 2019; Selwyn, 2019; Traoré, 2024).

AI was perceived as an effective aid in classroom management, with students recognizing that tools helped "keep track of tasks," "organize assignments," and even "group us for projects". Again, Spain scored significantly higher (M = 4.45) than Chile (M = 4.15, $p < .01$). This suggests that AI's predictive and scheduling capacities are most impactful when embedded in cohesive classroom workflows (Gobierno de España, 2021). In contrast, Chilean educators often reported infrastructural inconsistencies, leading to fragmented implementation (Morrell, 2008; Wang & Xue, 2024).

The most revealing contrast emerged in Emotional Support: Spain (M = 4.41) vs. Chile (M = 4.07, $p < .001$). These findings align with broader concerns in AI ethics: that AI lacks empathy and must not replace human relational labor (Akgun & Greenhow, 2022; Luckin et al., 2016; Luckin, 2022).

Table 4. Descriptive statistics (quantitative study, students by country)

	Chile			Spain			Total
TTI Domain	**Mean (Std)**	**Min**	**Max**	**Mean (Std)**	**Min**	**Max**	
Classroom Organization	4.15 (0.185)	3.63	4.64	4.45 (0.209)	3.8	4.88	60
Emotional Support	4.07 (0.182)	3.71	4.47	4.41 (0.198)	3.99	5.0	60
Instructional Support	4.22 (0.199)	3.88	4.74	4.51 (0.152)	4.21	4.92	60

As outlined in Table 4, the Instructional Support domain received the highest scores overall, consistent with qualitative teacher reports. Emotional Support, while positive in both countries, showed the largest discrepancy.

To examine differences in teacher–student interaction quality, quantitative comparisons were made using both parametric (Welch's t-tests) and non-parametric (Mann–Whitney U tests). As shown in Table 5, Welch's t-tests indicated that Spanish students rated all three domains significantly higher than their Chilean counterparts, with p-values ranging from p = 0.01 to p = 0.03. Mann–Whitney U tests were also conducted, confirming statistically significant differences across all domains.

Effect sizes were substantial across all comparisons: for Instructional Support, Cohen's d = 1.996; for Classroom Organization, d = 1.514; and for Emotional Support, d = 1.990. These results suggest not only statistically reliable differences, but also practically meaningful impacts of AI integration on classroom dynamics when mediated by effective teacher practices.

Taken together, these findings provide strong empirical support for the argument that AI tools, when purposefully integrated and scaffolded by educators, enhance student perceptions of instructional clarity, emotional connection, and classroom management.

Table 5. T-test table: Mean differences (Welch t-tests / Mann–Whitney, effect sizes + 95% CI) using the TTI framework

	Chile	**Spain**	**p-value**
TTI Domain	**(Mean)**	**(Mean)**	
Classroom Organization	4.15	4.45	0.02*
Emotional Support	4.07	4.41	0.03*
Instructional Support	4.22	4.51	0.01**

Note: N = 60 per country; *p < .05, **p < .01)

Thus, these results affirm that when AI tools are used to support—rather than replace—teacher interaction, the quality of student experience improves measurably across cognitive, structural, and emotional domains.

Regarding the observed correlations among TTI domains, additional analysis revealed strong, positive relationships between perceived usefulness of AI and core interactional domains. Notably, we appreciated AI usefulness and perceived instructional clarity or support (r = 0.69), AI usefulness and classroom organization (r = 0.64), and AI usefulness (or instructional support) and perceived teacher fairness (r = 0.59).

To sum up, these findings support the augmentative role of AI tools in reinforcing traditional TTI domains when properly scaffolded by teacher interaction. Below (see Figure 1) is the bar chart that synthesizes the findings from both descriptive and inferential analysis, contextualized within the TTI framework and cross-national dynamics of AI integration in K–12 education. It illustrates that Spanish students reported higher levels of support across all three domains.

Figure 1. TTI domain mean (bar chart, Chile vs. Spain)

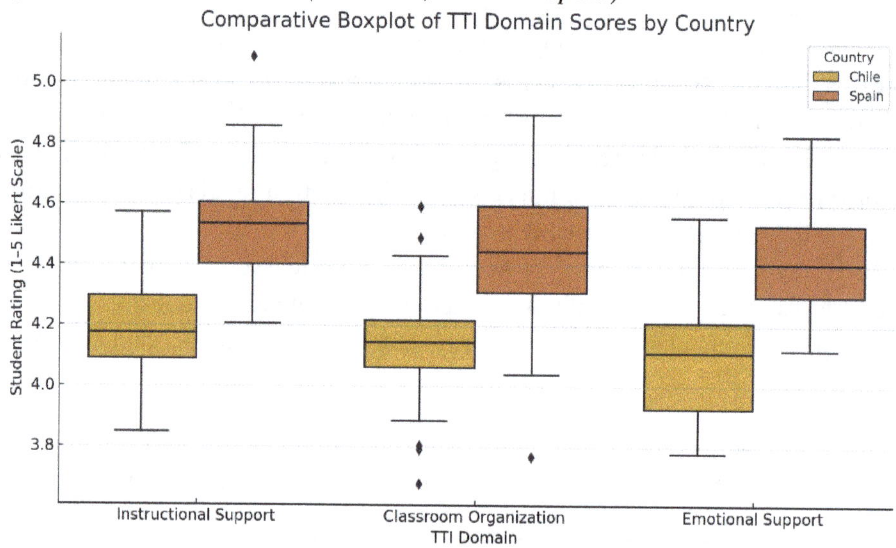

Finally, a boxplot for a cross-country comparison of TTI domain scores by country is described (see Figure 2). The boxplot shows that Spain consistently scores higher than Chile across all three domains.

Figure 2. Comparative boxplots by country

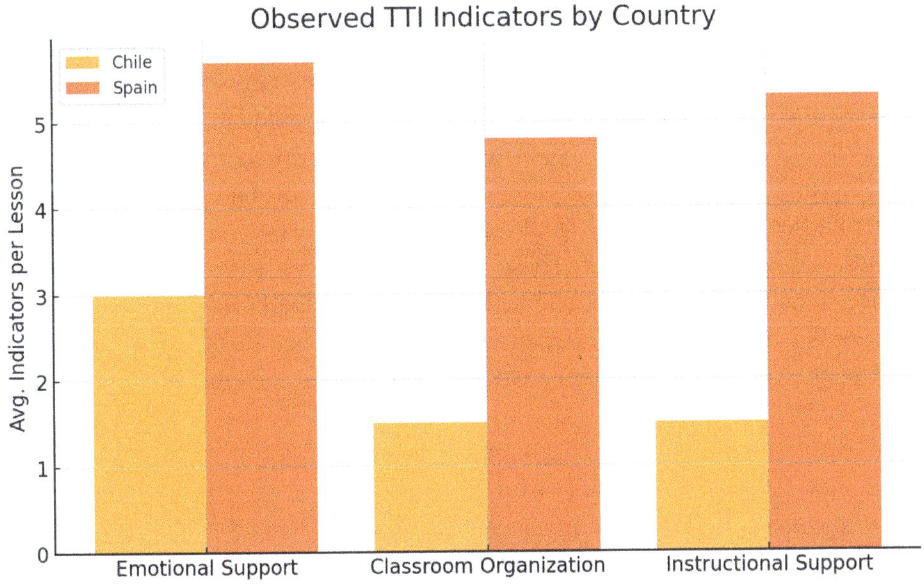

4.3. RQ3 – What systemic, institutional, cultural, and contextual factors enable or constrain AI integration?

This subsection addresses RQ3 by linking findings to systemic and institutional conditions.-The observation rubric was as follows (table 6):

Table 6. TTI Observation Rubric

TTI Domain	Rubric Focus Areas	Indicators Observed
Emotional Support	Teacher warmth, responsiveness, emotional and peer support, student comfort during AI use.	Verbal praise, checking emotional state post-AI task, relational follow-up.
Classroom Organization	Use of AI for transitions, time management, behavior guidance, engagement with digital tasks.	AI-assisted grouping, clear directions, time-efficient rotations, low downtime.
Instructional Support	Integration of AI into explanations, teacher scaffolding based on AI feedback, conceptual development.	Teacher references to AI data, elaboration based on AI results, responsive questioning.

4.3.1. Field Observations: Chile and Spain

As shown in table 6, in Spanish schools, notably those in Barcelona and Madrid, teachers maintained consistent eye contact and verbal responsiveness during AI-based activities. Observers coded frequent “emotionally attuned scaffolding”, where teachers used data from tools like *EmoTrack* or learning dashboards to check in with struggling students. For example, in one 6th-grade math class in Madrid, a teacher paused automated quiz feedback to kneel beside a student and offered clarification, affirming their effort. These moments were recorded as high-frequency emotional support moves that augmented AI tool outputs. By contrast, Chilean classrooms exhibited lower observed emotional presence during AI tool use. In Valparaiso and Temuco, teachers tended to monitor from a distance while students worked independently.

Observations in Spanish classrooms highlighted efficient classroom routines supported by AI. Teachers used virtual whiteboards and adaptive grouping algorithms to rotate tasks smoothly, managing transitions with minimal downtime. In one case, a teacher used AI-generated groupings based on recent performance to rotate students across reading stations. The resulting structure minimized behavioral disruptions and maximized task engagement—both indicators of high Classroom Organization within the TTI rubric.

In Chile, organizational patterns were more heterogeneous. In urban schools like Santiago, teachers occasionally used AI tools (e.g., lesson generators) to support instruction, but transitions were often manually orchestrated, with less fluidity. In rural schools, inconsistent connectivity often forces teachers to revert to analog methods mid-lesson, disrupting pacing and group cohesion. Observers coded several moments where instructional delays (due to tech troubleshooting) led to off-task behavior, compromising overall classroom organization. Chilean teachers showed competence in content delivery but tended to use AI tools in parallel rather than integrated ways. For instance, in Temuco school, the virtual tutor provided automated feedback, but the teacher did not reference this in follow-up discussion. Instruction proceeded in a more linear fashion, with AI acting as a side tool rather than an interactive agent (see table 7).

Table 7. TTI Observation Coding Matrix

Observation Code	Description	Chile (avg./lesson)	Spain (avg./lesson)
ES-CheckIn	Teacher checks in emotionally after AI task	1.2	2.5
ES-Praise	Teacher gives verbal/emotional praise	1.8	3.2
CO-GroupAI	AI used to form instructional groups	0.6	2.1
CO-Transition	Smooth AI-mediated transition	0.9	2.7
IS-AIData	Teacher responds to AI dashboard data	0.8	2.8
IS-Elaborate	Teacher elaborates on concept from AI result	0.7	2.5

In addition, instructional quality in Spain reflected strong AI–teacher integration. Teachers interacted with student outputs, shaping questioning and clarifications. In one science class, a simulation was paused when AI flagged misunderstandings; the teacher reframed the concept with a real-world analogy, coded as "responsive elaboration." Moreover, the cross-country comparison revealed a consistent trend: Spanish classrooms showed higher levels of teacher-mediated orchestration, particularly in dynamic instructional adaptation and affective responsiveness (see Figure 3). Chilean classrooms displayed professionalism but faced infrastructural challenges that limited integration.

Figure 3. Observed TTI indicators by country (field observations)

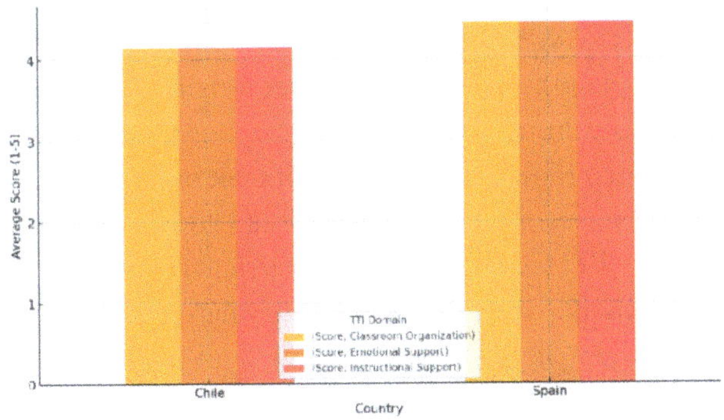

4.4. RQ4 – What strategies can be proposed to ensure that AI integration enhances, rather than undermines, relational pedagogy in K–12 classrooms? Barriers, Enablers, and Strategies for AI Integration through the TTI Framework

Finally, RQ4 is addressed by synthesizing barriers, enablers, and evidence-based strategies identified in the study:

- Barriers: In Chile, digital infrastructure gaps, lack of localized content, and limited teacher training constrained adoption.
- Enablers: In Spain, institutional support, predictive analytics, and professional development fostered teacher confidence.
- Strategies:
  - *Instructional Support*: Use adaptive AI for real-time feedback, but with teacher override.
  - *Classroom Organization*: Employ dashboards for grouping and pacing, while maintaining teacher-led routines.
  - *Emotional Support*: Deploy sentiment-analysis tools only as early warning systems, with follow-up anchored in teacher empathy.

4.4.1. Barriers to AI Integration

In Chilean schools, particularly those in areas such as Temuco and Valparaiso, key challenges included limited digital infrastructure, sporadic internet connectivity, and insufficient access to AI-compatible devices. Moreover, many Chilean teachers reported minimal exposure to professional development centered on AI tools. Language localization and culturally relevant content were also lacking, particularly in indigenous and bilingual regions. These barriers not only constrained instructional efficacy but also impacted on students' emotional support and engagement—two critical domains in the TTI framework. Thus, barriers to effective AI use were most visible in how they disrupted or constrained teacher–student interactions in each TTI domain:

- Instructional Support: Teachers often faced challenges in aligning AI-generated content with national curricular standards. Tools lacked flexibility, and formative feedback functions were not consistently reliable in Spanish, limiting the ability to scaffold students' higher-order thinking. Even when platforms were available (e.g., chatbot tutors or adaptive quiz generators), their alignment with national curriculum standards was inconsistent, often requiring significant manual adaptation.

- Classroom Organization: AI systems were underused for behavior tracking, adaptive grouping, or task management due to hardware shortages and inconsistent Wi-Fi access, especially in rural areas like Temuco.
- Emotional Support: Students expressed that while AI could provide fast responses or grades, it did not "understand their needs" in the way a teacher did. The absence of emotionally intelligent design and lack of localized emotional analytics tools limited the domain's development.

4.4.2. Enablers in Successful Contexts to AI Integration

By contrast, Spanish schools demonstrated more favorable conditions for AI integration. Enablers included multi-level support from regional education ministries, widespread access to predictive analytics dashboards, and schoolwide professional development initiatives focusing on "AI-literacy for educators". Teachers actively used AI not as a replacement but as a pedagogical amplifier. Importantly, these tools were interpreted through a human-in-the-loop model, where teachers maintained interpretive and relational control, reinforcing both Classroom Organization and Emotional Support domains. Furthermore, AI implementation was often scaffolded through community-informed design and data privacy frameworks (Teo et al., 2021). These conditions created an ecosystem where AI enhanced relational pedagogy rather than replacing it.

In sum, the Spanish schools studied leveraged AI in ways that amplified TTI-aligned teacher–student interaction:

- Instructional Support: Adaptive AI tools were embedded in daily practice, offering individualized practice pathways while teachers interpreted student dashboards to plan follow-ups and differentiate instruction.
- Classroom Organization: Predictive analytics tools were used to pre-emptively group students and assign roles in collaborative tasks.
- Emotional Support: Platforms like EmoTrack enabled teachers to monitor fluctuations in student motivation and well-being.

4.4.3. Evidence-Based Strategies for Scalable and Culturally Sensitive Adoption

Ultimately, the findings confirm that AI tool integration cannot be isolated from broader social, pedagogical, and infrastructural contexts. Success depends less on the sophistication of the tools themselves and more on their orchestration by informed, empowered educators within equitable and culturally responsive learning environments.

Drawing on the TTI domains, a strategic matrix was developed to guide AI adoption (table 8).

Table 8. Strategy aligned to TTI domains

TTI Domain	Scalable Strategy	Alignment
Instructional Support	Implement AI tools that provide real-time feedback and content adaptation but allow teacher override.	Respects teacher autonomy and enables scaffolding of cognitive demand.
Classroom Organization	Use AI dashboards for formative grouping and behavior signals, paired with teacher-led classroom routines.	Supports fluid transitions and goal-oriented instruction.
Emotional Support	Introduce emotionally aware AI tools only as early detectors; teacher empathy must remain primary.	Maintains student–teacher relational bonds and trust.

Drawing from these comparative insights, several key strategies emerge:

- Blended Orchestration Models. Rather than viewing AI as autonomous or instructional, the most effective practices were those where teachers used AI to scaffold human interaction, e.g., preparing formative assessments, adapting lesson pacing, or flagging at-risk students.
- Localized and Inclusive Design: AI tools must account for cultural, linguistic, and curricular contexts.
- Teacher-Centered Professional Development: Sustained training programs—not one-off workshops—are essential. Teachers must learn not just tool functions, but how AI interacts with pedagogy, classroom culture, and ethical boundaries.
- Equity-Oriented Infrastructure Investment: In Chile, gaps in student perception correlated with material disparities (devices, bandwidth). Equity-based funding and partnerships with public–private actors (e.g., Fundación Telefónica) were cited as vital by some rural schools.
- Ethical and Interpretive Autonomy: Maintaining the teacher's role as ethical filter and emotional connector is non-negotiable. In both countries, students trusted AI-enhanced environments only when teachers retained interpretive control and remained visibly engaged.

To sum up, AI integration in Spain is structured and institutionalized, supported by centralized policy, whereas in Chile it is innovative but uneven due to infrastructural and training gaps. Both cases show that AI works best as an augmentative tool, not a substitute for relational teaching.

While these strategies provide actionable insights, their effectiveness must be critically examined in light of the study's comparative findings and global policy debates

5. DISCUSSION, CONCLUSIONS, RECOMMENDATIONS, LIMITATIONS, AND FUTURE RESEARCH

5.1. Discussion

These findings set the stage for a broader discussion, where we interpret the comparative evidence through global policy debates.

Regarding RQ1: How are AI tools being integrated into K–12 classrooms in Chile and Spain? The study revealed that AI integration patterns differ markedly across the two contexts, reflecting their governance and infrastructural landscapes. Spain demonstrates a top-down, policy-driven model, where national and EU frameworks foster systematic adoption through learning management systems, predictive dashboards, and state-sponsored training. Chile illustrates a more bottom-up, grassroots approach, where teachers and schools experiment with locally developed or adapted tools such as UmmIA or SmartPal.

A central tension highlighted by this study is the gap between the rapid pace of technological innovation and the slower adaptation of teacher professional development systems. While AI tools evolve quickly, professional training frameworks in both Chile and Spain remain uneven and, in many cases, reactive. The OECD (Misiejuk et al., 2025) has warned that unless teacher capacity is systematically upgraded, AI integration risks becoming fragmented and inequitable, with educators left to improvise their own solutions. This divergence illustrates the challenge of aligning technological change with human capital development — a challenge echoed in global policy debates.

Another key tension lies in the equity implications of AI adoption. UNESCO (2023) repeatedly emphasizes that AI in education must serve as a force for inclusion rather than exclusion. These cases illustrate UNESCO's concern that without explicit equity safeguards, AI may inadvertently widen — rather than close — learning gaps across diverse school systems.

Finally, the question of teacher agency and responsibility is particularly salient. The U.S. Department of Education (UNESCO, 2023) underscores the importance of human oversight, transparency, and trust in AI-enhanced classrooms. Our findings show that teachers in both Chile and Spain remain cautious about allowing AI to mediate relational dimensions of teaching, especially emotional support. This resonates with international guidance that AI should function as an augmentative partner rather than a substitute. By foregrounding teacher interpretive authority, both countries highlight a globally relevant principle: sustainable AI integration depends not on the sophistication of algorithms alone, but on the preservation of human judgment and relational trust.

Regarding RQ2: How do participants perceive the impact of AI on teacher–student interactions? Across both contexts, perceptions were consistently positive but uneven. Survey and interview data demonstrated that Spanish teachers reported higher satisfaction, more frequent AI use, and greater confidence. Students in Spain perceived AI as improving instructional clarity and classroom organization, often citing dashboards and feedback tools as supports. Chilean students, by contrast, described AI as "occasional" and sometimes frustrating—particularly when tools lacked cultural or linguistic sensitivity (e.g., Mapuche variants).

These findings highlight a tension between technological promise and emotional trust. Teachers and students alike emphasized that relational warmth cannot be automated. AI tools contributed most effectively to Instructional Support and Classroom Organization, but Emotional Support remained contingent on teacher mediation (Luckin, 2022; Misiejuk et al., 2025).

Regarding RQ3: What systemic, institutional, cultural, and contextual factors enable or constrain AI integration? The comparative analysis surfaces three diverging conditions:

1. Infrastructure: Chile's rural–urban disparities limit consistency, while Spain benefits from EU-funded connectivity and tools.
2. Professional development: Chile relies on voluntary or ad-hoc training, while Spain institutionalizes digital. competence frameworks.
3. Tool origin: Chile often draws on grassroots or NGO-led initiatives, while Spain adopts EU-aligned institutional platforms.

The discussion also raises a critical point: equity. Without deliberate safeguards, AI integration risks widening existing gaps—between urban and rural schools in Chile, or between schools with more versus less digital maturity in Spain.

Regarding RQ4: What strategies can ensure AI integration enhances, rather than undermines, relational pedagogy? Findings suggest that a hybrid approach is most promising—one that combines Spain's policy coherence with Chile's innovation ethos. Practical strategies include:

- Blended orchestration: using AI to flag at-risk students or automate tasks but keeping teachers as relational mediators.

- Localized design: ensuring linguistic and cultural adaptation to avoid alienating learners.
- Teacher-centered PD: moving from one-off workshops to longitudinal, collaborative, and ethically grounded training.
- Equity-oriented investment: particularly in Chile, where connectivity and hardware gaps remain a first-order barrier.

To sum up, the TTI framework highlights that AI's role is augmentative, not substitutive, and that ethical, cultural, and pedagogical considerations must be prioritized alongside technical ones. In line with UNESCO and OECD guidance, the findings from Chile and Spain illustrate broader global dynamics: AI integration advances inclusion only when paired with safeguards for equity, teacher readiness, and cultural adaptation. Spain shows how centralized frameworks can promote coherence, while Chile demonstrates the risks of uneven access but also the value of grassroots innovation.

These insights directly inform the conclusions outlined below. Together, they reinforce the principle that AI must augment, not replace, human-centered pedagogy.

5.2. Conclusions

Through the lens of the TTI framework, this chapter has mapped how Chilean and Spanish educators negotiate the complex terrain of AI tool usage, balancing efficiency with care, and personalization with equity. Key conclusions include:

1. Instructional Support is the domain most enhanced by AI, as adaptive feedback and formative assessments strengthen clarity and pacing.
2. Classroom Organization also benefits, when AI dashboards and grouping algorithms are paired with teacher responsiveness.
3. Emotional Support remains AI's weakest domain; tools can flag signals, but trust and empathy remain uniquely human functions.
4. Teacher agency is decisive: meaningful integration occurs only when teachers maintain interpretive and relational control.

To sum up, a balanced strategy —Spain's structured governance plus Chile's creative adaptation— may provide the most sustainable path for scaling AI responsibly. Building on these conclusions, we propose several recommendations for policymakers, educators, and technology designers.

5.3. Recommendations

This chapter contributes actionable insights for policymakers, school leaders, educators, and EdTech designers. Based on the comparative findings and TTI-based analysis, the following recommendations are proposed to guide effective and equitable AI integration in K–12 settings:

- For policymakers, they should embed TTI domains into AI curricula, including AI ethics in teacher certification, and foster cross-national policy labs (e.g., Ibero-American EdTech Consortium) to co-develop equitable AI tools and pedagogy guidelines.
    - For school leaders, it is important to designate AI-pedagogical liaisons to pilot and mentor peers, implement micro-certifications (e.g., emotional AI ethics, adaptive curriculum design) and apply TTI as an audit framework for EdTech procurement.
- For teachers, it is recommended to co-design routines reflecting AI's role in each TTI domain, use dashboards for metacognitive reflection, and document/share AI practices. Focus on AI tools that support teaching tasks (lesson planning, feedback) rather than replacing engagement.

Furthermore, in Latin America, AI can support large classrooms by identifying learning gaps (e.g., math, science), allowing teachers to focus on guidance and mentorship. Teachers must safeguard student data, address bias, and ensure AI vendors comply with privacy laws to maintain trust, and adopt AI incrementally to streamline planning and differentiation, using customized resources to improve engagement. By focusing on these strategies, teachers in both Chile and Spain can effectively integrate AI into their classrooms, enhancing educational processes while addressing the diverse needs of their students (Gobierno de España, 2021; Molina et al., 2024).

- For technology developers, they must co-design culturally and linguistically relevant AI with educators; usability and cultural fit are key for adoption.

In this sense, some international agencies such as UNESCO (2023) and the Gobierno de España (2021) stress equity, transparency, and teacher-centered AI. Chile's grassroots creativity and Spain's policy coherence reflect these debates, showing how national approaches contribute to global AI governance in education.

5.4. Limitations and Future Research

While these recommendations are actionable, they must be understood alongside the study's limitations. Although the sample offers rich insights, limitations include potential variability in AI tool exposure and reliance on self-reported data:

- The small purposive sample (120 students, 10 teachers in six schools) limits generalization, and self-reported questionnaires risk social desirability bias. However, triangulation with interviews and observations strengthens reliability.
- Observations were time-limited and may not represent habitual practices. Moreover, the study focused on widely available AI tools without disaggregating by brand or model type, so tool-specific effects were not measured.
- In terms of differences between countries, Chile and Spain differ in policies, infrastructure, and teacher training, which may confound perceptions of AI. In addition, in this research schools were selected for AI exposure, limiting generalization.

These limitations point toward several directions for future research. Regarding directions for future research, the main considerations are the following:

- Future work should investigate the long-term influence of AI-enhanced teaching on student learning outcomes, classroom climate, and teacher instructional evolution, ideally through longitudinal mixed-methods designs spanning academic years.
- Also, comparative studies should examine how different AI types (e.g., chatbots, emotion recognition) affect each TTI domain.
- Another direction for research is oriented to assess whether AI tools widen or narrow equity gaps, particularly for students with disabilities, multilingual learners, or those from socioeconomically disadvantaged backgrounds. Focus should include algorithmic bias and accessibility in educational AI design.
- Future studies could investigate how students develop trust, skepticism, or dependency on AI tools, and whether age, cultural context, or classroom climate mediate these attitudes. Integrating media literacy and AI ethics curricula may be a promising intervention.
- Research should also examine how AI integration affects teachers' professional identity, autonomy, and emotional labor in co-instructional settings.

REFERENCES

Akgun, S., & Greenhow, C. (2022). Artificial intelligence in education: Addressing ethical challenges in K-12 settings. *AI and Ethics*, *2*(3), 431–440. DOI: 10.1007/s43681-021-00096-7

Alemdag, E. (2023). The effect of chatbots on learning: A meta-analysis of empirical research. *Journal of Research on Technology in Education*, *55*(1), 1–23. DOI: 10.1080/15391523.2023.2255698

Alvarez-Garcia, M., Arenas-Parra, M., & Ibar-Alonso, R. (2024). Uncovering student profiles. An explainable cluster analysis approach to PISA 2022. *Computers & Education*, *223*, 105166. DOI: 10.1016/j.compedu.2024.105166

Anderson, J. R., Corbett, A. T., Koedinger, K. R., & Pelletier, R. (1995). Cognitive tutors: Lessons learned. *Journal of the Learning Sciences*, *4*(2), 167–207. DOI: 10.1207/s15327809jls0402_2

Asagar, M. S. (2025). Digital Competence in Education: A Comparative Analysis of Frameworks and Conceptual Foundations. *Synergy: International Journal of Multidisciplinary Studies*, *2*(1), 9–23. DOI: 10.63960/synergyint.j.multidiscip.stud.v2i1.34

Ayala-Pazmiño, M. (2023). Inteligencia artificial en la educación: Explorando los beneficios y riesgos potenciales. *593 Digital Publisher CEIT*, 8(3), 892-899. https://doi.org/DOI: 10.33386/593dp.2023.3.1827

Baker, R. S., & Inventado, P. S. (2014). Educational data mining and learning analytics. In Larusson, J., & White, B. (Eds.), *Learning analytics* (pp. 61–75). Springer., DOI: 10.1007/978-1-4614-3305-7_4

Barragán-Torres, M. (2022). A comparative study of mathematics classroom practices in Chile, Colombia, and Mexico. UCLA. ProQuest ID: BarraganTorres_ucla_0031D_20584. Merritt ID: ark:/13030/m5fn878g. https://escholarship.org/uc/item/91r8m44r

Becker, B., & Park, K. (2011). Effects of integrative approaches among science, technology, engineering, and mathematics (STEM) subjects on students' learning. *Journal of STEM Education: Innovations and Research*, *12*(5), 23–37. https://eric.ed.gov/?id=EJ943196

Buckingham Shum, S., & Ferguson, R. (2012). Social learning analytics. *Journal of Educational Technology & Society*, *15*(3), 3–26. https://www.jstor.org/stable/jeductechsoci.15.3.3

Burchinal, M., Zaslow, M., & Tarullo, L. (2016). Quality thresholds, features, and dosage in early care and education: Secondary data analyses of child outcomes. *Monographs of the Society for Research in Child Development*, *81*(2), 1–126. https://www.jstor.org/stable/45106669

Carella, G., Italia, M., Conte, M., & Parolini, F. (2024). How to adopt strategic design inside universities: Transforming research in educational formats. In: *ICERI2024 Proceedings*. https://re.public.polimi.it/handle/11311/1278942

Chen, L., Chen, P., & Lin, Z. (2020). Artificial Intelligence in Education: A Review. *IEEE Access : Practical Innovations, Open Solutions*, *8*, 75264–75278. DOI: 10.1109/ACCESS.2020.2988510

Dellepiane, P., & Guidi, P. (2023). La inteligencia artificial y la educación: Retos y oportunidades desde una perspectiva ética. *Question/Cuestión, 3*(76), e859. https://doi.org/DOI: 10.24215/16696581e859

Demszky, D., Liu, J., Hill, H. C., Jurafsky, D., & Piech, C. (2023). Can Automated Feedback Improve Teachers' Uptake of Student Ideas? Evidence From a Randomized Controlled Trial in a Large-Scale Online Course. [Original work published in 2024]. *Educational Evaluation and Policy Analysis*, *46*(3), 483–505. DOI: 10.3102/01623737231169270

European Commission. (2020). *Digital Education Action Plan 2021–2027*. https://education.ec.europa.eu/focus-topics/digital/digital-education-action-plan

Feng, M., Heffernan, N. T., & Koedinger, K. R. (2009). Addressing the assessment challenge with an online system that tutors as it assesses. *User Modeling and User-Adapted Interaction*, *19*(3), 243–266. DOI: 10.1007/s11257-009-9063-7

Fonseca, A., Ferreira, A., Ribeiro, L., Moreira, S., & Duque, C. (2024). Embracing the future—Is artificial intelligence already better? A comparative study of artificial intelligence performance in diagnostic accuracy and decision-making. *European Journal of Neurology*, *31*(4), 16195. DOI: 10.1111/ene.16195

Gobierno de España. (2021). *Plan Nacional de Competencias Digitales*. https://avance.digital.gob.es/es-es/espana digital./210127_plan_nacional_de_competencias_digital.es.pdf

Hadas, E., & Hershkovitz, A. (2025). Assessing Creativity Across Multi-Step Intervention Using Generative AI Models. *Journal of Learning Analytics*, *12*(1), 91–109. DOI: 10.18608/jla.2025.8571

Hamre, B. K., Pianta, R. C., Downer, J. T., DeCoster, J., Mashburn, A. J., Jones, S. M., Brown, J. L., Cappella, E., Atkins, M., Rivers, S. E., Brackett, M. A., & Hamagami, A. (2013). Teaching through interactions: Testing a developmental framework of teacher effectiveness in over 4,000 classrooms. *The Elementary School Journal, 113*(4), 461–487. DOI: 10.1086/669616

Holmes, W., Bialik, M., & Fadel, C. (2022). *Artificial intelligence in education: Promises and implications for teaching and learning.* Center for Curriculum Redesign. https://www.researchgate.net/publication/332180327

Holstein, K., McLaren, B. M., & Aleven, V. (2019). Co-Designing a Real-Time Classroom Orchestration Tool to Support Teacher–AI Complementarity. *Journal of Learning Analytics, 6*(2), 27–52. DOI: 10.18608/jla.2019.62.3

Kapoor, V., & Bakhshi, A. K. (2025). Artificial Intelligence and the Future of Education. Indian. *Journal of Educational Technology, 7*(1), 389–397. https://journals.ncert.gov.in/IJET/article/view/837

Lampropoulos, G., & Papadakis, S. (2025). The Educational Value of Artificial Intelligence and Social Robots. In Lampropoulos, G., & Papadakis, S. (Eds.), *Social Robots in Education. Studies in Computational Intelligence* (Vol. 1194, pp. 3–15). Springer., DOI: 10.1007/978-3-031-82915-4_1

Lavidas, K., Papadakis, S., Manesis, D., Grigoriadou, A. S., & Gialamas, V.Lectures and Lab Classes. (2022a). The effects of social desirability on students' self-reports in two social contexts: Lectures vs. lectures and lab classes. *Information (Basel), 13*(10), 491. DOI: 10.3390/info13100491

Lavidas, K., Petropoulou, A., Papadakis, S., Apostolou, Z., Komis, V., Jimoyiannis, A., & Gialamas, V. (2022b). Factors affecting response rates of the web survey with teachers. *Computers, 11*(9), 127. DOI: 10.3390/computers11090127

Lekan, K., & Pardos, Z. A. (2025). AI-Augmented Advising: A Comparative Study of GPT-4 and Advisor-based Major Recommendations. *Journal of Learning Analytics, 12*(1), 110–128. DOI: 10.18608/jla.2025.8593

Leyva, D., Weiland, C., Barata, M., Yoshikawa, H., Snow, C., Treviño, E., & Rolla, A. (2015). Teacher–Child Interactions in Chile and Their Associations with Prekindergarten Outcomes. *Child Development, 86*(3), 781–799. DOI: 10.1111/cdev.12342

Luckin, R. (2022). *Machine learning and human intelligence: The future of education for the 21st century.* UCL Press. https://eric.ed.gov/?id=ED584840

Luckin, R., Holmes, W., Griffiths, M., & Forcier, L. B. (2016). *Intelligence unleashed: An argument for AI in education*. Pearson Education. https://static.googleusercontent.com/media/edu.google.com/en//pdfs/Intelligence-Unleashed-Publication.pdf

Matos, T., Santos, W., Zdravevski, E., Coelho, P. J., Pires, I. M., & Madeira, F. (2025). A systematic review of artificial intelligence applications in education: Emerging trends and challenges. *Decision Analytics Journal, 15*, 100571. DOI: 10.1016/j.dajour.2025.100571

Means, B., Toyama, Y., Murphy, R., Bakia, M., & Jones, K. (2009). *Evaluation of evidence-based practices in online learning*. U.S. Department of Education. https://eric.ed.gov/?id=ED505824

Miller, D., & Robertson, D. (2010). Using games console in the primary classroom: Effects of 'Brain Training' programme on computation and self-esteem. *British Journal of Educational Technology, 41*(2), 242–255. DOI: 10.1111/j.1467-8535.2008.00918.x

Misiejuk, K., López-Pernas, S., Kaliisa, R., & Saqr, M. (2025). Mapping the Landscape of Generative Artificial Intelligence in Learning Analytics: A Systematic Literature Review. *Journal of Learning Analytics, 12*(1), 12–31. DOI: 10.18608/jla.2025.8591

Molina, E., Cobo, C., Pineda, J., & Rovner, H. (2024). *AI revolution in education: What you need to know.* World Bank. www.worldbank.org

Morrell, E. (2008). *Critical Literacy and Urban Youth: Pedagogies of Access, Dissent, and Liberation* (1st ed.). Routledge., DOI: 10.4324/9780203937914

O'Neil, C., & Schutt, R. (2013). *Doing data science*. O'Reilly Media.

Papadakis, S., Lytvynova, S. H., Ivanova, S. M., & Selyshcheva, I. A. (2024b). *Advancing lifelong learning with AI-enhanced ICT: A review of 3L-Person 2024.* In *CEUR Workshop Proceedings (9th International Workshop on Professional Retraining and Life-Long Learning using ICT: Person-oriented Approach — 3L-Person 2024, Lviv, Ukraine, September 25, 2023).* CEUR-WS.org.

Papadakis, S., Striuk, A. M., Kravtsov, H. M., Shyshkina, M. P., Marienko, M. V., & Danylchuk, H. B. (2024a). *Embracing digital innovation and cloud technologies for transformative learning experiences.* In *Proceedings of the 11th Workshop on Cloud Technologies in Education (CTE 2023), Kryvyi Rih, Ukraine, December 22, 2023.* CEUR Workshop Proceedings.

Pianta, R. C. (2016). Teacher–Student Interactions: Measurement, Impacts, Improvement, and Policy. *Policy Insights from the Behavioral and Brain Sciences, 3*(1), 98–105. DOI: 10.1177/2372732215622457

Pianta, R. C., & Hofkens, T. (2023). Defining early education quality using CLASS-observed teacher–student interaction. *Frontiers in Psychology, 14*, 1110419. Advance online publication. DOI: 10.3389/fpsyg.2023.1110419

Pianta, R. C., La Paro, K. M., & Hamre, B. K. (2008). *CLASS manual: K–3*. Paul H. Brookes Publishing.

Possaghi, I., Vesin, B., Zhang, F., Sharma, K., Knudsen, C., Bjørkum, H., & Papavlasopoulou, S. (2025). Integrating multi-modal learning analytics dashboard in K-12 education: Insights for enhancing orchestration and teacher decision-making. *Smart Learning Environments, 12*(1), 53. DOI: 10.1186/s40561-025-00410-4

Pozdniakov, S., Brazil, J., Mohammadi, M., Dollinger, M., Sadiq, S., & Khosravi, H. (2025). AI-Assisted Co-Creation: Bridging Skill Gaps in Student-Generated Content. *Journal of Learning Analytics, 12*(1), 129–151. DOI: 10.18608/jla.2025.8601

ProFuturo Foundation. (2022). *Annual impact report*. https://profuturo.education/wp-content/uploads/2023/06/Memoria_ProFuturo_2022_DIGITAL.pdf

Redecker, C. (2017). *European Framework for the Digital Competence of Educators (DigCompEdu)*. EU Science Hub., DOI: 10.2760/159770

Romero, C., & Ventura, S. (2020). Educational data mining and learning analytics: An updated survey. *Wiley Interdisciplinary Reviews. Data Mining and Knowledge Discovery, 10*(3), e1355. DOI: 10.1002/widm.1355

Rundquist, R., Holmberg, K., Rack, J., Mohseni, Z., & Masiello, I. (2024). Use of Learning Analytics in K–12 Mathematics Education: Systematic Scoping Review of the Impact on Teaching and Learning. *Journal of Learning Analytics, 11*(3), 174–191. DOI: 10.18608/jla.2024.8299

Saha, P., Hossain, M., Roy, N. C., Masud, A. A., & Amin, R. (2025). Unlocking the power of AI in education: Students' intentions and AI tool use driving learning success in an emerging economy. *On the Horizon, 33*(1), 126–144. DOI: 10.1108/OTH-10-2024-0066

Schmid, R. F., Bernard, R. M., Borokhovski, E., Tamim, R. M., Abrami, P. C., Surkes, M., Wade, A., & Woods, J. (2014). The effects of technology use in postsecondary education: A meta-analysis of classroom applications. *Computers & Education, 72*, 271–291. DOI: 10.1016/j.compedu.2013.11.002

Selwyn, N. (2019). *Should robots replace teachers? AI and the future of education*. Political Press.

Singh, Y., & Phoolka, S. (2025). Hybrid education in the age of Education 5.0- A study of engagement and innovations in the Indian education system amidst covid-19. *Indian Journal of Educational Technology*, *7*(1), 309–328. https://journals.ncert.gov.in/IJET/article/view/848

Tang, Z., & Zhang, P. (2023). Comparative Analysis of AI Applications in Libraries: A Systematic Literature Review. *Proceedings of the Association for Information Science and Technology*, *60*(1), 1146–1148. DOI: 10.1002/pra2.973

Teo, T., Unwin, S., Scherer, R., & Gardiner, V. (2021). Initial teacher training for twenty-first century skills in the Fourth Industrial Revolution (IR 4.0): A scoping review. *Computers & Education*, *170*, 104223. DOI: 10.1016/j.compedu.2021.104223

Traoré, D. (2024). Integration of Artificial Intelligence in Education: Challenges and Prospects. *Revista Internacional de Pedagogía e Innovación Educativa*, *4*(2), 329–342. DOI: 10.51660/ripie42221

Tudino, G., & Qin, Y. (2024). A corpus-driven comparative analysis of AI in academic discourse: Investigating ChatGPT-generated academic texts in social sciences. *Lingua*, *312*, 103838. DOI: 10.1016/j.lingua.2024.103838

UNESCO. (2023). *Generative AI and the futures of education*. UNESCO., DOI: 10.54675/HOXG8740

VanLehn, K. (2011). The Relative Effectiveness of Human Tutoring, Intelligent Tutoring Systems, and Other Tutoring Systems. *Educational Psychologist*, *46*(4), 197–221. DOI: 10.1080/00461520.2011.611369

Varghese, C., Vernon-Feagans, L., & Bratsch-Hines, M. (2019). Rural classroom environments as contexts for teacher-child relationships. *The Journal of Educational Research*, *112*(3), 411–420. DOI: 10.1080/00220671.2018.1545214

Vygotsky, L. S. (1978). *Mind in society: The development of higher psychological processes*. Harvard University Press.

Wang, P., Yin, K., Zhang, M., Zheng, Y., Zhang, T., Kang, Y., & Feng, X. (2025). The effect of incorporating large language models into the teaching on critical thinking disposition: An "AI+Constructivism Learning Theory" attempt. *Education and Information Technologies*, *30*(9), 11625–11647. DOI: 10.1007/s10639-024-13244-3

Wang, S., Wang, F., Zhu, Z., Wang, J., Tran, T., & Du, Z. (2024). Artificial intelligence in education: A systematic literature review, *Expert Systems with Applications*, 252. *Expert Systems with Applications*, *124167*, 124167. Advance online publication. DOI: 10.1016/j.eswa.2024.124167

Wang, Y., & Chuang, Y. (2024). Artificial Intelligence Self-Efficacy: Scale Development and Validation. *Education and Information Technologies, 29*(4), 4785–4808. DOI: 10.1007/s10639-023-12015-w

Wang, Y., & Xue, L. (2024). Using AI-driven chatbots to foster Chinese EFL students' academic engagement: An intervention study. *Computers in Human Behavior, 159*, 108353. DOI: 10.1016/j.chb.2024.108353

Wiese, L. J., Patil, I., Schiff, D. S., & Magana, A. J. (2025). AI ethics education: A systematic literature review. *Computers and Education: Artificial Intelligence, 8*, 100405. DOI: 10.1016/j.caeai.2025.100405

Williamson, B. (2024). The Social life of AI in Education. *International Journal of Artificial Intelligence in Education, 34*(1), 97–104. DOI: 10.1007/s40593-023-00342-5

Williamson, B., Macgilchrist, F., & Potter, J. (2023). Re-examining AI, automation and datafication in education. *Learning, Media and Technology, 48*(1), 1–5. DOI: 10.1080/17439884.2023.2167830

Woolf, B. P. (2008). *Building Intelligent Interactive Tutors: Student-centered strategies for revolutionizing e-learning*. Morgan Kaufmann Publishers Inc.

Xu, Z. (2024). AI in education: Enhancing learning experiences and student outcomes. *Applied and Computational Engineering, 51*(1), 104–111. DOI: 10.54254/2755-2721/51/20241187

Yang, L. (2024). From Tradition to Innovation: A Comparative Analysis of Education Systems in China and Finland. *Journal of International Education and Development.*, *8*(07), 112–118. DOI: 10.47297/wspiedWSP2516-250018.20240807

Yue, M., Dai, Y., Siu-Yung, M., & Chai, C.-S. (2021). An Analysis of K-12 Artificial Intelligence Curricula in Eight Countries. In: Rodrigo, M. M. T. et al. (Eds.). *Proceedings of the 29th International Conference on Computers in Education*. Asia-Pacific Society for Computers in Education. https://library.apsce.net/index.php/ICCE/article/view/4335

Zawacki-Richter, O., Marín, V. I., Bond, M., & Gouverneur, F. (2019). Systematic Review of Research on Artificial Intelligence Applications in Higher Education—Where Are the Educators? *International Journal of Educational Technology in Higher Education, 16*(1), 39. DOI: 10.1186/s41239-019-0171-0

Zhang, J., & Zhang, Z. (2024). AI in teacher education: Unlocking new dimensions in teaching support, inclusive learning, and digital literacy. *Journal of Computer Assisted Learning, 40*(4), 1871–1885. DOI: 10.1111/jcal.12988

Chapter 14
Future Trends and Innovations in AI-Powered Education

Debaditya Kundu
http://orcid.org/0009-0008-2338-9967
Indian Institute of Information Technology, Dharwad, India

Krishnendu Ghosh
http://orcid.org/0000-0003-4287-8383
Indian Institute of Information Technology, Dharwad, India

ABSTRACT

Artificial Intelligence is transforming education through personalized learning, intelligent tutoring, automated assessments and predictive analytics. AI tools enhance engagement, adapt content to learners' needs and ease educators' workload by automating routine tasks. Intelligent Tutoring Systems offer real-time support and AI-driven grading improves efficiency and fairness. However, AI integration poses challenges, including data privacy, algorithmic bias and ethical issues in automated decisions. The digital divide also limits access to AI tools in underserved areas due to economic and infrastructure gaps. This chapter explores trends and innovations in AI-driven education, discussing real-world applications, key technologies like machine learning, natural language processing and learning analytics. Ethical considerations and future directions are also examined. By analyzing current advancements and limitations, this chapter offers insights for educators, researchers, and policymakers to effectively use AI in creating inclusive, efficient and adaptive learning environments.

DOI: 10.4018/979-8-2600-0101-1.ch014

1. INTRODUCTION

The global education landscape is undergoing a profound transformation, catalyzed by rapid advancements in Artificial Intelligence (AI). Once confined to experimental pilots, AI technologies are now deeply embedded into K–12 and higher education ecosystems, offering intelligent functionalities such as adaptive learning systems (O'Sullivan et al., 2020), automated assessments, intelligent tutoring, natural language interaction, and predictive analytics. These innovations hold the potential to democratize access to education, enhance student engagement, and optimize instructional delivery at scale, with particular implications for the unique developmental and pedagogical needs of K–12 learners (Lampropoulos & Papadakis, 2025).

AI's unique capacity to tailor learning trajectories to individual students, analyze behavior in real time, and support multimodal content delivery reflects a paradigm shift toward learner-centered and competency-based education. In K–12 classrooms, platforms such as DreamBox (mathematics), Lexia Core5 (literacy), and Duolingo for Schools (language learning) exemplify how intelligent automation can create adaptive pathways that respect age, developmental stage, and curriculum requirements. These systems not only disseminate content but also actively model learner understanding, recommend personalized pathways, and adjust difficulty levels based on analytics of engagement and mastery (Pane et al., 2015; Roschelle et al., 2016).

Recent research by Ghosh et al. (2022, 2025) has added important depth to this vision. Their AI frameworks augment recorded video lectures with community-generated question-answer content, automatically identify off-topic segments, and suggest supplementary multimodal resources. These features ensure that learners not only stay on track but engage with the material in a more coherent and contextually enriched manner. By integrating deep learning and natural language processing (NLP) techniques, these systems are capable of curating content in ways that promote continuity, conceptual clarity, and deeper cognitive engagement. Building on this line of inquiry, Ghosh and Das (2023) proposed methods for the automatic generation of algebraic representations for physics problems—demonstrating AI's emerging role in symbolic reasoning and abstraction, domains that have traditionally resisted automation due to their complexity and need for deep cognitive modeling.

In parallel, ensemble-based models for automatic short-answer grading, as proposed by Sahu and Bhowmick (2019), represent another frontier in intelligent evaluation. These models aim to replicate human evaluative behavior by leveraging semantic understanding and contextual judgment, offering fair, explainable, and scalable solutions to one of the most labor-intensive educational tasks. Similarly, Krishna et al. (2015) and Roy & Bhowmick (2016) focused on automatic question generation aligned to course topics, especially in the context of MOOCs. These

AI-powered assessment tools not only support large-scale formative evaluation but also enhance the personalization of feedback and learning materials.

Scholarly literature in international platforms like the *International Journal of Artificial Intelligence in Education (IJAIED)* and *IEEE Transactions on Learning Technologies (TLT)* has documented the increasing sophistication of AI systems in educational contexts. Studies highlight applications in diagnostic feedback, emotional state recognition, and metacognitive scaffolding. For instance, Holmes, 2020 demonstrated that AI-based adaptive systems significantly outperform static models in identifying and correcting learner misconceptions. Their work illustrates how dynamic learning paths, informed by continuous assessment and learner modeling, can guide students toward conceptual mastery. Likewise, Luckin & Holmes (2016) called for a reimagining of educational AI through the lens of "co-intelligent" systems—AI tools that work alongside, rather than in place of, educators to foster deeper engagement and support. These co-intelligent systems aim to augment teacher insight by automating routine analytics, thus enabling educators to focus on more complex, creative, and socio-emotional aspects of teaching.

Despite these advances, AI's expansion into education is not without substantial challenges. The digital divide remains one of the most significant barriers to equitable access. In low-resource contexts, the deployment of AI-driven systems is hindered by infrastructure limitations, bandwidth constraints, and lack of digital literacy. This technological inequity risks reinforcing existing educational disparities and must be addressed through inclusive design and policy interventions. Moreover, as Williamson, B., & Eynon, R. (2020) argue, unchecked deployment of AI in educational contexts can inadvertently exacerbate algorithmic bias, reduce student agency, and amplify surveillance concerns under the guise of personalization and efficiency. Without thoughtful governance, these technologies may privilege metrics over meaning and control over creativity.

Among the most pressing concerns is the issue of algorithmic opacity. AI systems are typically trained on historical datasets that may encode latent biases related to socioeconomic status, race, gender, or geography. These biases, once embedded into recommendation engines, assessment algorithms, or dropout prediction models, can lead to discriminatory outcomes and perpetuate systemic inequalities. Binns et al., 2018 caution that the perceived fairness of algorithmic decisions is often undermined by a lack of transparency—particularly when learners do not understand or cannot contest decisions made by opaque, automated systems. Similarly, Williamson and Eynon (2020) warn that datafied learning environments, while seemingly objective, may erode learner autonomy and prioritize behavioral conformity over critical inquiry. When learning becomes a set of metrics to optimize rather than a process of exploration, the essence of education is at risk.

Compounding these concerns is the reality that many AI tools are designed with minimal pedagogical input. The mere presence of intelligent functionality does not ensure educational efficacy. As Woolf et al. (2013) argue, the success of AI in educational contexts depends on the extent to which these tools are aligned with well-established cognitive science principles, instructional design strategies, and learner variability. Without such alignment, AI tools may inadvertently reinforce surface-level learning, neglect affective development, or ignore culturally specific learning contexts. A critical lesson from decades of intelligent tutoring system (ITS) research is that learning outcomes improve most significantly when AI systems are deeply embedded into coherent pedagogical strategies, rather than treated as bolt-on technologies.

To address these issues, several mitigation strategies are being explored across the AI in education community. One such approach is Explainable AI (XAI), which aims to make AI decisions more transparent and interpretable to end users—especially learners and educators. Huang et al., 2021 demonstrated that integrating visual explanations and interpretable decision models into intelligent tutoring systems can foster user trust, promote agency, and encourage deeper reflection. Yet, XAI remains a developing field, often struggling to reconcile interpretability with the complexity of deep learning models, particularly in high-stakes educational scenarios.

Fairness-aware machine learning represents another line of defense against algorithmic bias. These approaches involve adjusting training data, loss functions, or decision thresholds to ensure that models perform equitably across diverse user groups. However, as Veale and Brass (2019) caution, technical fairness metrics may fail to capture the broader social, historical, and ethical dynamics of educational settings. A model that achieves statistical parity may still fail to address culturally relevant pedagogy, learner motivation, or localized epistemologies. Thus, technical solutions must be complemented by participatory design and policy oversight.

Another promising but complex approach is the use of privacy-preserving techniques, such as federated learning. This method enables machine learning models to be trained on decentralized data sources—like student devices—without transferring sensitive data to centralized servers. Kairouz et al., 2021 argue that federated learning can empower learners to maintain control over their own data while still benefiting from intelligent services. Nonetheless, these systems demand significant computational infrastructure and robust coordination protocols, which may be infeasible in under-resourced educational environments.

Concurrently, there is a growing consensus that AI should enhance—not replace—human educators. As highlighted by Luckin & Holmes (2016), the most effective AI systems are those that serve as co-pilots to teachers—automating the analytics, not the artistry, of teaching. These systems can alert instructors to students at risk, recommend timely interventions, and surface patterns that inform instructional design.

However, such co-intelligence requires a corresponding investment in professional development. Teachers must be supported not just as users of AI, but as co-designers and critical evaluators of these systems. A shift of this magnitude demands systemic support, participatory governance, and a rethinking of teacher education programs.

Equally vital is the establishment of robust ethical governance frameworks. The UNESCO (2022) Recommendation on the Ethics of Artificial Intelligence in Education emphasizes the need for transparent impact assessments, inclusive stakeholder consultations, and mechanisms for ongoing oversight. These recommendations aim to safeguard human rights, promote digital equity, and prevent the commodification of learner data. They also encourage institutions to build AI literacy among students, empowering them to critically engage with, rather than passively consume, algorithmically mediated learning environments.

Taken together, these developments underscore the dual nature of AI's role in education—as both an unprecedented opportunity and a profound ethical challenge. If thoughtfully designed and responsibly deployed, AI has the potential to reimagine educational practice and address long-standing inequities. However, if misapplied or left unregulated, it may exacerbate existing problems and introduce new risks that undermine trust, transparency, and the core human values of education. By blending state-of-the-art research with applied insights, this chapter seeks to equip researchers, practitioners, and policymakers with a clear understanding of how to responsibly and effectively implement AI in modern educational systems.

2. BACKGROUND

The application of Artificial Intelligence (AI) in education has evolved dramatically over the past five decades. From the early days of symbolic logic-based tutoring systems to today's sophisticated deep learning-powered platforms, AI has undergone multiple paradigm shifts. These changes have not only enhanced the capabilities of educational technologies but also fundamentally reshaped how learners interact with content, instructors, and peers.

The earliest implementations of AI in education emerged in the 1970s and 1980s, when systems such as SCHOLAR and SOPHIE attempted to emulate the Socratic method through rule-based dialogue trees. These *expert systems* were built on hardcoded domain knowledge and inference engines, enabling limited forms of tutoring in narrow topics like geography or electronics. However, their utility was constrained by their brittle logic and inability to adapt to diverse learner responses (Carbonell, 2007; Nwana, 1990). Figure 1 illustrates the chronological evolution of AI applications in education, from early expert systems like SCHOLAR to modern deep learning-powered adaptive platforms. This timeline helps contextualize key technological milestones that shaped AI's pedagogical role (Graesser et al., 2005; Koedinger et al., 1997; D'Mello et al., 2017).

Figure 1. Evolution of AI in Education: A timeline showing key milestones from rule-based expert systems in the 1970s to deep learning-driven personalized platforms in the 2020s. Adapted and synthesized from Graesser et al. (2005), Koedinger et al. (1997), and D'Mello et al. (2017).

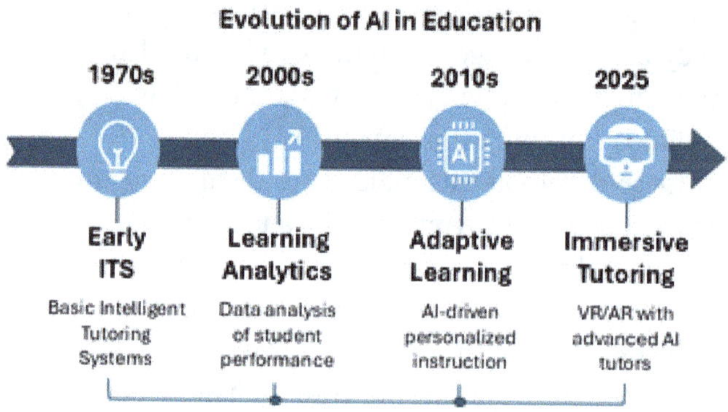

In the 1990s, the field transitioned into the era of *machine learning*, enabling systems to move beyond rigid rule sets and begin adapting to data. One prominent development was the creation of *Intelligent Tutoring Systems (ITS)*, which provided real-time feedback, student modeling, and curriculum adaptation. Systems like AutoTutor (Graesser et al., 2005) and Cognitive Tutor (Koedinger et al., 1997) demonstrated measurable gains in student performance, particularly in mathematics and science instruction. These systems could trace student errors, infer misconceptions, and personalize instruction—laying the groundwork for many modern adaptive learning tools.

The 2000s saw a surge in *Natural Language Processing (NLP)*, allowing AI to handle unstructured text, interpret student queries, and assess written responses. NLP was instrumental in automating processes such as *short-answer grading, chatbot-based tutoring, and content summarization*. Tools like ETS's e-rater and Rajeshwari et al., 2020 demonstrated how AI could process learner-generated language at scale. More recent work, such as that of Sahu and Bhowmick (2019), has advanced NLP-based *ensemble models* for evaluating free-text responses, achieving reliability comparable to human graders.

With the advent of *deep learning* in the 2010s, AI in education entered a new era. Deep neural networks, particularly *convolutional neural networks (CNNs)* and *transformers*, enabled systems to analyze complex multimodal data—text, audio, video, and behavioral logs. This innovation supported the rise of *multimodal learning analytics*, where AI analyzes not just what learners do, but how they do it, identifying patterns in facial expression, voice tone, clickstream behavior, and more (Blikstein, 2013; D'Mello et al., 2017). Deep learning also empowered intelligent content recommendation engines, as seen in platforms like Coursera and edX, which use user profiles and historical engagement to serve relevant courses and resources dynamically.

In parallel, the rise of *Big data analytics* has provided the backbone for large-scale educational data mining. Learning Management Systems (LMS) like Moodle, Canvas, and Blackboard now log vast amounts of data—time on task, frequency of participation, peer collaboration, and assessment results. AI systems harness this data to power *Predictive analytics*, helping institutions identify at-risk students and intervene early. Institutions like Georgia State University have used AI-based predictive models to improve retention rates by as much as 20% (Means et al., 2020).

Another critical development has been in *Recommender Systems* for learning. Ghosh et al. (2022, 2025) have contributed notably by developing frameworks that augment textbook and video content with curated community question-answer data, enhancing conceptual continuity. These systems integrate deep learning, semantic similarity models, and graph-based representations to provide targeted and context-aware content augmentation.

At present, AI technologies are also being combined with *Virtual Reality (VR) and Augmented Reality (AR)*, producing immersive learning environments that engage multiple senses and simulate real-world contexts. For instance, VR-based medical training systems powered by AI are being used to train surgical students, offering personalized guidance and error correction in real-time. These applications combine computer vision, sensor fusion, and reinforcement learning, making AI a central component in next-generation experiential learning.

Across these technological transitions, several core AI technologies now serve as the foundation for educational applications:

- **Machine Learning (ML):** Enables pattern recognition and model training on educational data to personalize content and feedback.
- **Natural Language Processing (NLP):** Powers essay scoring, chatbots, text summarization, speech recognition, and semantic search in learning environments.
- **Deep Learning (DL):** Facilitates multimodal analysis, recommendation engines, video segmentation, and adaptive assessment.
- **Big Data Analytics:** Supports learning analytics dashboards, student performance prediction, and institutional decision-making.

Table 1. Key milestones in the development of AI applications in education from 1970 to present.

Year/ Period	Milestone	Key Innovation	Impact	References
1970s–80s	Rule-Based Systems	SCHOLAR, SOPHIE	Early AI tutoring in narrow domains	Carbonell (1970); Nwana (1990)
1990s	Intelligent Tutoring Systems	AutoTutor, Cognitive Tutor	Personalized instruction using student modeling	Koedinger et al. (1997)
2000s	NLP in Assessment	e-rater, chatbot tutors	Text processing for essay scoring, Q&A	Graesser et al. (2005); Burstein et al. (2004); Sahu & Bhowmick (2019)
2010s	Deep Learning & Big Data	Coursera recommender, edX logs	Multimodal learning analytics, dropout prediction	Blikstein (2013); Means et al. (2020)
2020s	AI Ethics & VR Integration	XAI, federated learning, AI-VR	Equity, interpretability, immersive pedagogy	Huang et al. (2021); Papakostas et al. (2024)

In summary, the background of AI in education is a story of increasing intelligence, flexibility, and human-centered design. As AI continues to mature, the focus is shifting from mere automation to augmentation—supporting human learners and educators through systems that adapt, explain, and collaborate. These foundational advancements have laid the groundwork for the more futuristic and context-aware applications explored in subsequent sections of this chapter.

3. LITERATURE REVIEW AND THEORETICAL FOUNDATIONS

The integration of Artificial Intelligence (AI) into education cannot be fully understood without grounding in established learning theories. Constructivist principles (Piaget & Inhelder, 2019; Vygotsky, 1978) emphasize that learners actively build knowledge through interaction, which resonates with AI-driven adaptive and interactive systems. Vygotsky's concept of the Zone of Proximal Development (ZPD), for example, aligns with Intelligent Tutoring Systems (ITS) that scaffold learners just beyond their current ability.

Cognitive Load Theory (Sweller, 2011) further underscores the importance of adaptive personalization. AI systems that dynamically adjust difficulty levels or offer multimodal resources can reduce extraneous cognitive load, enabling deeper engagement with core learning materials. Similarly, Bloom's taxonomy, revised by Anderson & Krathwohl (2001), provides a useful framework for understanding how AI can facilitate progression from knowledge recall to higher-order thinking.

Social learning theory (Bandura, 1986) complements these perspectives by framing AI as a tool for collaborative and observational learning. For example, AI-powered discussion forums or peer recommendation engines support students in modeling behaviors and strategies from others. Together, these frameworks provide a robust pedagogical foundation, ensuring that AI adoption does not merely automate tasks but enhances meaningful, developmentally aligned learning experiences.

Recent studies further enrich the theoretical and empirical landscape of AI in education, particularly within K–12 contexts. Lampropoulos and Papadakis (2025) highlight the educational value of AI and social robots, emphasizing their role in fostering interactive, student-centered learning experiences. Complementing this, Uğraş et al. (2024) demonstrate how ChatGPT-supported education in primary schools can contribute to sustainable practices, while Uğraş et al. (2024) provide teacher perspectives on the integration of ChatGPT into early childhood STEM education, underscoring both opportunities and pedagogical challenges. Beyond the design of AI tools, student perceptions and data collection practices also warrant careful attention. Lavidas et al. (2022a) show how social desirability bias affects student self-reports across different learning contexts, raising concerns about the reliability of learner-generated data that often underpin AI analytics. Similarly, Lavidas et al. (2022b) identify factors influencing teacher survey response rates, reminding us that the quality of teacher feedback—central to AI training datasets—depends on contextually sensitive research design. Collectively, these studies underscore that AI's successful adoption in K–12 education requires not only technological innovation but also sustainable practices, ethical data use, and robust alignment with teacher and learner perspectives.

4. AI IN K-12 CLASSROOMS

While much of the early adoption of AI in education has been concentrated in higher education and MOOCs, recent developments demonstrate significant impact in primary and secondary schools. Intelligent tutoring systems like Carnegie Learning's Cognitive Tutor have been integrated into middle and high school curricula, showing measurable gains in mathematics achievement (Koedinger et al., 1997). Similarly, DreamBox Learning has been widely used in elementary schools, adapting math content in real time based on individual student responses.

In literacy, Lexia Core5 provides adaptive reading interventions, supporting differentiated instruction for diverse learners, including English language learners and students with dyslexia. Duolingo for Schools exemplifies how gamified AI applications support language acquisition for younger learners. Beyond content delivery, AI-based analytics are increasingly used by K–12 school districts to flag early signs of absenteeism, disengagement, or at-risk performance, allowing timely teacher interventions.

A critical factor in successful adoption is teacher readiness and AI literacy. Teachers require not only technical skills but also pedagogical frameworks to integrate AI tools meaningfully into daily instruction. Professional development programs focused on AI pedagogy are essential to ensure that teachers act as co-designers and evaluators of these technologies rather than passive implementers.

5. GLOBAL AI ADOPTION IN EDUCATION

AI adoption in education varies significantly across regions, shaped by infrastructure, policy, and cultural contexts. In Africa, mobile-based adaptive tutoring systems are being piloted to address gaps in teacher availability and improve access in rural communities (Mhlanga, 2023). In Latin America, AI has been integrated into literacy and numeracy programs to supplement limited classroom resources. In India, platforms such as BYJU'S leverage AI-powered personalization to scale learning access for millions of schoolchildren, particularly in mathematics and science.

International organizations such as UNESCO and OECD emphasize the importance of equity, ethics, and inclusion in AI adoption. UNESCO's 2022 Recommendation on the Ethics of Artificial Intelligence highlights the need for impact assessments, transparency, and capacity-building for teachers, while OECD policy papers underscore strategies for balancing innovation with protection of student rights (UNESCO, 2022; Huang et al., 2021).

6. DOMAINS OF AI INNOVATION IN EDUCATION

AI-powered Intelligent Tutoring Systems are among the most established and impactful applications of AI in education. These systems aim to replicate the adaptive and responsive behavior of a human tutor by offering individualized support in real-time. They deliver feedback, guide problem-solving, and scaffold knowledge acquisition based on a learner's ongoing performance.

For instance, *AutoTutor*, developed by Graesser et al. (2005), engages learners in natural language conversations to promote deeper learning in STEM domains. Similarly, *Carnegie Learning's MATHia* uses cognitive models to adapt instruction in mathematics, often showing better outcomes than conventional instruction. Rajeshwari et al., 2020 leverages natural language processing and domain-specific knowledge graphs to respond meaningfully to student queries, tailoring content based on the learner's conceptual understanding.

ITS has been shown to significantly improve student learning outcomes. A meta-analysis by VanLehn (2011) revealed that ITS can achieve effect sizes close to those of human tutors, especially in well-structured domains. Their scalable architecture allows deployment across thousands of learners simultaneously, making high-quality tutoring accessible even in under-resourced settings.

However, challenges remain in making ITS emotionally responsive and pedagogically flexible. Many ITS systems struggle to detect and appropriately respond to learner frustration or disengagement. Integrating *affective computing*, as suggested by Woolf et al. (2009), offers a way forward, allowing systems to detect non-verbal cues and adjust instructional strategies accordingly.

Table 2. Key applications of AI in education, corresponding technologies, use cases, and tools.

AI Domain	**Core Technologies**	**Educational Use Cases**	**Notable Tools**	**References**
Intelligent Tutoring Systems (ITS)	NLP, Knowledge Graphs, Bayesian Models	Real-time feedback, personalized instruction	AutoTutor, MATHia, Squirrel AI	VanLehn (2011); Graesser et al. (2005)
Automated Assessment	NLP, ML, Ensemble Models	Essay grading, short-answer scoring, peer review support	ETS e-rater, Turnitin, Coursera Grader	Burstein et al. (2004); Sahu & Bhowmick (2019)
Predictive Analytics	Deep Learning, Logistic Regression, Learning Analytics	Dropout prediction, adaptive interventions	Georgia State Predictive Model, Purdue Signals	Arnold & Pistilli (2012); Kurzweil (2015)
Personalized Learning	Reinforcement Learning, User Modeling, Recommendation Systems	Curriculum adaptation, course suggestions	Khan Academy AI Tutor, Duolingo, Coursera	Settles & Meeder (2016); Anderson et al. (2014)
Emotion-aware Learning	Affective Computing, Facial Recognition, Voice Analysis	Frustration detection, motivation tracking	AutoTutor Emotion Tracker	D'Mello & Graesser (2013)
Immersive Learning (VR/AR)	Computer Vision, Sensor Fusion, Reinforcement Learning	Simulation-based learning, 3D experiments	Labster, zSpace	Barsom et al. (2016); Radianti et al. (2020)

6.1. AI-Powered Intelligent Tutoring Systems (ITS):

AI-powered Intelligent Tutoring Systems are among the most established and impactful applications of AI in education. These systems aim to replicate the adaptive and responsive behavior of a human tutor by offering individualized support in real-time. They deliver feedback, guide problem-solving, and scaffold knowledge acquisition based on a learner's ongoing performance.

For instance, *AutoTutor*, developed by Graesser et al. (2005), engages learners in natural language conversations to promote deeper learning in STEM domains. Similarly, *Carnegie Learning's MATHia* uses cognitive models to adapt instruction in mathematics, often showing better outcomes than conventional instruction. Rajeshwari et al., 2020 leverages natural language processing and domain-specific knowledge graphs to respond meaningfully to student queries, tailoring content based on the learner's conceptual understanding.

ITS has been shown to significantly improve student learning outcomes. A meta-analysis by VanLehn (2011) revealed that ITS can achieve effect sizes close to those of human tutors, especially in well-structured domains. Their scalable architecture allows deployment across thousands of learners simultaneously, making high-quality tutoring accessible even in under-resourced settings.

However, challenges remain in making ITS emotionally responsive and pedagogically flexible. Many ITS systems struggle to detect and appropriately respond to learner frustration or disengagement. Integrating *affective computing*, as suggested by Woolf et al. (2009), offers a way forward, allowing systems to detect non-verbal cues and adjust instructional strategies accordingly.

6.2. Automated Grading & AI-Based Assessment:

Assessment is a cornerstone of education, and AI is increasingly being used to automate the grading of assignments, essays, code, and even multimedia submissions. These systems aim to reduce instructor workload, ensure consistency, and deliver instant feedback to learners. They range from traditional rule-based models to deep learning algorithms capable of assessing complex and open-ended tasks.

AI-based graders such as the *e-rater* system developed by ETS are now standard in high-stakes exams like TOEFL. They evaluate grammar, coherence, and argumentation in student essays, allowing quicker turnaround without compromising on quality. Platforms like *Turnitin* use machine learning not only to detect plagiarism but also to assess the quality of writing based on rubrics.

In MOOCs and large university settings, AI assessment tools scale grading across thousands of students. Tools like *Peergrade* and Coursera's AI grader enable robust peer-review workflows, where machine learning models provide rubric-based assistance to improve peer evaluation accuracy.

However, these systems are not without limitations. As noted by Sahu and Bhowmick (2019), while ensemble methods improve accuracy in grading short answers, challenges remain in evaluating nuanced reasoning and contextual interpretation. There are ongoing concerns that AI graders may penalize creativity or reward formulaic responses if not appropriately calibrated. This highlights the importance of hybrid approaches that combine automated scoring with human oversight in sensitive or high-stakes evaluations.

6.3. Predictive Analytics & Student Retention:

Another domain where AI is proving transformative is predictive analytics, particularly in identifying students at risk of dropping out or underperforming. These models analyze behavioral logs, assessment data, demographic profiles, and platform usage to flag disengagement or academic struggles early in the learning process.

At *Georgia State University*, AI-driven predictive models have helped reduce dropout rates by over 21% by identifying at-risk students and triggering personalized interventions (Kurzweil, 2015). *Purdue University's Signals system* uses learning management system data to provide real-time risk alerts to students, encouraging proactive behavioral change.

The construction of these predictive models involves complex feature engineering and validation. Lykourentzou et al. (2009) showed that learner engagement metrics could accurately predict 70% of dropouts in e-learning environments. More recent models use deep learning to capture temporal patterns and interactions that traditional models may miss.

Despite these successes, predictive analytics in education faces ethical concerns. Models may reflect historical biases or over-rely on sensitive demographic attributes. Tools must be transparent and explainable to both educators and learners to build trust. As Adadi and Berrada (2018) emphasize, *Explainable AI (XAI)* is vital in such contexts, allowing users to interrogate predictions and understand the rationale behind alerts.

6.4. AI in Virtual & Augmented Reality (VR/AR) Learning:

The integration of AI with immersive technologies like VR and AR has opened new frontiers in experiential learning. These environments provide learners with rich, interactive experiences that enhance engagement, visualization, and retention.

AI enhances VR/AR systems by personalizing the experience based on real-time learner data. For example, in *AI-powered surgical simulators*, computer vision tracks hand movements, while machine learning algorithms assess skill proficiency and adapt the training scenario accordingly. Similarly, *AR-based chemistry labs* like those from *Labster* or *zSpace* allow students to manipulate virtual molecules, with AI adjusting task complexity based on performance.

Papakostas et al. (2024) showed that students trained in AI-VR environments retained knowledge better than those in traditional classrooms. Radianti et al. (2020) emphasized that such immersive systems are particularly effective in complex STEM domains where visualization is critical.

However, barriers such as high hardware costs, limited content availability, and accessibility constraints pose challenges to broader adoption. Research is increasingly focused on developing *lightweight AI-driven immersive solutions* that can run on mobile devices, thereby democratizing access to these advanced tools.

6.5. Learner Experiences with AI Tutors

Beyond technical effectiveness, student perceptions of AI-powered tools are critical for sustained adoption. Studies show that while many learners appreciate personalized feedback and adaptive pathways, concerns remain around trust, anxiety, and reduced autonomy. Vistorte et al. (2024) found that students' emotional states, such as frustration or motivation, significantly influenced their interactions with AI tutors. Moreover, transparency in AI decisions has been linked to higher trust and engagement (Luckin & Holmes, 2016).

Importantly, research suggests that when students view AI as a supportive partner rather than a replacement for teachers, their motivation and autonomy increase. Designing AI systems that promote learner agency and metacognition, while also addressing usability and cultural relevance, is therefore crucial to positive educational outcomes.

6.6. Ethical AI & Bias Reduction in Education:

As AI becomes embedded in core educational processes, its ethical implications become more pronounced. Bias in algorithms, lack of transparency, and data privacy concerns are critical issues that must be addressed to ensure equitable outcomes for all learners.

If not thoughtfully designed, AI systems in education risk perpetuating and even exacerbating existing societal biases. As Binns et al., 2018 caution, the lack of transparency in algorithmic decision-making often compromises fairness, particularly when learners are unable to interpret or contest the outcomes produced by these systems. Similarly, Williamson and Eynon (2020) argue that the increasing datafication of education may lead to the commodification of student behavior, thereby undermining learner autonomy and diminishing trust in educational technologies.

Efforts to address these issues include *fairness-aware learning*, which modifies algorithms to ensure equitable treatment across groups, and *interpretable models* that provide human-understandable explanations for decisions. The UNESCO Recommendation on the Ethics of AI (2021) calls for continuous impact assessments, stakeholder participation, and inclusive governance to guide AI deployment in education.

Practical steps include using *differential privacy* to protect student data, developing *bias detection audits*, and involving diverse stakeholders in system design. Moreover, integrating *value-sensitive design* principles ensures that AI tools align with pedagogical values and human rights.

Table 3. Common ethical challenges in AI-based educational systems and corresponding mitigation strategies.

Ethical Issue	Description	Technical Solution	Governance Approach	References
Algorithmic Bias	Unequal model outcomes across race, gender, SES	Fairness-aware ML, Data balancing	Inclusive dataset curation	Veale & Brass (2019); Binns et al. (2018)
Opacity (Black-box models)	Difficulty in understanding AI decisions	Explainable AI (e.g., LIME, SHAP)	Human-in-the-loop oversight	Adadi & Berrada (2018); Huang et al. (2021)
Privacy Violations	Leakage of sensitive learner data	Federated Learning, Differential Privacy	GDPR, FERPA compliance	Kairouz et al. (2021); UNESCO (2022)
Over-Surveillance	Excessive behavior tracking and profiling	Data minimization, consent protocols	Ethical audits, transparency reports	Williamson & Eynon (2020)
Misalignment with Pedagogy	Poor integration of cognitive science principles	Teacher-involved co-design	Educator training, curriculum alignment	Woolf et al. (2013); Luckin & Holmes (2016)

AI systems in education raise complex legal and ethical concerns that go beyond algorithmic fairness. Legal safeguards such as GDPR (EU), FERPA (USA), and COPPA specifically regulate how student data, especially that of minors, may be collected, processed, and shared. These regulations are particularly critical in K–12 contexts, where learners lack full autonomy and require enhanced protection (Livingstone et al., 2019).

To ensure ethical compliance and legal accountability, institutions must:

- Conduct *impact assessments* before deployment of AI systems (UNESCO, 2022)
- Ensure *transparency and explainability* of AI decisions (Adadi & Berrada, 2018)
- Involve *educators, students, parents, and policymakers* in the design and oversight processes (Veale & Brass, 2019)
- Embed *privacy-by-design* strategies such as federated learning and differential privacy (Kairouz et al., 2021)
- Align AI implementation with *Universal Design for Learning (UDL) and child digital rights frameworks* (Al-Azawei et al., 2016)

Institutions and developers must be jointly responsible for *ethical alignment, legal compliance*, and *educational effectiveness*, balancing innovation with protection.

6.7. Ethical & Policy Considerations in K–12

The integration of Artificial Intelligence (AI) into education raises a wide spectrum of ethical, legal, and policy challenges. While issues of algorithmic bias, transparency, and data governance are relevant across all educational levels, the K–12 context introduces unique considerations because of the developmental stage of learners, their limited autonomy, and the heightened need for child protection.

In K–12 contexts, ethical concerns extend beyond generic debates about fairness and bias to include the rights and protections of minors. Regulations such as the Children's Online Privacy Protection Act (COPPA) in the United States, the Family Educational Rights and Privacy Act (FERPA), and the EU's General Data Protection Regulation–Kids (GDPR-K) set strict boundaries on how children's data may be collected, processed, and shared (Livingstone et al., 2019).

Parental consent, teacher oversight, and transparent communication with families are therefore central to AI adoption in schools. Teachers must be supported to act not only as implementers but as co-designers and ethical gatekeepers of AI tools. Embedding principles of explainable AI, fairness-aware machine learning, and child digital rights frameworks is essential to safeguarding learners while fostering trust among parents and communities.

An often-overlooked opportunity is AI's potential to support diverse learners in K–12 contexts. Adaptive platforms can personalize content for students with learning disabilities, such as dyslexia or ADHD, by offering multimodal inputs and scaffolds. AI-driven speech recognition tools aid language acquisition for English language learners, while affective computing can monitor emotional cues to support students on the autism spectrum.

The framework of Universal Design for Learning (UDL) emphasizes flexibility in how content is presented and how learners demonstrate understanding. When aligned with AI, UDL principles ensure that personalization extends to accessibility and equity (Al-Azawei et al., 2016). This dimension of AI adoption is critical to closing gaps for students who are often marginalized by traditional educational systems.

Furthermore, effective governance in K–12 requires active stakeholder engagement, including input from teachers, school administrators, parents, and child advocacy groups. Co-design processes should be implemented to ensure AI tools reflect pedagogical goals, protect child rights, and account for cultural and developmental needs. Transparent reporting practices and community consultations foster trust and legitimacy, especially when AI impacts assessment, placement, or disciplinary interventions (UNESCO, 2022; Veale & Brass, 2019).

7. SOLUTIONS AND RECOMMENDATIONS

The integration of AI-powered solutions in education has led to significant transformations in learning methodologies, assessment techniques, and student engagement strategies. These advancements are shaping the future of education by improving personalized learning, increasing accessibility, enabling real-time diagnostics, and streamlining administrative tasks. However, the successful adoption of AI in education hinges on addressing several critical challenges, such as ensuring data privacy, mitigating algorithmic bias, and making AI-driven educational tools accessible across socio-economic boundaries.

This section explores some of the most impactful AI-powered solutions currently deployed across educational contexts. Each solution is presented with examples from real-world implementations, supported by recent academic insights, and followed by a discussion on limitations and future directions.

7.1. Personalized Learning with AI

AI-driven adaptive learning systems tailor content delivery based on a learner's proficiency, pace, and prior knowledge. Platforms like Khan Academy deploy AI tutors that analyze learner interactions to personalize quizzes and videos, reportedly improving proficiency by over 30% (Khan Academy, 2021). Duolingo applies reinforcement learning and spaced repetition algorithms to enhance language retention, achieving recall rates 60% higher than traditional methods (Settles & Meeder, 2016). Coursera's recommendation engine customizes course suggestions based on learner history, increasing completion rates by 35% (Anderson et al., 2014). Research by Pane et al., 2015 showed students using personalized platforms gained 8 percentile points more in mathematics. Brusilovsky & Millán (2007) emphasized the role of intelligent learner modelling in personalizing recommendations. While these platforms enhance engagement and outcomes, challenges like algorithmic bias and data privacy persist. Future systems could integrate emotion-aware AI to respond to learner frustration or disengagement, as suggested by D'Mello & Graesser (2013).

7.2 AI-Powered Intelligent Tutoring Systems (ITS)

ITS provide on-demand, adaptive tutoring by detecting learner knowledge gaps and offering contextual feedback. For example, IBM Watson Tutor uses NLP to simulate Socratic dialogue, reducing learning gaps by up to 40% (Rajeshwari et al., 2020). Carnegie Learning's MATHia applies cognitive models to improve algebra proficiency by 38% (Pane et al., 2014), while Squirrel AI in China uses reinforcement learning to improve student test scores by 32% (Zhou et al., 2020). As shown in Figure 2, a typical ITS consists of interconnected modules including domain knowledge, a learner model, natural language processing (NLP) components, and a feedback engine—collectively enabling dynamic personalization and learner adaptation (Graesser et al., 2005; Woolf et al., 2009).

Figure 2. Architecture of a modern Intelligent Tutoring System. The block diagram includes core components such as domain knowledge, learner model, NLP interface, decision engine, and feedback generator. Inspired by Graesser et al. (2005) and Woolf et al. (2009).

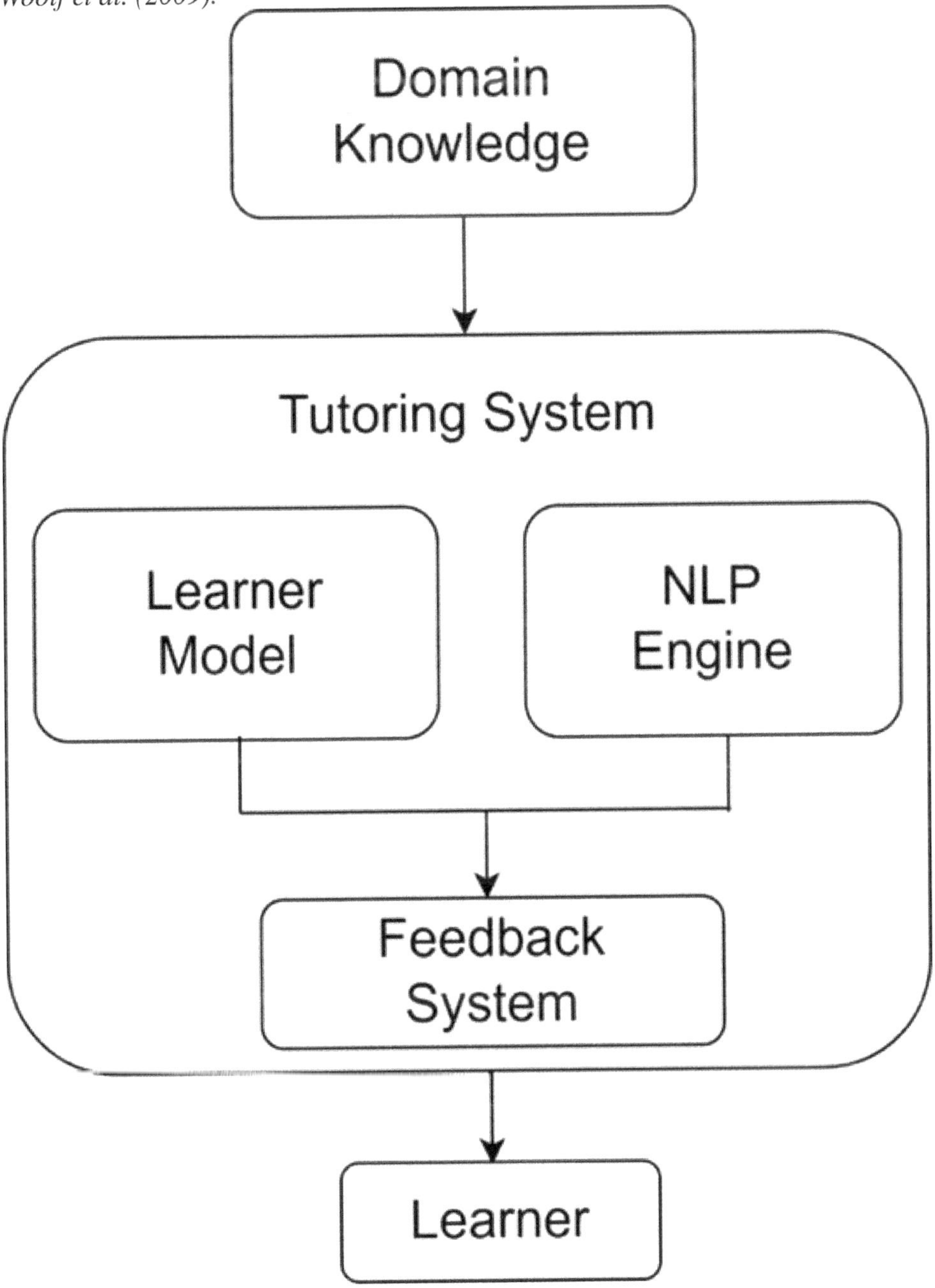

Meta-analyses by VanLehn (2011) confirm ITS can match the effectiveness of human tutors in structured domains. Systems like AutoTutor (Graesser et al., 2005) and Wayang Outpost have demonstrated consistent performance across diverse learner profiles. However, most ITS struggle to respond to emotional states. Affective computing approaches, such as those proposed by Woolf et al. (2009), offer ways to detect non-verbal cues and improve emotional responsiveness.

Table 4. Comparative analysis of notable AI Powered Education Frameworks and Models

Framework/Model	Scope	Strengths	Limitations	Reference
AutoTutor	Conversational ITS	Natural dialogue, deep reasoning	Limited subject flexibility	Graesser et al. (2005)
MATHia	Cognitive tutor for algebra	Mastery-based learning, skill modeling	Focused on math only	Pane et al. (2014)
Coursera Recommendation Engine	MOOC personalization	Scale, relevance, completion rate gains	Cold start for new users	Anderson et al. (2014)
Georgia State Predictive Model	Student success analytics	Real-world impact, risk alerts	Requires rich longitudinal data	Kurzweil (2015)
OpenAI GPT Models in EdTech	Generative AI for tutoring & Q&A	Language fluency, scalability	Needs guardrails for fairness	OpenAI (2023)

7.3 AI in Automated Assessments

Automated assessment tools powered by AI offer scalable, objective, and instant evaluation of student work. Systems like Turnitin assess grammar, coherence, and argumentation, achieving 96% grading accuracy (Roe et al., 2023). ETS's e-rater, used in TOEFL exams, increases grading efficiency by 50% (Burstein et al., 2004), and Coursera's AI grader supports scalable peer-review frameworks for MOOCs (Piech et al., 2012). Research by Sahu & Bhowmick (2019) demonstrated the superiority of ensemble models in short-answer grading. Reimann et al. (2013) highlighted the robustness of AI-assisted evaluation when paired with rubric-based scoring. Despite the speed and scalability benefits, AI assessments can misinterpret nuanced arguments or creative expressions. Future grading systems must include deep semantic analysis and human-in-the-loop workflows to mitigate bias and ensure fairness.

7.4. AI for Predictive Analytics & Student Retention

Predictive analytics models leverage behavioral and performance data to identify students at risk of dropout or failure. Georgia State University reduced dropout rates by 21% using such models to trigger early interventions (Kurzweil, 2015), while Purdue University's Signals system improved graduation rates by 20% by alerting students to academic risks (Arnold & Pistilli, 2012). Studies like Lykourentzou et al. (2009) have shown 70% predictive accuracy using engagement metrics, while Clow (2013) emphasized incorporating motivational and behavioral data for dropout prediction. Although powerful, these tools raise concerns about data accuracy, bias, and transparency. Adadi & Berrada (2018) advocate for Explainable AI (XAI) to clarify model decisions and build user trust. Ensuring ethical use of predictive analytics involves combining technical transparency with inclusive intervention strategies.

7.5. AI-Enhanced Virtual & Augmented Reality (VR/AR) Learning

The fusion of AI with immersive VR/AR environments facilitates experiential learning that is interactive, personalized, and context-rich. In surgical training, AI-powered VR simulators improve skill acquisition by 75% through real-time feedback (Barsom et al., 2016). Platforms like zSpace and Labster offer AR-based science labs that adapt experiment difficulty based on student performance, improving inquiry-based learning (Deng et al., 2024). Radianti et al. (2020) found immersive learning significantly enhanced retention in complex STEM subjects. Papakostas et al. (2024) confirmed that AI-supported VR instruction outperforms both traditional and face-to-face modalities. Yet, high hardware costs and accessibility issues remain major barriers. Future directions include developing mobile-compatible immersive platforms and designing inclusive, low-cost AR/VR solutions.

7.6. Ethical AI & Addressing Bias in Education

As AI adoption grows, ensuring fairness, transparency, and ethical use is paramount. Bias in training data and opaque algorithms can lead to unfair outcomes. Binns et al. (2018) emphasized that learners must understand and contest algorithmic decisions. Williamson & Eynon (2020) warned that over-reliance on data-driven decision-making may commodify student behavior and reduce learner autonomy. Initiatives like OpenAI's efforts to reduce bias by 35% in GPT-4 (OpenAI, 2023) and the UNESCO AI Ethics Guidelines (2021) exemplify best practices in ethical deployment. Fairness-aware machine learning, stakeholder participation, and privacy-preserving techniques like differential privacy are essential. Embedding ethical principles into the design, governance, and evaluation of educational AI systems will be critical to building equitable learning futures. Figure 3 presents a layered ethical framework for AI in education, distinguishing between technical-level algorithmic fairness, institutional safeguards, and policy-level interventions aligned with global guidelines such as UNESCO (2022).

Figure 3. Ethical AI in Education: A multi-layered framework highlighting ethical concerns and mitigation strategies across technical, institutional, and policy levels. Reflects design principles advocated by UNESCO (2022) and Adadi & Berrada (2018).

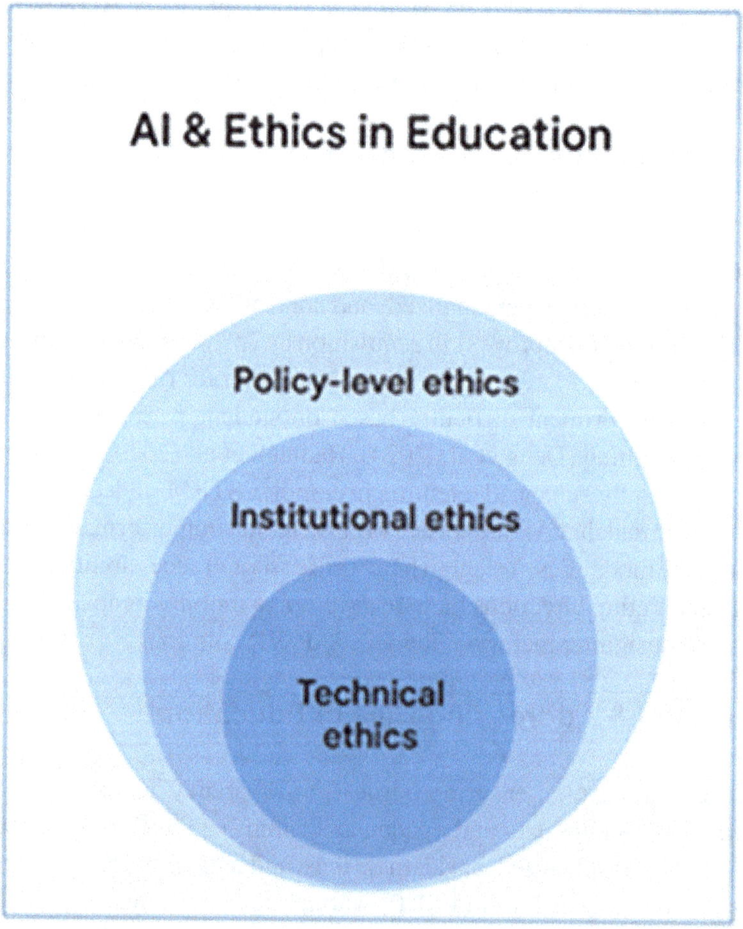

8. FUTURE RESEARCH DIRECTIONS

As the deployment of Artificial Intelligence in education accelerates, there is a growing need to explore *emerging research directions* that can enhance the *transparency, trustworthiness, inclusivity, and effectiveness* of AI-driven educational systems. While current applications have shown promise in automating and personalizing instruction, new challenges have surfaced, particularly around explainability, emotional intelligence, and the secure management of academic credentials. This section highlights *three pivotal frontiers* in AI research education that warrant focused attention from both researchers and developers.

8.1. Explainable AI (XAI) in Education

One of the critical challenges in AI adoption in education is the *"black box" nature* of many machine learning models. While these models may be highly accurate, their internal reasoning processes are often opaque to users, including students, teachers, and administrators. This *lack of interpretability undermines trust, accountability, and pedagogical utility*, particularly in high-stakes scenarios such as admissions, grading, or intervention targeting.

Explainable AI (XAI) refers to a set of techniques designed to *make the decision-making of AI systems transparent and understandable* to humans. In educational contexts, XAI can enhance decision-making by allowing users to examine why a particular student was flagged as at-risk, how a personalized learning (Baird et al., 2017) path was generated, or why a response received a specific grade.

Recent studies have begun to address this issue. For example, Huang et al. (2021) discuss how visual explanations and local feature importance models can help teachers interpret AI recommendations. Similarly, Adadi and Berrada (2018) propose model-agnostic tools like LIME and SHAP that can be applied to intelligent tutoring systems (Jing et al., 2020) to explain both predictions and feedback logic.

However, a trade-off often exists between model performance and explainability. Deep learning models—particularly transformers and recurrent networks—may offer state-of-the-art accuracy but are inherently less interpretable. Future research must explore *hybrid approaches*, combining rule-based systems with black-box models, or developing *intrinsically interpretable architectures* (e.g., decision trees, attention maps) tailored to educational settings.

Furthermore, user-centered XAI research is essential—what is explainable to a data scientist may not be meaningful to a teacher or student. *Human-in-the-loop evaluations*, usability studies, and participatory design will be critical to creating XAI systems that serve real educational needs.

8.2. AI-Driven Emotional Intelligence

Another important frontier in AI-powered education is the development of systems capable of *recognizing and responding to students' emotional states*—a field commonly referred to as *affective computing*. Emotion plays a fundamental role in learning: engagement, frustration, boredom, and motivation all influence cognitive processing and knowledge retention. Current AI systems often fail to consider these emotional dimensions, limiting their effectiveness in promoting sustained learner engagement.

AI-driven emotional intelligence systems aim to detect emotions using multimodal inputs such as facial expressions, voice tone, body language, and even physiological data (e.g., heart rate, eye movement). Once recognized, AI can adapt instructional strategies, offering encouragement during frustration, slowing down during confusion, or introducing challenges to re-engage bored learners.

Several studies have demonstrated the feasibility of this approach. D'Mello and Graesser (2013) developed the AutoTutor Emotion Tracker, which integrates facial expression and dialogue features to infer learner emotions in real time. More recently, Calvo and D'Mello (2010) emphasized the importance of context-aware emotion recognition, where AI systems consider not only affective cues but also task difficulty and prior learner behavior.

Future research should explore *multimodal fusion techniques* that combine visual, auditory, and contextual data for robust emotion detection. Additionally, *ethical concerns* around surveillance and emotional manipulation must be addressed—particularly in systems deployed to minors. Privacy-preserving emotion detection methods, along with transparent consent mechanisms, are critical for responsible development.

There is also room to investigate *emotion-adaptive content delivery models*, where AI dynamically modifies learning environments to support positive affective states. Such models could incorporate narrative gamification, peer interactions, or ambient feedback to sustain motivation and well-being.

8.3. Blockchain and AI for Secure Credential Verification

In parallel with AI's growth in instruction and assessment, another frontier is the *secure management of educational credentials and academic records*. Credential fraud, transcript manipulation, and the rising complexity of cross-institutional verification, especially in global and online learning contexts, necessitate innovative solutions. This is where the integration of *Blockchain and AI technologies* holds significant promise.

Blockchain technology provides a *decentralized, tamper-proof, and transparent ledger system*, ideal for storing and verifying certificates, diplomas, micro-credentials, and learning badges. By combining blockchain with AI-driven verification mechanisms, institutions can create *smart contracts* that automatically validate a learner's progress and competencies based on authenticated data.

Initiatives like the *MIT Digital Diploma Project* and *Blockcerts* have already demonstrated the viability of blockchain-based credentialing. AI can augment these systems by analyzing learning behavior and performance data to *generate real-time skill assessments*, which can then be recorded immutably on a blockchain.

Such integration not only enhances security but also *supports lifelong learning ecosystems*, where learners accumulate modular credentials from various platforms (e.g., Coursera, edX, university systems) into a unified, verifiable portfolio.

Future research should focus on *scaling blockchain implementations* in low-resource educational settings, minimizing environmental impact, and improving interoperability across institutional systems. Standards must also be developed to ensure *privacy protection, auditability, and inclusivity*, especially for non-traditional learners or those in informal learning environments.

Transparent deployment of AI in education must be coupled with *inclusive stakeholder engagement*, ensuring that *educators, students, parents, and policymakers* are involved in design, deployment, and feedback cycles. Participatory co-design processes and continuous feedback loops foster not only trust but also ensure context-sensitive adaptation of AI tools (UNESCO, 2022; Veale & Brass, 2019).

8.4. AI Governance and Policy Research for Education

As AI becomes integral to education, future research must also address *system-wide governance frameworks*. This includes:

- Developing national AI-in-education strategies aligned with ethical guidelines (UNESCO, 2022)
- Designing *institutional governance bodies* responsible for AI audits, ethical oversight, and stakeholder consultation
- Exploring *legal standards for algorithmic accountability*, such as impact assessments and algorithmic registers
- Ensuring *global interoperability* of legal and data standards to accommodate cross-border online education

Such frameworks will be crucial in enabling AI to deliver on its promise while safeguarding learner rights and societal values.

9. CONCLUSION

Artificial Intelligence has moved beyond its early promise to become a powerful and pervasive force in modern education. From *intelligent tutoring systems and automated assessments to predictive analytics, immersive learning environments, and personalized content delivery*, AI is reshaping how knowledge is imparted, acquired, and assessed. This chapter has explored the *evolution of AI in education*, outlined its *core innovations*, and discussed both the *opportunities and complexities* that define its present and future.

The insights presented throughout this chapter reaffirm the *transformative potential of AI* to create more personalized, inclusive, and efficient learning systems. Adaptive platforms now allow learners to progress at their own pace, intelligent tutors provide instant feedback at scale, and AI-powered assessments reduce human bias while improving turnaround time. Predictive analytics help institutions retain more students, while emotion-aware systems are beginning to understand and respond to the affective needs of learners. Emerging technologies like blockchain promise secure and verifiable credentialing, enabling lifelong and cross-institutional learning pathways.

Yet, as we embrace this future, it is equally important to remain vigilant of AI's limitations and risks. Issues such as *algorithmic bias, opaque decision-making, lack of pedagogical grounding, digital inequity, and threats to student privacy* pose serious challenges. These are not merely technical problems but *socio-ethical dilemmas* that demand thoughtful solutions, participatory design, and responsible deployment.

Ethical AI is not an optional add-on, it is the foundation upon which trust, fairness, and long-term impact in education must rest. The use of explainable AI (XAI), fairness-aware machine learning, privacy-preserving techniques, and inclusive datasets must become standard practice in both academic research and industry innovation.

REFERENCES

Adadi, A., & Berrada, M. (2018). Peeking inside the black-box: A survey on explainable artificial intelligence (XAI). *IEEE Access : Practical Innovations, Open Solutions*, *6*, 52138–52160. DOI: 10.1109/ACCESS.2018.2870052

Al-Azawei, A., Parslow, P., & Lundqvist, K. (2016). Barriers and opportunities of e-learning implementation in Iraq: A case of public universities. *International Review of Research in Open and Distance Learning*, *17*(5). Advance online publication. DOI: 10.19173/irrodl.v17i5.2501

Al-Azawei, A., Serenelli, F., & Lundqvist, K. (2016). Universal Design for Learning (UDL): A content analysis of peer reviewed journals from 2012 to 2015. *The Journal of Scholarship of Teaching and Learning*, *16*(3), 39–56. DOI: 10.14434/josotl.v16i3.19295

Anderson, A., Huttenlocher, D., Kleinberg, J., & Leskovec, J. (2014, April). Engaging with massive online courses. In *Proceedings of the 23rd international conference on World wide web* (pp. 687-698).

Anderson, L. W., & Krathwohl, D. R. (2001). *A taxonomy for learning, teaching, and assessing: A revision of Bloom's taxonomy of educational objectives: complete edition*. Addison Wesley Longman, Inc.

Arnold, K. E., & Pistilli, M. D. (2012, April). Course signals at Purdue: Using learning analytics to increase student success. In *Proceedings of the 2nd international conference on learning analytics and knowledge* (pp. 267-270). DOI: 10.1145/2330601.2330666

Baird, M. D., Pane, J. F., Steiner, E. D., Hamilton, L. S., & Pane, J. D. (2017). Informing Progress: Insights on Personalized Learning Implementation and Effects.

Bandura, A. (1986). Social foundations of thought and action. *Englewood Cliffs, NJ, 1986*(23-28), 2.

Barsom, E. Z., Graafland, M., & Schijven, M. P. (2016). Systematic review on the effectiveness of augmented reality applications in medical training. *Surgical Endoscopy*, *30*(10), 4174–4183. DOI: 10.1007/s00464-016-4800-6 PMID: 26905573

Binns, R., Van Kleek, M., Veale, M., Lyngs, U., Zhao, J., & Shadbolt, N. (2018, April). 'It's Reducing a Human Being to a Percentage' Perceptions of Justice in Algorithmic Decisions. In *Proceedings of the 2018 Chi conference on human factors in computing systems* (pp. 1-14). DOI: 10.31235/osf.io/9wqxr

Blikstein, P. (2013, April). Multimodal learning analytics. In *Proceedings of the third international conference on learning analytics and knowledge* (pp. 102-106). DOI: 10.1145/2460296.2460316

Brusilovsky, P., & Millán, E. (2007). User models for adaptive hypermedia and adaptive educational systems. In *The adaptive web: methods and strategies of web personalization* (pp. 3–53). Springer Berlin Heidelberg. DOI: 10.1007/978-3-540-72079-9_1

Burstein, J., Chodorow, M., & Leacock, C. (2004). Automated essay evaluation: The Criterion online writing service. *AI Magazine*, *25*(3), 27–27.

Calvo, R. A., & D'Mello, S. (2010). Affect detection: An interdisciplinary review of models, methods, and their applications. *IEEE Transactions on Affective Computing*, *1*(1), 18–37. DOI: 10.1109/T-AFFC.2010.1

Carbonell, J. R. (1970). *Mixed-initiative man-computer instructional dialogues* (Doctoral dissertation, Massachusetts Institute of Technology).

Carbonell, J. R. (2007). AI in CAI: An artificial-intelligence approach to computer-assisted instruction. *IEEE Transactions on Man-Machine Systems*, *11*(4), 190–202. DOI: 10.1109/TMMS.1970.299942

Clow, D. (2013). An overview of learning analytics. *Teaching in Higher Education*, *18*(6), 683–695. DOI: 10.1080/13562517.2013.827653

D'Mello, S., Dieterle, E., & Duckworth, A. (2017). Advanced, analytic, automated (AAA) measurement of engagement during learning. *Educational Psychologist*, *52*(2), 104–123. DOI: 10.1080/00461520.2017.1281747 PMID: 29038607

D'mello, S., & Graesser, A. (2013). AutoTutor and affective AutoTutor: Learning by talking with cognitively and emotionally intelligent computers that talk back. [TiiS]. *ACM Transactions on Interactive Intelligent Systems*, *2*(4), 1–39. DOI: 10.1145/2395123.2395128

Deng, W., Wang, L., & Deng, X. (2024). Exploring Interactive Learning Environments Based on Augmented Reality Technology. *International Journal of Interactive Mobile Technologies*, *18*(12), 15–29. DOI: 10.3991/ijim.v18i12.49911

Ghosh, K. (2025). Recommending Personalized Video Lecture Augmentations with Tagged Community Question Answers. *International Journal of Artificial Intelligence in Education*, *35*(4), 1–48. DOI: 10.1007/s40593-025-00459-9

Ghosh, K., & Das, S. (2023). Automatic Generation of Algebraic Representation for Physics Problems. *TAM METİN BİLDİRİ KİTABI*, 91.

Ghosh, K., Nangi, S. R., Kanchugantla, Y., Rayapati, P. G., Bhowmick, P. K., & Goyal, P. (2022). Augmenting video lectures: Identifying off-topic concepts and linking to relevant video lecture segments. *International Journal of Artificial Intelligence in Education, 32*(2), 382–412. DOI: 10.1007/s40593-021-00257-z

Graesser, A. C., Chipman, P., Haynes, B. C., & Olney, A. (2005). AutoTutor: An intelligent tutoring system with mixed-initiative dialogue. *IEEE Transactions on Education, 48*(4), 612–618. DOI: 10.1109/TE.2005.856149

Holmes, W. (2020). Artificial intelligence in education. In *Encyclopedia of education and information technologies* (pp. 88–103). Springer International Publishing. DOI: 10.1007/978-3-030-10576-1_107

Huang, C., Samek, T., & Shiri, A. (2021). AI and ethics: Ethical and educational perspectives for LIS. *Journal of Education for Library and Information Science, 62*(4), 351–365. DOI: 10.3138/jelis-62-4-2020-0106

Jing, S., Tang, Y., Liu, X., Gong, X., Cui, W., & Liang, J. (2020, October). A parallel education based intelligent tutoring systems framework. In *2020 IEEE International Conference on Networking, Sensing and Control (ICNSC)* (pp. 1-6). IEEE. DOI: 10.1109/ICNSC48988.2020.9238052

Kairouz, P., McMahan, H. B., Avent, B., Bellet, A., Bennis, M., Bhagoji, A. N., ... & Zhao, S. (2021). Advances and open problems in federated learning. *Foundations and trends® in machine learning, 14*(1–2), 1-210.

Koedinger, K. R., Anderson, J. R., Hadley, W. H., & Mark, M. A. (1997). Intelligent tutoring goes to school in the big city. *International Journal of Artificial Intelligence in Education, 8*, 30–43.

Koedinger, K. R., Anderson, J. R., Hadley, W. H., & Mark, M. A. (1997). Intelligent tutoring goes to school in the big city. *International Journal of Artificial Intelligence in Education, 8*, 30–43.

Krishna, A., Bhowmick, P., Ghosh, K., Sahu, A., & Roy, S. (2015, March). Automatic generation and insertion of assessment items in online video courses. In *Companion Proceedings of the 20th International Conference on Intelligent User Interfaces* (pp. 1-4). DOI: 10.1145/2732158.2732183

Kurzweil, M., & Wu, D. D. (2015). *Building a Pathway to Student Success: at Georgia State University*. ITHAKA S+ R.

Lampropoulos, G., & Papadakis, S. (2025). The educational value of artificial intelligence and social robots. In *Social robots in education* (pp. 3–15). Springer. DOI: 10.1007/978-3-031-82915-4_1

Lampropoulos, G., & Papadakis, S. (2025). The educational value of artificial intelligence and social robots. In *Social robots in education* (pp. 3–15). Springer. DOI: 10.1007/978-3-031-82915-4_1

Lavidas, K., Papadakis, S., Manesis, D., Grigoriadou, A. S., & Gialamas, V.Lectures and Lab Classes. (2022). The effects of social desirability on students' self-reports in two social contexts: Lectures vs. lectures and lab classes. *Information (Basel), 13*(10), 491. DOI: 10.3390/info13100491

Lavidas, K., Petropoulou, A., Papadakis, S., Apostolou, Z., Komis, V., Jimoyiannis, A., & Gialamas, V. (2022). Factors affecting response rates of the web survey with teachers. *Computers, 11*(9), 127. DOI: 10.3390/computers11090127

Livingstone, S., Stoilova, M., & Nandagiri, R. (2019). Children's data and privacy online. *Technology, 58*(2), 157–165.

Luckin, R., & Holmes, W. (2016). Intelligence unleashed: An argument for AI in education.

Lykourentzou, I., Giannoukos, I., Nikolopoulos, V., Mpardis, G., & Loumos, V. (2009). Dropout prediction in e-learning courses through the combination of machine learning techniques. *Computers & Education, 53*(3), 950–965. DOI: 10.1016/j.compedu.2009.05.010

Nwana, H. S. (1990). Intelligent tutoring systems: An overview. *Artificial Intelligence Review, 4*(4), 251–277. DOI: 10.1007/BF00168958

O'Sullivan, P., Forgette, C., Monroe, S., & England, M. T. (2020). Student perceptions of the effectiveness of adaptive courseware for learning. *Current Issues in Emerging Elearning, 7*(1), 5.

Pane, J. F., Griffin, B. A., McCaffrey, D. F., & Karam, R. (2014). Effectiveness of cognitive tutor algebra I at scale. *Educational Evaluation and Policy Analysis, 36*(2), 127–144. DOI: 10.3102/0162373713507480

Pane, J. F., Steiner, E. D., Baird, M. D., & Hamilton, L. S. (2015). *Continued Progress: Promising Evidence on Personalized Learning*. Rand Corporation. DOI: 10.7249/RR1365

Papakostas, C., Troussas, C., & Sgouropoulou, C. (2024). Review of the literature on AI-enhanced augmented reality in education. *Special Topics in Artificial Intelligence and Augmented Reality: The Case of Spatial Intelligence Enhancement*, 13-50.

Piaget, J., & Inhelder, B. (2019). *The Psychology Of The Child.*

Piech, C., Sahami, M., Koller, D., Cooper, S., & Blikstein, P. (2012, February). Modeling how students learn to program. In *Proceedings of the 43rd ACM technical symposium on Computer Science Education* (pp. 153-160).

Radianti, J., Majchrzak, T. A., Fromm, J., & Wohlgenannt, I. (2020). A systematic review of immersive virtual reality applications for higher education: Design elements, lessons learned, and research agenda. *Computers & Education, 147*, 103778. DOI: 10.1016/j.compedu.2019.103778

Rajeshwari, M., & Krishna Prasad, K. (2020). IBM watson industry cognitive education methods. [IJCSBE]. *International Journal of Case Studies in Business, IT, and Education*, *4*(1), 38–50.

Reimann, P., & Yacef, K. (2013). Using process mining for understanding learning. *Handbook of design in educational technology*, 472-481.

Roe, J., Renandya, W. A., & Jacobs, G. M. (2023). A review of AI-powered writing tools and their implications for academic integrity in the language classroom. *Journal of English and Applied Linguistics*, *2*(1), 3. DOI: 10.59588/2961-3094.1035

Roschelle, J., Feng, M., Murphy, R. F., & Mason, C. A. (2016). Online mathematics homework increases student achievement. *AERA Open*, *2*(4), 2332858416673968. DOI: 10.1177/2332858416673968

Roy, S., & Bhowmick, P. K. (2016). Augmenting Online Video Lectures with Topically Relevant Assessment Items. In *ICCE*. DOI: 10.58459/icce.2016.1167

Sahu, A., & Bhowmick, P. K. (2019). Feature engineering and ensemble-based approach for improving automatic short-answer grading performance. *IEEE Transactions on Learning Technologies*, *13*(1), 77–90. DOI: 10.1109/TLT.2019.2897997

Settles, B., & Meeder, B. (2016, August). A trainable spaced repetition model for language learning. In *Proceedings of the 54th annual meeting of the association for computational linguistics* (volume 1*: long papers)* (pp. 1848-1858). DOI: 10.18653/v1/P16-1174

Sweller, J. (2011). Cognitive load theory. [). Academic Press.]. *Psychology of Learning and Motivation*, *55*, 37–76. DOI: 10.1016/B978 0 12 387691-1.00002-8

Uğraş, H., Uğraş, M., Papadakis, S., & Kalogiannakis, M. (2024). ChatGPT-supported education in primary schools: The potential of ChatGPT for sustainable practices. *Sustainability (Basel)*, *16*(22), 9855. DOI: 10.3390/su16229855

Uğraş, H., Uğraş, M., Papadakis, S., & Kalogiannakis, M. (2025). Innovative Early Childhood STEM Education with ChatGPT: Teacher Perspectives. *Technology. Knowledge and Learning*, *30*(2), 809–831. DOI: 10.1007/s10758-024-09804-8

Unesco. (2022). *Recommendation on the ethics of artificial intelligence*. United Nations Educational, Scientific and Cultural Organization.

VanLehn, K. (2011). The relative effectiveness of human tutoring, intelligent tutoring systems, and other tutoring systems. *Educational Psychologist*, *46*(4), 197–221. DOI: 10.1080/00461520.2011.611369

Veale, M., & Brass, I. (2019). Administration by algorithm? Public management meets public sector machine learning. *Public management meets public sector machine learning*.

Vistorte, A. O. R., Deroncele-Acosta, A., Ayala, J. L. M., Barrasa, A., López-Granero, C., & Martí-González, M. (2024). Integrating artificial intelligence to assess emotions in learning environments: A systematic literature review. *Frontiers in Psychology*, *15*, 1387089. DOI: 10.3389/fpsyg.2024.1387089 PMID: 38966729

Vygotsky, L. S. (1978). *Mind in society: The development of higher psychological processes* (Vol. 86). Harvard university press.

Williamson, B., & Eynon, R. (2020). Historical threads, missing links, and future directions in AI in education. *Learning, Media and Technology*, *45*(3), 223–235. DOI: 10.1080/17439884.2020.1798995

Woolf, B., Burleson, W., Arroyo, I., Dragon, T., Cooper, D., & Picard, R. (2009). Affect-aware tutors: Recognising and responding to student affect. *International Journal of Learning Technology*, *4*(3-4), 129–164. DOI: 10.1504/IJLT.2009.028804

Woolf, B. P., Lane, H. C., Chaudhri, V. K., & Kolodner, J. L. (2013). AI grand challenges for education. *AI Magazine*, *34*(4), 66–84. DOI: 10.1609/aimag.v34i4.2490

Compilation of References

Abar, C. A. A. P., Dos Santos, J. M. D. S., & de Almeida, M. V. (2024). *Contribuciones de la integración entre el pensamiento computacional y la inteligencia artificial para la educación matemática*. Springer., DOI: 10.1007/978-3-031-54256-5_27

Acharya, D. B., Kuppan, K., & Divya, B. (2025). Agentic AI: Autonomous intelligence for complex Goals—A comprehensive survey. *IEEE Access : Practical Innovations, Open Solutions*, *13*, 18912–18936. DOI: 10.1109/ACCESS.2025.3532853

Adadi, A., & Berrada, M. (2018). Peeking inside the black-box: A survey on explainable artificial intelligence (XAI). *IEEE Access : Practical Innovations, Open Solutions*, *6*, 52138–52160. DOI: 10.1109/ACCESS.2018.2870052

Adams, C., Pente, P., Lemermeyer, G., & Rockwell, G. (2023). Ethical principles for artificial intelligence in K-12 education. *Comput. Educ. Artif. Intell.*, *4*, 100131. DOI: 10.1016/j.caeai.2023.100131

Adams, D., & Thompson, P. (2025). Transforming School Leadership with Artificial Intelligence: Applications, Implications, and Future Directions. *Leadership and Policy in Schools*, *24*(1), 77–89. DOI: 10.1080/15700763.2024.2411295

Adel, A., Ahsan, A., & Davison, C. (2024). ChatGPT promises and challenges in education: Computational and ethical perspectives. *Education Sciences*, *14*(8), 814. Advance online publication. DOI: 10.3390/educsci14080814

Agkathidis, A. (2015). Generative Design Methods - Implementing Computational Techniques in Undergraduate Architectural Education. *Proceedings of the 33th International Conference on Education and Research in Computer Aided Architectural Design in Europe (eCAADe) [Volume 2]*.

Akgun, S., & Greenhow, C. (2022). Artificial intelligence in education: Addressing ethical challenges in K-12 settings. *AI and Ethics*, *2*(3), 431–440. DOI: 10.1007/s43681-021-00096-7

Akhtar, G., & Shah, W. (2025). AI in Mathematics and STEAM Learning: A Design-Based Research Approach to Enhancing Digital Education. DOI: 10.13140/RG.2.2.29554.82885

Akpan, I. J., Kobara, Y. M., Owolabi, J., Akpan, A. A., & Offodile, O. F. (2025). Conversational and generative artificial intelligence and human–chatbot interaction in education and research. *International Transactions in Operational Research*, *32*(3), 1251–1281. DOI: 10.1111/itor.13522

Al Darayseh, A. (2023). Acceptance of artificial intelligence in teaching science: Science teachers' perspective. *Computers and Education: Artificial Intelligence*, *4*, 100132. DOI: 10.1016/j.caeai.2023.100132

Al Nabhani, F., Hamzah, M., & Abuhassna, H. (2025). The role of artificial intelligence in personalizing educational content: Enhancing the learning experience and developing the teacher's role in an integrated educational environment. *Contemporary Educational Technology*, *17*(2), ep573. DOI: 10.30935/cedtech/16089

Al-Azawei, A., Parslow, P., & Lundqvist, K. (2016). Barriers and opportunities of e-learning implementation in Iraq: A case of public universities. *International Review of Research in Open and Distance Learning*, *17*(5). Advance online publication. DOI: 10.19173/irrodl.v17i5.2501

Al-Azawei, A., Serenelli, F., & Lundqvist, K. (2016). Universal Design for Learning (UDL): A content analysis of peer reviewed journals from 2012 to 2015. *The Journal of Scholarship of Teaching and Learning*, *16*(3), 39–56. DOI: 10.14434/josotl.v16i3.19295

Albadarin, Y., Saqr, M., Pope, N., & Tukiainen, M. (2024). A systematic literature review of empirical research on ChatGPT in education. *Discover Education*, *3*(1), 60. DOI: 10.1007/s44217-024-00138-2

Al-Badi, A., & Khan, A. & Eid-Alotaibi (2022).Perceptions of Learners and Instructors towards Artificial Intelligence in Personalized Learning. *Procedia Computer Science*, 201, 445-451. ISSN 1877-0509, Doi:DOI: 10.1016/j.procs.2022.03.058

Albornoz-De Luise, R. S., Arnau-González, P., Serrano-Mamolar, A., Solera-Monforte, S., & Wu, Y. (2024). *Balancing innovation with ethics.*, DOI: 10.1002/9781394257744.ch11

Alemdag, E. (2023). The effect of chatbots on learning: A meta-analysis of empirical research. *Journal of Research on Technology in Education*, *55*(1), 1–23. DOI: 10.1080/15391523.2023.2255698

Aleven, V., Baraniuk, R., Brunskill, E., Crossley, S., Demszky, D., Fancsali, S., . . . Xing, W. (2023, June). *Towards the future of AI-augmented human tutoring in math learning*. In R. Luckin (Ed.), *Artificial intelligence in education: Proceedings of the 24th International Conference on Artificial Intelligence in Education (AIED 2023)* (pp. 26-31). Springer Nature Switzerland. DOI: 10.1007/978-3-031-36336-8_3

Alfaro-Salas, H., & Díaz, J. A. (2024). Percepciones y Aplicaciones de la IA entre Estudiantes de Secundaria. *Revista Docentes 2.0, 17*(1), 200–215. https://doi.org/ DOI: 10.37843/rted.v17i1.458

Alhazzani, N. S. (2024). Enhancing mathematics teachers' pedagogical skills by using ChatGPT. *International Journal of Innovative Research and Scientific Studies*, 7(4), 1614–1626. DOI: 10.53894/ijirss.v7i4.3460

Alier Forment, M., Garcia Peñalvo, F., Casañ Guerrero, M. J., Pereira, J. A., & Llorens Largo, F. (2024). *Manifiesto para una IA Segura en la Educación* (Versión 0.4.0). *Manifiesto para una IA Segura en la Educación*. https://manifesto.safeaieducation.org

Al-kfairy, M., Mustafa, D., Kshetri, N., Insiew, M., & Alfandi, O. (2024). Ethical challenges and solutions of generative AI: An interdisciplinary perspective. *Informatics (MDPI), 11*(3), 58. DOI: 10.3390/informatics11030058

Alkhasawneh, S. N., Lampropoulos, G., & Hernández-Leo, D. (2025). Generative AI in Learning Design: A Systematic Review. In *International Conference on Artificial Intelligence in Education* (pp. 17-30). Springer, Cham. DOI: 10.1007/978-3-031-98459-4_2

Almuhanna, M. A. (2024). Teachers' perspectives of integrating AI-powered technologies in K-12 education for creating customized learning materials and resources. *Education and Information Technologies*. Advance online publication. DOI: 10.1007/s10639-024-13257-y

Alvarez-Garcia, M., Arenas-Parra, M., & Ibar-Alonso, R. (2024). Uncovering student profiles. An explainable cluster analysis approach to PISA 2022. *Computers & Education, 223*, 105166. DOI: 10.1016/j.compedu.2024.105166

Álvarez-Herrero, J. F. (2023). Análisis de 5 recursos de Inteligencia Artificial capaces de generar Situaciones de Aprendizaje. In: *Libro de Actas de las X Jornadas Iberoamericanas de Innovación Educativa en el ámbito de las TIC y las TAC* (pp. 103-110). Aplicaciones Tecnológicas para la Enseñanza de las TIC (ATETIC), Universidad de Las Palmas de Gran Canaria.

Álvarez-Herrero, J. F. (2024). Opinion of Spanish Teachers About Artificial Intelligence and Its Use in Education. In S. Papadakis (Ed.), *IoT, AI, and ICT for Educational Applications. Technologies to Enable Education for All* (pp. 163-172). EAI/Springer Innovations in Communication and Computing. Springer, Cham. DOI: 10.1007/978-3-031-50139-5_8

Alwaqdani, M. (2024). Investigating teachers' perceptions of artificial intelligence tools in education: Potential and difficulties. *Education and Information Technologies, 30*(3), 2737–2755. DOI: 10.1007/s10639-024-12903-9

Al-Zahrani, A. M. (2024). From Traditionalism to Algorithms: Embracing Artificial Intelligence for Effective University Teaching and Learning. *IgMin Research, 2*(2), 102–112. DOI: 10.61927/igmin151

Al-Zahrani, A., Khalil, I., Awaji, B., & Mohsen, M. (2024). AI technologies in STEAM education for students: Systematic literature review. *Journal of Ecohumanism, 3*(4), 3380–3394. DOI: 10.62754/joe.v3i4.3855

Amershi, S., Weld, D., Vorvoreanu, M., Fourney, A., Nushi, B., Collisson, P., Suh, J., Iqbal, S., Bennett, P. N., Inkpen, K., Teevan, J., Kikin-Gil, R., & Horvitz, E. (2019). Guidelines for Human-AI interaction. *Proceedings of the 2019 CHI Conference on Human Factors in Computing Systems*. DOI: 10.1145/3290605.3300233

Amo-Filva, D., ... (2024). Empowering Student Data Privacy in Schools Through Open Educational Resources. García-Peñalvo, F.J., Sein-Echaluce, M.L., Fidalgo-Blanco, Á. (eds) *Innovation and Technologies for the Digital Transformation of Education. Lecture Notes in Educational Technology*. Springer, Singapore. Doi:DOI: 10.1007/978-981-97-2468-0_25

Amran, M. S., Bakar, K. A., Surat, S., Mahmud, S. N. D., & Shafie, A. A. B. M. (2021). Assessing preschool teachers' challenges and needs for creativity in STEM education. *Asian Journal of University Education, 17*(3), 99–108. DOI: 10.24191/ajue.v17i3.14517

Anderson, A., Huttenlocher, D., Kleinberg, J., & Leskovec, J. (2014, April). Engaging with massive online courses. In *Proceedings of the 23rd international conference on World wide web* (pp. 687-698).

Anderson, J. R., Boyle, C. F., & Reiser, B. J. (1985). Intelligent tutoring systems. *Science, 228*(4698), 456–462. DOI: 10.1126/science.228.4698.456

Anderson, J. R., Corbett, A. T., Koedinger, K. R., & Pelletier, R. (1995). Cognitive tutors: Lessons learned. *Journal of the Learning Sciences, 4*(2), 167–207. DOI: 10.1207/s15327809jls0402_2

Anderson, L. W., & Krathwohl, D. R. (2001). *A taxonomy for learning, teaching, and assessing: A revision of Bloom's taxonomy of educational objectives: complete edition*. Addison Wesley Longman, Inc.

Anjum, G., Choubey, J., Kushwaha, S., & Patkar, V. (2023). AI in Education: Evaluating the Efficacy and Fairness of Automated Grading Systems. *International Journal of Innovative Research in Science, Engineering and Technology*, *12*(06), 1–14. DOI: 10.15680/IJIRSET.2023.1206161

Annamalai, N. (2025). Factors affecting English language high school teachers switching intention to ChatGPT: A Push-Pull-Mooring theory perspective. *Interactive Learning Environments*, *33*(2), 1367–1384. DOI: 10.1080/10494820.2024.2371928

Ansari, A. N., Ahmad, S., & Bhutta, S. M. (2024). Mapping the global evidence around the use of ChatGPT in higher education: A systematic scoping review. *Education and Information Technologies*, *29*(9), 11281–11321. DOI: 10.1007/s10639-023-12223-4

An, X., Chai, C. S., Li, Y., Zhou, Y., Shen, X., Zheng, C., & Chen, M. (2023). Modeling English teachers' behavioral intention to use artificial intelligence in middle schools. *Education and Information Technologies*, *28*(5), 5187–5208. DOI: 10.1007/s10639-022-11286-z

Aparicio, W. O. (2023). La Inteligencia Artificial y su Incidencia en la Educación: Transformando el Aprendizaje para el Siglo XXI. *Revista Internacional de Pedagogía e Innovación Educativa*, *3*(2), 217–229. DOI: 10.51660/ripie.v3i2.133

Aravantinos, S., Lavidas, K., Voulgari, I., Papadakis, S., Karalis, T., & Komis, V. (2024). Educational Approaches with AI in Primary School Settings: A Systematic Review of the Literature Available in Scopus. *Education Sciences*, *14*(7), 744. DOI: 10.3390/educsci14070744

Arefian, M. H., Çomoğlu, I., & Dikilitaş, K. (2024). Understanding EFL teachers' experiences of ChatGPT-driven collaborative reflective practice through a community of practice lens. *Innovation in Language Learning and Teaching*, •••, 1–16. DOI: 10.1080/17501229.2024.2412769

Arifin, M. Z., Zulkarnain, I., & Ansori, H. (2025). The influence of artificial intelligence on critical thinking ability in mathematics: A systematic literature review. *Indonesian Journal of Science and Mathematics Education*, *8*(1), 82–92. DOI: 10.24042/ijsme.v8i1.24352

Arnold, K. E., & Pistilli, M. D. (2012, April). Course signals at Purdue: Using learning analytics to increase student success. In *Proceedings of the 2nd international conference on learning analytics and knowledge* (pp. 267-270). DOI: 10.1145/2330601.2330666

Asagar, M. S. (2025). Digital Competence in Education: A Comparative Analysis of Frameworks and Conceptual Foundations. *Synergy: International Journal of Multidisciplinary Studies, 2*(1), 9–23. DOI: 10.63960/synergyint.j.multidiscip.stud.v2i1.34

Asencio, G., Medina, R., Coto, L., Gómez, M., López, P., Contreras, V., & Muñoz, A. (2024). Libro de Memorias proyecto de investigación latinoamericana 100 investigadores. En *Libro de Memorias proyecto de investigación latinoamericana, 8*(3).

Aslam, U., & Abbas, A. (2025). Ethical AI and ICT integration in mathematics education: Enhancing lifelong learning through blended synchronous learning. DOI: 10.13140/RG.2.2.30393.68969

Atiq, Z., & Batra, R. (2024). How do first-year engineering students' emotions change while working on programming problems? ACM Transactions on Computing Education, 24(2). *Article, 24*(2), 1–30. DOI: 10.1145/3643865

Awang, L. A., Yusop, F. D., & Danaee, M. (2025). Current practices and future direction of artificial intelligence in mathematics education: A systematic review. *International Electronic Journal of Mathematics Education, 20*(2), em0823. Advance online publication. DOI: 10.29333/iejme/16006

Awidi, I. T. (2024). Comparing expert tutor evaluation of reflective essays with marking by generative artificial intelligence (AI) tool. *Computers and Education: Artificial Intelligence, 6*, 100226. DOI: 10.1016/j.caeai.2024.100226

Ayala-Pazmiño, M. (2023). Inteligencia artificial en la educación: Explorando los beneficios y riesgos potenciales. *593 Digital Publisher CEIT,* 8(3), 892-899. https://doi.org/DOI: 10.33386/593dp.2023.3.1827

Ayanwale, M. A., Sanusi, I. T., Adelana, O. P., Aruleba, K. D., & Oyelere, S. S. (2022). Teachers' readiness and intention to teach artificial intelligence in schools. *Computers and Education: Artificial Intelligence, 3*(August), 100099. DOI: 10.1016/j.caeai.2022.100099

Ayeni, O. O., Al Hamad, N. M., Chisom, O. N., Osawaru, B., & Adewusi, O. E. (2024). AI in education: A review of personalized learning and educational technology. *GSC Advanced Research and Reviews, 18*(2), 261–271. DOI: 10.30574/gscarr.2024.18.2.0062

Ayuso-del Puerto, D. A., & Gutiérrez-Esteban, P. G. (2022). La Inteligencia Artificial como recurso educativo durante la formación inicial del profesorado. *RIED-Revista Iberoamericana de Educación a Distancia*, *25*(2), 347–358. DOI: 10.5944/ried.25.2.32332

Azzahra, I. M., Diana, R. R., Nirwana, E. S., Wiranata, R. R. S., & Andriani, K. M. (2022). Learning facilities and infrastructure based on the characteristics of Children with Special Needs in inclusive education. Al-Athfaal. *Jurnal Ilmiah Pendidikan Anak Usia Dini*, *5*(2), 169–190. DOI: 10.24042/ajipaud.v5i2.14432

Babushkina, D. (2023). Are we justified attributing a mistake in diagnosis to an AI diagnostic system? *AI and Ethics*, *3*(2), 567–584. DOI: 10.1007/s43681-022-00189-x

Bahroun, Z., Anane, C., Ahmed, V., & Zacca, A. (2023). Transforming education: A comprehensive review of generative artificial intelligence in educational settings through bibliometric and content analysis. *Sustainability (Basel)*, *15*(17), 12983. DOI: 10.3390/su151712983

Baïdoo-Anu, D., & Ansah, L. O. (2023). Education in the era of generative artificial intelligence (AI): Understanding the potential benefits of ChatGPT in promoting teaching and learning. *Journal of AI*, *7*(1), 52–62. DOI: 10.61969/jai.1337500

Baig, M. I., & Yadegaridehkordi, E. (2024). ChatGPT in the higher education: A systematic literature review and research challenges. *International Journal of Educational Research*, *127*, 102411. DOI: 10.1016/j.ijer.2024.102411

Baird, M. D., Pane, J. F., Steiner, E. D., Hamilton, L. S., & Pane, J. D. (2017). Informing Progress: Insights on Personalized Learning Implementation and Effects.

Baker, R. S., & Hawn, A. (2022). Algorithmic Bias in Education. *International Journal of Artificial Intelligence in Education*, *32*(4), 1052–1092. DOI: 10.1007/s40593-021-00285-9

Baker, R. S., & Inventado, P. S. (2014). Educational data mining and learning analytics. In Larusson, J., & White, B. (Eds.), *Learning analytics* (pp. 61–75). Springer., DOI: 10.1007/978-1-4614-3305-7_4

Balalle, H., & Pannilage, S. (2025). Reassessing academic integrity in the age of AI: A systematic literature review on AI and academic integrity. *Social Sciences & Humanities Open*, vol.11, 101299, ISSN 2590-2911. Doi:DOI: 10.1016/j.ssaho.2025.101299

Bandura, A. (1986). Social foundations of thought and action. *Englewood Cliffs, NJ, 1986*(23-28), 2.

Baniata, L. H., & Kang, S. (2024). Switching self-attention text classification model with innovative reverse positional encoding for right-to-left languages: A focus on Arabic dialects. *Mathematics, 12*(6), 865. DOI: 10.3390/math12060865

Barakova, E., Väänänen, K., Kaipainen, K., & Markopoulos, P. (2023). Benefits, challenges and research recommendations for social robots in education and learning: A Meta-Review. *2023 32nd IEEE International Conference on Robot and Human Interactive Communication (RO-MAN)*, 2555–2561. DOI: 10.1109/RO-MAN57019.2023.10309345

Bardin, L. (1991). *Análisis de contenido* (Vol. 89). Ediciones Akal.

Barragán-Torres, M. (2022). A comparative study of mathematics classroom practices in Chile, Colombia, and Mexico. UCLA. ProQuest ID: BarraganTorres_ucla_0031D_20584. Merritt ID: ark:/13030/m5fn878g. https://escholarship.org/uc/item/91r8m44r

Barsom, E. Z., Graafland, M., & Schijven, M. P. (2016). Systematic review on the effectiveness of augmented reality applications in medical training. *Surgical Endoscopy, 30*(10), 4174–4183. DOI: 10.1007/s00464-016-4800-6 PMID: 26905573

Bateman, T. (2025). Teacher perspectives of ChatGPT as a pedagogical tool in the K-12 setting: A case study. *Quality Assurance in Education, 33*(2), 203–217. DOI: 10.1108/QAE-02-2024-0042

Batista, J., Mesquita, A., & Carnaz, G. (2024). Generative AI and Higher Education: Trends, Challenges, and Future Directions from a Systematic Literature Review. *Information (Basel), 15*(11), 676. DOI: 10.3390/info15110676

Bauschard, S., & Quidwai, S. (2024). From Insight to Implementation: How to Create Your AI School Guidance. In SSRN *Electronic Journal* (Issue July). DOI: 10.2139/ssrn.4784207

Baylor, A. L., & Kim, Y. (2005). Simulating instructional roles through pedagogical agents. *International Journal of Artificial Intelligence in Education, 15*(2), 95–115. DOI: 10.3233/IRG-2005-15(2)02

Becker, B., & Park, K. (2011). Effects of integrative approaches among science, technology, engineering, and mathematics (STEM) subjects on students' learning. *Journal of STEM Education: Innovations and Research, 12*(5), 23–37. https://eric.ed.gov/?id=EJ943196

Behera, G., Meenakshi, S., Rajini, J., Pravin, T., Boopathi, S., & Associates. (2025). Entrepreneurial Insights From Higher Education: Startup Business Ventures. In Real-World Tools and Scenarios for Entrepreneurship Exploration (pp. 101–132). IGI Global.

Belpaeme, T., Kennedy, J., Ramachandran, A., Scassellati, B., & Tanaka, F. (2018). Social robots for education: A review. *Science Robotics*, *3*(21), eaat5954. Advance online publication. DOI: 10.1126/scirobotics.aat5954

Belpaeme, T., & Tanaka, F. (2021). Social robots as educators. In *OECD digital education outlook 2021 pushing the frontiers with artificial intelligence, blockchain and robots: Pushing the frontiers with artificial intelligence, blockchain and robots* (p. 143). OECD Publishing Paris. DOI: 10.1787/589b283f-en

Benhadj, Y., El Messaoudi, M., & Nfissi, A. (2019). Artificial intelligence in education: Integrating serious gaming into the language class classdojo technology for classroom behavioral management. *IAES International Journal of Artificial Intelligence*, *8*(4), 382. DOI: 10.11591/ijai.v8.i4.pp382-390

Benzizoune, O. (2024). Enhancing Classroom Management and Student Engagement: The Role of ClassDojo and Gamification in Education. *Journal of English Language Teaching and Applied Linguistics*, *6*(3), 106–114. DOI: 10.32996/jeltal.2024.6.3.13

Berlian, Z., & Huda, M. (2022). Reflecting culturally responsive and communicative teaching (CRCT) through partnership commitment. *Education Sciences*, *12*(5), 295. DOI: 10.3390/educsci12050295

Besnoy, K. D. (2021). Creating A Sustainable Digital Ecosystem for the Gifted Education Classroom. In *Methods and Materials for Teaching the Gifted* (pp. 629–662). Routledge., DOI: 10.4324/9781003236603-23

Bettayeb, A. M., Abu Talib, M., Sobhe Altayasinah, A. Z., & Dakalbab, F. (2024). Exploring the impact of ChatGPT: Conversational AI in education. *Frontiers in Education*, *9*, 1379796. DOI: 10.3389/feduc.2024.1379796

Beyer, S. (2014). Why are women underrepresented in computer science? Gender differences in stereotypes, self-efficacy, values, and interests and predictors of future CS course-taking and grades. *Computer Science Education*, *24*(2–3), 153–192. DOI: 10.1080/08993408.2014.963363

Biagini, G. (2025). Towards an AI-Literate Future: A Systematic Literature Review Exploring Education, Ethics, and Applications. *International Journal of Artificial Intelligence in Education*, *35*(4), 2616–2666. Advance online publication. DOI: 10.1007/s40593-025-00466-w

Binhammad, M. H. Y., Othman, A., Abuljadayel, L., Al Mheiri, H., Alkaabi, M., & Almarri, M. (2024). Investigating how generative AI can create personalized learning materials tailored to individual student needs. *Creative Education, 15*(7), 1499–1523. DOI: 10.4236/ce.2024.157091

Binns, R., Van Kleek, M., Veale, M., Lyngs, U., Zhao, J., & Shadbolt, N. (2018, April). 'It's Reducing a Human Being to a Percentage' Perceptions of Justice in Algorithmic Decisions. In *Proceedings of the 2018 Chi conference on human factors in computing systems* (pp. 1-14). DOI: 10.31235/osf.io/9wqxr

Blikstein, P. (2013, April). Multimodal learning analytics. In *Proceedings of the third international conference on learning analytics and knowledge* (pp. 102-106). DOI: 10.1145/2460296.2460316

Bloomberg. (2023). Generative AI to become a $1.3 trillion market by 2032, research finds. Bloomberg. https://www.bloomberg.com/company/press/generative-ai-to-become-a-1-3-trillion-market-by-2032-research-finds/

Bohara, D. K., & Rana, K. (2024). Unmasking teachers' proficiency in harnessing Artificial Intelligence (AI) for transformative education. *SN Social Sciences, 4*(11), 203. DOI: 10.1007/s43545-024-01003-7

Boie, M. A. K., Dalsgaard, C., & Caviglia, F. (2024). Digital instinct—A keyword for making sense of students' digital practice and digital literacy. *British Journal of Educational Technology, 55*(2), 668–686. DOI: 10.1111/bjet.13398

Borah, A. R. T. N., N., & Gupta, S. (2024). Improved learning based on GenAI. *2024 2nd International Conference on Intelligent Data Communication Technologies and Internet of Things (IDCIoT),* Bengaluru, India, 1527-1532. DOI: 10.1109/IDCIoT59759.2024.10467943

Borah, P., & Borah, A. C.Dr. Pratibha BorahDr. Anil Chandra Borah. (2024). A Review of use of artificial intelligence in teaching and learning of mathematics. *IJSAT-International Journal on Science and Technology, 15*(4), 1190. Advance online publication. DOI: 10.71097/IJSAT.v15.i4.1190

Bosch, C., & Kruger, D. (2024). AI chatbots as Open Educational Resources: Enhancing student agency and Self-Directed Learning. *Italian Journal of Educational Technology, 32*(1), 53–68.

Bougdira, A., & Al Murshidi, G. (2025). Generative AI as a Tool for Personalized STEAM K-12 Education. In *Prompt Engineering and Generative AI Applications for Teaching and Learning* (pp. 387–410). IGI Global Scientific Publishing., DOI: 10.4018/979-8-3693-7332-3.ch023

Boulay, B. (2022). Artificial Intelligence in Education and Ethics. Olaf Zawacki-Richter, Insung Jung (Eds), *Handbook of Open, Distance and Digital Education,* 1-16. https://goo.su/RcMdU

Bower, M., Torrington, J., Lai, J. W. M., Petocz, P., & Alfano, M. (2024). How should we change teaching and assessment in response to increasingly powerful generative Artificial Intelligence? Outcomes of the ChatGPT teacher survey. *Education and Information Technologies*. Advance online publication. DOI: 10.1007/s10639-023-12405-0

Bozkurt, A. (2023). Unleashing the potential of generative AI, conversational agents and chatbots in educational praxis: A systematic review and bibliometric analysis of GenAI in education. In *Open Praxis* (No. 4; Vol. 15, pp. 261–270). International Council for Open; Distance Education Oslo, Norway. DOI: 10.55982/openpraxis.15.4.609

Bozkurt, A., Junhong, X., Lambert, S., Pazurek, A., Crompton, H., Koseoglu, S., Farrow, R., Bond, M., Nerantzi, C., & Honeychurch, S.. (2023). Speculative futures on ChatGPT and generative artificial intelligence (AI): A collective reflection from the educational landscape. *Asian Journal of Distance Education, 18*(1), 53–130.

Braun, V., & Clarke, V. (2006). Using thematic analysis in psychology. Qualitative research in psychology. *Qualitative Research in Psychology, 3*(2), 77–101. DOI: 10.1191/1478088706qp063oa

Braze (2019). *Artificial Intelligence Trends 2019 Roundup*. Braze, New York. https://bit.ly/RoundUP19

Breazeal, C., Dautenhahn, K., & Kanda, T. (2016). Social robotics. In *Springer handbooks* (pp. 1935–1972). DOI: 10.1007/978-3-319-32552-1_72

Breazeal, C. (2003). Toward sociable robots. *Robotics and Autonomous Systems, 42*(3-4), 167–175. DOI: 10.1016/S0921-8890(02)00373-1

Breazeal, C. (2004). *Designing sociable robots.* MIT press.

Brenneman, K., Lange, A., & Nayfeld, I. (2019). Integrating STEM into Preschool Education; Designing a Professional Development Model in Diverse Settings. *Early Childhood Education Journal, 47*(1), 15–28. DOI: 10.1007/s10643-018-0912-z

Brusilovsky, P., & Millán, E. (2007). User models for adaptive hypermedia and adaptive educational systems. In *The adaptive web: methods and strategies of web personalization* (pp. 3–53). Springer Berlin Heidelberg. DOI: 10.1007/978-3-540-72079-9_1

Brynjolfsson, E., Li, D., & Raymond, L. R. (2023). *Generative AI at work (No. w31161)*. National Bureau of Economic Research. DOI: 10.3386/w31161

Brynjolfsson, E., & Mcafee, A. (2017). Artificial intelligence, for real. *Harvard Business Review*, *1*, 1–31.

Buckingham Shum, S., & Ferguson, R. (2012). Social learning analytics. *Journal of Educational Technology & Society*, *15*(3), 3–26. https://www.jstor.org/stable/jeductechsoci.15.3.3

Bughin, J., & Hazan, E. (2017). The new spring of artificial intelligence: A few early economies. *McKinsey Global Institute*. https://goo.su/tEftfT

Burchinal, M., Zaslow, M., & Tarullo, L. (2016). Quality thresholds, features, and dosage in early care and education: Secondary data analyses of child outcomes. *Monographs of the Society for Research in Child Development*, *81*(2), 1–126. https://www.jstor.org/stable/45106669

Burstein, J., Chodorow, M., & Leacock, C. (2004). Automated essay evaluation: The Criterion online writing service. *AI Magazine*, *25*(3), 27–27.

Cai, Z., Liu, L., Chen, B., & Wang, Y. (2021). *Artificial intelligence: From beginning to date*. World Scientific. DOI: 10.1142/11921

Calvo, R. A., & D'Mello, S. (2010). Affect detection: An interdisciplinary review of models, methods, and their applications. *IEEE Transactions on Affective Computing*, *1*(1), 18–37. DOI: 10.1109/T-AFFC.2010.1

Canonigo, A. M. (2024). Levering AI to enhance students' conceptual understanding and confidence in mathematics. *Journal of Computer Assisted Learning*, *40*(6), 3215–3229. DOI: 10.1111/jcal.13065

Carbonell, J. R. (1970). *Mixed-initiative man-computer instructional dialogues* (Doctoral dissertation, Massachusetts Institute of Technology).

Carbonell, J. R. (2007). AI in CAI: An artificial-intelligence approach to computer-assisted instruction. *IEEE Transactions on Man-Machine Systems*, *11*(4), 190–202. DOI: 10.1109/TMMS.1970.299942

Carella, G., Italia, M., Conte, M., & Parolini, F. (2024). How to adopt strategic design inside universities: Transforming research in educational formats. In: *ICERI2024 Proceedings*. https://re.public.polimi.it/handle/11311/1278942

Casal-Otero, L., Catala, A., Fernández-Morante, C., Taboada, M., Cebreiro, B., & Barro, S. (2023). AI literacy in K-12: A systematic literature review. *International Journal of STEM Education, 10*(1), 29. Advance online publication. DOI: 10.1186/s40594-023-00418-7

Caspersen, M. E., & Nowack, P. (2013). Computational thinking and practice—A generic approach to computing in Danish high schools. In Grønbæk, D., & Irgens, S. (Eds.), *Proceedings of the Fifteenth Australasian Computing Education Conference (ACE 2013)* (pp. 137–143). Australian Computer Society.

Celik, I. (2023). Towards Intelligent-TPACK: An empirical study on teachers' professional knowledge to ethically integrate artificial intelligence (AI)-based tools into education. *Computers in Human Behavior, 138*(May 2022), 107468. DOI: 10.1016/j.chb.2022.107468

Celik, I., Dindar, M., Muukkonen, H., & Järvelä, S. (2022). The Promises and Challenges of Artificial Intelligence for Teachers: A Systematic Review of Research. *TechTrends, 66*(4), 616–630. DOI: 10.1007/s11528-022-00715-y

Cengage Group. (2023, August). Generative AI in Higher Education Research Findings. Retrieved from https://www.cengagegroup.com/news/perspectives/2023/higher-ed-gen-ai-faculty-research-findings/

Cetin, Y., Taş, Ö., Alakuş, H., & Kaplan, H. İ. (2024). Examining School Principals' and Teachers' Perceptions of Using ChatGPT in Education. *Educational Process International Journal, 13*(3). Advance online publication. DOI: 10.22521/edupij.2024.133.5

Chai, C. S., Liang, S., & Wang, X. (2024). A survey study of chinese teachers' continuous intentions to teach artificial intelligence. *Education and Information Technologies, 29*(11), 14015–14034. DOI: 10.1007/s10639-023-12430-z

Chan, C. K. Y. (2023). A comprehensive AI policy education framework for university teaching and learning. *International Journal of Educational Technology in Higher Education, 20*(1), 38. DOI: 10.1186/s41239-023-00408-3

Chan, C. K. Y., & Hu, W. (2023). Students' voices on generative AI: Perceptions, benefits, and challenges in higher education. *International Journal of Educational Technology in Higher Education, 20*(1), 43. Advance online publication. DOI: 10.1186/s41239-023-00411-8

Chan, W. (2023). AI chatbots and liberal education. *AI & Society*, •••, 1–3.

Chaturvedi, R., Verma, S., Das, R., & Dwivedi, Y. K. (2023). Social companionship with artificial intelligence: Recent trends and future avenues,Technological Forecasting and Social Change,Volume 193, 122634, ISSN 0040-1625. Doi: DOI: 10.1016/j.techfore.2023.122634

Cheng, E. C. K., & Wang, T. (2023). Leading digital transformation and eliminating barriers for teachers to incorporate artificial intelligence in basic education in Hong Kong. *Computers and Education: Artificial Intelligence*, *5*, 100171. DOI: 10.1016/j.caeai.2023.100171

Chen, J. J. (2024). A scoping study on AI affordances in early childhood education: Mapping the global landscape, identifying research gaps, and charting future research directions. *Journal of Artificial Intelligence Research*, *81*, 701–740. DOI: 10.1613/jair.1.16882

Chen, L., Chen, P., & Lin, Z. (2020). Artificial intelligence in education: A review. *IEEE Access : Practical Innovations, Open Solutions*, *8*, 75264–75278. DOI: 10.1109/ACCESS.2020.2988510

Chen, X., Xie, H., & Hwang, G.-J. (2020). A multi-perspective study on artificial intelligence in education: Grants, conferences, journals, software tools, institutions, and researchers. *Computers and Education: Artificial Intelligence*, *1*, 100005. DOI: 10.1016/j.caeai.2020.100005

Chen, X., Xie, H., Zou, D., & Hwang, G.-J. (2020). Application and theory gaps during the rise of artificial intelligence in education. *Computers and Education: Artificial Intelligence*, *1*, 100002. DOI: 10.1016/j.caeai.2020.100002

Chen, X., Zou, D., Xie, H., Cheng, G., & Liu, C. (2022). Two decades of artificial intelligence in education. *Journal of Educational Technology & Society*, *25*(1), 28–47.

Chignell, M., Wang, L., Zare, A., & Li, J. (2023). The evolution of HCI and human factors: Integrating human and artificial intelligence. *ACM Transactions on Computer-Human Interaction*, *30*(2), 1–30. DOI: 10.1145/3557891

Chiu, T. K. F. (2024a). Future research recommendations for transforming higher education with generative AI. *Computers and Education: Artificial Intelligence*, *6*, 100197. DOI: 10.1016/j.caeai.2023.100197

Chiu, T. K. F. (2024b). The impact of generative AI (GenAI) on practices, policies and research direction in education: A case of ChatGPT and midjourney. *Interactive Learning Environments*, *32*(10), 6187–6203. DOI: 10.1080/10494820.2023.2253861

Chiu, T. K. F., Xia, Q., Zhou, X., Chai, C. S., & Cheng, M. (2023). Systematic literature review on opportunities, challenges, and future research recommendations of artificial intelligence in education. *Computers and Education: Artificial Intelligence, 4*, 100118. DOI: 10.1016/j.caeai.2022.100118

Chomutare, T., Tejedor, M., Svenning, T. O., Marco-Ruiz, L., Tayefi, M., Lind, K., Godtliebsen, F., Moen, A., Ismail, L., Makhlysheva, A., & Ngo, P. D. (2022). Artificial Intelligence Implementation in Healthcare: A Theory-Based Scoping Review of Barriers and Facilitators. *International Journal of Environmental Research and Public Health, 19*(23), 16359. DOI: 10.3390/ijerph192316359

Chounta, I.-A., Bardone, E., Raudsep, A., & Pedaste, M. (2022). Exploring Teachers' Perceptions of Artificial Intelligence as a Tool to Support their Practice in Estonian K-12 Education. *International Journal of Artificial Intelligence in Education, 32*(3), 725–755. DOI: 10.1007/s40593-021-00243-5

Christyodetaputri, J. H., & Marwa, N. (2024). Sinergi International Journal of Islamic Studies. *Zakat Management Practices and Sustainable Development in Indonesia Ernil, 2*(1), 24–37. https://doi.org/https://doi.org/10.61194/education.v2i3.590

Chua, I. S., Gaziel-Yablowitz, M., Korach, Z. T., Kehl, K. L., Levitan, N. A., Arriaga, Y. E., Jackson, G. P., Bates, D. W., & Hassett, M. (2021). Artificial intelligence in oncology: Path to implementation. *Cancer Medicine, 10*(12), 4138–4149. DOI: 10.1002/cam4.3935

Chukwuere, J. E., & Handoko, B. L. (2024). The future of generative AI chatbots in higher education. *Journal of Emerging Technologies, 4*(1), 36–44.

Chytas, D., Noussios, G., Paraskevas, G., Vasiliadis, A. V., Giovanidis, G., & Troupis, T. (2025). Can ChatGPT play a significant role in anatomy education? A scoping review. *Morphologie, 109*(365), 100949. DOI: 10.1016/j.morpho.2025.100949 PMID: 39813897

Çiftçi, A., & Topçu, M. S. (2022). Pre-service early childhood teachers' challenges and solutions to Planning and Implementing STEM education–based activities. *Canadian Journal of Science, Mathematics and Technology Education = Revue Canadienne de l'Enseignement des Sciences, des Mathématiques et de la Technologie, 22*(2), 422–443. DOI: 10.1007/s42330-022-00206-5

Cirneanu, A. L., & Moldoveanu, C. E. (2024). Use of digital technology in integrated mathematics education. *Applied System Innovation, 7*(4), 66. DOI: 10.3390/asi7040066

Clarizia, F., Colace, F., Lombardi, M., Pascale, F., & Santaniello, D. (2018). Chatbot: An education support system for student. In *Lecture notes in computer science* (pp. 291–302). DOI: 10.1007/978-3-030-01689-0_23

Clark, L., Pantidi, N., Cooney, O., Doyle, P., Garaialde, D., Edwards, J., Spillane, B., Gilmartin, E., Murad, C., Munteanu, C., Wade, V., & Cowan, B. R. (2019). What makes a good conversation? *Proceedings of the 2019 CHI Conference on Human Factors in Computing Systems*, 1–12. DOI: 10.1145/3290605.3300705

Cleto, B. (2023). Exploração de algumas ferramentas de Inteligência Artificial numa Unidade Curricular de Multimédia. *RE@D - Revista de Educação a Distância e Elearning*, 6, 2. https://revistas.rcaap.pt/lead_read/article/view/32673/23517

Clow, D. (2013). An overview of learning analytics. *Teaching in Higher Education, 18*(6), 683–695. DOI: 10.1080/13562517.2013.827653

Cohen, J. (1988). *Statistical power analysis for the behavioral sciences* (2nd ed.). Lawrence Erlbaum Associates.

Cohen, L., Manion, L., & Morrison, K. (2007). *Research methods in education.* Routledge. DOI: 10.4324/9780203029053

Coltri, M. A. (2024). The Ethical Dilemma with Open AI ChatGPT: Is it Right or Wrong to prohibit it?. *Athens Journal of Law*, *10*(1), 121, 119-130.

Common Sense. (2025). *Social AI Companions.* https://www.commonsensemedia .org/ai-ratings/social-ai-companions?gate=riskassessment

Conati, C. (2009). Intelligent tutoring systems: New challenges and directions. *Twenty-First International Joint Conference on Artificial Intelligence.*

Conti, D., Cirasa, C., Di Nuovo, S., & Di Nuovo, A. (2020). Robot, tell me a tale! *Interaction Studies: Social Behaviour and Communication in Biological and Artificial Systems, 21*(2), 220–242. DOI: 10.1075/is.18024.con

Contreras, E. (2024, 15 mayo). Retos para los docentes con la llegada de la IA. *Uninpahu.* https://uninpahu.edu.co/retos-para-los-docentes-con-la-llegada-de-la-ia/

Cooper, G. (2023). Examining science education in ChatGPT: An exploratory study of generative artificial intelligence. *Journal of Science Education and Technology, 32*(3), 444–452. DOI: 10.1007/s10956-023-10039-y

Costa, A., Sánchez-Gómez, M., & Martín, M. (Eds.). (2020). *La Práctca de la investgación cualitatva: ejemplifcación de estudios (2ª parte).* Ludomedia.

Cotta, G. M., Davel, M., Rocha, M., Lozório, M. Z. A., Angelo, R. N. F. da S., Andrião, S. Z., & Dalvi, Z. M. de V. (2024). Personalised learning with artificial intelligence: A new paradigm for the school curriculum. *Revista Ibero-Americana de Humanidades. Ciência & Educação (Bauru)*, *10*(10), 4024–4041. DOI: 10.51891/rease.v10i10.16399

Coursera. (2024). *Global Skills Report 2024*. Retrieved from https://www.coursera.org/skills-reports/global

Coutinho, C. (2013). *Metodologia de investigação em ciências sociais e humanas: teoria e prática*. Almedina.

Crawford, K. (2021). *Atlas of AI Power, Politics, and The Planetary Costs of Artificial Intelligence*. Yale University Press.

Creely, E., & Blannin, J. (2025). Creative partnerships with generative AI. Possibilities for education and beyond. *Thinking Skills and Creativity*, *56*, 101727. DOI: 10.1016/j.tsc.2024.101727

Creswell, J. W. (2014). *A concise introduction to mixed methods research*. SAGE publications.

Crockett, K., Latham, A., & Whitton, N. (2017). On predicting learning styles in conversational intelligent tutoring systems using fuzzy decision trees. *International Journal of Human-Computer Studies*, *97*, 98–115. DOI: 10.1016/j.ijhcs.2016.08.005

Crompton, H. & Burke, D. (2024). Artificial Intelligence Applications in Higher Education: Theories, Ethics, and Case Studies for Universities. *STEMPS Faculty Books*. 13.

Crompton, H., & Burke, D. (2022). Affordances and challenges of artificial intelligence in K-12 education: A systematic review. *Journal of Research on Technology in Education*, *56*(3), 248–268. DOI: 10.1080/15391523.2022.2121344

Crompton, H., & Song, D. (2021). The potential of artificial intelligence in higher education. *RVUCN*, *62*(62), 1–4. DOI: 10.35575/rvucn.n62a1

Crosthwaite, P., Smala, S., & Spinelli, F. (2024). Prompting for pedagogy? Australian F-10 teachers' generative AI prompting use cases. *Australian Educational Researcher*. Advance online publication. DOI: 10.1007/s13384-024-00787-0

Cukurova, M., Miao, X., & Brooker, R. (2023). Adoption of Artificial Intelligence in Schools: Unveiling Factors Influencing Teachers' Engagement. *Lecture Notes in Computer Science (Including Subseries Lecture Notes in Artificial Intelligence and Lecture Notes in Bioinformatics), 13916 LNAI*, 151–163. DOI: 10.1007/978-3-031-36272-9_13

Cukurova, M. (2025). The interplay of learning, analytics and artificial intelligence in education: A vision for hybrid intelligence. *British Journal of Educational Technology, 56*(2), 469–488. DOI: 10.1111/bjet.13514

Cumming, T. M., & Rose, M. C. (2022). Exploring universal design for learning as an accessibility tool in higher education: A review of the current literature. *Australian Educational Researcher, 49*(5), 1025–1043. DOI: 10.1007/s13384-021-00471-7

Czerkawski, B. (2024). Designing language learning experiences with generative AI tools. *Advances in Educational Technologies and Instructional Design Book Series,* 324-341. .DOI: 10.4018/979-8-3693-0872-1.ch015

D'Mello, S., Dieterle, E., & Duckworth, A. (2017). Advanced, analytic, automated (AAA) measurement of engagement during learning. *Educational Psychologist, 52*(2), 104–123. DOI: 10.1080/00461520.2017.1281747 PMID: 29038607

D'mello, S., & Graesser, A. (2013). AutoTutor and affective AutoTutor: Learning by talking with cognitively and emotionally intelligent computers that talk back. [TiiS]. *ACM Transactions on Interactive Intelligent Systems, 2*(4), 1–39. DOI: 10.1145/2395123.2395128

Dabingaya, M. (2022). Analyzing the effectiveness of AI-powered adaptive learning platforms in mathematics education. *Interdisciplinary Journal Papier Human Review, 3*(1), 1–7. DOI: 10.47667/ijphr.v3i1.226

Dangol, A., Lewis, A., Suh, H., Hong, X., Meadan, H., Fogarty, J., & Kientz, J. A. (2025, April). "I Want to Think Like an SLP": A Design Exploration of AI-Supported Home Practice in Speech Therapy. In Proceedings of the 2025 CHI Conference on Human Factors in Computing Systems (pp. 1-22).

Danyaro, A., Aladesusi, A. G., Ajamu, A. O., Adegbite, A. F., & Attah, J. O. (2024). Pre-Service Teachers' Awareness and Attitude Towards the Use of Open Educational Resources for Learning in Kano State, Nigeria. *Suluh: Jurnal Bimbingan Dan Konseling, 9*(2), 76–80. DOI: 10.33084/suluh.v9i2.6989

Dar, Z., Muhammad, R., Usman, B., Akhtar, J., Alazawi, A., Ali, H., & Hameed, E. (2024). Advanced generative AI methods for academic text summarization. .DOI: 10.1109/ICMI60790.2024.10585622

Darveau, P. (2023). Decision Trees: Modeling with fast intuition and slow, deliberate analysis.

Dash, A., Ye, J., & Wang, G. (2023). A review of generative adversarial networks (GANs) and its applications in a wide variety of disciplines: From medical to remote sensing. *IEEE Access : Practical Innovations, Open Solutions.*

Davar, N. F., Dewan, M. A. A., & Zhang, X. (2025). AI Chatbots in Education: Challenges and Opportunities. *Information (Basel), 16*(3), 235. DOI: 10.3390/info16030235

Davis, E. (2024). Mathematics, word problems, common sense, and artificial intelligence. *Bulletin of the American Mathematical Society, 61*(2), 287–303. DOI: 10.1090/bull/1828

Davoodi, A. (2024). Crafting innovative paths in non-linear professional learning for bilingual education: The role of connectivism in the age of AI. *Professional Development in Education*, •••, 1–17. DOI: 10.1080/19415257.2024.2421492

De Mántaras, R. L., & Crosa, P. B. (2023). *¿Qué es la inteligencia artificial? Papeles de relaciones ecosociales y cambio global*, (164), 13-21.

de Oliveira, F. B., & Stoltz, T. (2020). Social and Affective Interaction of Gifted Students. *Socio-emotional Development and Creativity of Gifted Students, 139.* Advance online publication. DOI: 10.14195/978-989-26-1770-1

Dehouche, N. (2021). Plagiarism in the age of massive generative pre-trained transformers (GPT-3). *Ethics in Science and Environmental Politics, 21*, 17–23. DOI: 10.3354/esep00195

Dellepiane, P., & Guidi, P. (2023). La inteligencia artificial y la educación: Retos y oportunidades desde una perspectiva ética. *Question/Cuestión, 3*(76), e859. https://doi.org/DOI: 10.24215/16696581e859

Demircan, H. Ö. (2022). How am I supposed to do this on my own? A case study on perspectives of preschool teachers regarding integrative STEM practices. *Journal of Early Childhood Research, 20*(1), 93–112. DOI: 10.1177/1476718X211052749

Demszky, D., Liu, J., Hill, H. C., Jurafsky, D., & Piech, C. (2023). Can Automated Feedback Improve Teachers' Uptake of Student Ideas? Evidence From a Randomized Controlled Trial in a Large-Scale Online Course. [Original work published in 2024]. *Educational Evaluation and Policy Analysis, 46*(3), 483–505. DOI: 10.3102/01623737231169270

Denga, E. M., & Denga, S. W. (2024). Revolutionizing education: The power of technology. In *Revolutionizing Curricula through Computational Thinking, Logic, and Problem Solving* (pp. 167-188). IGI Global. DOI: 10.4018/979-8-3693-1974-1.ch010

Deng, W., Wang, L., & Deng, X. (2024). Exploring Interactive Learning Environments Based on Augmented Reality Technology. *International Journal of Interactive Mobile Technologies, 18*(12), 15–29. DOI: 10.3991/ijim.v18i12.49911

Deng, X., & Yu, Z. (2023). A Meta-Analysis and systematic review of the effect of chatbot technology use in sustainable education. *Sustainability (Basel), 15*(4), 2940. DOI: 10.3390/su15042940

Denner, J., Werner, L., Campe, S., & Ortiz, E. (2014). Pair programming: Under what conditions is it advantageous for middle school students? *Journal of Research on Technology in Education, 46*(3), 277–296. DOI: 10.1080/15391523.2014.888272

Díaz, B., & Nussbaum, M. (2024). Artificial intelligence for teaching and learning in schools: The need for pedagogical intelligence. *Computers & Education, 217*(April), 105071. DOI: 10.1016/j.compedu.2024.105071

Dimeli, M., & Kostas, A. (2025). The Role of ChatGPT in Education: Applications, Challenges: Insights From a Systematic Review. *Journal of Information Technology Education, 24*, 2. DOI: 10.28945/5422

Ding, A. C. E., Shi, L., Yang, H., & Choi, I. (2024). Enhancing teacher AI literacy and integration through different types of cases in teacher professional development. *Computers and Education Open, 6*, 100178. DOI: 10.1016/j.caeo.2024.100178

Dogan, S., Nalbantoglu, U. Y., Celik, I., & Agacli Dogan, N. (2025). Artificial intelligence professional development: A systematic review of TPACK, designs, and effects for teacher learning. *Professional Development in Education, 51*(3), 1–28. DOI: 10.1080/19415257.2025.2454457

Done, P. (2022). *The Art of Teaching Children: All I Learned from a Lifetime in the Classroom*. Simon and Schuster.

Dong, S., Wang, P., & Abbas, K. (2021). A survey on deep learning and its applications. *Computer Science Review, 40*, 100379. DOI: 10.1016/j.cosrev.2021.100379

Dong, Z., An, J., & Liu, L. (2023). Leveraging Emotion Recognition for Enhancing Arts Education: A Classroom Behavior Analysis Approach. *In 2023 International Conference on Information Education and Artificial Intelligence (ICIEAI 2023)*, 6 pages. DOI: 10.1145/3660043.3660081

Donley, K. (2024). Teaching with ChatGPT as a linguistically responsive tool for multilingual learners. *Technology in Language Teaching & Learning*, *6*(3), 1719. DOI: 10.29140/tltl.v6n3.1719

Dos Santos, M. G. (2024). The Impact of Artificial Intelligence on Teaching Carreer: Pedagogical, Administrative and Ethical Challenges and Opportunities. *International Journal of Advanced Research*, *12*(10), 854–866. DOI: 10.21474/IJAR01/19705

Dovgyi, S., Babiichuk, S., Davybida, L., & Biletska, M. (2024). TEACHERS' AND STUDENTS' ATTITUDES TOWARDS THE USE OF ARTIFICIAL INTELLIGENCE: ALL-UKRAINIAN RESEARCH. *Information Technologies and Learning Tools*, *104*(6), 197–215. DOI: 10.33407/itlt.v104i6.5890

Drachsler, H., & Greller, W. (2016). *Privacy and analytics: It's a DELICATE issue*. In *LAK '16: Proceedings of the 6th International Conference on Learning Analytics & Knowledge* (pp. 89–98). https://doi.org/DOI: 10.1145/2883851.2883893

Duan, Y., Edwards, J. S., & Dwivedi, Y. K. (2019). Artificial intelligence for decision making in the era of big data - evolution, challenges and research agenda. *International Journal of Information Management*, *48*, 63–71. DOI: 10.1016/j.ijinfomgt.2019.01.021

Duckworth, A. (2016). *Grit: The power of passion and perseverance* (Vol. 234). Scribner.

Du, H., Sun, Y., Jiang, H., Islam, A. Y. M. A., & Gu, X. (2024). Exploring the effects of AI literacy in teacher learning: An empirical study. *Humanities & Social Sciences Communications*, *11*(1), 559. DOI: 10.1057/s41599-024-03101-6

Dwivedi, Y. K., Kshetri, N., Hughes, L., Slade, E. L., Jeyaraj, A., Kar, A. K., Baabdullah, A. M., Koohang, A., Raghavan, V., Ahuja, M., Albanna, H., Albashrawi, M. A., Al-Busaidi, A. S., Balakrishnan, J., Barlette, Y., Basu, S., Bose, I., Brooks, L., Buhalis, D., & Wright, R. (2023). "So what if ChatGPT wrote it?" Multidisciplinary perspectives on opportunities, challenges and implications of generative conversational AI for research, practice and policy. *International Journal of Information Management*, *71*, 102642. DOI: 10.1016/j.ijinfomgt.2023.102642

Ecker, J., Eckert, G., & Cummings, E. (2025). Augmenting gifted education through artificial intelligence: A four-dimensional framework for AI tutoring integration. *Journal of Advanced Academics*, *36*(1), 1–18. DOI: 10.1177/1932202X251356326

Egara, F. O., Mosimege, M., & Mosia, M. (2025). Secondary school students' perceptions of their usage of artificial intelligence-based ChatGPT in mathematics learning. *Journal of Education (University of KwaZulu-Natal)*, (98), 124-146. DOI: 10.17159/2520-9868/i98a07

Egara, F. O., & Mosimege, M. (2024). Exploring the integration of artificial intelligence-based ChatGPT into mathematics instruction: Perceptions, challenges, and implications for educators. *Education Sciences*, *14*(7), 742. DOI: 10.3390/educsci14070742

Ehsan, U., & Riedl, M. O. (2024). Explainability pitfalls: Beyond dark patterns in explainable AI. *Patterns (New York, N.Y.)*, *5*(6), 100971. DOI: 10.1016/j.patter.2024.100971 PMID: 39005480

Elijah, O. (2024). Innovative pedagogical practices in mathematics education. In *Impacts of Globalization and Innovation in Mathematics Education* (pp. 67–96). IGI Global., DOI: 10.4018/979-8-3693-2873-6.ch004

Elmore, R. (2023). *Guide to Prompt Engineering*. https://builtin.com/artificial-intelligence/prompt-engineering

Engelbrecht, J., & Borba, M. C. (2024). Recent developments in using digital technology in mathematics education. *ZDM Mathematics Education*, *56*(2), 281–292. DOI: 10.1007/s11858-023-01530-2

Engeström, Y. (1987). *Learning by expanding: An activity-theoretical approach to developmental Research.* Orienta-Konsultit.

Ertel, W. (2018). *Introduction to artificial intelligence*. Springer.

Estrada Carrera, F. M. L., Loor Zambrano, H. Y., & Viteri Rade, L. Y. (2022). Reemplazo de personal humano por inteligencia artificial: Ventajas y desventajas. *Revista Investigación y Negocios*, *15*(25), 31–38. DOI: 10.38147/invneg.v15i25.213

Etaat, F. (2024). The Effect of AI-Based Applications on EFL Writing Skill Development: An Inquiry into Integration of AI into Language Learning (Master's thesis, UiT Norges arktiske universitet).

European Commission. (2020). Digital Education Action Plan (2021–2027): Resetting education and training for the digital age. Publications Office of the European Union. https://education.ec.europa.eu/focus-topics/digital/education-action-plan

European Commission. (2020). *Digital Education Action Plan 2021–2027*. https://education.ec.europa.eu/focus-topics/digital/digital-education-action-plan

European Commission. (2021a). 2030 Digital Compass: The European way for the Digital Decade (COM/2021/118 final). Publications Office of the European Union. https://eur-lex.europa.eu/legal-content/EN/TXT/?uri=CELEX:52021DC0118

European Commission. (2022). *Ethical guidelines on the use of artificial intelligence (AI) and data in teaching and learning for educators.* Publications Office of the European Union. https://data.europa.eu/doi/10.2766/153756

European Commission. (2022). Ethical guidelines on the use of artificial intelligence (AI) and data in teaching and learning for educators. Publications Office of the European Union. https://education.ec.europa.eu/document/ethical-guidelines-on-the-use-of-ai-and-data-in-teaching-and-learning-for-educators

European Commission. (2023a). Report on the state of the Digital Decade 2023 (COM(2023) 570 final). https://eur-lex.europa.eu/legal-content/EN/TXT/?uri=CELEX:52023DC0570

European Commission. (2023b). DESI methodological note—Digital Decade report 2023. https://digital-strategy.ec.europa.eu/en/library/desi-methodological-note-digital-decade-report-2023

European Parliament & Council of the European Union. (2024). Regulation (EU) 2024/1689 of the European Parliament and of the Council of 13 June 2024 laying down harmonised rules on artificial intelligence (Artificial Intelligence Act) and amending certain Union legislative acts. *Official Journal of the European Union, L, 202*, 1–102. https://eur-lex.europa.eu/legal-content/EN/TXT/?uri=CELEX:32024R1689

Eurydice. (2023). Greece: Embracing change and technology – The Open School reform in elementary and secondary education. European Education and Culture Executive Agency. https://eurydice.eacea.ec.europa.eu/news/greece-embracing-change-and-technology-open-school-reform-elementary-and-secondary-education

Fadillah, M. A., Usmeldi, U., Lufri, L., Mawardi, M., & Festiyed, F. (2024). Exploring user perceptions: The impact of ChatGPT on high school students' physics understanding and learning. *Advances in Mobile Learning Educational Research, 4*(2), 1197–1207. DOI: 10.25082/AMLER.2024.02.013

Faisal, E. (2024, April). Unlock the potential for Saudi Arabian higher education: a systematic review of the benefits of ChatGPT. In *Frontiers in Education* (Vol. 9, p. 1325601). Frontiers Media SA. https://doi.org/DOI: 10.3389/feduc.2024.1325601

Fakhar, S., Baber, J., Bazai, S. U., Marjan, S., Jasinski, M., Jasinska, E., Chaudhry, M. U., Leonowicz, Z., & Hussain, S. (2022). Smart Classroom Monitoring Using Novel Real-Time Facial Expression Recognition System. *Applied Sciences (Basel, Switzerland)*, *12*(23), 1–18. DOI: 10.3390/app122312134

Familoni, B. T., & Onyebuchi, N. C.Babajide Tolulope FamiloniNneamaka Chisom Onyebuchi. (2024). Advancements and Challenges in Ai Integration for Technical Literacy: A Systematic Review. *Engineering Science & Technology Journal*, *5*(4), 1415–1430. DOI: 10.51594/estj.v5i4.1042

Fang, X., Ng, D. T. K., & Yuen, M. (2025). Effects of geogebra-enhanced scratch computational thinking instruction on fifth-grade students' motivation, anxiety, cognitive load. *Education and Information Technologies*, *30*(1), 377–402. DOI: 10.1007/s10639-024-13052-9

Fanni, S. C., Febi, M., Aghakhanyan, G., & Neri, E. (2023). Natural language processing. In *Introduction to Artificial Intelligence* (pp. 87–99). Springer International Publishing. DOI: 10.1007/978-3-031-25928-9_5

Farooqi, M. T. K., Amanat, I., & Awan, S. M. (2024). Ethical Considerations and Challenges in the Integration of Artificial Intelligence in Education: A Systematic Review. *Journal of Excellence in Management Sciences*, *3*(4), 35–50. DOI: 10.69565/jems.v3i4.314

Farrelly, T., & Baker, N. (2023). Generative artificial intelligence: Implications and considerations for higher education practice. *Education Sciences*, *13*(11), 1109. Advance online publication. DOI: 10.3390/educsci13111109

Fauzi, F., Tuhuteru, L., Sampe, F., Ausat, A. M., & Hatta, H. R. (2023). Análisis del papel de ChatGPT en la mejora de la productividad de los estudiantes en la educación superior. *Review of Education*, *5*(4), 14886–14891. DOI: 10.31004/joe.v5i4.2563

Feine, J., Gnewuch, U., Morana, S., & Maedche, A. (2019). A taxonomy of social cues for conversational agents. *International Journal of Human-Computer Studies*, *132*, 138–161. DOI: 10.1016/j.ijhcs.2019.07.009

Felix, C. (2020). The role of the teacher and AI in education. Sengupta, Enakshi, Blessinger, Patrick, Makhanya, Mandla (Eds.), International perspectives on the role of technology in humanizing higher education, 33. *Emerald Publishing Limited*, Leeds, 33-48. DOI: 10.1108/S2055-364120200000033003

Feng, M., Heffernan, N. T., & Koedinger, K. R. (2009). Addressing the assessment challenge with an online system that tutors as it assesses. *User Modeling and User-Adapted Interaction*, *19*(3), 243–266. DOI: 10.1007/s11257-009-9063-7

Fenta, A. A. (2025). A review on enhancing education with AI: Exploring the potential of ChatGPT, Bard, and generative AI. *Discover Education*, *4*(1), 38. DOI: 10.1007/s44217-025-00426-5

Ferrara, E. (2023). Fairness and bias in artificial intelligence: A brief survey of sources, impacts, and mitigation strategies. *Sci*, *6*(1), 3. DOI: 10.3390/sci6010003

Feuerriegel, S., Hartmann, J., Janiesch, C., & Zschech, P. (2024). Generative AI. *Business & Information Systems Engineering*, *66*(1), 111–126. DOI: 10.1007/s12599-023-00834-7

Floridi, L. (2020). AI and Its New Winter: From Myths to Realities. *Philosophy & Technology*, *33*(1), 1–3. DOI: 10.1007/s13347-020-00396-6

Fong, T., Nourbakhsh, I., & Dautenhahn, K. (2003). A survey of socially interactive robots. *Robotics and Autonomous Systems*, *42*(3-4), 143–166. DOI: 10.1016/S0921-8890(02)00372-X

Fonseca, A., Ferreira, A., Ribeiro, L., Moreira, S., & Duque, C. (2024). Embracing the future—Is artificial intelligence already better? A comparative study of artificial intelligence performance in diagnostic accuracy and decision-making. *European Journal of Neurology*, *31*(4), 16195. DOI: 10.1111/ene.16195

Foshee, C. M., Elliott, S. N., & Atkinson, R. K. (2016). Technology-enhanced learning in college mathematics remediation. *British Journal of Educational Technology*, *47*(5), 893–905. DOI: 10.1111/bjet.12285

Frasson, C., & Chalfoun, P. (2010). Managing learner's affective states in intelligent tutoring systems. In *Studies in computational intelligence* (pp. 339–358). DOI: 10.1007/978-3-642-14363-2_17

Froebel, F. (1887). *The education of man*. A. Lovell & Company.

Fui-Hoon Nah, F., Zheng, R., Cai, J., Siau, K., & Chen, L. (2023). Generative AI and ChatGPT: Applications, challenges, and AI-human collaboration. *Journal of Information Technology Case and Application Research*, *25*(3), 277–304. DOI: 10.1080/15228053.2023.2233814

Fundi, M., Sanusi, I. T., Oyelere, S. S., & Ayere, M. (2024). Advancing AI education: Assessing Kenyan in-service teachers' preparedness for integrating artificial intelligence in competence-based curriculum. *Computers in Human Behavior Reports*, *14*, 100412. DOI: 10.1016/j.chbr.2024.100412

Fütterer, T., Goldberg, P., Bühler, B., Sikimić, V., Trautwein, U., Gerjets, P., Stürmer, K., & Kasneci, E. (2023). *Artificial Intelligence in Classroom Management: A Systematic Review on Educational Purposes, Technical Implementations, and Ethical Considerations* (Issue June). DOI: 10.31219/osf.io/wfazn

Fu, Y., & Weng, Z. (2024). Navigating the ethical terrain of AI in education: A systematic review on framing responsible human-centered AI practices. *Computers and Education: Artificial Intelligence*, *7*, 100306. DOI: 10.1016/j.caeai.2024.100306

Gagné, F. (2004). Differentiating giftedness and talent: The DMGT as a conceptual framework. In Sternberg, R. J., Davidson, J. E., & Kaufman, J. C. (Eds.), *The international handbook of giftedness* (pp. 99–119). Cambridge University Press.

Gallardo, E., Tomás-Rojas, A., Bossio, J., & Freundt-Thurne, U. (2023). Evidence of validity and reliability of the DigCompEdu CheckIn in teachers at a private Peruvian university. *Publicaciones*, *53*, 49–88. DOI: 10.30827/publicaciones.v53i2.26817

García-López, I. M., González, C. S. G., Ramírez-Montoya, M. S., & Molina-Espinosa, J. M. (2025). Challenges of implementing ChatGPT on education: Systematic literature review. *International Journal of Educational Research Open*, *8*, 100401. DOI: 10.1016/j.ijedro.2024.100401

García-López, I. M., & Trujillo-Liñán, L. (2025). Ethical and regulatory challenges of Generative AI in education: A systematic review. *Frontiers in Education*, *10*, 1565938. DOI: 10.3389/feduc.2025.1565938

García-Peñalvo, F. J. (2024). Cómo afecta la inteligencia artificial generativa a los procesos de evaluación. *Revista científica comunicación y educación y educación, 4(54),* 106-170.

George, B., & Wooden, O. (2023). Managing the strategic transformation of higher education through artificial intelligence. *Administrative Sciences*, *13*(9), 196. DOI: 10.3390/admsci13090196

Getenet, S. (2024). Pre-Service Teachers and ChatGPT in Multistrategy Problem-Solving: Implications for Mathematics Teaching in Primary Schools. *International Electronic Journal of Mathematics Education*, *19*(1), em0766. Advance online publication. DOI: 10.29333/iejme/14141

Ghimire, A., & Edwards, J. (2024). Generative AI Adoption in the Classroom: A Contextual Exploration Using the Technology Acceptance Model (TAM) and the Innovation Diffusion Theory (IDT). *2024 Intermountain Engineering. Technology and Computing, IETC*, *2024*, 129–134. DOI: 10.1109/IETC61393.2024.10564292

Ghojogh, B., & Ghodsi, A. (2020). Attention mechanism, transformers, BERT, and GPT: Tutorial and survey.

Ghosh, K., & Das, S. (2023). Automatic Generation of Algebraic Representation for Physics Problems. *TAM METİN BİLDİRİ KİTABI*, 91.

Ghosh, K. (2025). Recommending Personalized Video Lecture Augmentations with Tagged Community Question Answers. *International Journal of Artificial Intelligence in Education*, *35*(4), 1–48. DOI: 10.1007/s40593-025-00459-9

Ghosh, K., Nangi, S. R., Kanchugantla, Y., Rayapati, P. G., Bhowmick, P. K., & Goyal, P. (2022). Augmenting video lectures: Identifying off-topic concepts and linking to relevant video lecture segments. *International Journal of Artificial Intelligence in Education*, *32*(2), 382–412. DOI: 10.1007/s40593-021-00257-z

Giannakos, M., Azevedo, R., Brusilovsky, P., Cukurova, M., Dimitriadis, Y., Hernandez-Leo, D., Järvelä, S., Mavrikis, M., & Rienties, B. (2024). The promise and challenges of generative AI in education. *Behaviour & Information Technology*, •••, 1–27. DOI: 10.1080/0144929X.2024.2394886

Gil, A. C. (1999). *Métodos e técnicas de pesquisa social.* Atlas.

Gill, S. S., Xu, M., Patros, P., Wu, H., Kaur, R., Kaur, K., Fuller, S., Singh, M., Arora, P., Parlikad, A. K., Stankovski, V., Abraham, A., Ghosh, S. K., Lutfiyya, H., Kanhere, S. S., Bahsoon, R., Rana, O., Dustdar, S., Sakellariou, R., & Buyya, R. (2024). Transformative effects of ChatGPT on modern education: Emerging era of AI chatbots. *Internet of Things and Cyber-Physical Systems*, *4*, 19–23. DOI: 10.1016/j.iotcps.2023.06.002

Glover, E. (2023). What is an AI hallucination? https://builtin.com/artificial-intelligence/ai-hallucination

Glynn, S. M., Brickman, P., Armstrong, N., & Taasoobshirazi, G. (2011). Science Motivation Questionnaire II: Validation with science majors and nonscience majors. *Journal of Research in Science Teaching*, *48*(10), 1159–1176. DOI: 10.1002/tea.20442

Gnanaprakasam, J., & Lourdusamy, R. (2024). The Role of AI in Automating Grading: Enhancing Feedback and Efficiency. In *Artificial Intelligence and Education-Shaping the Future of Learning* (pp. 1–18). IntechOpen., DOI: 10.5772/intechopen.1005025

Gobert, J. D., Sao Pedro, M. A., & Betts, C. G. (2023). An AI-based teacher dashboard to support students' inquiry: Design principles, features, and technological specifications. In *Handbook of research on science education* (pp. 1011–1044). Routledge. DOI: 10.4324/9780367855758-37

Gobierno de España. (2021). *Plan Nacional de Competencias Digitales*. https://avance.digital.gob.es/es-es/espana_digital./210127_plan_nacional_de_competencias_digital.es.pdf

Gökçearslan, S., Tosun, C., & Erdemir, Z. G. (2024). Benefits, challenges, and methods of artificial intelligence (AI) chatbots in education: A systematic literature review. *International Journal of Technology in Education*, *7*(1), 19–39. https://eric.ed.gov/?id=EJ1415037. DOI: 10.46328/ijte.600

Goksel, N., & Bozkurt, A. (2019). Artificial intelligence in education. In Sisman-Ugur, S., & Kurubacak, G. (Eds.), *Handbook of research on learning in the age of transhumanism* (pp. 224–236). IGI Global., DOI: 10.4018/978-1-5225-8431-5.ch014

Gong, X., Tang, Y., Liu, X., Jing, S., Cui, W., Liang, J., & Wang, F. Y. (2020, October). K-9 artificial intelligence education in Qingdao: Issues, challenges and suggestions. In *2020 IEEE international Conference on networking, Sensing and control (ICNSC)* (pp. 1-6). IEEE.

Goodwin, B., Rouleau, K., Abla, C., Baptiste, K., Gibson, T., & Kimball, M. (2022). *The new classroom instruction that works: The best research-based strategies for increasing student achievement*. ASCD.

Gouseti, A., James, F., Fallin, L., & Burden, K. (2025). The ethics of using AI in K-12 education: A systematic literature review. *Technology, Pedagogy and Education*, *34*(2), 161–182. DOI: 10.1080/1475939X.2024.2428601

Govender, R. (2024). A reflection on the use of artificial intelligence tools for the meaningful learning of mathematics. *Pythagoras-Journal of the Association for Mathematics Education of South Africa*, *45*(1), 831. DOI: 10.4102/pythagoras.v45i1.831

Goyal, R., Kumar, P., & Singh, V. P. (2023). A systematic survey on automated text generation tools and techniques: Application, evaluation, and challenges. *Multimedia Tools and Applications*, *82*(28), 43089–43144. DOI: 10.1007/s11042-023-15224-0

Graesser, A. C., Conley, M. W., & Olney, A. (2012). Intelligent tutoring systems. In *APA educational psychology handbook, vol 3: Application to learning and teaching*. (pp. 451–473). DOI: 10.1037/13275-018

Graesser, A. C., Hu, X., & Sottilare, R. (2018). Intelligent tutoring systems. In *International handbook of the learning sciences* (pp. 246–255). DOI: 10.4324/9781315617572-24

Graesser, A. C., Chipman, P., Haynes, B. C., & Olney, A. (2005). AutoTutor: An intelligent tutoring system with mixed-initiative dialogue. *IEEE Transactions on Education, 48*(4), 612–618. DOI: 10.1109/TE.2005.856149

Graesser, A. C., Li, H., & Forsyth, C. (2014). Learning by communicating in natural language with conversational agents. *Current Directions in Psychological Science, 23*(5), 374–380. DOI: 10.1177/0963721414540680

Gross, S., Mokbel, B., Hammer, B., & Pinkwart, N. (2015). Learning feedback in intelligent tutoring systems. *KI - Künstliche Intelligenz, 29*(4), 413–418. DOI: 10.1007/s13218-015-0367-y

Grover, S., & Pea, R. (2018). Computational thinking: A competency whose time has come. *Computer Science Education, 28*(1), 70–74. DOI: 0.5040/9781350057142.ch-003

Grugeon-Allys, B., & Pilet, J. (2024). The algebraic learning of middle school students' evolution during a school year: A statistical large-scale study based on results in mathematics didactics. *Educational Studies in Mathematics, 117*(3), 533–564. DOI: 10.1007/s10649-024-10347-z

Gubareva, R., & Lopes, R. P. (2020). Virtual assistants for learning: A systematic literature review. *Proceedings of the 12th International Conference on Computer Supported Education*, 97–103. DOI: 10.5220/0009417600970103

Guerrero, L. P. M., Molina, P. M. E., & Molina, S.Leticia Paulina Martínez GuerreroPaulina Mercedes Erazo MolinaSofía del Pilar Erazo MolinaAngela Guillermina Molina Molina. (2025). Hacia una enseñanza personalizada: El rol de la inteligencia artificial en la educación básica. *Revista Imaginario Social, 8*(1), 15–25. DOI: 10.59155/is.v8i1.259

Guerrero-Solé, F. (2023). El impacto de la inteligencia artificial generativa en la disciplina de la comunicación. *Hipertext.net, 1-9.* .DOI: 10.31009/hipertext.net.2023.i26.01

Guijarro, A. de L. Á. A. (2024). Impact of artificial intelligence on educational assessment and feedback. *RETOS PARA LA INVESTIGACIÓN, 3*(1), 19–32. https://doi.org/https://doi.org/10.62465/rri.v3n1.2024.72

Guilbault, K. M., Wang, Y., & McCormick, K. M. (2025). Using ChatGPT in the Secondary Gifted Classroom for Personalized Learning and Mentoring. *Gifted Child Today, 48*(2), 93–103. DOI: 10.1177/10762175241308950

Guilherme, A. (2019). AI and education: The importance of teacher and student relations. *AI & Society, 34*(1), 47–54. DOI: 10.1007/s00146-017-0693-8

Gujjula, R., & Sanghera, K. (2023). *Ethical considerations and data privacy in AI education. Journal of Student-Scientists' Research*, 5. https://doi.org/DOI: 10.13021/jssr2023.3958

Gunawan, J., Aungsuroch, Y., & Montayre, J. (2024). ChatGPT integration within nursing education and its implications for nursing students: A systematic review and text network analysis. *Nurse Education Today*, *106323*, 106323. Advance online publication. DOI: 10.1016/j.nedt.2024.106323 PMID: 39068726

Güneyli, A., Burgul, N. S., Dericioğlu, S., Cenkova, N., Becan, S., Şimşek, Ş. E., & Güneralp, H. (2024). Exploring Teacher Awareness of Artificial Intelligence in Education: A Case Study from Northern Cyprus. *European Journal of Investigation in Health, Psychology and Education*, *14*(8), 2358–2376. DOI: 10.3390/ejihpe14080156 PMID: 39194950

Guo, Y. R., & Goh, D. H.-L. (2015). Affect in embodied pedagogical agents. *Journal of Educational Computing Research*, *53*(1), 124–149. DOI: 10.1177/0735633115588774

Hadas, E., & Hershkovitz, A. (2025). Assessing Creativity Across Multi-Step Intervention Using Generative AI Models. *Journal of Learning Analytics*, *12*(1), 91–109. DOI: 10.18608/jla.2025.8571

Haenlein, M., & Kaplan, A. (2019). A brief history of artificial intelligence: On the past, present, and future of artificial intelligence. *California Management Review*, *61*(4), 5–14. DOI: 10.1177/0008125619864925

Halomoan, H., Hakiki, M., Ramadhan, M. A., Hidayah, Y., Fakhri, J., Aljamaliah, S. N. M., & Abi Hamid, M. (2024). Integrating Principal Leadership and Teacher Roles with AI-Based "Merdeka" Curriculum Innovation: The Quantitative Research. *TEM Journal*, 3397–3404. https://doi.org/DOI: 10.18421/TEM134-73

Hamre, B. K., Pianta, R. C., Downer, J. T., DeCoster, J., Mashburn, A. J., Jones, S. M., Brown, J. L., Cappella, E., Atkins, M., Rivers, S. E., Brackett, M. A., & Hamagami, A. (2013). Teaching through interactions: Testing a developmental framework of teacher effectiveness in over 4,000 classrooms. *The Elementary School Journal*, *113*(4), 461–487. DOI: 10.1086/669616

Han, X., Zhang, Z., Ding, N., Gu, Y., Liu, X., Huo, Y., Qiu, J., Yao, Y., Zhang, A., Zhang, L., Han, W., Huang, M., Jin, Q., Lan, Y., Liu, Y., Liu, Z., Lu, Z., Qiu, X., Song, R., & Zhu, J. (2021). Pre-trained models: Past, present and future. *AI Open*, *2*, 225–250. DOI: 10.1016/j.aiopen.2021.08.002

Han, Z., Battaglia, F., Udaiyar, A., Fooks, A., & Terlecky, S. R. (2024). An explorative assessment of ChatGPT as an aid in medical education: Use it with caution. *Medical Teacher*, *46*(5), 657–664. DOI: 10.1080/0142159X.2023.2271159 PMID: 37862566

Hardt, M., & Recht, B. (2021). Patterns, predictions, and actions: A story about machine learning. arXiv preprint arXiv:2102.05242.

Hartsock, I., & Rasool, G. (2024). Vision-language models for medical report generation and visual question answering: A review. *Frontiers in Artificial Intelligence*, *7*, 1430984. DOI: 10.3389/frai.2024.1430984

Hays, L., Jurkowski, O., & Sims, S. K. (2024). ChatGPT in K-12 Education. *TechTrends*, *68*(2), 281–294. DOI: 10.1007/s11528-023-00924-z

Heald, J. B., Lengyel, M., & Wolpert, D. M. (2023). Contextual inference in learning and memory. *Trends in Cognitive Sciences*, *27*(1), 43–64. DOI: 10.1016/j.tics.2022.10.004 PMID: 36435674

Hegel, F., Muhl, C., Wrede, B., Hielscher-Fastabend, M., & Sagerer, G. (2009). Understanding social robots. *2009 Second International Conferences on Advances in Computer-Human Interactions*, 169–174. DOI: 10.1109/ACHI.2009.51

Heidig, S., & Clarebout, G. (2011). Do pedagogical agents make a difference to student motivation and learning? *Educational Research Review*, *6*(1), 27–54. DOI: 10.1016/j.edurev.2010.07.004

Hemachandran, K., Verma, P., Pareek, P., Arora, N., Rajesh Kumar, K. V., Ahanger, T. A., Pise, A. A., & Ratna, R. (2022). Artificial intelligence: A universal virtual tool to augment tutoring in higher education. *Computational Intelligence and Neuroscience*, *2022*, 1–8. DOI: 10.1155/2022/1410448

Henkel, O., Horne-Robinson, H., Kozhakhmetova, N., & Lee, A. (2024, July). Effective and Scalable Math Support: Experimental Evidence on the Impact of an AI-Math Tutor in Ghana. In C. Rodrigo, A. Mitrovic, & A. Wise (Eds.), *Artificial intelligence in education: Proceedings of the 25th International Conference on Artificial Intelligence in Education (AIED 2024)* (pp. 373-381). Springer Nature Switzerland. DOI: 10.1007/978-3-031-64315-6_34

Henriksen, D., Mehta, R., & Mehta, S. (2019). Design thinking gives STEAM to teaching: A framework that breaks disciplinary boundaries. *STEAM education. Theory into Practice*, •••, 57–78. DOI: 10.1007/978-3-030-04003-1_4

Hinojo-Lucena, F.-J., Aznar-Díaz, I., Cáceres-Reche, M.-P., & Romero-Rodríguez, J.-M. (2019). Artificial intelligence in higher education: A bibliometric study on its impact in the scientific literature. *Education Sciences*, *9*(1), 51. DOI: 10.3390/educsci9010051

Hintze, A. (13 November 2016). Understanding the four types of AI, from reactive robots to self-aware beings. The Conversation. https://bit.ly/theconversation2016

Hirschberg, J., & Manning, C. D. (2015). Advances in natural language processing. *Science*, *349*(6245), 261–266. DOI: 10.1126/science.aaa8685

Hirsh-Pasek, K., Golinkoff, R. M., Berk, L. E., & Singer, D. G. (2009). *A mandate for playful learning in preschool: Presenting the evidence*. Oxford University Press.

Hobert, S., & Meyer von Wolff, R. (2019). Say hello to your new automated tutor–a structured literature review on pedagogical conversational agents. *Proceedings of the 14th International Conference on Wirtschaftsinformatik*.

Hoel, T., & Chen, W. (2018). Privacy and data protection in learning analytics should be motivated by an educational maxim—Towards a proposal. *Research and Practice in Technology Enhanced Learning*, *13*(1), 20. DOI: 10.1186/s41039-018-0086-8 PMID: 30595748

Hojeij, Z., Kuhail, M. A., & ElSayary, A. (2024). Investigating in-service teachers' views on ChatGPT integration. *Interactive Technology and Smart Education*. Advance online publication. DOI: 10.1108/ITSE-04-2024-0094

Holmes, W., & Porayska-Pomsta, K. (2023). *The ethics of artificial intelligence in education*. Lontoo: Routledge, 621-653.

Holmes, W., Bialik, M., & Fadel, C. (2022). *Artificial intelligence in education: Promises and implications for teaching and learning*. Center for Curriculum Redesign. https://www.researchgate.net/publication/332180327

Holmes, W. (2020). Artificial intelligence in education. In *Encyclopedia of education and information technologies* (pp. 88–103). Springer International Publishing. DOI: 10.1007/978-3-030-10576-1_107

Holmes, W. (2023). The Unintended Consequences of Artificial Intelligence and Education. In *Education International*. Issue October., https://www.ei-ie.org/en/item/28115:the-unintended-consequences-of-artificial-intelligence-and-education

Holmes, W., Bialik, M., & Fadel, C. (2019). *Artificial intelligence in education promises and implications for teaching and learning*. Center for Curriculum Redesign.

Holmes, W., Bialik, M., & Fadel, C. (2020). *Artificial intelligence in education: Promises and implications for teaching and learning*. Center for Curriculum Redesign.

Holmes, W., Porayska-Pomsta, K., Holstein, K., Sutherland, E., Baker, T., Shum, S. B., & Koedinger, K. R. (2022). Ethics of AI in education: Towards a community-wide framework. *International Journal of Artificial Intelligence in Education, 32*(3), 504–526.

Holstein, K., McLaren, B. M., & Aleven, V. (2018). Student learning benefits of a mixed-reality teacher awareness tool in AI-enhanced classrooms. In *Artificial Intelligence in Education: 19th International Conference, AIED 2018, London, UK, June 27–30, 2018* [Springer International Publishing.]. *Proceedings, 19*(Part I), 154–168.

Holstein, K., McLaren, B. M., & Aleven, V. (2019). Co-Designing a Real-Time Classroom Orchestration Tool to Support Teacher–AI Complementarity. *Journal of Learning Analytics, 6*(2), 27–52. DOI: 10.18608/jla.2019.62.3

Hopcan, S., Türkmen, G., & Polat, E. (2024). Exploring the artificial intelligence anxiety and machine learning attitudes of teacher candidates. *Education and Information Technologies, 29*(6), 7281–7301. DOI: 10.1007/s10639-023-12086-9

Hopfenbeck, T. N., Zhang, Z., Sun, S. Z., Robertson, P., & McGrane, J. A. (2023). Challenges and opportunities for classroom-based formative assessment and AI: A perspective article. *Frontiers in Education, 8*(November), 1–9. DOI: 10.3389/feduc.2023.1270700

Hosseini, S., & Seilani, H. (2025). The role of agentic AI in shaping a smart future: A systematic review. *Array (New York, N.Y.), 26*, 100399. DOI: 10.1016/j.array.2025.100399

Huang, A. Y. Q., Lu, O. H. T., & Yang, S. J. H. (2023). Effects of artificial Intelligence–Enabled personalized recommendations on learners' learning engagement, motivation, and outcomes in a flipped classroom. *Computers and Education, 194*(November 2022), 104684. DOI: 10.1016/j.compedu.2022.104684

Huang, C., Samek, T., & Shiri, A. (2021). AI and ethics: Ethical and educational perspectives for LIS. *Journal of Education for Library and Information Science, 62*(4), 351–365. DOI: 10.3138/jelis-62-4-2020-0106

Huang, L. (2023). Ethics of artificial intelligence in education: Student privacy and data protection. *Science Insights Education Frontiers, 16*(2), 2577–2587. DOI: 10.15354/sief.23.re202

Huang, W., Jiang, J., King, R. B., & Fryer, L. K. (2025). Chatbots and student motivation: A scoping review. *International Journal of Educational Technology in Higher Education*, *22*(1), 26. DOI: 10.1186/s41239-025-00524-2

Hussain, A., & Rizwan, R. (2024). Strategic AI adoption in SMEs: A Prescriptive Framework. *Computers and Society*. https://doi.org/https://doi.org/10.48550/arXiv.2408.11825

Hutson, J. (2024). Rethinking plagiarism in the era of generative AI. *Journal of International Communication*, *4*(1), 619. DOI: 10.54963/jic.v4i1.220

Hwang, G. J., & Chen, N. S. (2023). Exploring the potential of generative artificial intelligence in education: Applications, challenges, and future research directions. *Journal of Educational Technology & Society*, *26*(2). Advance online publication. DOI: 10.30191/ETS.202304_26(2).0014

Hwang, G.-J. (2003). A conceptual map model for developing intelligent tutoring systems. *Computers & Education*, *40*(3), 217–235. DOI: 10.1016/S0360-1315(02)00121-5

Hwang, G.-J., & Chang, C.-Y. (2023). A review of opportunities and challenges of chatbots in education. *Interactive Learning Environments*, *31*(7), 4099–4112. DOI: 10.1080/10494820.2021.1952615

Hwang, G.-J., Xie, H., Wah, B. W., & Gašević, D. (2020). Vision, challenges, roles and research issues of artificial intelligence in education. *Computers and Education: Artificial Intelligence*, *1*, 100001. DOI: 10.1016/j.caeai.2020.100001

Hwang, G., & Tu, Y. (2021). Roles and Research Trends of Artificial Intelligence in Mathematics Education: A Bibliometric Mapping Analysis and Systematic Review. *Mathematics*, *9*(6), 584. DOI: 10.3390/math9060584

Ifenthaler, D., & Schumacher, C. (2016). Student perceptions of privacy principles for learning analytics. *Educational Technology Research and Development*, *64*(5), 923–938. DOI: 10.1007/s11423-016-9477-y

Ilene R. Berson, Michael J. Berson & Wenwei Luo. (2025). Innovating responsibly: ethical considerations for AI in early childhood education. https://doi.org/DOI: 10.1007/s44436-025-00003-5

Imran, M., & Almusharraf, N. (2023). Analyzing the role of ChatGPT as a writing assistant at higher education level: A systematic review of the literature. *Contemporary Educational Technology*, *15*(4), ep464. DOI: 10.30935/cedtech/13605

Inside Higher Ed. (2024, June). Survey: How Are Profs, Staff Using AI? Retrieved from https://www.insidehighered.com/news/student-success/academic-life/2024/06/28/one-third-college-instructors-are-using-genai-heres

Institute of Educational Policy (IEP). (2024). Curricula for secondary education 2024–2025. https://www.iep.edu.gr/2024-2025-3/

Instituto Nacional de Tecnologías Educativas y de Formación del Profesorado (INTEF). (2022). *Escuela de Pensamiento Computacional e Inteligencia Artificial 2021/22. De la formación docente al cambio metodológico. Resultados de la investigación.* https://code.intef.es/wp-content/uploads/2022/11/09_22_Experimentacion_Investigacion-EPCIA-21-22_Investigacion-R3.pdf

Intriago, K. E. C., Rodríguez, L. M. A., & Cevallos, L. A. T. (2021). Specific learning difficulty: Autism, dyscalculia, dyslexia and dysgraphia. International Research Journal of Engineering. *IT and Scientific Research*, *7*(3), 97–106.

Ioannidou, A., Chatzilari, E., Nikolopoulos, S., & Kompatsiaris, I. (2017). Deep learning advances in computer vision with 3D data: A survey. *ACM Computing Surveys*, *50*(2), 1–38. DOI: 10.1145/3042064

Ipek, Z. H., Gozum, A. C., Papadakis, S., & Kallogianakis, M. (2023). Educational applications of the ChatGPT AI system: A systematic review research. *Educational Process: International Journal*, *12*(3), 26–55. DOI: 10.22521/edupij.2023.123.2

Iskender, A. (2023). Holy or Unholy? Interview with Open AI's ChatGPT. *European Journal of Tourism Research*, *34*, 1–11. DOI: 10.54055/ejtr.v34i.3169

Ismail, I. & Aloshi, J. (2025). Data Privacy in AI- Driven Education An In-Depth Exploration Into the Data Privacy Concerns and Potential Solutions. Doi: .DOI: 10.4018/979-8-3693-5443-8.ch008

Itzin, C. (2024). Ageism awareness training: a model for group work. In *Dependency and Interdependency in Old Age* (pp. 114–126). Routledge. DOI: 10.4324/9781032715940-12

Jang, H., & Choi, H. (2025). A Double-Edged Sword: Physics Educators' Perspectives on Utilizing ChatGPT and Its Future in Classrooms. *Journal of Science Education and Technology*, *34*(2), 267–283. DOI: 10.1007/s10956-024-10173-1

Jaramillo, J. D. F., & Olivera, N. R. N. (2024). Application on artificial intelligence in education in Latin America: Trends, benefits and challenges. *Revista Veritas de Difusão Científica*, *5*(1), 01–21. https://doi.org/https://doi.org/10.61616/rvdc.v5i1.52 Aplicación

Jeon, J., & Lee, S. (2024). Can learners benefit from chatbots instead of humans? A systematic review of human-chatbot comparison research in language education. *Education and Information Technologies*, *29*(17), 1–32. DOI: 10.1007/s10639-024-12725-9

Jing, S., Tang, Y., Liu, X., Gong, X., Cui, W., & Liang, J. (2020, October). A parallel education based intelligent tutoring systems framework. In *2020 IEEE International Conference on Networking, Sensing and Control (ICNSC)* (pp. 1-6). IEEE. DOI: 10.1109/ICNSC48988.2020.9238052

Jita, T., Jita, L. C., & Omoniyi, A. A. (2025). Mathematics education in the AI era: Preparing teachers for evolving classroom demands. *International Journal of Learning. Teaching and Educational Research*, *24*(10), 417–434. DOI: 10.26803/ijlter.24.10.19

Johal, W. (2020). Research trends in social robots for learning. *Current Robotics Reports*, *1*(3), 75–83. DOI: 10.1007/s43154-020-00008-3

Johnson, W. L., Rickel, J. W., & Lester, J. C.. (2000). Animated pedagogical agents: Face-to-face interaction in interactive learning environments. *International Journal of Artificial Intelligence in Education*, *11*(1), 47–78.

Jong, M. S. Y., Zhai, X., & Chen, W. (2024). Innovative uses of technologies in science, mathematics and STEM education in K-12 contexts. *International Journal of Science and Mathematics Education*, *22*(S1), 1–9. DOI: 10.1007/s10763-024-10530-x

Joshi, A., Dabre, R., Kanojia, D., Li, Z., Zhan, H., Haffari, G., & Dippold, D. (2025). Natural language processing for dialects of a language: A survey. *ACM Computing Surveys*, *57*(6), 1–37. DOI: 10.1145/3712060

Joshi, S. (2025). *Strategic Integration of Artificial Intelligence in U. S. K – 12 Education : A Comprehensive Review and Policy Roadmap*. https://doi.org/http://dx.doi.org/10.20944/preprints202506.0301.v1

Joshi, S., Sharma, M., Das, R. P., Rosak-Szyrocka, J., Żywiołek, J., Muduli, K., & Prasad, M. (2022). Modeling Conceptual Framework for Implementing Barriers of AI in Public Healthcare for Improving Operational Excellence: Experiences from Developing Countries. *Sustainability (Basel)*, *14*(18), 11698. DOI: 10.3390/su141811698

Jusoh, S., & Kadir, R. A. (2025). *Chatbot in education: trends, personalisation, and techniques*. Multimed Tools Appl., DOI: 10.1007/s11042-025-20659-8

Kadaruddin, K. (2023). Empowering education through generative AI: Innovative instructional strategies for tomorrow's learners. *International Journal of Business, Law, and Education*, *4*(2), 618–625. DOI: 10.56442/ijble.v4i2.215

Kaddouri, M., Mhamdi, K., Jabri, A., Boukare, M., & Jmad, S. (2025). Generative Artificial Intelligence and Assessment of Learning: Challenges and Perspectives. In Gregory, S. (Ed.), *Effective Instructional Design Informed by AI* (pp. 277–326). IGI Global Scientific Publishing. DOI: 10.4018/979-8-3693-6527-4.ch010

Kahlke, R., Lee, M., & Eva, K. W. (2023). Building Blocks for Critical Reviews in Health Professions Education. *Journal of Graduate Medical Education*, *15*(April), 186–189. https://doi.org/DOI. DOI: 10.4300/JGME-D-23-00155.1

Kairouz, P., McMahan, H. B., Avent, B., Bellet, A., Bennis, M., Bhagoji, A. N., ... & Zhao, S. (2021). Advances and open problems in federated learning. *Foundations and trends® in machine learning, 14*(1–2), 1-210.

Kalligeropoulos, D., & Vasileiadou, S. (2008). The homeric automata and their implementation. In *Science and technology in homeric epics* (pp. 77–84). Springer Netherlands.

Kalobo, L., & Setlalentoa, W. (2024). Navigating Challenges in Gifted Education: A Teacher's Perspective on Overcoming Barriers. *Athens Journal of Education*, *11*(4), 269–287. DOI: 10.30958/aje.11-4-1

Kamalov, F., Calonge, D. S., Smail, L., Azizov, D., Thadani, D. R., Kwong, T., & Atif, A. (2025). *Evolution of AI in education: Agentic workflows* (Preprint on ArXiv No. 2504.20082). DOI: 10.48550/ARXIV.2504.20082

Kaplan, A., & Haenlein, M. (2019). Siri, siri, in my hand: Who's the fairest in the land? On the interpretations, illustrations, and implications of artificial intelligence. *Business Horizons*, *62*(1), 15–25. DOI: 10.1016/j.bushor.2018.08.004

Kaplan-Rakowski, R., Grotewold, K., Hartwick, P., & Papin, K. (2023). Generative AI and teachers' perspectives on its implementation in education. *Journal of Interactive Learning Research*, *34*(2), 313–338. DOI: 10.70725/815246mfssgp

Kapoor, V., & Bakhshi, A. K. (2025). Artificial Intelligence and the Future of Education. Indian. *Journal of Educational Technology*, *7*(1), 389–397. https://journals.ncert.gov.in/IJET/article/view/837

Karan, B. (2024). Integration of artificial intelligence by the Central Board of Secondary Education in India: Towards innovative teaching and learning practices. *Technology, Pedagogy and Education*, *33*(4), 455–474. DOI: 10.1080/1475939X.2024.2337924

Karataş, F., Eriçok, B., & Tanrikulu, L. (2025). Reshaping curriculum adaptation in the age of artificial intelligence: Mapping teachers' AI -driven curriculum adaptation patterns. *British Educational Research Journal, 51*(1), 154–180. DOI: 10.1002/berj.4068

Karnes, F. A., & Bean, S. M. (Eds.). (2021). *Methods and materials for teaching the gifted* (4th ed.). Routledge., DOI: 10.4324/9781003236603

Karthikeyan, M., Madan, B. S., Suchitra, V., Varshini, E. S. A., Sarkar, R., & Boopathi, S. (2025). Flipped Classroom Methods for Enhanced Student Engagement and Knowledge Developments in Indian Higher Education. In Global Practices in Inclusive Education Curriculum and Policy (pp. 313–342). IGI Global.

Kavitha, K., & Joshith, V. P. (2025). Artificial Intelligence Powered Pedagogy: Unveiling Higher Educators' Acceptance with Extended TAM. *Journal of University Teaching & Learning Practice, 21*(8). Advance online publication. DOI: 10.53761/s1pkk784

Kaymakci, G., & Can, S. (2023). Bibliometric Analysis of the Articles on STEM/STEAM Education in Gifted Students. *Uluslararası Türk Eğitim Bilimleri Dergisi, 2023*(21), 275–308. DOI: 10.46778/goputeb.1258457

Kayyali, M. (2025). E-Learning Platforms and Their Influence on Lifelong Learning. In Impact of Digitalization on Education and Social Sustainability (pp. 155-176). IGI Global.

Kayyali, M. (2022). Equity, Equality, Diversity, and Inclusion as Key Performance Indicators in Higher Education. *Online Submission, 3*(5), 1–3.

Kazim, T., & Tomlinson, J. (2023). Automation bias and the principles of judicial review. *Judicial Review, 28*(1), 9–16. DOI: 10.1080/10854681.2023.2189405

Keleş, A., Ocak, R., Keleş, A., & Gülcü, A. (2009). ZOSMAT: Web-based intelligent tutoring system for teaching–learning process. *Expert Systems with Applications, 36*(2), 1229–1239. DOI: 10.1016/j.eswa.2007.11.064

Kewalramani, S., Kidman, G., & Palaiologou, I. (2021). Using Artificial Intelligence (AI)-interfaced robotic toys in early childhood settings: A case for children's inquiry literacy. *European Early Childhood Education Research Journal, 29*(5), 652–668. DOI: 10.1080/1350293X.2021.1968458

Khairuddin, Z., Shahabani, N. S., Ahmad, S. N., Ahmad, A. R., & Zamri, N. A. (2024). Students' Perceptions on The Artificial Intelligence (AI) Tools As Academic Support. [MJSSH]. *Malaysian Journal of Social Sciences and Humanities, 9*(11), e003087. DOI: 10.47405/mjssh.v9i11.3087

Khalil, M., Shakya, R., & Liu, Q. (2025). *Towards privacy-preserving data-driven education: The potential of federated learning. arXiv preprint* 2503.13550. https://doi.org//arXiv.2503.13550DOI: 10.1109/ICTCS65341.2025.10989403

Khamparia, A., & Singh, K. M. (2019). A systematic review on deep learning architectures and applications. *Expert Systems: International Journal of Knowledge Engineering and Neural Networks, 36*(3), e12400. DOI: 10.1111/exsy.12400

Khan, S. (2024). *Brave New Words: How AI Will Revolutionize Education (and why That's a Good Thing)*. Penguin.

Khasawneh, M. A. S. (2024). Teacher Opinions on the Role of Educational Robots in Enhancing Programming Skills among Hearing-Impaired Students. *International Journal of Learning. Teaching and Educational Research, 23*(5), 309–322. DOI: 10.26803/ijlter.23.5.16

Khazanchi, R., Di Mitri, D., & Drachsler, H. (2025). The effect of AI-based systems on mathematics achievement in rural context: A quantitative study. *Journal of Computer Assisted Learning, 41*(1), e13098. DOI: 10.1111/jcal.13098

Khogali, H. O., & Mekid, S. (2023). The blended future of automation and AI: Examining some long-term societal and ethical impact features. *Technology in Society, 73*, 102232. DOI: 10.1016/j.techsoc.2023.102232

Khosrawi-Rad, B., Rinn, H., Schlimbach, R., Gebbing, P., Yang, X., Lattemann, C., Markgraf, D., & Robra-Bissantz, S. (2022). Conversational agents in education - a systematic literature review. *Thirtieth European Conference on Information Systems (ECIS)*.

Kim, J. (2024). Leading teachers' perspective on teacher-AI collaboration in education. *Education and Information Technologies, 29*(7), 8693–8724. DOI: 10.1007/s10639-023-12109-5

Kim, J. (2024). Types of teacher-AI collaboration in K-12 classroom instruction: Chinese teachers' perspective. *Education and Information Technologies, 29*(13), 17433–17465. DOI: 10.1007/s10639-024-12523-3

Kim, J., Lee, H., & Cho, Y. H. (2022). Learning design to support student-AI collaboration: Perspectives of leading teachers for AI in education. *Education and Information Technologies, 27*(5), 6069–6104. DOI: 10.1007/s10639-021-10831-6

Kim, N. J., & Kim, M. K. (2022). Teacher's Perceptions of Using an Artificial Intelligence-Based Educational Tool for Scientific Writing. *Frontiers in Education, 7*, 755914. DOI: 10.3389/feduc.2022.755914

Kim, T. W. (2023). Application of artificial intelligence chatbots, including ChatGPT, in education, scholarly work, programming, and content generation and its prospects: A narrative review. *Journal of Educational Evaluation for Health Professions*, *20*, 38. Advance online publication. DOI: 10.3352/jeehp.2023.20.38 PMID: 38148495

Kim, Y., & Baylor, A. L. (2006a). A Social-Cognitive framework for pedagogical agents as learning companions. *Educational Technology Research and Development*, *54*(6), 569–596. DOI: 10.1007/s11423-006-0637-3

Kim, Y., & Baylor, A. L. (2006b). Pedagogical agents as learning companions: The role of agent competency and type of interaction. *Educational Technology Research and Development*, *54*(3), 223–243. DOI: 10.1007/s11423-006-8805-z

Kirby, R., Forlizzi, J., & Simmons, R. (2010). Affective social robots. *Robotics and Autonomous Systems*, *58*(3), 322–332. DOI: 10.1016/j.robot.2009.09.015

Koedinger, K. R., Anderson, J. R., Hadley, W. H., & Mark, M. A. (1997). Intelligent tutoring goes to school in the big city. *International Journal of Artificial Intelligence in Education*, *8*, 30–43.

Kohnke, S., & Zaugg, T. (2025). Artificial Intelligence: An Untapped Opportunity for Equity and Access in STEM Education. *Education Sciences*, *15*(1), 68. DOI: 10.3390/educsci15010068

Kokoç, M. (2024). Factors influencing K-12 teachers' experiences of using Generative AI Tools: Opportunities and barriers. *Journal of E-Learning and Knowledge Society, Vol 20 No 3*, 101-111 Pages. DOI: 10.20368/1971-8829/1136039

Konar, A. (2018). *Artificial intelligence and soft computing: Behavioral and cognitive modeling of the human brain*. CRC Press.

Kong, S. C., & Yang, Y. (2024). A human-centered learning and teaching framework using generative artificial intelligence for self-regulated learning development through domain knowledge learning in K–12 settings. *IEEE Transactions on Learning Technologies*, *17*, 1562–1573. DOI: 10.1109/TLT.2024.3392830

Konkus, Ö. C., & Topsakal, Ü. U. (2022). The Effects of STEAM-Based Activities on Gifted Students' STEAM Attitudes, Cooperative Working Skills and Career Choices. *Journal of Science Learning*, *5*(3), 398–410. DOI: 10.17509/jsl.v5i3.46215

Kontorovich, I., & Ovadiya, T. (2023). How narratives about the secondary-tertiary transition shape undergraduate tutors' sense-making of their teaching. *Educational Studies in Mathematics*, *113*(1), 125–146. DOI: 10.1007/s10649-023-10211-6

Kooli, C. (2023). Chatbots in education and research: A critical examination of ethical implications and solutions. *Sustainability (Basel), 15*(7), 5614. DOI: 10.3390/su15075614

Korucu-Kış, S. (2024). Zone of proximal creativity: An empirical study on EFL teachers' use of ChatGPT for enhanced practice. *Thinking Skills and Creativity, 54,* 101639. DOI: 10.1016/j.tsc.2024.101639

Kossow, N., Windwehr, S., & Jenkins, M. (2022). *Algorithmic transparency and accountability*. Transparency International.

Kothari, P., Mehta, P., Patil, S., & Hole, V. (2024). InterviewEase: AI-powered interview assistance. DOI: 10.21203/rs.3.rs-3964944/v1

Krakowski, S. (2025). Human-AI agency in the age of generative AI. *Information and Organization, 35*(1), 100560. DOI: 10.1016/j.infoandorg.2025.100560

Krämer, N. C., & Bente, G. (2010). Personalizing e-learning. The social effects of pedagogical agents. *Educational Psychology Review*, *22*(1), 71–87. DOI: 10.1007/s10648-010-9123-x

Krishna, A., Bhowmick, P., Ghosh, K., Sahu, A., & Roy, S. (2015, March). Automatic generation and insertion of assessment items in online video courses. In *Companion Proceedings of the 20th International Conference on Intelligent User Interfaces* (pp. 1-4). DOI: 10.1145/2732158.2732183

Krishnamoorthy, N., Chandrasekar, J., Saqib, M., Therasa, P., Ganesh, C. S., & Boopathi, S. (2025). The Role of CO-PO Mapping in NBA Accreditation Assessments: Enhancing Educational Quality and Outcomes. In Hispanic Leadership in Higher Education (pp. 89–118). IGI Global.

KucuKakin, P. M., & Demir, Ü. C. G. (2021). The Relationship Between Classroom Management and Students' Learning: A Systematic Review. *Nevşehir Hacı Bektaş Veli Üniversitesi SBE Dergisi, 11*(2), 843–861. DOI: 10.30783/nevsosbilen.894503

Kuhail, M. A., Alturki, N., Alramlawi, S., & Alhejori, K. (2023). Interacting with educational chatbots: A systematic review. *Education and Information Technologies*, *28*(1), 973–1018. DOI: 10.1007/s10639-022-11177 3

Kulik, J. A. (1994). Meta-analytic studies of findings on computer-based instruction. In *Technology assessment in education and training* (pp. 9–33). Lawrence Erlbaum Associates, Inc.

Kulik, J. A., & Fletcher, J. D. (2016). Effectiveness of intelligent tutoring systems. *Review of Educational Research*, *86*(1), 42–78. DOI: 10.3102/0034654315581420

Kumar, J. A. (2021). Educational chatbots for project-based learning: Investigating learning outcomes for a team-based design course. *International Journal of Educational Technology in Higher Education, 18*(1), 65. DOI: 10.1186/s41239-021-00302-w PMID: 34926790

Kumar, R., & Raman, R. (2022). Student Perceptions on Artificial Intelligence (AI) in higher education. *IEEE Integrated STEM Education Conference (ISEC)*, Princeton, 450-454. Doi: DOI: 10.1109/ISEC54952.2022.10025165

Kurzweil, M., & Wu, D. D. (2015). *Building a Pathway to Student Success: at Georgia State University*. ITHAKA S+ R.

Labadze, L., Grigolia, M., & Machaidze, L. (2023). Role of AI chatbots in education: Systematic literature review. *International Journal of Educational Technology in Higher Education, 20*(1), 56. Advance online publication. DOI: 10.1186/s41239-023-00426-1

Lalar, S., Kumar, T., Kumar, R., & Kumar, S. (2025). Unlocking Potential: The Role of Artificial Intelligence in Revolutionizing Special Education for Inclusive Learning. In Impacts of Generative AI on the Future of Research and Education (pp. 201-232). IGI Global.

Lameras, P., & Arnab, S. (2022). Power to the Teachers: An Exploratory Review on Artificial Intelligence in Education. *Information (Basel), 13*(1), 14. DOI: 10.3390/info13010014

Lampropoulos, G. (2023). Augmented reality and artificial intelligence in education: Toward immersive intelligent tutoring systems. In *Augmented reality and artificial intelligence* (pp. 137–146). DOI: 10.1007/978-3-031-27166-3_8

Lampropoulos, G. (2025a). Combining artificial intelligence with augmented reality and virtual reality in education: Current trends and future perspectives. *Multimodal Technologies and Interaction, 9*(2), 11. DOI: 10.3390/mti9020011

Lampropoulos, G. (2025b). Social robots in education: Current trends and future perspectives. *Information (Basel), 16*(1), 29. DOI: 10.3390/info16010029

Lampropoulos, G., & Papadakis, S. (2025). The Educational Value of Artificial Intelligence and Social Robots. In Lampropoulos, G., & Papadakis, S. (Eds.), *Social Robots in Education. Studies in Computational Intelligence* (Vol. 1194). Springer., DOI: 10.1007/978-3-031-82915-4_1

Lampropoulos, G., & Papadakis, S. (2025). *The Educational Value of Artificial Intelligence and Social Robots. Social Robots in Education*. Springer.

Lata, P. (2024). Towards Equitable Learning: Exploring Artificial Intelligence in Inclusive Education.

Lau, W. W. F., & Yuen, A. H. K. (2011). Modelling programming performance: Beyond the influence of learner characteristics. *Computers & Education*, *57*(1), 1202–1213. DOI: 10.1016/j.compedu.2011.01.002

Lave, J., & Wenger, E. (1991). *Situated learning: Legitimate peripheral participation.* Cambridge University Press. DOI: 10.1017/CBO9780511815355

Lavidas, K., Papadakis, S., Manesis, D., Grigoriadou, A. S., & Gialamas, V.Lectures and Lab Classes. (2022a). The effects of social desirability on students' self-reports in two social contexts: Lectures vs. lectures and lab classes. *Information (Basel)*, *13*(10), 491. DOI: 10.3390/info13100491

Lavidas, K., Petropoulou, A., Papadakis, S., Apostolou, Z., Komis, V., Jimoyiannis, A., & Gialamas, V. (2022b). Factors affecting response rates of the web survey with teachers. *Computers*, *11*(9), 127. DOI: 10.3390/computers11090127

Lee, S. J., & Kwon, K. (2024). A systematic review of AI education in K-12 classrooms from 2018 to 2023: Topics, strategies, and learning outcomes. *Computers and Education: Artificial Intelligence*, *6*(October 2023), 100211. DOI: 10.1016/j.caeai.2024.100211

Lee, C. C., & Low, M. Y. H. (2024). Using GenAI in education: The case for critical thinking. *Frontiers in Artificial Intelligence*, *7*, 1452131. DOI: 10.3389/frai.2024.1452131

Lee, D., Arnold, M., Srivastava, A., Plastow, K., Strelan, P., Ploeckl, F., Lekkas, D., & Palmer, E. (2024). The impact of generative AI on higher education learning and teaching: A study of educators' perspectives. *Computers and Education: Artificial Intelligence*, *6*, 100221. DOI: 10.1016/j.caeai.2024.100221

Lee, I., & Perret, B. (2022). Preparing High School Teachers to Integrate AI Methods into STEM Classrooms. *Proceedings of the AAAI Conference on Artificial Intelligence*, *36*(11), 12783–12791. Advance online publication. DOI: 10.1609/aaai.v36i11.21557

Lcc, K.-F. (2019). *As Superpotências da Inteligência Artificial. A China, Silicon Valley e a Nova Ordem Mundial*. Relógio d'Água.

Lee, K.-F., & Qiufan, C. (2023). *Inteligência Artificial 2041*. Relógio de Água.

Lee, R. S. (2023). Major NLP applications. In *Natural Language Processing: A Textbook with Python Implementation* (pp. 199–239). Springer Nature Singapore.

Lee, Y.-J., Davis, R. O., & Ryu, J. (2024). Korean in-Service Teachers' Perceptions of Implementing Artificial Intelligence (AI) Education for Teaching in Schools and Their AI Teacher Training Programs. *International Journal of Information and Education Technology (IJIET)*, *14*(2), 214–219. DOI: 10.18178/ijiet.2024.14.2.2042

Leite, I., Martinho, C., & Paiva, A. (2013). Social robots for Long-Term interaction: A survey. *International Journal of Social Robotics*, *5*(2), 291–308. DOI: 10.1007/s12369-013-0178-y

Lekan, K., & Pardos, Z. A. (2025). AI-Augmented Advising: A Comparative Study of GPT-4 and Advisor-based Major Recommendations. *Journal of Learning Analytics*, *12*(1), 110–128. DOI: 10.18608/jla.2025.8593

Lenke, M., & Tenberge, C. (2022). Future Primary Teacher Education: Computational Thinking and STEAM. *PATT*, *39*, 428.

Lester, J., Branting, K., & Mott, B. (2004). Conversational agents. *The Practical Handbook of Internet Computing*, 220–240.

Lewis, C. M., Yasuhara, K., & Anderson, R. E. (2011). Deciding to major in computer science: A grounded theory of students' self-assessment of ability. In *Proceedings of the Seventh International Computing Education Research Workshop* (pp. 3–10). ACM. DOI: 10.1145/2016911.2016915

Leyva, D., Weiland, C., Barata, M., Yoshikawa, H., Snow, C., Treviño, E., & Rolla, A. (2015). Teacher–Child Interactions in Chile and Their Associations with Prekindergarten Outcomes. *Child Development*, *86*(3), 781–799. DOI: 10.1111/cdev.12342

Li, Z., Dhruv, A., & Jain, V. (2024). Ethical considerations in the use of AI for higher education: A comprehensive guide. In *2024 IEEE 18th International Conference on Semantic Computing (ICSC)* (pp. 218-223). IEEE. DOI: 10.1109/ICSC59802.2024.00041

Li, B., Lowell, V. L., Wang, C., & Li, X. (2024). A systematic review of the first year of publications on ChatGPT and language education: Examining research on ChatGPT's use in language learning and teaching. *Computers and Education: Artificial Intelligence*, *100266*, 100266. Advance online publication. DOI: 10.1016/j.caeai.2024.100266

Li, D., & Du, Y. (2017). *Artificial intelligence with uncertainty*. CRC press., DOI: 10.1201/9781315366951

Li, M. (2024). Integrating Artificial Intelligence in Primary Mathematics Education: Investigating Internal and External Influences on Teacher Adoption. *International Journal of Science and Mathematics Education*. Advance online publication. DOI: 10.1007/s10763-024-10515-w

Lim, J., Lee, U., Koh, J., Jeong, Y., Lee, Y., Byun, G., Jung, H., Jang, Y., Lee, S., & Moon, J. (2025). Development and implementation of a generative artificial intelligence-enhanced simulation to enhance problem-solving skills for pre-service teachers. *Computers & Education, 232*, 105306. DOI: 10.1016/j.compedu.2025.105306

Lim, W. M., Gunasekara, A., Pallant, J. L., Pallant, J. I., & Pechenkina, E. (2023). Generative AI and the future of education: Ragnarök or reformation? A paradoxical perspective from management educators. *International Journal of Management Education, 21*(2), 100790. DOI: 10.1016/j.ijme.2023.100790

Lin, C.-C., Huang, A. Y. Q., & Lu, O. H. T. (2023). Artificial intelligence in intelligent tutoring systems toward sustainable education: A systematic review. *Smart Learning Environments, 10*(1), 41. Advance online publication. DOI: 10.1186/s40561-023-00260-y

Lin, J. C., Younessi, D. N., Kurapati, S. S., Tang, O. Y., & Scott, I. U. (2023). Comparison of GPT-3.5, GPT-4, and human user performance on a practice ophthalmology written examination. *Eye (London, England), 37*(17), 1–2. DOI: 10.1038/s41433-023-02564-2 PMID: 37156862

Lin, T., & Riccomini, P. (2025). Inclusive Education in rural settings: Leveraging technology for improved math learning outcomes among students with disabilities. *Journal of Special Education Technology, 40*(2), 219–226. DOI: 10.1177/01626434241263045

Li, R. (2020). *Artificial intelligence revolution: How AI will change our society, economy, and culture*. Simon and Schuster.

Li, T., Ji, Y., & Zhan, Z. (2024). Expert or machine? Comparing the effect of pairing student teacher with in-service teacher and ChatGPT on their critical thinking, learning performance, and cognitive load in an integrated-STEM course. *Asia Pacific Journal of Education, 44*(1), 45–60. DOI: 10.1080/02188791.2024.2305163

Liu, Q., Shakya, R., Khalil, M., & Jovanovic, J. (2025). *Advancing privacy in learning analytics using differential privacy. arXiv preprint* 2501.01786. https://doi.org//arXiv.2501.01786DOI: 10.1145/3706468.3706493

Livingstone, S., Stoilova, M., & Nandagiri, R. (2019). Children's data and privacy online. *Technology*, *58*(2), 157–165.

Li, W., Zhang, X., Li, J., Yang, X., Li, D., & Liu, Y. (2024). An explanatory study of factors influencing engagement in AI education at the K-12 Level: An extension of the classic TAM model. *Scientific Reports*, *14*(1), 1–17. DOI: 10.1038/s41598-024-64363-3

Li, X., Gould, T., & Zaki, R. (2024). The impact of artificial intelligence on learners and teachers: A mathematics education perspective. In Bakken, J. P., Obiakor, F. E., & Rotatori, A. F. (Eds.), *Education, development and intervention: Toward participatory and integrated solutions* (pp. 133–148). Springer Nature Switzerland., DOI: 10.1007/978-3-031-60713-4_9

Llurba, C., & Palau, R. (2024). Real-Time Emotion Recognition for Improving the Teaching–Learning Process: A Scoping Review. *Journal of Imaging*, *10*(12), 313. DOI: 10.3390/jimaging10120313

Lo, A. W. (2025). The educational affordances and challenges of generative AI in Global Englishes-oriented materials development and implementation: A critical ecological perspective. *System*, *130*, 103610. DOI: 10.1016/j.system.2025.103610

Loaiza Galeano, C. D. (2024). *Un análisis a las lecciones aprendidas en etapa de inversión en tres proyectos de transformación digital en empresas de Pereira y el Norte del Valle, haciendo uso de inteligencia artificial generativa.* [Tesis de Maestría, Universidad EAFIT]. https://hdl.handle.net/10784/34547

Lo, C. K. (2023). What is the impact of ChatGPT on education? A rapid review of the literature. *Education Sciences*, *13*(4), 410. DOI: 10.3390/educsci13040410

Lo, C. K., & Hew, K. F. (2023). A review of integrating AI-based chatbots into flipped learning: New possibilities and challenges. *Frontiers in Education*, *8*, 1175715. DOI: 10.3389/feduc.2023.1175715

Lo, C. K., Yu, P. L. H., Xu, S., Ng, D. T. K., & Jong, M. S. Y. (2024). Exploring the application of ChatGPT in ESL/EFL education and related research issues: A systematic review of empirical studies. *Smart Learning Environments*, *11*(1), 50. DOI: 10.1186/s40561-024-00342-5

Lo, L. S. (2023). The CLEAR path: A framework for enhancing information literacy through prompt engineering. *Journal of Academic Librarianship*, *49*(4), 4. DOI: 10.1016/j.acalib.2023.102720

López Gómez, S., Martín Gómez, S., & Vidal Esteve, M. I. (2021). Análisis de aplicaciones móviles dirigidas a la infancia: Características técnicas, pedagógicas, de diseño y contenido. *Revista Iberoamericana de Educación*, *85*(1), 81–100. DOI: 10.35362/rie8514013

Luckin, R. (2022). *Machine learning and human intelligence: The future of education for the 21st century*. UCL Press. https://eric.ed.gov/?id=ED584840

Luckin, R., & Holmes, W. (2016). Intelligence unleashed: An argument for AI in education.

Luckin, R., Holmes, W., Griffiths, M., & Forcier, L. B. (2016). *Intelligence unleashed: An argument for AI in education*. Pearson Education. https://static.googleusercontent.com/media/edu.google.com/en//pdfs/Intelligence-Unleashed-Publication.pdf

Luckin, R. (2018). *Machine Learning and Human Intelligence. The future of education for the 21st century*. UCL Institute of Education Press.

Luckin, R., Cukurova, M., Kent, C., & Du Boulay, B. (2022). Empowering educators to be AI-ready. *Computers and Education: Artificial Intelligence*, *3*, 100076.

Luzano, J. (2024). An integrative review of AI-Powered STEM education. *International Journal of Academic Pedagogical Research*, *8*(4), 113–118.

Lykourentzou, I., Giannoukos, I., Nikolopoulos, V., Mpardis, G., & Loumos, V. (2009). Dropout prediction in e-learning courses through the combination of machine learning techniques. *Computers & Education*, *53*(3), 950–965. DOI: 10.1016/j.compedu.2009.05.010

Maanu, V., Boateng, F. O., & Larbi, E. (2025). AI-assisted instructions in collaborative learning in mathematics education: A qualitative approach. *American Journal of STEM Education*, *7*, 11–36. DOI: 10.32674/68zzkz60

Maclure, J. (2020). The new AI spring: A deflationary view. *AI & Society*, *35*(3), 747–750. DOI: 10.1007/s00146-019-00912-z

Magat, R. J. B., & Sangalang, E. M. (2024). Teachers' Familiarity, Perceptions, and Training Needs on the Use of ChatGPT in Mathematics Instruction. *International Journal of Education in Mathematics, Science and Technology*, 1471–1487. DOI: 10.46328/ijemst.4332

Mahdi, H., Akgun, S. A., Saleh, S., & Dautenhahn, K. (2022). A survey on the design and evolution of social robots — Past, present and future. *Robotics and Autonomous Systems*, *156*, 104193. DOI: 10.1016/j.robot.2022.104193

Mahmoud, C. F., & Sørensen, J. T. (2024). Artificial Intelligence in Personalized Learning with a Focus on Current Developments and Future Prospects. *Research and Advances in Education, 3*(8), 25–31. DOI: 10.56397/RAE.2024.08.04

Mahsun, M., Ali, M., Ekaningrum, I. R., & Ibda, H. (2024). Trend of Using ChatGPT in Learning Process and Character Education: A Systematic Literature Review. *International Journal of Learning. Teaching and Educational Research, 23*(5), 387–402. DOI: 10.26803/ijlter.23.5.20

Maina, A. M., & Kuria, J. (2024). Building an AI Future: Research and Policy Directions for Africa's Higher Education. *2024 IST-Africa Conference. IST-Africa, 2024*(November), 1–9. DOI: 10.23919/IST-Africa63983.2024.10569692

Maita, I., Saide, S., Putri, A. M., & Muwardi, D. (2024). ProsCons of Artificial Intelligence-ChatGPT Adoption in Education Settings: A Literature Review and Future Research Agendas. *IEEE Engineering Management Review, 52*(3), 27–42. Advance online publication. DOI: 10.1109/EMR.2024.3394540

Makinde, A. I., Adeleye, S. A., Oronti, A. O., & Jimoh, I. T. (2024). Revolutionizing education. In Rao, K. R., & Dastidar, R. G. (Eds.), *Artificial intelligence for wireless communication systems: Technology and applications* (p. 103). CRC Press., DOI: 10.1201/9781003517689-5

Malik, R., Abdi, D., Wang, R., & Demszky, D. (2025). Scaffolding middle school mathematics curricula with large language models. *British Journal of Educational Technology, 56*(3), 999–1027. DOI: 10.1111/bjet.13571

Mananay, J. A. (2024). Integrating Artificial Intelligence (AI) in Language Teaching: Effectiveness, Challenges, and Strategies. *International Journal of Learning. Teaching and Educational Research, 23*(9), 361–382. DOI: 10.26803/ijlter.23.9.19

Mann, S., Calvin, A., Lenhart, A., & Robb, M. B. (2025). *The Common Sense census: Media use by kids zero to eight, 2025*. Common Sense Media.

Mao, J., Chen, B., & Liu, J. C. (2024). Generative artificial intelligence in education and its implications for assessment. *TechTrends, 68*(1), 58–66. DOI: 10.1007/s11528-023-00911-4

Maphalala, M. C., & Ajani, O. A. (2025). Leveraging artificial intelligence as a learning tool in higher education. *Interdisciplinary Journal of Education Research, 7*(1), a01–a01. DOI: 10.38140/ijer-2025.vol7.1.01

Marino, M. T., Vasquez, E., Dieker, L., Basham, J., & Blackorby, J. (2023). The future of artificial intelligence in special education technology. *Journal of Special Education Technology, 38*(3), 404–416. DOI: 10.1177/01626434231165977

Martin, F., Zhuang, M., & Schaefer, D. (2024). Systematic review of research on artificial intelligence in K-12 education (2017–2022). *Computers and Education: Artificial Intelligence, 6*(December 2023). DOI: 10.1016/j.caeai.2023.100195

Martins, I., & Baptista, M. (2024). Teacher professional development in integrated STEAM education: A study on its contribution to the development of the PCK of physics teachers. *Education Sciences, 14*(2), 164. DOI: 10.3390/educsci14020164

Marzano, D. (2025). Generative Artificial Intelligence (GAI) in Teaching and Learning Processes at the K-12 Level: A Systematic Review. *Technology, Knowledge and Learning*. DOI: 10.1007/s10758-025-09853-7

Master, A., Cheryan, S., & Meltzoff, A. N. (2016). Computing whether she belongs: Stereotypes undermine girls' interest and sense of belonging in computer science. *Journal of Educational Psychology, 108*(3), 424–437. DOI: 10.1037/edu0000061

Matli, W. (2024). Extending the theory of information poverty to deepfake technology. *International Journal of Information Management Data Insights*, vol. 4, 2, 100286, ISSN 2667-0968. Doi: DOI: 10.1016/j.jjimei.2024.100286

Matos, T., Santos, W., Zdravevski, E., Coelho, P. J., Pires, I. M., & Madeira, F. (2025). A systematic review of artificial intelligence applications in education: Emerging trends and challenges. *Decision Analytics Journal, 15*, 100571. DOI: 10.1016/j.dajour.2025.100571

Maulida, L., Nurossobah, P., Aura, B. A., Nengsih, E. D., & Rasilah, R. (2024). Improving The effectiveness of mathematics learning through artificial intelligence: Literature review. *Journal of General Education and Humanities, 3*(4), 323–338. DOI: 10.58421/gehu.v3i4.267

Maung, B. M., McBride, K., Lucas, J. S., Tabar, M., & Lee, D. (2024). Generative AI disproportionately harms long tail users. *Computer, 57*(11), 82–85. DOI: 10.1109/MC.2024.3408594

Ma, W., Adesope, O. O., Nesbit, J. C., & Liu, Q. (2014). Intelligent tutoring systems and learning outcomes: A meta-analysis. *Journal of Educational Psychology, 106*(4), 901–918. DOI: 10.1037/a0037123

Mayer, R. E. (2005). *The Cambridge Handbook of Multimedia Learning*. Cambridge University Press. DOI: 10.1017/CBO9780511816819

Means, B., Toyama, Y., Murphy, R., Bakia, M., & Jones, K. (2009). *Evaluation of evidence-based practices in online learning*. U.S. Department of Education. https://eric.ed.gov/?id=ED505824

Mehta, P., Chillarge, G. R., Sapkal, S. D., Shinde, G. R., & Kshirsagar, P. S. (2023). Inclusion of children with special needs in the educational system, artificial intelligence (AI). In *AI-assisted special education for students with exceptional needs* (pp. 156–185). IGI Global. DOI: 10.4018/979-8-3693-0378-8.ch007

Meng, N., Dhimolea, T. K., & Ali, Z. (2022). AI-enhanced education: Teaching and learning reimagined. In *Bridging human intelligence and artificial intelligence* (pp. 107–124). Springer International Publishing., DOI: 10.1007/978-3-030-84729-6_7

Meylani, R. (2024). Artificial Intelligence in the Education of Teachers: A Qualitative Synthesis of the Cutting-Edge Research Literature. *Journal of Computer and Education Research*, *12*(24), 600–637. DOI: 10.18009/jcer.1477709

Michel-Villarreal, R., Vilalta-Perdomo, E., Salinas-Navarro, D. E., Thierry-Aguilera, R., & Gerardou, F. S. (2023). Challenges and opportunities of generative AI for higher education as explained by ChatGPT. *Education Sciences*, *13*(9), 856. DOI: 10.3390/educsci13090856

Mikeladze, T., Meijer, P. C., & Verhoeff, R. P. (2024). A comprehensive exploration of artificial intelligence competence frameworks for educators: A critical review. *European Journal of Education*, *59*(3), e12663. DOI: 10.1111/ejed.12663

Milakis, E. D. (2025). Collaborative project-based learning as a pedagogical strategy for inclusion in gifted STEAM education: Teachers perspectives from mixed-ability classrooms. *International Journal of Multidisciplinary Trends*, *7*(5), 92–105. DOI: 10.22271/multi.2025.v7.i5b.690

Milakis, E. D., Argyrakou, C. C., Melidis, A., & Vrettaros, J. (2025). ChatGPT and AI Chatbots in Education: An Umbrella Review of Systematic Reviews, Scoping Reviews, and Meta-Analyses. *International Journal of Education and Information Technologies*, *19*, 100–119. DOI: 10.46300/9109.2025.19.11

Miller, W. (2024). Adapting to AI: Reimagining the Role of Assessment Professionals. Intersection: A Journal at the Intersection of Assessment and Learning. *A Journal at the Intersection of Assessment and Learning*, *5*(4), 99–113. https://scholar.google.com/scholar?hl=en&as_sdt=0%2C5&q=2.+Adapting+to+AI%3A+Reimagining+the+Role+of+Assessment+Professionals+WIll+Miller&btnG=

Miller, D., & Robertson, D. (2010). Using games console in the primary classroom: Effects of 'Brain Training' programme on computation and self-esteem. *British Journal of Educational Technology*, *41*(2), 242–255. DOI: 10.1111/j.1467-8535.2008.00918.x

Mills, A., Bali, M., & Eaton, L. (2023). How do we respond to generative AI in education? Open educational practices give us a framework for an ongoing process. *Journal of Applied Learning and Teaching*, *6*(1), 16–30.

Ministry of Education and Religious Affairs. (2023). *Informatics curriculum reform: Government Gazette FEK B/2951/2023*. Hellenic Republic.

Mishra, P., Warr, M., & Islam, R. (2023). TPACK in the age of ChatGPT and Generative AI. *Journal of Digital Learning in Teacher Education, 39*(4), 235–251. DOI: 10.1080/21532974.2023.2247480

Misiejuk, K., López-Pernas, S., Kaliisa, R., & Saqr, M. (2025). Mapping the Landscape of Generative Artificial Intelligence in Learning Analytics: A Systematic Literature Review. *Journal of Learning Analytics, 12*(1), 12–31. DOI: 10.18608/jla.2025.8591

Mittal, U., Sai, S., Chamola, V., & Sangwan, D. (2024). A comprehensive review on generative AI for education. *IEEE Access : Practical Innovations, Open Solutions, 12*, 142733–142759. DOI: 10.1109/ACCESS.2024.3468368

Mogali, S. R. (2023). Initial impressions of ChatGPT for anatomy education. *Anatomical Sciences Education, 17*(2), 444–447. DOI: 10.1002/ase.2261 PMID: 36749034

Mohamed, M. Z. B., Hidayat, R., & Mahmud, M. K. H. B. (2022). Artificial Intelligence in Mathematics Education: A Systematic Literature Review. *International Electronic Journal of Mathematics Education, 17*(3), em0694. Advance online publication. DOI: 10.29333/iejme/12132

Mohamudally-Boolaky, A., & Padachi, K. (2024). Leveraging technology for math education: A systematic literature review. *Creative Education, 15*(8), 1692–1704. DOI: 10.4236/ce.2024.158102

Mohandoss, K. (2023). The Omnipotent and Omnipresent Inevitability of Artificial Intelligence (AI): AI Is All about Creating a Win-Win Situation. In Artificial intelligence in Pharmaceutical Sciences (pp. 1-17). CRC Press.

Molina, E., Cobo, C., Pineda, J., & Rovner, H. (2024). *AI revolution in education: What you need to know.* World Bank. www.worldbank.org

Mollick, E., & Mollick, L. (2023). Assigning AI: Seven approaches for students, with prompts. arXiv preprint arXiv:2306.10052.

Montenegro-Rueda, M., Fernández-Cerero, J., Fernández-Batanero, J. M., & López-Meneses, E. (2023). Impact of the implementation of ChatGPT in education: A systematic review. *Computers, 12*(8), 153. DOI: 10.3390/computers12080153

Montessori, M. (1967). *The absorbent mind.* Holt, Rinehart and Winston.

Montessori, M. (1988). *The discovery of the child.* Ballantine Books.

Moreno-Guerrero, A. J., Marín-Marín, J. A., Dúo-Terrón, P., & López-Belmonte, J. (2022). Chatbots in education: A systematic review of the science literature. *Artificial Intelligence in Higher Education*, 81-94. DOI: 10.1201/9781003184157-4

Moreno, R., Mayer, R. E., Spires, H. A., & Lester, J. C. (2001). The case for social agency in Computer-Based teaching: Do students learn more deeply when they interact with animated pedagogical agents? *Cognition and Instruction, 19*(2), 177–213. DOI: 10.1207/S1532690XCI1902_02

Morrell, E. (2008). *Critical Literacy and Urban Youth: Pedagogies of Access, Dissent, and Liberation* (1st ed.). Routledge., DOI: 10.4324/9780203937914

Moura, A & Tchiang, Van Man, I. (2025). Curipod's Artificial Intelligence Assistant in the Proofreading Process: An Exploratory Study. In Moreira, Filipe T. & Teles, Rui Oliva, *Improving Student Assessment with Emerging AI Tools.* IGI Global Book, 143-168.

Moura, A. & Carvalho, A. A. (2023b). Literacia de Prompts para Potenciar o Uso da Inteligência Artificial na Educação. *RE@D-Revista de Educação a Distância e Elearning,* 6 (2): e202308, 1-26.

Moura, A. (2024). Inteligência Artificial na Educação: perceções dos professores participantes numa oficina de formação. Carvalho, A. A. A., Schlemmer, E., Area, M., Marques, C. G., Santos, I. L., Guimarães, D., Cruz, S., Moura, A., Reis, C. S., Rebelo, P. V. (Orgs) (2024). *Atas do 6º Encontro Internacional sobre Jogos e Mobile Learning.* Centro de Estudos Interdisciplinares, 184-193.

Moura, A., & Carvalho, A. A. (2023a). Inteligência Artificial para Ensinar e para Aprender. In Alves, L. (Org.), *Inteligência Artificial (IA) e Educação: refletindo sobre os desafios contemporâneos.* Salvador: Editora EDUFBA, 155-168.

Mousavinasab, E., Zarifsanaiey, N., & Niakan Kalhori, R., S., Rakhshan, M., Keikha, L., & Ghazi Saeedi, M. (. (2021). Intelligent tutoring systems: A systematic review of characteristics, applications, and evaluation methods. *Interactive Learning Environments, 29*(1), 142–163. DOI: 10.1080/10494820.2018.1558257

Mudau, S. P., & Nzima, D. R. (2023). Teacher perspectives on the use of augmentative and alternative communication systems for learners with complex communication needs. *South African Journal of Education, 43*(4), 2170. DOI: 10.15700/saje.v43n4a2170

Mukherjee, A., & Chang, H. (2023). Managing the Creative Frontier of Generative AI: The Novelty-Usefulness Tradeoff. *California Management Review.*

Mumm, J., & Mutlu, B. (2011). Designing motivational agents: The role of praise, social comparison, and embodiment in computer feedback. *Computers in Human Behavior*, *27*(5), 1643–1650. DOI: 10.1016/j.chb.2011.02.002

Murugesan, S. (2025). The rise of agentic AI: Implications, concerns, and the path forward. *IEEE Intelligent Systems*, *40*(2), 8–14. DOI: 10.1109/MIS.2025.3544940

Mustafa, M. Y., Tlili, A., Lampropoulos, G., Huang, R., Jandrić, P., Zhao, J., Salha, S., Xu, L., Panda, S., Kinshuk, , López-Pernas, S., & Saqr, M. (2024). A systematic review of literature reviews on artificial intelligence in education (AIED): A roadmap to a future research agenda. *Smart Learning Environments*, *11*(1), 59. Advance online publication. DOI: 10.1186/s40561-024-00350-5

Naida, R., Berezovska, L., Bulgakova, O., Kravets, N., & Savchenkova, M. (2024). Integrating innovative pedagogical technologies into Early Childhood education training programs: A comparative analysis. *Conhecimento & Diversidade*, *16*(41), 568–595. DOI: 10.18316/rcd.v16i41.11551

Naik, D., Naik, I., & Naik, N. (2024). The AI Engine of Creation: Exploring the Capabilities of AI Chatbots based on Generative AI, Large Language Models and Large Multimodal Models. *TechRxiv,* November 19, 2024, 1-32. DOI: 10.36227/techrxiv.173198336.68543189/v1

Naseri, R. N. N., & Abdullah, M. S. (2024). Understanding AI Technology Adoption in Educational Settings: A Review of Theoretical Frameworks and their Applications. *Information Management and Business Review, 16*(3), 174–181. https://doi.org/https://doi.org/10.22610/imbr.v16i3(i).3963

Naveed, H., Khan, A. U., Qiu, S., Saqib, M., Anwar, S., Usman, M., . . . Mian, A. (2023). A comprehensive overview of large language models. *arXiv preprint,* arXiv:2307.06435.

Neal, T. M. (2025). Creating Academically Advanced Learning Environments for Gifted Students Through Artificial Intelligence. In *Transforming Special Education Through Artificial Intelligence* (pp. 165–192). IGI Global., DOI: 10.4018/979-8-3693-5538-1.ch006

Nee, C. K., Rahman, M. H. A., Yahaya, N., Ibrahim, N. H., Razak, R. A., & Sugino, C. (2023). Exploring the trend and potential distribution of chatbot in education: A systematic review. *International Journal of Information and Education Technology (IJIET)*, *13*(3), 516–525. DOI: 10.18178/ijiet.2023.13.3.1834

Ng, A. (2017). Andrew Ng on why Artificial Intelligence is the New Electricity. *InsideHPC.* https://insidehpc.com/2017/03/andrew-ng-artificial-intelligence-new-electricity/

Nguyen, A. (2024). Addressing Inequities: The Struggle for Quality Education and Life for Disabled and Marginalized Youth.

Nguyen, T. H. C. (2024). Exploring the Role of Artificial Intelligence-Powered Facilitator in Enhancing Digital Competencies of Primary School Teachers. *European Journal of Educational Research, volume–13–2024*(volume–13–issue–1–january–2024), 219–231. DOI: 10.12973/eu-jer.13.1.219

Nguyen, A., Kremantzis, M., Essien, A., Petrounias, I., & Hosseini, S. (2024). Enhancing student engagement through artificial intelligence (AI): Understanding the basics, opportunities, and challenges. *Journal of University Teaching & Learning Practice, 21*(06). Advance online publication. DOI: 10.53761/caraaq92

Nitto, H., Taniyama, D., & Inagaki, H. (2017). Social acceptance and impact of robots and artificial intelligence. *Nomura Res. Inst. Pap, 211*, 1–5.

Nonju, K. D. S., & Ihua-Maduenyi, A. B. (2024). The Impact of Artificial Intelligence on Privacy Laws. *International Journal of Research and Innovation in Social Science, VIII*(IX), 2150–2174. DOI: 10.47772/IJRISS.2024.8090178

Noor, S., & Ali, K. (2025). Ethical AI and Multimodal Semiotic Reasoning: Redefining mathematics and STEAM education in the digital era. DOI: 10.13140/RG.2.2.14455.33443

Noroozi, O., Soleimani, S., Farrokhnia, M., & Banihashem, S. K. (2024). Generative AI in Education: Pedagogical, Theoretical, and Methodological Perspectives. *International Journal of Technology in Education, 7*(3), 373–385. DOI: 10.46328/ijte.845

Nourian, P., Azadi, S., & Oval, R. (2023). Generative design in architecture: From mathematical optimization to grammatical customization. In *Computational Design and Digital Manufacturing* (pp. 1–43). Springer International Publishing. DOI: 10.1007/978-3-031-21167-6_1

Núñez-Michuy, C. M., Veloz-Segura, V. T., Agualongo-Chela, L. M., & Bayas-Romero, E. L. (2023). Integración de la Inteligencia Artificial en la Educación para el Desarrollo Sostenible: Oportunidades y Desafíos. *Magazine de las Ciencias: Revista de Investigación e Innovación, 8*(4), 96–108. DOI: 10.33262/rmc.v8i4.2959

Nunnally, J. C., & Bernstein, I. H. (1994). *Psychometric theory* (3rd ed.). McGraw-Hill.

Nwana, H. S. (1990). Intelligent tutoring systems: An overview. *Artificial Intelligence Review*, *4*(4), 251–277. DOI: 10.1007/BF00168958

O'Neil, C., & Schutt, R. (2013). *Doing data science*. O'Reilly Media.

O'Sullivan, P., Forgette, C., Monroe, S., & England, M. T. (2020). Student perceptions of the effectiveness of adaptive courseware for learning. *Current Issues in Emerging Elearning*, *7*(1), 5.

Ocaña-Fernández, Y., Valenzuela-Fernández, L. A., & Garro-Aburto, L. L. (2019). Inteligencia artificial y sus implicaciones en la educación superior. *Propósitos Y Representaciones, 7*(2), 536–568. DOI: 10.20511/pyr2019.v7n2.274

OECD. (2019). OECD Principles on Artificial Intelligence. Organisation for Economic Co-operation and Development. https://oecd.ai/en/ai-principles

OECD. (2019). *Recommendation of the Council on Artificial Intelligence*. OECD Legal Instruments. https://oecd.ai/en/assets/files/OECD-LEGAL-0449-en.pdf

OECD. (2021). *OECD AI Principles*. OECD Publishing. https://oecd.ai/en/ai-principles

OECD. (2025). *Empowering learners for the age of AI: An AI literacy framework for primary and secondary education (Review draft)*. OECD. Paris. https://ailiteracyframework.org

Ogoke, C. J., Anyanwu, A., Okolie, A., Onuoha, E., & Vivian, D. O. (2025). Application of artificial intelligence in the teaching and learning of mathematics: Implication for achievement and retention. *Eureka: Journal of Educational Research*, *3*(2), 134–141. DOI: 10.56773/ejer.v3i2.62

Okonkwo, C. W. & Ade-Ibijola, A. (2021). Chatbots applications in education: A systematic review. *Computers and Education: Artificial Intelligence*, 2.

Okonkwo, C. W., & Ade-Ibijola, A. (2021). Chatbots applications in education: A systematic review. *Computers and Education: Artificial Intelligence*, 2, 100033. DOI: 10.1016/j.caeai.2021.100033

Ooi, K.-B., Tan, G. W.-H., Al-Emran, M., Al-Sharafi, M. A., Capatina, A., Chakraborty, A., Dwivedi, Y. K., Huang, T.-L., Kar, A. K., Lee, V.-H., Loh, X.-M., Micu, A., Mikalef, P., Mogaji, E., Pandey, N., Raman, R., Rana, N. P., Sarker, P., Sharma, A., & Wong, L.-W. (2023). The potential of generative artificial intelligence across disciplines: Perspectives and future directions. *Journal of Computer Information Systems*, •••, 1–32. DOI: 10.1080/08874417.2023.2261010

OpenAI at ASU. (2023). Retrieved from https://ai.asu.edu/openAI

Opesemowo, O. A. G. (2025). Artificial Intelligence in Mathematics Education: The Pros and Cons. In *Encyclopedia of Information Science and Technology, Sixth Edition* (pp. 1-18). IGI Global.

Opesemowo, O. A., & Ndlovu, M. (2024). Artificial intelligence in mathematics education: The good, the bad, and the ugly. *Journal of Pedagogical Research, 8*(3), 333–346. DOI: 10.33902/JPR.202426428

Ortega-Ochoa, E., Arguedas, M., & Daradoumis, T. (2024). Empathic pedagogical conversational agents: A systematic literature review. *British Journal of Educational Technology, 55*(3), 886–909. DOI: 10.1111/bjet.13413

Owoseni, A., Kolade, O., & Egbetokun, A. (2024). Generative AI and Its Implications for Higher Education Students and Educators. In *Generative AI in Higher Education: Innovation Strategies for Teaching and Learning* (pp. 1–25). Springer Nature Switzerland. DOI: 10.1007/978-3-031-60179-8_1

Özgür, E. G., & Bekiroğlu, N. (2025). Can ChatGPT be used as an education assistant in the field of health sciences? Examining with the integration of meta-analysis and co-citation analysis. *Heliyon, 11*(3), e41925. Advance online publication. DOI: 10.1016/j.heliyon.2025.e41925 PMID: 39981362

Page, M. J., McKenzie, J. E., Bossuyt, P. M., Boutron, I., Hoffmann, T. C., Mulrow, C. D., Shamseer, L., Tetzlaff, J. M., Akl, E. A., Brennan, S. E., Chou, R., Glanville, J., Grimshaw, J. M., Hróbjartsson, A., Lalu, M. M., Li, T., Loder, E. W., Mayo-Wilson, E., McDonald, S., & Moher, D. (2021). The PRISMA statement: An updated guideline for reporting systematic reviews. *BMJ (Clinical Research Ed.)*, (71), n71. Advance online publication. DOI: 10.1136/bmj.n71 PMID: 33782057

Paiz, J. M. (2024). *Droids don't teach, we do: Addressing AI anxiety in language teaching and learning*. The FLTMag. https://www.doi.org/10.69732/VFPR7648

Paliwal, V., & Patel, S. (2025). Can artificial intelligence facilitate mathematics instruction? In Nagar, S., & Kumar, M. (Eds.), *Transforming Special Education through Artificial Intelligence* (pp. 223–244). IGI Global., DOI: 10.4018/979-8-3693-5538-1.ch008

Palmer, Z. B., & Oswal, S. K. (2024). Constructing websites with generative AI tools: The accessibility of their workflows and products for users with disabilities. *Journal of Business and Technical Communication, 0*(0). Advance online publication. DOI: 10.1177/10506519241280644

Pane, J. F., Griffin, B. A., McCaffrey, D. F., & Karam, R. (2014). Effectiveness of cognitive tutor algebra I at scale. *Educational Evaluation and Policy Analysis, 36*(2), 127–144. DOI: 10.3102/0162373713507480

Pane, J. F., Steiner, E. D., Baird, M. D., & Hamilton, L. S. (2015). *Continued Progress: Promising Evidence on Personalized Learning*. Rand Corporation. DOI: 10.7249/RR1365

Pang, S., Nol, E., & Heng, K. (2025). Generative AI as a Personal Tutor for English Language Learning: A Review of Benefits and Concerns. *International Journal of Changes in Education*. DOI: 10.47852/bonviewIJCE52023724

Panigrahi, A., Malladi, S., Xia, M., & Arora, S. (2023). Trainable transformer in transformer. *arXiv preprint,* arXiv:2307.01189.

Panit, N. M. (2024). Can critical thinking and AI work together? Observations of science, Mathematics, and language instructors. *Environment and Social Psychology, 9*(11), 1–16. DOI: 10.59429/esp.v9i11.3141

Panjwani, M. M.Mubashir Moosa Panjwani. (2024). Impact of AI in teaching and learning of CS in low-resourced schools. *International Journal of Science and Research Archive, 12*(2), 1933–1939. DOI: 10.30574/ijsra.2024.12.2.1451

Papadakis, S., Lytvynova, S. H., Ivanova, S. M., & Selyshcheva, I. A. (2024b). *Advancing lifelong learning with AI-enhanced ICT: A review of 3L-Person 2024.* In *CEUR Workshop Proceedings (9th International Workshop on Professional Retraining and Life-Long Learning using ICT: Person-oriented Approach — 3L-Person 2024, Lviv, Ukraine, September 25, 2023).* CEUR-WS.org.

Papadakis, S., Lytvynova, S., Mintii, I. S., Ivanova, S., & Iryna A Selyshcheva, S. O. Semerikov. (2024b). *Advancing lifelong learning with AI-enhanced ICT: A review of 3L-Person 2024. (2024). CEUR Workshop Proceedings, 1–9.* https://ceur-ws.org/Vol-3781/paper00.pdf

Papadakis, S., Semerikov, S. O., & Striuk, A., Hennadiy M Kravtsov, Mariya Shyshkina, Maiia Volodymyrivna Marienko, Hanna Danylchuk. (2024). *Embracing digital innovation and cloud technologies for transformative learning experiences.* In *Proceedings of the 11th Workshop on Cloud Technologies in Education (CTE 2023), Kryvyi Rih, Ukraine, December 22, 2023.* CEUR Workshop Proceedings.

Papadakis, S., Striuk, A. M., Kravtsov, H. M., Shyshkina, M. P., Marienko, M. V., & Danylchuk, H. B. (2024a). *Embracing digital innovation and cloud technologies for transformative learning experiences.* In *Proceedings of the 11th Workshop on Cloud Technologies in Education (CTE 2023), Kryvyi Rih, Ukraine, December 22, 2023.* CEUR Workshop Proceedings.

Papakostas, C., Troussas, C., & Sgouropoulou, C. (2024). Review of the literature on AI-enhanced augmented reality in education. *Special Topics in Artificial Intelligence and Augmented Reality: The Case of Spatial Intelligence Enhancement*, 13-50.

Pardo, A., & Siemens, G. (2014). Ethical and privacy principles for learning analytics. *British Journal of Educational Technology, 45*(3), 438–450. DOI: 10.1111/bjet.12152

Pascual, J. (2019). Innovación Educativa: Un proceso construido sobre relaciones de poder. *Revista Educación Política y Sociedad, 4*(2), 9–30. DOI: 10.15366/reps2019.4.2.001

Paul, A., Yu, C. L., Susanto, E. A., Lau, N. W. L., & Meadows, G. I. (2024). *AgentPeerTalk: Empowering students through Agentic-AI-Driven discernment of bullying and joking in peer interactions in schools* (Preprint on ArXiv No. 2408.01459). DOI: 10.48550/ARXIV.2408.01459

Pawar, S. (2024). Advancing interview preparation: An AI-driven approach. *Indian Scientific Journal of Research in Engineering and Management, 8*(2), 1–13. DOI: 10.55041/IJSREM28705

Payadnya, I. P. A. A., Putri, G. A. M. A., Suwija, I. K., Saelee, S., & Jayantika, I. G. A. N. T. (2025). Cultural integration in AI-enhanced mathematics education: Insights from Southeast Asian educators. *Journal for Multicultural Education, 19*(1), 58–72. DOI: 10.1108/JME-09-2024-0119

Pedro, F., Subosa, M., Rivas, A., & Valverde, P. (2019). *Artificial intelligence in education: Challenges and opportunities for sustainable development.*

Pekrun, R. (2006). The control–value theory of achievement emotions: Assumptions, corollaries, and implications for educational research and practice. *Educational Psychology Review, 18*(4), 315–341. DOI: 10.1007/s10648-006-9029-9

Pekrun, R., Goetz, T., Frenzel, A. C., Barchfeld, P., & Perry, R. P. (2011). Measuring emotions in students' learning and performance: The Achievement Emotions Questionnaire (AEQ). *Contemporary Educational Psychology, 36*(1), 36–48. DOI: 10.1016/j.cedpsych.2010.10.002

Pekrun, R., & Linnenbrink-Garcia, L. (2012). Academic emotions and student engagement. In Christenson, S. L., Reschly, A. L., & Wylie, C. (Eds.), *Handbook of research on student engagement* (pp. 259–282). Springer., DOI: 10.1007/978-1-4614-2018-7_12

Pekrun, R., & Perry, R. P. (2014). Control–value theory of achievement emotions. In Pekrun, R., & Linnenbrink-Garcia, L. (Eds.), *International handbook of emotions in education* (pp. 120–141). Routledge. DOI: 10.4324/9780203148211

Pellas, N. (2023). The influence of sociodemographic factors on students' attitudes toward AI-generated video content creation. *Smart Learning Environments*, *10*(1), 57. DOI: 10.1186/s40561-023-00276-4

Peña, A. A. R. (2019). Robot-Proof: Higher Education in the age of artificial intelligence. *Innovación Educativa (México, D.F.)*, *19*(80), 181–183.

Peña-Fernández, S., Meso Ayerdi, K., Larrondo Ureta, A., & Díaz Noci, J. (2023). Sin periodistas, no hay periodismo: La dimensión social de la inteligencia artificial generativa en los medios de comunicación. *El Profesional de la Información*, *32*(2), e320227. DOI: 10.3145/epi.2023.mar.27

Peres, R., Schreier, M., Schweidel, D., & Sorescu, A. (2023). On ChatGPT and beyond: How generative artificial intelligence may affect research, teaching, and practice. *International Journal of Research in Marketing*, *40*(2), 269–275. DOI: 10.1016/j.ijresmar.2023.03.001

Pérez-Marín, D. (2021). A review of the practical applications of pedagogic conversational agents to be used in school and university classrooms. *Digital*, *1*(1), 18–33. DOI: 10.3390/digital1010002

Peters, M. A., Jackson, L., Papastephanou, M., Jandrić, P., Lazaroiu, G., Evers, C. W., Cope, B., Kalantzis, M., Araya, D., Tesar, M., Mika, C., Chen, L., Wang, C., Sturm, S., Rider, S., & Fuller, S. (2023). AI and the future of humanity: ChatGPT-4, philosophy and education–Critical responses. *Educational Philosophy and Theory*, *56*(9), 828–862. DOI: 10.1080/00131857.2023.2213437

Peters, S. J., Gentry, M., Whiting, G. W., & McBee, M. T. (2019). Who gets served in gifted education? Demographic representation and a call for action. *Gifted Child Quarterly*, *63*(4), 273–287. DOI: 10.1177/0016986219833738

Piaget, J., & Inhelder, B. (2019). *The Psychology Of The Child.*

Pianta, R. C. (2016). Teacher–Student Interactions: Measurement, Impacts, Improvement, and Policy. *Policy Insights from the Behavioral and Brain Sciences*, *3*(1), 98–105. DOI: 10.1177/2372732215622457

Pianta, R. C., & Hofkens, T. (2023). Defining early education quality using CLASS-observed teacher–student interaction. *Frontiers in Psychology, 14,* 1110419. Advance online publication. DOI: 10.3389/fpsyg.2023.1110419

Pianta, R. C., La Paro, K. M., & Hamre, B. K. (2008). *CLASS manual: K–3.* Paul H. Brookes Publishing.

Piech, C., Sahami, M., Koller, D., Cooper, S., & Blikstein, P. (2012, February). Modeling how students learn to program. In *Proceedings of the 43rd ACM technical symposium on Computer Science Education* (pp. 153-160).

Pikhart, M., & Al-Obaydi, L. H. (2025). Reporting the potential risk of using AI in higher education: Subjective perspectives of educators. *Computers in Human Behavior Reports, 18*, 100693. DOI: 10.1016/j.chbr.2025.100693

Pintrich, P. R. (2000). The role of goal orientation in self-regulated learning. In M. Boekaerts. P.R. Pintrich & M. Zeidner (Eds.), Handbook of Self-Regulation, (pp. 451–502). Academic Press. DOI: 10.1016/B978-012109890-2/50043-3

Pörn, R., Braskén, M., Wingren, M., & Andersson, S. (2024). Attitudes towards and expectations on the role of artificial intelligence in the classroom among digitally skilled Finnish K-12 mathematics teachers. *LUMAT: International Journal on Math. Science and Technology Education, 12*(3). Advance online publication. DOI: 10.31129/LUMAT.12.3.2102

Possaghi, I., Vesin, B., Zhang, F., Sharma, K., Knudsen, C., Bjørkum, H., & Papavlasopoulou, S. (2025). Integrating multi-modal learning analytics dashboard in K-12 education: Insights for enhancing orchestration and teacher decision-making. *Smart Learning Environments, 12*(1), 53. DOI: 10.1186/s40561-025-00410-4

Pozdniakov, S., Brazil, J., Mohammadi, M., Dollinger, M., Sadiq, S., & Khosravi, H. (2025). AI-Assisted Co-Creation: Bridging Skill Gaps in Student-Generated Content. *Journal of Learning Analytics, 12*(1), 129–151. DOI: 10.18608/jla.2025.8601

Prestoza, M. J. R., & Banatao, J. C. M. (2024). Exploring the efficacy of AI passion-drivenpedagogy in enhancing student engagement and learning outcomes: A case study inphilippines. *Asian Journal of Assessment in Teaching and Learning, 14*(1), 45–54. DOI: 10.37134/ajatel.vol14.1.5.2024

ProFuturo Foundation. (2022). *Annual impact report.* https://profuturo.education/wp-content/uploads/2023/06/Memoria_ProFuturo_2022_DIGITAL.pdf

Qadir, J. (2023). *Engineering education in the era of ChatGPT: Promise and pitfalls of generative AI for education. 2023 IEEE Global Engineering Education Conference (EDUCON),* IEEE. DOI: 10.1109/EDUCON54358.2023.10125121

Radianti, J., Majchrzak, T. A., Fromm, J., & Wohlgenannt, I. (2020). A systematic review of immersive virtual reality applications for higher education: Design elements, lessons learned, and research agenda. *Computers & Education, 147*, 103778. DOI: 10.1016/j.compedu.2019.103778

Rajeshwari, M., & Krishna Prasad, K. (2020). IBM watson industry cognitive education methods. [IJCSBE]. *International Journal of Case Studies in Business, IT, and Education, 4*(1), 38–50.

Ramírez, R. A., & Layret, I. R. R. (2024). Co-designing the future with generative AI: cultivating student digital competencies for tomorrow. In *ICERI2024 Proceedings* (pp. 7756-7762). IATED. DOI: 10.21125/iceri.2024.1896

Rane, N. (2023). Role and challenges of ChatGPT and similar generative artificial intelligence in human resource management. *Available at SSRN,* 4603230. DOI: 10.2139/ssrn.4603230

Ranoliya, B. R., Raghuwanshi, N., & Singh, S. (2017). Chatbot for university related FAQs. *2017 International Conference on Advances in Computing, Communications and Informatics (ICACCI)*, 1525–1530. DOI: 10.1109/ICACCI.2017.8126057

Ransom, K. L. (2023). *How Do Parental Experiences During the IEP Process Impact or Inform Education Plans for Their Children and Education Leaders to Improve IEP Processes?* Temple University.

Ravšelj, D., Keržič, D., Tomaževič, N., Umek, L., Brezovar, N., Iahad, N. A., & Aristovnik, A. (2025). Higher education students' perceptions of ChatGPT: A global study of early reactions. *PLoS One, 20*(2), e0315011. DOI: 10.1371/journal.pone.0315011 PMID: 39908277

Real Decreto 95/2022, de 1 de febrero, por el que se establece la ordenación y las enseñanzas mínimas de la Educación Infantil. *Boletín Oficial del Estado*, 28, de 2 de febrero de 2022. https://www.boe.es/eli/es/rd/2022/02/01/95/con

Redecker, C. (2017). *European Framework for the Digital Competence of Educators (DigCompEdu).* EU Science Hub., DOI: 10.2760/159770

Reich, J. (2020). *Failure to disrupt. Why technology alone can't transform education* Harvard University Press., DOI: 10.2307/j.ctv322v4cp

Reimann, P., & Yacef, K. (2013). Using process mining for understanding learning. *Handbook of design in educational technology*, 472-481.

Reina-Parrado, M., Román-Graván, P., & Hervás-Gómez, C. (2025). Integration of Artificial Intelligence and Machine Learning in Education: A Systematic Review. *International Journal of Educational Methodology*, *11*(2), 203–216. DOI: 10.12973/ijem.11.2.203

Renzulli, J. S. (2021). The three-ring conception of giftedness: A developmental model for promoting creative productivity. In Sternberg, R. J., & Ambrose, D. (Eds.), *Conceptions of giftedness* (3rd ed., pp. 335–357). Cambridge University Press., DOI: 10.1007/978-3-030-56869-6_19

Riemer, K., & Peter, S. (2024). Conceptualizing generative AI as style engines: Application archetypes and implications. *International Journal of Information Management*, *79*, 102824. DOI: 10.1016/j.ijinfomgt.2024.102824

Riga, A., & Malafantis, K. (2023). Gifted students within the Greek educational context: Challenges and perspectives in the frame of contemporary inclusive European education. *European Journal of Education and Pedagogy*, *4*(1), 112–118. DOI: 10.24018/ejedu.2023.4.1.568

Riggs, V. (2025). Impact of AI literacy professional development on teaching: Evaluating changes in perceptions and classroom practices. *American Journal of STEM Education*, *7*, 37–50. DOI: 10.32674/rbajg012

Rivas, A., Buchbinder, N., & Barrenechea, I. (2023). El futuro de la inteligencia artificial en educación en América Latina. *Innovación Educativa (México, D.F.)*, *24*(96).

Rizvi, S., Waite, J., & Sentance, S. (2023). Artificial Intelligence teaching and learning in K-12 from 2019 to 2022: A systematic literature review. *Computers and Education: Artificial Intelligence*, *4*(January), 100145. DOI: 10.1016/j.caeai.2023.100145

Rodríguez, A., Orozco, K., García, J., Rodríguez, S., & Barros, H. (2023). La Implementación de la Inteligencia Artificial en la Educación: Análisis Sistemático. *Dominio De Las Ciencias*, *9*(3), 2162–2178. DOI: 10.23857/dc.v9i3.3548

Roe, J., Renandya, W. A., & Jacobs, G. M. (2023). A review of AI-powered writing tools and their implications for academic integrity in the language classroom. *Journal of English and Applied Linguistics*, *2*(1), 3. DOI: 10.59588/2961-3094.1035

Rogers, E. M. (2003). *Diffusion of Innovations* (5th ed.). Free Press.

Romero, C., & Ventura, S. (2020). Educational data mining and learning analytics: An updated survey. *Wiley Interdisciplinary Reviews. Data Mining and Knowledge Discovery*, *10*(3), e1355. DOI: 10.1002/widm.1355

Roschelle, J., Feng, M., Murphy, R. F., & Mason, C. A. (2016). Online mathematics homework increases student achievement. *AERA Open*, *2*(4), 2332858416673968. DOI: 10.1177/2332858416673968

Roy, S., & Bhowmick, P. K. (2016). Augmenting Online Video Lectures with Topically Relevant Assessment Items. In *ICCE*. DOI: 10.58459/icce.2016.1167

Ruane, E., Birhane, A., & Ventresque, A. (2019). Conversational AI: Social and ethical considerations. *AICS*, *2563*, 104–115.

Rundquist, R., Holmberg, K., Rack, J., Mohseni, Z., & Masiello, I. (2024). Use of Learning Analytics in K–12 Mathematics Education: Systematic Scoping Review of the Impact on Teaching and Learning. *Journal of Learning Analytics*, *11*(3), 174–191. DOI: 10.18608/jla.2024.8299

Russell, S. (2021). *Inteligência artificial a nosso favor: Como manter o controle sobre a tecnologia*. Companhia das Letras.

Sadykova, G., & Kayumova, A. (2024). Educators' Perception of Artificial Intelligence as Instructional Tool. *TEM Journal*, 3194–3204. https://doi.org/DOI: 10.18421/TEM134-54

Sætra, H. S. (2023). Generative AI: Here to stay, but for good? *Technology in Society*, *75*, 102372. DOI: 10.1016/j.techsoc.2023.102372

Safi, R. (2025). Plagiarism in the age of generative AI: An exploratory experiment. *Communications of the Association for Information Systems*, *56*(1), 594–612. DOI: 10.17705/1CAIS.05624

Safiulina, E., Vintere, A., & Panova, O. (2024). Exploring AI-based mathematics learning platforms and applications. In *EDULEARN24 Proceedings* (pp. 6861-6865). IATED. DOI: 10.21125/edulearn.2024.1629

Sağdıç, A., Elumar-Efe, E., & Sani-Bozkurt, S. (2024). GenAI, robots, and inclusive special education: Autism spectrum disorder in the age of generative AI. In *Transforming Education with Generative AI: Prompt Engineering and Synthetic Content Creation* (pp. 309-326). IGI Global.

Saha, P., Hossain, M., Roy, N. C., Masud, A. A., & Amin, R. (2025). Unlocking the power of AI in education: Students' intentions and AI tool use driving learning success in an emerging economy. *On the Horizon*, *33*(1), 126–144. DOI: 10.1108/OTH-10-2024-0066

Sahu, A., & Bhowmick, P. K. (2019). Feature engineering and ensemble-based approach for improving automatic short-answer grading performance. *IEEE Transactions on Learning Technologies, 13*(1), 77–90. DOI: 10.1109/TLT.2019.2897997

Sakamoto, M., Tan, S., & Clivaz, S. (2024). Social, cultural and political perspectives of generative AI in teacher education: Lesson planning in Japanese teacher education. In M. Searson, E. Langran & J. Trumle (Eds.), *Exploring new horizons: Generative artificial intelligence and teacher education* (pp. 178-209). Association for the Advancement of Computing in Education (AACE). https://www.learntechlib.org/p/223928/

Salih, S., Husain, O., Hamdan, M., Abdelsalam, S., Elshafie, H., & Motwakel, A. (2024). Transforming Education with AI: A Systematic Review of ChatGPT's Role in Learning, Academic Practices, and Institutional Adoption. *Results in Engineering, 103837*. Advance online publication. DOI: 10.1016/j.rineng.2024.103837

Salta, K., & Koulougliotis, D. (2015). Assessing motivation to learn chemistry: Adaptation and validation of the Science Motivation Questionnaire II with Greek secondary school students. *Chemistry Education Research and Practice, 16*(2), 237–250. DOI: 10.1039/C4RP00196F

Samala, A. D., Rawas, S., Wang, T., Reed, J. M., Kim, J., Howard, N.-J., & Ertz, M. (2025). Unveiling the landscape of generative artificial intelligence in education: A comprehensive taxonomy of applications, challenges, and future prospects. *Education and Information Technologies, 30*(3), 3239–3278. DOI: 10.1007/s10639-024-12936-0

Samuel, I. R., & Salisu, A. D. (2025). Shaping the future of STEM education in Nigeria through artificial intelligence. *Journal of African Innovation and Advanced Studies*. DOI: 10.70382/ajaias.v7i2.011

Sandu, N., & Gide, E. (2019). Adoption of AI-Chatbots to enhance student learning experience in higher education in india. *2019 18th International Conference on Information Technology Based Higher Education and Training (ITHET)*. DOI: 10.1109/ITHET46829.2019.8937382

Sangarsu, R. R. (2023). Enhancing Student Engagement in Learning with Modern Web and AI Technologies. [IJSR]. *International Journal of Science and Research (Raipur, India), 12*(10), 1439–1442. DOI: 10.21275/SR231017100712

Sanusi, I. T., Agbo, F. J., Dada, O. A., Yunusa, A. A., Aruleba, K. D., Obaido, G., Olawumi, O., & Oyelere, S. S.Centre for Multidisciplinary Research and Innovation (CEMRI). (2024). Stakeholders' insights on artificial intelligence education: Perspectives of teachers, students, and policymakers. *Computers and Education Open, 7*, 100212. DOI: 10.1016/j.caeo.2024.100212

Sanusi, I. T., Olaleye, S. A., Oyelere, S. S., & Dixon, R. A. (2022). Investigating learners' competencies for artificial intelligence education in an African K-12 setting. *Computers and Education Open*, *3*, 100083. Advance online publication. DOI: 10.1016/j.caeo.2022.100083

Saputra, I., Kurniawan, A., Yanita, M., Yeni Putri, E., & Mahniza, M. (2024). The Evolution of Educational Assessment: How Artificial Intelligence is Shaping the Trends and Future of Learning Evaluation. *The Indonesian Journal of Computer Science*, *13*(6), 9056–9074. DOI: 10.33022/ijcs.v13i6.4465

Sarkar, R., Mahamuni, V. S., Chitra, M., Vijayakumar, M., Jefferson, K., & Boopathi, S. (2025). Integrating Innovation Tools and Technology in Educational Management. In Planning Tools for Policy, Leadership, and Management of Education Systems (pp. 121–154). IGI Global.

Sarkar, R., Parmar, D. V., Trivedi, N. B., Prabakaran, S., Chandra, S., & Boopathi, S. (2025). Pedagogical Contents Developments and Specialized Training for Teaching Careers. In Global Practices in Inclusive Education Curriculum and Policy (pp. 187–216). IGI Global.

Sarker, I. H. (2021). Machine learning: Algorithms, real-world applications and research directions. *SN Computer Science*, *2*(3), 160. DOI: 10.1007/s42979-021-00592-x

Sartor, G., & Lagioia, F. (2020). *The impact of the General Data Protection Regulation (GDPR) on artificial intelligence*. European Parliament. [10.2861/293]

Saúde, S., Barros, J. P., & Almeida, I. (2024). Impacts of generative artificial intelligence in higher education: Research trends and students' perceptions. *Social Sciences (Basel, Switzerland)*, *13*(8), 410. DOI: 10.3390/socsci13080410

Schmid, R. F., Bernard, R. M., Borokhovski, E., Tamim, R. M., Abrami, P. C., Surkes, M., Wade, A., & Woods, J. (2014). The effects of technology use in postsecondary education: A meta-analysis of classroom applications. *Computers & Education*, *72*, 271–291. DOI: 10.1016/j.compedu.2013.11.002

Schmidt, T., & Strasser, T. (2022). Artificial Intelligence in Foreign Language Learning and Teaching A CALL for Intelligent Practice. *Anglistik*, *33*(1), 165–184. DOI: 10.33675/ANGL/2022/1/14

Schneider, J. (2025). *Generative to agentic AI: Survey, conceptualization, and challenges* (Preprint on ArXiv No. 2504.18875). DOI: 10.48550/ARXIV.2504.18875

Schroeder, N. L., & Adesope, O. O. (2014). A systematic review of pedagogical agents' persona, motivation, and cognitive load implications for learners. *Journal of Research on Technology in Education, 46*(3), 229–251. DOI: 10.1080/15391523.2014.888265

Schroeder, N. L., & Craig, S. D. (2021). Learning with virtual humans: Introduction to the special issue. *Journal of Research on Technology in Education, 53*(1), 1–7. DOI: 10.1080/15391523.2020.1863114

Selwyn, N. (2019). *Should robots replace teachers? AI and the future of education.* Political Press.

Semwaiko, G. S., Chao, W.-H., & Yang, C.-Y. (2024). Transforming K-12 education: A systematic review of AI integration. *International Journal of Educational Technology and Learning, 17*(2), 43–63. DOI: 10.55217/101.v17i2.847

Serin, H. (2023). The role of technology in mathematics education: Promoting student achievement. *International Journal of Social Sciences & Educational Studies, 10*(2), 390–395. DOI: 10.23918/ijsses.v10i2p390

Sethi, S. S., & Jain, K. (2024). AI technologies for social emotional learning: Recent research and future directions. *Journal of Research in Innovative Teaching & Learning, 17*(2), 213–225. DOI: 10.1108/JRIT-03-2024-0073

Settles, B., & Meeder, B. (2016, August). A trainable spaced repetition model for language learning. In *Proceedings of the 54th annual meeting of the association for computational linguistics* (volume 1*: long papers)* (pp. 1848-1858). DOI: 10.18653/v1/P16-1174

Shabbir, J., & Anwer, T. (2018). Artificial intelligence and its role in near future. *arXiv preprint*, arXiv:1804.01396.

Shan, Y., Qiao, H., & Yu, B. (2024). Applied Mathematics and Nonlinear Sciences A Practical Discussion of Artificial Intelligence Technology for Efficient Classroom. *Applied Mathematics and Nonlinear Sciences, 9*(1), 1–17. https://doi.org/doi.org/10.2478/amns-2024-3586

Sharples, M. (2023). Towards social generative AI for education: Theory, practices and ethics. *Learning: Research and Practice, 9*(2), 159–167. DOI: 10.1080/23735082.2023.2261131

Shavit, Y., Agarwal, S., Brundage, M., Adler, S., O'Keefe, C., Campbell, R., Lee, T., Mishkin, P., Eloundou, T., Hickey, A., ... (2023). Practices for governing agentic AI systems. *Research Paper, OpenAI.*

Shiri, A. (2024). Artificial intelligence literacy: A proposed faceted taxonomy. *Digital Library Perspectives*, *40*(4), 681–699. DOI: 10.1108/DLP-04-2024-0067

Shneiderman, B. (2022). *Human-centered AI*. Oxford University Press. DOI: 10.1093/oso/9780192845290.001.0001

Sh, U. A., & Supriyono, N. M. R. P.SH. (2023). Optimizing Learning Through Artificial Intelligence: Evaluating the Impact of Adaptive Learning Technologies on Student Outcomes. *Sinergi International Journal of Education*, *1*(3), 138–149. DOI: 10.61194/education.v1i3.584

Shum, H.-Y., He, X.-D., & Li, D. (2018). From Eliza to XiaoIce: Challenges and Opportunities with Social Chatbots. *Frontiers of Information Technology & Electronic Engineering*, *19*(1), 10–26. DOI: 10.1631/FITEE.1700826

Shute, V. J., & Zapata-Rivera, D. (2007). Adaptive technologies. *ETS Research Report Series*, *2007*(1), 1–34. DOI: 10.1002/j.2333-8504.2007.tb02047.x

Siegle, R. F., Schroeder, N. L., Lane, H. C., & Craig, S. D. (2023). Twenty-five years of learning with pedagogical agents: History, barriers, and opportunities. *TechTrends*, *67*(5), 851–864. DOI: 10.1007/s11528-023-00869-3

Silva, G., Godwin, G., & Jayanagara, O. (2023). The impact of AI on personalized learning. Journal of Learning Sciences. *International Transactions on Education Technology (ITEE), 3*(1), 36–46. https://doi.org/https://doi.org/10.33050/itee.v3i1.669

Singh, H., Chauhan, U., Chauhan, S. P. S., Saxena, A., & Kumari, P. (2024). Adaptive and personalized learning in industry 5.0 education. In *Infrastructure Possibilities and Human-Centered Approaches With Industry 5.0* (pp. 1–19). IGI Global Scientific Publishing. DOI: 10.4018/979-8-3693-0782-3.ch001

Singh, P. H.Harpreet Paramjeet Singh. (2025). The Transformative Potential of AI in Educational Settings: From Personalized Learning to Global Access. *Journal of Computer Science and Technology Studies*, *7*(4), 507–514. DOI: 10.32996/jcsts.2025.7.4.59

Singh, S. (2023). Leadership challenges and strategies in the era of ai transformation. In *2023 International Conference on Computational Science and Computational Intelligence (CSCI)* (pp. 119-124). IEEE. https://doi.org/DOI: 10.1109/CSCI62032.2023.00025

Singh, V., & Ram, S. (2024). Impact of Artificial Intelligence on Teacher Education. *Shodh Sari-An International Multidisciplinary Journal*, *03*(01), 243–266. DOI: 10.59231/SARI7669

Singh, Y., & Phoolka, S. (2025). Hybrid education in the age of Education 5.0- A study of engagement and innovations in the Indian education system amidst covid-19. *Indian Journal of Educational Technology*, *7*(1), 309–328. https://journals.ncert.gov.in/IJET/article/view/848

Sit, C., Srinivasan, R., Amlani, A., Muthuswamy, K., Azam, A., Monzon, L., & Poon, S. D. (2020). Attitudes and perceptions of UK medical students towards artificial intelligence and radiology: A multicentre survey. *Insights Into Imaging*, *11*(1), 14. DOI: 10.1186/s13244-019-0830-7 PMID: 32025951

Skapura, D. M. (1996). *Building neural networks*. Addison-Wesley Professional.

Slade, S., & Prinsloo, P. (2013). Learning analytics: Ethical issues and dilemmas. *The American Behavioral Scientist*, *57*(10), 1510–1529. DOI: 10.1177/0002764213479366

Sleeman, D., & Brown, J. S. (1982). *Intelligent tutoring systems*. Academic Press.

Slimi, Z., Benayoune, A., & Alemu, A. E. (2025). Students' perceptions of artificial intelligence integration in higher education. *European Journal of Educational Research*, *14*(2), 471–484. DOI: 10.12973/eu-jer.14.2.471

Smakman, M., Vogt, P., & Konijn, E. A. (2021). Moral considerations on social robots in education: A multi-stakeholder perspective. *Computers & Education*, *174*, 104317. DOI: 10.1016/j.compedu.2021.104317

Smolansky, A., Cram, A., Raduescu, C., Zeivots, S., Huber, E., & Kizilcec, R. F. (2023, July). Educator and student perspectives on the impact of generative AI on assessments in higher education. In *Proceedings of the tenth ACM conference on Learning@ Scale* (pp. 378–382). DOI: 10.1145/3573051.3596191

Song, D., Oh, E. Y., & Rice, M. (2017). Interacting with a conversational agent system for educational purposes in online courses. *2017 10th International Conference on Human System Interactions (HSI)*, 78–82. DOI: 10.1109/HSI.2017.8005002

Song, P., & Wang, X. (2020). A bibliometric analysis of worldwide educational artificial intelligence research development in recent twenty years. *Asia Pacific Education Review*, *21*(3), 473–486. DOI: 10.1007/s12564-020-09640-2

Song, Y., Huang, L., Zheng, L., Fan, M., & Liu, Z. (2025). Interactions with generative AI chatbots: Unveiling dialogic dynamics, students' perceptions, and practical competencies in creative problem-solving. *International Journal of Educational Technology in Higher Education*, *22*(1), 12. DOI: 10.1186/s41239-025-00508-2

Srinivasan, R., & Uchino, K. (2021, March). Biases in generative art: A causal look from the lens of art history. In *Proceedings of the 2021 ACM Conference on Fairness, Accountability, and Transparency* (pp. 41-51). DOI: 10.1145/3442188.3445869

Stambaugh, T., & Wood, S. M. (2021). *Serving gifted students in rural settings.* Routledge., DOI: 10.4324/9781003237938

Starks, A. C., & Reich, S. M. (2023). "What about special ed?": Barriers and enablers for teaching with technology in special education. Computers & Education, 193, 104665.

Steenbergen-Hu, S., & Cooper, H. (2014). A meta-analysis of the effectiveness of intelligent tutoring systems on college students' academic learning. *Journal of Educational Psychology, 106*(2), 331–347. DOI: 10.1037/a0034752

Sternberg, R. J. (2003). *Wisdom, intelligence, and creativity synthesized.* Cambridge University Press., DOI: 10.1017/CBO9780511509612

Stock-Homburg, R., & Nguyen, M. A. (2023). See No evil, hear No evil: How users blindly overrely on robots with automation bias.

Stöhr, C., Ou, A. W., & Malmström, H. (2024). Perceptions and usage of AI chatbots among students in higher education across genders, academic levels and fields of study. *Computers and Education: Artificial Intelligence*, *7*, 100259. DOI: 10.1016/j.caeai.2024.100259

Stokel-Walker, C. (2022, December 9). AI bot ChatGPT writes smart essays-should academics worry? *Nature*. Advance online publication. DOI: 10.1038/d41586-022-04397-7

Stone, B. W. (2024). Generative AI in Higher Education: Uncertain Students, Ambiguous Use Cases, and Mercenary Perspectives. *Teaching of Psychology*, •••, 00986283241305398.

Stone, P., Brooks, R., Brynjolfsson, E., Calo, R., Etzioni, O., Hager, G., Hirschberg, J., Kalyanakrishnan, S., Kamar, E., Kraus, S., Leyton-Brown, K., Parkes, D., Press, W., Saxenian, A., Shah, J., Tambe, M., & Teller, A. (2016). *Artificial intelligence and life in 2030: The one hundred year study on artificial intelligence.* DOI: 10.48550/ARXIV.2211.06318

Strelkova, O., & Pasichnyk, O. (2017). *Three Types of Artificial Intelligence*. Khmelnitsky National University.

Su, J., Guo, K., Chen, X., & Chu, S. K. W. (2024). Teaching artificial intelligence in K–12 classrooms: A scoping review. *Interactive Learning Environments, 32*(9), 5207–5226. DOI: 10.1080/10494820.2023.2212706

Su, J., & Yang, W. (2022). Artificial intelligence in early childhood education: A scoping review. *Computers and Education: Artificial Intelligence, 3*, 100049. DOI: 10.1016/j.caeai.2022.100049

Su, J., & Yang, W. (2023). Unlocking the power of ChatGPT: A framework for applying generative AI in education. *ECNU Review of Education, 6*(3), 355–366. DOI: 10.1177/20965311231168423

Su, J., Zhong, Y., & Ng, D. T. K. (2022). A meta-review of literature on educational approaches for teaching AI at the K-12 levels in the Asia-Pacific region. *Computers and Education: Artificial Intelligence, 3*(March), 100065. DOI: 10.1016/j.caeai.2022.100065

Sukackė, V. (2019). Towards Extending the Original Technology Acceptance Model (Tam) for a Better Understanding of Educational Technology Adoption. *Society Integration Education. Proceedings of the International Scientific Conference, 5*, 525–549. DOI: 10.17770/sie2019vol5.3798

Sullivan, M., Kelly, A., & McLaughlan, P. (2023). ChatGPT in higher education: Considerations for academic integrity and student learning. *Journal of Applied Learning & Teaching, 6*(1), 31–40.

Sun, J. C., & Pratt, T. L. (2024). Navigating AI Integration in Career and Technical Education: Diffusion Challenges, Opportunities, and Decisions. *Education Sciences, 14*(12), 1285. DOI: 10.3390/educsci14121285

Sun, L., & Zhou, L. (2024). Does generative artificial intelligence improve the academic achievement of college students? A meta-analysis. *Journal of Educational Computing Research, 62*(7), 1896–1933. DOI: 10.1177/07356331241277937

Susilo, T. (2024). The Role of Artificial Intelligence in Personalizing Learning for Each Student. *Journal International of Lingua and Technology, 3*(2), 229–242. https://doi.org/https://doi.org/10.55849/jiltech.v3i1.632. DOI: 10.55849/jiltech.v3i2.632

Sweller, J. (2011). Cognitive load theory. [). Academic Press.]. *Psychology of Learning and Motivation, 55*, 37–76. DOI: 10.1016/B978-0-12-387691-1.00002-8

Tam, W., Huynh, T., Tang, A., Luong, S., Khatri, Y., & Zhou, W. (2023). Nursing education in the age of artificial intelligence powered Chatbots (AI-Chatbots): Are we ready yet? *Nurse Education Today, 129*(July), 105917. DOI: 10.1016/j.nedt.2023.105917

Tan, D. Y., & Cheah, C. W. (2021). Developing a gamified AI-enabled online learning application to improve students' perception of university physics. *Computers and Education: Artificial Intelligence*, *2*, 100032. DOI: 10.1016/j.caeai.2021.100032

Tang, K. H. D. (2024). Implications of Artificial Intelligence for Teaching and Learning. *Acta Pedagogia Asiana*, *3*(2), 65–79. DOI: 10.53623/apga.v3i2.404

Tang, L., & Su, Y. S. (2024). Ethical Implications and Principles of Using Artificial Intelligence Models in the Classroom: A Systematic Literature Review. *International Journal of Interactive Multimedia and Artificial Intelligence*, *8*(5), 25–36. DOI: 10.9781/ijimai.2024.02.010

Tang, Z., & Zhang, P. (2023). Comparative Analysis of AI Applications in Libraries: A Systematic Literature Review. *Proceedings of the Association for Information Science and Technology*, *60*(1), 1146–1148. DOI: 10.1002/pra2.973

Tan, Q., & Tang, X. (2025). Unveiling AI literacy in K-12 education: A systematic literature review of empirical research. *Interactive Learning Environments*, *33*(9), 1–17. DOI: 10.1080/10494820.2025.2482586

Tao, Y. (2019). Kindergarten teachers' attitudes toward and confidence for Integrated STEM Education. *Journal for STEM Education Research*, *2*(2), 154–171. DOI: 10.1007/s41979-019-00017-8

Tapalova, O., & Zhiyenbayeva, N. (2022). Artificial Intelligence in Education: AIEd for Personalised Learning Pathways. *Electronic Journal of e-Learning*, *20*(5), 639–653. DOI: 10.34190/ejel.20.5.2597

Tarisayi, K. S. (2024). A Theoretical Framework for Interrogating the Integration of Artificial Intelligence in Education. *Research on Education and Media*, *16*(1), 38–44. DOI: 10.2478/rem-2024-0006

Tashtoush, M. A., Qasimi, A. B., Shirawia, N. H., & Hussein, L. A. (2025). The efficacy of utilizing artificial intelligence techniques in developing critical thinking in mathematics among secondary school students and their attitudes toward it. *Iraqi Journal for Computer Science and Mathematics*, *6*(1), 3. DOI: 10.52866/2788-7421.1231

Tashtoush, M. A., Wardat, Y., Al Ali, R., & Saleh, S. (2024). Artificial Intelligence in Education: Mathematics Teachers' Perspectives, Practices and Challenges. *Iraqi Journal for Computer Science and Mathematics*, *5*(1), 60–77. DOI: 10.52866/ijcsm.2024.05.01.004

Teo, T., Unwin, S., Scherer, R., & Gardiner, V. (2021). Initial teacher training for twenty-first century skills in the Fourth Industrial Revolution (IR 4.0): A scoping review. *Computers & Education, 170*, 104223. DOI: 10.1016/j.compedu.2021.104223

Tlili, A., Shehata, B., Adarkwah, M. A., Bozkurt, A., Hickey, D. T., Huang, R., & Agyemang, B. (2023). What if the devil is my guardian angel: ChatGPT as a case study of using chatbots in education. *Smart Learn. Environ., 10*(1), 15. DOI: 10.1186/s40561-023-00237-x

Topali, P., Haelermans, C., Molenaar, I., & Segers, E. (2025). Pedagogical considerations in the automation era: A systematic literature review of AIEd in K-12 authentic settings. *British Educational Research Journal, 51*(May), 1–33. DOI: 10.1002/berj.4200

Topali, P., Ortega-Arranz, A., Rodríguez-Triana, M. J., Er, E., Khalil, M., & Akçapınar, G. (2025). Designing human-centered learning analytics and artificial intelligence in education solutions: A systematic literature review. *Behaviour & Information Technology, 44*(5), 1071–1098. DOI: 10.1080/0144929X.2024.2345295

Torres-Peña, R. C., Peña-González, D., Chacuto-López, E., Ariza, E. A., & Vergara, D. (2024). Updating calculus teaching with AI: A classroom experience. *Education Sciences, 14*(9), 1019. DOI: 10.3390/educsci14091019

Towfek, S. K., Khodadadi, N., Abualigah, L., & Rizk, F. H. (2024). AI in higher education: Insights from student surveys and predictive analytics using PSO-guided WOA and linear regression. *Journal of Artificial Intelligence in Engineering Practice, 1*(1), 1–17. DOI: 10.21608/jaiep.2024.354003

Tran, T. T., Pham, T. T., & Le, T. T. (2024). Transformative Interactions: ChatGPT's Role in Facilitating Professional Development Among Vietnamese English as a Foreign Language Teachers. *Higher Learning Research Communications, 14*(2). Advance online publication. DOI: 10.18870/hlrc.v14i2.1558

Traoré, D. (2024). Integration of Artificial Intelligence in Education: Challenges and Prospects. *Revista Internacional de Pedagogía e Innovación Educativa, 4*(2), 329–342. DOI: 10.51660/ripie42221

Tudino, G., & Qin, Y. (2024). A corpus-driven comparative analysis of AI in academic discourse: Investigating ChatGPT-generated academic texts in social sciences. *Lingua, 312*, 103838. DOI: 10.1016/j.lingua.2024.103838

Turing, D. (2018). *The Story of Computing*. Arcturus Publishing.

Tyton Partners. (2023, October). GenAI in Higher Education: Fall 2023 Update of Time for Class Study.

U.S Department of Education Office of Educational Technology. (2023). *Artificial intelligence and the future of teaching and learning: Insights and recommendations.* (Issue 1). https://www2.ed.gov/documents/ai-report/ai-report.pdf

Uğraş, H., Uğraş, M., Papadakis, S., & Kalogiannakis, M. (2024b). Innovative Early Childhood STEM Education with ChatGPT: Teacher Perspectives. *Technology, Knowledge and Learning*, 1-23.

Uğraş, H., Uğraş, M., Papadakis, S., & Kalogiannakis, M. (2024b). Innovative Early Childhood STEM Education with ChatGPT: Teacher Perspectives. *Technology, Knowledge and Learning*, 1-23. https://doi.org/DOI: 10.1007/s10758-024-09758-3

Uğraş, H., Uğraş, M., Papadakis, S., & Kalogiannakis, M. (2024a). ChatGPT-supported education in primary schools: The potential of ChatGPT for sustainable practices. *Sustainability (Basel)*, *16*(22), 9855. DOI: 10.3390/su16229855

Uğraş, H., Uğraş, M., Papadakis, S., & Kalogiannakis, M. (2024b). Innovative Early Childhood STEM Education with ChatGPT: Teacher Perspectives. *Technology. Knowledge and Learning*, *30*(2), 809–831. DOI: 10.1007/s10758-024-09804-8

Uğraş, H., Uğraş, M., Papadakis, S., & Kalogiannakis, M. (2025). Innovative early childhood STEM education with ChatGPT: Teacher perspectives. Technology. *Knowledge and Learning*, *30*(2), 809–831.

Unesco. (2022). *Recommendation on the ethics of artificial intelligence*. United Nations Educational, Scientific and Cultural Organization.

UNESCO. (2023). *Currículos de IA para la enseñanza preescolar, primaria y secundaria: un mapeo de los currículos de IA aprobados por los gobiernos*. París, France. https://unesdoc.unesco.org/ark:/48223/pf0000380602_spa

UNESCO. (2023). *Generative AI and the futures of education*. UNESCO., DOI: 10.54675/HOXG8740

UNESCO. (2023). *Guidance for generative AI in education and research*. UNESCO Publishing.

UNESCO. (2023). *Less than 10% of Schools and Universities have formal Guidance on AI*. Unesco Survey. https://www.unesco.org/en/articles/unesco-survey-less-10-schools-and-universities-have-formal-guidance-ai

UNESCO. (2024). Greece's Digital Education Transformation Initiative. Paris: UNESCO. Retrieved from https://www.unesco.org/en/dtc-financing-toolkit/greeces-digital-education-transformation-initiative

Urban, M., Brom, C., Lukavský, J., Děchtěrenko, F., Hein, V., Svacha, F., Kmoníčková, P., & Urban, K. (2025). "ChatGPT can make mistakes. Check important info." Epistemic beliefs and metacognitive accuracy in students' integration of ChatGPT content into academic writing. *British Journal of Educational Technology*, *56*(5), 1897–1918. DOI: 10.1111/bjet.13591

Urdaneta-Ponte, M. C., Mendez-Zorrilla, A., & Oleagordia-Ruiz, I. (2021). Recommendation systems for education: Systematic review. *Electronics (Basel)*, *10*(14), 1611. DOI: 10.3390/electronics10141611

Valeri, F., Nilsson, P., & Cederqvist, A. M. (2025). Exploring students' experience of ChatGPT in STEM education. *Computers and Education: Artificial Intelligence*, *8*, 100360. DOI: 10.1016/j.caeai.2024.100360

Vallor, S., & Vierkant, T. (2024). Find the gap: AI, responsible agency and vulnerability. *Minds and Machines*, *34*(3), 20. DOI: 10.1007/s11023-024-09674-0 PMID: 38855350

Van Den Berg, G. (2024). Generative AI and Educators: Partnering in Using Open Digital Content for Transforming Education. *Open Praxis*, *16*(2), 130–141. DOI: 10.55982/openpraxis.16.2.640

van Dis, E. A. M., Bollen, J., Zuidema, W., van Rooij, R., & Bockting, C. L. (2023). ChatGPT: Five priorities for research. *Nature*, *614*(7947), 224–226. DOI: 10.1038/d41586-023-00288-7

Van, H. N., Thanh, D. T., & Dinh, V. P. (2025). Bringing AI into Teaching : Understanding Vietnamese Teachers ' Perspectives and Pedagogical Challenges. [Introduction]. *International Journal of Educational Methodology*, *11*(3), 335–347. https://doi.org/https://doi.org/10.12973/ijem.11.3.335. DOI: 10.12973/ijem.11.3.335

Vanhaelen, Q., Lin, Y. C., & Zhavoronkov, A. (2020). The advent of generative chemistry. *ACS Medicinal Chemistry Letters*, *11*(8), 1496–1505. DOI: 10.1021/acsmedchemlett.0c00088 PMID: 32832015

VanLehn, K. (2006). The behavior of tutoring systems. *International Journal of Artificial Intelligence in Education*, *16*(3), 227–265. DOI: 10.3233/IRG-2006-16(3)02

VanLehn, K. (2011). The relative effectiveness of human tutoring, intelligent tutoring systems, and other tutoring systems. *Educational Psychologist*, *46*(4), 197–221. DOI: 10.1080/00461520.2011.611369

Varghese, C., Vernon-Feagans, L., & Bratsch-Hines, M. (2019). Rural classroom environments as contexts for teacher-child relationships. *The Journal of Educational Research*, *112*(3), 411–420. DOI: 10.1080/00220671.2018.1545214

Vásquez, E. D. C., Loza, R. F. N., Cherrez, A. M. F., & Montes, R. E. T. (2024). Use of Artificial Intelligence in the Personalisation of Learning. *Conocimiento Global, 9*(1), 75–83. https://conocimientoglobal.org/revista/index.php/cglobal/article/view/339/216

Vaswani, A. (2017). Attention is all you need. *Advances in Neural Information Processing Systems.*

Vazhayil, A., Shetty, R., Bhavani, R. R., & Akshay, N. (2019). Focusing on Teacher Education to Introduce AI in Schools: Perspectives and Illustrative Findings. *Proceedings - IEEE 10th International Conference on Technology for Education, T4E 2019, January 2023*, 71–77. DOI: 10.1109/T4E.2019.00021

Veale, M., & Brass, I. (2019). Administration by algorithm? Public management meets public sector machine learning. *Public management meets public sector machine learning.*

Veletsianos, G., & Russell, G. S. (2014). Pedagogical agents. In *Handbook of research on educational communications and technology* (pp. 759–769). DOI: 10.1007/978-1-4614-3185-5_61

Vella, O. (2025). *The Future of Maths Learning: Personalised and AI-Driven.* eBookIt.com.

Venkatasubramanian, V., Chitra, M., Sudha, R., Singh, V. P., Jefferson, K., & Boopathi, S. (2024). Examining the Impacts of Course Outcome Analysis in Indian Higher Education: Enhancing Educational Quality. In Challenges of Globalization and Inclusivity in Academic Research (pp. 124–145). IGI Global Scientific Publishing.

Venkatesh, V. (2022). Adoption and use of AI tools: A research agenda grounded in UTAUT. *Annals of Operations Research, 308*(1), 641–652. DOI: 10.1007/s10479-020-03918-9

Viberg, O., Cukurova, M., Feldman-Maggor, Y., Alexandron, G., Shirai, S., Kanemune, S., Wasson, B., Tømte, C., Spikol, D., Milrad, M., Coelho, R., & Kizilcec, R. F. (2024). What Explains Teachers' Trust in AI in Education Across Six Countries? *International Journal of Artificial Intelligence in Education.* Advance online publication. DOI: 10.1007/s40593-024-00433-x

Vidal, Q., Vincent-Lancrin, S., & Yun, H. (2023). Emerging governance of generative AI in education. In *OECD Digital Education Outlook.* OECD.

Vistorte, A. O. R., Deroncele-Acosta, A., Ayala, J. L. M., Barrasa, A., López-Granero, C., & Martí-González, M. (2024). Integrating artificial intelligence to assess emotions in learning environments: A systematic literature review. *Frontiers in Psychology, 15*, 1387089. DOI: 10.3389/fpsyg.2024.1387089 PMID: 38966729

Vivar, J. M. F., & Peñalvo, F. J. G. (2023). Reflexiones sobre la ética, potencialidades y retos de la Inteligencia Artificial en el marco de la Educación de Calidad (ODS4). *Comunicar: Revista cientifica de comunicacion y educacion*, (74), 37-47.

Voulgari, I., Lavidas, K., Aravantinos, S., Sypsa, S., & Sfyroera, M. (2024). Exploring the Role, Implementation, and Educational Implications of AI in Early Childhood Education. In Olney, A. M., Chounta, I.-A., Liu, Z., Santos, O. C., & Bittencourt, I. I. (Eds.), *Artificial Intelligence in Education. Posters and Late Breaking Results, Workshops and Tutorials, Industry and Innovation Tracks, Practitioners, Doctoral Consortium and Blue Sky* (pp. 29–37). Springer Nature Switzerland., DOI: 10.1007/978-3-031-64312-5_4

Voulodimos, A., Doulamis, N., Doulamis, A., & Protopapadakis, E. (2018). Deep learning for computer vision: A brief review. *Computational Intelligence and Neuroscience, 2018*(1), 7068349. DOI: 10.1155/2018/7068349

Vygotsky, L. S. (1978). *Mind in society: The development of higher psychological processes* (Cole, M., John-Steiner, V., Scribner, S., & Souberman, E., Eds.). Harvard University Press.

Wager, E., & Kleinert, S. (2012). Cooperation between research institutions and journals on research integrity cases: Guidance from the committee on publication ethics. *Saudi Journal of Anaesthesia, 6*(2), 155–160. DOI: 10.4103/1658-354X.97030

Wallace, R. (2022). How AI founders on adversarial landscapes of fog and friction. *The Journal of Defense Modeling and Simulation, 19*(3), 519–538. DOI: 10.1177/1548512920962227

Wang, D., Churchill, E., Maes, P., Fan, X., Shneiderman, B., Shi, Y., & Wang, Q. (2020). From Human-Human collaboration to Human-AI collaboration. *Extended Abstracts of the 2020 CHI Conference on Human Factors in Computing Systems*, 1–6. DOI: 10.1145/3334480.3381069

Wang, B., Rau, P. L. P., & Yuan, T. (2023). Measuring user competence in using artificial intelligence: Validity and reliability of artificial intelligence literacy scale. *Behaviour & Information Technology, 42*(9), 1324–1337. DOI: 10.1080/0144929X.2022.2072768

Wang, G., Chen, X., Zhang, D., Kang, Y., Wang, F., & Su, M. (2022). Development and application of an intelligent assessment system for mathematics learning strategy among high school students—Take Jianzha county as an example. *Sustainability (Basel), 14*(19), 12265. DOI: 10.3390/su141912265

Wang, K., Chai, C.-S., Liang, J.-C., & Sang, G. (2024). Exploring teachers' behavioural intentions to design artificial intelligence-assisted learning in Chinese K–12 education. *Technology, Pedagogy and Education, 33*(5), 629–645. DOI: 10.1080/1475939X.2024.2369241

Wang, N., Wang, X., & Su, Y.-S. (2024). Critical analysis of the technological affordances, challenges and future directions of generative AI in education: A systematic review. *Asia Pacific Journal of Education, 44*(1), 139–155. DOI: 10.1080/02188791.2024.2305156

Wang, P., Yin, K., Zhang, M., Zheng, Y., Zhang, T., Kang, Y., & Feng, X. (2025). The effect of incorporating large language models into the teaching on critical thinking disposition: An "AI+Constructivism Learning Theory" attempt. *Education and Information Technologies, 30*(9), 11625–11647. DOI: 10.1007/s10639-024-13244-3

Wang, S., Wang, F., Zhu, Z., Wang, J., Tran, T., & Du, Z. (2024). Artificial intelligence in education: A systematic literature review. *Expert Systems with Applications, 252*, 124167. DOI: 10.1016/j.eswa.2024.124167

Wang, T., & Cheng, E. C. K. (2021). An investigation of barriers to Hong Kong K-12 schools incorporating Artificial Intelligence in education. *Computers and Education: Artificial Intelligence*, 2, 100031. DOI: 10.1016/j.caeai.2021.100031

Wang, Y., & Chuang, Y. (2024). Artificial Intelligence Self-Efficacy: Scale Development and Validation. *Education and Information Technologies, 29*(4), 4785–4808. DOI: 10.1007/s10639-023-12015-w

Wang, Y., Herron, L., & Tiwary, P. (2022). From data to noise to data for mixing physics across temperatures with generative artificial intelligence. *Proceedings of the National Academy of Sciences of the United States of America, 119*(32), e2203656119. DOI: 10.1073/pnas.2203656119

Wang, Y., & Xue, L. (2024). Using AI-driven chatbots to foster Chinese EFL students' academic engagement: An intervention study. *Computers in Human Behavior, 159*, 108353. DOI: 10.1016/j.chb.2024.108353

Wardat, Y., Tashtoush, M. A., AlAli, R., & Jarrah, A. M. (2023). ChatGPT: A revolutionary tool for teaching and learning mathematics. *Eurasia Journal of Mathematics, Science and Technology Education*, *19*(7), em2286. Advance online publication. DOI: 10.29333/ejmste/13272

Ward, W., Cole, R., Bolaños, D., Buchenroth-Martin, C., Svirsky, E., Vuuren, S. V., Weston, T., Zheng, J., & Becker, L. (2011). My science tutor. *ACM Transactions on Speech and Language Processing*, *7*(4), 1–29. DOI: 10.1145/1998384.1998392

Waring, R. (2024). Microcultures of collaboration: entangled artistic pedagogies for students and educator (Doctoral dissertation, Bournemouth University).

Weber, F., Wambsganss, T., Rüttimann, D., & Söllner, M. (2021). Pedagogical agents for interactive learning: A taxonomy of conversational agents in education. *Forty-Second International Conference on Information Systems (ICIS)*.

Weigand, H. G., Trgalova, J., & Tabach, M. (2024). Mathematics teaching, learning, and assessment in the digital age. *ZDM Mathematics Education*, *56*(4), 525–541. DOI: 10.1007/s11858-024-01612-9

Wenger, E. (1998). Communities of practice: Learning as a social system. *The Systems Thinker*, *9*(5), 2–3.

Weng, X., Ye, H., Dai, Y., & Ng, O. (2024). Integrating Artificial Intelligence and Computational Thinking in Educational Contexts: A Systematic Review of Instructional Design and Student Learning Outcomes. *Journal of Educational Computing Research*, *62*(6), 1420–1450. DOI: 10.1177/07356331241248686

Whalen, J., Grube, W., Xu, C., & Trust, T. (2025). K-12 Educators' Reactions and Responses to ChatGPT and GenAI During the 2022–2023 School Year. *TechTrends*, *69*(1), 125–137. DOI: 10.1007/s11528-024-01028-y

White, S. V., Childs, J., Koshy, S., & Scott, A. (2024). Policy Implementation in the Era of Responsible Artificial Intelligence (AI) use in K-12 Education. *RESPECT 2024 - Proceedings of the Conference for Research on Equitable and Sustained Participation in Engineering, Computing, and Technology*, 81–85. DOI: 10.1145/3653666.3656097

Wiese, L. J., Patil, I., Schiff, D. S., & Magana, A. J. (2025). AI ethics education: A systematic literature review. *Computers and Education: Artificial Intelligence*, *8*, 100405. DOI: 10.1016/j.caeai.2025.100405

Williamson, B. (2024). The Social life of AI in Education. *International Journal of Artificial Intelligence in Education*, *34*(1), 97–104. DOI: 10.1007/s40593-023-00342-5

Williamson, B., Bayne, S., & Shay, S. (2020). The datafication of teaching in higher education: Critical issues and perspectives. *Teaching in Higher Education, 25*(4), 351–365. DOI: 10.1080/13562517.2020.1748811

Williamson, B., & Eynon, R. (2020). Historical threads, missing links, and future directions in AI in education. *Learning, Media and Technology, 45*(3), 223–235. DOI: 10.1080/17439884.2020.1798995

Williamson, B., Macgilchrist, F., & Potter, J. (2023). Re-examining AI, automation and datafication in education. *Learning, Media and Technology, 48*(1), 1–5. DOI: 10.1080/17439884.2023.2167830

Williams, R., Park, H. W., Oh, L., & Breazeal, C. (2019). PopBots: Designing an Artificial Intelligence Curriculum for Early Childhood Education. *Proceedings of the AAAI Conference on Artificial Intelligence, 33*(1), 9729–9736. DOI: 10.1609/aaai.v33i01.33019729

Williyan, A., Fitriati, S. W., Pratama, H., & Sakhiyya, Z. (2024). AI AS CO-CREATOR: EXPLORING INDONESIAN EFL TEACHERS' COLLABORATION WITH AI IN CONTENT DEVELOPMENT. *Teaching English With Technology, 2024*(2). Advance online publication. DOI: 10.56297/vaca6841/LRDX3699/RZOH5366

Wing, J. M. (2006). Computational Thinking. *Communications of the ACM, 49*(3), 33–35. DOI: 10.1145/1118178.1118215

Winkler, R., Hobert, S., Salovaara, A., Söllner, M., & Leimeister, J. M. (2020). Sara, the lecturer: Improving learning in online education with a Scaffolding-Based conversational agent. *Proceedings of the 2020 CHI Conference on Human Factors in Computing Systems*, 1–14. DOI: 10.1145/3313831.3376781

Winkler, R., & Soellner, M. (2018). Unleashing the potential of chatbots in education: A State-Of-The-Art analysis. *Proceedings - Academy of Management, 2018*(1), 15903. DOI: 10.5465/AMBPP.2018.15903abstract

Wollny, S., Schneider, J., Di Mitri, D., Weidlich, J., Rittberger, M., & Drachsler, H. (2021). Are we there yet? - a systematic literature review on chatbots in education. *Frontiers in Artificial Intelligence, 4*, 654924. Advance online publication. DOI: 10.3389/frai.2021.654924

Wong, J. M. S., Liu, P. H. C., & Yip, C. W. H. (2025). Navigating the Digital Shift: Early Childhood Educators' Attitudes Towards Generative Artificial Intelligence and Emerging Technologies. In Cheng, E. C. K. (Ed.), *Innovating Education with AI. AETS 2024. Lecture Notes in Educational Technology*. Springer. DOI: 10.1007/978-981-96-4952-5_6

Woo, H., LeTendre, G. K., Pham-Shouse, T., & Xiong, Y. (2021). The use of social robots in classrooms: A review of field-based studies. *Educational Research Review, 33*, 100388. DOI: 10.1016/j.edurev.2021.100388

Woolf, B. P. (2008). *Building Intelligent Interactive Tutors: Student-centered strategies for revolutionizing e-learning*. Morgan Kaufmann Publishers Inc.

Woolf, B. P. (2015). AI and education: Celebrating 30 years of marriage. *International Conference on Artificial Intelligence In Education.* Cham: Springer, 4, 38-47.

Woolf, B. P., Lane, H. C., Chaudhri, V. K., & Kolodner, J. L. (2013). AI grand challenges for education. *AI Magazine, 34*(4), 66–84. DOI: 10.1609/aimag.v34i4.2490

Woolf, B., Burleson, W., Arroyo, I., Dragon, T., Cooper, D., & Picard, R. (2009). Affect-aware tutors: Recognising and responding to student affect. *International Journal of Learning Technology, 4*(3-4), 129–164. DOI: 10.1504/IJLT.2009.028804

World Bank. (2023). *Generative artificial intelligence. (Emerging Technologies Curation Series No. 5)*. World Bank.

Worrell, F. C., Subotnik, R. F., Olszewski-Kubilius, P., & Dixson, D. D. (2019). Gifted students. *Annual Review of Psychology, 70*(1), 551–576. DOI: 10.1146/annurev-psych-010418-102846 PMID: 30089229

Wu, R., & Yu, Z. (2024). Do <scp>AI</scp> chatbots improve students learning outcomes? Evidence from a meta-analysis. *British Journal of Educational Technology, 55*(1), 10–33. DOI: 10.1111/bjet.13334

Xavier, B. (2025). Biases within AI: Challenging the illusion of neutrality. *AI & Society, 40*(3), 1545–1546. DOI: 10.1007/s00146-024-01985-1

Xiao, P., Chen, Y., & Bao, W. (2023). Waiting, banning, and embracing: An empirical analysis of adapting policies for generative AI in higher education. *arXiv preprint,* arXiv:2305.18617.

Xin, J. J. (2024). Investigating EFL teachers' use of generative AI to develop reading materials: A practice and perception study. *Language Teaching Research, 13621688241303321*, 13621688241303321. Advance online publication. DOI: 10.1177/13621688241303321

Xu, Y., Prado, Y., & Severson, R. L. Lovatom & S., Cassell, J. (2025). Growing Up with Artificial Intelligence: Implications for Child Development. Christakis, D.A., Hale, L. (eds) *Handbook of Children and Screens*. Springer, Cham. Doi: DOI: 10.1007/978-3-031-69362-5_83

Xu, W., Dainoff, M. J., Ge, L., & Gao, Z. (2021). *Transitioning to human interaction with AI systems: New challenges and opportunities for HCI professionals to enable human-centered AI* (Preprint on ArXiv No. 2105.05424). DOI: 10.48550/ARXIV.2105.05424

Xu, Z. (2024). AI in education: Enhancing learning experiences and student outcomes. *Applied and Computational Engineering*, *51*(1), 104–111. DOI: 10.54254/2755-2721/51/20241187

Xu, Z., Wijekumar, K., Ramirez, G., Hu, X., & Irey, R. (2019). The effectiveness of intelligent tutoring systems on k-12 students' reading comprehension: A meta-analysis. *British Journal of Educational Technology*, *50*(6), 3119–3137. DOI: 10.1111/bjet.12758

Y, M. N., H, L. P., & N, S. (2024). Revolutionizing Education : Harnessing AI for Personalized Learning Pathways and Student Success. *International Journal for Multidisciplinary Research (IJFMR)*, *6*(5), 1–11. https://doi.org/https://doi.org/10.36948/ijfmr.2024.v06i05.28371

Yadav, S. (2025). Leveraging AI to enhance teaching and learning in education: The role of artificial intelligence in modernizing classroom practices. In Singh, A. K., & Sharma, R. (Eds.), *Optimizing Research Techniques and Learning Strategies with Digital Technologies* (pp. 211–238). IGI Global Scientific Publishing., DOI: 10.4018/979-8-3693-7863-2.ch008

Yampolskiy, R. V. (2024). *AI: Unexplainable, unpredictable, uncontrollable*. CRC Press. DOI: 10.1201/9781003440260

Yang, Z. Q., Cao, J., Li, X., Wang, K., Zheng, X., Poon, K. C. F., & Lai, D. (2024). DMP_AI: An AI-Aided K-12 System for Teaching and Learning in Diverse Schools. *Lecture Notes in Computer Science (Including Subseries Lecture Notes in Artificial Intelligence and Lecture Notes in Bioinformatics)*, *14797 LNCS*, 117–130. DOI: 10.1007/978-981-97-4442-8_9

Yang, L. (2024). From Tradition to Innovation: A Comparative Analysis of Education Systems in China and Finland. *Journal of International Education and Development.*, *8*(07), 112–118. DOI: 10.47297/wspiedWSP2516-250018.20240807

Yang, X. (2023). A historical review of collaborative learning and cooperative learning. *TechTrends*, *67*(4), 718–728. DOI: 10.1007/s11528-022-00823-9 PMID: 36711122

Yang, Y., Sun, W., Sun, D., & Salas-Pilco, S. Z. (2024). Navigating the AI-Enhanced STEM education landscape: A decade of insights, trends, and opportunities. *Research in Science & Technological Education*, •••, 1–25. DOI: 10.1080/02635143.2024.2370764

Yannier, N., Hudson, S. E., & Koedinger, K. R. (2020). Active learning is about more Than Hands-On: A mixed-reality AI system to support STEM education. *International Journal of Artificial Intelligence in Education*, *30*(1), 74–96. DOI: 10.1007/s40593-020-00194-3

Yau, K. W., Chai, C. S., Chiu, T. K., Meng, H., King, I., & Yam, Y. (2023). A phenomenographic approach on teacher conceptions of teaching Artificial Intelligence (AI) in K-12 schools. *Education and Information Technologies*, *28*(1), 1041–1064. DOI: 10.1007/s10639-022-11161-x

Yenduri, G., Ramalingam, M., Selvi, G. C., Supriya, Y., Srivastava, G., Maddikunta, P. K. R., Raj, G. D., Jhaveri, R. H., Prabadevi, B., Wang, W., Vasilakos, A. V., & Gadekallu, T. R. (2024). GPT (Generative Pre-trained Transformer)–A comprehensive review on enabling technologies, potential applications, emerging challenges, and future directions. *IEEE Access : Practical Innovations, Open Solutions*, *12*, 54608–54649. DOI: 10.1109/ACCESS.2024.3389497

Yeo, M. (2023). Academic integrity in the age of Artificial Intelligence (AI) authoring apps. *TESOL Journal*, *14*(3), e716. Advance online publication. DOI: 10.1002/tesj.716

Yeo, S., Moon, J., & Kim, D. J. (2024). Transforming mathematics education with AI: Innovations, implementations, and insights. *The Mathematics Educator*, *63*(2), 387–392. DOI: 10.63311/mathedu.2024.63.2.387

Yildirim-Erbasli, S., Bulut, O., Epp, C. D., & Cui, Y. (2025). Advancing higher education students' assessment experiences with conversational agents. *Educational Technology Research and Development*, *73*(3), 1811–1834. Advance online publication. DOI: 10.1007/s11423-025-10472-3

Yıldırım, Ö., & Demir, S. B. (2022). Inside the black box: Do teachers practice assessment as learning? *International Journal of Assessment Tools in Education*, *9*(Special Issue), 46–71. DOI: 10.21449/ijate.1132923

Yilmaz, R., & Yilmaz, F. G. K. (2023). The effect of generative artificial intelligence (AI)-based tool use on students' computational thinking skills, programming self-efficacy and motivation. *Computers and Education: Artificial Intelligence,* vol.4, 100147, ISSN 2666-920X. Doi:DOI: 10.1016/j.caeai.2023.100147

Yılmaz, Z., Galanti, T. M., Naresh, N., & Kanbir, S. (2025). Exploring the interactions among instructors, prospective teachers and AI in facilitating mathematics learning. *School Science and Mathematics.* Advance online publication. DOI: 10.1111/ssm.18341

Yim, I. H. Y., & Su, J. (2025). Artificial intelligence literacy education in primary schools: A review. *International Journal of Technology and Design Education, 35*(5), 2175–2204. Advance online publication. DOI: 10.1007/s10798-025-09979-w

Yongqi, D., Xingmin, L., Ruohan, L., Wei, S., Bart, V. A., & Farah, H. (2023). Intelligent anomaly detection for lane rendering using transformer with self-supervised pre-training and customized fine-tuning. *arXiv.org, abs/2312.04398.* https://doi.org//arxiv.2312.04398DOI: 10.48550

You, H. S., Kim, K., Black, K., & Min, K. W. (2018). Assessing science motivation for college students: Validation of the SMQ-II using the Rasch–Andrich rating scale model. *Eurasia Journal of Mathematics, Science and Technology Education, 14*(4), 1161–1173. DOI: 10.29333/ejmste/81821

Younas, A., Subramanian, K. P., Al-Haziazi, M., Hussainy, S. S., & Al Kindi, A. N. S. (2023). Influence of Psychological Well-Being and School Factors on Delinquency, During the Covid-19 Period Among Secondary School Students in Selected Schools in Nakuru County : Kenya. [IJRISS]. *Iternational Journal of Research and Innovation in Social Science, 7*(8), 1175–1189. DOI: 10.47772/IJRISS

Young, J. R. (2023). The role of technology in enhancing urban mathematics education. *Journal of Urban Mathematics Education, 16*(2), 1–13. DOI: 10.21423/jume-v16i2a589 PMID: 37525688

Youvan, D. C. (2024). Amplification Through Progression: From Analog Signals to Artificial Intelligence.

Yue, M., Dai, Y., Siu-Yung, M., & Chai, C.-S. (2021). An Analysis of K-12 Artificial Intelligence Curricula in Eight Countries. In: Rodrigo, M. M. T. et al. (Eds.). *Proceedings of the 29th International Conference on Computers in Education.* Asia-Pacific Society for Computers in Education. https://library.apsce.net/index.php/ICCE/article/view/4335

Yue, M., Jong, M. S. Y., & Ng, D. T. K. (2024). Understanding K–12 teachers' technological pedagogical content knowledge readiness and attitudes toward artificial intelligence education. In *Education and Information Technologies* (Vol. 29, Issue 15). Springer US. DOI: 10.1007/s10639-024-12621-2

Yu, H., & Guo, Y. (2023). Generative artificial intelligence empowers educational reform: Current status, issues, and prospects. *Frontiers in Education*, *8*, 1183162. Advance online publication. DOI: 10.3389/feduc.2023.1183162

Yunianto, W., Lavicza, Z., Kastner-Hauler, O., & Houghton, T. (2024). Investigating the use of ChatGPT to solve a GeoGebra based mathematics+computational thinking task in a geometry topic. *Journal on Mathematics Education*, *15*(3), 1027–1052. DOI: 10.22342/jme.v15i3.pp1027-1052

Yusuf, A., Bello, S., Pervin, N., & Tukur, A. K. (2024). Implementing a proposed framework for enhancing critical thinking skills in synthesizing AI-generated texts. *Thinking Skills and Creativity*, *53*, 101619. DOI: 10.1016/j.tsc.2024.101619

Yusuf, A., Pervin, N., Román-González, M., & Noor, N. M. (2024). Generative AI in education and research: A systematic mapping review. *Review of Education*, *12*(2), e3489. DOI: 10.1002/rev3.3489

Yusuf, H., Money, A., & Daylamani-Zad, D. (2025). Pedagogical AI conversational agents in higher education: A conceptual framework and survey of the state of the art. *Educational Technology Research and Development*, *73*(2), 815–874. DOI: 10.1007/s11423-025-10447-4

Yuwono, E. I., Tjondronegoro, D., Riverola, C., & Loy, J. (2024). Co-creation in action: Bridging the knowledge gap in artificial intelligence among innovation champions. *Computers and Education: Artificial Intelligence*, *7*(May), 100272. DOI: 10.1016/j.caeai.2024.100272

Zaidi, S. A. Z., Ahmad, E., & Shukla, N. (2024). Ethical Considerations in the Use of Artificial Intelligence (AI) for Education and Research: A Review. *International Journal of Innovations in Science. Engineering And Management*, *3*(2), 156–167. DOI: 10.69968/ijisem.2024v3si2156-167

Zapata-Ros, M. (2023). Inteligencia Artificial Generativa Y Aprendizaje Inteligente. *EdArXiv*, 27 June 2023. DOI: 10.35542/osf.io/86ykm

Zawacki-Richter, O., & Latchem, C. (2018). Exploring four decades of research in computers & education. *Computers & Education*, *122*, 136–152. DOI: 10.1016/j.compedu.2018.04.001

Zawacki-Richter, O., Marín, V. I., Bond, M., & Gouverneur, F. (2019). Systematic review of research on artificial intelligence applications in higher education – where are the educators? *International Journal of Educational Technology in Higher Education, 16*(1), 1–27. DOI: 10.1186/s41239-019-0171-0

Zeng, Z., Dai, H., Zhang, D. J., Zhang, H., Zhang, R., Xu, Z., & Shen, Z. J. M. (2023). The impact of social nudges on user-generated content for social network platforms. *Management Science, 69*(9), 5189–5208. DOI: 10.1287/mnsc.2022.4622

Zhai, C., Wibowo, S., & Li, L. D. (2024). The effects of over-reliance on AI dialogue systems on students' cognitive abilities: A systematic review. *Smart Learn. Environ., 11*(1), 28. DOI: 10.1186/s40561-024-00316-7

Zhai, X. (2024). Transforming teachers' roles and agencies in the era of generative ai: Perceptions, acceptance, knowledge, and practices. *Journal of Science Education and Technology, 2024*, 1–11. DOI: 10.1007/s10956-024-10174-0

Zhai, X., Chu, X., Chai, C. S., Jong, M. S. Y., Istenic, A., Spector, M., Liu, J.-B., Yuan, J., & Li, Y. (2021). A review of artificial intelligence (AI) in education from 2010 to 2020. *Complexity, 2021*(1), 1–18. DOI: 10.1155/2021/8812542

Zhai, X., Nyaaba, M., & Ma, W. (2024). Can generative AI and ChatGPT outperform humans on cognitive-demanding problem-solving tasks in science? *Science & Education*, •••, 1–22.

Zhang, S., Xu, J., & Alvero, A. (2024, September 20). Generative AI meets open-ended survey responses: Participant use of AI and homogenization.

Zhang, Z., & Wasie, S. (2023). Educational Technology in the Post-Pandemic Era: Current Progress, Potential, and Challenges. *Proceedings of the 15thInternational Conference on Education Technology and Computers*, 40-46. Doi: DOI: 10.1145/3629296.3629303

Zhang, J., & Zhang, Z. (2024). AI in teacher education: Unlocking new dimensions in teaching support, inclusive learning, and digital literacy. *Journal of Computer Assisted Learning, 40*(4), 1871–1885. DOI: 10.1111/jcal.12988

Zhang, P., & Kamel Boulos, M. N. (2023). Generative AI in Medicine and Healthcare: Promises, Opportunities and Challenges. *Future Internet, 15*(9), 286. DOI: 10.3390/fi15090286

Zhang, P., & Tur, G. (2024). A systematic review of ChatGPT use in K-12 education. *European Journal of Education, 59*(2), e12599. DOI: 10.1111/ejed.12599

Zhao, Z., Alzubaidi, L., Zhang, J., Duan, Y., & Gu, Y. (2023). A comparison review of transfer learning and self-supervised learning: Definitions, applications, advantages and limitations. *Expert Systems with Applications*, •••, 122807.

Zhu, W., Huang, L., Zhou, X., Li, X., Shi, G., Ying, J., & Wang, C. (2025). Could AI ethical anxiety, perceived ethical risks and ethical awareness about AI influence university students' use of generative AI products? An ethical perspective. *International Journal of Human-Computer Interaction, 41*(1), 742–764. DOI: 10.1080/10447318.2024.2323277

Zickafoose, A., Ilesanmi, O., Diaz-Manrique, M., Adeyemi, A. E., Walumbe, B., Strong, R., Wingenbach, G., Rodriguez, M. T., & Dooley, K. (2024). Barriers and challenges affecting quality education (Sustainable Development Goal# 4) in sub-Saharan Africa by 2030. *Sustainability (Basel), 16*(7), 2657. DOI: 10.3390/su16072657

Zimmerman, B. J. (2002). Becoming a Self-Regulated Learner: An Overview. *Theory into Practice, 41*(2), 64–70. DOI: 10.1207/s15430421tip4102_2

Zoph, B., Ghiasi, G., Lin, T.-Y., Cui, Y., Liu, H., Cubuk, E. D., & Le, Q. (2020). Rethinking pre-training and self-training. *Advances in Neural Information Processing Systems, 33*, 3833–3845.

Zreik, M. (2024). Redefining mathematics education in the age of artificial intelligence: Challenges and opportunities. *Impacts of Globalization and Innovation in Mathematics Education*, 19-40. DOI: 10.4018/979-8-3693-2873-6.ch002

Zulianti, H., Hastuti, H., Nurchurifiani, E., Hastomo, T., Maximilian, A., & Ajeng, G. D. (2024). Enhancing Novice EFL Teachers' Competency in AI-Powered Tools Through a TPACK-Based Professional Development Program. *World Journal of English Language, 15*(3), 117. DOI: 10.5430/wjel.v15n3p117

About the Contributors

Stamatios Papadakis is an Assistant Professor in Educational Technology at the Department of Preschool Education at the University of Crete, Greece. His scientific and research interests focus on integrating EdTech apps in preschool and primary education, novice programming environments, mobile learning, and the application of generative AI in education. His work aims to enhance early childhood learning experiences through innovative technologies. Dr. Papadakis has been a prolific researcher and editor, contributing to numerous books and journals in educational technology. He was recognised for his significant contributions and was included in the world's most outstanding scientists ranking in 2020, 2021, 2022, and 2023. This prestigious ranking places him among the top 100,000 scientists globally or in the top 2% of his sub-field.

***

Juan Francisco Álvarez-Herrero Regarding his training, he holds a degree in Chemistry, specializing in fundamental sciences and branching out in Organic Chemistry, from the University of Valencia (UV). He holds a Master's degree in Educational Technology: e-learning and knowledge management, as well as a PhD in Educational Technology: e-learning and knowledge management (with distinction) from the Rovira i Virgili University of Tarragona. He also holds a Master's degree in educational center management from the Catholic University of Valencia (UCV) and a University Expert in Internet and its Applications from the National University of Distance Education (UNED). In the teaching field, he was a secondary school teacher in the areas of Physics and Chemistry, and Biology and Geology at the ACI Educational Foundation – Esclavas SCJ Alcoy from 1994 to September 2020. From 2014 to 2017, he also served as the school's director. At the Catholic University of Valencia, he was a contract professor for the subjects: ICT and Classroom Management and ICT and School Management for the Master's

Degree in Technological Innovation in Education, from 2014 to September 2020. He has also supervised more than 25 Master's Final Projects and has served on Master's Thesis defense panels. At the University of Alicante, he was an Associate Professor in the Department of General and Specific Didactics of the Faculty of Education from the 2016-2017 academic year until September 2020. From September 2020 to September 2024, he was an Assistant Professor. He is currently a Permanent Lecturer (PPL) and teaches Curriculum Development and Digital Classrooms, and Teaching Knowledge of the Natural Environment in the Teaching Degree, specializing in Early Childhood Education. He also directs Final Projects (FDPs) for this degree, as well as Final Projects (FPMs) for the Master's Degree in Secondary Education Teaching. He has also been and is the coordinator and author of two courses from the National Institute of Educational Technologies and Teacher Training (INTEF), specifically: The Performance of the Management Function and Updating Management Competencies. He was previously the tutor and coordinator of the courses: PBL in Secondary and Baccalaureate Education and PLE. He has been and continues to be a trainer for various CEFIREs in the Valencian Community and teacher training centers throughout Spain. He has also been a speaker at numerous national and international meetings, conferences, and congresses. He has also been invited to provide training at various universities both in Spain and abroad, as well as at numerous educational centers at all educational levels.

Spyridon Aravantinos is a primary school teacher, a postgraduate student at the Department of Educational Sciences and Early Childhood Education at University of Patras, Greece and holds a master's degree in educational leadership and school administration. His scientific and research interests include preschool and primary education, educational leadership, teacher professional development and the use of artificial intelligence in education.

Constantina Corazon Argyrakou is a Ph.D. candidate in Cultural Geography at Harokopio University of Athens, with a solid academic foundation that includes a Master's degree in Cultural Studies and Education from the National and Kapodistrian University of Athens and a Bachelor's degree in Geography from Harokopio University of Athens. She also holds a Diploma in Byzantine Music from the School of Byzantine Music "Priest Paul the Scopelite". As a Senior Lecturer in the field of Education, Constantina has taught a wide range of undergraduate and postgraduate modules spanning early childhood education, interdisciplinary curriculum design, counselling psychology in education, and special needs education. Her teaching expertise includes subjects such as project-based learning, curriculum theory and practice, educational arts, and educational research methodology. Constantina has published numerous books, book chapters, articles in international journals, and conference presentations. Her research interests encompass cultural geography, immigration, multicultural education, music education, interdisciplinary education, and the integration of technology in teaching.

Luis Manuel Cerdá Suárez Associate professor and researcher in the Faculty of Business and Communication (UNIR), Spain. His academic expertise lies at the intersection of digital education, teacher training, and the integration of emerging technologies in educational contexts. He has contributed to multiple national and international projects focused on pedagogical innovation, learning analytics, and digital competencies in K–12 and higher education.

Alejandro De la Hoz Serrano Graduate in Primary Education, currently pursuing a PhD in the Department of Experimental Science and Mathematics Education With professional development and training in Educational Technology (Robotics, AI, Computational Thinking), his research focuses on the use of technology in teaching science and mathematics content, digital literacy, teacher training, and learning analysis using mixed research methodologies.

RADINAL FADLI is a lecturer and researcher at Universitas Lampung, Department of Information Technology Education. His academic focus centers on the integration of technology in education, with research interests spanning Technology Enhanced Learning, digital learning, online learning, mobile learning, educational media, network technology, and cybersecurity. Through his work, he aims to advance innovative learning environments and contribute to the development of secure and effective digital education systems.

Krishnendu Ghosh is currently working as an Assistant Professor at the Department of Computer Science and Engineering at Indian Institute of Information Technology Dharwad. He completed his B.Tech in Computer Science from WBUT in 2008 and M.S. from IIT Kharagpur in 2012 under the supervision of Prof. Krothapalli Sreenivasa Rao, focusing on Text Analysis for Bengali Text-to-speech Synthesis System. He completed his Ph.D. from IIT Kharagpur in 2021 under supervision of Dr. Plaban Kumar Bhowmick and Dr. Pawan Goyal, working on the topic: Augmenting Learning Materials to Support Integrated and Multimodal Learning. Dr. Ghosh has 5+ year's teaching experience working at IIIT Dharwad, Techno International New Town, SOA University, KiiT University, NIT Sikkim, and GNIPST and 11+ year's research experience. His research domains are speech processing, natural language processing, artificial intelligence, information retrieval, and educational technology.

Anik Ghufron is a professor at Yogyakarta State University, Indonesia. He is providing lecturing services in the department of educational sciences and is the coordinator of the Graduate School. Ghufron has published several research articles and participated in diverse conferences. His research area cuts across the curriculum and educational technology.

Deepak Gupta is a distinguished academician with over 20 years of teaching experience and expertise in Computer Science and Engineering. He holds a Ph.D. in Computer Engineering and has an extensive research portfolio, including many international journal papers, multiple conference proceedings, and several books. His research interests span machine learning, artificial intelligence, and data mining. Currently, Dr. Gupta serves as an Associate Professor and Head of Department of CSE (Emerging Branches) at ITM Gwalior, MP, India. He has also contributed significantly to the field through patents and copyrights and actively engages as a reviewer, conference chair and editor.

Beltrán Gutiérrez Jiménez Associate Professor and researcher in the Universidad Internacional de La Rioja, Spain. His academic expertise lies at the intersection of digital education, teacher training, and the integration of emerging technologies in educational contexts. He has contributed to multiple national and international projects focused on pedagogical innovation, learning analytics, and digital competencies in K–12 and higher education.

Loyiso Currell Jita is the Dean of the Faculty of Education, University of the Free State, South Africa. He is also the Chair, SANRAL in Science, Mathematics and Technology Education. He holds a PhD in Curriculum Studies, Science Teaching and Education Policy Studies from Michigan State University, USA. His research interests centre around classroom reform and instructional leadership in science and mathematics education.

Thuthukile Jita is a Professor in the Department of Curriculum Studies and Higher Education at the University of the Free State (UFS), South Africa. She is the Programme Director for Teaching Practice/Practicum and Research Coordinator of the Instructional Leadership and Curriculum Implementation Studies (ILCIS) group. Her research focuses on curriculum studies, pre-service teacher education, digital technologies in teaching and learning, Work-Integrated Learning (WIL), and science education. She has published in high-impact international journals, presented at national and global conferences, and supervised Master's and Doctoral students to completion. Prof Jita also serves as Co-Chair of the International Perspectives SIG at the SITE conferences (2026–2027).

Thanassis Karalis is Professor of Lifelong Learning and Adult Education at the Department of Educational Science and Early Childhood Education, University of Patras, Greece. He is the coordinator of the Center for Teaching and Learning and a former member of the Quality Assurance Unit of the University of Patras. He is the vice-president of the Hellenic Adult Education Association and scientific collaborator to the Labour Institute, Greek General Confederation of Workers (INE GSEE).

Harpominder Kaur is currently serving as an Assistant professor in the school of Business studies, Department of management at Chandigarh University. I earned my Ph.D from Desh Bhagat university in 2019. With over 16 years of experience in academia. I held various academic and administrative positions in reputed colleges and universities.I had taught a wide range of management subjects to both undergraduate and postgraduate students. I have published numerous research paper in national and international journals.I hold 5 parents and also participated in multiple national and international conferences.

Vasilis Komis is a Professor at the Department of Educational Sciences and Early Childhood Education, University of Patras, with a specialization in Computer Science Education and the Applications of Information and Communication Technologies in Education. His research interests focus on the integration of Digital Technologies into teaching and learning across all levels of education and training. He has thirty years of teaching experience at both undergraduate and postgraduate level in various universities in Greece and abroad. He has published extensively in international journals and conferences.

Debaditya Kundu is currently pursuing a Ph.D. in Computer Science and Engineering at the Indian Institute of Information Technology (IIIT), Dharwad, Karnataka, India. He holds a Master of Engineering (M.E.) degree in Information Technology from the West Bengal University of Technology, Kolkata and a Bachelor of Engineering (B.E.) degree in Information Technology from Siliguri Institute of Technology under the University of North Bengal. With over 18 years of academic experience, he has been serving as an Assistant Professor at Siliguri Institute of Technology, West Bengal, India since 2006. His teaching and research interests include Operating Systems, Computer Networks, Network Security, and Natural Language Processing. He has also served as a lecturer and part-time faculty at various institutes in the early stages of his career. Mr. Kundu is an active member of several professional bodies including the Computer Society of India (CSI), the Institution of Engineers (India), the Cryptology Research Society of India, and the International Association of Computer Science and Information Technology (IACSIT). He also holds the title of Chartered Engineer (India). His research contributions include publications in international conferences and journals, notably in the areas of face recognition, video-based face tracking, and optimization techniques in numerical computation.

Georgios Lampropoulos is a Postdoctoral Researcher at the Department of Applied Informatics at the University of Macedonia, Greece and at the Department of Preschool Education at the University of Crete, Greece. Additionally, he is a Visiting Lecturer at the Department of Education at the University of Nicosia, Cyprus. His research focuses on educational technology and his research interests include learning technologies, extended reality technologies, artificial intelligence, learning analytics, gamification, serious games, and robotics.

Konstantinos Lavidas, Greece, University of Patras, Assistant Professor at the Department of Educational Science and Early Childhood Education. He holds a PhD in mathematics education. He teaches methodology of educational research and statistics. His research interests focus on methodology of educational research, statistics education, ICT use in the teaching and learning of mathematics, and STEM education.

Emmanouil D. Milakis is a Ph.D. candidate in Education Sciences at the European University Cyprus, with a robust academic background that includes a Master of Arts in Technologies of Learning & Communication and an integrated Master's/Bachelor's in Electrical and Computer Engineering, specializing in Informatics. He holds certifications in pedagogical and teaching competence, as well as adult education training qualifications. As a Special Education IT Instructor and researcher, Emmanouil brings extensive experience in teaching IT in diverse educational settings, including special and gifted education. Emmanouil has published numerous articles in international journals, with research interests that include educational technology, STEAM education, special education, and the integration of AI in teaching methodologies.

Adelina Moura has got a degree in Portuguese and French teaching, a certificate in School Management and a Master's degree in Education. She earned her Ph.D. in Educational Technologies, from the University of Minho. She has been involved in academic research in "Mobile Learning", having done several publications in conference proceedings and book chapters. She also teaches Educational Technology in Master Degrees. She is a member of the research group, Games Interaction Learning Technologies (GILT), hosted in the School of Engineering of Porto, Portugal. She is a member of the National Reading Plan, and a tutor of e-learning training courses.

Adebayo Akinyinka Omoniyi holds a Ph.D. in Mathematics Education from the University of South Africa and is currently a postdoctoral research fellow hosted by the SANRAL Chair in Science, Mathematics, and Technology Education, Office of the Dean, Faculty of Education (Bloemfontein Campus), University of the Free State (UFS), South Africa. His research primarily focuses on mathematics education, teacher education, and curriculum studies, with an emphasis on identifying, developing and validating effective pedagogical practices that enhance student learning in mathematics.

Santiago Pozo Sánchez is Doctor cum laude in Educational Sciences from the University of Granada. He holds a Master's degree from the University of Granada, as well as the Bachelor of Music History and Sciences from the University from La Rioja. It also has the Master of Teachers in Secondary Education by the Alfons X el Sabio University, the Degree in Spanish: Language and Literature and the Degree in History and Heritage from the University of Burgos. He works as a teacher both in the field of secondary education and in the field of higher education, being professor at the International University of La Rioja within the Master's Degree in Teaching in the Faculties of Education and Social Sciences and Humanities. Member of AREA Research Group (HUM-672) of the University of Granada.

Nuria Puente Domínguez holds a PhD in Communication Sciences from Antonio de Nebrija University, where she also earned a Master's degree in Digital Marketing and Advertising. She holds a degree os Audiovisual Communication from the University of Burgos and a postgraduate degree in Innovation Management from the International University of La Rioja (UNIR). She currently works as University Professor at UNIR and is the Academic Deputy Director of the Postgraduate Area in Marketing and Communication. She is part of the Academic Innovation in Online Teaching in Spanish research project, aimed at improving online higher education through the use of advanced technologies, data, and artificial intelligence. Her academic expertise lies at the intersection of digital education, teacher training, and the integration of emerging technologies in educational contexts. She has contributed to multiple projects focused on pedagogical innovation, learning analytics, and digital competencies.

Carolina Ramirez holds a Master of Mathematical Education and is a primary school teacher. Her research interests include mathematics education and the applications of Artificial Intelligence in education

Agariadne Dwinggo Samala is a professional educator, futurist, and dedicated researcher, currently serving as an Associate Professor at the Faculty of Engineering, Universitas Negeri Padang (UNP), Indonesia, and an affiliated Tutor at Universitas

Terbuka, Indonesia. His academic journey began with a bachelor's degree in Computer Engineering from Universitas Andalas, Indonesia (2015), followed by a master's degree in Technology and Vocational Education from UNP, specializing in Informatics Engineering Education (2018). In 2023, he completed his doctoral studies at UNP, focusing on integrating technology in education. With over five years of experience, Agariadne excels in applying digital technology to enhance educational practices. He actively contributes to the academic community as a member of several professional associations, including APTEKINDO (Association of Technology and Vocational Education of Indonesia), APTIKOM (Association of Higher Education in Informatics and Computers), the Digital Society Lab at the Institute for Philosophy and Social Theory, the International Society for Engineering Pedagogy (IGIP) in Austria, the International Association of Engineers (IAENG), Ikatan Ilmuwan Indonesia Internasional (I4), and the Association for Computing Machinery (ACM). Agariadne's collaborative efforts extend internationally as an external collaborator with the Digital Society Lab at the Institute for Philosophy and Social Theory (IFDT), University of Belgrade, Serbia. His research interests include technology-enhanced learning (TEL), educational technology, bibliometrics, immersive learning applications and experiences, digital learning, microlearning, and emerging technologies in educational contexts.

Shazia Shaikh received her Ph.D. in Computer Science & Information Technology in 2021, her M.Sc. degree in Computer Science in 2011, and her M.Phil. degree in Computer Science in 2015 from the Department of Computer Science & Information Technology, Dr. Babasaheb Ambedkar Marathwada University, Aurangabad, India. She is currently affiliated with the College of Computer Science, King Khalid University, Saudi Arabia. She has over 11 years of combined teaching and research experience. Her research interests include Biomedical Image Processing, Cyber Security, and Artificial Intelligence.

S.Sivaiah is presently working as a Professor of Mathematics at Vidya Jyothi Institute of Technology(A),Hyderabad. He did his M.Sc and obtained Ph.D.,in 2004 from Sri Krishnadevaraya University, Anantapur. He had brilliant and strong academic career while obtaining first division and rank in the board and university examinations. Under his supervision one Ph.D., and four M.Phil.,degrees awarded in the area of Fluid Dynamics from various Universities .He has authored four text books namely 'Mathematical Methods' and 'Engineering Mathematics' 'Optimization Techniques' and 'Foundations of Data Science' for the students of Engineering, He was successfully completed UGC Minor Research Project on "Heat & Mass Transfer Problems in MHD Flows by Finite Element Method" during 2015-2018.Apart from the main stream, he also completed multi disciplinary courses like M.Tech (Computer Science) and MBA during his career. He has more than 34 years of teaching experience in various institutions at different levels including Principal. He was published more than 30 research publications in various national and International Journals. He has also published three patents in the research area and to update knowledge he had attended more than 50 National and International conferences and workshops. Apart from his major area of Mathematics, his interests include Probability & statistics,Operational Research,Optimization techniques and Computer Science too.

Herman Dwi Surjono, Professor of Information Technology, Faculty of Engineering at Yogyakarta State University, Indonesia. Working as a lecturer at the Department of Informatics Engineering Education and lecturer at the Graduate School Yogyakarta State University. Currently serving as Head of Study Program of Doctoral Engineering Sciences of Yogyakarta State University. Areas of expertise: e-learning, multimedia learning, adaptive hypermedia, learning of information technology.

Mukesh Kumar Tripathi received a Ph.D. in Computer Science and Engineering from VTU, Belagavi. He also received a B.E. in Information Technology from Guru Nanak Dev Engineering College, Bidar, India and M.Tech. Computer Science and Engineering from SCET, JNTUH University in 2013. He has 13 years of teaching and administrative experience. He has authored or co-authored more than ten publications and over 250 citations. He is working as an assistant professor with the Department of Computer Science and Engineering, Vardhaman College of Engineering, Hyderabad, India. His research interests include machine learning, intelligent systems and computer vision. He can be contacted at email: mukeshtripathi016@gmail.com

Johnson Upahi is an Assistant Professor at Universiti Brunei Darussalam, Brunei Darussalam. He is also a Senior Research Associate at the Centre for Advanced Learning Technologies in Science, Technology, Engineering, Arts and Mathematics (CALTSTEAM), University of Johannesburg, South Africa. His research endeavors focus on context- and problem-based learning, the nature of science (NOS), and scientific literacy, as well as science document analysis. His recent research efforts focus on inquiry-based science education, learning progressions in science, science teachers' pedagogical content knowledge (PCK), and integrating immersive technologies into science education. He is interested in developing students' understanding of NOS as scientifically literate citizens in diverse contexts. He has published some of his research endeavours in quartile one (Q1) journals such as Research in Science Education (RISE), Chemistry Education

Research and Practice (CERP), Science and Education (S & E), and School Science and Mathematics (SSM).

Abdulnassir Yassin is an educator and a researcher in instructional technology, currently an Assistant Lecturer in the Department of Curriculum and Instruction at the Islamic University in Uganda (IUIU). He is the associate editor of the Interdisciplinary Journal of Education (IJE) at IUIU. He holds a master's degree in Education, specializing in Instructional Technology from IUIU, and is pursuing a doctoral degree in Educational Sciences with a focus on Instructional Technology at Yogyakarta State University in Indonesia. His research work spans: Pedagogical Innovations, AI in Education, E-Learning, and Tech-Enhanced Learning.

Index

A

C

F

G

H

I

K

L

M

O

P

R

S

T

U

V

www.ingramcontent.com/pod-product-compliance
Lightning Source LLC
LaVergne TN
LVHW081319300926
849161LV00008B/1813